Reports of the Research Committee

of the

Society of Antiquaries of London

No. XXXII

# Excavations at Portchester Castle

Volume I : Roman

By

## Barry Cunliffe, M.A., Ph.D., F.S.A.

with sections by

T. Ambrose, B.A., A. Eastham, B.A., M. Fulford, B.A., A. Grant, M.A.,
M. Guido, M.A., F.S.A., R. Harcourt, M.Sc., D. B. Harden, Ph.D., F.S.A.,
M. Henig, D.Phil., F.S.A., B. Hooper, Joanna Morris, B.A., P. Murphy, B.A.,
R. Reece, D.Phil., F.S.A., J. M. Renfrew, M.A., J. Webster, B.A.

Published by
The Society of Antiquaries of London
Distributed by
Thames and Hudson Ltd
1975

PRINTED IN ENGLAND BY
ADLARD AND SON LTD,
BARTHOLOMEW PRESS, DORKING

# CONTENTS

# LIST OF FIGURES

## LIST OF PLATES (at end)

# GENERAL BIBLIOGRAPHY

(Note: detailed bibliographies will be found with several of the specialist reports)

BERSU, G. 1964. *Die spätrömische Befestigung 'Bürgle' bei Gundremmingen*. München.

BUSHE-FOX, J. P. 1932. 'Some notes on coast defences.' *J.R.S.* xxii, 60–72.

BUTLER, R. M. 1955. 'A Roman gateway at Portchester Castle?' *Antiq. J.* xxxv, 219–22.

CLARK, J. G. D. 1934. 'Derivative forms of the *petit tranchet* in Britain.' *Arch. J.* xci, 32–58.

COLLINGWOOD, R. G. and RICHMOND, I. A. 1969. *The Archaeology of Roman Britain*. London.

COTTON, M. A. and GATHERCOLE, P. W. 1958. *Excavations at Clausentum, Southampton 1951–1954*. HMSO, London.

CUNLIFFE, B. W. 1963. 'Excavations at Portchester Castle, Hants, 1961–3. First Interim Report.' *Antiq. J.* xliii, 218–27.

CUNLIFFE, B. W. 1966. 'Excavations at Portchester Castle, Hants, 1963–5. Second Interim Report.' *Antiq. J.* xlvi, 39–49.

CUNLIFFE, B. W. 1967. 'Excavations at Gatcombe, Somerset, in 1965 and 1966.' *Proc. Univ. Bristol Spelaeol. Soc.* xi, 126–60.

CUNLIFFE, B. W. 1968. *Fifth Report on the Excavations of the Roman Fort at Richborough, Kent*. Oxford.

CUNLIFFE, B. W. 1969. 'Excavations at Portchester Castle, Hants, 1966–8. Third Interim Report.' *Antiq. J.* xlix, 62–74.

CUNLIFFE, B. W. 1970. 'The Saxon culture-sequence at Portchester Castle.' *Antiq. J.* l, 67–85.

CUNLIFFE, B. W. 1971. 'The Tudor store-house at Portchester Castle, Hants.' *Post-Med. Arch.* v, 188–90.

CUNLIFFE, B. W. 1972. 'Excavations at Portchester Castle, Hants, 1969–71. Fourth Interim Report.' *Antiq. J.* lii, 70–83.

FRERE, S. S. 1967. *Britannia: a History of Roman Britain*. London.

GRENIER, A. 1931. *Manuel d'archéologie gallo-romaine*. Paris.

HAWKES, S. C. and DUNNING, G. C. 1961. 'Soldiers and settlers in Britain, fourth to fifth century'. *Med. Arch.* v, 1–70.

JOHNSON, J. S. 1970. 'The date of the construction of the Saxon shore fort at Richborough.' *Britannia*, i, 240–8.

MacMULLEN, R. 1967. *Soldier and Civilian in the Later Roman Empire*. Harvard.

MARASOVIĆ, J. and MAROSOVIĆ, T. 1968. *Der Diokletianspalast*. Zagreb.

MERTENS, J. 1962. 'Oudenburg et le Litus Saxonicum en Belgique.' *Helinium*, ii, 51–62.

MORRIS, A. J. and HAWKES, C. F. C. 1961. 'The fort of the Saxon shore at Burgh Castle, Suffolk.' *Arch. J.* cvi, 66–9.

MYRES, J. N. L. 1969. *Anglo-Saxon Pottery and the Settlement of England*. Oxford.

NASH WILLIAMS, V. E. 1954. *The Roman Frontier in Wales*. Cardiff.

PEERS, C. 1952. *Pevensey Castle, Sussex*. HMSO, London.

PETRIKOVITS, H. VON 1971. 'Fortifications in the north-western Roman empire from the third to fifth centuries A.D.' *J.R.S.* lxi, 178–218.

PHILP, B. 1969. *The Roman Fort at Reculver*. West Wickham.

PHILP, B. 1971. 'The discovery of the 'Classis Britannica' and 'Saxon shore' forts at Dover. An interim report.' *Kent Arch. Rev.* xxiii, 74–86.

RIGOLD, S. E. 1966. 'Recent investigations into the earliest defences of Carisbrooke Castle, Isle of Wight.' Taylor, A. J. (ed.), *Château Gaillard Colloque*, iii, 128–38.

ROACH SMITH, C. 1850. *The Antiquities of Richborough, Reculver and Lympne*. London.

ROACH SMITH, C. 1852. *The Roman Castrum at Lympne in Kent*. London.

ST. JOSEPH, J. K. 1936. 'The Roman fort at Brancaster.' *Antiq. J.* xvi, 444–60.

STEVENS, C. E. 1941. 'The British sections of the 'Notitia Dignitatum'.' *Arch. J.* xcvii, 125–54.

WAINWRIGHT, G. J. 1972. 'The excavation of a Neolithic settlement on Broome Heath, Ditchingham, Norfolk, England.' *Proc. Prehist. Soc.* xxxviii, 1–97.

WAINWRIGHT, G. J. and LONGWORTH, I. H. 1971. *Durrington Walls Excavations 1966–1968*. London.

WARD, J. H. 1973. 'The British sections of the *Notitia Dignitatum*: an alternative interpretation'. *Britannia*, iv, 253–63.

WHEELER, R. E. M. 1924. *Segontium and the Roman Occupation of Wales*. Cardiff.

WHITE, D. A. 1961. *Litus Saxonicum*. Wisconsin.

# PREFACE

THE first phase of excavation at Portchester Castle, which began in June 1961, came to a close in July 1972. This report is the first volume of a series which will cover the development of the site from prehistoric times until the early nineteenth century. Twelve years of excavation have necessarily involved the efforts and goodwill of a large number of people; sadly only a few can be mentioned by name here.

Permission for the excavation was given by the Department of the Environment, the guardians of the site, with the willing co-operation of the landowners, the Southwick Estate and the Fareham Urban District Council. The kindly co-operation of the Department's inspectors responsible for the monument, Messrs R. Gilyard-Beer, S. E. Rigold and A. Saunders, has at all times ensured the smooth and untroubled running of the excavation. With their encouragement and the active assistance of the area superintendent, Mr W. Taylor, and of the successive site foremen, Messrs R. Sanders and A. Pearce, the administrative and practical difficulties which so often accompany large-scale excavation were easily eliminated.

Generous grants towards the cost of excavation were made annually by the Department of the Environment, the Society of Antiquaries, the British Academy, and the Haverfield Trust. Addititional financial support came from the Hampshire Field Club, the Libraries and Museums Committee of the Portsmouth City Council and the Joint Archaeological Committee (of South-east Hampshire and South-west Sussex). It need hardly be said that without the support of these bodies the excavation would not have been possible. In all £9950 was spent on excavation between 1961 and 1972.

The work was under my direction with assistance from two or three site supervisors a year. To all of them, Tim Ambrose, David Baker, Brendan O'Connor, Fred Ferguson, Mike Fulford, Patrick Greene, Tony Norton, Mike Parrington, Bill Startin, Nigel Sunter and Alyson Taylor I wish to record my grateful thanks. The debt of every excavation director to the efficiency and accuracy of his supervisors is considerable: the speed with which the first volume was created is a measure of their highly organized site records.

The very large quantity of material which was recovered each year was admirably organized on site by a succession of lady assistants, including Mrs Frances Cunliffe, Miss Alyson Taylor, Miss Pauline Winstanley, Mrs Jo Chaplin and Miss Karen Lawrence, while site photography was in the hands of David Baker, David Leigh, Nick Bradford and Mike Rouillard. Only the writer can have a full appreciation of the importance of their support.

The preparation of this report also involved the efforts of a not inconsiderable team of co-workers. For the last year Mrs Judi Startin has performed the invaluable function of general organizer, at all times knowing where everything was and, even more important, being able to produce any object at a moment's notice. The relative ease with which (I hope) this report can be used owes much to her efficient and understanding organization. Even a cursory examination of the following pages will show how much labour has been expended on illustration. All the pottery was drawn by Miss Jane Holdsworth, all the small finds and diagrams by Mike Rouillard, while the writer has been responsible for plans and sections. Our great debt to Miss Holdsworth and Mr Rouillard needs no emphasis; their published work will serve as a constant reminder of their invaluable contribution. All the photographs were produced at short notice by Mr R. Wilkins with the assistance of Miss Lorna Llewellyn. The site photographs were printed from the negatives provided by the excavation photographer, but all the object photography was undertaken in Mr Wilkins' department in the Institute of Archaeology at Oxford.

The specialist reports which form such an important part of this volume are all credited to their authors. To single out any particular contribution for comment would be impossible but anyone who has handled quantities of archaeological material will be able to appreciate the immense labour and expertise involved. The good-natured response of all the contributors to my constant, but I hope gentle, pressures to meet deadlines was very gratefully received.

The unstinted efforts of the small team who worked so hard as the deadline for this report approached will remain a vivid memory. Miss Angela Blanch produced the entire typescript in a neat and unbelievably accurate form, from a jumble of scribblings, with the utmost speed and efficiency, while Tim Ambrose, Mike Rouillard, Lorna Llewellyn and Bob Wilkins worked long hours to ensure that everything was ready on time. Without their dedicated efforts this volume would have been long delayed.

The work involved in preparation for publication was no less arduous or costly than the excavation itself. That it could be attempted at all is entirely the result of two generous grants, one from the Pilgrim Trust for conservation work, the other from the Gulbenkian Trust for specialist preparation. The farsighted response of these bodies puts us all firmly in their debt. All the archaeological material from the Roman levels at Portchester is now in the Portsmouth City Museum.

These words are being written as the second phase of excavation at Portchester begins, a programme of excavations designed to explore the medieval castle. The subsequent volumes of this series dealing with the medieval period must necessarily await the completion of the exploration, but in the meantime work is in hand on the second volume covering the Saxon occupation.

Barry Cunliffe

Institute of Archaeology, Oxford
5 July 1973

# I. INTRODUCTORY SECTIONS

## GENERAL INTRODUCTION

PORTCHESTER CASTLE lies at the head of Portsmouth Harbour (pl. I), an almost landlocked expanse of water, triangular in shape, with its apex providing a narrow exit to the open water of the Solent. The first major structure to be erected on the site was a $8\frac{1}{2}$ acre (3·4 hectare) shore fort of late Roman date, which was occupied from the 280s. Occupation continued throughout the Saxon period and in the early tenth century Portchester was used as a burgh, fortified against threat of Viking attack. Towards the end of the eleventh century, the old Roman enclosure was used once more, this time as the outer bailey of a Norman castle built in the north-west corner. Early in the twelfth century, an Augustinian Priory was established in the south-east quarter, but it was abandoned within a few years, the monks moving to a more congenial site at Southwick, 3 miles (4·8 km.) away. Their church, however, has remained in use as the parish church ever since.

The Norman castle continued to be fortified until the fourteenth century, the last phase being represented by the outer earthwork thrown up to protect the approaches to the castle at the time of the French raids along the south coast in the early fourteenth century. Thereafter, the site declined in military significance with the growth of Portsmouth, lying at the entrance to the harbour.

Towards the end of the fourteenth century, a massive programme of rebuilding was carried out at Portchester, in an attempt to turn the castle into a comfortable fortified residence for Richard II, but the removal of the king from power in 1399 left the new work unfinished. Thereafter, a series of constables continued to maintain the fabric until the building was finally sold by Charles I in 1632. Before then, the site had been used several times as a mustering base for troops. The most famous occasion was in 1415 in the days before Agincourt. There had also been an attempt to turn it into a naval store base early in the sixteenth century by the erection of a vast storehouse, but the castle was too inconveniently sited in relation to Portsmouth and the attempt failed.

In the last phase of its life, Portchester served as a prison camp, first during the Dutch wars in the seventeenth century and later during the wars with France, reaching a peak in the period from 1793 to 1814. After a brief and mercifully unsuccessful attempt to turn the castle into a hospital for veterans from the Crimean war, the site was abandoned to more rural pursuits, and indeed was farmed until the Office of Works assumed responsibility for the monument in 1926.

The early antiquarians took little notice of Portchester, presumably because of its continued use as a military installation until as late as the early nineteenth century. Then followed a number of accounts, many somewhat romantic and most of little value.[1] The

---

[1] Among the more interesting or amusing descriptions are: E. King, *Munimenta Antiqua*, 2 (1801), 22–35; J. H. Cooke, *Portchester Castle—its Romance in Tradition and History* (Portsmouth, 1928); J. D. Henderson, *Guide and History of* *Portchester Castle* (Portsmouth, *c.* 1890); Rev. Canon Vaughan, *A Short History of Portchester Castle* (local, pre-1923); Anon., *Portchester Castle, its Origin, History and Antiquity, interspersed with anecdotes of its occupation during the late French wars* (local, 1845).

first scholarly description was published in the Victoria County History in 1908, covering both the historical and architectural development of the site. The descriptive sections of the work were not superseded until the appearance of the official Guide Book; the historical account remained the standard work until the publication of *The King's Works* in 1963.[1]

Before 1961, when the present series of excavations began, little archaeological attention had been paid to the site. The massive clearance works undertaken in the 1920s and 30s were ill recorded and the bulk of the large collection of artifacts recovered was stacked into a cupboard in the site hut, and there remained until it was re-discovered in 1961. Unfortunately, by that time most of the bags and labels had rotted, or had been eaten by rodents, and the individual groups had been reduced to an amorphous heap. A few of the small finds and all of the coins had, however, been removed to the Ministry of Works soon after the excavation, allowing some passing reference to be made to the coin sequence by Bushe-Fox in his general paper on Shore Forts published in 1932 (see General Bibliography).

The watergate received some attention in 1955 when Dr R. M. Butler suggested it to be basically a Roman structure, a view originally hinted at by Sir Mortimer Wheeler 20 years earlier (Wheeler, 1935). Subsequent excavation has suggested that a late Saxon date would be more appropriate. Finally, in 1956, a single trial trench was cut across the outer Roman ditch, south of the road leading to the entrance, by the Ministry of Works at a time when a proposal to build a public lavatory in the area was under discussion.

The present series of excavations was planned in 1960 with two objectives in mind; to examine the nature of the Roman defences and to test the possibility of settlement continuity in the south-west quarter of the fort, but before work could be begun, the need arose to excavate a large area inside the west wall south of the landgate, where it was expected that the public lavatory was to be built. This excavation was carried out in 1961, and exposed part of the Roman west gate.

From 1962–4, the original objectives were reinstated, with the examination of the east and west gates and several of the bastions (Easter 1962–Easter 1963), the sectioning of the Roman ditches (June 1963), the sectioning of the outer earthwork (Easter 1964), and the digging of test trenches in the south-west quarter of the fort (Easter 1964). By 1964 the work on the defences was largely accomplished, but the opportunity was later taken to cut two further sections through the outer earthwork (July 1968 and July 1972).

The test trenches in the interior of the fort had demonstrated the survival of archaeological features spanning the period from the late third to the early nineteenth century, but showing at the same time that limited excavation was less than useless in interpreting the features exposed. It was therefore decided to attempt the large scale stripping of a continuous area in the south-west quarter of the fort. Work began in 1965 and continued annually each summer until 1972, by which time an area measuring some 300 by 150 ft. (91 by 46 m.) had been cleared. The completion of the first stage of this programme presents the occasion for the production of this report.[2]

In parallel with the area excavation, work began on the examination of the Priory and

[1] H. Colvin, *The King's Works* (1963), 783–92.

[2] Interim reports have been published from time to time. These include: Cunliffe 1963, 1966, 1969, 1970, 1971, 1972.

the Castle. This project is still in operation, and is expected to take several years to complete. At that stage it will be decided whether or not to undertake a further programme of area excavation.

# INTRODUCTION TO THE REPORT

The present volume deals with Roman features and material derived from the excavations of 1961–72, taking note of earlier discoveries. The post-Roman finds will appear in subsequent volumes: Volume 2: Saxon, is to appear shortly, followed by Volume 3, concerning the medieval outer bailey and the Priory.

In the sections to follow, an account is first given of the scattered finds pre-dating the late Roman fort. Then follows a detailed description of structures representing the shore fort, prefaced by a short consideration of the post-depositional history of the Roman levels, necessary to understand the limitation of the evidence. The description is divided into four parts: the fortifications which includes all standing structures, the ditch system, and the results of the excavations relevant to the defences; an introduction to the chronological sequence inside the fort, with a summary of the evidence on which it is based; a description of all features found in the main area excavation; and a description of the results of excavations elsewhere inside the fort.

The rest of the volume is devoted to specialist reports on the material, with a concluding chapter summarizing the results of the work in a historical and regional perspective.

In order to facilitate cross-referencing, several procedures have been adopted. All section illustrations have been relegated to the end of the volume, and are provided with their own commentary. Wherever they are relevant in the text, cross-reference is made. One great advantage of arranging the sections in this way is that they can be folded out beyond the text to facilitate use.

A second procedure concerns the treatment of small finds, including coins. To list them all together would be unnecessary and difficult to use. Here we have given detailed lists only in relation to well stratified features and layers: these lists include all objects recovered, even formless scraps of metal. In the small finds report, only identifiable small finds are dealt with, and then on a typological basis. Both lists are cross-referenced.

Much the same procedure is used for the pottery and bone. Both groups of material are dealt with in their own right, but cross-referenced summaries are attached to the descriptions of individual features.

# THE SITE AND THE ENVIRONMENT
### (figs. 1 and 2)

Portchester lies at the head of one of a series of harbours formed originally by the drowning of the Hampshire coastal plain in the period following the regression of the last ice sheet. By the Roman period, the relationship of the land to the sea must have been not dissimilar to the present situation, allowing for a retreat of the shore line through erosion. The solid geology hereabouts consists of chalk overlaid by thin and often discontinuous marl capped by a consistent layer of fine yellow silty clay, called brickearth. The depth of the chalk below the surface of the brickearth varies from about 1 ft. (0·31 m.) to 5 ft. (1·5 m.), the surface of the chalk being highly irregular and penetrated by pipes and fissures filled with marl. Copious springs can be tapped at a depth of about 10 ft. (3·1 m.).

The promontory upon which the fort was built stands at present at a height of 16 ft. (4·9 m.) above Ordnance Datum. The sea lapped the east wall at high tide until the modern retaining wall was built to prevent damage by undercutting, but extensive erosion can still be

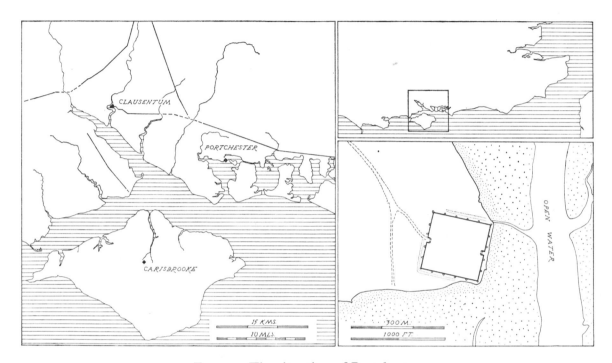

FIG. 1.   The situation of Portchester

observed along the south shore of the promontory. Several feet of land have been lost in some places since the excavation began, and it can only be supposed that encroachment by the sea has gone on over a long period of time. Documentary accounts record serious erosion and flooding during turbulent weather in the early decades of the fourteenth century.

The position of the Roman shore line cannot now be established, but to the east it probably lay close to the deep water channel 500 ft. (152 m.) from the east wall, while to the south it could well have lain even further from the present shore. Thus the fort would probably have been sited a little inland, but close to open navigable water represented by the present channel which is unlikely to have changed position substantially.

The fort must once have been linked to the Roman road system. No trace of a service

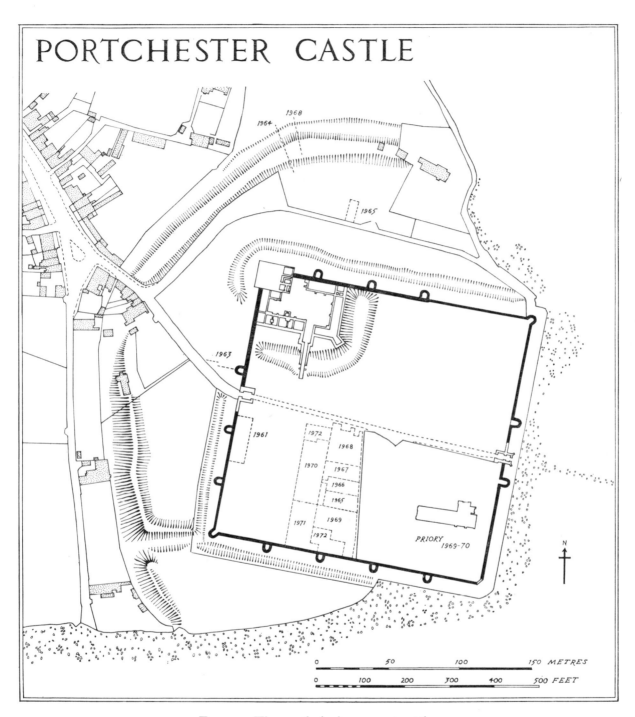

FIG. 2.   The castle in its present setting

road survives, but the outline of the main road system is well established with an east–west road from Chichester to *Clausentum*, branching at Wickham to Winchester. Portchester was divided from the east–west road by the ridge of Portsdown which presented a steep ascent. One possible approach to the main road lies west from Portchester along the coast to Fareham and then north to join the system at Wickham, but until positive evidence of the line is produced, the matter must remain open.

Little is known of the Roman settlement pattern around Portchester. The coastal plain does not appear to have been densely settled and villas are absent, a fact which emphasizes the relatively inhospitable nature of the tertiary sands and clays, and the expanses of river gravel, which blanket much of the area to the west. The brickearth and the chalk ridge of Portsdown presented a more congenial environment which appears to have been settled by peasant farmsteads.

Pottery was made at Rowlands Castle, 6 miles (9·7 km.) to the east, while pottery and tiles were made at Botley, 8 miles (12·9 km.) north-west, but neither area appears to have been in major production by the time that Portchester was founded, although a few Rowlands Castle types did find their way to the site. The only other natural commodity produced locally was salt, which was extracted from sea water at a number of sites around the Solent shores. Other attractions would have included shell-fish, marsh birds and fish.

# PRE-ROMAN OCCUPATION

The Portchester promontory was sporadically used in the pre-Roman period. The earliest occupation of the area dates to the Mesolithic and Neolithic periods. Several locations have been discovered around the north shores of Portsmouth harbour, where flint debris suggests the presence of camp sites used in the period spanning the seventh to third millennia, possibly by hunting parties engaged in the collection of wild fowl, fish and molluscs from the rich coastal environment.

During the excavation, a number of struck flint flakes were found on the original ground surface, most of them made from iron-stained flint of the kind which occurs in quantity around the shore. No concentrations came to light and the impression gained is that occupation was scattered and sporadic, although the possibility of the existence of more substantial camp sites nearby cannot be ruled out. Only four implements were recovered, including a fragment of a polished flint axe of Neolithic date (fig. 3, no. 2).

A complete polished axe of greenstone (fig. 3, no. 1) was found in the flint metalling of the Roman main N–S road leading to the south postern gate. How it came to be in this position is uncertain, but one possibility is that it was picked up from fields somewhere on the chalk downs along with the flints for the metalling and carted to the fort in the Roman period.

The only evidence of use during the second and first millennia B.C. was provided by a single sherd of pre-Roman Iron Age pottery (fig. 4). The absence of other traces is a reasonable indication that the site, or that part of it which has been excavated, was not occupied during this period.

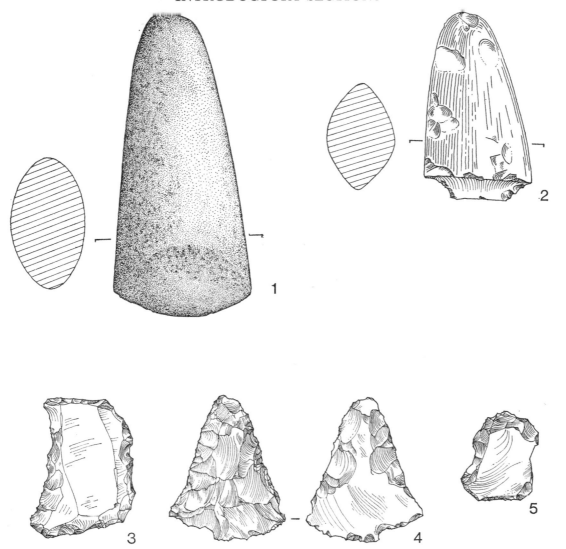

FIG. 3. Neolithic and early Bronze Age finds (pp. 7, 8).
Scales: nos. 1 and 2, ½, nos. 3–5, ⅟₁

*Small finds*[1] (fig. 3)

1. Polished stone axe. Greenstone ungrouped.
   Trench 91 layer 46 (1315).
2. Polished flint axe. Broken and stained with iron salts.
   Trench P9 layer 12 (1237).[2]
3. Hollow scraper with abrupt marginal retouch on all edges. The edge working is least steep within the hollow. No clear wear patterns can be seen. The raw material is probably

[1] The description of the flint implements was contributed by Richard Bradley, Dr David Peacock kindly sectioned the greenstone axe.

[2] Trench P9 was sited in the Priory grounds in the south-east corner of the fort. The axe was found in a Roman context.

derived from the chalk. The type is one which has a long history and this general form is present on both Mesolithic and late Neolithic sites in the immediate area. In the absence of earlier material here, the later date could be the more likely.

Trench 93 layer 6 (1328).

4. Transverse arrow-head with scale flaking on the upper surface and shallow inverse retouch. Abrasion is confined to the edges and the base and might suggest secondary use as a cutting implement. The raw material is probably derived from the chalk.

The form is closest to Clark's type G (Clark, 1934, especially fig. 12, 45), but the working of either edge and the scale flaking of the whole upper surface are unusual features. The associations discussed by Clark (1934) and by Wainwright and Longworth (1972, 170–3, 257–9) are predominantly late Neolithic and related forms seem to be particularly associated with Grooved Ware.

Trench 54 layer 7 (219).

5. End scraper on small irregular flake with possible wear on the right-hand edge. The raw material is possibly derived from gravel or beach flint. The type is not really dateable, but small irregular scrapers of similar form are often evidenced in Beaker contexts (for example Wainwright, 1972, 61-6).

Trench 54 layer 14 (87).

FIG. 4.   Iron Age pot sherd (p. 8). Scale ¼

*Iron Age pottery* (fig. 4)

Single sherd of the rim of a jar in sandy fabric tempered with crushed flint. Fired reddish brown on the surface: surface smoothed.

Trench 97 layer 12.

Vessels of this kind are difficult to date with precision but appear to have been in use during the fourth to third century.


## EARLY ROMAN OCCUPATION

A group of early Roman pottery was found in a restricted area of some 200 ft² (18·6 m²) just beyond the west end of the E–W road 1, an area much disturbed by late Saxon buildings. The pottery was found generally scattered in the churned-up Roman occupation level and in several post-Roman features. There was no level which could be identified as pre-late third century, nor is it possible to isolate early Roman post holes from the greater mass of postholes hereabouts.

A few sherds of contemporary material were found close to the main E–W road, and a single coin of Claudius (no. 2072) was recovered unstratified from the same area.

All the material belongs to the middle years of the first century A.D., and is best explained as a temporary settlement representing the transient use of the site by a very small group of people. The total absence of material dating to the period *c.* A.D. 50–280 points to lack of occupation until the late Roman fort was constructed.

*Pottery*
(fig. 5)

*Bead rimmed jars; nos.* 1–14

Wheel-turned, made in a variety of grey sandy wares. 2, 6 and 12 contain crushed flint grits. All have a well-smoothed surface which tends to be fired darker grey than the core. 14 is in a hard light grey ware with a light grey slipped surface burnished below the shoulder.

Provenances: 1, 56 layer 8; 2, 98 layer 22; 3, 55 layer 6; 4, 55 layer 6; 5, 58 layer 9; 6, 56 layer 7; 7, 75 layer 25; 8, 34 layer 12; 9, 58 layer 9; 10, 58 layer 9; 11, 55 layer 13; 12, 56 layer 5; 13, 56 layer 6; 14, 63 layer 4.

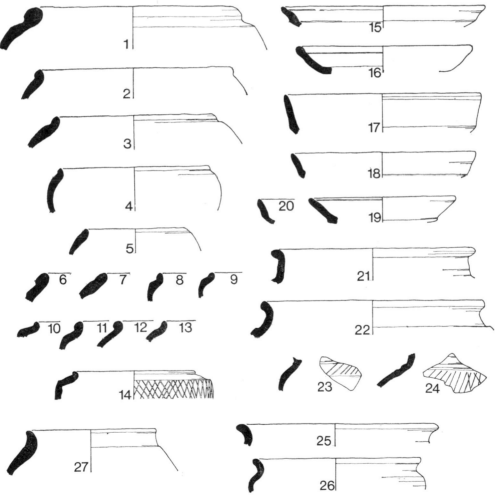

Fig. 5.   Early Roman pottery (pp. 9–10). Scale ¼

*Dishes and/or lids; nos.* 15–20

Wheel-turned grey sandy wares with smoothed surfaces.

Provenances: 15, 56 layer 7; 16, 104 layer 8 and 58 layers 3 and 6; 17, 58 layer 7; 18, 55 layer 6; 19, 58 layers 5 and 6; 20, 58 layer 13.

*Shouldered jars; nos.* 21–24

Wheel-turned grey sandy wares with smoothed surfaces. 21 is a light grey ware, 22 dark grey with black burnished surface, 23 hard light grey with bluish slip, 24 soft light grey.

The basic form is of a jar with upstanding neck, sharp shoulder, sometimes with a cordon at the junction of the neck and shoulder.

Provenances: 21, 98 layer 30; 22, 56 layer 6; 23, 58 layer 9; 24, 58 layer 9.

*Miscellaneous jars; nos.* 25–27

25: grey flint gritted ware; 26: light grey sandy ware; 27: dark grey sandy ware, all wheel-turned with the possible exception of 25.

Provenances: 25, unstratified; 26, 56 layer 7; 27, 55 layer 5.

Pottery of the types represented above was commonly in use during the first half of the first century A.D., the forms originating in the preceding century. By *c.* A.D. 40 ± 20 years, the fabrics were usually hard and sandy, the vessels almost invariably being wheel turned. The absence of associated imports prevents a closer dating of the Portchester group.

## THE NATURE OF THE SURVIVING LATE ROMAN REMAINS

Towards the end of the third century, part of the Portchester promontory was enclosed by a massive masonry wall fronted by a double ditch system. Within the enclosure lay a series of metalled roads, together with timber buildings and probably isolated masonry structures.

The surviving evidence for the internal layout is discussed in detail below (pp. 38–186): it is derived entirely from excavation, since no trace of the Roman features now survives above ground. After the end of the Roman period, large areas of the fort were subjected to ploughing, which continued sporadically from Saxon times to the post-medieval period, interspersed with periods of intense building activity. The combination of these two processes has ensured that no Roman building survives above the impressions made by their basal timbers. The remaining Roman levels are now buried beneath between 1 and 3 ft. (0·3 and 0·9 m.) of later soil accumulation. While no masonry buildings were discovered in the area excavated, fragments of building material survived, often re-used in Saxon contexts. It seems likely therefore that some Roman masonry buildings existed, but were probably robbed of their re-usable building material in Saxon times.

The enclosing wall, 10 ft. (3·1 m.) wide and 20 ft. (6·1 m.) high, together with its 20 forward projecting bastions and four gates, survived substantially intact into the Saxon period, although the double ditch system had largely silted up by then. During the Saxon period, part of the gatehouse of the west gate (landgate) was pulled down, leaving only the front wall in position, which was subsequently partly rebuilt using the original greensand blocks set in clay (to be discussed in Vol. 2). The gatehouse of the east gate (watergate) was also removed to its foundation level in Saxon times, probably to provide stone for structures built inside the fort. In the late Saxon period a new, smaller, gate was erected within the gap left by the removal of the Roman structure.

The first major changes to the Roman walls were carried out in the late eleventh and early twelfth century, at the time when the fort was converted into a Norman castle, for which the Roman wall served as the outer bailey. The two Roman postern gates were stripped of their greensand facing and blocked with flint and mortar masonry, while a new gatehouse was built to replace the ruined west gate. An inner bailey was created in the north-west corner of the fort, surrounding a keep which lay over the site of the north-west corner bastion (bastion 3): bastions 2 and 4 were probably heightened and used as integral parts of the Norman fortifications at this time.

The Norman building project required enormous quantities of building material, some of which, e.g. the Binstead limestone used for facing, was imported, while the rest, mainly flint for the rubble cores of the walls, was quarried from the internal face of the Roman fort wall. In most areas, up to 5 ft. (1·5 m.) of the original thickness was removed in this way. Three points of detail suggest that the quarrying was Norman. In the first place, the reduced thickness was exactly matched by that of the new blocking wall attached to the Norman landgate; secondly, the level to which the quarrying was taken was equivalent to the Norman ground surface; and thirdly, the only part of the Roman wall which was allowed to retain its former thickness was that part incorporated in the inner bailey where defensive strength was required.

By the twelfth century the ground surface had risen both inside and outside the walls to about 3 ft. (1 m.) above the Roman offset level, largely as the result of soil accumulation combined with the gradual erosion of the Roman masonry. The effect of this was to protect the original Roman facing. Inside the fort, except in the inner bailey, the post-Roman accumulation remains uncleared, but around the outside, on the berm between the wall and the inner ditch, the overburden was removed in the 1920s to foundation level. A close examination of the outer face often shows the position of the old ground surface as a horizontal line between the original Roman facing below and the refaced wall above.

Throughout the medieval period, the wall was subjected to patching and refacing. Considerable expenditure is recorded on this work in the documentary records and reference to undermining by the sea occurs more than once. It was during this period that bastions 7, 9 and 12 disappeared, and large stretches of the east wall seem to have been substantially rebuilt. Practically the whole length of the wall was heightened, and refaced in characteristic coursed masonry incorporating contrasting bands of flint and limestone rubble.

After the middle of the fourteenth century, little renovation appears to have been carried out, until the castle began to be used on a large scale as a prisoner of war camp throughout the eighteenth and early nineteenth centuries. During this period, extensive patching of the east wall was undertaken, with more limited refacing elsewhere, the new work often incorporating large squared blocks of limestone and bricks.

Finally, after the site was taken into guardianship by the then Office of Works in 1926, clearance began. The inner Roman ditch was cleared out and the level of the berm lowered approximately to the Roman surface. A concrete sea wall was built around the east side, and the space between it and the Roman wall filled with spoil. Since then, work has been limited to the repointing of weakened areas of the wall face.

The extent of the survival of the Roman levels within the fort was largely conditioned by the Saxon and medieval use to which the area was put. In the north-west corner, for example, the foundation of the medieval castle and the ditch fronting the inner bailey wall have destroyed large areas of the Roman surface. Similarly, in the south-east corner, the early medieval priory and the extensive graveyard which grew up around it have removed virtually all trace of the archaeological levels. The north-east and south-west quarters were however undisturbed. Since the north-east quarter is now used as a cricket pitch, the areas selected for large scale excavation lay in the south-west quarter.

# II. THE FORTIFICATIONS
(fig. 6)

THE Roman wall encloses an almost square area measuring internally 600 by 614 ft. (183 by 187·1 m.) — an area of 8·48 acres (3·43 hectares). Major gates were provided in the centres of the east and west walls, with postern gates occupying central positions in the north and south walls. Originally, the walls were protected by 20 forward-projecting hollow D-shaped bastions, of which 14 still survive. Outside the west wall, a pair of closely spaced ditches was discovered. In all probability, such a system once enclosed the fort, but medieval recutting and early twentieth-century excavation have together obscured the original plan.

## THE WALLS
(pls. II–VI)

The Roman wall was 10 ft. (3·1 m.) wide above ground and stood to a height of at least 20 ft. (6·1 m.). The outer face was vertical (pl. II). The treatment of the inner face is less certain. It may have been stepped in at intervals to reduce the wall width, but the possibility that it too was vertical cannot be ruled out. The highest remaining section of the back face lies behind bastion 1 where the original facing flints survived to a height of 10 ft. (3·1 m.) above the present ground surface. In view of this it would seem unlikely that any reduction in width was attempted.

The wall is now provided with a parapet and wall-walk, which, where the style of the masonry can be dated, can be shown to be early medieval. Nevertheless there can be little reasonable doubt that the Roman wall was once capped by a wall-walk not dissimilar to the medieval structure. Some idea of the original arrangement can be gained by reference to the better preserved wall of Pevensey where the parapet is reasonably complete in part (fig. 7).

The structure of the wall appears to have been uniform throughout. At one point on the south wall between bastions 16 and 17, where a Saxon pit had undermined the wall, it was possible to examine the footings in some detail. The results of these observations, together with the evidence derived from a trial trench excavated in front of the wall, are incorporated in fig. 8, from which it is possible to work out the processes involved in construction. To begin with, a foundation trench 5 ft. (1·5 m.) deep and 15 ft. (4·6 m.) wide was dug through the brickearth and coombe rock down to the solid chalk. Within the trench, a foundation consisting of tightly packed and rammed layers of flint and chalk was prepared to a thickness of some 2 ft. (0·6 m.). The possibility of the existence of vertical piles within or below the foundation was investigated, but none were found. While piles offered an obvious advantage on sites where the bedrock lacked rigidity, for example at Clausentum and Pevensey,[1] the solidity of the natural chalk at Portchester would have rendered piling unnecessary.

---

[1] The piles at Clausentum were incorrectly interpreted by the excavator as a stockade; Cotton and Gathercole, 1958, fig. 7. For Pevensey see Bushe-Fox, 1932, fig. 7.

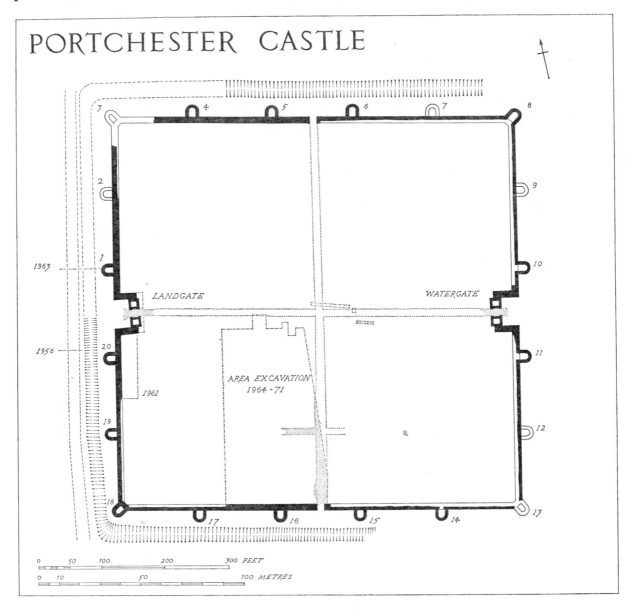

FIG. 6.   The Roman fort

The next stage entailed the construction of the basal raft of timber and flint. Timber baulks 1 ft. (0·3 m.) square were laid on a mortar bedding parallel to the wall faces. Cross members were placed at right angles with the intervening spaces cross braced (fig. 9). The spaces between the timbers were filled with flints and mortar, and the lateral timbers were faced externally with 1 ft. (0·3 m.) of flint and mortar masonry. The most extensive exposure of timbers (or more correctly the voids where the timbers once were) was between bastions 14 and 15, where medieval pits and structures in the grounds of the Priory had destroyed part ot the Roman masonry, allowing a section of the Roman footings to be examined. Further traces of timbering appeared in a similar area of destruction immediately to the east of the south postern gate.

Timbering of precisely this kind is recorded from Pevensey and from Richborough (fig. 10), suggesting that it may well have been a normal constructional technique, at least in late Roman defensive architecture. It is difficult to explain functionally, but presumably reflects the same reasoning as is implied by the use of corduroys of horizontal timbers beneath earthen ramparts. The more sophisticated timbering of the masonry forts would have imparted an element of lateral strengthening to the wall, greatly reducing the possibility of subsidence cracks.

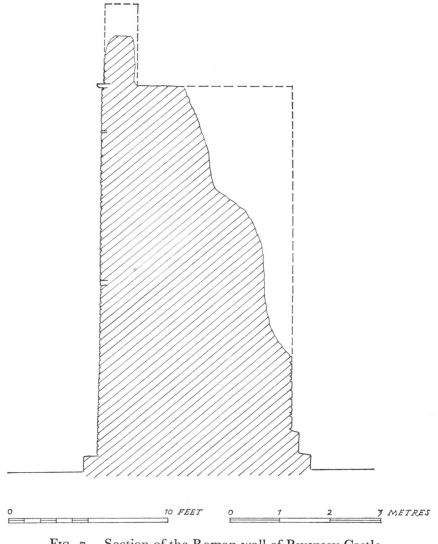

Fig. 7.   Section of the Roman wall of Pevensey Castle

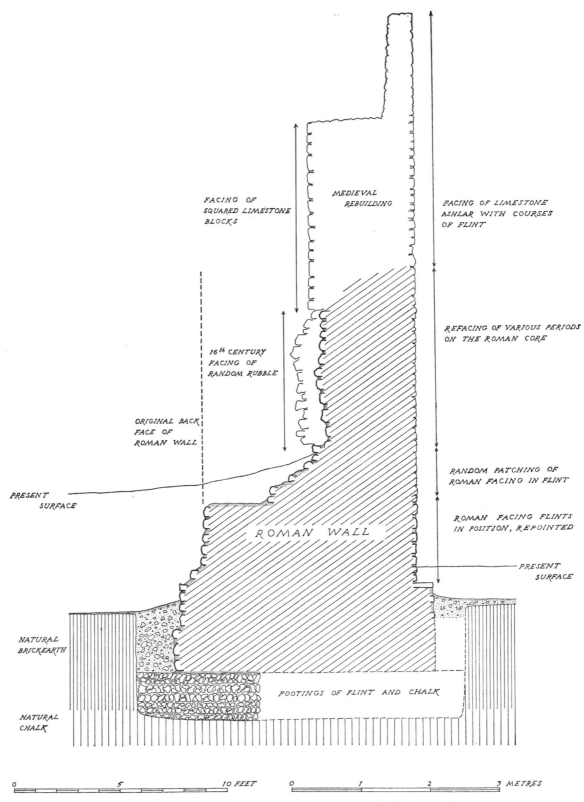

FACING OF
SQUARED LIMESTONE
BLOCKS

MEDIEVAL
REBUILDING

FACING OF LIMESTONE
ASHLAR WITH COURSES
OF FLINT

16th CENTURY
FACING OF
RANDOM RUBBLE

REFACING OF VARIOUS PERIODS
ON THE ROMAN CORE

ORIGINAL BACK
FACE OF
ROMAN WALL

RANDOM PATCHING OF
ROMAN FACING IN FLINT

PRESENT
SURFACE

ROMAN FACING FLINTS
IN POSITION, REPOINTED

ROMAN   WALL

PRESENT
SURFACE

NATURAL
BRICKEARTH

FOOTINGS OF FLINT AND CHALK

NATURAL
CHALK

0        5        10 FEET        0        1        2        3 METRES

FIG. 8. Section through the south wall of the Roman fort

Upon the strengthened basal course the wall was continued up to the contemporary ground surface at a width of 12 ft. (3·7 m.). At this stage, the front face was set back 9 in. (23 cm.), the resulting offset being faced with limestone slabs. The inner face was reduced in two stages until the wall standing above ground reached a standard thickness of 10 ft. (3·1 m.). The inner offsets were less regularly finished, and were evidently intended to be hidden with banked-up soil.

The faced external offset seems to have been a consistent feature around the entire circuit of the walls. For the most part it can now be seen as the result of soil clearance carried out

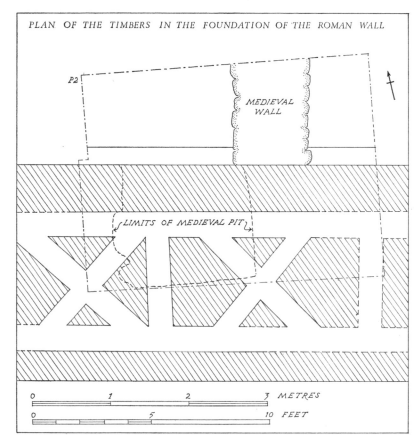

PLAN OF THE TIMBERS IN THE FOUNDATION OF THE ROMAN WALL

FIG. 9. Roman wall structure as exposed in a trench dug in the grounds of the priory

by the Office of Works in the 1920s, but along some lengths, particularly the east wall, it is still covered by post-Roman overburden. Between bastions the offset maintained an exact horizontal level, but since it was intended to be a ground level offset it was necessary for it to be stepped down along the north wall, so as to conform to the slope of the land, the change of level taking place at the bastions.

The internal offsets are less consistent, but for the most part a 12–15 in.- (30·5–38·1 cm.-) wide offset was created a little above ground level with a second offset varying in width below ground (figs. 211, 212).

3

The main body of the superstructure, 10 ft. (3·1 m.) wide and about 20 ft. (6·1 m.) high, was built in horizontal courses of flint and sometimes chalk laid on thick beddings of cream-coloured chalky mortar. The process of construction must have been gradual. First of all, the previous layer of mortar was allowed to dry sufficiently to allow the builders to walk on the surface. (At one point in area D the hobnail impression of a builder's boot was recorded on one of the grouting surfaces.) The builders then laid the next course of flints, packing them closely together, quite often choosing elongated nodules which could be placed at an angle leaning against neighbouring flints. When the placing of the course had been completed, a thick layer of mortar was spread over the surface, the consistency being such that the mortar oozed down into the interstices between the flints; even so air spaces remained.

PEVENSEY (foundation)                    RICHBOROUGH (superstructure)

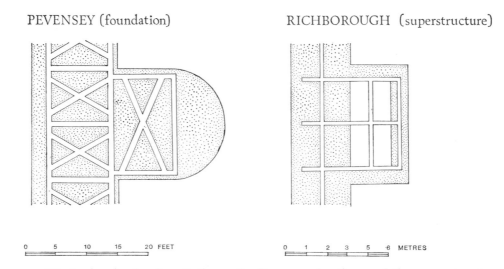

FIG. 10.   Timbering in the foundations of a Pevensey bastion and the superstructure of a bastion from Richborough

A building technique of this kind created certain inherent instabilities, not the least of which was that the face was subjected to lateral pressures from the weight of the core. To reduce the problem, the flints chosen for the facing were usually longer, up to 1 ft. (0·3 m.) long, so that they could be more easily bonded back into the core. Additional strength was provided for the outer face by the laying of horizontal bonding courses of tile or limestone extending into the core to a depth of 15–18 in. (38–46 cm.) from the face (see below p. 20). While these measures would ultimately have given sufficient strength to the structure to prevent the facing flints from peeling away from the core, they could not have overcome instabilities in the building stage before the mortar had hardened. Simply stated, the stresses inherent in a vertical-faced construction of this kind would have tended to cause a slumping of the exterior stones all the time that the mortar acted as a fluid. The problem could however have been overcome by strengthening the structure while the mortar was hardening. Evidence for strengthening is provided by the discovery of a number of voids running horizontally through the wall core, representing the positions of wooden poles 2 in. (5·1 cm.) in diameter. An examination of the largest area of exposed wall core, the interior face between bastions 19 and 20, showed that the poles were inserted during the construction phase in horizontal rows 5 ft. (1·5 m.) apart, the poles in each row being set at a distance of about 5½ ft. (1·68 m.) from each other. Since pole holes never show where the original facing is intact, it must be supposed that either the poles did not penetrate the faces or, if they did, that they were later cut off and the hole plugged with flint. There are two possible explanations for the poles, the simplest being that they were employed to give a rigidity to the structure while it was drying, thus reducing the risk of slumping. An alternative is that the poles projected beyond the wall face and served as points of attachment for shuttering. Against this second explanation it could be pointed out that, wherever the wall faces survived in protected situations, there were signs of careful trowel pointing. Such a finish could not have been achieved had the face been encased in timber shuttering. The Roman work contrasts noticeably with the Norman masonry blocking the south postern gate, where shuttering was used. Here, the mortar had begun to fill up the space between the flints and the timber, giving a characteristic finish. The Roman technique must have entailed the laying and pointing of the facing flints separately, in order to retain the core work. Thus, although the face and core were of the same material, the building technique was similar to that employed in stone-faced, and not in shuttered concrete, construction.

The walls of Portchester, like those of the other shore forts, notably Richborough and Pevensey, were built in sections by different groups of workmen, the junctions between the work of each gang appearing as vertical breaks in the continuity of the facing. At Portchester, the constant refacing and repointing to which the Roman work has been subjected has tended to obscure most of the junctions, but some can still be traced (pl. III), giving the general impression that each gang was responsible for one bastion, most of the curtain wall on one side of their bastion, and a short length on the other. The apportionment must have varied at the gates and on the corners.

The most obvious of the junctions lay on the south side of bastion 20. It was first noticed during the excavation of area D in 1961, appearing as a sloping but nearly vertical discontinuity in the coursing of the flint and mortar core. Not only did the rows of flints not line up, but the actual grouting surfaces could be seen to be on different levels. The section of wall on the north side of the junction had been built first. So that the courses should be level, a stack of limestone blocks had first been mortared into position at the end of the section, presumably to serve as guides for the builders' levelling strings. In the building trade, the blocks would now be referred to as 'dead men'. A similar pile of spacers had been laid at the outer face. Both stacks can still be seen, but those on the outer face are somewhat obscured by later repointing and their significance might not have been recognized had it not been for the exposure of the original inner face by excavation.

As the wall increased in height, it would have been necessary to provide some kind of scaffolding to enable men to reach the working surface with their materials. A series of seven postholes, presumably for scaffolding, were found along the inner face of the south wall west of the postern gate (pl. V*a*). They would have supported posts some 8–9 in. (20–23 cm.) in diameter, placed in larger holes, packed with flints, dug into the first phase of the lower clay bank (p. 41) which had been thrown up at the time of construction. Additional tips of clay dating to the end of the construction phase were spread around the standing posts.

Although only seven posts were discovered, it seems probable that others once continued the line to the west. Their absence here and in area D can however be explained by the destructive effects of the later pits which concentrate in the area behind the walls.[1]

The use of bonding courses of tiles and stones in the outer face of the wall has already been mentioned. Various materials were employed for this purpose, including blocks of limestone up to 5 in. (12·7 cm.) in thickness, slabs of limestone 1½–2 in. (3·8–5·1 cm.) thick, used either in single or double courses, and tiles usually used in double courses but sometimes in single. No great consistency can be traced, except that different materials are not mixed in a single course. Otherwise it would appear that the builders used whatever material came to hand. There are, however, several recurring features which imply that the builders were working to a preconceived design; for example, a course of limestone blocks formed the basal layer immediately above the offset. The next course was normally at about 5 ft. (1·5 m.) above the offset with a third at 10 ft. (3·1 m.). Above the 10 ft. (3·1 m.) level, where the evidence survives, the courses tend to be spaced at 18 in. (46 cm.) intervals. While these generalities are broadly correct, there is much variation in detail, as for example between bastions 3 and 4, where a course at 2 ft. 6 in. (0·76 m.) is interposed. The extent of the refacing to which the wall was subjected has rendered a detailed description of the surviving fragments of dubious value, but some impression of the Roman work can be obtained from the illustrations (pls. V–XI).

The range of building material was limited to flint, chalk, limestone, upper greensand, lower greensand and tile, the greensand being restricted in use to the gates. Flint was by far the commonest material, accounting for about 90% of the bulk of the walls. The nodules used were large and fresh: they showed no sign of rolling or staining and must therefore have been collected from the chalk, either from Portsdown or from the downs further inland. Chalk was used sparingly, but in the core of the wall between bastions 16 and 18 exceptional amounts were substituted for flint. Chalk would however have been consumed in quantity for the production of mortar. In all probability the chalk used was quarried on Portsdown, where a series of old workings, which might well date back to the Roman period, can still be seen a mile (1·6 km.) to the north of the fort. The limestone, of Tertiary origins, would have been brought in by boat from the Isle of Wight, collected from the convenient outcrops which occur along parts of the coast. Some of the blocks have the appearance of having been water worn, but this might be the result of later weathering. Limestone was generally restricted to use in bonding courses, but the north inturned wall of the east gate, bastion 20 and the adjacent wall to the north incorporate quantities of rough lumps in place of flint.

The upper greensand which was used as facing stone in the construction of the guard chamber of the main gates and the jambs of the posterns, does not appear to have been used elsewhere, but a ferruginous sandstone of the lower greensand origin which was probably used in the superstructure of the gates (p. 31) turns up in small quantities in courses between bastions 14 and 15, where it served not as bonding material, but simply as rubble (pl. XIa). The fragments may well be offcuts from the shaping of the gate blocks. Both the upper and

---

[1] The possibility was considered that these posts formed part of a timber building erected along the wall. This, however, seems unlikely because of the absence of corresponding timbers to form the north side.

lower greensand are of Wealden origin, but extensive outcrops occur in the Isle of Wight as well as the Sussex Weald. The shortness of the distance and the ease with which stone can be transported by boat would favour the Isle of Wight as the source.

## THE BASTIONS
### (pls. VII–XIII)

The fort was originally provided with 20 bastions, one at each corner and four regularly spaced along each side: 14 now survive. One (no. 2) was pulled down soon after 1790, no. 13 was lost at about the same time, no. 3 was removed in the eleventh century when the keep was constructed, while the remaining three, nos. 7, 9 and 12, fell during the medieval period, possibly as the result of undermining by the sea — a process known to have caused considerable damage to the walls in the fourteenth century.

The bastions are all of similar plan, and are built of coursed flint masonry with walls averaging 5 ft. (1·5 m.) thick. Each was bonded with the fort wall, and was built on a rectangular foundation platform which was laid at the same time as the wall footings. They were originally hollow, presumably with a timber fighting platform at wall-walk level. To overcome the problem of rain water accumulation, drains were provided at ground level to allow water to escape on to the berm.

In the descriptions to follow, details derived from visual examination are combined with the results of limited excavation.

### Bastion 1

The face of the squared foundation was seen in the trench cut to examine the fort ditches (p. 37). Upon this the foundation course of large squared blocks had been laid, incorporating a tile drain on the north side 3 ft. 8 in. (1·1 m.) from the wall face. The lower 10 ft. (3·1 m.) of the Roman facing survives, but above this the core has been refaced with random limestone. On the south side double tile courses occurred at c. 7 ft. and 8 ft. 6 in. (2·1 and 2·6 m.) above foundation. The tiles used were standard 12 by 18 in. (30·5 by 45·7 cm.) type. A hole cut through the south side showed that the bonding course, here of stone slabs, penetrated the thickness of the bastion wall.

### Bastion 2 (fig. 11)

The bastion, heightened in the medieval period, was illustrated in an engraving of c. 1790, but was subsequently demolished to foundation level. The foundations were exposed by the Ministry of Works in 1950 and carefully repointed.

Within the upper part of the foundation course two baulks of timber 1 ft. (0·3 m.) square had been incorporated on the same level as the timbering beneath the main wall. Although the bastion walls no longer survive, it is evident from the reconstruction that the timbers were so placed as to underly the north and south walls. The possibility of the previous existence of a third timber beneath the front of the bastion cannot be ruled out: destruction has however removed all trace. One block belonging to the lowest course of the bastion superstructure survives in position where the south side joined the fort wall.

*Bastion* 3

Corner bastion destroyed late in the eleventh century when the keep was built.

*Bastion* 4

This bastion was extensively refaced above the medieval ground surface 4 ft. (1·2 m.) above the Roman level. Below this the original Roman pointing survives. The bonding courses, where they are visible, are of limestone slabs.

*Bastion* 5 (pl. VIII)

Well-preserved bastion, retaining much of its original Roman facing. The basal course of stone blocks incorporates a drain on the east side, constructed of two imbrex tiles. The first bonding course of stone slabs occurs after 11 flint courses. Thereafter there are bonding courses of tile and stone at intervals of two or three flint courses.

The well-preserved state of the upper levels suggested that a limited excavation of the earth-filled interior would be of interest. The bastion proved to have been filled to the top with clay and soil in the medieval period (dated on the basis of the stratified pottery). The filling preserved an internal offset to the Roman work some 14 in. (35·6 cm.) wide, sufficient to have supported the joists of a timber floor or fighting platform (pl. VIII*b*). Below the offset the original Roman pointing remained intact.

*Bastion* 6

This bastion has been extensively refaced, but Roman core-work is exposed to a height of 18 ft. (5·5 m.). No foundation offset is visible, but bonding courses of stone and tile can be seen at intervals.

*Bastion* 7 (fig. 11 and pls. X–XI*a*)

No trace of the bastion now survives above ground level, but slight irregularities in the refacing of the fort wall indicate its former position.

A single trench (trench 31) 3 ft. (0·9 m.) wide was dug along the wall face to examine the bastion foundations at their point of junction with the wall. Natural brickearth was discovered at a depth of 4 ft. 4 in. (1·3 m.). The foundation offset of the fort wall, capped with limestone slabs, was 1 ft. 6 in. (0·46 m.) above natural and 6 in. (15 cm.) above the level of the flint-built foundation platform of the bastion. One basal stone block survived at the junction of the bastion and wall.

The difference in level between the natural clay and the foundation offset had been made up with tips of mortar and flint surfaced with redeposited natural clay. Such a treatment was necessary to compensate for a fall in the natural ground level towards the sea. If it is assumed that the foundation offset was laid level with the ground surface at the base of bastion 6, the natural slope in this sector must be 1 in 70.

The superstructure of the bastion had been totally removed in the medieval period, but the face of the Roman wall which would have been within the bastion still bears the marks of the original pointing trowel where the Roman work survives below the level of the medieval refacing (pl. XI*a*).

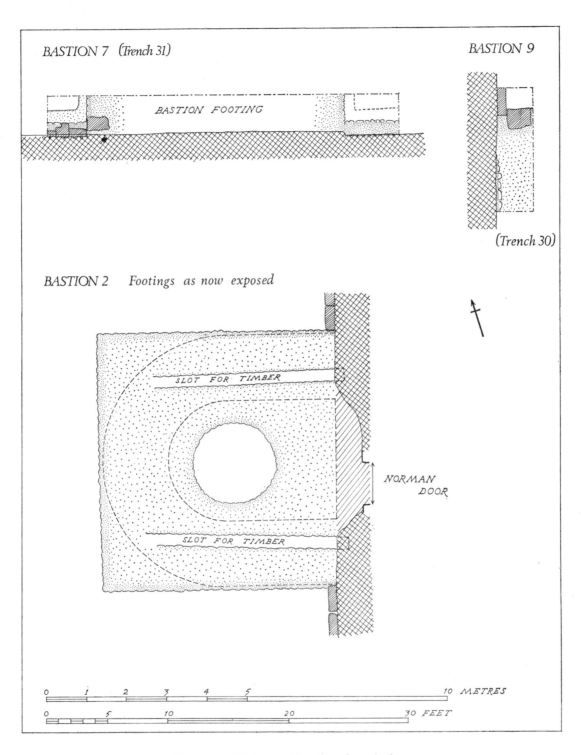

BASTION 7 (Trench 31)

BASTION FOOTING

BASTION 9

(Trench 30)

BASTION 2    Footings as now exposed

SLOT FOR TIMBER

SLOT FOR TIMBER

NORMAN DOOR

| 0 | 1 | 2 | 3 | 4 | 5 | | 10 METRES |

| 0 | 5 | 10 | 20 | 30 FEET |

FIG. 11.   Details of bastion foundations

*Bastion* 8

Corner bastion, extensively repointed and refaced in the post-Roman period. Two bonding courses of thick stone blocks appear at 2 ft. 6 in. (0·76 m.) and 4 ft. (1·2 m.) above foundation level.

*Bastion* 9 (fig. 11, pl. IX)

The bastion was demolished to foundation level in the medieval period and the wall refaced. To test its existence a small trench (trench 30) was dug where the north side of the bastion should have joined the fort wall. The angle was discovered, the edge of the bastion footing being marked by a large limestone block on the same level as the offset of the wall.

The entire overburden derived from the 1920s levelling, and represented infilling behind the newly constructed concrete sea wall. Before then the bastion footings were washed by the sea, as the thin spread of shingle hereabouts shows. Some years after the excavation, a drawing of this junction came to light among the Irvine papers in the Bath Reference Library. It appears that the architect James Irvine visited Portchester in 1875 and faithfully recorded the surviving bastion footing, correctly interpreting it.

*Bastion* 10

Largely refaced and repointed in the post-Roman period.

*Bastion* 11

Extensively refaced in the post-Roman period, although the remains of three tile courses are visible on the south side.

*Bastion* 12

No trace of the bastion now survives above ground.

*Bastion* 13

The corner bastion was probably destroyed in the late eighteenth century, at which time the gap left by its removal was blocked with masonry.

*Bastion* 14

The upper levels have been extensively patched, but the basal blocks are Roman. Traces of three double tile courses occur at 18 in. (0·46 m.) intervals above 12 ft. (3·7 m.).

*Bastion* 15

The Roman work has been repointed and patched, but the basal blocks can be seen together with a bonding course of stone slabs at 5 ft. (1·5 m.) and another at 10 ft. (3·1 m.).

*Bastion* 16 (pl. VIIa)

Much of the Roman masonry is visible, although in places it has been extensively repointed. A tile drain at ground level can be seen in the west face. Above this, bonding courses of tiles and stone blocks survive. It would appear that the course of stone blocks had been laid only in the west side, while several of the tile courses seem to be limited in extent to the front curved face, and do not continue far around the sides.

The tiles used for the external facing of the bonding courses were standard bricks of 12 by 18 in. (31–46 cm.) size, but inside the bastion *tegulae* were employed instead.

## Bastion 17

The lower courses of the Roman work are well preserved. The basal blocks can be seen, with a bonding course of stone blocks at a height of 5 ft. (1·5 m.); above this traces of two tile courses survive.

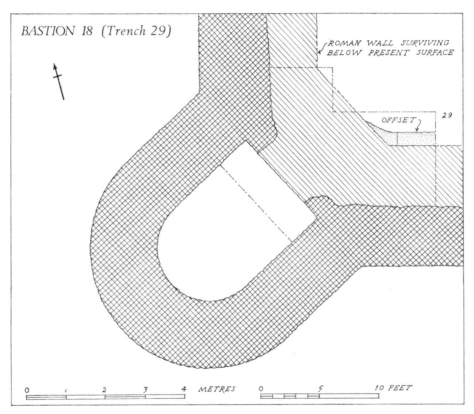

FIG. 12.  The south-west corner bastion

## Bastion 18 (fig. 12, pls. XII–XIIIa)

Corner bastion almost entirely refaced. Only the basal blocks and part of one tile course can be seen of the original Roman work. Inside, however, the Roman facing is well preserved.

A limited trial trench (trench 29) was dug to examine the treatment of the back face of the wall behind a corner bastion. As the plan will show (fig. 12), the wall continued diagonally, the only difference being that no foundation offset was provided for the diagonal section. A small area was cleared within the bastion down to the mortar surface of the foundation platform. The 4 ft.- (1·2 m.-) thick accumulation within was entirely of mortar and flints which had eroded from the superstructure. The wall of the bastion was provided with a single tile course at 3 ft. 3 in. (1 m.) above the foundations.

### Bastion 19

The repointed and patched Roman work is well preserved, with the basal blocks visible and tile and stone courses showing at intervals.

### Bastion 20 (pl. VIIb)

This bastion is one of the best preserved at Portchester. Although the face has been repointed and the uppermost courses rebuilt, the bonding courses still survive largely intact, together with areas of facing flints laid in herring-bone fashion. All the bonding courses are of tile, but the basal blocks are limestone.

# POSTERN GATES

Two Roman postern gates have been identified, one in the centre of the north wall, the other in the centre of the south. Both were blocked in the Norman period, but the north postern was partially re-opened in later medieval times and still functions as a gate.

### The North Postern Gate (Trenches 20 and 21) (fig. 13, pls. XIIIb, XIV)

The Roman north postern gate consisted of a simple 10 ft.- (3 m.-) wide opening through the thickness of the Roman wall. Originally the walls of the opening were lined with blocks of upper greensand pointed with pink mortar. Although only the basal course now survives, this facing would once have been continued up both sides of the passage and presumably over the top as a vault. Inside the fort, the greensand masonry projected beyond the wall face, on both sides of the passage, for a distance of 15 in. (38 cm.). How this feature was treated visually is uncertain, but the projections could have been made to appear as pilasters supporting an arch. The total destruction of the superstructure and the removal of the greensand blocks prior to blocking in the Norman period prevent further assessment.

Little of the area of the road was exposed by excavation, but where a small area was examined close to the west side of the postern, no metalling survived above the builders' spread of mortar and greensand chippings which lay at a depth of 4 ft. 2 in. (1·3 m.) from the present surface. A layer of grey clayey soil 2–3 in. (5–8 cm.) thick had accumulated over this before the Norman blocking wall was built.

### The South Postern Gate (Trenches 28 and 91) (figs. 13, 14, pl. XV)

Limited trial trenching was carried out behind the postern gate in 1962 (trench 28), and the entire area was stripped in 1969 (trench 91).

The gate, like the north postern, was a simple 10 ft.- (3 m.-) wide gap once lined with greensand blocks and presumably once arched. One significant difference, however, is that there were no internal projections, nor was there any evidence of pink mortar rendering.

Most of the greensand blocks had been prised out in the Norman period when the blocking wall was inserted.

Little of the original Roman stratigraphy survived the foundation pit for the Norman blocking, but a thin layer of cobbles representing the Roman road was traced across the footings beneath the Norman building spread. Below the cobbles was found a coin of Gallienus (A.D. 233–68).

Nothing is known of the gate structures themselves, all trace having been obscured in both cases by the Norman masonry, but in all probability the gates opened inwards behind responds.

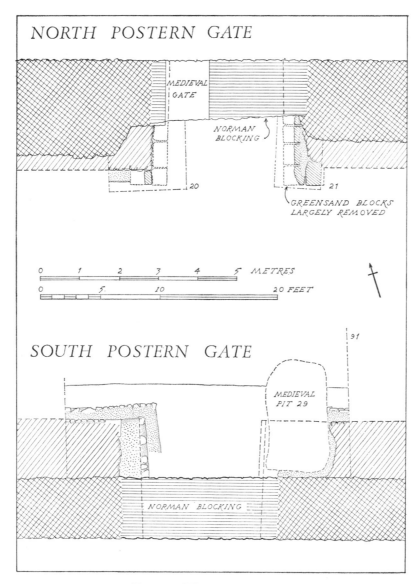

FIG. 13. The postern gates.

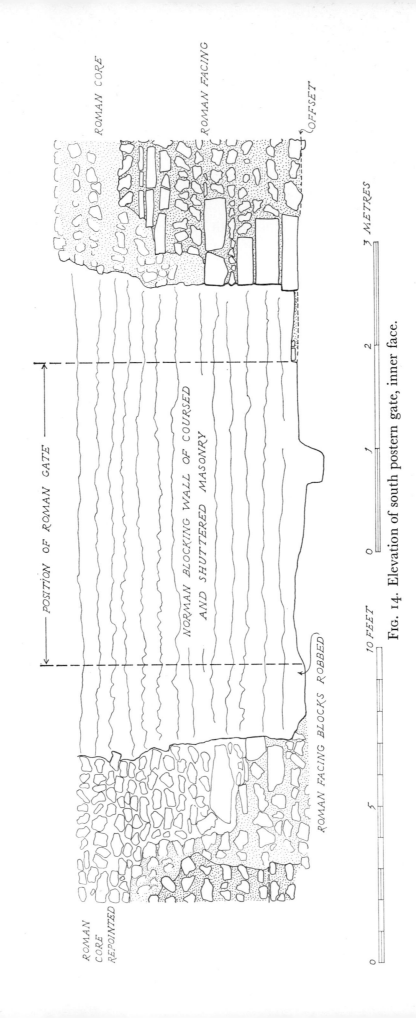

ROMAN CORE

ROMAN FACING

OFFSET

POSITION OF ROMAN GATE

NORMAN BLOCKING WALL OF COURSED
AND SHUTTERED MASONRY

ROMAN
CORE
REPOINTED

ROMAN FACING BLOCKS ROBBED

10 FEET

5

0

0

1

2

3 METRES

FIG. 14. Elevation of south postern gate, inner face.

# THE MAIN GATES

The two main gates lay in the centres of the east and west walls of the fort: both were later incorporated into the medieval gatehouses, serving the outer bailey, and both have continued to be used ever since. Excavation has brought to light a considerable amount of information relevant to all periods from the third to the fourteenth centuries. In the discussion below, only the Roman features are described; the Saxon and medieval phases will be considered in detail in subsequent volumes.

## The West Gate (Landgate) (figs. 15, 16, 209, pls. XVI–XXI)

The site of the Roman west gate is now partly occupied by the landgate, a Norman structure with later additions and modifications. The Norman gatehouse covers only part of the site of the Roman gate. A cursory examination of the exterior wall of the gatehouse and its adjacent curtain wall shows a marked vertical change in structure some 30 ft. (9 m.) south of the south jamb of the gate (pl. XVI). This denotes the junction between the original Roman wall and a Norman blocking wall constructed in one with the gatehouse to fill the gap between it and the standing Roman masonry. In 1961 an excavation behind the wall at this point exposed part of the Roman gate and demonstrated for the first time the nature of the relationship between the Roman and Norman work (pl. XVII). In the following year a number of small trial trenches were cut to elucidate further details of the Roman structure. Work, however, was limited by the constant use of the landgate by traffic to and from the church, and by the presence of a public lavatory, which occupied the corner between the gate and the curtain wall. In 1969 the lavatory was demolished, allowing part of the site to be excavated: the work was eventually completed in 1972.

The Roman gate complex consisted of three elements: a gatehouse, a courtyard in front of it measuring 44 ft. 9 in. (13·64 m.) by 22 ft. (6·71 m.), and the walls flanking the courtyard, which were created by inturning the fort wall for a distance of 36 ft. (11 m.). The form of the gate can best be appreciated by reference to fig. 15.

## The Inturned Flanking Walls (pls. XVIII, XIX)

The entire length of the southern flanking wall, some 9 ft. 8 in. (2·95 m.) thick, was uncovered in the excavations of 1961, 1962 and 1969. It was built entirely of coursed flint set in cream-coloured mortar surviving now to a height of nine courses above the external offset. The eighth course was a bonding course of stone slabs set into the outer (north) face and the end (east) face. The slabs were only superficial and did not penetrate the core of the wall. The inside face of the wall was provided with two foundation offsets continuous with those of the main curtain wall. The outer face had only one offset at ground level, surfaced with slabs of limestone, which was continuous with the offset at the foot of the main fort wall. The trial trench (trench 6), dug at the junction between the Norman blocking wall with the Roman work, showed that the external angle of the Roman wall was slightly rounded, while the offset slabs were sharply angled (pl. XVIIb). The offset was continued for the full length of the inturn, beyond the point at which the guard chamber abutted.

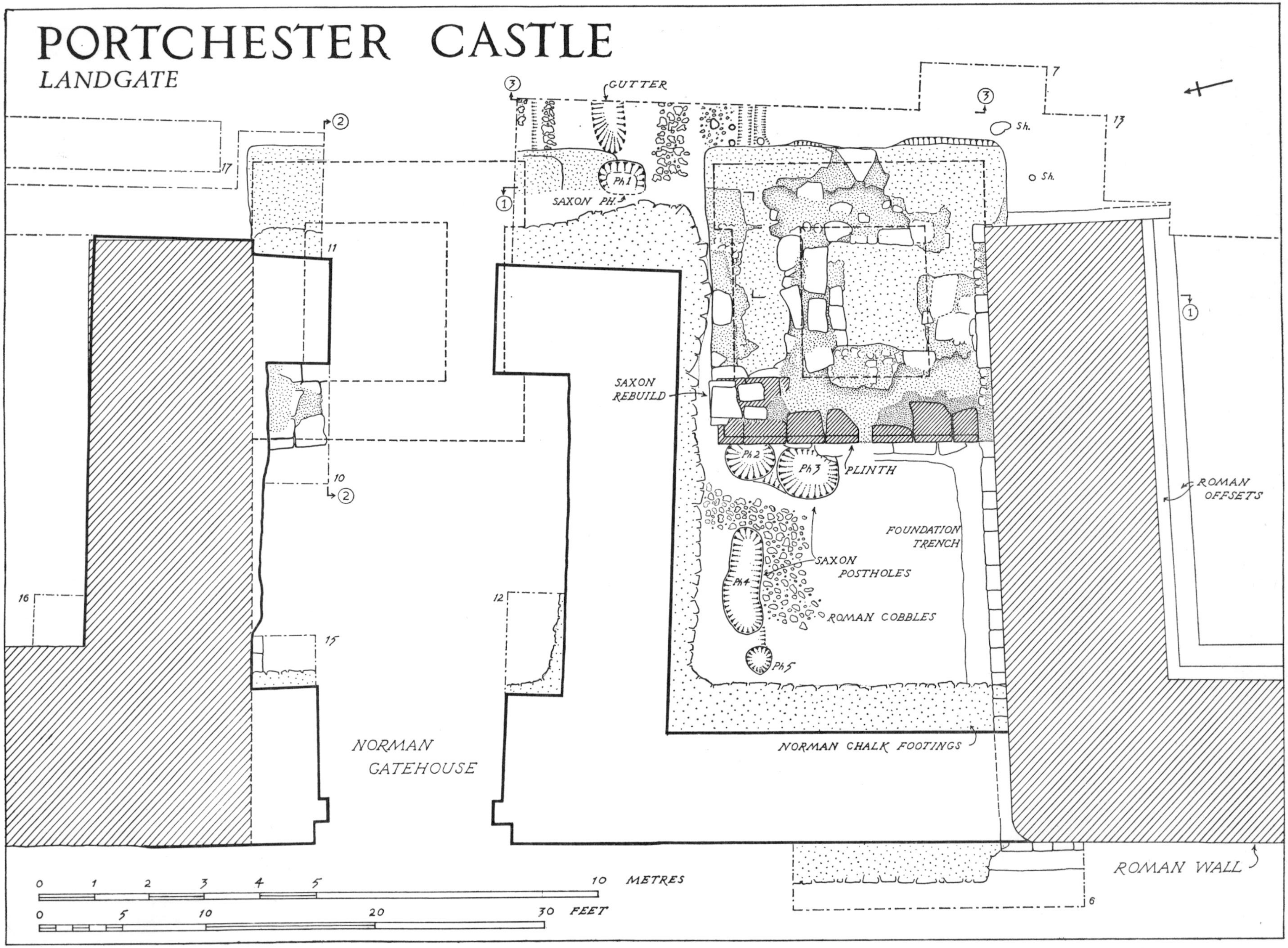
PORTCHESTER CASTLE
LANDGATE
GUTTER
SAXON PH.
Ph1
Ph2
Ph3
Ph4
Ph5
Sh.
Sh.
SAXON REBUILD
PLINTH
FOUNDATION TRENCH
SAXON POSTHOLES
ROMAN COBBLES
ROMAN OFFSETS
NORMAN CHALK FOOTINGS
NORMAN GATEHOUSE
ROMAN WALL
0 1 2 3 4 5 10 METRES
0 5 10 20 30 FEET

Fig. 15

The northern flanking wall is now incorporated in the north wall of the Norman gate. In the inner corner, the Roman work is still visible several feet above present ground level. A trial trench (trench 16) dug in the corner angle showed that the faces of the original Roman work were well preserved below the recent ground surface. Trench 15 demonstrated the existence of an external slab-surfaced offset at a depth of 3 ft. (0·9 m.) below the modern road. The only other point at which the Roman work was exposed was in trench 11, dug against the east end of the inturn, where six courses of Roman masonry survived below the level of the Norman refacing. The north-east corner of the inturn was built in limestone slabs, but no bonding courses showed in the five now remaining. In all probability the Roman core survives to a considerable height encased within the Norman refacing.

*The Gatehouse* (pls. XX, XXI)

The gatehouse was set back between the internal flanking walls. It consisted of two rectangular guard-chambers, between which ran a roadway 10 ft. (3·1 m.) wide. The road would have been spanned by a vault which would have allowed a second storey to the gatehouse, providing a fighting platform on its roof.

Each guard-chamber was built on a platform of tightly rammed chalk and clay laid in a foundation pit more than 2 ft. (0·6 m.) deep: the platforms measured approximately 18 ft. (5·5 m.) square, and were finished at a uniform flat surface between 8 and 11 in. (20–28 cm.) below the level of the natural brickearth.

The southern guard-chamber, which was totally excavated, provided details of the next stage of construction. Around the west, north and east side of the platform a wide foundation course was laid, composed of blocks of greensand and chalk set in cream-coloured mortar. The foundation butted up to the inturned wall, and its top was level with the surface of the natural brickearth. The space enclosed was then partially filled with layers of greensand chippings and clay, leaving a gap along the face of the inturned wall which was later packed with greensand rubble and mortar to form a solid base for the south wall of the guard chamber. On the new platform thus created, the first course of the superstructure was laid.

The only part of the superstructure now to survive is the basal course of the west wall of the southern guard-chamber, consisting of neatly cut greensand blocks, with chamfered corners, forming a plinth. The line of the wall face was set back, its position still recognizable by the fact that rain water with iron salts in solution had dripped on to the exposed plinth, discolouring it brown, leaving the area once beneath the wall fresh in colour and unweathered. The observation also implies that ferruginous sandstone was used in the superstructure, presumably to provide a decorative effect. Fragments of sandstone were found in the collapsed rubbish filling the guard-chamber.

The nature of the superstructure is a matter for speculation. It might be supposed, however, that a second storey, provided with windows, was surmounted by an embattled roof, the details being picked out in tiles, while the basic building material was flint. Some idea of how the structure may have appeared is given in fig. 16.

The interior of the guard-chamber was floored with trampled greensand chippings, and was provided with a single hearth. The door leading into the ground floor of the chamber must have been in the east wall, but no trace of it now survives, except for an area of wear on the surface outside. Presumably a ladder provided access to the first floor.

FIG. 16. Roman landgate: axonometric reconstruction.

Only a small part of the northern guard-chamber was available for excavation, but it would appear that much of the superstructure had been robbed, except for the western wall close to the inturned wall where three courses of greensand blocks of the foundation level still survived.

There is little to be said of the form of the gates themselves, although it is clear that projecting responds would have required the front gates to be set back by some 2 ft. (0·6 m.). If similar responds were provided at the rear of the entrance passage, the recesses created would have been of sufficient size to allow half gates to swing back into them, thus providing unimpeded passage.

It will be evident from the above description and from the plan (fig. 15) that the guard-chambers were built after the inturned curtain wall. Several points, however, suggest that no significant period of time elapsed between the two acts. Some element of planning is implied by the fact that the basal blocks in the inturned wall were not continued far beyond the point at which the guard-chamber was abutted. Since basal blocks were a consistent feature throughout, wherever the wall face was exposed to wear, their deliberate omission might be thought to suggest that the builders were aware of the impending gatehouse construction. A second point of importance is that the foundation trench for both the in-turned wall and the south guard-chambers was continuous, while the mortar spills and builders' debris derived from the erection of the guardhouse were indistinguishable from mortar slopping dropped when the inturned walls were built. Had there been a time lag one would have expected an erosion level or even soil accumulation to separate the two phases. A final point suggestive of the same conclusion is that the mortar rendering of the inturned wall, where it was protected by the abutted guard-chamber, was in a completely unweathered condition, in contrast to the exposed wall face, where different degrees of erosion are apparent.

The evidence for a broad contemporaneity is therefore impressive. The most reasonable explanation for the differences both in building technique and phasing is that gate building was reserved for a more specialist group of workmen, who began their task after the wall building gangs had completed the flanking walls. Such a division of labour is well within the realms of credibility.

## The Courtyard and the Road

The area around the gatehouse was covered with greensand chippings and spills of mortar dropped and trampled at the time of construction: indeed, so much waste survives that it must be supposed that the greensand blocks for the superstructure of the gatehouse were trimmed on the spot. The courtyard was covered to a thickness of 3–6 in. (7·6–15 cm.), between the gatehouses the depth increased to almost 1 ft. (30 cm.), while on the east side of the gate the thickness averaged 1–3 in. (2·5–7·6 cm.). One obvious advantage of leaving such a layer in position was that it would have improved the drainage of the entrance, at the same time serving as an efficient bonding material for the road metalling spread on top of it.

Very little of the metalling now survives, but between the gates it consists of a single layer of large flint nodules packed in finer gravel. Metalling of a similar kind was spread out across the courtyard, leaving the inner corners unsurfaced. There is no evidence of large scale remetalling, but limited patching may have been undertaken: absence of evidence is not significant in an area so disturbed by later features. Once inside the fort, the road was metalled with large flints, and was provided with a central gutter which ended in line with the inner face of the gatehouse.

## Occupation and Destruction Levels associated with the Gate

On the east side of the north guard chamber a thick layer of occupation material had been allowed to accumulate to a depth of about 1 ft. 6 in. (0·46 m.). A similar layer was found to the east of the south guard-chamber associated with two shallow gullies flanking the road and a series of stake holes (fig. 15). Within the south guard-chamber a 9 in.- (23 cm.-) thick layer of grey soil mixed with occupation debris (layer 4) was sealed between the floor and the mortar rubble representing the collapse of the superstructure. A similar layer also occurred in the south-east angle of the courtyard, where rubbish reached a thickness of

4

8 in. (20·3 cm.). In all three areas, the occupation layer must have formed during the period between the construction of the fort and the time when the superstructure began to disintegrate. It therefore represents a continuous process uninterrupted by any major phase of building activity. Taken together with the absence of any evidence for structural alterations or even reflooring, the strong impression is given that the gate, once built, remained untouched throughout its life.

After a period of time during which the superstructure eroded and partly collapsed, giving rise to a thick layer of mortary rubble, the walls of the gatehouse were robbed of much of the greensand masonry. A sherd of grass-tempered pottery found in the robber trench confirms that the robbing was not undertaken before the Saxon period.

### Small Finds from the West Gate

*From occupation layers against north face of Roman gate* (11 layer 3 and 17 layer 3).

| Bronze coin | (31) | Constantius I (A.D. 306–37) |
| | (32) | Gratian (A.D. 367–87) |
| Shale bracelet | (33) | decorated, fig. 122, no. 139 |
| Shale spindle whorl | (35) | not illustrated |

*From collapsed rubble outside east wall of south guard chamber* (110 layers 4 and 16).

| Bronze coin | (2573) | Valentinian II (A.D. 388–92) |
| | (2584) | House of Theodosius (A.D. 388–402) |
| Bronze spoon handle | (2575) | not illustrated |
| Bronze fragments | (2576, 2586, 2587) | not illustrated |

*From collapsed rubble in the guard chamber* (110 layer 12).

| Bronze coin | (2569) | House of Constantine (A.D. 350–60) |

*From occupation level in the guard chamber* (110 layer 13).

| Bronze coin | (2567) | Constantine I (A.D. 330–5). |

### The East Gate (Watergate) (figs. 17, 210 and pls. XXII, XXIII)

The site of the Roman east gate is now partly occupied by the watergate, a structure erected first in the late Saxon period and modified in the fourteenth century. The late Saxon gatehouse made use of one wall of the Roman structure, but was otherwise built within the courtyard fronting the Roman gatehouse, a short length of curtain wall being necessary to join the Saxon work to the Roman fort wall.

Above ground, there is little to suggest the existence of a Roman gate, since the junction between the Saxon and Roman work has been obscured by medieval repointing and refacing. It was at one time argued that the late Saxon gatehouse was in fact a standing Roman structure up to the level of the top of the arch (Butler, 1955). The only hint, before excavation, that this was unlikely to be so was provided by a consideration of the spacing of the gate in relation to the bastions. That it was eccentric in an otherwise regular structure might have suggested a post-Roman date.

Excavations carried out in 1962 and 1963 exposed the north guard-chamber of the Roman

# PORTCHESTER CASTLE

## WATERGATE

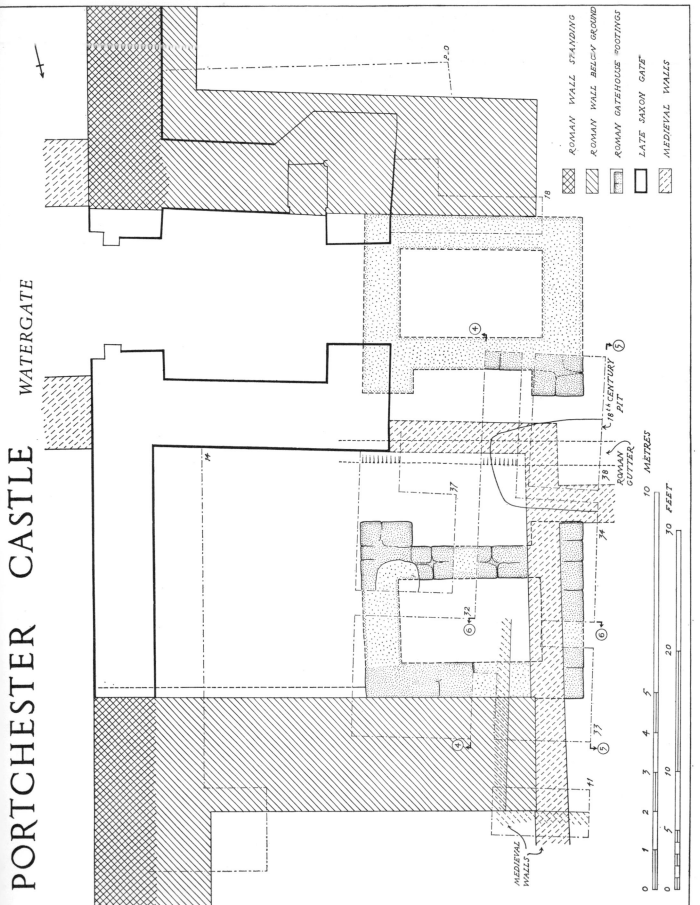

ROMAN WALL STANDING
ROMAN WALL BELOW GROUND
ROMAN GATEHOUSE FOOTINGS
LATE SAXON GATE
MEDIEVAL WALLS

FIG. 17

gate, together with the adjacent inturned wall, and established the position of the south guard chamber. A limited excavation undertaken in the churchyard in 1969 uncovered part of the south inturned wall.

The Roman east gate, like the west gate, consisted of three elements, the gatehouse, a fronting courtyard, and flanking walls inturned at right angles to the fort wall.

## The Inturned Flanking Walls (pls. XXII, XXIII)

The full width of the fort wall was inturned into the fort for a distance of 37 ft. (11·3 m.), to form the flanking walls of the courtyard. They were built of coursed flint, chalk and limestone rubble, with a basal layer of limestone blocks and a ground level foundation offset capped with limestone slabs. A double bonding course of flanged roof tiles was provided in the north inturned wall at a height of 6 ft. (1·8 m.) above the offset. The external corners of the inturns were constructed in limestone quoins.

## The Gatehouse

The two guard chambers of the gatehouse were built on a continuous platform of rammed chalk blocks, 19 ft. (5·8 m.) wide, running between the flanking walls. The greensand blocks constituting the lowest course of the superstructure were laid directly on the foundation, set in a bedding of cream-coloured mortar. Although subsequent robbing had totally removed the superstructure, the impressions of the blocks could still be traced in their mortar bedding and in places small fragments of greensand were found to be adhering to it. The plan of the guard-houses, thus obtained, showed them to be rectangular with their inner walls recessed so as to accommodate inward swinging gates.

The interior of the northern guard-chamber was made up with a layer of greensand chippings (layer 20), upon which lay a hearth of tiles associated with a thin occupation layer (layer 19). The hearth was later heightened by the addition of clay packing, and another surfacing of tiles (layer 18). Thereafter, soil containing occupation material accumulated (layers 17 and 15), interspersed with a lens of mortary rubble (layer 16).

The presence of a roadway still in use running through the late Saxon gatehouse prevented the excavation of the southern guard-chamber.

## Comparison between the East and West Gates

Sufficient will have been said to show that the two gates were closely similar in size, plan and constructional detail. The west gate was, however, built at a slight angle to the wall, possibly as the result of an error in the initial laying out of the inturned walls. Another difference appears in the form of the foundation work for the gatehouses: individual platforms were laid for each of the west gate guard-chambers, whereas a single continuous foundation sufficed at the east gate. At the west gate the top of the foundation platform seems to have been too low, with the result that a foundation course of greensand blocks had to be laid before the basal course. The error was not repeated at the east gate. Apart from these small differences, the gates show striking similarities.

The discovery that ironstone was used at the west gate raises the possibility that the ironstone incorporated in the late Saxon watergate may have been derived from its Roman predecessor. While the possibility must remain, it cannot be proved.

*Small Finds from the East Gate*

*From occupation layers within the guard chamber*

| Bone pin | (37) | fig. 116, no. 81 | (32 layer 12) |
|---|---|---|---|
|  | (38) | fig. 116, no. 83 | (33 layer 9) |
|  | (39) | fig. 116, no. 89 | (34 layer 18) |

# THE DITCHES

## (figs. 6 and 218)

The Roman fort is at present defended on the north, south and part of the west sides by a ditch which was dug in the 1930s to follow as closely as possible the line of the Roman ditch. In the region around the keep, however, medieval recutting and realignment had obviously confused the situation.

To test the reliability of the pre-war clearing operations, a single trench was cut across the line of the ditch where its filling was undisturbed in front of bastion 1. The trench (trench 42) showed that the Roman ditch had been recut as a wide flat bottomed structure early in the medieval period, leaving only the lowest 2 ft. (0·6 m.) of the Roman ditch intact. Sufficient survived, however, to demonstrate that the Roman ditch was originally 6 ft. 6 in. (2 m.) deep and 14 ft. (4·3 m.) wide.

The trench was extended (as trench 43) further to the west to reveal a second Roman ditch which had escaped recutting. This outer ditch measured 6 ft. (1·8 m.) deep by 14 ft. (4·3 m.) wide. The primary filling (4 layer 4) consisted of washed-in gravelly clay, overlaid by a soil accumulation (layer 3) containing fragments of greensand, tile, limestone bonding slabs and large flints. Above this came a layer of clayey soil (layer 2) representing a long period of secondary silting. The layer produced two coins (nos. 42 and 43), one of Licinius (A.D. 309–24) and one of Constantius Chlorus (A.D. 293–306).

The outer ditch was sectioned in front of bastion 20 by the Ministry of Works in 1956. The drawn section (unpublished) shows that it had been 14 ft. (4·3 m.) wide, but only 4 ft. (1·2 m.) deep, with a flat bottom. It is possible, however, that the true bottom was not reached. The section was extended sufficiently far west of the outer ditch lip to show that there was no third ditch.

It is not yet known whether the double ditch system extended around the north and south sides of the fort, but in all probability it did. The treatment of the east side remains a problem, for the sea has washed away most of the evidence. Trial trenching on the sea shore was inconclusive, but it seems likely that the fort, as originally designed, was defended by its double ditch system on all four sides, and may indeed have been sited some distance from the contemporary shore line.

No evidence survives to demonstrate the nature of the ditch crossings at the main gates: the presence of a modern road through the landgate rules out the possibility of excavation, but if the 1930s clearance work can be trusted to follow accurately the Roman inner ditch, any exit from the postern gates would have been by bridge. A similar arrangement might well have existed at the main gates.

# III. THE INTERIOR AREA: ESTABLISHMENT OF A SEQUENCE

## INTRODUCTION

THE largest area to be excavated lay within the south-west quarter of the walled enclosure, immediately adjacent to the Roman street leading from the centre of the fort to the south postern gate. Between 1964 and 1972 some 40,600 ft². (3772 m.²) were cleared, leaving only occasional baulks between one season's work and another. The area had been intensively occupied from the end of the third century until the second decade of the nineteenth century, the post-Roman activity resulting in considerable disturbance of the earlier levels. An indication of the overall complex of features is given by fig. 18 which should be compared with fig. 20, upon which only Roman features are shown.

For ease of description, the area has been divided into three sections: A, B and C. Area A occupies the area adjacent to the fort wall, where the Roman levels are best preserved; Area B has been affected by Saxon ploughing, which has left little of the Roman stratigraphy intact, while Area C, close to the main through road, has suffered considerably from ploughing, pit digging and the destructive effects of wheeled traffic (pl. XXVIII*b*). Thus Area A is of crucial importance for the establishment of a dated sequence within the Roman period, while areas B and C have relatively little to add.

In the sections to follow, the sequence in Area A is described in two parts, first the layers against the wall, and second the roads and make-up layers which can be related to them. After each section a complete list of small finds is given together with details of the stratified pottery: the animal bones are described elsewhere (pp. 378–408). The discussion of Area A is completed with a list of stratified coins and a summary of the dating evidence (p. 59).

The assessments of sequence in areas B and C are much shorter. Since the only stratigraphy is related to individual features rather than to layers, discussion of the stratified finds is reserved for later consideration. Over most of these areas the Roman occupation level, where it survives, is unsealed and often shows signs of disturbance by ploughing and other agricultural activities, as well as by pit digging. Finds and pottery from this general layer are not separately listed, but appear in the specialist discussions.

## AREA A: THE BUILD-UP OF LAYERS AGAINST THE FORT WALL
### (figs. 22, 23)

The principal evidence for the establishment of a chronological sequence within the Roman period comes from the series of closely stratified layers which accumulated against the inner face of the south wall of the Roman fort. The survival of, in some places, up to 5 ft. (1·5 m.) of undisturbed Roman deposits is due to three factors: the deliberate tipping of clay at certain times during the occupation; the constant spreading of refuse in the area; and the sporadic

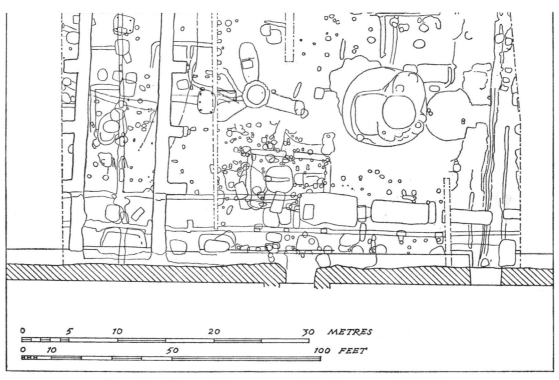

0        5       10                 20                      30     METRES

0      10                50                       100  FEET

FIG. 18.   General plan summarizing features of all dates

*facing p.* 38

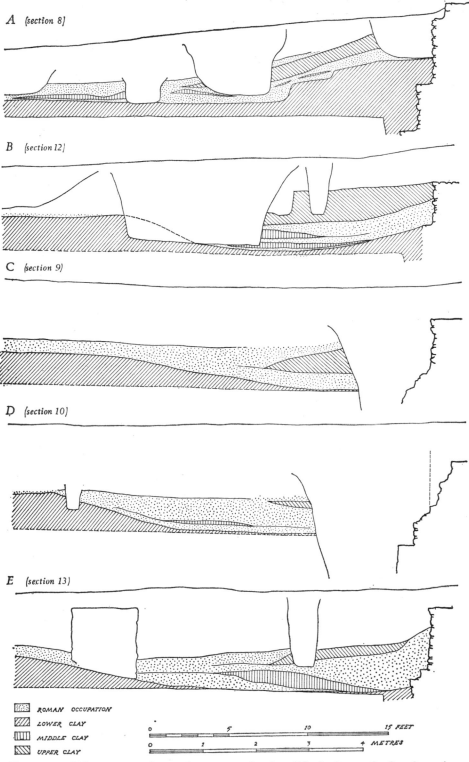

A (section 8)

B (section 12)

C (section 9)

D (section 10)

E (section 13)

ROMAN OCCUPATION
LOWER CLAY
MIDDLE CLAY
UPPER CLAY

0        5        10        15 FEET
0    1    2    3    4 METRES

FIG. 19.   Diagrammatic sections, greatly simplified, through the deposits
against the south wall of the fort

collapse of sections of the wall facing. Added to this is the fact that agricultural activity in the Saxon and medieval period had, of necessity, to leave the area immediately adjacent to the wall unploughed to provide sufficient room for the headlands.

The sequence of levels is best understood by reference to the five simplified diagrammatic sections (fig. 19) which emphasize, above all, the considerable variability over the area excavated. Broadly speaking, there were three periods during which layers of clay were laid down, each followed by a time when occupation rubbish accumulated.

### Period 1: the Lower Clay Bank (pl. XXVIb)

A consistent layer of redeposited brickearth and chalk marl covered most of the area. The bulk of this material was presumably derived from the digging of the foundation trench for the wall — a process which would have yielded some $9 \cdot 3$ yd³. of spoil for every linear yard of wall footing. In trenches 102 and 103 this clay was heaped up to form a low bank not exceeding 2 ft. 6 in. ($0 \cdot 76$ m.) high and of maximum width 20 ft. (6 m.). To some extent it compensated for the natural slope of the land, creating a level platform which suddenly sloped off towards the wall along its southern extremity. This arrangement was maintained right up to the edge of the road leading to the south postern gate, but closer to the road (in trenches 107 and 91) additional thicknesses of clay and marl were piled up between the initial bank and the back face of the wall so that (in section A for example) the bank, instead of sloping off towards the wall, actually increased in thickness to form a rampart piled against the wall face. Although the nature of the tip lines show that there were two distinct phases in the construction process, there was no significant time gap between them, both being carried out as part of a unified plan. The additional volume of material needed to create this 'rampart' may have been derived from the digging of the ditches, since it could easily have been brought in through the gate.

Wherever the original ground surface was examined beneath the clay layer, it was found to be without trace of disturbance or occupation, with the exception of a single area in trenches 88 and 89. Here the tail of the lower clay was found to overly an irregular quarry hollow (later substantially destroyed by the Saxon well, pit 135). The quarry consisted of a series of intercut scoops dug to depths averaging 2 ft. 6 in. to 3 ft. 6 in. ($0 \cdot 75-1 \cdot 1$ m.), filled with redeposited brickearth, occasional flints and a few sherds of coarse ware. The simplest explanation of this feature is that it represents an operation aimed at the collection of suitable brickearth for the manufacture of the daub walls of timber and daub buildings erected at the time of the fort's construction.

To summarize, the sequence of work involved in the building programme was:

(a) the quarrying of clay, probably for building;
(b) the digging of the foundation trench for the wall and the spreading of the spoil in a low bank;
(c) the construction of the wall;
(d) the creation of a low rampart between the bank and the wall close to the postern gate.

As we have said, this work is likely to have been part of a continuous process and to have occupied only a short period of time.

Absolute dating is dependent upon two pieces of direct evidence: the first is a coin of Gallienus (no. 1373) found in the filling of the quarry hollow, thus dating the construction to in or after the bracket A.D. 260–8. The second depends on the interpretation of the layers sealing the clay bank in the area of trench 108 (see section B). Here, in the hollow between the bank and the wall, a very thin layer of soil was allowed to accumulate, representing little more than an erosion surface on which some mortar and occupation material had fallen: in all the layer (108 layer 231) seldom exceeded 2 in. (5 cm.) at its thickest, and for the most part was usually $\frac{1}{2}$ in. (1 cm.) thick. It was sealed by a mass of clean clay (108 layers 225, 230), reaching a maximum thickness of 4 ft. (1·22 m.) in the centre of trench 108, but thinning out to nothing at the east and west edges (in section B it just appears). One observation of some significance is that the clay was deposited around the scaffold posts (p. 19). which were still standing at the time. It is reasonable then to suggest that the clay was tipped into position at a very early stage in the fort's existence, possibly as the last act in the construction process following the completion of the wall. Adding this to the phasing given above, we have:

(e)   completion of construction work;
(f)   deposition of clay to fill part of the hollow against the wall.

Phase (e) (that is, 108 layer 231) produced two coins, one of Tetricus I (2602), the other of Carausius (2603).

## Period 2: the Lower Occupation

Following the construction phase, tips of occupation material were allowed to accumulate over the period 1 clay bank, varying in thickness from place to place. It was during this period that pits 222, 223, 230, 234, serving largely as cesspits, were dug into the lower clay. An isolated timber structure belonging to this period was discovered in trench 102. It consisted of two vertical stakes 6 in. (15 cm.) in diameter and 4 ft. (1·22 m.) apart rammed into the clay bank to a depth of 1 ft. (0·31 m.). To the north of them was the seating for two horizontal timbers. If all four are part of the same structure, it may be supposed that the verticals were intended to support the ends of the horizontals. Suitably boarded across, this framework could have functioned as a projecting platform sited so as to facilitate the tipping of rubbish in the immediate vicinity.

Dating depends upon the interpretation of the single coin of Tetricus I found in the general occupation spread together with the coin of Licinius from pit 222, the two coins, one of Crispus and one of Constantine I from pit 223, and the coin of Constantine I from pit 230; the evidence is discussed in some detail on pp. 59–61 in relation to the coin sequences from the other related layers.

## Period 3: the Middle Clay

The spread of decaying occupation rubbish and open cesspits which lay at its deepest in the hollow between the clay bank and the fort wall was soon partly sealed by a layer of clean redeposited brickearth averaging 1 ft. to 1 ft. 6 in. (0·31–0·46 m.  at its thickest. Its extent can best be appreciated by reference to fig. 19.

The section of clay bank in trench 107 (i.e. approaching the postern gate), where no hollow existed in the preceding period, was covered only with discontinuous lenses of clay of the same period as the main deposit. It was in this area that a simple rectangular timber structure had been erected, terraced partly into the slope of the clay bank (fig. 20). The six posts of which it was built were set in holes varying in depth from 1 ft. to 1 ft. 6 in. (0·31–0·46 m.). Each row of three timbers presumably formed the structure to which some kind of vertical planking was attached. Outside the southern wall, the space between the wall itself and the cut back face of the clay bank was packed with flints and sealed by a layer of clean clay. The area outside the northern wall was spread with an area of similar clay.

The function of the structure is impossible to discern from internal evidence, but its position in relation to the road and postern might suggest that it served as some kind of guard chamber.

### Period 4: the Middle Occupation

The period following the deposition of the middle clay saw the accumulation of the greatest quantity of occupation rubbish against the wall. Even in its rotted down and compacted state, in some places it exceeded $1\frac{1}{2}$ ft. (0·46 m.) in thickness. It was in this period that pits 195, 209, 224, 225, 227, 228 and 229 were dug. The content of this massive rubbish accumulation included a great deal of broken pottery, masses of animal bones, oyster shells and occasional fragments of tile. The relative lack of building material and the great preponderance of kitchen debris strongly suggest that the layer represents a period of intensive occupation, but one during which little or no rebuilding was undertaken.

Four coins were recovered from the general layer: one of Carausius or Allectus and three of Constantine I. Pit 227 produced a coin of Constantine I.

### Period 5: the Upper Clay

A major tidying up operation followed with the deposition of a considerable volume of clean brickearth forming a seal overlying the rubbish. The general effect of this action was to complete the filling of the hollow against the wall and to create a uniform sloping rampart.

### Period 6: the Upper Occupation

After the final attempt to impose some order in this otherwise squalid region of the fort, more occupation material was eventually allowed to accumulate. The extent of this layer will however never be known, since there is likely to have been extensive post-Roman disturbance of the uppermost levels, particularly on the sloping rampart where the natural agencies of rain and weathering would have caused erosion.

The upper occupation material produced no less than 12 coins, including four of the late third century, six dating to A.D. 300–40 and one issue each of Gratian (A.D. 367–75) and the House of Theodosius (A.D. 388–402).

### List of Finds from Layers against the Fort Wall

The finds are listed below according to their period. At the beginning of each list a schedule of the component trench and layer numbers is given. The number in brackets is the small find number.

*Period* 1 : *occupation lens within the lower clay* — trench 108 layer 231.

| | | | |
|---|---|---|---|
| Bronze coin | (2602) | Tetricus I (A.D. 270–3) | (trench 108 layer 231) |
| Bronze coin | (2603) | Carausius (A.D. 286–93) | (trench 108 layer 231) |

*Period* 2 : *the Lower Occupation* — trench 91 layers 51, 55
trench 102 layers 32, 66
trench 103 layer 87
trench 107 layer 61
trench 108 layers 205, 202

| | | | |
|---|---|---|---|
| Bronze coin | (2484) | Tetricus I (A.D. 270–3) | (107 layer 61) |
| Bronze fragment | (2585) | not illustrated | (108 layer 205) |
| Bone pin | (2294) | as nos. 81–5, not illustrated | (103 layer 87) |
| | (2585) | as nos. 81–5, not illustrated | (108 layer 205) |
| | (2552) | as nos. 81–5, not illustrated | (108 layer 205) |
| Iron knife | (2295) | fig. 126, no. 196 | (103 layer 87) |

*Period* 3 : *the Middle Clay* — trench 91 layer 50
trench 102 layers 28, 65
trench 103 layers 85, 86
trench 107 layers 53, 73
trench 108 layers 225, 230, 206, 210

| | | | |
|---|---|---|---|
| Bone pin | (2123) | shaft only, not illustrated | (102 layer 65) |
| | (2480) | shaft only, not illustrated | (107 layer 53) |
| Worked antler | (2436) | roughly shaped tine, pl. XXXIII*f* | (107 layer 53) |
| Whetstone | (2609) | not illustrated: no. 348 | (108 layer 225) |

*Period* 4 : *the Middle Occupation* — trench 91 layers 48, 49
trench 102 layers 24, 25, 26, 27, 60, 63
trench 103 layers 77
trench 107 layers 52, 60
trench 108 layers 124, 163, 187.

| | | | |
|---|---|---|---|
| Bronze coin | (2118) | Carausius or Allectus (A.D. 286–96) | (102 layer 63) |
| Bronze coin | (2457) | Constantine I (A.D. 310–7) | (107 layer 52) |
| | (2508) | Constantine I (A.D. 321–4) | (108 layer 124) |
| | (2461) | Constantine I (A.D. 310–7) | (107 layer 52) |
| Bronze bracelet | (2526) | twisted wire type, not illustrated | (108 layer 163) |
| | (2531) | twisted wire type, not illustrated | (108 layer 163) |
| Bronze fragments | (2148) | | |
| | (2150, | | |
| | 2117, | | |
| | 2149, | | |
| | 2158, | | |
| | 2116) | not illustrated | (102 layer 60) |
| | (2119) | not illustrated | (102 layer 63) |
| | (2463) | not illustrated | (107 layer 52) |
| | (2555) | not illustrated | (108 layer 163) |

| Bone pin | (2598) | as nos. 81–5, not illustrated | (108 layer 163) |
|---|---|---|---|
| | (2551) | as nos. 81–5, not illustrated | (108 layer 163) |
| | (2455) | as nos. 81–5, not illustrated | (107 layer 52) |
| | (2443) | as nos. 81–5, not illustrated | (107 layer 52) |
| | (2439) | as nos. 81–5, not illustrated | (107 layer 52) |
| | (2456) | as no. 87, not illustrated | (107 layer 52) |
| | (2553) | fig. 116, no. 95 | (108 layer 163) |
| | (2544) | as above, not illustrated | (108 layer 163) |
| Bone bracelet | (2147) | fig. 117, no. 99 | (102 layer 63) |
| Antler object | (2460) | tine cut with basal perforation, pl. XXXIII*b* | (107 layer 52) |
| | | Also sawn antler from trench 108 layer 163 | |
| Shale bracelet | (2120) | plain, external dia. 7·7 cm., not illustrated | (102 layer 63) |
| Iron awl | (2122) | fig. 128, no. 213 | (102 layer 60) |
| Whetstone | (2458) | not illustrated, no. 350 | (107 layer 52) |
| Nails | | 1, 5·1 cm.+ | (102 layer 63) |
| Daub | | see p. 73 | (108 layer 163) |
| Painted plaster | | see p. 73 | (102 layer 60) |

*Period 5: the Upper Clay* — trench 91 layer 35
trench 102 layers 22, 62
trench 103 layers 46, 74
trench 107 layer 50
trench 108 layer 111

| Bronze spoon | (2450) | bowl only, not illustrated | (107 layer 50) |
|---|---|---|---|
| Bronze bracelet | (2438) | horizontal strip type, not illustrated | (107 layer 50) |
| Shale bracelet | (2459) | plain fragment, not illustrated | (107 layer 50) |
| Iron leaf hook | (2520) | fig. 128, no. 217 | (108 layer 111) |
| Whetstone | (2293) | not illustrated, no. 352 | (103 layer 74) |

*Period 6: the Upper Occupation layer* — trench 91 layer 26
trench 102 layers 33, 44, 46, 48
trench 103 layer 23
trench 107 layer 21, 31, 41, 44
trench 108 layers 62, 72, 73, 86, 90, 95, 99, 100, 118

| Bronze coin | (2403) | Galerius (A.D. 303–9) | (107 layer 41) |
|---|---|---|---|
| | (2481) | Victorinus (A.D. 268–70) | (108 layer 62) |
| | (2500) | Constantine I (A.D. 310–17) | (108 layer 62) |
| | (2521) | Tetricus II (A.D. 270–3) | (108 layer 100) |
| | (2074) | Carausius (A.D. 286–93) | (102 layer 33) |
| | (2096) | Carausius (A.D. 286–93) | (102 layer 48) |
| | (2075) | Constantine I (A.D. 335–7) | (102 layer 33) |
| | (2098) | Constans (A.D. 335–7) | (102 layer 48) |
| | (2209) | Constantine II (A.D. 335–7) | (103 layer 23) |
| | (2222) | Urbs Roma (A.D. 330–45) | (103 layer 23) |

|  |  |  |  |
|---|---|---|---|
|  | (2477) | Gratian (A.D. 367–75) | (108 layer 86) |
|  | (2105) | House of Theodosius (A.D. 388–402) | (102 layer 48) |
| Bronze bracelet | (2115) | strip type: not illustrated | (102 layer 48) |
|  | (2483) | strip type: not illustrated | (108 layer 62) |
|  | (2077) | strip type: not illustrated | (102 layer 44) |
|  | (2214) | wire type: not illustrated | (103 layer 23) |
| Bronze tweezers | (2482) | not illustrated | (107 layer 31) |
| Bronze buckle | (2106) | fig. 110, no. 21 | (102 layer 48) |
| Bronze pin | (2279) | fig. 114, no. 71 | (103 layer 23) |
| Bronze discs | (2505) | fig. 110, no. 23 | (108 layer 99) |
| Bronze ring | (2407) | fig. 112, no. 47 | (107 layer 41) |
| Bronze strip | (2224) | 7 cm. long, plain: not illustrated | (103 layer 23) |
| Bronze rod | (2411) | 5 cm. long: not illustrated | (107 layer 44) |
| Bronze fragment | (2223) | sheet: not illustrated | (103 layer 23) |
| Bone pin | (2410) | as no. 84, not illustrated | (107 layer 44) |
| Bone pin | (2406) | shaft, not illustrated | (107 layer 41) |
| Bone pin | (2280) | shaft, not illustrated | (103 layer 23) |
| Bone spindle-whorl | (2405) | fig. 117, no. 106 | (107 layer 41) |
| Antler | | sawn fragments from 102 layer 46, 107 layer 31, 108 layers 72, 90 and 99. | |
| Shale bracelet | (2518) | plain fragment, not illustrated | (108 layer 90) |
| Iron ring and tie | (2499) | fig. 129, no. 226 | (108 layer 62) |
| Iron chisel? | (2412) | fig. 131, no 262 | (107 layer 44) |
| Iron spear or arrow | (2104) | fig. 124, no. 179 | (102 layer 48) |
| Iron fragments | (2408) | not illustrated | (107 layer 41) |
|  | (2432) | not illustrated | (107 layer 44) |
|  | (2282) | not illustrated | (103 layer 23) |
| Iron slag | | not illustrated (p. 265) | (108 layer 99) |
| Lead sheet | (2100) | 7·7 by 2·8 cm. with a perforation at each end; not illustrated | (102 layer 48) |
| Whetstone | (2431) | not illustrated, no. 359 | (107 layer 44) |
| Whetstone | (2097) | not illustrated, no. 349 | (102 layer 48) |
| Whetstone | (2283) | not illustrated, no. 362 | (103 layer 23) |
| Glass vessels | | cf. fig. 197, no. 9 | (103 layer 23) |
| Window glass | | fig. 199, no. 23 | (103 layer 23) |

*List of Pottery from the Layers against the Fort Wall*

by MICHAEL FULFORD

A quantitative assessment of the pottery from the stratified layers behind the fort wall is given below, together with a general comment on each group. The layers constituting each level have been listed above (pp. 43–5). The type numbers in italics indicate sherds drawn in the main type series. For discussions of the fabrics and grouping according to production centre, see pp. 280–301.

*Period 1 : from the lower clay bank*

*New Forest:* 22.1–5; weight, 20 g.; 16·0%.
*Oxford:* 15.1.
*Hand-made, fabric A:* 123(2); weight, 105 g.; 84·0%.
Total weight: 125 g.

This is the earliest group from the fort, and unfortunately the smallest. It dates from the construction of the fort and is important in that it shows the presence of not only the crude 'grog' tempered wares from the late third century, but also the New Forest and Oxford fabrics.

*Period 2 : the lower occupation*

*New Forest:* Fabric 1: *2/10.18*, 2/10.21, 23, 22.1–5(5); weight, 260 g.; 3·10%.
Fabric 2: 43(4); weight, 450 g.; 5·36%.
Fabric 3: 49, *56.2*, *66.1*; weight, 330 g.; 3·93%.
Total weight: 1040 g.; 12·38%.
*Oxford:* Fabric 1: 30.2, 43, 58; weight, 90 g.; 1·07%.
Fabric 2: 14.
Fabric 3: weight, 40 g.; 0·48%.
Total weight: 130 g.; 1·54%.
*Misc.:* 46, *68.1*; weight, 15 g.; 0·18%.
*Hand-made, fabric A:* 86(7), *88.4*, 107(4), 123(8); weight, 2320 g.; 27·62%.
*Black-burnished:* 85(3), 107(4), 126(8); weight, 1,540 g.; 18·33%.
*Grey fabrics:* 77, 85(6), *86.6*, 107(2), 117.2(3), 119, 127(6), 128(2), 129(4), 129.4, 131.3, 132, 133(2), 137.2, 139, 140(2), 145; weight, 3355 g.; 39·94%.
Total weight of all fabrics: 8400 g.

This represents the rubbish accumulation against the wall from *c.* A.D. 300–*c.* A.D. 325, and, with pit 230, is the only pottery that can securely be dated to this phase.

*Period 3 : the middle clay*

*New Forest:* Fabric 1: 2/10.22–25(3), 19.1–3, 22.1–5, 43, sherd of 49; weight, 260 g.; 7·2%
Fabric 2: 43; Weight, 40 g.; 1·1%.
Fabric 3: weight: 10 g.; 0·27%.
Total weight: 310 g.; 8·57%.
*Oxford:* 15.1.
*Hand-made, fabric A:* 86, 107(2), 123; weight, 1460 g.; 40·9%.
*Black-burnished:* 85, 107(2), 126; weight, 375 g.; 10·5%.
*Grey fabrics:* 76.6, 85(2), 103.1, 127(2), 129(3), 136, 137.2, 139, 140, 142.1–3(2), 145, 148; weight, 1420 g.; 39·8%.
Total weight: 3565 g.

This group seals the lower occupation and is in turn sealed by the middle occupation.

*Period 4 : the middle occupation*

*TS:* Dr. 33, Central Gaul, Antonine; Central Gaulish fragment, Hadrianic–early Antonine.
*New Forest:* Fabric 1: 3.1–2(3), 2/10.16, 2/10.20, 2/10.22–25(2), 13(4), 19.1–3(2), 20.1, 21.1(2), 55.10–11; weight, 1840 g.; 4·63%.

Fabric 2: 29(9), 43(11), 61; weight, 1930 g.; 4·86%.

Fabric 3: 11.1–2(2), 11.3, 48, 49(5), 53.1 (sherds of the same vessel in the layer above make-up and the upper occupation), 64(2), 65(2) (one with a join in upper occupation), 66(4); weight, 1860 g.; 4·68%.

Total weight: 5630 g.; 14·17%.

*Oxford:* Fabric 1: 35.9, 40(3), 57, 58(4); weight, 650 g.; 1·64%.

Fabric 2: 14(3), 17.10(2); weight, 25 g.; 0·06%.

Fabric 3: 63.4, 63(5); weight, 580 g.; 1·46%.

Total weight: 1255 g.; 3·16%.

*Misc.:* 1.1, 4, 7.2, 16, 27, 31.7 (with joining sherds in pit 223 and upper clay), 56.2, 55.17, 137.7, 144.2 (sherds of same vessel in upper clay), 144.3 (sherds of same vessel in upper occupation), 144.4; weight, 550 g.; 1·38%.

*Hand-made fabric A:* 86(30), 107(11), 123(24), 133(5); weight, 11,260 g.; 28·34%.

*Black-burnished:* 85(13), 107(15), 117(3), 126(18), 175; weight, 8450 g.; 21·27%.

*Grey fabrics:* 76.2, 76.4, 77.4, 77.8, 85(26), 94(2), 98.2, 100.2, 107(7), 111.3, 117.2(4), 118, 119(3), 120.2–3, 127(22), 128(2), 129(4), 129.4(9), 131.4, 131.6, 134, 136(3), 137.1, 137.2, 138, 139, 140(11), 142.1–3(4), 145(5), 152.2 (sherds of same vessel in upper clay), 153.4, 153.8, 154.6, 157, 158, 159.1–2, 159.4–5(5), 159.10, 159.7–13(2) 169, 172(2), 175(2), 178; Weight, 12,490 g.; 31·44%.

*Fabric D:* sherds only; weight, 95 g.; 0·24%.

Total Weight: 39,730 g.

These layers represent the accumulation of rubbish between *c.* A.D. 325 and *c.* A.D. 345 at the latest, though an earlier date is possible. The middle occupation is important for the small amounts of both the Oxfordshire and 'D' fabrics, and is crucial for the dating of their types.

## Period 5: *the upper clay*

*New Forest:* Fabric 1: 2/10.1, 2/10.17, 2/10.20, 21.7, 22.1–5(3); weight, 540 g.; 5·03%.

Fabric 2: 29, 29.6–7, 43(3); weight, 340 g.; 3·17%.

Fabric 3: sherds only; weight, 375 g.; 3·49%.

Total weight: 1255 g.; 11·69%.

*Oxford:* Fabric 1: 40(3) (sherds of one vessel in the upper occupation), 42, 43, 58(2); weight, 540 g.; 5·03%.

Fabric 2: 15.1–2(2); weight, 80 g.; 0·75%.

Fabric 3: no sherds.

Total weight: 620 g.; 5·78%.

*Misc.:* 30.7, 31.7, 55.2–3, 144.2 (sherds of same vessel in the middle occupation); weight, 55 g.; 0·51%.

*Hand-made, fabric A:* 86(4), 107(2), 123(14); weight, 3050 g.; 28·41%.

*Black-burnished:* 85(6), 107(2), 117.1, 126(9); weight, 2840 g.; 26·46%.

*Grey fabrics:* 76.2(2), 85(8), 94, 106, 107, 127(6), 129, 129.4(2), 129.6, 137.1, 138, 139(2), 140(5), 142.1–3(2), 142.4–5, 145, 152 (sherds of same vessel in the middle occupation), 154.6, 159.4–5; weight, 2770 g.; 25·80%.

*Fabric D:* sherds only; 145 g.; 1·35%.

Total weight: 10,735 g.

## Period 6: *the upper occupation*

*TS:* central Gaulish fragment, C2; Dr. 31, Central Gaul, Hadrianic–Antonine.

*Argonne:* Chenet 326 and 328.

*New Forest:* Fabric 1: 2/10.2, 2/10.9, 2/10.17, 2/10.19, 2/10.20, 2/10.22–25(2), 10.2–3, 13(7), 18.7, 19.1–3(2), 21.1(2), 22.1–5(8), 22.8, 52.5, 55.12, 55.20; weight, 1490 g.; 5·84%.

　　Fabric 2: 29(6), 29.6–7, 39.2, 43.9, 43(16), 44.2, 47, 50.4, 58.4; weight, 1935 g.; 7·58%.

　　Fabric 3: 49, 53.1 (sherds of same vessel in the layer above the make-up and in the middle occupation), 64(2), 65(2) (one has join in the middle occupation), 66, 105.4; weight, 640 g.; 2·51%.

Total weight: 4065 g.; 15·92%.

*Oxford:* Fabric 1: 30.6, 30.8, 34.2, 35.6, 35.8, 35.9, 36.2, 36.5, 36.16, 36.17, 42, 43.10–12(2), 43(6), 57(2), 58(6); weight, 1515 g.; 5·93%.

　　Fabric 2: 17.6, 18.2; weight, 290 g.; 1·14%.

　　Fabric 3: 63(4), 63.4(3); weight, 460 g.; 1·80%.

Total weight: 2265 g.; 8·87%.

*Pevensey:* 35.15, 42; weight, 55 g.; 0·22%.

*Misc.:* 30.2(2), 55.2–3, 56.2, 137.7, 144.3 (sherds of same vessel in middle occupation); weight, 50 g.; 0·20%.

*Hand-made, fabric A:* 86(15), 88.4, 107(11), 123(44); weight, 6045 g.; 23·68%.

*Black-burnished:* 85(20), 107(15), 117.1(2), 126(22); weight, 5240 g.; 20·52%.

*Grey fabrics:* 76.4, 76.5, 80.1, 85(9), 87.1(2), 87.5, 92, 94, 103.2, 107(10), 109.1–3(2), 117(5), 118, 119, 124.2, 127(17), 128(2), 129(5), 129.4(2), 129.5, 131.4(3), 132(2), 133(2), 134.4, 136(2), 137.2, 138, 140(8), 141, 142.1–3(8), 142.4–5, 145(3), 157, 159.3, 159.4–5, 159.11, 159.11–13(2), 160, 166.1, 172(2), 175, 176.2, 176.4, 177.1, 177.6, 179.2; weight, 7445 g.; 29·16%.

*Fabric D:* 87.2, 137.4–6(4); weight, 365 g.; 1·43%.

Total weight: 25,530 g.

　　The pottery from this group represents the rubbish accumulating above the upper clay seal after *c.* A.D. 345. It is not a sealed group and while the majority of the coins are not later than *c.* 345, there are two which put the latest date of deposition of rubbish to the very end of the fourth century. This is a surprisingly small number, and raises the possibility that the upper occupation largely represents material deposited soon after 345 rather than a gradual accumulation over half a century. In this respect it should be remembered that the upper part of the layer has been extensively eroded (p. 42). As regards the pottery, the relative quantities of each fabric are not very different from the ratios in the middle occupation and upper clay groups. As has been observed already, the latter have very little Oxfordshire and 'D' fabric types, whereas, a proportion of the pits do have these fabrics and types which fit better with those present in the upper occupation group. Furthermore, the latter group has only a little more than half the amount of material as the middle occupation group, and this would fit better the explanation that the rubbish deposits of the upper occupation largely represent a date range *c.* 340–50, rather than a gradual accumulation extending to the end of the century. From the pottery, therefore, it would be more satisfactory to see the majority of the material against the wall dating up to *c.* 345–50, with the deposition of the upper clay dating before the end of the *c.* 330–45 phase.

# AREA A: THE SEQUENCE OF ROADS AND THE MAKE-UP LAYERS

The northern half of Area A produced evidence of a simple stratified sequence which can be linked directly to the phases of the clay bank, to the remetallings of the road running to the south postern gate and to the gravel spread which lies to the west. Since these make-up layers and roads are described in some detail below (pp. 63–5) it is necessary here only to refer to their relationship to the main sequence.

## Period 1

The earliest layers, contemporary with the first clay bank, were varied in their characteristics as fig. 22 will show. In the centre was a layer of fine white chalky mortar, usually between ½ and 1 in. (1·3–2·5 cm.) in thickness, lying immediately upon the surface of the natural clay (pl. XXVII). The fact that the mortar is closely similar to that used in the fort wall strongly suggests that the layer represents the remnants of a mortar mixing area in use during the construction period. To the east and south the mortar merged with a layer of clayey gravel and chalk marl which was continuous with the tail of the clay bank in its first phase. It was this layer which sealed the filled-in quarry pits (p. 40). Further east the marl and gravel disappeared save for an occasional scatter of pebbles trampled into the natural brickearth.

In the eastern part of the site two substantial spreads of pebble metalling survived; one stretched along the slope of the clay bank, the other lay to the north of it. These layers were quite thin, consisting of water-worn pebbles, usually up to 1 in. (2·5 cm.) in diameter, trampled into natural brickearth. The layer seldom exceeded 1½ in. (3·8 cm.) in thickness and was normally even thinner.

The main road leading to the postern gate was metalled in a similar material. As it approached the gate the road metalling spread over the slope of the adjacent early period clay bank, showing that the two must be part of the same construction process, there being no time lag between the construction of the bank and the laying of the metalling. Beneath the early metalling, at the point where it ran over the footing of the wall through the gate, a coin of Gallienus was found. At all points where the relationship survived, these layers can be shown to be primary and contemporary with the early bank.

## Periods 2–4

Overlying the early make-up and gravel layers was a spread of occupation material associated with pits, gullies, hearths, and other structures described below (pp. 73–187). This activity must be contemporary with the lower occupation, middle clay and middle occupation. Seven coins were found stratified in layers of this period: one of Tetricus II; three of Carausius; one of Diocletian; and two Constantinopolis issues. Thus no coin issued after A.D. 330–5 was recovered in contexts predating period 5.

## Period 5

After the phase of occupation represented by the layers and features of periods 2–4, came a phase of constructional activity during which the main N–S road and the metalled areas

5

lying towards the western part of the site were re-surfaced (p. 64 and fig. 23). To the west of the road were found a series of discontinuous spreads of redeposited brickearth, mortar and gravel, the extent and relationship of which are best illustrated by fig. 23. The chalky mortar immediately adjacent to the road was associated with a timber building (described below p. 67). The rest appear to have limited structural significance: all the layers were thin, usually no more than 1 in. (2·5 cm.) thick, and except where they were cut by later features they were without distinctive edges.

The remetalling of the road can be shown to be stratigraphically of the same phase as the deposition of the upper clay, and since the adjacent spreads of mortar, chalk marl and clay can similarly be linked to the road resurfacing, it is possible to regard all these elements as part of the same general process of reorganization.

## *Period* 6

The make-up and metalling layers of period 5 were sealed by a deposit of general occupation material which was associated with a number of pits, gullies and minor irregular hollows. This occupation must, by definition, be broadly contemporary with the upper occupation over the clay bank, since both follow the period 5 make-up levels. It will be argued below, on the basis of the coin evidence, that period 5 should be dated to *c*. A.D. 340–5. Of the 26 coins from the period 6 occupation levels, 24 belong to the period up to *c*. 370, with only two, one of Gratian and one of Theodosius I, belonging to the later years of the fourth century. The implication would seem to be that while most of the period 6 activity took place in the 30 years of A.D. 240–70, some later occupation is clearly indicated. It must however be stressed that the period 6 levels are not sealed by distinct early Saxon deposits, although features of the fifth and sixth centuries cut through them. Indeed, over most of the area, ploughing of both the Saxon and medieval period has considerably disturbed the uppermost Roman levels. One further proviso must be added: it is not always possible to distinguish between the occupation levels of periods 2–4 and period 6 in places where the intervening deposits of period 5 are absent. This applies particularly to the western part of the area. In such cases, where only one level of occupation material is distinguishable, the finds from it have been treated with those of period 6. The potential effect of such an unavoidable procedure is to increase the apparent percentage of early material in the latest level. The extent of this is reflected in the list of coins from period 6 (p. 60) which includes six coins minted before 320. The remaining 20 minted after 320 can all reasonably be expected to have been in common use during period 6, from 345 onwards. Even the six early coins could well have remained in circulation after 340. If, then, the coins offer a reasonable guide, the amount of early material assessed with deposits of period 6 is not likely to be excessive.

### *List of Finds relating to the Roads and Make-up Layers*

For the sake of convenience four lists are offered, two relating to the make-up layers and two to the road metallings. The unique small find number of each object is given in brackets first, the trench and layer number appears later.

*Periods* 2, 3, 4: *from layers below the upper road surface* (trenches 87 and 91)

| | | | |
|---|---|---|---|
| Bronze coin | (1354) | Tetricus II (A.D. 270–3) | (87 layer 50) |
| | (1356) | Carausius (A.D. 286–93) | (91 layer 64) |
| | (1341) | Carausius (A.D. 286–93) | (91 layer 64) |
| | (1355) | Diocletian (A.D. 294–305) | (87 layer 48) |
| | (1106) | Constantinopolis type (A.D. 330–5) | (87 layer 39) |
| Silver ring | (1270) | fig. 112, no. 49 | (87 layer 48) |
| Bronze fragment | (1347) | nondescript: not illustrated | (87 layer 48) |
| Iron cleat | (1349) | much corroded: not illustrated | (87 layer 48) |
| Iron clamp | (1370) | fragment, L-shaped: not illustrated | (87 layer 48) |
| Iron rod | (1348) | shank? of nail: not illustrated | (87 layer 48) |
| Iron sheet | (1346) | fragment; not illustrated | (87 layer 48) |
| Bone pin | (1029) | shank, no head: not illustrated | (87 layer 20) |
| Bone pin | (1345) | as nos. 81–5: not illustrated | (91 layer 64) |
| Antler | (1366) | fragment showing cut marks; pl. XXXIII | (91 layer 67) |
| Whetstone | (1339) | not illustrated, no. 360 | (91 layer 65) |
| Window glass | (1362) | cf. fig. 199, no. 24 | (87 layer 50) |
| Nails | | 1, 8·25, bent; 1, 5·1, bent; 1, 8·9, bent; | |
| (measurements in cm.) | | 1, 6·35; 1, 7·6, bent; 1, 3·8 | (87 layer 10) |
| | | 1, 7·0; 1, 3·8 | (87 layer 39) |
| | | 1, 2·55+ | (87 layer 50) |
| | | 1, 6·35: head 4·453×·8 shape, 1·25 thick | (91 layer 64) |

*Periods* 2, 3, 4: *from layers beneath the upper make-up* (trenches 88, 89, 90)

| | | | |
|---|---|---|---|
| Bronze coin | (1038) | Carausius (A.D. 286–93) | (88 layer 14) |
| Bronze coin | (1368) | Constantinopolis type (A.D. 330–5) | (88 layer 50) |
| Bronze buckle | (1036) | fig. 110, no. 15 | (88 layer 14) |
| Bone pin | (1334) | shaft only; not illustrated | (88 layer 67) |
| Shale bracelet | (1304) | oval section 7 × 5 mm., external diameter 7 cm.; | |
| | | not illustrated | (88 layer 68) |
| Iron shears | (1317) | not illustrated | (89 layer 58) |
| Iron horseshoe | (1320) | not illustrated | (89 layer 58) |
| Iron knife | (1318) | not illustrated | (89 layer 58) |
| Iron rods | (1319) | two corroded together, one 8·3 cm., the other 4·2 cm., | |
| | | square cross-section; not illustrated | (89 layer 58) |
| Nails | | 1, 6·35; 1, 3·85; | (88 layer 14) |
| (measurements in cm.) | | 1, 17·8 +, shaft 1·25 thick; 1, 7·65 +; 1, 7·00; | |
| | | 1, 1·25+ | (88 layer 67) |
| | | 1, 11·45+ | (88 layer 17) |
| | | 1, 4·45 | (89 layer 67) |

*Period* 6: *from layers immediately above or cutting into upper road surface* (trenches 87 and 91)

| | | | |
|---|---|---|---|
| Bronze coin | (1096) | Carausius (A.D. 286–93) | (87 layer 27) |
| | (1019) | Constantine I (A.D. 310–13) | (87 layer 13) |
| | (1054) | Constantine I (A.D. 319) | (87 layer 27) |
| | (1081) | Constantine I (A.D. 324) | (87 layer 34) |

|  | (1290) | Constantine I (A.D. 320–4) | (87 layer 54) |
|---|---|---|---|
|  | (1084) | Crispus (A.D. 324) | (87 layer 14) |
|  | (1061) | Constans (A.D. 333–5) | (87 layer 9) |
|  | (1041) | Constantinopolis (A.D. 330–5) | (87 layer 9) |
|  | (1274) | Constantine II (A.D. 330–5) | (91 layer 46) |
|  | (1024) | Constantine II (A.D. 330–5) | (87 layer 9) |
|  | (1023) | Constantius II (A.D. 337–41) | (87 layer 9) |
|  | (1280) | Valens (A.D. 364–78) | (91 layer 46) |
|  | (1006) | Gratian (A.D. 378–83) | (87 layer 9) |
| Bronze spoon | (1337) | not illustrated | (91 layer 63) |
| Bronze fish hook | (1293) | fig. 114, no. 63 | (91 layer 52) |
| Bronze ring | (1313) | fig. 112, no. 46 | (91 layer 46) |
| Bronze pin | (1005) | fig. 113, no. 51 | (87 layer 9) |
| Bronze ring | (1042) | made of wire 1 mm. diameter; not illustrated | (87 layer 13) |
| Bronze comb | (1027) | fig. 115, no. 79 | (87 layer 9) |
| Bronze bracelet | (1305) | fig. 111, no. 24 | (91 layer 56) |
|  | (1272) | decorated, fig. 112, no. 35 | (91 layer 46) |
|  | (1288) | strip type, as nos. 40–2; not illustrated | (91 layer 46) |
|  | (1289) | two strand twisted wire; not illustrated | (91 layer 46) |
|  | (1296) | two strand twisted wire; not illustrated | (91 layer 52) |
|  | (1062) | two strand twisted wire; not illustrated | (87 layer 34) |
| Bronze sheet | (1007) | fragment; not illustrated | (87 layer 9) |
| Bronze sheet | (1282) | fragment; not illustrated | (91 layer 43) |
| Bronze strip | (1300) | fragment of plain strip 6 cm. wide | (91 layer 46) |
| Bronze rod | (1316) | 10 cm. long; not illustrated | (91 layer 53) |
| Bronze strip/rod | (1015) | 4 cm. long; not illustrated | (87 layer 9) |
| Bronze wire | (1002) | not illustrated | (87 layer 9) |
| Bronze rod | (1297) | not illustrated | (91 layer 52) |
| Bone pin | (1321) | fig. 116, no. 82 | (91 layer 46) |
| Bone pin | (1246) | as nos. 81–5; not illustrated | (91 layer 19) |
| Bone handle | (1111) | fig. 118, no. 112 associated with much corroded lumps of bronze | (87 layer 27) |
| Bone handle | (1475) | fig. 119, no. 120 | (91 layer 46) |
| Bone spatula | (1003) | fig. 119, no. 123 | (87 layer 9) |
| Shale vessel | (1389) | small fragment of base angle; not illustrated | (87 layer 9) |
| Shale bracelet | (1022) | decorated, fig. 122, no. 138 | (87 layer 9) |
| Shale bracelet | (1026) | external diameter 5·0 cm.; circular cross section; not illustrated | (87 layer 9) |
| Antler |  | sawn fragment | (91 layer 46) |
| Glass bead | (1277) | not illustrated, no. 160 | (91 layer 46) |
| Glass beads | (1298) | three, not illustrated, no. 154 | (91 layer 52) |
| Glass bead | (1133) | not illustrated, no. 153 | (87 layer 44) |
| Iron knife | (1351) | fig. 125, no. 186 | (87 layer 47) |
| Iron ladle | (1278) | fig. 131, no. 251 | (91 layer 46) |
| Iron sword tip | (1299) | fig. 124, no. 168 | (91 layer 52) |
| Iron strip or horseshoe | (1032) | fig. 130, no. 241 | (87 layer 9) |
| Iron knife | (1132) | fig. 125, no. 184 | (87 layer 41) |

| | | | |
|---|---|---|---|
| Iron ring | (1057) | fig. 131, no. 253 | (87 layer 33) |
| Iron tie | (1033) | fig. 129, no. 228 | (87 layer 9) |
| Iron chopper | (1292) | fig. 126, no. 197 | (91 layer 52) |
| Iron looped terminal | (1275) | fig. 131, no. 257 | (91 layer 46) |
| Iron fragments | (1097) | | |
| | (1134, | | |
| | 1021, | | |
| | 1058, | | |
| | 1273, | | |
| | 1291) | miscellaneous, much corroded; not illustrated | (various) |
| Iron slag | | not illustrated | (91 layer 53) |
| Polished stone axe | (1315) | Neolithic, fig. 3, no. 1 | (91 layer 46) |
| Whetstone? | (1367) | not illustrated, no. 346 | (91 layer 73) |
| Nails | | 2, 8·85+; 2, 7·6; 1, 7·6+; 1, 5·1+; 2, 5·1 | (87 layer 27) |
| (measurements in cm.) | | 1, 5·1+ | (87 layer 26) |
| | | 1, 5·1+ | (87 layer 40) |
| | | 2, 5·1, one without head | (87 layer 18) |
| | | 1, 5·1 | (87 layer 34) |
| | | 1, 6·35; 2, 3·8; 1, 1·25+; 2, 4·65; 1, 7·6; 1, 1·9+ | (87 layer 9) |
| | | 1, 3·2 | (87 layer 13) |
| | | 1, 8·9 | (91 layer 43) |
| | | 1, 12·75; 1, 8·9; 1, 8·3; 1, 6·4; 11, 5·1; 2, 3·8 | (91 layer 46) |
| | | 1, 8·3 broken in two; 1, 5·1 | (91 layer 53) |
| | | 1, 7·6; 1, 8·9; 1, 4·5; 1, 3·75 | (91 layer 55) |
| Glass vessels | | cf. fig. 197, no. 6 | (87 layer 27) |
| | | cf. fig. 197, no. 9 | (91 layer 47) |
| | | fig. 198, no. 20 | (91 layer 52) |

*Period* 6: *from layers above or cutting into the upper make-up* (trenches 88–90)

| | | | |
|---|---|---|---|
| Bronze coin | (1137) | barbarous radiate (A.D. 270–90) | (89 layer 23) |
| | (1053) | Carausius (A.D. 286–93) | (88 layer 5) |
| | (1206) | Licinius (A.D. 310–13) | (90 layer 30) |
| | (1014) | Constantine I (A.D. 310–13) | (88 layer 10) |
| | (1044) | Constantine I (A.D. 319–20) | (88 layer 10) |
| | (996) | Constantine I (A.D. 330–5) | (88 layer 5) |
| | (1153) | Urbs Roma (A.D. 330–7) | (89 layer 23) |
| | (1034) | House of Constantine (A.D. 330–45) | (88 layer 10) |
| | (1129) | Constantine II (A.D. 335–7) | (89 layer 23) |
| | (1025) | Valens (A.D. 364–78) | (88 layer 10) |
| | (1180) | Valentinian I (A.D. 364–75) | (89 layer 38) |
| | (1219) | Valentinian I (A.D. 364–75) | (90 layer 29) |
| | (997) | Theodosius I (A.D. 388–95) | (88 layer 6) |
| Bronze penannular brooch | (977) | fig. 109, no. 7 | (88 layer 5) |
| | (1000) | fig. 109, no. 6 | (88 layer 6) |
| Bronze strip bracelet | (1012) | fig. 111, no. 29 | (88 layer 6) |
| | (969) | fig. 111, no. 33 | (88 layer 5) |

| | | | |
|---|---|---|---|
| | (1147) | fig. 112, no. 37 | (89 layer 21) |
| | (1204) | fragment, not illustrated | (90 layer 29) |
| | (1156) | not illustrated | (89 layer 33) |
| | (1194) | plain; not illustrated | (90 layer 29) |
| Bronze sheet, decorated | (1168) | fig. 110, no. 18 | (89 layer 38) |
| Bronze bracelet | (1150) | two strand twisted; not illustrated | (89 layer 33) |
| | (1253) | two strand twisted; not illustrated | (90 layer 30) |
| | (1140) | two strand twisted; not illustrated | (89 layer 21) |
| Bronze fibula pin | (1125) | not illustrated | (89 layer 21) |
| Bronze tweezers | (1209) | not illustrated | (90 layer 30) |
| Bronze pin | (1052) | fragment, not illustrated | (88 layer 10) |
| Bronze ring | (1043) | plain, 2 cm. diameter; not illustrated | (88 layer 10) |
| Bronze sheet | (1269) | fragment, not illustrated | (90 layer 26) |
| Bronze fragments | (1010, 1157, 1165) | miscellaneous, not illustrated | |
| Lead sheet | (1018) | c. 9 cm. square, folded; not illustrated | (88 layer 10) |
| Bone plaque | (998) | fig. 119, no. 121 | (88 layer 5) |
| Bone spindlewhorl | (1163) | fig. 118, no. 108 | (89 layer 21) |
| | (1141) | fig. 117, no. 107 | (89 layer 21) |
| Bone pin | (1011) | fig. 116, no. 88 | (88 layer 6) |
| | (1294) | as nos. 81–5; not illustrated | (90 layer 30) |
| | (1332) | fragment, not illustrated | (88 layer 10) |
| Bone bracelet | (1158) | fragment, not illustrated | (89 layer 36) |
| Shale bowl | (1390) | fig. 122, no. 143 | (88 layer 10) |
| Shale bracelet | (1388) | fig. 122, no. 137 | (89 layer 21) |
| Shale spindlewhorl | (1030) | fig. 121, no. 127 | (88 layer 10) |
| Iron spur | (990) | fig. 125, no. 180 | (88 layer 5) |
| Iron horseshoe | (991) | fig. 125, no. 183 | (88 layer 5) |
| Iron shears | (1177) | fig. 127, no. 200 | (89 layer 38) |
| Iron knife | (1210) | fig. 125, no. 187 | (90 layer 30) |
| Iron tripod ?candlestick | (1218) | fig. 131, no. 250 | (90 layer 30) |
| Iron handle | (1095) | fig. 131, no. 260 | (88 layer 62) |
| Iron binding | (1205) | fig. 130, no. 242 | (90 layer 30) |
| Iron split pin | (1127) | fig. 129, no. 223 | (89 layer 21) |
| Iron rod | (1138) | square cross-section, 26 cm. long; not illustrated | (89 layer 21) |
| Iron rod | (1159) | shank of long nail; not illustrated | (89 layer 21) |
| Iron plate | (1139) | fig. 131, no. 256 | (89 layer 21) |
| Iron ?tang | (1028) | fig. 131, no. 259 | (88 layer 10) |
| Iron strip | (1605) | fig. 130, no. 239 | (88 layer 10) |
| Iron ring | (1343) | 4 cm. diameter; not illustrated | (88 layer 92) |
| Iron fragments | (999, (1016, 1017, 1020, 1045, | | |

|  |  |  |  |
|---|---|---|---|
| | 1124, | | |
| | 1126, | | |
| | 1136, | | |
| | 1142, | | |
| | 1143, | | |
| | 1155, | | |
| | 1166, | | |
| | 1195) | miscellaneous, not illustrated | |
| Iron slag | | see p. 265 | (89 layer 31) |
| Whetstone | (1189) | not illustrated, no. 347 | (89 layer 38) |
| | (1009) | not illustrated, no. 340 | (88 layer 5) |
| | (1148) | not illustrated, no. 353 | (89 layer 23) |
| | (1152) | not illustrated, no. 345 | (89 layer 21) |
| | (1187) | fragment; not illustrated, no. 358 | (89 layer 35) |
| Glass vessels | | cf. fig. 197, no. 1 | (88 layer 10) |
| | | fig. 197, no. 9 | (88 layer 6) |
| | | cf. fig. 198, no. 18 | (88 layer 10) |
| Window glass | | cf. fig. 199, no. 24 | (88 layer 53) |
| | | fig. 199, no. 25 | (88 layer 10) |
| Painted plaster | | see p. 73 | (88 layer 10) |
| Nails | | 1, 11·5+; 1, 7·6; 1, 4·5+; 1, 8·9; 2, 7·6, bent; | |
| (measurements in cm.) | | 1, 5·1; 1, 3·85 | (88 layer 5) |
| | | 1, 7·6 | (88 layer 20) |
| | | 1, 10·2; 1, 7·0; 2, 5·1; 1, 3·85 | (88 layer 62) |
| | | 1, 8·9, no head; 2, 8·25; 2, 7·0; 3, 7·6; 2, 5·75; | |
| | | 1, 5·1; 1, 5·1, bent; 1, 3·85 | (88 layer 10) |
| | | 1, 5·75+ | (88 layer 46) |
| | | 2, 8·25; 1, 5·1; 1, 2·55; 1, 8·9; 1, 7·6; 1, 6·35 | (89 layer 38) |
| | | 1, 3·85 | (89 layer 36) |
| | | 1, 8·25; 1, 7·6; 1, 6·35+; 2, 5·75; 1, 5·1; 3, 3·85, | |
| | | two without heads | (89 layer 21) |
| | | 1, 5·75; 1, 7·0; 1, 11·5; 1, 10·2, bent; 1, 7·6, bent | (90 layer 29) |
| | | 1, 10·2; 1, 10·2, bent | (90 layer 30) |
| | | 1, 3·2; 1, 1·95 | (90 layer 32) |

## List of Pottery relating to the Roads and Make-up Layers

### by MICHAEL FULFORD

A quantitative assessment of the pottery from the stratified layers behind the fort wall is given below, together with a general comment on each group. The layers constituting each level have been listed above (pp. 43–5). The numbers in italics indicate sherds drawn in the main type series. For discussions of the fabrics and grouping according to production centre, see pp. 280–301.

*Periods 2, 3, 4: layers below the upper road surface*

*Argonne:* Chenet 320, rim only.

*New Forest:* Fabric 1: 3.1–2, 2/10.22–25(3), 10.2–3(2), 13, 19.1–3, 20.3, 22.1–5(4); weight, 630 g.; 8·19%.

Fabric 2: 40.2, 43(5); weight, 455 g.; 5·91%.

Fabric 3: 10.1, 55.8–9(2), 65; weight, 410 g.; 5·33%.

Total weight: 1495 g. (19·43%) + 100 g. from a layer where no division was made between individual New Forest fabrics.

*Oxford:* Fabric 1: 31, 40, 42, 43(3), 57, 58; weight, 380 g.; 4·94%.

Fabric 2: 14, 15.1.

Fabric 3: 63(2); weight, 235 g.; 3·05%.

Total weight: 615 g.; 7·99%.

*Misc.:* 24, 56.2.

*Hand-made, fabric A:* 86(8), 107(6), 114, 123(13); weight, 1765 g.; 22·94%.

*Black-burnished:* 85(6), 107(9), 126(10); weight, 1380 g.; 17·93%.

*Grey fabrics:* 85(4), 103.1, 109.1–3, 127(4), 129(5), 129.6(2), 132(4), 136(2), 140(6), 142.1–3(3), 143, 145(3), 149.1, 153.8(2), 159.1–5(2); weight, 2340 g.; 30·41%.

*Fabric D:* 87.2.

Total weight: 7695 g.

This group has only limited use in dating as it could represent the gradual accumulation of rubbish on the first road surface from *c.* A.D. 300 until the new surface was laid in about 345. But although residual material must be present in the group, it is probable that the majority of the pottery represents rubbish loss in the stages immediately prior to the building of the new road, since it is unlikely that much rubbish would have been allowed to gather whilst it was in general use. Moreover, the sherds do not, in most cases, show that degree of abrasion and wear which both foot and vehicular traffic might cause.

In many respects the variation between the main fabric groups is similar to that in the pottery from the upper occupation, and indeed from above the road surface. This is wholly consistent with the view that the bulk of the rubbish on the lower road does not pre-date period 5 by very long.

*Periods 2, 3, 4: from layers beneath the upper make-up*

*New Forest:* Fabric 1: 3.1–2, 19.1–3(3); weight, 70 g.; 3·44%.

Fabric 2: 43(2); weight, 50 g.; 2·46%.

Fabric 3: sherds only; weight, 80 g.; 3·93%.

Total weight: 200 g. (9·83%), + 300 g. from layers where no division was made between individual New Forest fabrics; 25·06%.

*Oxford:* Fabric 1: 40, 43(2); weight, 60 g.; 2·95%.

Fabric 2: 15.1.

Fabric 3: weight, 5 g.; 0·25%.

Total weight: 65 g.; 3·19%.

*Hand-made, fabric A:* 86, 123(2); weight, 320 g.; 15·72%.

*Black-burnished:* 85(2), 107(3), 126; weight, 490 g.; 24·08%.

*Grey fabrics:* 127(3), 129.4, 133, 139, 141, 142.1–3; weight, 660 g.; 32·43%.

Total weight: 2035 g.

The same reservations about the group below the upper road surface apply to this. The pottery could represent the gradual accumulation of rubbish up to *c.* A.D. 345 with a large residual element, although it would be more reasonable to see the bulk of the pottery dating from *c.* 330. The ratios of the various fabrics suggests comparability with the middle to upper occupation layers against the wall. Against a firm conclusion should be set the size of the group, which is the same as that of an average pit, and smaller than most of the non-pit groups.

*Period 6: from layers immediately above or cutting into the upper make-up*

*TS:* Dr. 31, East Gaul, later second to mid third century A.D.
*Argonne:* Chenet 320 with stamp nos. 303, 324, 329; weight, 10 g.; 0·07%.
*New Forest:* Fabric 1: 2/10.17, 2/10.21, 2/10.22–25, 6(2), 6.3, 10.2–3, 13(4), 19.4(2), 19.1–3(2), 21.4–5(2), 22.1–5(7), 22.6–7(2), 22.8, 55.5–7; weight, 970 g.; 7·08%. Another 2060 g. were recorded from layers where no coarse ware body sherds had been kept.

Fabric 2: 29(6), 41.3, 43(15), 57.2, 57.3, 57.4, 60; weight, 1020 g.; 7·44%. Another 1010 g. were recorded from layers where no coarse ware body sherds had been kept.

Fabric 3: 48, 49(3), 53.1 (sherds of same vessel in middle occupation/upper occupation), 64, 65(2), 66, 105.1; weight, 700 g.; 5·11%. Another 710 g. were recorded, as above.
Total weight: 2690 (19·62%) + 3780 g.
*Oxford:* Fabric 1: 1, 30.9, 33.6, 33.11, 34.7, 35.1, 35.6, 35.10(2), 35.13(2), 35.14 (join in layers above the upper road surface), 36.1, 36.3, 36.9, 36.12, 40(7), 42, 43.10–12(3), 43(12), 53.2, 57(6), 57.5, 58(10), 58.6; weight, 495 g.; 3·61%. Another 3330 g. were recorded, as above.

Fabric 2: 14(3), 15.1(2), 17.7, 17.12; weight, 170 g.; but all from contexts with no coarse body sherds.

Fabric 3: 45(2), 63(4), 63.4(3); weight, 410 g.; 2·99%. Another 910 g. were recorded, as above.
Total weight: 905 (6·60%) + 4410 g.
*Pevensey:* 35.2, 37, 42, 43(2); weight, 15 g.; 0·11%.
*Misc.:* 18, 30.2, 31.6, 88.9, 137.7(2); weight, 25 g.; 0·18%.
*Hand-made, fabric A:* 86(30), 100.1, 107(12), 107.3(2), 107.4(2), 107.5(2), 114(3), 123(79), 125.1; weight, 3280 g.; 23·92%.
*Black-burnished:* 85(41), 88.2, 107(33), 117(4), 126(44), 154(2); weight, 3195 g.; 23·30%.
*Grey fabrics:* 76.1, 77(3), 79.1, 84.3, 85(10), 87.1(2), 91, 92, 94, 98.2, 100.3, 101(2), 103.1(4), 106, 107(5), 109.6(3), 109.7, 109.11, 117(10), 118(2), 119(2), 121, 122.2(4), 127(18), 128(3), 129(5), 129.4(7), 129.6(3), 131.1, 131.3, 133(5), 133.3, 134(12), 135(3), 136(6), 137.1, 137.2(7), 137.3, 137.8(6), 139(3), 140(7), 141(2), 142.1–3(4), 142.4–5(3), 145(3), 146, 148.2, 149.2(2), 149.3, 153.5, 153.6(3), 153.8(3), 153.9, 154.6, 157, 159.4–5, 172, 173, 174, 174.3, 175(2), 176.2, 177.1, 177.4, 177.6 (joining sherd in upper occupation), 178(2), 177/179.4; weight, 3560 g.; 25·97%.
*Fabric D:* 87.2, 109.8, 137.4–6(9), 173; weight 30 g.; 0·22%.
Total weight: 13,710 g. (excluding any pottery from layers where not all sherds were kept).

This group should be considered in the same way as the group from the layers above the upper Roman road surface.

*Period 6: from layers immediately above or cutting into upper road surface*

*TS:* Dr. 45, East Gaul, late second to mid third century A.D.

*Argonne:* Chenet 320 (rims only of two bowls), 328; weight, 5 g.; 0·02%.

*New Forest:* Fabric 1: 3.1(2), 3.5–6, 2/10.1, 2/10.10–11, 10.2–3, 13(5) 21.1(2), 21.4–5(2), 22.1–5(7), 22.6–7(3), 23.1–2, 24, 55.4, 55.5–7, 55.10–11, 55.13, 55.21; weight, 1510 g.; 5·82%. Another 400 g. were recorded from layers where no coarse ware body sherds were kept.

Fabric 2: 29(9), 32, 33.9, 34.1, 43.9, 43(9), 88.8, 174.4; weight, 670 g.; 2·58%. Another 330 g. were recorded from layers where no coarse ware body sherds were kept.

Fabric 3: 11.1–2, 49(4), 55.8–9, 64(3), 66, 68, 105.5; weight, 530 g.; 2·04%. Another 135 g. were recorded from layers where no coarse ware body sherds were kept.

Total weight: 2710 (10·45%) + 865 g. + 1680 g. from layers where no distinction was made between the individual NF fabrics.

*Oxford:* Fabric 1: 31, 34.3, 34.4, 34.5, 34.7(2),35.14 (join in layers above the upper make-up), 36.1(2), 36.7, 40(5), 41, 43(11), 57(2), 58(5); weight, 1485 g.; 5·72%. Another 750 g. were recorded from layers where no coarse ware sherds were kept.

Fabric 2: 14(5), 15.1(2), 15.2, 17.7(3), 17.8, 17.11, 18.8, 26; weight, 50 g.; 0·19%.

Fabric 3: 50.2, 63(5); weight, 430 g.; 1·66%. Another 270 g. were recorded from layers where no coarse ware sherds were kept.

Total weight: 1965 (7·57%) + 1020 g.

*Pevensey:* 37; weight, 5 g.; 0·02%.

*Misc.:* 55.2–3, 73, 74, 81, 88.9, 132.3, 134(8); weight, 40 g.; 0·15%.

*Hand-made, fabric A:* 86(28), 93.1(3), 107(17), 107.4, 107.5(3), 114(2), 123.5, 123.10, 123(81), 174.3; weight, 7440 g.; 28·68%.

*Black-burnished:* 85(34), 107(32), 117.1(2), 126(36), 175(4); weight, 4995 g.; 19·26%.

*Grey fabrics:* 76.1, 76.3, 77(2), 85(10), 87.1(2), 87.7, 89.4, 92, 94, 101, 107.12, 107.13, 107.14, 107(6), 109.5(2), 109.6, 117.2(2), 118.3, 118, 119, 120.3, 127(9), 128, 129(6), 129.4(4), 129.6, 131.3, 131.4(2), 131.6, 132(3), 133(5), 133.3, 136(6), 137.2(2), 140(12), 142.1–3(6), 143, 145(2), 149.3, 153.2, 153.8, 154.6, 155, 159.1–2, 159.4–5(5), 159.12, 159.14, 159.7–13(2), 161.1, 162, 163, 172(3), 175(2), 176.3, 177.1, 177.4, 178(2), 179.2; weight, 8490 g.; 32·73%.

*Fabric D:* 87.2, 137.4–6(8), 173; weight, 290 g.; 1·12%.

Total weight: 25,940 g. + 3565 g. (additional NF and Oxon, see above).

This represents the accumulation of rubbish above the latest Roman road surface from *c.* A.D. 345 until the close of 'Roman' occupation at Portchester. Since the group will contain pottery brought up by the digging of postholes, etc., into earlier layers, an amount of residual material is to be expected. Equally, as it is the latest Roman group from Portchester, it will, in any case carry proportionally more residual pottery than the preceding groups. It is hoped that this factor can be partly accounted for by the relative percentage of any one type in the post-345 groups, when compared with the earlier ones, provided that the general fabric trend respective to any type is considered as well.

# AREA A: SUMMARY LIST OF STRATIFIED COINS AS DATING EVIDENCE

Before considering the dating of the six periods in detail, it will be convenient to summarize the stratified coins.

*Correlation of coins with stratified layers against south wall*

*Lower clay bank* (period 1 phase a)

|       |       |
|-------|-------|
| (1373) | Gallienus (A.D. 260–8) |

(period 1 phase e)

|       |       |
|-------|-------|
| (2602) | Tetricus I (A.D. 270–3) |
| (2603) | Carausius (A.D. 286–93) |

*Lower occupation* (period 2)

|       |       |
|-------|-------|
| (2484) | Tetricus I (A.D. 270–3) |

*Middle clay* (period 3)

None

*Middle occupation* (period 4)

|       |       |
|-------|-------|
| (2118) | Carausius or Allectus (A.D. 286–96) |
| (2457) | Constantine I (A.D. 310–17) |
| (2461) | Constantine I (A.D. 310–17) |
| (2508) | Constantine I (A.D. 321–4) |

*Upper clay* (period 5)

None

*Upper occupation*

|       |       |
|-------|-------|
| (2481) | Victorinus (A.D. 268–70) |
| (2521) | Tetricus II (A.D. 270–3) |
| (2074) | Carausius (A.D. 289–93) |
| (2096) | Carausius (A.D. 286–93) |
| (2403) | Galerius (A.D. 303–5) |
| (2500) | Constantine I (A.D. 310–17) |
| (2222) | Urbs Roma (A.D. 330–45) |
| (2075) | Constantine I (A.D. 335–7) |
| (2098) | Constans (A.D. 335–7) |
| (2209) | Constantine II (A.D. 335–7) |
| (2477) | Gratian (A.D. 367–75) |
| (2105) | House of Theodosius (A.D. 388–402) |

*Correlation of coins with stratified 'make-up' and road levels*

*Below lower road* (period 1)

|       |       |
|-------|-------|
| (37) | Gallienus (A.D. 260–8) |

*Below upper 'make-up' and road* (periods 2, 3, 4)

|       |       |
|-------|-------|
| (1345) | Tetricus II (A.D. 270–3) |
| (1356) | Carausius (A.D. 286–93) |
| (1341) | Carausius (A.D. 286–93) |

    (1038)    Carausius (A.D. 286–93)
    (1355)    Diocletian (A.D. 294–305)
    (1106)    Constantinopolis (A.D. 330–5)
    (1368)    Constantinopolis (A.D. 330–5)

*Above upper 'make-up' and road* (period 6)

    (1137)    barbarous radiate (A.D. 270–90)
    (1053)    Carausius (A.D. 286–93)
    (1096)    Carausius (A.D. 286–93)
    (1206)    Licinius (A.D. 310–13)
    (1014)    Constantine I (A.D. 310–13)
    (1019)    Constantine I (A.D. 310–13)
    (1044)    Constantine I (A.D. 319–20)
    (1054)    Constantine I (A.D. 319)
    (1081)    Constantine I (A.D. 324)
    (1290)    Constantine I (A.D. 320–24)
    (1084)    Crispus (A.D. 324)
    (996)    Constantine I (A.D. 330–5)
    (1061)    Constans (A.D. 333–5)
    (1153)    Urbs Roma (A.D. 330–7)
    (1041)    Constantinopolis (A.D. 330–5)
    (1034)    House of Constantine (A.D. 330–45)
    (1274)    Constantine II (A.D. 330–5)
    (1024)    Constantine II (A.D. 330–5)
    (1129)    Constantine II (A.D. 335–7)
    (1023)    Constantine II (A.D. 337–41)
    (1025)    Valens (A.D. 364–78)
    (1280)    Valens (A.D. 364–78)
    (1180)    Valentinian I (A.D. 364–75)
    (1219)    Valentinian I (A.D. 364–75)
    (1006)    Gratian (A.D. 378–83)
    (997)    Theodosius I (A.D. 388–95)

Since the other artifacts are not closely datable, any assessment of date must rest entirely upon the coin sequence.

### Period 1 (*construction period*)

The coin of Gallienus found beneath the earliest road where it passes through the postern gate, together with a coin of the same emperor from the quarry hollow, provide a *terminus post quem* of A.D. 260–8 for the construction of the fort. The fact that coins of Tetricus I (270–3) and Carausius (286–93) were recovered from the period 1e occupation layer, which must lie within the first few years of the fort's life, strongly suggests that construction took place in the 270s or early 280s. On balance a date early in the reign of Carausius is preferred.

### Periods 2–4

It is most convenient to take the evidence for all three periods together. The latest coins are two Constantinopolis issues of A.D. 330–5, representing the last in a group of only 12 coins.

In view of the range of coins in Period 6, it would be reasonable to suggest that period 4 came to an end soon after the appearance of the Constantinopolis issues, thus dating to about 340–5. The date span of periods 2–4 would therefore be 285/90–340/5.

Apart from a single coin of Tetricus from a Period 2 layer, one coin of Constantine I (310–17) came from the filling of a contemporary pit (pot 230). A coin of Licinius (310–17) was recovered from a period 3 layer in pit 222, while from the layers of silt covering a clay sealing of period 3, low in the filling of pit 223, came two coins, one of Crispus (321–3) and one of Constantine I (320–4). This sequence implies that period 2 continued until about 325, terminating with the deposition of the layer of clay representing period 3 at about that time.

Period 4 is represented by four coins from general layers, two from pit 223 mentioned above, and one from pit 230. Six of the seven were minted between 310 and 324, a fact consistent with a date range of 325–45 for period 4.

*Periods 5 and 6*

The deposition of clay, make-up and metalling which represents period 5 probably took place, for reasons given above, in about A.D. 345. Thereafter until *c.* 370 occupation seems to have continued at some intensity, being represented by 35 coins. Three coins, one of Gratian (378–83) and two of the House of Theodosius (388–402) hint at the continued use of the site but on a much reduced scale in the closing decades of the fourth century.

The following chronological outline may be offered:

| | | |
|---|---|---|
| Period 1: | construction | A.D. 285/90 |
| Period 2: | lower occupation | A.D. 285/90–325 |
| Period 3: | middle clay | A.D. 325 |
| Period 4: | middle occupation | A.D. 325–45 |
| Period 5: | upper clay | A.D. 345 |
| Period 6: | upper occupation | A.D. 345–70 (some continuation afterwards) |

# AREA B: EVIDENCE FOR PHASES
## (fig. 24)

The only stratigraphical distinctions which occur in area B relate to the areas of metalling. The main road leading to the postern gate, and the side roads (E–W1) branching from it, shows two distinct phases of metalling; a lower metalling of small pebbles trampled into the surface of the natural brickearth, and an upper metalling, usually composed of large flint cobbles packed tightly together. Where the two layers survive, there is usually a lens of occupation rubbish between them containing quantities of broken pottery and animal bones. E–W road 2 was constructed at the time of the later metalling.

The upper cobbles are discontinuous and vary in quality. In some areas, e.g. between pits 40 and 41, the individual flints are smaller and tightly packed, but the patch immediately to the north of this is much looser, the flints being packed in occupation debris. Beneath this layer was found a coin of Valentinian I (A.D. 364–75) (small find no. 211). Evidently patching took place on more than one occasion. Further evidence of sequence is shown, in this area, by the two pits 40 and 41, which cut through the metalling, pit 41 being subsequently sealed by two hearths which may well be Roman, since the hearths and the adjacent metalling were together scored by Saxon plough ruts. There is no dating evidence to calibrate the sequence.

The amorphous expanse of gravel metalling which covers much of the western part of the area was also subject to patching, particularly in the region between pits 142 and 210, but no dating evidence was obtained. The metalling was also cut by a series of gullies (gullies 23–6), one of which, gully 25, contained a coin of the House of Constantius (350–60).

# AREA C: EVIDENCE FOR PHASES
## (fig. 25)

Evidence for phasing on a stratigraphic basis in area C is non-existent. The features are isolated and without direct relationships to general stratigraphy, except where pits can be seen to cut each other or into spreads of gravel. Pit 103, however, deserves mention here: it was probably dug to provide clay for construction purposes and later served as a demolition pit for the remains of dismantled timber buildings (p. 115) early in the life of the fort. It was subsequently sealed by a general occupation layer. No evidence for the absolute dating of this sequence is forthcoming.

# IV. THE INTERIOR: THE PLAN AND THE STRUCTURES

## INTRODUCTION

IT will be immediately apparent from the simplified plan (fig. 20) that the Roman features are somewhat haphazardly arranged and very incomplete. Three factors contribute to this: the extent of the post-Roman disturbance, the very insubstantial nature of the structural remains (with the exception of the pits and wells, which survived unscathed), and the fact that the activities of 100 years of Roman occupation are superimposed. All three factors must be clearly borne in mind and due allowance made for them.

The post-Roman history of the site has ensured the destruction of most superficial structural remains over the northern two-thirds of the area; thus the likely positions of buildings can only be worked out, and then very tentatively, from the spacing of the pits which seem to leave certain areas clear, possibly because they were occupied. That little trace of structures survives need occasion no surprise when it is realized that the form of construction employed was a sill beam principle, which entailed the use of horizontal timbers into which verticals were slotted. The actual surviving remains of such buildings, even under ideal conditions, (pp. 67–8) are very slight. The different periods represented can be allowed for in the southern part of the site (mainly area A) where it is possible to separate the different phases stratigraphically into primary structures, of period 1, and features relating to the period 5 make-up and remetalling.

The structures and features which constitute the main evidence for Roman occupation include roads and gravel spreads together with their gutters, buildings with associated structures such as hearths, ovens and eavesdrip gullies, wells, cesspits, and drainage gullies. Each of these categories will be described separately.

## ROADS AND GRAVEL SPREADS
### (pls. XXIV–XXVI)

*The Roads: Early Phase*

The best preserved of the roads is the main N–S road which runs from the centre of the fort to the south postern gate. In its earliest phase (period 1) it consisted of a 3 in. (7·6 cm.) layer of metalling composed of pebbles, presumably collected from the sea shore, laid directly on the original ground surface. There is no evidence at this stage of a central gutter, but one might have existed only to be subsequently destroyed in the second phase of remetalling.

In the first period one road, E–W road 1, joined the main N–S road at right angles; it was metalled in an identical manner to the main N–S road, and measured 9 ft. 6 in. (2·9 m.) wide, surviving for a distance of 48 ft. (14·6 m.), beyond which late Saxon disturbance had totally destroyed any further trace. The similarity of the primary metalling of the two roads, together with the stratigraphic evidence, leaves little doubt that they were laid out as part of the same plan. A further point of some relevance is that the western edge of the main N–S road occupies a different line on either side of E–W road 1, giving the impression that the roads were constructed together in relation to standing structures.

### The Roads: Late Phase

The first remetalling of the roads probably took place at the same time, equivalent to period 5 dated to *c.* A.D. 345 (p. 61). The metalling varied in quality and extent, but for the most part consisted of flint nodules and occasional fragments of tile packed together on top of the layer of occupation material which had accumulated over the earlier road surfaces.

The main N–S road (pl. XXIV*a*) seems to have been remetalled throughout its entire length and provided with a central gutter (gully 10).[1] Although the slot in which the gutter had been constructed had been widened and made irregular by subsequent erosion, sufficient survived to show that the gutter, presumably of timber planking, was about 1 ft. wide and 1 ft. deep (0·31 m.). As the road approached the south postern gate, it passed between the ends of the clay bank behind the fort wall. The drainage problems posed by this arrangement were overcome by constructing two side gutters, each some 9 in. (23 cm.) wide, flanking the road for a distance of 40 ft. (12·2 m.), restricting its effective width to 10 ft. (3·1 m.). The metalling, however, extended beyond the side gutters (fig. 22), ending somewhat irregularly.

E–W road 1 (pl. XXIV*b*) was also remetalled with flints laid over occupation material, on a line exactly following that of the earlier road surface. The late metalling appears to be of one period, but had suffered considerably from Saxon building activity. No gutters were provided.

A new road, E–W road 2, was constructed at about this time. It measured 14 ft. wide (4·3 m.) with a central gutter of the same proportions as that of the N–S road. Two types of metalling were apparent: tightly packed flints averaging 2–3 in. (5–8 cm.) across, which surfaced the southern part of the road, and larger flints more loosely packed, representing much of the northern part, giving the impression of being a patch of later remetalling. Beneath the looser flints was a coin of Valentinian I. The southern part of the road had been cut into by pits 40 and 41, and two hearths (hearths 2 and 3) were later created on its line. How far west the road originally extended must remain unknown.

The evidence for the late fourth-century remetalling of part of E–W road 2 is matched by similar evidence along the line of the main N–S road, where it is clear that hollows forming by wear were being constantly patched with hardcore of flints and tiles. It seems that wherever a puddle formed someone shovelled rubble into it. There is no independent dating evidence for these patchings, but presumably the process was continuous throughout the latter half of the fourth century.

Eventually repair was abandoned, rubbish accumulated over the road surface, and the timber gutters were left to rot and clog up. The latest coins from the area imply that this process of decay followed the 370s, but it may indeed have begun before.

---

[1] The small finds from this gulley are listed together with those from the upper occupation layers (pp. 51–3): they include nos. 1291, 1292, 1293, 1296, 1297, 1298, 1299, 1301.

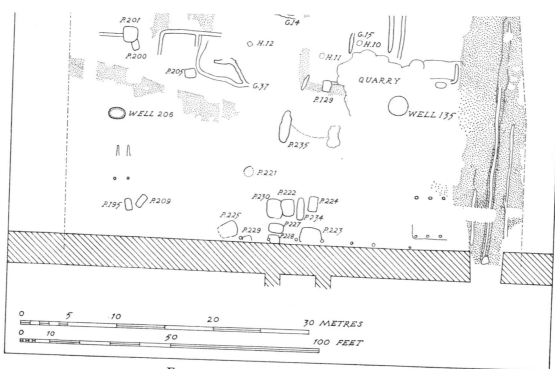

FIG. 20.  Plan of all Roman features

*The Gravel Spread West of the Roads* (pls. XXV–XXVI)

Extensive but discontinuous spreads of gravel metalling blanketed much of the western part of the site, an area of approximately 80 ft. by 200 ft. (24 m. by 61 m.) (figs. 22–4). The discontinuous nature of the spread can best be explained by the destructive effects of post-Roman activity in the area, a point emphasized by the fact that the remaining patches of metalling survive almost wholly in slight hollows where they have escaped disturbance. The nature of the metalling varies from small pebbles and flint cobbles to rather larger flints in the area between pits 77 and 79. In all cases the metalling can be shown to have been laid immediately on the original ground surface, and therefore belongs to the construction phase of the fort. There are, however, several areas which show signs of remetalling, usually with large flints and fragments of tile. One such occurred in area A (fig. 23) and continued into the southern part of area B (fig. 24); another lay to the north of gully 23. How extensive the remetalling originally was it is impossible to say, nor is it possible to be sure on how many separate occasions remetalling took place. In all probability, rubble was laid only when the need arose to fill muddy patches.

The limits of the metalled area are difficult to define with precision. To the south, it may originally have joined with the metalling on the clay bank (see below); its eastern limit seems to extend up to the timber buildings and the three major groups of cesspits; at the northern extremity it presumably joined with the main E–W road, but the point is incapable of proof: the western limit may well lie beyond the excavated area.

The possible function of the metalling will be discussed below (p. 426); here it is sufficient to underline the implication that much of the western part of the site remained an open area throughout the life of the fort, and was maintained as such by occasional remetalling and by the digging of drainage ditches.

*The Gravel Metalling on the Clay Bank*

The northern slope of the clay bank retains evidence of two phases of metalling, the extent of which is shown on figs. 22 and 23. The northern edge of the metalling appears to mark a deliberate limit, but the southern edge is completely arbitrary, since it has been created by the denuding effects of Saxon ploughing, vivid evidence for which was provided by the discovery of plough ruts scoring the adjacent surface of the clay bank. If, however, it is supposed that the metalling was originally more extensive, perhaps surfacing much of the clay bank, then it could have served as an E–W road joining up with the main N–S road close to the south postern gate.

The two phases of metalling, each of flint cobbles, can be related to the make-up layers of periods 1 and 5 respectively.

# THE BUILDINGS AND ASSOCIATED STRUCTURES
## (pls. XXVII, XXIX, XXX)

The recognition of buildings poses serious problems, not the least of which is the method of construction employed. Basically it would appear that horizontal sill beams were placed on the unprepared original ground surface to serve as the basis for the superstructure.

Occasionally, e.g. building R5, the indentation made by the beams on the original surface can be traced. In another case, building R4, sloppings of mortar dropped during construction mark the positions of timbers in negative, but more often traces of the actual buildings are non-existent, the only indication of their presence being either a clear space uncluttered by pits or gravel metalling, or drainage gullies dug to collect the eavesdrips.

### Building R1 (fig. 22; pl. XXVIIa)

Building R1 is represented now only by the eavesdrip gullies, which together define two rectangular areas, one measuring approximately 22 by 18 ft. (6·7 by 5·5 m.), the other 25 ft. by approximately 20 ft. (7·6 by 6·1 m.). Beyond this, interpretation is difficult. One of the E–W gullies shows signs of recutting, and it could therefore be argued that the two parallel N–S gullies are similarly of different dates: alternatively, they may represent contemporary drains on either side of an alley-way dividing two separate structures. Difficulty also attaches to the interpretation of the two L-shaped gullies which appear to demarcate the north-east and south-east corners of the building: it may be that they belong to a separate phase. The arrangement, however, was such that free access was allowed from the supposed building to the main N–S street without the necessity of having to step over the gutter.

The drainage gullies were all similar in form, consisting of roughly straight slots of U-shaped sections averaging 4 in. (10 cm.) deep. They were all filled with black soil containing sherds of pottery and animal bones. Their irregular profiles and lack of strict rectangularity in plan prohibit the possibility of their being slots for sill beams.

The form of the structure erected within the drains is even less clear than its plan, but possibly it was of sill beam construction with a raised timber floor.[1] Two postholes (ph 675 and 1087) belong to the early phase and might well have been part of the original structure, but they could be later since their only stratigraphical relationship to the slots is that both features were sealed by the upper make-up. Around the building, particularly on the east and west sides, thin spreads of gravel had been laid: along the southern side was the edge of the clay bank cut by a later well (pit 135).

The dating of the building depends on the fact that the drainage gullies were dug into the natural clay immediately after the construction period and were sealed by the upper make-up which is dated to c. A.D. 345 (p. 61). The upper make-up at this point consists of a spread of broken chalky mortar and daub up to 3 in. (8 cm.) thick, which blankets the area. The nature of the layer is highly suggestive of building debris, and could thus have derived from the decay or demolition of the structure standing there.

### Building R2 (fig. 22)

Building R2, like the structure just described, is also represented only by its drainage gullies, which define two rectangular areas each approximately 10 by 16 ft. (3 by 5 m.). The gully delimiting the southern side is more substantial than the others, measuring some 1 ft. 6 in. (0·46 m.) across and 9 in. (0·23 m.) deep. The reason for this increased size may

---

[1] An equally plausible alternative is that the gullies drained the area around tents.

well be that, in such a position, it would have had to collect and contain surface water running off the metalled slope of the adjacent clay bank.

Of the structure itself, there is little to be said. No trace of walls survive, but in the general occupation level sealing the area, a few fragments of daub were recovered. The building butts up to the clay bank on the south side, whilst the area to the north of it is heavily metalled and shows signs of considerable wear.

A date soon after the construction period of the fort is suggested for the erection of building R2 by the fact that the gullies cut through a builder's mortar spread of the earliest period, and appear to be respected by the gravel metalling laid immediately upon it. One of the gullies is sealed by a gravel metalling equivalent to the upper make-up, while at the same time the site was cut by two of the late gullies (gully 37). The building is therefore likely to have gone out of use by the 340s.

### Building R3 (fig. 22)

The evidence for building R3 is even more tenuous than that for buildings R1 and R2, and indeed the very existence of the structure must be regarded as open to debate. All that survives is a single length of gully roughly aligned with the northern gully of building R2. To the north of it, however, is an open area devoid of gravel metalling and cesspit digging, but occupied by an oven (oven 4) and an elongated pit associated with it (p. 69). It could be argued that the oven lay within a building sited here, but in the absence of further positive evidence, the problem is best left open.

### Building R4 (figs. 23 and 24)

Building R4 lies at the junction of the main N–S road and E–W road 1. The ghost of the structure owes its survival to the fact that mortar was dropped at the time of construction between a series of sill beams placed on the original ground surface. The positions of the beams are therefore marked by the absence of mortar. The rear (western) part of the building is indistinct, largely because the mortar spilling did not extend to this area.

The surviving traces show that the beams were almost exactly 1 ft. (31 cm.) wide and defined a structure measuring overall 20 ft. (6 m.) long by about 18 ft. (5·5 m.) wide. Across the front ran a verandah or corridor 5 ft. (1·5 m.) wide. The substantial room behind might have been divided into two by a cross partition. To the west of the building were traces of two further walls set at right angles to each other with a post at the corner.

The nature of the superstructure is purely speculative, but in all probability the sill beams supported walls of wattle and daub. The floor poses a problem, since the mortar spread shows signs of two fires having been lit on it. This could mean either that the mortar served as the floor surface or that the fires pre- or post-dated the construction of a raised timber floor. Both explanations are equally possible.

The northern side of the building is bounded by a shallow V-sectioned gully, 8 in. (20·3 cm.) deep, which bends slightly to negotiate the corner of the structure. This point alone would suggest that the gully was probably contemporary with the building and may have served to drain off surface water accumulating on the street surface.

The relationship of building R4 to building R1 is demonstrated by the superimposition of the mortar spread and sill beams of building R4 on the gully belonging to building R1. The fact that the remetalling of the main N–S road was evidently carried out in relation to building R4 further supports the view that building R4 belongs to a late stage in the history of the fort, and should be correlated with period 5 (*c.* 345). No independent dating evidence survived the extensive disturbance to which this area was subjected in the post-Roman period.

### Building R5 (fig. 24, pl. XXIX*a*)

The rectangular area created by the remetalling of the main N–S road and E–W roads 1 and 2 could have accommodated a building equivalent in size to building R4. The area had been very disturbed by Saxon and medieval features, but the position of a single sill beam could still be traced as a shallow indentation in the surface of the natural clay no more than ¼ in. (0·6 cm.) deep. In spite of an extremely careful examination of the surrounding areas no further beam positions could be located. The only other features of Roman date in the immediate area were an oven (oven 1) and a hearth (hearth 1), neither of which need necessarily relate to the building.

No dating evidence survives, but the way in which the late metalling of the adjacent roads appears to respect the supposed building would suggest that it too, like building R4, belonged to the period 5 rebuilding.

### Building R6 (fig. 20)

Close to the south postern gate, fronting on to the main N–S road was a rectangular post-built structure measuring 14 by 11 ft. (4 by 3·4 m.). It was terraced into the lower clay bank and associated with tips of the 'middle clay', which was used as a packing material outside the rows of posts representing the walls. The positions of six posts were recovered, each averaging 8–12 in. (20–31 cm.) in diameter and 1–1½ ft. (31–46 cm.) deep. The nature of the superstructure is otherwise unknown.

From its position, the building might well have served as a guard chamber, controlling passage through the south postern gate. It is dated by its association with the middle clay to *c.* A.D. 325, and was out of use by the time the upper clay was spread over the area, *c.* 345 (pp. 49–50).

### Other Possible Buildings

The northern part of the excavated area has been so decimated by later earth-disturbing activities that not the slightest trace of a building survives. The grouping of the pits, however, would allow for the one-time existence of structures fronting on to the main N–S road, the pits being sited either behind or between the buildings. Similarly, it could be argued that gullies 41–3, 39 and 40, defined building plots. In the absence of firm evidence it would be unwise to speculate further, except to say that the existence of buildings here, while likely, is unproven.

### Ovens

Within the excavated area four ovens have been found, all of which could in theory have been sited within buildings or in yards close by. That no ovens were found in the area occupied by the gravel spreads supports the view that domestic activities were restricted to certain well-defined parts of the fort.

### Oven 1 (trench 60)

Oven 1 was constructed of clay and set in a shallow excavation cut into the natural brick-earth. A ledge had been provided along one side some 2 in. (5 cm.) above the level of the oven floor. Partially cut away by pit 37.

### Oven 2 (trench 74)

Oven 2 was constructed of clay strengthened with fragments of tile. The floor had been cut a few inches below the level of the adjacent natural. Beside it was an elongated trench, 3 ft. long by 1 ft. wide (0·91 by 0·31 m.) cut to a depth of 3 in. (7·6 cm.) into the natural clay. It was filled with black soil (layer 83). The surface of the natural clay around the oven was heavily scorched.

### Oven 3 (trench 77)

A small oven constructed of clay. Badly mutilated by a post hole and cut by pit 104. The natural clay nearby was heavily burnt.

### Oven 4 (trench 100)

A well-constructed oven, built of tiles set horizontally in a chalky mortar (pl. XXIX*b*). The floor was composed of limestone slabs. It was filled with a mixture of black earth mixed with fragments of collapsed superstructure (layer 51). The stoke hole has been partly cut away by a later posthole. Beside the oven was an elongated trench, 6 ft. long by 1 ft. 6 in. wide (1·83 by 0·46 m.) and 1 ft. 2 in. (0·36 m.) deep. It was filled with grey soil containing fragments of tiles, some bone and an iron ring (2274). The natural clay in front of the slot was heavily burnt.

### Hearths

In all, some 13 hearths were found, ranging from well-built tile structures to little more than patches of burning. As with the ovens, the distribution of hearths is closely related to the supposed sitings of buildings, leaving the gravel area totally unencumbered.

### Hearth 1 (trench 60)

Patch of burnt natural clay *c.* 1 ft. 6 in. (0·46 m.) across.

### Hearth 2 (trench 62)

Patch of burnt clay 1–1½ in. (2·5–3·8 cm.) thick and 1 ft. 6 in. (0·46 m.) across, laid over the filling of pit 41. Possibly early Saxon in date.

*Hearth* 2 (trench 62)

Rectangular patch of burnt clay 2 ft. 6 in. (0·76 m.) by 3 ft. 3 in. (1 m.), and 3 in. (7·6 cm.) thick. It lies partly on the natural clay surface and partly over the filling of pit 41. It has been cut by a plough furrow. Possibly early Saxon in date.

*Hearth* 4 (trench 65)

Hearth built largely of complete tiles laid directly on the surface of the natural clay (pl. XXX*b*). The surface had been subjected to considerable heat.

*Hearths* 5 *and* 6 (trench 76)

Two discontinuous patches of burnt clay, inset with fragments of tiles and laid on the surface of the natural brickearth. The hearths had been mutilated by later disturbances.

*Hearth* 7 (trenches 77 and 78)

Area of burning on the surface of the natural clay, covering an area of 5–6 ft. (1·5–1·83 m.) in diameter. Cut by the Napoleonic fence trench.

*Hearth* 8 (trench 88)

Area of broken tiles set in clay and laid horizontally on the surface of layer 13, which was burnt in its vicinity.

*Hearth* 9 (trench 88)

Area of burnt clay laid on the surface of layer 13, which showed signs of burning nearby.

*Hearth* 10 (trench 89)

Area of burnt clay *c.* 3 ft. square (0·9 m.) and 2 in. (5 cm.) thick, with a fragment of tile set in it, lying on layer 41 and cut by a posthole.

*Hearth* 11 (trench 89)

Area of burnt marl with a few tile fragments set into it. This is strictly a continuation of layer 41.

*Hearth* 12 (trench 90)

Small hearth measuring about 2 ft. by 1 ft. (0·6 by 0·3 m.) composed of tiles set in baked clay, and laid on the surface of the natural clay.

*Hearth* 13 (trench 99)

Fragmentary remains of a hearth built of complete tiles set in clay and laid on the surface of the natural clay. Mutilated by later features, but originally at least 6 ft. (1·83 m.) wide.

## STRUCTURAL EVIDENCE OUT OF POSITION

The description above has been concerned with traces of buildings and their ancillary features found *in situ*. Another class of evidence which throws some light on the problem of the internal buildings is loose finds such as nails, daub, painted plaster, tiles, bricks and window glass.

### Bricks and Tiles (pl. XXXI)

Fragments of a wide range of bricks and tiles were found scattered in occupation layers, in pits and re-used in post-Roman structures. The only tiles to be found *in situ* were used in hearths (pp. 69–70) or as bonding courses in the fort walls (pp. 13–20).

### Tegulae

The most common type of tile was the tegula made in two fabrics, a hard red sandy ware and a softer orange-red fabric with large inclusions. Size appears to have been uniform, but two standards were adopted for the flanges, one 2 cm. wide and upturned by 2 cm., the other 1·5 cm. wide and upturned by the same amount. The smaller sizes were invariably made in the orange-red fabric.

Finishing was restricted to finger grooving in the angle of the flange and finger drawn arcs at one end. Rarely rough combing in the form of a cross was found in place of the arcs.

Provenance: generally scattered throughout, but particularly numerous in the large pit 103.

### Imbrices

Fragments of imbrex tiles were numerous, the only distinctive feature being the comb decorations on the end of one fragment.

Provenance: generally scattered throughout, but occurring in quantity in pit 103 as the result of the demolition of a nearby roof.

### Bricks

Standard size Roman bricks were fairly common, measuring 26–30 cm. by *c.* 45 cm. Two thicknesses are recorded, 3·7 cm. and 4·7 cm., the former being the more common. Both the red sandy and orange fabrics were used for bricks.

Two examples were found tapering in thickness; this type would have been made for the construction of arches.

Provenance: from all parts of the site.

### Hypocaust tiles

Three types were recovered:

Pilae *tiles*, measuring 20·5 cm. square. Four, all in orange fabric with inclusions, were recovered from trench 90. Fragments of others may well have passed unnoticed.

Pilae *bases*. Squarish tiles measuring 26·5 by 28 cm. and 3·5 cm. thick. These were found in various parts of the site. Again, fragments would not have been distinguished. Tiles of this kind were sometimes used as the base for *pilae* built of the smaller tiles, and sometimes for the capping, helping to span the spaces between *pilae*.

*Hypocaust bricks*. Large bricks 5·5 cm. thick and approximately 44 cm. square. The upper surface was usually scored with a comb in a simple Union Jack pattern. Tiles of this size were usually employed as a final capping to hypocausts, the *pilae* being so spaced that tiles placed centrally upon them would have butted up to each other.

Provenance: various occupation layers, Roman pits 79, 103 and 147, and Saxon Well (pit 135). Also from layers below and above upper make-up.

### Box Tiles (pl. XXXI)

Fragments of box tiles occurred widely; the most common measured 18·5 by 17 cm. in section. Since no complete tiles were found, the length remains unknown. Some examples were provided with rectangular vents in the sides, others with triangular openings. Several were stained with soot internally. The surfaces were decorated with combing in three basic arrangements, roughly vertical, Union Jack fashion, or vertical and wavy.

A fragment of one example of a wedge-shaped voussoir box tile was recovered with rectangular side vents and a combed surface.

Provenance: widely distributed: Roman pits 48, 51, 166, 186, and several post-Roman pits. Also from layers above the upper make-up and road surface.

### Circular Tiles

One fragment of a circular tile 5 cm. thick was found. Its upper surface was comb decorated.

Provenance: trench 32 layer 5: watergate.

It will be apparent from the above description that two types of building construction were represented by the tiles: structures with tiled roofs and a building (or buildings) with hypocausts. Since all the relevant material was found out of its original context it is impossible to go further, except to draw attention to the small bath suites found in the shore forts of Richborough and Lympne. That a building of this kind probably existed at Portchester seems likely on the available evidence.

### Window Glass

The window glass is discussed in detail by Dr Harden on p. 373. Here it is necessary merely to record that fragments have been found in pits 66, 103, 121, in the layers below the upper road, and in the layers above the upper make-up and the upper occupation, together with a few pieces from general and post-Roman layers. Although the quantity is small, there is sufficient to suggest that glazed windows were not uncommon at Portchester.

### Nails

Large numbers of iron nails of different sizes were discovered in most levels reflecting the widespread occurrence of timber structures. Numbers and sizes have been recorded under the individual groups.

### Daub

A small quantity of chalky daub was found, much of it showing the marks of wattles, 1·5 cm. in diameter, or laths about 4 cm. wide. Some fragments would have come from timber-framed walls 8–10 cm. thick.

Daub is recorded from the following contexts: pits 47, 61, 62, 65, 86, 92, 119, 121, 130, 187, and from the middle occupation (trench 108 layer 163). Two of the fragments from pit 86 were painted red on their roughly smoothed surfaces (small finds 361 and 640). It is perhaps significant that all the daub belongs to period 4 (325–45) which is therefore likely to be a time when timber structures were being replaced on a substantial scale.

### Painted Plaster (fig. 21)

A few fragments of white sandy mortar, 1–3 cm. thick, were found. The outer surface was invariably smooth and either left white or painted in stripes of red or ochre. Plaster has been recovered from:

Pit 103: fragments include some that are coarsely moulded with vertical V-shaped grooves (fig. 21, no. 1).

Pit 195: fragment 2 cm. thick with lath marks on the back: white surface with a red band (fig. 21, no. 3).

Middle occupation (trench 102 layer 60): fragments including a piece from a window embrasure moulded around laths and painted red on the surface (fig. 21, no. 2).

Layer above make-up (trench 88 layer 10): fragment.

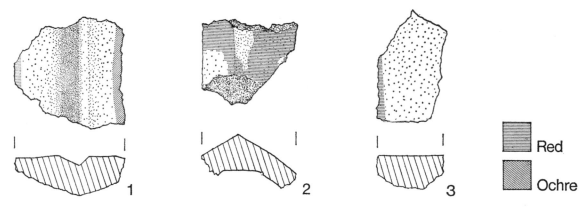

FIG. 21.  Painted plaster. Scale ½

# DRAINAGE GULLIES

The drainage gullies can be divided into two groups: those related to the buildings described above (pp. 66–8), and those which appear to have been dug to drain the gravel spread. To this latter group belong two major systems: gully 37 draining the southern area of the gravel spread, and gullies 23–6 which run across the centre of the gravel area. In addition, there are a number of isolated lengths in various parts of the site. A third system of gullies (nos. 41–3) occupying the eastern part of the site are of uncertain date, but since they contain only Roman material they will be described here. It is possible that this group served to drain the environs of timber buildings which have since disappeared.

### Gully 14 (90 layer 55)

Short irregular gully dug to a maximum depth of 9 in. (23 cm.) below the top of the upper make-up and cutting into the natural clay to a maximum depth of 5 in. (13 cm.). Filled with black occupation material.

### Gully 15 (89 layer 35)

Short length of gully cut through the upper make-up to a depth of 8 in. (20·3 cm.). Filled with black occupation material.
*Small finds:* Whetstone (1187): not illustrated, no. 358.

### Gully 23 (96 layers 26, 47 and 68)

Irregular gully running across the gravelled area. It varies in depth from 5 to 9 in. (13 to 23 cm.). Gullies 24, 25, 26, all appear to be part of the same system, but the relationship of gully 24 cannot be tested because of a later disturbance at the junction. Filled with black occupation material.

### Gully 24 (96 layers 53 and 54)

Irregular gully crossing the gravelled area. Its depth averages 5 in. (13 cm.). The relationship to gully 23 has been destroyed. Filled with brown loamy soil.

### Gully 25 (96 layer 72)

Short length of gully, running into gully 23. Cut through cobbles to a depth of 2 in. (5 cm.). Filled with black soil.
*Small finds:* Bronze coin (1808): House of Constantine (A.D. 350–60).

### Gully 26 (96 layer 61)

Very irregular gully expanding into a shallow hollow (pit 155). Filled with occupation debris mixed with brickearth.

### Gully 37 (90 layers 73, 74; trench 101 layers 122, 123, 141)

Two irregular gullies running into each other. They are cut through the upper make-up and appear to be laid out so as to drain the upper layer of cobble metalling. The maximum depth to which they are dug below the contemporary surface is 4 in. (10 cm.). Filled with black soil mixed with occupation material.

### Gully 39 (76 layer 28)

Short length of gully 8 in. (20·3 cm.) deep. Filled with grey–brown loamy soil.
*Small finds:* Iron ring (534): not illustrated; lead cuttings (535): not illustrated.

*Gully 40* (76 layer 11)

Gully on the same alignment as gully 39. Filled with dark grey loamy soil.

*Gully 41* (65 layer 7 and 70 layer 10)

Long regular gully cut through the top filling of pit 60 and through the surface of the main N–S road. The depth below the top of natural brickearth averages 8 in. (20·3 cm.).

Filled with greenish-grey loam mixed with some occupation material. Because of its relationship to pit 60 the gully is likely to belong to the second half of the fourth century or later. Since it produced only Roman material it is described here, but a date in the early Saxon period cannot be totally overlooked.

*Small finds:* Iron fragment (372): not illustrated.

*Gully 42* (70 layer 11)

Long regular gully dug to a depth of 8 in. (20·3 cm.) below the original ground level. Filled with greenish-grey loam mixed with some occupation material. The relationship of the gully to pit 51 could not be determined. The gully appears to belong to the same system as gully 41. A further length of gully on the same alignment occurs, after a gap, to the south.

*Gully 43* (65 layer 15)

Straight length of gully 3 in. (7·6 cm.) deep. Filled with greenish-grey soil with some oyster shells and bones. It is possibly part of the system to which gullies 41 and 42 belong.

*Gully 44* (71 layer 16)

Curved section of gully dug to a depth of 4 in. (10 cm.). Filled with greenish-grey marl containing pottery and oyster shells. The gully was cut through the cobbled surface.

*Gully 45* (89 layer 60)

Short length of gully dug to a depth of 3 in. (7·6 cm.) below the top of the upper make-up. Filled with occupation rubbish.

## WELLS

Altogether, six wells of Roman date were found. In the site recording system they were numbered together with the pits since the distinction between pits and wells was not apparent at the surface clearing stage. The wells are therefore recorded as pits 121, 135, 144, 164, 206 and 236.

The siting of the wells appears to have been planned. None was constructed within the zone occupied by the buildings, but nos. 135 and 121 lay close to the extremities of the area. The rest were arranged in a north–south line across the gravelled area.

All showed certain characteristics in common: they were constructed in circular or sub-rectangular well pits and must all have been lined with timber to retain the clay packed between the lining and the edge of the well pit. Nothing of the timber lining now survives, but since the actual shafts were all circular in section, the lining must have been of vertical planking, perhaps a series of barrel-like structures set one upon the other.[1]

The subsequent history of the wells varies. No. 135 continued in use into the Saxon period, no. 206 was deliberately filled with flints and clay, and no. 164 was also deliberately filled with soil and clay. The remaining three, nos. 121, 144 and 236, were allowed to fill up with occupation rubbish, of which they contained prolific amounts. Datable material from the shafts shows that there is no reason why the deliberate filling should not be Roman, although it cannot be closely dated. The coins from no. 121 would allow the tipping of rubbish to have filled the shaft by the 330s or 340s. The filling of no. 144 was not completed until a decade or two later, if the coin evidence can be taken as a reasonable guide. No. 236 was largely filled by the 340s to 350s, the uppermost soil accumulation probably forming in the 360s.

*Summary of Coins from the Wells*

| | | | |
|---|---|---|---|
| Well (pit) 121 | (816) | Constantine I (A.D. 308–17) | layer 36 |
| | (868) | Crispus (A.D. 322–4) | layer 36 |
| | (879) | Constantine I (A.D. 308–17) | layer 53 |
| | (883) | Galerius (A.D. 295–305) | layer 58 |
| | (937) | follis (?) (c. A.D. 295) | layer 68 |
| Well (pit) 144 | (1665) | Constans (A.D. 337–41) | layer 92 |
| | (1711) | corroded, 3rd–4th century | layer 92 |
| | (1745) | Helena (A.D. 324–30) | layer 134 |
| Well (pit) 236 | (2619) | Constantinopolis (A.D. 330–5) | layer 91 |
| | (2620) | Constantinopolis (A.D. 330–5) | layer 91 |
| | (2618) | Constantine II (A.D. 353–6) | layer 91 |
| | (2617) | Constantine II (A.D. 337–40) | layer 105 |
| | (2616) | House of Constantine (A.D. 322–4) | layer 109 |
| | (2615) | Carausius (A.D. 286–93) | layer 115 |

# THE PITS

## (pls. XXVIII, XXX)

Altogether some 83 Roman structures have been recorded as pits. Within this general category, six turned out on excavation to be wells (p. 75) and at least 42 were cesspits, the remainder being a miscellaneous group, composed largely of shallow scoops or hollows filled with occupation debris. It is evident that the majority of the cesspits fall into five distinct groups:

Group A: pits 178, 182, 183, 184, 185, 186, 231.
Group B: pits 85, 86, 87, 88, 90, 92, 94.
Group C: pits 60a, 60b, 61, 62, 63, 64, 65, 66.
Group D: pits 43, 46, 47, 48, 49, 52, 54.
Group E: pits 222, 223, 224, 225, 227, 228, 229, 235,

---

[1] Well 236, however, may have been lined with flints, although it is a distinct possibility that the flints were packed behind a timber lining.

Each group occupies a well defined area and each comprises between six and nine pits dug in a restricted series of almost standard sizes. The implication would seem to be that each group of pits was dug over a limited period of years in distinct areas, set aside for such purposes quite probably between and behind contemporary buildings. The apparent adherence to a series of standards, including 3½ by 3½ ft. (1·07 by 1·07 m.), 3 by 5 ft. (0·91 by 1·52 m.) and 4 by 7 ft. (1·22 by 2·13 m.) goes some way towards hinting at an element of military precision. In simple functional terms the small square pits could have served as single seat latrines, while the larger elongated structures were more suitable for two-seaters.

Most of the cesspits were allowed to fill practically to the top before being sealed by a thick deposit of clay and marl. How often, if at all, they were emptied before the final sealing it is impossible to say, but on balance it is more likely that a new pit was dug each time the old pit was filled. In theory it would be possible, by simple mathematics, to work out the capacity of each group in terms of man days, but such an exercise would be open to many variables. It is simpler to suppose that the life of each group was short, but not so short as to prevent the occasional accident of a new pit being cut into the side of an old one.

The dating of the cesspit groups depends upon the coins found in them. These may conveniently be summarized:

Group A:  pit 178   (1972)   Constantine I (A.D. 310–13)
Group B:  pit 86    ( 629)   Constantine I (A.D. 308–17)
          pit 92    (671)    Constantine I (A.D. 307–17)
                    (707)    Constantine I (A.D. 317–22)
                    (661)    House of Constantine (A.D. 335–45)
Group C:  pit 60a   (278)    Constantine I (A.D. 308–17)
                    (375)    Constantine I (A.D. 317–23)
          pit 62    (259)    Carausius (A.D. 286–93)
                    (275)    Constantine I? (c. A.D. 300–17)
          pit 63    (418)    Constantine I (A.D. 308–17)
                    (319)    Constantine I (A.D. 323–30)
                    (393)    Gratian (A.D. 367–78)
                    (395)    Gratian (A.D. 367–78)     ⎧From the uppermost fill of the pit, from
                    (404)    Valentinian (A.D. 364–75) ⎨late occupation rubbish
          pit 66    (297)    Valentinian I (A.D. 364–75) ⎩From uppermost fill
Group D:  pit 46    (197)    Tetricus I (A.D. 270–3)
                    (174)    Crispus (A.D. 317–24)
Group E:  pit 222   (2538)   Licinius (A.D. 310–17)
          pit 223   (2532)   Crispus (A.D. 321–3)
                    (2534)   Constantine I (A.D. 320–4)
          pit 227   (2550)   Constantine I (A.D. 310–17)
          pit 230   (2565)   Constantine I (A.D. 310–17)

The evidence speaks for itself. Apart from the late fourth-century coins from the very top of pits 63 and 66, from layers representing late rubbish accumulations, all the coins fall within a group which might reasonably have been in circulation in the 330s and 340s. This is precisely the period which the coin evidence in general indicates to be one of unusual activity (p. 196).

Three of the isolated pits outside the main groups produced coins:

Pit 103   (825) unidentifiable
Pit 138 (1621) Constantine II (A.D. 337–40)
Pit 187 (1982) Carausius (A.D. 286–93)
          (983) Constantine I (A.D. 319–22)

This group is also consistent with a dating in the 330s and 340s.

While it must be admitted that the evidence is not conclusive, the strong impression given by the above coin lists is that pit digging was restricted to a limited period of time and presumably therefore represents a particular kind of usage in one phase of the fort's life.

One further group of pits deserves mention, the two large pits close to the main E–W road, pits 103 and 187. As the detailed accounts will show, both were large and sub-rectangular, with irregular bottoms. Pit 103 had been filled with tips of building material derived from the demolition of timber buildings, but it had not necessarily been dug primarily as a demolition pit, although this explanation is possible. Pit 187 was of similar form, but the filling was largely of soil accumulation. Both show signs of having been left open for some time. While their purpose must remain unproven, various explanations are possible. It could be argued that they were quarry pits to provide brickearth for building. Another alternative is that the pits were dug as ponds. Both were close to wells, and conveniently sited for the watering of livestock. Such an explanation might at first sight appear far-fetched for a military installation, but the possible context for it and further implications will be examined in more detail below.

In the pages to follow, details of the filling and contents of each pit will be given. All small finds are listed, together with a simple statistical assessment of the pottery and comments on the animal bones.

The figures for the pottery are the work of Michael Fulford, whose general consideration of the pottery from the pits appears on pp. 272–5. The numbers given in italics refer to sherds illustrated in the type series.

The assessment of the animal bones is by Annie Grant. A detailed discussion of the bones appears below. The number following the name of the species is the percentage of the total number of fragments identified, excluding ribs and skull fragments (but including upper jaws with teeth present and horn cores). The main bone report includes a discussion of different methods for determining percentages of species represented and an assessment of their relative values. Where no percentage is given the animal forms less than 0·5% of the total. Percentages are generally corrected to the nearest whole number (and consequently do not always add up to 100). Where no percentages are given for a pit, it was considered that too few fragments were found for such an analysis to be meaningful. It should be noted that the significance of the percentages is proportional to the number of fragments identified, and percentages of species in pits where relatively few bones have been identified should be treated with caution. In all cases the order of species given is the order of their importance in the pit.

### Pit 40 (PC 66, trench 62, layer 7, Pit A)

Rectangular pit 3 by 2 ft. 9 in. (0·9 × 0·84 m.) at the top, with almost vertical sides, 4 ft deep (1·22 m.).

The upper fill consisted of black occupation soil containing quantities of large flint nodules, tiles and bones. The lower fill of crumbly brown soil, with oyster shells, bones and tiles thrown in, represented the original cesspit filling.

The pit was cut through the adjacent layer of cobbles.

PIT 40

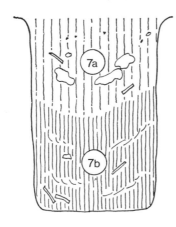 

ONE METRE

TWO METRES

THREE FEET — SECTIONS

SIX FEET — PLANS

FIG. 26

*Nails* (measurement in cm., as also for pits below)

From layer 7:

  1, 8·9; 1, 8·9 +; 1, 8·25; 4, 6·35: 1, 10·2 +; 1, 5·1 +; 1, 2·55.

*Pottery*

From layer 7:

  *New Forest*; body sherds in fabrics 1, 2 and 3; weight, 60 g.; 2·51%.
  *Oxford;* as 63·7, and body sherds of ?Oxford beakers; weight, 40 g.; 1·67%.
  *Hand-made fabric A;* 86 (5), 123 (5); weight, 1200 g.; 50·21%.
  *Black-burnished:* 85, 107, 126 (3); weight; 680 g.; 28·45%.
  *Grey fabrics:* as 76·1, 119, 133 (2), 140, 148, 159·3; weight, 370 g.; 15·48%.
  *Fabric D:* 40 g.; 1·67%.
  Total weight: 2390 g.

*Animal Bones*

  457 fragments identified (including 145 ribs and 54 skull fragments).
  Species represented: ox, 60; sheep, 18; pig, 16; bird, 2; dog, 1; red deer, 1; horse, 1; cat, 1.

### *Pit 41* (PC 66, trench 62, layer 12, Pit B)

Approximately rectangular pit measuring 4 ft. 3 in. by 5 ft. (1·30 × 1·52 m.). The sides sloped in gradually to a flat bottom 1 ft. (0·3 m.) below the level of the natural.

The uniform filling consisted of black soil mixed with oyster shells and animal bones.

The pit was cut through the adjacent layer of cobbles but was sealed by two Roman hearths.

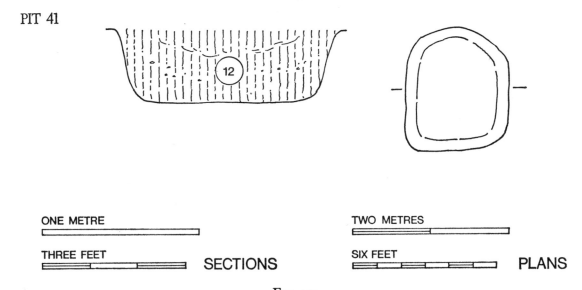

FIG. 27

### Nails

From layer 12:

1, 10·2, bent; 2, 5·1 +; 1, 5·1; 1, 7·6; 1, 3·85.

### Pottery

From layer 12:

*TS:* Dr. 31R, Central or East Gaul, second to mid third century.
*New Forest:* 2/*10.10* and *11*, 22.1–5 (2); 43 (2); weight, 150 g.; 7·69%.
*Oxford:* *15.4, 17.4,* as 31 and? Oxford *30.4;* weight, 225g; 11·54%
*Hand-made, fabric A:* 86 (2), 123, *123.7;* weight, 810 g.; 41·54%.
*Black-burnished:* 85, 107 (2), 117.1, 126 (2); weight, 460 g.; 23·59%.
*Grey fabrics:* as 109.6, 129 (2), 159.1; weight, 305 g.; 15·64%.
Total weight: 1950 g.

### Animal Bones

177 fragments identified (including 47 ribs and 22 skull fragments).
Species represented: ox, 62; pig, 18; sheep, 15; bird, 6.

### *Pit 43* (PC 66, trench 62, layer 14, Pit D)

Square pit 2 ft. 9 in. by 2 ft. 10 in. (0·84 × 0·86 m.) cut to a depth of 2 ft. 2 in. (0·66 m.). The filling contained some oysters and was of a uniform greenish clayey soil, representing its use as a cesspit.

Pit 43 was cut by pit 42 (late Saxon).

PIT 43

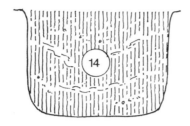 

ONE METRE

TWO METRES

THREE FEET    SECTIONS

SIX FEET    PLANS

Fig. 28

*Animal Bones*

58 fragments identified (including 16 ribs and 7 skull fragments).
Species represented: ox, 48; pig, 29; sheep, 20; dog, 3.

### *Pit 46* (PC 66, trench 63, layers 7, 7a, 7b, Pit Λ)

Rectangular pit with sloping sides measuring 4 ft. 3 in. by 7 ft. 4 in. (1·30 × 2·24 m.) at the top decreasing to 2 ft. 3 in. by 5 ft 0 in. (0·69 × 1·52 m.) at the bottom; 5 ft. (1·52 m.) deep.

Lowest fill (layer 7b) was of crumbly green–grey soil representing its use as a cesspit. The upper fill (layer 7a) was similar but contained more lenses of charcoal, oyster shells and roof tiles.

The pit post-dated pit 59 which was sealed by layer 7a. It was cut by the wall slot of a Saxon building.

*Small Finds*

From layer 7:
Bronze coin    (174)    Crispus (A.D. 317–24)
Bronze coin    (197)    Tetricus I (A.D. 270–3)
Shale board    (198)    curved fragment, fig. 122, no. 150
Skin vessel    (200)    no. 321; pl. XXXIV*b*

7

PITS 49 and 46

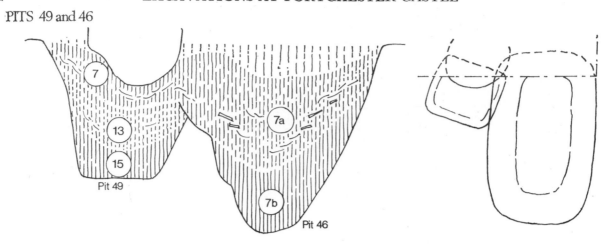

FIG. 29

Crucible        (199)    fragment, fig. 139, no. 336
Lead sheet      (204)    ⅛ in. thick, 1¾ in. wide, rolled into rough cylinder: not illustrated.
                         cf. fig. 123, no. 167.

### Nails

From layer 7:

    1, 8·9+; 2, 11·5; 1, 7·6, head 3·85 dia.; 1, 9·95 +; 1, 7·6 +; 1, 8·9; 1, 10·2; 2, 6·35; 2, 6·35 +;
    1, 7·0; 4, 5·1 +; 3, 3·85; 4, 3·85 +; 1, 7·6; 2, 2·55.

### Pottery

From layer 7:

    *New Forest:* as 2/10.21, 13 (2), *19.1–3, 20.2,* 22–1–5 (2), 32, 43, 43·8; weight, 360 g.; 4·26%.
    *Oxford: 17.11, 18.9,* as *34·6, 35·4, 36·8, 40·3,* 43, 58, 63 (2); weight, 880 g.; 10·41%.
    *Hand-made, fabric A:* 86 (3), 107 (2), 107·5, 123 (8), *123.8;* weight, 3085 g.; 36·49%.
    *Black-burnished:* 85 (7), 107 (6), 117.1, *126.3,* 126 (10); weight, 2810 g. 33·23%.
    *Grey fabrics:* 85, 127 (2), 129, *131.3, 142.1, 159.7, 159.8, 159.9, 178;* weight, 1300 g.; 15·38%.
    *Fabric D:* 20 g.; 0·24%.
    Total weight: 8455 g.

### Animal Bones

    291 fragments identified (including 87 ribs and 19 skull fragments).
    Species represented: ox, 54; pig, 16; sheep, 13; bird, 8; cat, 4; dog, 2; horse, 2; fish, 1; red deer, 1.
    Two almost complete ox skulls were found in this pit.
    The pig bones included part of a young animal.

*Human Bones*

Part of one infant burial.

*Pit 47* (PC 66, trench 63, layers 8, 9, 9a, Pit B)

Square pit, 3 ft. 9 in. (1·14 m.) across with almost vertical sides, 5 ft 2 in. (1·57 m.) deep.

The lowest fill (layer 9a) consisted of crumbly green–brown cesspit fill together with a quantity of animal bone. Above this (layer 9) came a thick deposit of the same material but with lenses of charcoal and oyster shells. The pit was sealed by a layer of burnt clay (8) mixed with lenses of soil and other burnt material. Fragments of daub were recovered from layer 9.

The pit was cut by a Saxon or medieval posthole.

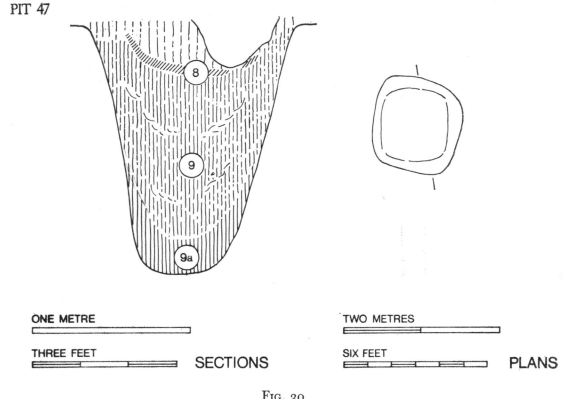

PIT 47

ONE METRE

THREE FEET          SECTIONS

TWO METRES

SIX FEET          PLANS

FIG. 30

*Small Finds*

From layer 9:

| | | |
|---|---|---|
| Bronze stylus | (168) | decorated, fig. 114, no. 64 |
| Bronze sheet | (179) | three fragments; not illustrated |
| Bone spindlewhorl | (195) | decorated, fig. 118, no. 109 |

Lead, melted but not re-formed.

*Glass Vessels*

From layer 9:
  fig. 198, no. 12.

*Nails*

From layer 9:
  1, 8·25; 2, 6·35; 1, 7·6 +; 1, 7·6 +, bent; 1, 4·5 +, bent; 1, 3·2 +; 1, 3·85; 2, 5·11.

*Pottery*

From layer 9:
  *New Forest:* 2/10.5, 22.1–5 (2), *29.2*; weight, 180 g.; 6·50%.
  *Oxford:* 31, other sherds of fabric 4; weight, 75 g.; 2·70%.
  *Hand-made, fabric A:* 86 (2), 107, 123; weight, 850 g.; 30·70%.
  *Black-burnished:* 85 (2), 107 (2), 126; weight, 850 g.; 30·70%.
  *Grey fabrics:* 85 (2), 92, 94, *119.1* (sherds of same vessel in pit 48) 127, 132, 140 (2), *154.5*; weight, 785 g.; 28·50%.
  *Fabric D:* 69; weight, 25 g.; 0·90%.
  Total weight: 2765 g.

*Animal Bones*

  309 fragments identified (including 50 ribs and 36 skull fragments).
  Species represented: ox, 37; cat, 30; bird, 14; pig, 9; sheep, 8; red deer, 2; dog; fish.
  This pit contained a higher than usual percentage of cat and bird bones. The cat bones included one almost complete animal and part of at least three others.
  The pig bones included part of a new-born animal.

*Human Bones*

  Infant tibia.

### Pit 48 (PC 66, trench 63, layers 14 and 14a, Pit D)

Rectangular pit 6 ft. 7 in. by 4 ft. (2·0 × 1·22 m.) with slightly insloping sides, 4 ft. 2 in. (1·27 m.) deep.

The lowest layer (layer 14a) was of crumbly green–brown cesspit filling containing quantities of animal bones. Above this was a greenish-grey soil of similar texture mixed with flints, oyster shells and lenses of charcoal.

The pit was cut by a shallow late Saxon feature.

*Small Finds*

From layer 14:
|  |  |  |
|---|---|---|
| Bone bracelet | (183) | fragment, fig. 117, no. 101 |
| Bone handle | (177) | fragment, fig. 119, no. 118 |
| Ceramic object | (175) | fig. 139, no. 334 |
| Ceramic spindle whorl | (176) | fig. 139, no. 332 |
| Lead, net weight | (2655) | fig. 123, no. 167 |
| Lead, melted but not re-formed. | | |

PIT 48

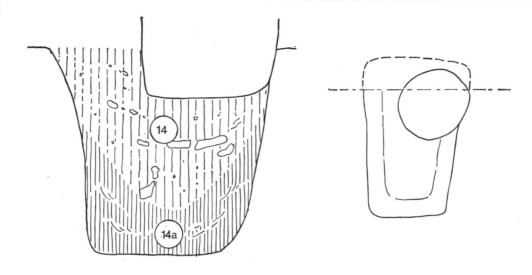

ONE METRE

TWO METRES

THREE FEET          SECTIONS          SIX FEET          PLANS

FIG. 31

## Nails

From layer 14:
  1, 10·2 +; 1, 8·9 +; 2, 5·1 +; 3, 3·85.

## Pottery

From layer 14:
  *New Forest:* 3.6, 2/10.22–25, 11, 22.1–5, 38.2, 43, 49.6; weight, 400 g.; 6·20%.
  *Oxford:* 15.1, sherds of of fabric 4; weight, 50 g.; 0·78%
  *Hand-made fabric A:* 86 (3), 107, 123 (11); weight, 1850 g.; 28·68%.
  *Black-burnished:* 85 (4), 107 (2), 126 (5); weight, 2300 g.; 35·66%.
  *Grey fabrics:* 85 (2), 92, 119.1 (sherds of same vessel in pit 47), 127 (6), 129, 129.4 (3), 141 (2),
        153.2, 175.2; weight, 1840 g.; 28·53%.
  *Fabric D:* 137; weight, 10 g.; 0·16%.
  Total weight: 6450 g.

## Animal Bones

  351 fragments identified (including 144 ribs and 10 skull fragments).
  Species represented: ox, 49; sheep, 21; pig, 20; bird, 9; cat, 1.
  The ox bones included part of an animal less than one year old.

### *Pit 49* (PC 66, trench 63, layers 13 and 15, Pit E)

Rectangular pit 3 ft. (0·91 m.) across and 2 ft. 9 in. (0·84 m.) deep.
The lowest layer (layer 15) was a crumbly green–grey cesspit filling. It was sealed by a layer

of chalk marl and soil (layer 13) presumably to act as a deliberate seal. Above this was layer 7, which represented the lateral extension of the filling of the adjacent pit 46.

Pit 49 pre-dated pit 46 on stratigraphical grounds.

*Pottery*

From layer 13:
  *New Forest:* 22.1–5; weight, 40 g.; 7·02%.
  *Hand-made, fabric A:* 123 (2); weight, 270 g.; 47·37%.
  *Black-burnished:* 85 (2) 126 (2); weight, 200 g.; 35·09%.
  *Grey fabrics:* 129, 132; weight, 60 g.; 10·53%.
  Total weight: 570 g.

*Animal Bones*

  45 fragments identified (including 18 ribs).
  Species represented: ox, sheep, bird, pig, cat, vole.

*Pit 51* (PC 66, trench 65, layer 11, Pit B; PC 67, trench 69, layer 19)

Rectangular pit 2 ft. 6 in. by 6 ft. 6 in. (0·76 × 1·98 m.), 1 ft. 7 in. deep (0·48 m.).

The filling was of a uniform grey soil mixed with quantities of charcoal.

The pit had been subjected to intense heat which scorched the sides and bottom, baking the clay red to a depth of 1 in. (2·5 cm.). It is possible that the pit was constructed for a process of some kind requiring heating: on abandonment it was filled with rubbish.

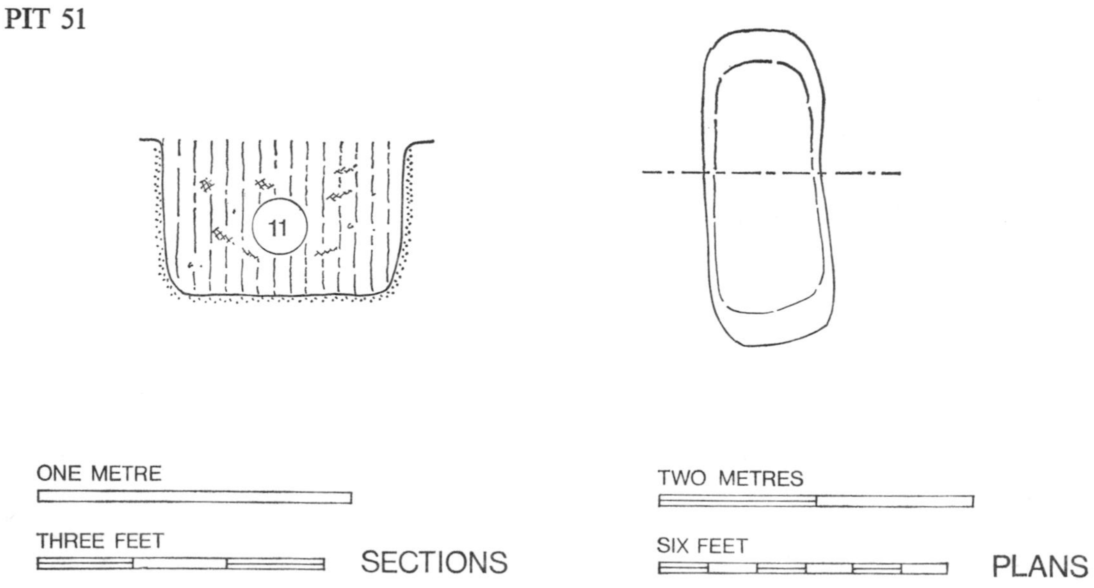

PIT 51

ONE METRE

TWO METRES

THREE FEET          SECTIONS

SIX FEET          PLANS

Fig. 32

*Small Finds*

From layer 11:
Bronze penannular brooch (212): much corroded, broken and distorted: the terminals do not survive and the object is without distinctive characteristics: not illustrated.

*Glass Vessel*

From layer 11:
fig. 198, no. 14.

*Nails*

From layer 11:
1, 7·6.

*Pottery*

From layer 11:
*New Forest:* 3.1–2, 43; weight, 120 g.; 13·72%.
*Oxford:* 43; weight, 10 g.; 1·14%.
*Hand-made, fabric A:* 123; weight, 140 g.; 16·0%.
*Black-burnished:* 107; weight, 80 g.; 9·14%.
*Grey fabrics: 109.1 and 2*; weight, 240 g.; 27·43%.
*Fabric D:* 97, *109.8*; weight, 225 g.; 25·71%.
*Misc.:* 156; weight, 60 g.; 6·86%.
Total weight: 875 g.

*Animal Bones*

57 fragments identified (including 8 ribs and 1 skull fragment).
Species represented: ox, 44; sheep, 40; pig, 10; bird, 4; cat, 2.

*Pit 52* (PC 66, trench 65, layer 12, Pit C)

Oval shaped pit 3 ft. by 4 ft. 6 in. (0·91 × 1·37 m.) dug to a depth of 2 ft 5 in. (0·74 m.). Uniform filling of grey soil, flints and occupation debris.
The pit was cut by pit 53 (late Saxon) and by the post pit of late Saxon date.

*Nails*

From layer 12:
1, 8·9; 1, 5·1; 1, 6·35.

*Pottery*

From layer 12:
*TS:* base, Dr. 31, Central Gaul, Antonine.
*New Forest:* 29, 43; weight, 60 g.; 2·63%.
*Oxford:* 31 (probably the same vessel as in pit 54), 57; weight, 200 g.; 8·77%.
*Hand-made, fabric A:* 107, *123.4*, 123 (3); weight, 960 g.; 42·11%.
*Black-burnished:* 85 (2), 126 (2); weight, 550 g.; 24·12%.

*Grey fabrics:* *85.1*, 85, 127, 134, 142; weight, 500 g.; 21·95%.
*Fabric D:* 87.2; weight, 10 g.; 0·44%.
Total weight: 2280 g.

## Animal Bones

96 fragments identified (including 41 ribs and 1 skull fragment).
Species represented: ox, 54; sheep, 20; pig, 18; red deer, 4; dog, 2; bird, 2.

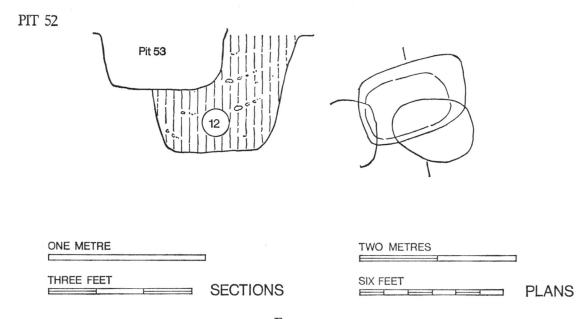

Fig. 33

*Pit 54* (PC 66, trench 65, layers 14 and 18, Pit E)

Roughly rectangular pit 2 ft. 9 in. by 3 ft. 9 in. (0·84 × 1·14 m.), 4 ft. 5 in. (1·35 m.) deep.
The lowest layer (layer 18) was of greenish-grey crumbly cesspit filling containing bones and oyster shells. The upper layer (layer 14) was grey soil containing occupation debris including charcoal.

## Small Finds

From layer 18:
   Iron key (181): fig. 129, no. 221.

## Nails

From layer 14:
   1, 7·6; 2, 5·1.
From layer 18:
   1, 10·2 +; 1, 5·1.

PIT 54

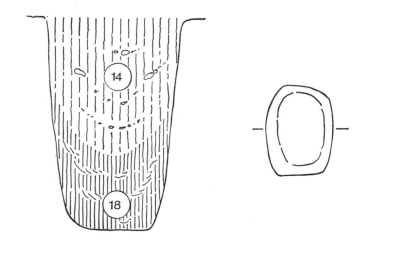

ONE METRE

TWO METRES

THREE FEET SECTIONS SIX FEET PLANS

Fig. 34

## Pottery

From layer 14:
*New Forest:* sherd of fabric 2; weight, 10 g.; 1·39%.
*Hand-made, fabric A:* 123 (3); weight, 170 g.; 23·61%.
*Black-burnished:* 107, 126 (3); weight, 180 g.; 25·0%.
*Grey fabrics:* 85, 127, 129, 145; weight, 250 g.; 34·72%.
*Fabric D:* 87.2; weight, 110 g.; 0·44%.
Total weight: 720 g.
From layer 18:
*New Forest:* sherds of fabric 1; weight, 20 g.; 1·53%.
*Oxford: 31.4* (probably the same vessel as in pit 52), 63; weight, 190 g.; 14·50%.
*Hand-made, fabric A:* 86, 123; weight, 440 g.; 33·59%.
*Black-burnished:* 85 (4), *107.8,* 126; weight, 310 g.; 23·66%.
*Grey fabrics: 127.3,* 127, 129, *131.2,* 140, *176.3;* weight, 350 g.; 26·72%.
Total weight: 1310 g.

## Animal Bones

95 fragments identified (including 30 ribs and 3 skull fragments).
Species represented: ox, 47; sheep, 26; pig, 16; bird, 11.

## Pits 6oa and b (PC 67, trench 68, layers 8a and 8b)

### Pit 6oa

Rectangular pit 6 ft. by 3 ft. 6 in. (1·83 × 1·07 m.), 2 ft. 10 in. (0·86 m.) deep.

The filling was completely uniform consisting of grey soil, flints and wads of yellow brick-earth all apparently thrown in at the same time.

The pit seems to have cut away most of the earlier pit 6ob.

PIT 60   A   and   B

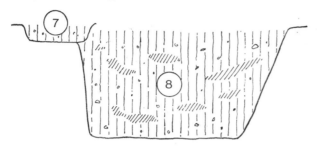
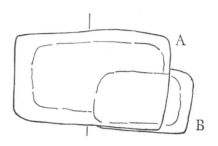

ONE METRE

TWO METRES

THREE FEET     SECTIONS

SIX FEET     PLANS

Fig. 35

### Pit 6ob

Rectangular pit 4 ft. by 2 ft. 6 in. (1·22 × 0·76 m.), 3 ft. (0·91 m.) deep.

The filling (layer 8b) consisted of dark grey soil and some lenses of clay difficult to distinguish from the filling of pit 6oa. Pit 6ob was apparently earlier than 6oa but the relationship was not indisputable. Pit 6ob was cut by a gully of early medieval date.

One possible explanation for this group of pits is that pit 6ob had been dug and filled before pit 6oa was laid out. After 6oa had been begun it was realized that it was cutting through the unconsolidated filling of an earlier structure and was accordingly abandoned and refilled.

Since there was difficulty in distinguishing between the two fillings it is better to regard all finds as belonging to the later pit.

### Pit 6oa

#### Small Finds

From layer 8:
Bronze coin   (278)   Constantine I (A.D. 308–17)
Bronze coin   (375)   Constantine I (A.D. 317–23)
Iron stylus   (273)   fig. 130, no. 243.

*Pottery*

From layer 8:
   *New Forest:* 19, 29, 43; weight, 110 g.; 2·59%.
   *Oxford:* sherds of fabrics 4 and 5; weight, 25 g.; 0·59%.
   *Misc.:* 15.
   *Hand-made, fabric A:* 86 (2), *107*.5, 123 (6); weight, 1660 g.; 39·01%.
   *Black-burnished:* 85 (2), 107 (2), 117.1, 126 (3); weight, 1060 g.; 24·91%.
   *Grey fabrics:* 77, 85, *87.3*, 119, 127, 129 *131*.5, 141, 159.7–13, 162, 172; weight, 1350 g.; 31·73%.
   *Fabric D:* 50 g.; 1·18%.
   Total weight: 4255 g.

*Animal Bones*

   219 fragments identified (including 73 ribs and 10 skull fragments).
   Species represented: ox, 54; sheep, 16; pig, 15; cat, 6; bird, 5; red deer, 2; dog, 1.
   The pig bones included part of a new-born animal.

*Human Bones*

Infant humerus.

## Pit 61 (PC 67, trench 68, layers 12, 23 and 24)

Rectangular pit 4 ft. by 2 ft. 6 in. (1·22 × 0·76 m.), 3 ft. (0·91 m.) deep.

The lower level (layer 24) was a greenish-grey crumbly soil representing the original filling of the cesspit. It was sealed by a thick layer of clean chalky marl (layer 23) which contained some flints. Above this was a layer of occupation rubbish (layer 12) consisting of grey soil, flints, chalk, oyster shells, bones and tile fragments. Fragments of daub were recovered from layer 23.

The pit was cut by a medieval gully.

*Small Finds*

From layer 12:
   Bronze bracelet   (245)   fragment, two-strand twisted wire; not illustrated.
   Shale bracelet   (244)   fragment, plain, external diameter 5·4 cm.; not illustrated.
   Iron knife   (272)   fig. 126, no. 190

*Pottery*

From layer 12:
   *New Forest:* sherd fabric 2; weight, 50 g.; 3·91%.
   *Oxford:* 14, 43, 58·3, *63*.7; weight, 250 g.; 19·53%.
   *Hand-made, fabric A:* 123; weight, 560 g.; 43·75%.
   *Black-burnished:* 107, 126; weight, 70 g.; 5·47%.
   *Grey fabrics:* 92, 119, *120*.2, 127, 140; weight, 350 g.; 27·34%.
   Total weight: 1280 g.

PIT 61

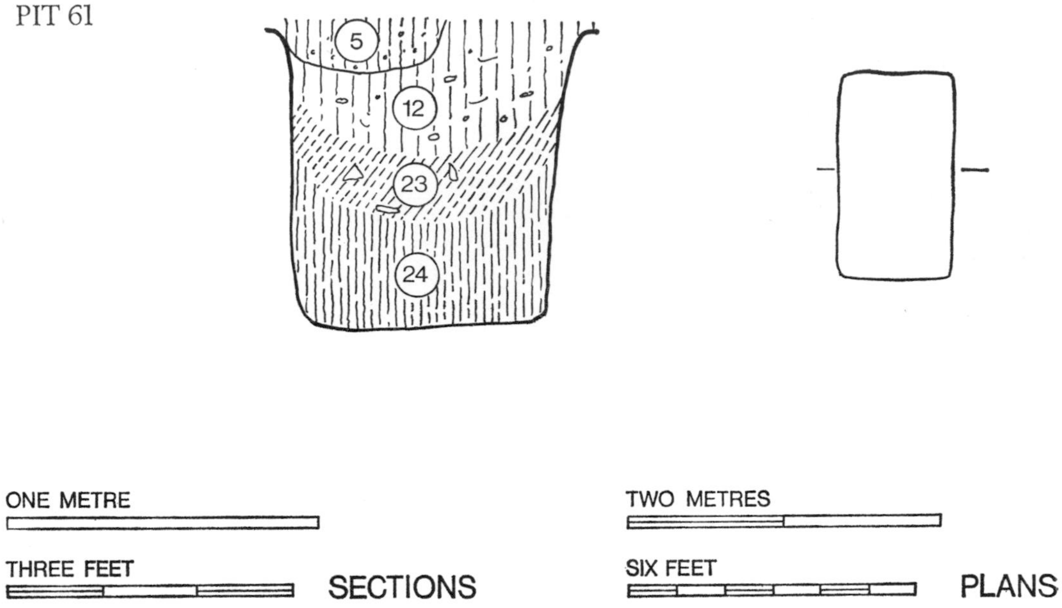

ONE METRE

THREE FEET                          SECTIONS

TWO METRES

SIX FEET                          PLANS

Fig. 36

From layer 23:
  *Oxford:* sherds of 14, as in 12; weight, 15 g.; 4·23%.
  *Hand-made, fabric A:* weight, 240 g.; 67·6%.
  *Black-burnished:* 126; weight, 10 g.; 2·82%.
  *Grey fabrics:* 127, *148.2*; weight, 80 g.; 22·54%.
  *Fabric D:* 10 g.; 2·82%.
  Total weight: 355 g.
From layer 24:
  *New Forest:* 29; weight, 10 g.; 10·0%.
  *Black-burnished:* weight, 20 g.; 20·0%.
  *Grey fabrics:* 84.1; weight, 70 g.; 70·0%.
  Total weight: 100 g.
  Weight from all the layers: 1735 g.

*Animal Bones*

  195 fragments identified (including 61 ribs and 15 skull fragments).
  Species represented: ox, 63; sheep, 21; pig, 14; badger, 2.

*Pit 62* (PC 67, trench 68, layers 13 and 22)

Rectangular pit 4 ft. 3 in. by 2 ft. 3 in. (1·29 × 0·69 m.), 3 ft. (0·91 m.) deep.

The lowest layer (layer 22) was a green–grey crumbly cesspit filling mixed with bones, oyster shells and some charcoal. This was sealed by a filling of grey soil (layer 13) which contained masses of bones, oyster shells and other occupation debris. At the bottom of this layer, sealing layer 22, was a discontinuous mass of yellow clay thrown in as shovelfuls to serve as a seal to the cesspit. Fragments of daub were recovered from layer 13.

The pit was cut by a medieval gully.

PIT 62

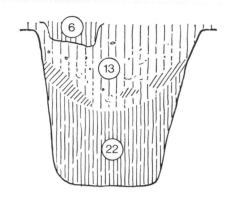
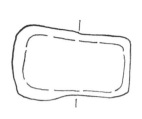

ONE METRE

TWO METRES

THREE FEET     SECTIONS

SIX FEET     PLANS

Fig. 37

## Small Finds

From layer 13:

| | | |
|---|---|---|
| Bronze coin | (259) | Carausius (A.D. 286–93) |
| Bronze coin | (275) | ?Constantine I (c. A.D. 300–17) |

## Pottery

From layer 13:

*New Forest:* sherd of fabric 2; weight, 5 g.; 0·48%.
*Hand-made, fabric A:* 86 (2), 123; weight, 620 g.; 59·90%.
*Black-burnished:* 85; weight, 100 g.; 9·66%.
*Grey fabrics:* 136 (2), ?175; weight, 300 g.; 28·99%.
*Mayen Ware: 151;* weight, 10 g.; 0·97%.
Total weight: 1035 g.

## Amimal Bones

227 fragments identified (including 65 ribs and 8 skull fragments).
Species represented: ox, 60; pig, 20; sheep, 16; bird, 3; cat, 1.

### *Pit 63* (PC 67, trench 70, layers 14, 29, 29a, 29b, 32, 35, 41, 42, 43, 44)

Large rectangular pit, 7 ft. by 4 ft. 6 in. (2·13 × 1·37 m.): 6 ft. 10 in. (2·08 m.) deep.
There were some traces of a timber lining composed of horizontal planking showing up against the face of the clay packing (layer 41) which survived in places around the upper levels of the pit. Originally this packing would have extended at least halfway down the pit sides, but following the removal or rotting of the lower planks during the Roman period it had eroded inwards (layers 42 and 43). In layer 41 carbonized remains of wood, possibly

from the planking, still survived. An alternative explanation is that the lower part of the pit was unlined, layers 42 and 43 representing the eroded sides rather than packing.

The lowest layer (layer 44) was a thin cesspit deposit of green–grey silt sealed by a similar material containing some pottery, bones and oyster shells (layer 35). Above this was a thick deposit of marl (layer 32) thrown in to seal the lower filling of the cesspit. On top of the marl lay a deposit of charcoal (layer 29b).

The next layers (29 and 29a) were of greenish-brown cesspit filling with lumps of flint, animal bones and oyster shells. Layer 29a contained more charcoal which had presumably been derived from the layer beneath (layer 29b). These cesspit fills were covered by a thick deposit of occupation rubbish (layer 14) containing tiles, bones, oysters, pottery, flints, etc., in a lens of black soil.

PIT 63

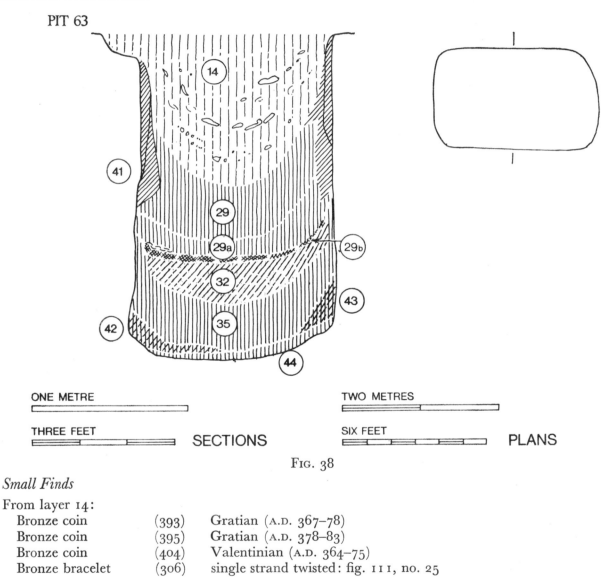

ONE METRE

TWO METRES

THREE FEET          SECTIONS          SIX FEET          PLANS

Fig. 38

*Small Finds*

From layer 14:

| | | |
|---|---|---|
| Bronze coin | (393) | Gratian (A.D. 367–78) |
| Bronze coin | (395) | Gratian (A.D. 378–83) |
| Bronze coin | (404) | Valentinian (A.D. 364–75) |
| Bronze bracelet | (306) | single strand twisted: fig. 111, no. 25 |

| | | |
|---|---|---|
| Bronze bracelet | (309) | single strand twisted; not illustrated |
| Bronze nail cleaner | (311) | fig. 113, no. 56 |
| Bronze bracelet | (411) | fragment of strip type; not illustrated |
| Bronze fragments | (312, 381, 382, 390, 394) | small nondescript corroded fragments; not illustrated |
| Iron object | (403) | fragment, not illustrated |
| Iron stylus | (296) | fig. 130, no. 244 |
| Iron nails | (407, 409, 410) | very fragmentary; not illustrated |
| Glass bead | (414) | not illustrated, no. 163 |
| Bone bracelet | (305) | fragment, not illustrated |
| Shale spindle whorl | (412) | not illustrated |

From layer 28:

| | | |
|---|---|---|
| Whetstone | (295) | not illustrated, no. 356 |

From layer 32:

| | | |
|---|---|---|
| Bronze coin | (319) | Constantine I (A.D. 323–30) |
| Bronze coin | (418) | Constantine I (A.D. 308–17) |

From layer 35:

| | | |
|---|---|---|
| Bronze fragment | (420) | corroded and nondescript; not illustrated |

## Nails

From layer 14:
1, 7·6; 1, 7·6 +; 1, 5·75; 1, 3·85.

## Pottery

From layer 14
(no weights are given for this layer as no body sherds were kept):
*New Forest:* 2/*10.13*, 29 (2), 32 (2), 41·3, 43.
*Oxford:* 34.6, *36*.3, 43 (3), 58 (2)
*Hand-made, fabric A:* 86 (2), 107, 123 (4)
*Black-burnished:* 85 (2), 126
*Grey fabrics:* 76, 85, 124 (3), 129 (3), 159.
*Fabric D:* 137.4–6.
From layer 29:
*New Forest:* 3.6, *10.1*; weight, 120 g.; 19·83%.
*Oxford:* 17.11; weight, 5 g.; 0·83%.
*Hand-made, fabric A:* 107 (2), 107.5, 123 (3); weight, 180 g.; 29·75%.
*Black-burnished:* 107; weight, 100 g.; 16·53%.
*Grey fabrics:* 77, 85 (2), 140, 148, 162.1; weight, 200 g.; 33·06%.
Total weight: 605 g.
From layer 35:
*New Forest:* 2/*10*.4–5, 43, 66; weight, 100 g.; 8·93%.
*Hand-made, fabric A:* 86, 123; weight, 320 g.; 28·57%.

*Black-burnished:* 85 (3), 126; weight, 420 g.; 37·5%.
*Grey fabrics:* 129 (3), 129.4, 132, 140 (2); weight, 280 g.; 25·0%.
Total weight: 1120 g.
From layer 41:
   *New Forest:* 49, sherds of fabric 1; weight, 15 g.; 3·9%.
   *Oxford:* sherd of fabric 4.
   *Hand-made, fabric A:* 123 (2); weight, 70 g.; 18·18%.
   *Black-burnished:* 107; weight, 50 g.; 12·99%.
   *Grey fabrics:* 129, 132, 140; weight, 250 g.; 64·94%.
   Total weight: 385 g.
   Weight from all the layers: 2110 g.

## Animal Bones

From layers 29a, 29, 32, 35:
   292 fragments identified (including 69 ribs and 14 skull fragments).
   Species represented: ox, 55; sheep, 16; pig, 13; bird, 12; red deer, 1·5; dog, 1; hare, 0·5; roe deer,
             0·5; cat, 0·5.
   Parts of a very young sheep and pig were recovered from this pit.

## Human Bones

   Infant ulna.

## Pit 64 (PC 67, trench 70, layers 19, 33 and 34)

Rectangular pit 5 ft. by 3 ft. 6 in. (1·52 × 1·07 m.), 3 ft. 1 in. (0·94 m.) deep.
  The lowest level (layer 34) was a greenish–grey cesspit fill containing some pottery, bones and oyster shells with a lens of charcoal towards the top. It was sealed by a thick layer of clayey marl (layer 33) above which lay a deposit of occupation debris (layer 19) consisting of black soil, tiles, bones, oysters and pottery.

## Small Finds

From layer 19:

| | | |
|---|---|---|
| Shale bracelet | (302) | undecorated fragment, external diameter 7·6 cm.; not illustrated. |
| Iron spear or arrow head | (299) | fig. 124, no. 177. |
| Iron key | (320) | fig. 129, no. 220. |
| Iron rod | (307) | ?part of a stylus handle; not illustrated. |
| Iron hook | (397) | fig. 130, no. 234. |

## Pottery

From layer 19:
   *New Forest:* 54.1; weight, 110 g.; 9·40%.
   *Misc.:* 15.1.
   *Hand-made, fabric A:* 123 (2); weight, 320 g.; 27·35%.
   *Black-burnished:* 107, 126 (2); weight, 150 g.; 12·82%.
   *Grey fabrics:* 85 (2), 129.4, 140, *153.8*; weight, 550 g.; 47·01%.
   *Fabric D:* 40 g.; 3·42%.
   Total weight: 1170 g.

PIT 64

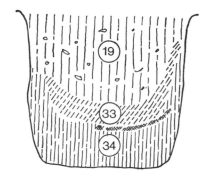
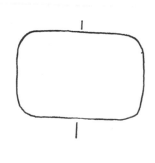

ONE METRE

TWO METRES

THREE FEET    SECTIONS        SIX FEET        PLANS

FIG. 39

From layer 33:
  *Hand-made, fabric A:* 107; weight, 10 g.; 33·33%.
  *Black-burnished:* weight, 20 g.; 66·67%.
  Total weight: 30 g.
From layer 34:
  *New Forest:* fabric 1; weight, 10 g.; 2·17%.
  *Hand-made, fabric A:* 86, 107, 123; weight, 150 g.; 32·61%.
  *Black-burnished:* 126; weight: 50 g.; 10·87%.
  *Grey fabrics:* weight, 250 g.; 54·35%.
  Total weight: 460 g.
  Weight from all the layers: 1660 g.

*Animal Bones*

  225 bones identified (including 55 ribs and 13 skull fragments).
  Species represented: ox, 50; sheep, 29; pig, 13; cat, 4; bird, 3; horse, 1.
  The sheep and pig bones both include a high percentage of young animals.

*Human Bones*

  Infant burial.

### *Pit 65* (PC 67, trench 70, layers 22, 36 and 37)

Rectangular pit 4 ft. 6 in. by 2 ft. 6 in. (1·37 × 0·76 m.): 4 ft. (1·22 m.) deep.
The lowest level (layer 37) was typical green–grey cesspit filling containing quantities of
bone, pottery and oyster shells. It was sealed by a thick layer of marl (layer 36) above which
was grey occupation soil (layer 22) mixed with bones, flints, oysters, pottery and charcoal.
The charcoal was denser towards the bottom. Fragments of daub were recovered from
layer 22.

8

PIT 65

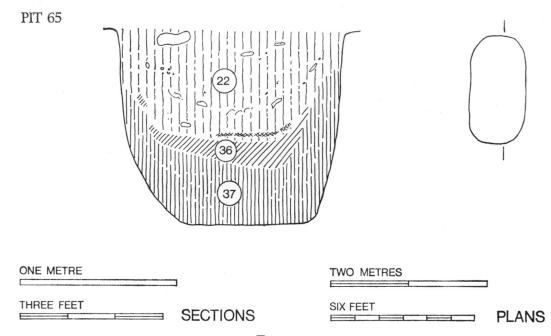

ONE METRE

THREE FEET    SECTIONS

TWO METRES

SIX FEET    PLANS

Fig. 40

*Small Finds*

From layer 37:
  Bone pin (323): fig. 116, no. 90.

*Pottery*

From layer 22:
  *New Forest: 13.4*; 43, weight, 50 g.; 3·64%.
  *Oxford: 40.4, 43.12, 58, 58.2*; weight, 70 g.; 5·09%.
  *Handmade, fabric A:* 86 (2); weight, 875 g.; 63·64%.
  *Black-burnished:* 126, ?175; weight, 170 g.; 12·36%.
  *Grey fabrics:* 107, 117.2, 127, 129 (2), 140; weight, 210 g.; 15·27%.
  Total weight, 1375 g.
From layer 36:
  *Black-burnished:* sherds.
From layer 37:
  *New Forest:* 22.1–5.
  *Hand-made, fabric A:* 123, weight, 60 g.; 11·11%.
  *Black-burnished:* 126.2; weight, 360 g.; 66·67%.
  *Grey fabrics:* 129.4, 140; weight, 120 g.; 22·22%.
  Total weight: 540 g.
  Weight from all the layers: 1915 g.

*Animal Bones*

  274 fragments identified (including 78 ribs and 22 skull fragments).
  Species represented: ox, 35; dog, 34; pig, 15; sheep, 13; bird, 2; red deer, 1.

The high percentage of dog bones recovered from this pit included one mature animal and one young animal of less than one year old. A large goat horn core was also found.

*Pit 66* (PC 67, trench 70, layers 23, 30 and 31)

Rectangular pit 4 ft. 6 in. by 3 ft. (1·37 × 0·91 m.), 3 ft. (0·91 m.) deep.

The lowest level (layer 31) was typical green–grey cesspit filling mixed with oyster shells and bone and interleaved with lenses of charcoal and clay. It was sealed by a thick layer of clayey marl (layer 30). Above this was occupation rubbish (layer 23) consisting of grey soil with flints, bone, tiles, oysters, etc.

PIT 66

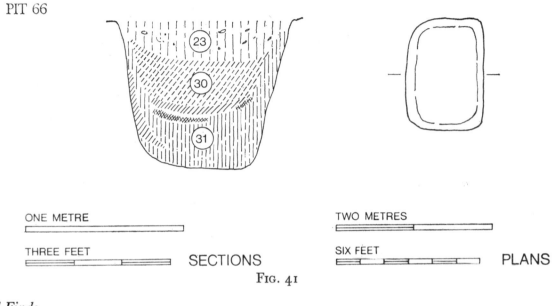

ONE METRE

TWO METRES

THREE FEET          SECTIONS          SIX FEET          PLANS

FIG. 41

*Small Finds*

From layer 23:
  Bronze coin                    (297)    Valentinian I (A.D. 364–75)
From layer 31:
  Bronze fragment                (382)    not illustrated.

*Window Glass*

From layer 23:
  Fragment, cf. fig. 199, no. 24.

*Nails*

From layer 23:
  1, 3·85.

*Pottery*

From layer 23:
  *New Forest:* 29, 43; weight, 50 g.; 4·50%.
  *Pevensey:* 37, weight, 20 g.; 1·80%.

*Hand-made, fabric A:* 86, 107, 123 (3); weight, 480 g.; 43·24%.
*Black-burnished:* 85, 107, 126; weight, 270 g.; 24·32%.
*Grey fabrics:* 107, 129, 136, 140; weight, 290 g.; 26·13%.
Total weight: 1110 g.
From layer 30:
    *Hand-made, fabric A:* sherds only; weight, 10 g.; 50·0%.
    *Black-burnished:* 126; weight, 10 g.; 50·0%.
    Total weight: 20 g.
From layer 31:
    *New Forest:* 29; weight, 80 g.; 19·51%.
    *Hand-made, fabric A:* 107, 123 (2); weight, 100 g.; 24·39%.
    *Black-burnished:* 126; weight, 70 g.; 17·07%.
    *Grey fabrics:* 140.5; weight, 160 g.; 39·02%.
    Total weight: 410 g.
    Weight from all the layers: 1540 g.

*Animal Bones*

From layers 30 and 31:
    81 fragments identified (including 39 ribs and 2 skull fragments).
    Species represented: ox, 65; pig, 18; sheep, 12; bird, 5.
From layer 23:
    82 fragments indentified (including 34 ribs and 4 skull fragments).
    Species represented: ox, 61; sheep, 20; pig, 11; bird, 9.

## *Pit 70* (PC 67, trench 69, layer 29)

Rectangular pit 3 ft. 6 in. by 4 ft. (1·07 × 1·22 m.), 1 ft. 7 in. (0·48 m.) deep.

The filling (layer 29) was uniform throughout consisting of black soil mixed with quantities of burnt clay and marl.

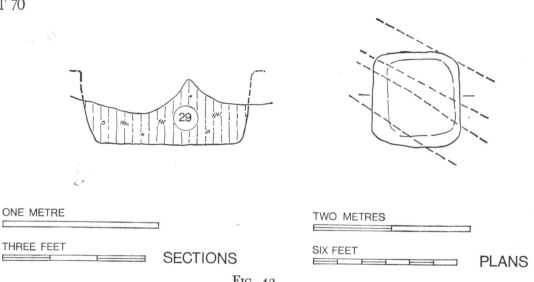

FIG. 42

*Small Finds*

From layer 29:

| | | |
|---|---|---|
| Iron nail | (315) | large nail, head 3·5 cm. diameter; not illustrated. |
| Iron nail | (316) | not illustrated. |
| Iron hobnails | (314) | 22 dome-headed hobnails, presumably from the sole of a shoe; not illustrated. |

*Pottery*

From layer 29:
 *New Forest:* base of fabric 2; weight, 70 g.; 17·95%.
 *Misc.:* 74.
 *Hand-made, fabric A:* weight 30 g.; 7·69%.
 *Black-burnished:* 107; weight, 110 g.; 28·21%.
 *Grey fabrics:* 107; weight, 180 g.; 46·15%.
 Total weight: 390 g.

*Animal Bones*

 74 fragments identified (including 12 ribs and 7 skull fragments).
 Species represented: ox, 53; pig, 27; sheep, 14; bird, 2; cat, 2; red deer, 2.

## *Pit 77* (PC 67, trench 71, layer 32)

Sub-rectangular pit 3 ft. 6 in. (1·07 m.) across and 1 ft. (0·31 m.) deep.
The filling was uniform consisting of grey soil mixed with chalky marl.
The pit appears to have been cut by the medieval drainage gullies.

*Small Finds*

From layer 32:
 Bone comb (353); fragment, fig. 117, no. 102.

PIT 77

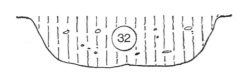 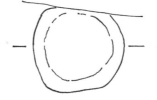

ONE METRE

THREE FEET          SECTIONS

TWO METRES

SIX FEET          PLANS

Fig. 43

*Pottery*

From layer 32:
    *New Forest:* 2/10.4–5, *22.1*, 43, 49; weight, 50 g.; 6·37%.
    *Oxford:* sherds of fabric 4; weight, 5 g.; 0·64%.
    *Hand-made, fabric A:* 86, 123 (4); weight, 300 g.; 38·22%.
    *Black-burnished:* 126; weight, 120 g.; 15·29%.
    *Grey fabrics:* 107, 129 (2); weight, 300 g.; 38·22%.
    *Fabric D:* 137, 4–6; weight, 10 g.; 1·27%.
    Total weight: 785 g.

*Animal Bones*

    57 fragments identified (including 20 ribs and 1 skull fragment)
    Species represented: ox, 36; sheep, 33; pig, 31.

### *Pit 79* (PC 68, trench 73, layer 14)

Irregular oval shaped pit dug to a maximum depth of 1 ft. 4 in. (0·41 m.) through a layer of Roman cobbles.

The filling was a uniform layer of black soil containing charcoal, oysters, cockles, winkles, animal bones and a few lumps of greensand.

PIT 79

ONE METRE

TWO METRES

THREE FEET        SECTIONS      SIX FEET        PLANS

FIG. 44

*Small Finds*

From layer 14:
    Iron cleat            (513)     fig. 129, no. 229.
    Iron fragments     (514)     two corroded fragments; not illustrated.
    Iron slag            (522)     p. 265.

*Nails*

From layer 14:
  1, 6.35.

*Pottery*

From layer 14:
  *New Forest:* 38, 49.1; weight, 110 g.; 61·11%.
  *Misc.:* 144.2; weight, 10 g.; 5·56%.
  *Hand-made, fabric A:* 86, 123, weight, 20 g.; 11·11%.
  *Black-burnished:* 85, 107; weight, 20 g.; 11·11%.
  *Grey fabrics:* 129, 129.3, 85; weight, 20 g.; 11·11%.
  Total weight: 180 g.

*Animal Bones*

  42 fragments identified (including 15 ribs and 1 skull fragment).
  Species represented: ox, sheep, pig.

### *Pit 83* (PC 68, trench 74, layer 19)

Sub-rectangular pit 4 by 3 ft. (1·22 × 0·91 m.), 2 ft. 8 in. (0·81 m.) deep.

The filling was of green–grey soil typical of cesspits. A discontinuous lens of charcoal and oyster shells occurred about halfway up the filling. A few flints had been thrown into the top.

PIT 83

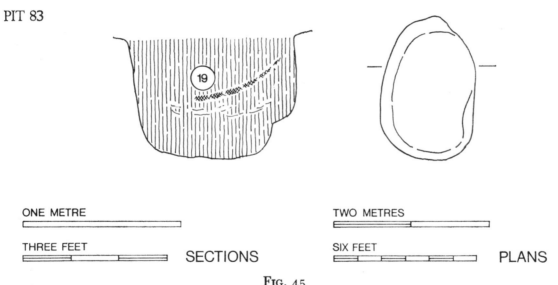

ONE METRE

THREE FEET            SECTIONS

TWO METRES

SIX FEET            PLANS

Fig. 45

*Small Finds*

From layer 19:
  Shale bracelet          (618)     4 by 5 mm. in cross-section, external diameter 6·8 cm.; not illustrated.
  Bronze fragments        (617, 619)     nondescript; not illustrated.

*Glass Vessel*

From layer 19:
  not illustrated, but similar to fig. 198, no. 14.

*Nails*

From layer 19:

1, 8·9; 1, 6·36 +, 1, 6·35, bent; 1, 11·5; 1, 10·2 +; 1, 7·6 +; 1, 7·0 +; 1, 5·75; 2, 5·1 +; 2, 5·1; 2, 3·85 +; 1, 3·85; 2, 2·55.

*Pottery*

From layer 19:

*New Forest:* 22.1–5; weight, 100 g.; 9·52%.
*Oxford:* 40; weight, 20 g.; 1·90%.
*Misc.:* 159.15.
*Hand-made, fabric A:* 107.5, 123 (2); weight, 350 g.; 33·33%.
*Black-burnished:* 107, 126 (2); weight, 180 g.; 17·14%.
*Grey fabrics:* 85, 98, 129 (2), 172; weight, 200 g.; 19·05%.
*Fabric D: 137.5,* 137; weight, 200 g.; 19·05%.
Total weight: 1050 g.

*Animal Bones*

43 fragments identified (including 14 ribs and 1 skull fragment).
Species represented: ox, sheep, bird, pig, cat.

## *Pit 84* (PC 68, trench 74, layer 22)

Square pit 2 ft. 9 in. (0·84 m.) across, 1 ft. (0·31 m.) deep.

The pit was completely filled with stones: small water-worn pebbles on top with large flints in the middle and pebbles in the bottom. The feature presumably represents a deliberately constructed base to support some kind of superstructure.

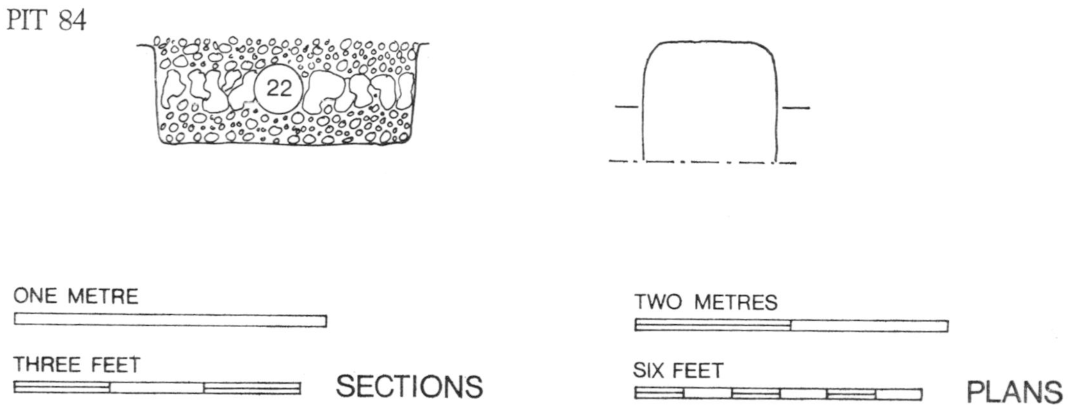

FIG. 46

## *Pit 85* (PC 68, trench 74, layers 24, 44 and 45)

Rectangular pit 4 ft. by 3 ft. 3 in. (1·22 × 0·99 m.) with inward sloping sides up to 5 ft. 10 in. (1·78 m.) deep.

The lowest level (layer 45) was of grey soil intermixed with chalky marl derived from the erosion of the pit sides and representing a typical cesspit filling. It was sealed by a layer of

PIT 85

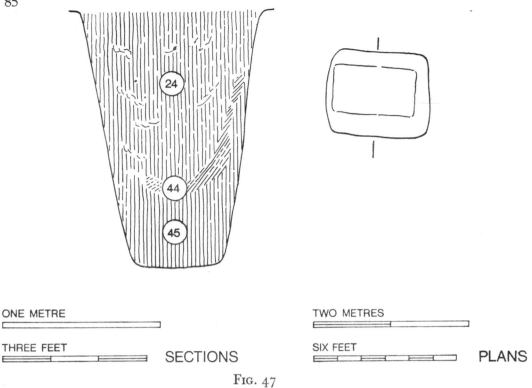

ONE METRE

TWO METRES

THREE FEET                    SECTIONS          SIX FEET              PLANS

FIG. 47

marl (layer 44) above which was another layer of greenish–grey cesspit filling mixed with charcoal, oysters and bone.

*Small Finds*

From layer 24:

| | | |
|---|---|---|
| Bronze fragments | (623, | nondescript; not illustrated. |
| | 625, | |
| | 626, | |
| | 648) | |
| Iron bucket rim | (646) | fig. 128, no. 208. |
| Iron hook | (647) | fig. 130, no. 233. |

*Glass Vessel*

From layer 44:
fig. 198, no. 13.

*Pottery*

From layer 24:
*New Forest:* 29, 52, *67,* base in fabric 2, with an incised cross on the outside; weight, 325 g.; 8·93%.
*Oxford: 31.5, 50.1* (sherd of same vessel in pit 86); weight, 25 g.; 0·69%.
*Misc.:* 15, metallic, grey–brown fabric with purple slip, not New Forest.

*Hand-made, fabric A:* 107, *107.6,* 123 (5); weight, 1550 g.; 42·58%.
*Black-burnished:* 85 (3), 107, *126.1, 126.4,* 126 (4); weight, 1120 g.; 30·77%.
*Grey fabrics:* 107 (2), 127, 129 (2), 153.8 (possibly the same vessel as in pit 64); weight, 620 g.;
　　　17·03%.
*Misc.: 179.1.*
Total weight: 3640 g.
From layer 44:
　*Black-burnished:* weight, 50 g.; 22·73%.
　*Grey fabrics:* 140; weight, 170 g.; 77·27%.
　Total weight: 220 g.
From layer 45:
　*Black-burnished:* 126; weight, 170 g.; 32·69%.
　*Grey fabrics: 128;* weight, 350 g.; 67·31%.
　Total weight: 520 g.
　Weight from all the layers: 4380 g.

## Animal Bones

229 fragments identified (including 90 ribs and 16 skull fragments).
Species represented: ox, 57; sheep, 22; pig, 14; bird, 5; horse, 1; red deer, 1.
The sheep and pig bones both included parts of animals of less than one year old.

### *Pit 86* (PC 68, trench 74, layers 27, 46, 47, 53 and 54)

Rectangular pit 4 ft. by 3 ft. 6 in. (1·22 × 1·07 m.), 4 ft 6 in. (1·37 m.) deep.

The lowest filling (layer 54) was a fine light grey-brown cesspit filling sealed by a thick lens of charcoal with some bone and pottery (layer 53). Above this lay a thick brown cesspit fill (layer 47) mixed with quantities of occupation material, including oyster shells, bones and pottery. The layer was capped with a sealing of chalky brickearth (layer 46). Above this was a grey silty layer (layer 27) containing flints, oysters, pottery and bone.

Fragments of daub were recovered from layers 27, 46 and 47.

## Small Finds

From layer 27:
　Bronze coin　　　　　　(629)　Constantine I (A.D. 307–17).
　Iron candle-holder　　　(652)　fig. 131, no. 249.
From layer 47:
　Bone pin　　　　　　　(639)　as nos. 81–5; not illustrated.
　Painted daub　　　　　(631,　clay–marl daub roughly faced and painted red.
　　　　　　　　　　　　(640)

## Nails

From layer 27:
　1, 7·6; 1, 5·1 +.
From layer 46:
　1, 2·55.
From layer 47:
　1, 3·85.

PIT 86

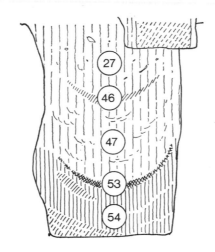 

ONE METRE

TWO METRES

THREE FEET      SECTIONS

SIX FEET      PLANS

FIG. 48

*Glass Vessel*
From layer 46:
    fig. 197, no. 6.

*Pottery*
From layer 27:
    *New Forest;* sherds of fabrics 1–3; weight, 120 g.; 6·86%.
    *Oxford:* 50.*1* (sherd of same vessel in pit 85) 58; weight, 160 g.; 9·14%.
    *Misc.:* 15.4.
    *Hand-made, fabric A:* 107 (2), 123 (2); weight, 620 g.; 35·43%.
    *Black-burnished:* 85, 126 (3); weight, 650 g.; 37·14%.
    *Grey fabrics:* 129, 159.4–5; weight, 200 g.; 11·43%.
    Total weight: 1750 g.
From layer 46:
    *New Forest:* sherd of fabric 1, 64; weight, 140 g.; 9·24%.
    *Hand-made, fabric A:* weight, 200 g.; 13·20%.
    *Black-burnished:* weight, 210 g.; 13·86%.
    *Grey fabric:* 85, *85.9,* 107, 129; weight, 965 g.; 63·70%.
    Total weight, 1515 g.
From layer 47:
    *New Forest:* sherd of fabric 3; weight, 15 g.; 2·63%.
    *Oxford:* 15.1.
    *Hand-made, fabric A:* 107; weight, 100 g.; 17·54%.

*Black-burnished:* 117, 123; weight, 400 g.; 70·18%.
*Grey fabrics:* 117.2; weight, 55 g.; 9·65%.
Total weight: 570 g.
Weight from all the layers: 3835 g.

## Animal Bones

296 fragments identified (including 101 ribs and 9 skull fragments).
Species represented: ox, 41; bird, 17; cat, 16; sheep, 12; pig, 12; horse, 2; dog, 1.
The pig bones included part of a young animal. The cat bones included one whole skull and at least two fairly complete animals. Like pit 47, this pit contained a higher than usual percentage of cat and bird bones.

## Human Bones

Infant radius.

### *Pit 87* (PC 68, trench 74, layers 28a, 31a, 31b, 31c, 32, 58, 59, 60)

Square pit 4 ft. across (1·2 m.) dug to a depth of 4 ft. 6 in. (1·4 m.).
The lowest level (layer 60) consisted of typical green–grey cesspit fill above which (layer 59) was a deposit of dark occupation material containing charcoal, bone and pottery. This was sealed by a layer of redeposited brickearth (layer 58). Then followed a mass of occupation rubbish (layer 32) sealed by another lens of brickearth (layer 31c). Above this the sequence was repeated with more occupation rubbish (layer 31b) and another seal of brickearth (layer 31a). In the top of the pit was a further layer of occupation material (layer 28a).

PIT 87

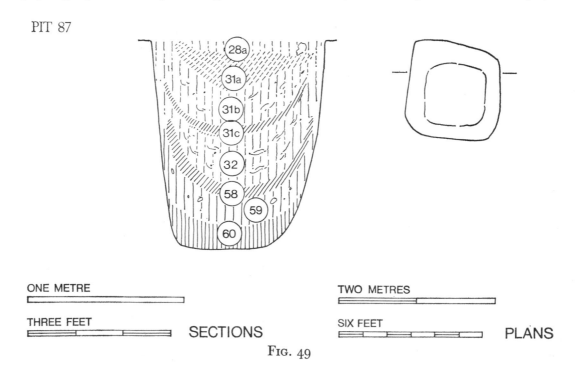

ONE METRE

TWO METRES

THREE FEET　　　　　SECTIONS　　　　SIX FEET　　　　PLANS

Fig. 49

*Pottery*

From layer 28a:
   *New Forest:* sherd of fabric 2; weight, 50 g.; 38·46%.
   *Oxford: 59.1*; weight, 80 g.; 61·54%.
   Total weight: 130 g.
From layer 31:
   *Hand-made:* weight, 10 g.; 9·52%.
   *Black-burnished:* weight, 60 g.; 57·14%.
   *Grey fabrics; 145.2*; weight, 35 g.; 33·33%.
   Total weight: 105 g.
From layer 32:
   *New Forest:* sherds of fabrics 1 and 2; weight, 70 g.; 18·91%.
   *Hand-made, fabric A:* weight, 50 g.; 13·51%.
   *Black-burnished:* weight, 110 g.; 29·72%.
   *Grey fabrics: 140, 145.2* (sherds of the same vessel as in 74/31); weight; 140 g.; 37·83%.
   Total weight: 370 g.
   Weight from all the layers: 605 g.

*Animal Bones*

   107 fragments identified (including 14 ribs and 6 skull fragments).
   Species represented: dog, 74; ox, 18; pig, 5; sheep, 3.
   The dog bones are all from one mature animal which was probably complete when placed in the pit.

### *Pit 88* (PC 68, trench 74, layer 42)

Circular pit 3 ft. 6 in. (1·07 m.) in diameter and 9 in. (0·23 m.) deep.
The filling was uniform consisting of greenish–grey soil mixed with occupation debris.

*Nails*

From layer 42:
   1, 6·35.

PIT 88

ONE METRE

TWO METRES

THREE FEET     SECTIONS     SIX FEET     PLANS

FIG. 50

*Animal Bones*

23 fragments identified (including 12 ribs).
Species represented: ox, bird, sheep, pig, horse.

### Pit 90 (PC 68, trench 74, layer 48)

Rectangular pit 3 ft. 6 in. by 2 ft. 6 in. (1·07 × 0·76 m.) cut to a depth of 2 ft. (0·61 m.). The filling consisted of black soil mixed with quantities of bone and pottery. The lower levels were slightly more clayey.

Pit 90 was cut by pit 91.

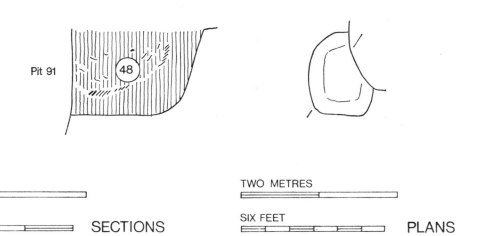

FIG. 51

*Small Finds*

From layer 48:
Lead trimming (660); not illustrated.

*Pottery*

From layer 48:
*New Forest:* sherd of fabric 1; weight, 10 g.; 3·08%.
*Hand-made, fabric A:* 123; weight, 220 g.; 67·69%.
*Black-burnished:* 126; weight, 40 g.; 12·31%.
*Grey fabrics:* 75.1; weight, 55 g.; 16·92%.
Total weight: 325 g.

*Animal Bones*

22 fragments identified (including 11 ribs).
Species represented: ox, sheep, pig.

### Pit 92 (PC 68, trench 74, layers 64, 65, 68, 70 and 71)

Rectangular pit 4 by 6 ft. (1·22 × 1·83 m.) with sloping sides, 4 ft. 6 in. (1·37 m.) deep. The lowest level (layer 71) consisted of a typical green–grey cesspit filling which, towards the top, was intermixed with more occupation material. This was sealed by a layer of orange brickearth (layer 70). Above came another thick deposit of greenish-brown soil (layer 68) containing marl, clay, stones and quantities of occupation material. The upper part of the pit (layer 65) was filled with black occupation soil which was cut by a shallow scoop filled with a similar black occupation deposit (layer 64). Fragments of daub were recovered from layer 64.

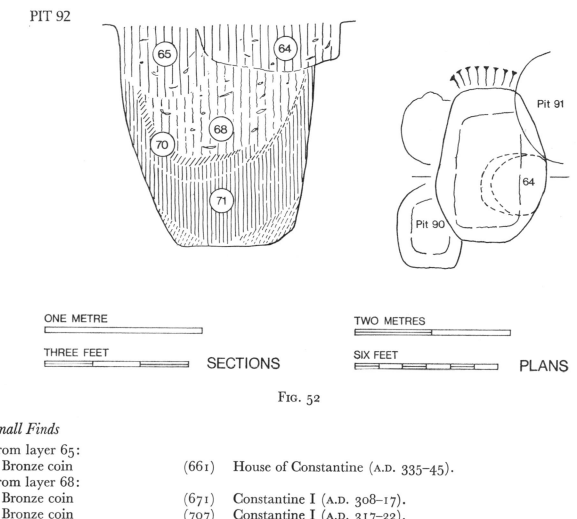

PIT 92

ONE METRE

THREE FEET            SECTIONS

TWO METRES

SIX FEET              PLANS

FIG. 52

## Small Finds

From layer 65:
  Bronze coin            (661)    House of Constantine (A.D. 335–45).
From layer 68:
  Bronze coin            (671)    Constantine I (A.D. 308–17).
  Bronze coin            (707)    Constantine I (A.D. 317–22).
  Shale bracelet         (689)    diam. uncertain; not illustrated.

## Nails

From layer 64:
  1, 10·2; 1, 2·55.
From layer 68:
  3, 7·0, one bent; 1, 2·55 +; 1, 2·55; 1, head only; 1, 5·1, broken.

*Pottery*

From layer 64:
  *New Forest:* 2/10.15, 2/10.17; weight, 30 g.; 2·80%.
  *Oxford:* 58; weight, 20 g.; 1·87%.
  *Misc.:* 24.
  *Hand-made, fabric A:* 123 (3); weight, 620 g.; 57·94%.
  *Black-burnished:* 107, 126 (2); weight, 180 g.; 16·82%.
  *Grey fabrics:* 129; weight, 200 g.; 18·69%.
  *Fabric D:* weight, 20 g.; 1·87%.
  Total weight: 1070 g.
From layer 68:
  *New Forest:* 22.8, ?25; weight, 70 g.; 4·05%.
  *Oxford:* 17.10; weight, 10 g.; 0·58%.
  *Hand-made, fabric A:* 107, 123 (2); weight, 660 g.; 38·15%.
  *Black-burnished:* 107, 126; weight, 320 g.; 18·50%.
  *Grey fabrics:* 129, *142.2*, 145, 175; weight, 670 g.; 38·73%.
  Total weight: 1730 g.
From layer 71:
  *New Forest: 52.4*; weight, 50 g.; 8·47%.
  *Oxford:* 15.1; weight, 10 g.; 1·69%.
  *Hand-made, fabric A:* 123 (same as in 74/68); weight, 300 g.; 50·85%.
  *Grey fabrics:* 132, 142.2 (sherds of same as in 74/68); weight, 230 g.; 38·98%.
  Total weight: 590 g.
  Weight from all the layers: 3390 g.


*Animal Bones*

  414 fragments identified (including 102 ribs and 14 skull fragments).
  Species represented: bird, 43; ox, 26; pig, 15; sheep, 8; cat, 7; red deer, 1; dog.
  This pit contained a high percentage of bird bones. The sheep bones included part of a young animal,
the pig bones one almost complete animal of about three weeks and part of another young animal, and
the cat bones recovered were all from one young animal.


*Human Bones*

  Infant burial.


## *Pit 94* (PC 68, trench 74, layer 69)

Oval-shaped pit 4 ft. 6 in. by 3 ft. (1·37 × 0·91 m.), 1 ft. 6 in. (0·45 m.) deep.
  The filling consisted of dark green-grey soil with a few large flints. Towards the top there
were patches of redeposited marl.
  Cut by pit 87.


*Small Finds*

From layer 69:
  Shale spindlewhorl           (679)     fig. 121, no. 128.

PIT 94

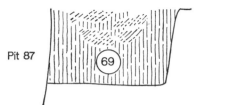

ONE METRE

THREE FEET   SECTIONS

TWO METRES

SIX FEET   PLANS

FIG. 53

*Pottery*

From layer 69:
    *Oxford: 59.1* (same vessel as in pit 87); weight, 5 g.; 1·61%.
    *New Forest: 95.2*; weight, 5 g.; 1·61%.
    *Hand-made, fabric A:* weight, 180 g.; 58·06%.
    *Black-burnished:* weight, 20 g.; 6·45%.
    *Grey fabrics: 87.7*; weight, 100 g.; 32·26%.
    Total weight: 310 g.

*Animal Bones*

    24 fragments identified (including 11 ribs and 2 skull fragments).
    Species represented: ox, sheep, pig.

### *Pit 95* (PC 68, trench 75, layers 22, 49 and 50)

Irregular pit 5 ft. 6 in. (1·68 m.) across, dug to a depth averaging 2 ft. (0·61 m.).
    The lowest filling (layer 50) consisted of washed-in lenses of brickearth containing some pot sherds. Above this came the main filling of fine black soil containing occupation rubbish (layer 49). In the top of the pit (layer 22) the occupation rubbish was distinguished by more charcoal and oyster shells.
    Pit 95 was cut by pit 119.

*Small Finds*

From layer 22:
| | | |
|---|---|---|
| Bronze fragments | (847, 873) | not illustrated |
| Iron ring | (848) | not illustrated. |
| Iron spearhead | (844) | fig. 124, no. 171. |
| Iron slag | | p. 265. |

9

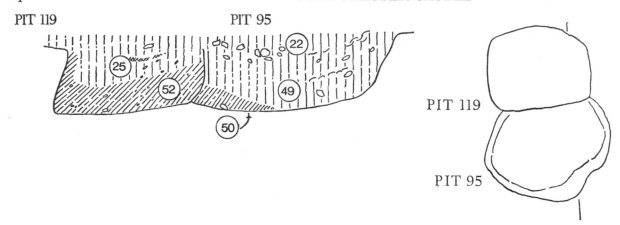

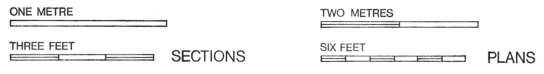

Fɪɢ. 54

From layer 50:
    Bronze bracelet

(850)   strip variety with ribbed decoration. Fragment only; not illustrated.

*Nails*

From layer 22:
    1, 6·35.
From layer 49:
    1, 8·9; 1, 4·5 +.
From layer 50:
    1, 6·35; 1, 3·85.

*Pottery*

From layer 22:
    *New Forest:* 22.1–5 (3); weight, 110 g.; 5·67%.
    *Oxford:* 15·1, sherds of fabrics 4 and 5; weight, 160 g.; 8·25%.
    *Hand-made, fabric A:* 86 (2), 123 (4); weight, 750 g.; 38·66%.
    *Black-burnished:* 126, 85 (3); weight, 300 g.; 15·46%.
    *Grey fabrics:* 129 (2), 142.1–3, *153.7,* 159.4–5; weight, 620 g.; 31·96%.
    Total weight: 1940 g.
From layer 49:
    *New Forest:* 49; weight, 5 g.; 1·82%.
    *Hand-made, fabric A:* weight, 120 g.; 43·64%.
    *Black-burnished:* 85; weight, 40 g.; 14·55%.
    *Grey fabrics:* weight, 110 g.; 40·0%.
    Total weight: 275 g.

From layer 50:
  *New Forest:* 64.2; weight, 30 g.; 5·08%.
  *Hand-made, fabric A:* 123 (2); weight, 240 g.; 40·68%.
  *Black-burnished:* 85, 107, 126; weight, 120 g.; 20·34%.
  *Grey fabrics:* 131·4; weight, 200 g.; 33·90%.
  Total weight, 590 g.
  Weight from all the layers: 2805 g.

## Animal Bones

162 fragments identified (including 35 ribs and 11 skull fragments).
Species represented: ox, 59; sheep, 27; pig, 11; red deer, 2; bird, 1.


*Pit 103* (PC 68, trench 78, layers 14, 15, 16 and 17; trench 79, layers 27, 28, 29, 33, 44)

Very large rectangular pit approximately 23 ft. (7 m.) square (pl. xxx). The bottom was irregular averaging 2–3 ft. (0·6–0·9 m.) deep but increasing to 4 ft. 3 in. (1·3 m.) in the centre.

The deepest part was filled with tips of brown soil and flints containing mortar and broken roof tiles together with lenses of charcoal (layer (79) 44). Above this and discontinuously covering the entire pit bottom was a layer of brown clayey soil composed largely of decomposed daub with occasional lumps of moulded wall plaster and thin films of white paint (layers (78) 17 and (79) 33). This layer must represent the decayed remains of painted daub walls. Above this were tips of Roman building rubble mixed with brown clayey soil (layers (78) 16 and (79) 29). The rubble was composed largely of fragments of broken roof tiles of tegula and imbrex type together with the fillets of mortar which would have joined the two. This rubble must originate from the systematic demolition of roofs from which all usable tiles had been carefully removed. Above this came layers of black soil mixed with daub (layers (78) 15 and (79) 28) which were sealed by black occupation rubbish containing flints, oyster shells and bones (layers (78) 14 and (79) 27). Fragments of painted plaster were recovered from (78)17 and (79) 29, 33.

## Small Finds

From 79 layer 27:
  Iron hook? (797) fig. 130, no. 232.
  Cut stone (784) not illustrated.
From 79 layer 28:
  Marble (831) not illustrated; fragment of a sheet of white marble with green/grey veins.
  Iron rod (859) 25 cm. long, square cross-section 5 mm. across; not illustrated.
From 79 layer 33:
  Bronze coin (825) unidentifiable.
  Worked antler (2290) fig. 120, no. 124.

## Window Glass

From 78 layer 14:
  cf. fig. 199, no. 25.

*Nails*

From 78 layer 14:
  1, 14·0; 1, 8.25; 1, 11.5, bent.
From 79 layer 27:
  1, 11·5 +; 1, 6·35 +; 1, 3·85 +; 1, 3·85, bent; 1, 3·85; 1, 4·5; 1, 5·1 +.
From 79 layer 28:
  1, 4·5.

*Pottery*

From 78 layer 15:
  *New Forest:* 2/10.20, *58.1*; weight, 110 g.; 32·35%.
  *Hand-made. fabric A:* 107; weight, 150 g.; 44·12%.
  *Grey fabrics:* weight, 80 g.; 23·53%.
  Total weight: 340 g.
From 78 layer 16:
  *New Forest:* sherds of fabric 1 and 2; weight, 20 g.; 8·70%.
  *Hand-made, fabric A:* weight, 50 g.; 21·74%.
  *Black-burnished:* weight, 50 g.; 21·74%.
  *Grey fabrics:* 127 (2); weight, 110 g.; 47·83%.
  Total weight: 230 g.
From 79 layer 27:
  *New Forest:* 3.2, 2/10.5, 2/10.17, *18.4*, 22.1–5, *33.5*, 43 (2); weight: 320 g.; 9·04%.
  *Oxford:* 34, 35.1, 40, 43.10–12, 58 (2), 63: weight, 200 g.; 5·65%.
  *Hand-made, fabric A:* 86 (2), 107, 123 (6); weight, 1400 g.; 39·55%.
  *Black-burnished:* 85 (2), 107 (3); weight, 300 g.; 8·47%.
  *Grey fabrics:* 75.2, *98.1*, 107 (2), 127 (2), 129 (2), 154.6, *161.3*; weight, 1200 g.; 33·90%.
  *Fabric D:* 137.4–6; weight, 120 g.; 3·39%.
  Total weight: 3540 g.
From 79 layer 28:
  *TS:* Dr. 36, Central Gaul, C2.
  *New Forest:* 2/*10.16*, 2/*10*.22, 22.1–5 (2), 43, *55.9*; weight, 550 g.; 10·68%.
  *Oxford:* 26, 40; weight, 25 g.; 0·49%.
  *Misc.:* 24.1.
  *Hand-made, fabric A:* 86 (4), 107, 123 (3); weight, 1825 g.; 35·44%.
  *Black-burnished:* 85 (2), 107 (3), 126 (3); weight, 840 g.; 16·31%.
  *Grey fabrics:* *98.1* (same as that in 79/27), 107 (2), *118.1*, *127.1*, 127 (2), 137 (2), 139, 140; weight,
            1870 g.; 36·31%.
  *Fabric D:* 137.4–6; weight, 40 g.; 0·78%.
  Total weight: 5150 g.
From 79 layer 33:
  *New Forest:* 3.1–2; weight, 150 g.; 3·94%.
  *Oxford:* 17.7, 63.4; weight, 30 g.; 0·79%.
  *Hand-made, fabric A:* 86, 107 (2), 123 (3); weight, 800 g.; 21·0%.
  *Black-burnished:* 85, *107.7*, 126; weight, 350 g.; 9·19%.
  *Grey fabrics:* 85, *107.11*, 127 (3), *140.3*, *159.5*, sherds of a storage jar; weight, 2480 g.; 65·09%.
  Total weight: 3810 g.

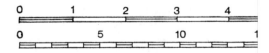

From 79 layer 44:
  *New Forest: 2/10.21, 22.1–5* (3); weight, 250 g.; 8·22%.
  *Misc.:* sherds and base in an orange sandy fabric; a join in pit 170; weight, 120 g.; 3·95%.
  *Hand-made, fabric A:* 123 (2); weight, 1050 g.; 34·54%.
  *Black-burnished:* 107, 126 (2); weight, 600 g.; 19·74%.
  *Grey fabrics:* 85 (2), 127 (5), 129, *140.3* (sherds from 79/33), *149.1*; weight, 1020 g.; 33·55%.
  Total weight: 3040 g.
  Weight from all the layers: 16,110 g.

*Animal Bones*

  756 fragments identified (including 356 ribs and 29 skull fragments).
  Species represented: ox, 55; pig, 18; dog, 13; sheep, 9; bird, 2; red deer, 2; fox, 1; horse, badger.
  The sheep bones included part of a young animal, and the pig bones included part of at least one very young animal. The fairly high percentage of dog bones comprised part of at least four individuals.

### *Pit 119* (PC 68, trench 75, layers 25 and 52)

  Roughly circular pit 4 ft. (1·22 m.) across and up to 3 ft. 6 in. (1·07 m.) deep.
  The lower filling (layer 52) consisted of a layer of redeposited clay sealed by an upper layer (layer 25) of dark grey occupation soil. Fragments of daub were recovered from layer 25.
  Pit 119 cut into pit 95.

*Small Finds*

From layer 25:
  Bronze fragments          (863)    not illustrated.

*Nails*

From layer 25:
  1, 3·85 +; 2, heads only.

*Pottery*

From layer 25:
  *New Forest:* sherds of fabrics 1 and 2; weight, 140 g.; 9·66%.
  *Oxford:* 58; weight, 20 g.; 1·38%.
  *Hand-made, fabric A:* 107, 123 (2); weight, 580 g.; 40·0%.
  *Black-burnished: 107.10,* 123; weight, 150 g.; 10·34%.
  *Grey fabrics:* 107, *118.2,* 127, *160*; weight, 360 g.; 24·83%.
  *Fabric D:* 137.4–6; weight, 200 g.; 13·79%.
  Total weight: 1450 g.
From layer 52:
  *New Forest:* sherds of fabrics 1 and 2; weight, 20 g.; 6·45%.
  *Oxford:* sherd of fabric 4; weight, 20 g.; 6·45%.
  *Hand-made, fabric A:* 123; weight, 130 g.; 41·94%.
  *Black-burnished:* 85; weight, 50 g.; 16·13%.
  *Grey fabrics:* weight, 90 g.; 29·03%.
  Total weight: 310 g.
  Weight from both layers: 1760 g.

*Animal Bones*

57 fragments identified (including 11 ribs and 2 skull fragments).
Species represented: ox, 43; sheep, 32; pig, 25.

*Human Bones*

Infant clavicle.

*Well (pit) 121* (PC 68 trench 79 layers 36, 37, 53, 58, 60, 61, 66, 67, 68)

Pit 121 is a circular well with a shaft diameter of 3 ft. 5 in. (1·04 m.). It had been constructed, presumably with a timber lining, in a pit some 4 ft. 6 in. (1·37 m.) across. Only the
shaft of the well was excavated, the packing being left in position. The bottom was not reached
at a depth of 13 ft. (4·0 m.): thereafter excavation was abandoned for reasons of safety. No
trace of the original timber lining survived, but the instability of the clay and marl through
which it had been dug leaves little doubt that some kind of lining must once have been
provided. The narrow diameter and the considerable depth meant that no vertical sections
could be retained, but depth measurements were taken at each change of layer. A summary
of layers, with measurements taken from the surface of the natural clay is offered here.

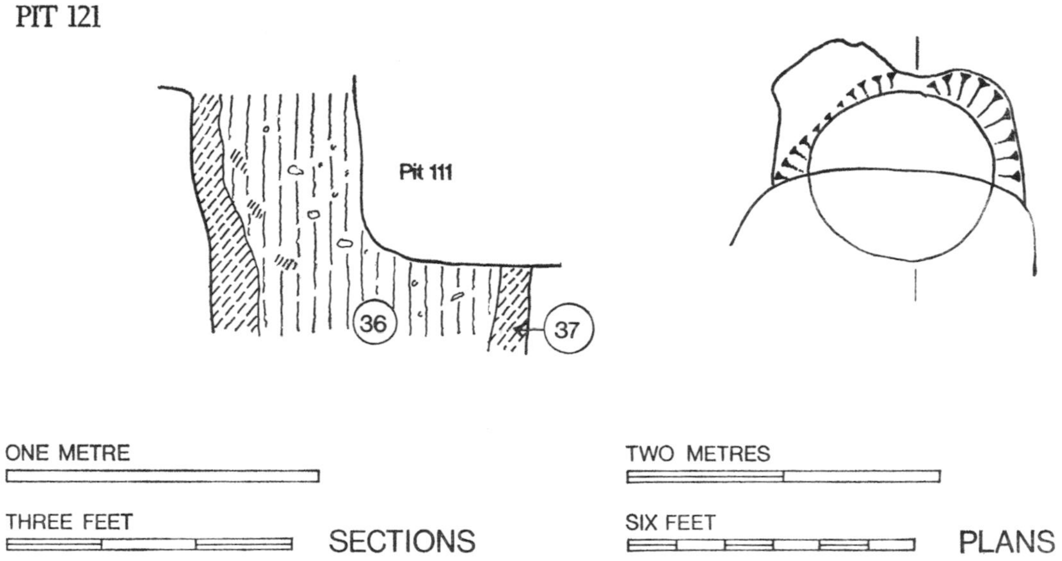

PIT 121

ONE METRE    TWO METRES

THREE FEET    SECTIONS    SIX FEET    PLANS

FIG. 56

Layer 68: 12 to 13 ft. (3·7–4·0 m.)
    Thick black clayey soil rich in occupation material (probing revealed that the layer
    continued for a further 3 ft. (0·91 m.) at least).
Layer 67: 11 ft. 10 in. to 12 ft. (3·61–3·66 m.)
    Thin lens of light grey clay.
Layer 66: 11 to 11 ft. 10 in. (3·35–3·61 m.)
    Black soil with occupation rubbish.

Layer 60: 8 to 11 ft. (2·44–3·35 m.)
Light grey chalky clay containing oyster shells and other occupation material.
Layer 58: 6 to 8 ft. (1·83–2·44 m.)
Brown clayey soil containing much brickearth eroded from the packing, together with occupation rubbish.
Layer 53: 4 to 6 ft. (1·22–1·83 m.)
Light brown marly soil intermixed with quantities of occupation rubbish.
Layer 36: 0–4 ft. (0–1·22 m.)
Black soil containing much occupation rubbish.

In addition to the filling of the shaft, the vertical packing between the sides of the well pit and the original lining was numbered as layers 37 and 61. Although this packing was not deliberately excavated, it began to fall away, particularly below about 8 ft. (2·44 m.), and had therefore to be partly removed. Fragments of daub were recovered from layer 60.

*Small Finds*

From layer 36:
| | | |
|---|---|---|
| Bronze coin | (816) | Constantine I (A.D. 308–17). |
| Bronze coin | (868) | Crispus (A.D. 322–4). |
| Bronze pin | (815) | cf. nos. 50, 51. |

From layer 53:
| | | |
|---|---|---|
| Bronze coin | (879) | Constantine I (A.D. 308–17). |
| Bronze fragment | (880) | not illustrated. |

From layer 58:
| | | |
|---|---|---|
| Bronze coin | (883) | Galerius (A.D. 295–305). |

From layer 60:
| | | |
|---|---|---|
| Bronze seal box | (891) | fragmentary; not illustrated. |
| Bronze chain | (893) | fig. 114, no. 65. |
| Bronze fragment | (892) | not illustrated. |
| Bone plaque | (898) | fig. 119, no. 122. |
| Bone pins | (894, 900, 905) | not illustrated. As nos. 81–5. |
| Lead sheet | (896) | fragment of sheet: not illustrated. |
| Iron key | (899) | fig. 129, no. 222. |
| Iron knife | (920a) | not illustrated, no. 188. |
| Iron paring chisel | (919) | fig. 128, no. 211. |
| Iron fragments | (901, 902) | not illustrated. |
| Whetstone | (908) | not illustrated, no. 357. |

From layer 68:
| | | |
|---|---|---|
| Bronze coin | (937) | corroded, either first or second century A.D. or a follis. |
| Iron ring | (911) | fragment 4·7 cm. external diameter: not illustrated. |
| Iron knife | (932) | fig. 126, no. 194. |
| Iron key | (917) | fig. 129, no. 219. |
| Iron binding | (918) | fig. 130, no. 240. |

| Iron spike loop | (912) | fig. 129, no. 224. |
| Iron eyelet spike | (920b) | fig. 129, no. 225. |
| Iron ring and tie | (922) | fig. 129, no. 227. |
| Bone pins | (909, | |
| | 910, | |
| | 923, | |
| | 931, | |
| | 936, | fig. 116, no. 84. |
| | 938, | |
| | 940) | |
| | (938, | are types 3; not illustrated. |
| | 910, | |
| | 940) | |
| Lead trimming | (924) | not illustrated. |

## Glass Vessels

From layer 60:
Fragment not illustrated but similar to fig. 197, no. 6.
From layer 68:
fig. 198, no. 11.
fig. 198, no. 17.

## Window Glass

From layer 68:
fig. 199, no. 24.

## Nails

From layer 36:
2, 10·2; 1, 7·6, bent; 1, 5·1; 1, 3·85, 1, 3·2 +; 1, 3·85 +.
From layer 58:
1, 1·3 +.
From layer 60:
3, 5·1, one bent; 2, 3·85 +; 2, 3·85; 1, 7·6; 2, heads only.
From layer 68:
1, 9·55; 1, 8·9 +; 2, 8·9; 2, 7·6 +; 2, 7·6; 1, 7·0; 3, 6·35 +; 2, 6·35; 4, 5·1 +; 13, 5·1; 2, 5·75; 5, 4·5; 3, 3·85 +; 12, 3·85; 8, 3·2; 2, 2·55 +; 5, 2·55; 2, 1·95; 4, 1·3 +; 4, heads only.

## Pottery

From layer 36:
*New Forest:* 13, 32, *39·3*; weight, 150 g.; 5·42%.
*Oxford:* 17.11, sherds of fabric 4; weight, 200 g.; 7·22%.
*Hand-made, fabric A:* 86 (2), 106, *107·5*, 107, 123 (5); weight, 1050 g.; 37·91%.
*Black-burnished:* 85 (3), 126 (4); weight, 630 g.; 22·74%.
*Grey fabrics:* 85, 107, 127, 129 (2), 137, *159·3*, *172·2*, *175·1*; weight, 740 g.; 26·71%.
Total weight: 2770 g.

From layer 58:
  *Hand-made, fabric A:* 123 (2); weight, 160 g.; 19·16%.
  *Black-burnished:* 107 (2), 117, 126 (2); weight, 450 g.; 53·89%.
  *Grey fabrics:* 85; weight, 225 g.; 26·95%.
  Total weight: 835 g.
From layer 60:
  *New Forest:* 43; weight, 250 g.; 11·36%.
  *Oxford: 14.3, 63.6;* weight, 100 g.; 4·55%.
  *Hand-made, fabric A:* 86, 123 (3); weight; 580 g.; 26·36%.
  *Black-burnished:* 85, *85.4,* 117; weight, 550 g.; 25·0%.
  *Grey fabrics:* 107; weight, 720 g.; 32·73%.
  Total weight: 2200 g.
From layer 66:
  *New Forest:* sherds of fabric 2; weight, 20 g.; 11·11%.
  *Hand-made, fabric A:* 123, *123.2;* weight, 100 g.; 55·56%.
  *Black-burnished:* weight, 50 g.; 27·78%.
  *Grey fabrics:* weight, 10 g.; 5·56%.
  Total weight: 180 g.
From layer 68:
  *TS:* Dr. 36, Central Gaul, second century.
  *New Forest: 2.2, 3.1–2* (2), *3.5–6, 22.1.5* (2), 32, 43, 66; weight, 950 g.; 7·06%.
  *Oxford:* 15.1, *18.1,* 58; weight, 700 g.; 5·20%.
  *Hand-made, fabric A; 123.1, 123.3, 123.9,* 123 (8); weight, 4600 g.; 34·20%.
  *Black-burnished:* 85 (4), 107 (5), 126 (8); weight, 4750 g.; 35·32%.
  *Grey fabrics: 76.2, 77.5, 94.1, 113,* 127 (3), 128, 129 (2), 145, *159.13,* 175; weight, 2450 g.; 18·22%.
  Total weight: 13,450 g.
  Weight from all the layers: 19,435 g.

*Animal Bones*

1343 fragments identified (including 463 ribs and 76 skull fragments).
Species represented: ox, 35; pig, 29; sheep, 24; dog, 4; bird, 4; cat, 3; red deer, 1; roe deer, badger, horse.
The sheep bones included part of at least two young animals, one under ten months and one under three months. The pig bones included a complete skull of an immature sow, and part of a new-born animal. The cat bones are from two animals, one mature and one immature, and include two whole skulls. A complete dog skull was also found. The red deer bones include a large skull fragment and both antlers of a mature animal. A very large number of pig jaws were found in this pit. 39% of all pig bones identified were jaws, compared with 18% of sheep bones (also fairly high), but only 10% of ox bones.

*Pit 122* (PC 68, trench 76, layer 39)

An irregularly shaped scoop 5 ft. (1·52 m.) across and up to 1 ft. (0·31 m.) deep. The filling was a uniform greenish–grey soil mixed with flints and occupation debris. The pit was cut by medieval gully 3.

PIT 122

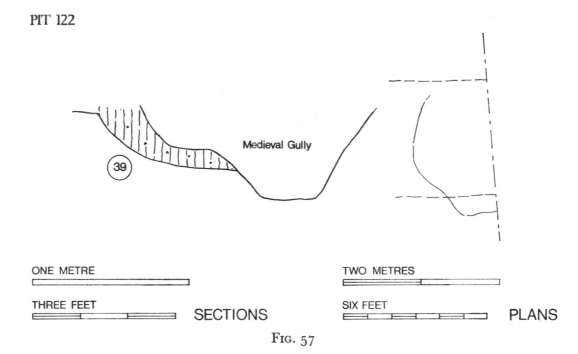

ONE METRE

TWO METRES

THREE FEET                          SECTIONS                    SIX FEET                          PLANS

FIG. 57

## Pottery

From layer 39:
   *Oxford:* 31; weight, 10 g.; 4·35%.
   *Hand-made, fabric A:* 86, 123 (2); weight, 180 g.; 78·26%.
   *Black-burnished:* weight, 20 g.; 8·70%.
   *Grey fabrics:* weight, 20 g.; 8·70%.
   Total weight: 230 g.

## Animal Bones

   10 fragments identified (including 4 ribs).
   Species represented: sheep, pig, ox.

### *Pit 125B* (PC 69, trench 88, layers 35, 36, 37, 38, 87)

Rectangular, 5 ft. by 2 ft. 9 in. (1·52 × 0·84 m.), dug to a depth of 3 ft. 3 in. (0·99 m.).
   The lowest layer (layer 87) was typical greenish cesspit filling containing animal bones. Above this (layer 38) was a similar layer mixed with chalk, a few flints and quantities of animal bones. This was sealed by a deposit (layer 37) of occupation rubbish including bones, shells, pottery and charcoal mixed with large flints and greyish soil. Next came a thin layer of small chalk lumps sealing the whole pit (layer 36), which was in turn covered by a mass of occupation rubbish in greenish–grey soil (layer 35).

## Small Finds

From layer 35:
   Bone plate                    (1055)  fig. 117, no. 105.

PIT 125b

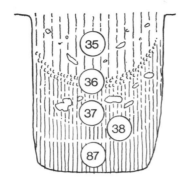

ONE METRE

TWO METRES

THREE FEET          SECTIONS

SIX FEET          PLANS

FIG. 58

*Pottery*

From layer 35:
    *New Forest:* weight, 30 g.; 7·14%.
    *Oxford:* *18.3,* 58; weight, 250 g.; 59·52%.
    *Hand-made, fabric A:* weight, 40 g.; 9·52%.
    *Black-burnished:* weight, 20 g.; 4·76%.
    *Grey fabrics:* 94; weight, 80 g.; 19·05%.
    Total weight: 420 g.
From layer 37:
    *New Forest:* 43: weight, 20 g.; 3·13%.
    *Oxford:* 35.1, sherds of beaker in 88/35; weight, 20 g.; 3·13%.
    *Hand-made, fabric A:* 86, 107 (2), 123 (2); weight, 350 g.; 54·69%.
    *Black-burnished:* 85, 107 (2); weight, 150 g.; 23·44%.
    *Grey fabrics:* 149·1; weight, 60 g. 9·38%.
    *Fabric D:* 137.4–6; weight, 40 g.; 6·25%.
    Total weight: 640 g.
From layer 38:
    *New Forest:* 2/10.21; weight, 30 g.; 3·75%.
    *Oxford:* *17.5, 33.3*; weight, 20 g.; 2·50%.
    *Hand-made, fabric A:* 86, 107, 123; weight, 450 g.; 56·25%.
    *Black-burnished:* 126; weight, 160 g.; 20·0%.
    *Grey fabrics:* 107; weight, 140 g.; 17·50%.
    Total weight 800 g.
    Weight from all the layers: 1860 g.

*Animal Bones*

239 fragments identified (including 24 ribs and 12 skull fragments).
Species represented: ox, 69; pig, 17; sheep, 12; bird, 1; horse, 1; cat, 1.

### *Pit 129* (PC 69, trench 89, layer 44)

Small rectangular pit 3 ft. by 3 ft. 6 in. (0·91 × 1·07 m.) dug to a depth of 1 ft. 1 in. (0·33 m.) through the layer of make-up.

The filling was of black soil mixed with charcoal, pottery, bones and a few large flints.

PIT 129

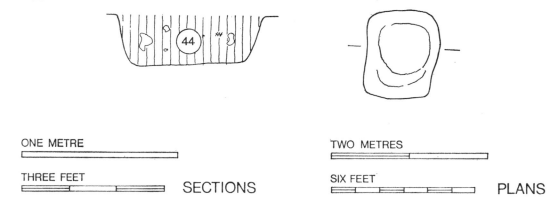

Fig. 59

*Pottery*

From layer 44:

*New Forest:* sherds of fabric 1; weight, 100 g.; 9·71%.
*Oxford:* 42, 57, 58, 63.4; weight, 250 g.; 24·27%.
*Hand-made, fabric A:* 86, 123; weight, 250 g.; 24·27%.
*Black-burnished:* 85; weight, 160 g.; 15·53%.
*Grey fabrics:* 87.1, 137.2; weight, 170 g.; 16·50%.
*Fabric D:* 137.4–6; weight, 100 g.; 9·71%.
Total weight: 1030 g.

*Animal Bones*

107 fragments identified (including 14 ribs and 14 skull fragments).
Species represented: ox, 62; sheep, 18; pig, 14; horse, 3; bird, 1; red deer, 1; dog, 1.
The pit contained one almost complete ox skull.

*Human Bones*

Part of an infant burial.

### *Pit 130A* (PC 69, trench 89, layers 50, 81 and 82)

Small rectangular pit 3 ft. by 3 ft. 3 in. (0·91 × 0·99 m.) dug to a depth of 2 ft. 3 in. (0·69 m.).

The lowest fill (layer 82) consisted of occupation rubbish including charcoal, chalk, flints, bones, shells, tiles and pottery mixed up in black soil. This was sealed by a layer of orange clay (layer 81) above which was another deposit of occupation rubbish (layer 50). Fragments of daub were recovered from layer 82.

The pit cut through a drainage gully.

PIT 130 a

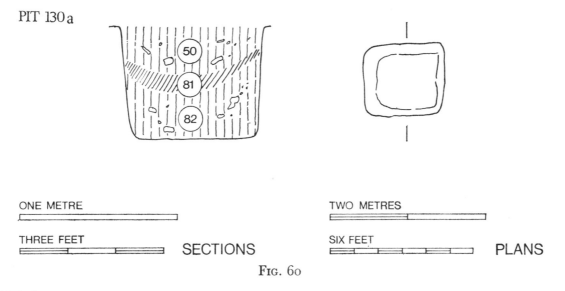

ONE METRE

THREE FEET                     SECTIONS

TWO METRES

SIX FEET                          PLANS

FIG. 60

*Small Finds*

From layer 82:

| | | |
|---|---|---|
| Shale spindlewhorl | (1229) | fig. 121, no. 129. |
| Bone bracelet | (1314) | 22 cm. in circumference, held together with small bronze rivet, now opened out into strip; not illustrated. |
| Bronze rivets | (1238) | corroded mass; not illustrated. |
| Iron fragment | (1239) | piece of a flat sheet; not illustrated. |

*Pottery*

From layer 50:
  *New Forest:* 22.1–5, 43; weight, 50 g.; 9·71%.
  *Pevensey:* 37; weight, 5 g.; 0·97%.
  *Hand-made, fabric A:* 86, 107, 123 (2); weight, 270 g.; 52·43%.
  *Black-burnished:* 85, 126; weight, 100 g.; 19·42%.
  *Grey fabrics:* 127, 137; weight: 90 g.; 17·48%.
  Total weight: 515 g.
From layer 81:
  *Hand-made, fabric A:* weight, 120 g.; 48·0%.
  *Black-burnished:* 85; weight, 130 g.; 52·0%.
  Total weight: 250 g.
From layer 82:
  *New Forest:* 2/10.17, 2/10.20, 22.1–5, 43 (2), 64, 66.5; weight, 560 g.; 17·83%.
  *Oxford:* 15.1, 15.2, 58 (2), 63; weight, 250 g.; 7·96%.

*Misc.:* 170.
*Hand-made, fabric A:* 86 (3), 107, 123 (2); weight, 750 g.; 23·89%.
*Black-burnished:* 85, 107 (2), 126 (3); weight, 400 g.; 12·74%.
*Grey fabrics:* 98, 107, 129 (3), 132 (2), 139, *139.5*; weight, 1180 g.; 37·58%.
Total weight: 3140 g.
Weight from all the layers: 3905 g.

### Animal Bones

392 fragments identified (including 104 ribs and 16 skull fragments).
Species represented: ox, 54; sheep, 22; pig, 19; bird, 2; dog, 1; horse, 1; fallow deer, 1; red deer, vole.
The pit contained a fairly complete sheep skull.

### Well (*pit*) *135* (PC 68, trench 88, layer 104)

Well 135 remained in use for a considerable period of time, probably starting as a Roman circular shaft, eroding out in the fifth century to become a muddy water-pit, and finally being redug and timber lined in the seventh century before being allowed to fill with rubbish. Most of the development lies within the Saxon period, and is therefore appropriate to volume 2, but the earliest phase must be considered here.

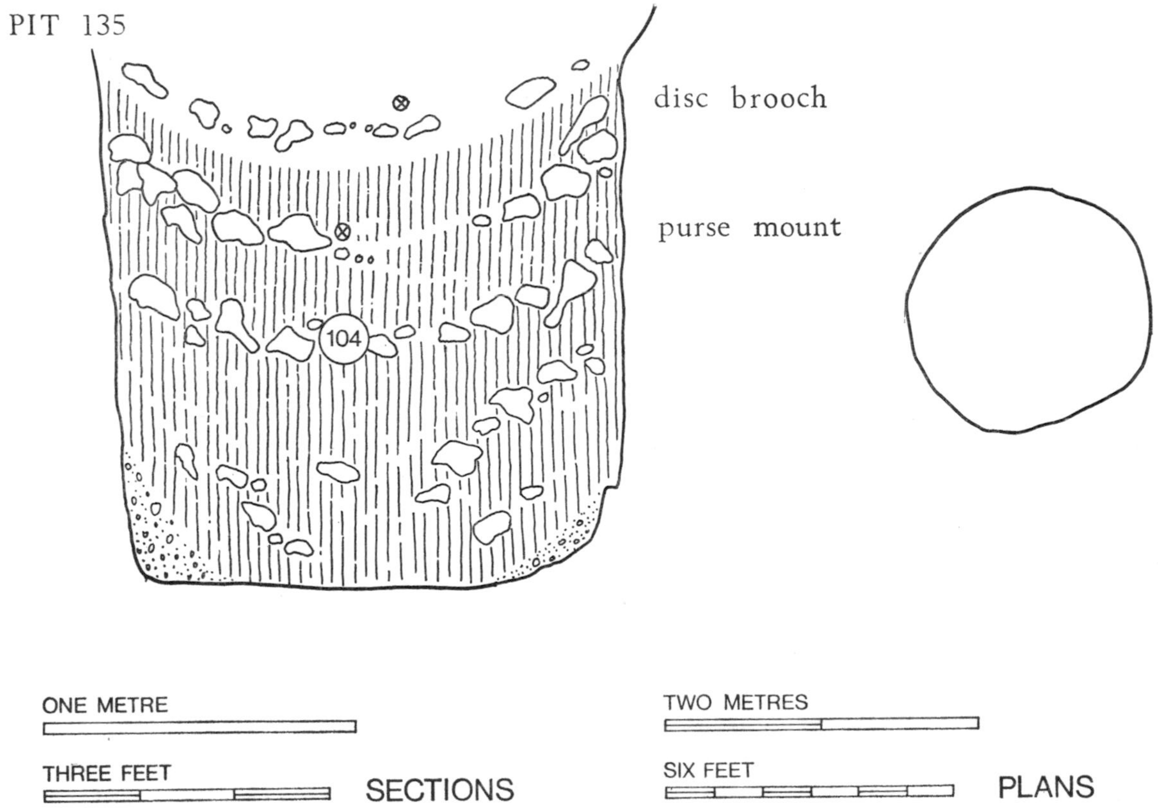

PIT 135

disc brooch

purse mount

ONE METRE

TWO METRES

THREE FEET          SECTIONS

SIX FEET          PLANS

Fig. 61

The first well was constructed in a circular shaft 5 ft. 6 in. (1·68 m.) in diameter. No trace of lining existed but it is possible that the original lining collapsed together with the packing behind it and was cleared out at some stage during or soon after the Roman period. Then followed a time during which black organic silt and flints were allowed to accumulate to a depth of 4 ft. 6 in. (1·37 m.), at which stage an iron purse mount of fifth-century date was dropped in. Thereafter mud continued to accumulate. It seems possible, but by no means certain, that the lowest level of silt belongs to the Roman period since it produced only Roman material, but the possibility must always remain that even the initial phases of the structure might date to the fifth century, the Roman finds being residual.

### Small Finds

From layer 104:

| | | |
|---|---|---|
| Iron hook | (1869) | not illustrated. |
| Bone bracelet | (1946) | plain, as fig. 117, no. 99; not illustrated. |
| Iron slag | | p. 265. |

### Animal Bones

103 fragments identified (including 8 ribs and 7 skull fragments).
Species represented: ox, 69; sheep, 10; pig, 10; red deer, 10.
Three large red deer antlers were found in the bottom layer of the well.

### Pit 138 (PC 70, trench 94, layers 91, 97, 98, 99, 100 and PC 71, trench 100, layers 33 and 46)

Rectangular pit in excess of 8 ft. 6 in. by 3 ft. 6 in. (2·59 × 1·07 m.), cut to a depth of 4 ft. 3 in. (1·29 m.).

Relatively little of the pit was excavated because a 2 ft. baulk had been left across the centre and a substantial part of it had been cut away by the foundations of the sixteenth-century storehouse.

The lowest layer (layer 99) consisted of a typical brownish cesspit filling mixed with charcoal and oyster shells. Layer 98 was a tip of black soil which extended down the west side of the pit and merged with the top of layer 99. Then came a sealing layer (layer 100) of yellow clay above which was a mass of general occupation debris (layer 97, and trench 100 layer 46), mixed with wads of redeposited natural brickearth which merged with layer 91 — a more clayey version of layer 97. The top of the pit was sealed by a mass of flints (trench 100 layer 33).

### Small Finds

From layer (100) 33:

| | | |
|---|---|---|
| Bronze coin | (1621) | Constantius II (A.D. 337–40) |
| Iron drill | (2067) | fig. 128, no. 216. |

### Pottery

From layer (94) 91:
*Argonne:* Chenet 328.
*Oxford:* sherds of fabric 4; weight, 25 g.; 10·64%.

PIT 138

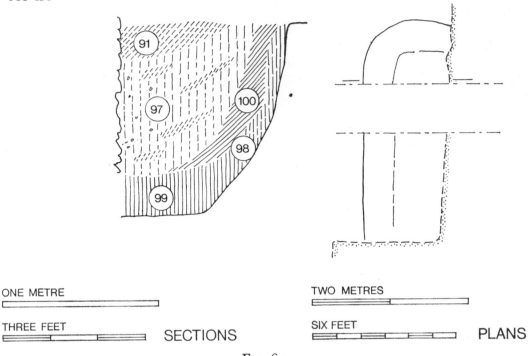

ONE METRE

THREE FEET　　　　　　SECTIONS

TWO METRES

SIX FEET　　　　　　PLANS

Fig. 62

*Pevensey:* sherds.
*Hand-made, fabric A:* 123; weight, 60 g.; 25·53%.
*Grey fabrics:* 85, 129, 146; weight, 150 g.; 63·83%.
Total weight: 235 g.
From layer (94) 97:
　*New Forest:* sherds of fabric 1; weight; 5 g.; 2·56%.
　*Hand-made, fabric A:* weight, 20 g.; 10·26%.
　*Grey fabrics:* sherds of a storage jar; weight, 150 g.; 76·92%.
　*Fabric D:* weight, 20 g.; 10·26%.
　Total weight: 195 g.
From layer (100) 33:
　*New Forest:* sherds of fabric 2; weight, 30 g.; 21·43%.
　*Oxford:* 40; weight, 50 g.; 35·71%.
　*Hand-made, fabric A:* 123; weight, 40 g.; 28·57%.
　*Grey fabrics:* 84.4; weight, 5 g.; 3·57%.
　*Fabric D:* 137.4–6; weight, 15 g.; 10·71%.
　Total weight: 140 g.
From layer (100) 46:
　*Oxford:* sherds of fabric 5; weight, 25 g.; 33·33%.
　*Grey fabrics;* weight, 50 g.; 66·67%.
　Total weight: 75 g.
　Weight from all the layers: 645 g.

*Animal Bones*

10 fragments identified (including 2 ribs and 1 skull fragment).
Species represented: pig, ox, sheep.

*Pit 140* (PC 70, trench 95, layers 78, 104, 105, 106, 107 and 108)

Rectangular pit cut by the footings of the sixteenth-century storebuilding. Dug to a depth of 4 ft. 5 in. (1·35 m.).

The lowest level (layer 107) was a typical greenish–grey cesspit filling. It was sealed by layers 106 and 108 which consisted of deposits of occupation debris, including burnt clay, bone, pottery and shells. These levels were sealed by a thick layer of marl (layer 105) above which was a deposit of brown soil with charcoal, burnt clay and tile fragments (layer 104), which was in turn sealed by another capping of marl (layer 78).

PIT 140

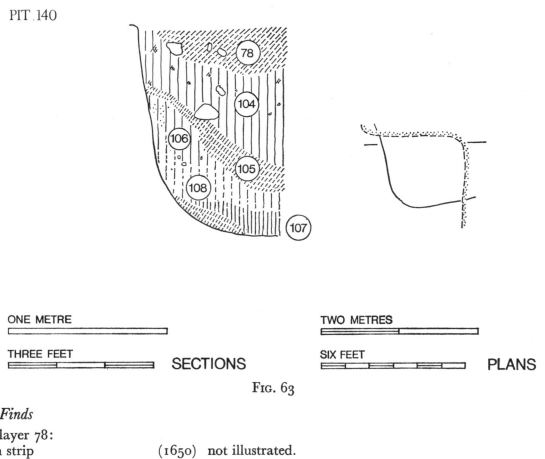

ONE METRE

TWO METRES

THREE FEET        SECTIONS       SIX FEET       PLANS

FIG. 63

*Small Finds*

From layer 78:
   Iron strip            (1650)  not illustrated.

*Pottery*

From layer 78:
  *New Forest:* sherds of fabric 2; weight, 5 g.; 3·23%.
  *Hand-made, fabric A:* 107; weight, 20 g.; 12·90%.

10

*Black-burnished* weight 10 g.; 6·45%.
*Grey fabrics:* weight, 80 g.; 51·61%.
*Fabric D:* weight, 40 g.; 25·81%.
Total weight: 155 g.

### Animal Bones

2 fragments identified.
Species represented: ox, sheep.

### *Pit 142* (PC 70, trench 94, layer 109)

Irregular pit or scoop, 3 ft. 6 in. by 2 ft. 3 in. (1·07 × 0·69 m.), cut to a depth of 10 in. (0·25 m.).

Filled with black soil containing bone, shells, brick, tile and pottery

PIT 142

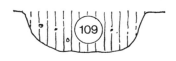 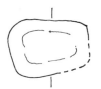

ONE METRE

THREE FEET     SECTIONS

TWO METRES

SIX FEET     PLANS

Fig. 64

### Pottery

From layer 109:
  *New Forest:* sherds of fabric 3; weight, 5 g.; 1·30%.
  *Hand-made, fabric A:* weight, 70 g.; 18·18%.
  *Black-burnished:* 85; weight, 70 g.; 18·18%.
  *Grey fabrics:* 85, weight, 240 g.; 62·34%.
  Total weight, 385 g.

### Animal Bones

23 fragments identified (including 5 ribs).
Species represented: ox, sheep, pig, red deer.

### *Well (pit) 144* (PC 70, trench 95, layers 92, 134, 141, 142, 148, 150, 151, 152)

A circular well shaft 3 ft. 6 in. (1·07 m.) in diameter set in a roughly rectangular well pit
4 ft. 6 in. (1·37 m.) across. The shaft would once have been lined with timber to retain the
clay and marl packing between the lining and the pit edge. The bottom of the well lay at

17 ft. (5·2 m.) below the surface of the natural clay. The shaft was completely excavated, but the clay packing was left in position.

The lowest filling (layers 148, 150, 151, 152) consisted of black organic mud interleaved with chalk lenses, from the bottom of the well at 17 ft. (5·2 m.) to 14 ft. (4·27 m.). Next came layer 142, between 13 and 14 ft. (3·96–4·27m): it consisted of grey clay containing large flints, masses of animal bone, oyster shells and pottery, together with well-preserved organic material.[1] Above, from 12 to 13 ft. (3·66–3·96 m.), was a similar layer (layer 141) but without the organic content preserved. From 10 to 12 ft. (3·05–3·66 m.) the same grey clay continued but contained quantities of crushed oysters (layer 134). The lowest 4 ft. (1·22 m.) of filling (layers 134, 141, 142) represent silting resulting from disuse with some sporadic tipping of rubbish. The upper 10 ft (3·05 m.) (layer 92) were a completely uniform tip of occupation rubbish consisting of loosely packed black soil containing tile, pottery, bone and shell. It appears to have been thrown in as part of a single act of refilling.

## Small Finds

From layer 92:

| | | |
|---|---|---|
| Bronze coin | (1665) | Constans (A.D. 337–41). |
| Bronze coin | (1711) | third or fourth century A.D.; very corroded. |
| Bronze bracelet | (1716) | fragment of strip type, plain; not illustrated. |
| Bronze bracelet | (1651) | two-strand twisted wire type; not illustrated. |
| Bronze sheet | (1674) | fragment, perforated; not illustrated. |
| Iron strip | (1672) | pointed, possibly shank of a nail; not illustrated. |
| Iron strip | (1673) | not illustrated. |
| Iron chisel | (1736) | fig. 128, no. 215. |

From layer 134:

| | | |
|---|---|---|
| Bronze coin | (1745) | Helena (A.D. 324–30). |

From layer 142:

| | | |
|---|---|---|
| Bone strip | (1990) | 1·1 cm. wide, 0·4 cm. thick, 5 cm. long (broken at both ends); not illustrated. |
| Leather shoes | (2280–2287) | fig. 136, nos. 367–74. |

From layer 148:

| | | |
|---|---|---|
| Whetstone | (1988) | laminated sandy limestone; not illustrated, no. 343. |

From layer 150:

| | | |
|---|---|---|
| Leather | (2660) | fig. 132, no. 264. |
| | (2676) | not illustrated, no. 280. |
| | (2678) | not illustrated, no. 281. |
| | (2714) | fig. 135, no. 318. |
| | (2715) | fig. 135, no. 319. |
| | (2716) | not illustrated, no. 320. |

From layer 151:

| | | |
|---|---|---|
| Antler ring | (2649) | roughly cut, fig. 120, no. 126. |
| Glass bead | (2650) | not illustrated, no. 155. |
| Wooden comb | (2651) | fig. 137, no. 322. |
| Wooden handle | (2652) | fig. 138, no. 329. |

---

[1] The faunal material preserved in the wells will be considered together with the Saxon evidence in volume 2.

PIT 144

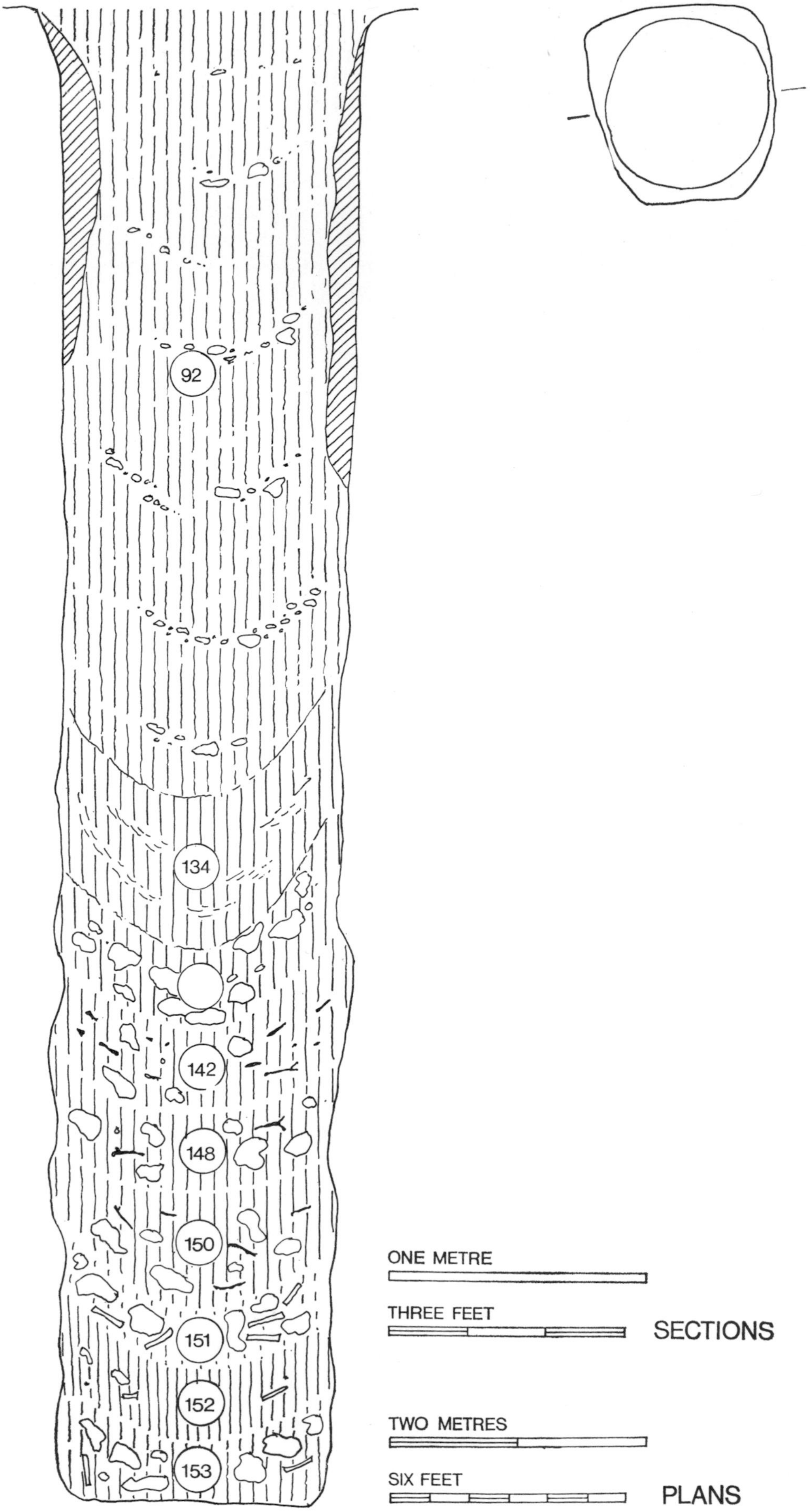

92

134

142

148

150

151

152

153

ONE METRE

THREE FEET                SECTIONS

TWO METRES

SIX FEET                   PLANS

FIG. 65

| Wooden handle | (2653) | fig. 138, no. 328. |
| Wooden block | (2654) | fig. 137, no. 325. |
| Leather shoes | (2288–2294) | fig. 136, nos. 375–81 |

## Nails

From layer 150:
1, 7·6 +.

## Pottery

From layer 92:
*New Forest:* 2/10, 1–2, 2/10.7, 6.1, 13, 13.2, 20.1, 22.1–5, 32 (2), 41.3, 43.8, 43 (2), 58 (2), 66.7; weight, 1000 g.; 9·78%.
*Oxford:* 14, 15.3, 30.9, 40, 43, 57, 58; weight, 280 g.; 2·74%.
*Misc.:* 11.4.
*Hand-made, fabric A:* 86 (6), 107 (2), 123 (6); weight, 2580 g.; 25·24%.
*Black-burnished:* 85 (4), 107 (2), 117.1, 117, 126 (3); weight, 3550 g.; 34·74%.
*Grey fabrics:* 80.2, 85, 103, 107 (2), 127 (3), 129 (4), 132 (2), 137.1, 137 (2), 141, 142.4, 148, 174.2; weight, 2760 g.; 27·01%.
*Fabric D:* 109.8; weight, 50 g.; 0·49%.
Total weight: 10,220 g.
From layer 134:
*New Forest:* 2/10.5, 43.6, 43; weight, 640 g.; 27·06%.
*Oxford:* 43, 58; weight, 200 g.; 8·46%.
*Hand-made, fabric A:* weight, 250 g.; 10·57%.
*Black-burnished:* 85, 107 (2); weight, 875 g.; 37·00%.
*Grey fabrics:* 127.2, 127, 134.2, 142, 159.4–5; weight, 390 g.; 16·49%.
*Fabric D:* weight, 10 g.; 0·42%.
Total weight: 2365 g.
From layer 141:
*TS:* Dr. 31, Central Gaul, Antonine.
*New Forest:* 3.1–2, 2/10.8, 10.2, 43 (2); weight, 350 g.; 13·46%.
*Oxford:* 40, 58; weight, 15 g.; 0·58%.
*Hand-made, fabric A:* 123; weight, 170 g.; 6·54%.
*Black-burnished:* 85 (sherd of same as in 134), 107 (2), 117, 126 (3); weight, 1270 g.; 48·85%.
*Grey fabrics:* 107 (2), 127, 175; base sherd with join in Pit 46; weight, 795 g.; 30·58%.
Total weight: 2600 g.
From layer 142:
*New Forest:* 29.5, 43; weight, 150 g.; 4·49%.
*Oxford:* 15 (possibly the same vessel as 15·3), 17.3; weight, 40 g.; 1·20%.
*Hand-made, fabric A:* 86, 123 (4); weight, 930 g.; 27·84%.
*Black-burnished:* 85 (2), 126 (3); weight, 1020 g.; 30·54%.
*Grey fabrics:* 76, 129, 129.4, 141.4; weight, 250 g.; 7·49%.
*Misc.:* sherds of type 179; weight, 950 g.; 28·44%.
Total weight: 3340 g.
From layer 148:
*New Forest:* 43; weight, 10 g.; 2·06%.
*Oxford:* more sherds of 15 and 17.3, as in 142, 15; weight, 10 g.; 2·06%.

*Hand-made, fabric A:* 123 (2); weight, 350 g.; 72·16%.
*Black-burnished:* 107, 126, weight, 100 g.; 20·62%.
*Grey fabrics:* weight, 15 g.; 3·09%.
Total weight: 485 g.
From layer 150:
   *New Forest:* sherds of fabric 1; weight, 120 g.; 13·41%.
   *Oxford:* sherds of 17.3, as above; weight, 5 g.; 0·56%.
   *Hand-made, fabric A:* 123 (2); weight, 270 g.; 30·17%.
   *Black-burnished:* 126; weight, 250 g.; 27·93%.
   *Grey fabrics:* weight, 250 g.; 27·93%.
   Total weight: 895 g.
From layer 151:
   *Oxford:* 58; weight, 70 g.; 21·88%.
   *Hand-made, fabric A:* weight, 80 g.; 25·0%.
   *Black-burnished:* 126; weight, 150 g.; 46·88%.
   *Grey fabrics: 103.1;* weight, 20 g.; 6·25%.
   Total weight: 320 g.
From layer 152:
   *TS:* Dr. 33, East Gaul, later second to mid third century A.D.
   *Oxford: 15.1.*
   *Hand-made, fabric A:* 107, 123; weight, 120 g.; 37·50%.
   *Black-burnished:* weight: 10 g.; 3·13%.
   *Grey fabrics:* 85, *159.6;* weight, 190 g.; 59·38%.
   Total weight: 320 g.
   Weight from all layers: 20,545 g.

## Animal Bones

1265 fragments identified (including 261 ribs and 142 skull fragments).
Species represented: ox, 47; dog, 22; sheep, 11; pig, 11; cat, 5; red deer, 3; horse, 1; roe deer, bird.
11 fairly complete ox skulls and more fragmentary remains of at least 6 others were found in this pit. The large number of dog bones included four complete skulls. The sheep bones included part of a very young, probably new born animal. The pig bones also included part of a young animal. The cat bones were the remains of two individuals and included two skulls.


## *Pit 147* (PC 70, trench 96, layers 27 and 32)

Irregular shaped pit *c.* 4 ft. 6 in. by 3 ft. 6 in. (1·37 × 1·07 m.) dug to a maximum depth of 1 ft. 10 in. (0·56 m.).

The lowest level (layer 32) consisted of greenish soil, mixed with charcoal and shells. Above (layer 27), the filling was of occupation rubbish, including shells, charcoal and bones mixed with brown soil.

## Small Finds

From layer 27:
   Bone strip                      (1746)  flat strip of bone, 1·7 cm. wide, 7·6 cm. long, and 0·4 cm. thick, complete; not illustrated.

PIT 147

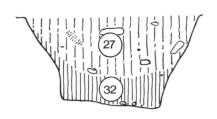

ONE METRE

TWO METRES

THREE FEET      SECTIONS

SIX FEET      PLANS

FIG. 66

## Pottery

From layer 27:
 *New Forest:* sherds of fabric 1, ?2/10. 15; weight, 80 g.; 4·88%.
 *Oxford: 36.5*, 43, 57, 58, 63; weight, 270 g.; 16·46%.
 *Pevensey: 35.15*, 37, weight, 10 g.; 0·61%.
 *Hand-made, fabric A:* 86, 123 (3); weight, 420 g.; 25·6%.
 *Black-burnished:* weight, 240 g.; 14·63%.
 *Grey fabrics: 87.6, 109.4*, 132, *137.8*; weight, 500 g.; 30·49%.
 *Fabric D:* weight, 120 g.; 7·32%.
 *Misc.: 179.2.*
 Total weight: 1640 g.
From layer 32:
 *New Forest:* sherd of fabric 1.
 *Hand-made, fabric A:* weight, 50 g.; 71·43%.
 *Black-burnished:* weight, 20 g.; 28·57%.
 Total weight: 70 g.
 Weight from both layers: 1710 g.

## Animal Bones

69 fragments identified (including 11 ribs and 2 skull fragments).
Species represented: ox, 66; pig, 18; sheep, 11; horse, 3; bird, 2.

### *Pit 155* (PC 70, trench 96, layer 56)

Irregular pit about 5 ft. (1·52 m.) across and up to 8 in. (0·20 m.) deep.
Filled with black soil containing occupation debris. It was cut by pit 151 and posthole
(layer 62) but appears to be later than the shallow scoop (layer 57).

PIT 155

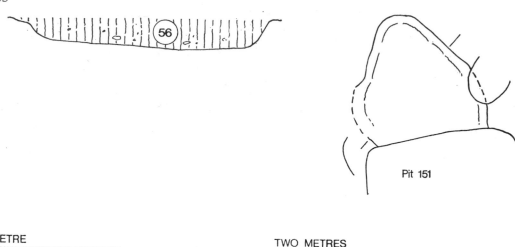

Pit 151

ONE METRE

THREE FEET          SECTIONS

TWO METRES

SIX FEET          PLANS

FIG. 67

*Pottery*

From layer 56:
   *Hand-made, fabric A:* weight, 30 g.; 20·0%.
   *Black-burnished:* 85, weight, 70 g.; 46·67%.
   *Grey fabrics:* 141 (possibly the same vessel as in pit 144); weight, 50 g.; 33·33%.
   Total weight: 150 g.

## Pit 157 (PC 70, trench 97, layer 28)

Rectangular pit of uncertain size largely cut away by the foundation of the sixteenth-century storehouse and the Napoleonic sewer; cut to a depth of 1 ft. 9 in. (0·53 m.).

The filling was uniform consisting of black soil containing occupation debris including charcoal, pottery, tile, oyster shells, etc.

*Pottery*

From layer 28:
   *New Forest:* 52.1–2; weight, 120 g.; 11·11%.
   *Oxford:* 18.1, 57; weight, 40 g.; 3·70%.
   *Hand-made, fabric A:* 123 (2); weight, 330 g.; 30·56%.
   *Black-burnished:* 85, 126; weight, 270 g.; 25·0%.
   *Grey fabrics:* 85 (2), 107, 127 (2), 140; weight, 320 g.; 29·63%.
   Total weight: 1080 g.

*Animal Bones*

   81 fragments identified (including 31 ribs and 3 skull fragments).
   Species represented: ox, 68; sheep, 15; pig, 11; horse, 4; dog, 2.

PIT 157

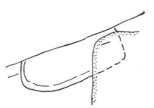

ONE METRE

THREE FEET     SECTIONS

TWO METRES

SIX FEET     PLANS

FIG. 68

*Pit 163* (PC 70, trench 98, layer 34)

Sub-rectangular pit 5 ft. by 4 ft. (1·52 × 1·22 m.) dug through the cobbles to a depth of 1 ft. 10 in. (0·56 m.).

The filling was uniform consisting of black soil containing fragments of tile and animal bones.

*Small Finds*

From layer 34:
  Bone pin            (1969) fig. 116, no. 98.

PIT 163

ONE METRE

THREE FEET     SECTIONS

TWO METRES

SIX FEET     PLANS

FIG. 69

*Pottery*

From layer 34:
    *New Forest:* 43; weight, 150 g.; 7·94%.
    *Hand-made, fabric A:* 107 (3), 123 (4); weight, 950 g.; 50·26%.
    *Black-burnished;* 85, 107 (2), 126; weight, 320 g.; 16·93%.
    *Grey fabrics:* 85, 107, 127 (4), *149.4*, 172; weight, 470 g.; 24·87%.
    Total weight: 1890 g.

*Animal Bones*

    10 fragments identified — all were ribs.

### *Well (pit) 164* (PC 70, trench 98, layers 50–54 and 69–75)

Circular well-shaft 3 ft. 3 in. (0·99 m.) in diameter set in a rectangular well pit about 5 ft. (1·52 m.) across. The well would originally have been lined with timber, the space between the lining and the edge of the well pit being packed with clay and marl. Excavated to a depth of 12 ft. (3·66 m.) but the bottom was not revealed.

The lowest levels reached (layers 69–75) consisted of dark brown soil mixed with occupation debris and interleaved with lenses of brickearth which had eroded in from the sides. Above the top of the layer 69, at 6 ft. (1·83 m.), the filling was uniform, consisting of brown soil mixed with flints, shells and charcoal. Above this came a layer of orange clayey soil containing patches of chalk marl (layer 52): this appeared to represent a deliberate packing. On top of this was a thickness of brown soil with some occupation debris (layer 51) which was eventually capped by a layer of brown soil containing pockets of redeposited material and lumps of mortar (layer 50).

The upper levels of the filling were cut by a later pit dug against one side of the well and filled with brown soil, mortar and wads of brickearth (layer 53).

*Small Finds*

From layer 50:
    Iron joiner's dog        (1981)  fig. 129, no. 230.

*Glass Vessels*

From layer 73:
    fig. 198, no. 19.
From layer 75:
    cf. fig. 198, no. 17.

*Pottery*

From layer 54:
    *New Forest:* sherd of fabric 1; weight, 5 g.; 1·33%.
    *Oxford:* 43; weight, 120 g.; 32·0%.
    *Misc.:* 82; weight, 40 g.; 10·67%.
    *Hand-made, fabric A:* 123 (2); weight, 100 g.; 26·67%.
    *Black-burnished:* 107, 126; weight, 60 g.; 16·0%.
    *Grey fabrics:* sherd with lightly scored chevron decoration; weight, 50 g.; 13·33%.
    Total weight: 375 g.

PIT 164

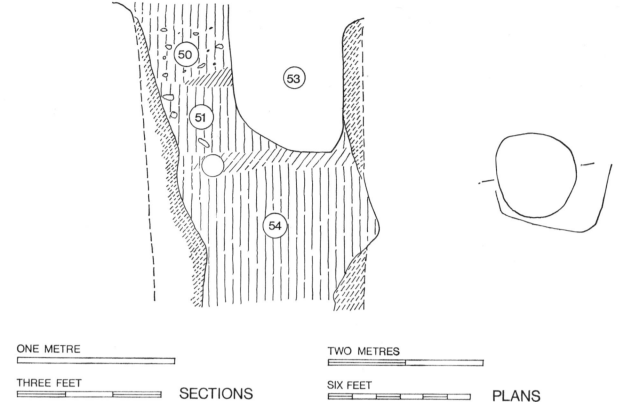

ONE METRE

THREE FEET · SECTIONS

TWO METRES

SIX FEET · PLANS

Fig. 70

From layer 69:
  *New Forest:* sherds of fabric 1; weight, 5 g.; 8·33%·
  *Black-burnished:* 126; weight, 50 g.; 83·33%·
  *Grey fabrics:* weight, 5 g.; 8·33%·
  Total weight, 60 g.
From layer 70:
  *New Forest:* 43; weight, 10 g.; 1·85%·
  *Hand-made, fabric A:* 123; weight, 160 g.; 29·63%·
  *Black-burnished:* weight, 230 g.; 42·59%·
  *Grey fabrics:* 129, 119; weight, 140 g.; 25·93%·
  Total weight: 540 g.
From layer 71:
  *New Forest:* sherds of fabrics 1 and 2; weight, 130 g.; 9·49%·
  *Hand-made, fabric A:* weight, 140 g.; 10·22%·
  *Black-burnished:* 107; weight, 250 g.; 18·25%·
  *Grey fabrics:* 77.3, 117.2, 129 (2), 148 (2), 159.4–5, 172.4; weight, 850 g.; 62·04%·
  Total weight: 1370 g.

From layer 72:
  *New Forest:* sherd of fabric 1; weight, 5 g.; 2·44%.
  *Hand-made, fabric A:* weight, 80 g.; 39·02%.
  *Black-burnished:* 85; weight, 120 g.; 58·54%.
  Total weight: 205 g.
From layer 73:
  *New Forest:* 2/10.20, *23.1* (2), 43; weight, 130 g.; 4·92%.
  *Oxford:* 58.5; weight, 120 g.; 4·55%.
  *Misc.:* *9.1*, 18; weight, 10 g.; 0·38%.
  *Hand-made, fabric A:* 86, 107, 123 (2); weight, 1250 g.; 47·35%.
  *Black-burnished:* 85 (2), 107, 126; weight, 800 g.; 30·30%.
  *Grey fabrics:* 103.1, 127, 139, 160, 175; weight, 320 g.; 12·12%.
  *Fabric D:* weight, 10 g.; 0·38%.
  Total weight: 2640 g.
From layer 74:
  *New Forest:* sherds of fabrics 1 and 2; weight, 5 g.; 0·41%.
  *Hand-made, fabric A:* 123; weight, 640 g.; 53·11%.
  *Black-burnished:* 126 (3); weight, 350 g.; 29·05%.
  *Grey fabrics:* 129, 139; weight, 210 g.; 17·43%.
  Total weight: 1205 g.
From layer 75:
  *Hand-made, fabric A:* 86, 107; weight, 400 g.; 68·97%.
  *Grey fabrics:* 129, 142, 177–9.3; weight, 180 g.; 31·03%.
  Total weight: 580 g.
  Weight from all the layers: 6975 g.

## Animal Bones

473 fragments identified (including 104 ribs and 40 skull fragments).
Species represented: ox, 75; sheep, 13; pig, 7; red deer, 2; bird, 1; dog, 1; cat, 1.
The pig bones included part of a new-born pig. The dog bones include a completed skull.

## Human Bones

Infant burial (4 bones).

### *Pit 166* (PC 70, trench 97, layer 58)

Oval shaped pit, 5 ft. by 3 ft. 6 in. (1·52 × 1·07 m.), dug to a depth of 2 ft. (0·61 m.).
  The filling consisted of dark brown soil containing redeposited brickearth, oyster shells, tile fragments and charcoal. The northern side of the pit was discoloured to a greenish colour.
  Cut by gullies 19 and 21.

## *Pottery*

From layer 58:
  *New Forest:* sherds of fabrics 1 and 2; weight, 50 g.; 20·0%.
  *Hand-made, fabric A:* 86, 123; weight, 70 g.; 28·0%.
  *Black-burnished:* 107; weight, 50 g.; 20·0%.
  *Grey fabrics:* 107, 127; weight, 80 g.; 32·0%.
  Total weight: 250 g.

PIT 166

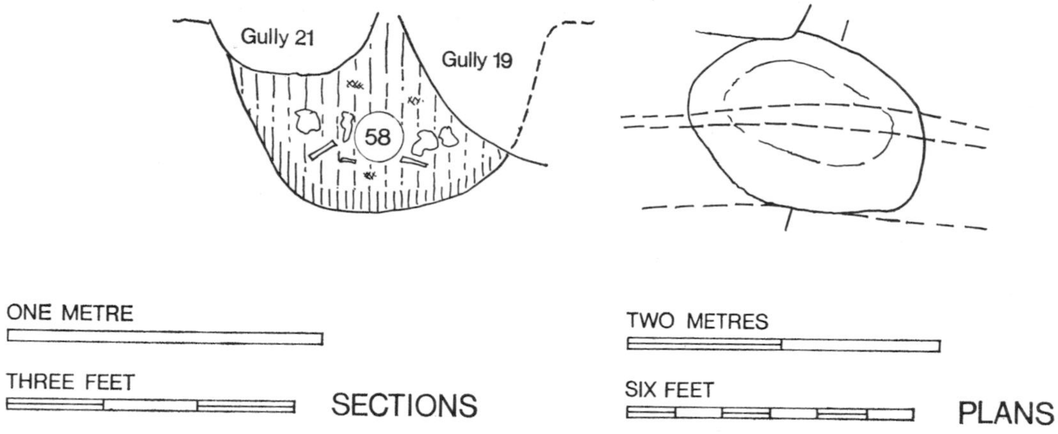

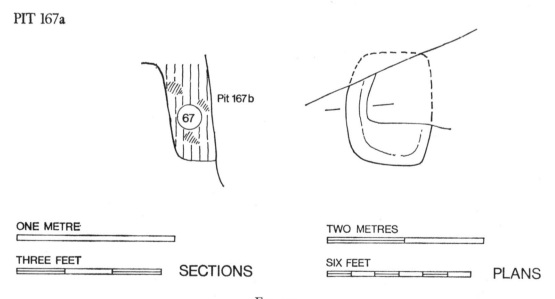

FIG. 71

*Pit 167A* (PC 70, trench 97, layer 67)

Sub-rectangular pit 3 ft. 6 in. (1·07 m.) wide and 2 ft. (0·61 m.) deep. Partially cut away by pit 167B and by the Napoleonic sewer.

The filling consisted of black soil mixed with redeposited brickearth, charcoal, oysters and fragments of tile.

PIT 167a

FIG. 72

*Pit 168* (PC 70, trench 99, layer 40)

Irregular pit 7 ft. (2·13 m.) across by 1 ft. 2 in. (0·36 m.) deep.

The filling consisted of brown soil mixed with wads of redeposited natural clay and flints together with some occupation debris.

Cut by pit 169.

PIT 168

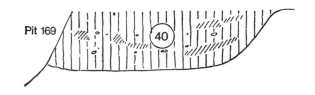
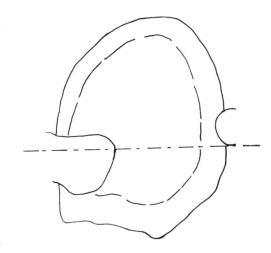

ONE METRE

THREE FEET                                      SECTIONS

TWO METRES

SIX FEET                                      PLANS

FIG. 73

*Pottery*

From layer 40:

    *New Forest:* 2/10.15, 6, 43; weight, 100 g.; 20.41%.
    *Oxford:* 35.4, *35.12*; weight, 50 g.; 10·20%.
    *Misc.: 108.*
    *Hand-made, fabric A:* 86, 123; weight, 160 g.; 32·65%.
    *Black-burnished:* 85, 107, 126; weight, 80 g.; 16·33%.
    *Grey fabrics:* 107, 129 (2); weight, 100 g.; 20·42%.
    Total weight: 490 g.

*Animal Bones*

    12 fragments identified (including 2 ribs).
    Species represented: ox, sheep, pig, bird, red deer.

*Pit 171* (PC 70, trench 99, layer 43)

Irregular pit 4 ft. (1·22 m.) across and 8 in. (0·20 m.) deep.
The filling consisted of black soil containing flints.

PIT 171

ONE METRE

TWO METRES

THREE FEET

SECTIONS

SIX FEET

PLANS

FIG. 74

## Pottery

From layer 43:
*New Forest:* 29; weight, 10 g.; 4·55%.
*Hand-made, fabric A:* 123; weight, 140 g.; 63·64%.
*Black-burnished:* weight, 70 g.; 31·82%.
Total weight: 220 g.

## Animal Bones

14 fragments identified (including 3 ribs).
Species represented: ox, sheep, pig.

### *Pit 178* (PC 70, trench 99, layer 76)

Rectangular pit 6 ft. (1·83 m.) long, partially cut away by the footings of the sixteenth-century storehouse; cut to a depth of 3 ft. 10 in. (1·17 m.).

The filling was uniform consisting of brown soil mixed with charcoal, flints, tile fragments, pottery, bone and shells. The natural clay around the edges of the pit had been stained green.

## Small Finds

From layer 76:

| | | |
|---|---|---|
| Bronze coin | (1972) | Constantine I (A.D. 310–13). |
| Shale bracelet | (1962) | rectangular cross-section 8 by 5 mm., 8·0 cm. in external diameter; not illustrated. |
| Shale bracelet | (1968) | rectangular cross-section 6 by 5 mm., 7·6 cm. in external diameter; not illustrated. |
| Bronze strip bracelet | (1970) | decorated, fig. 111, no. 31. |

PIT 178

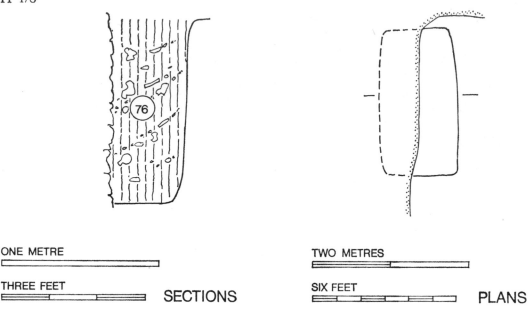

FIG. 75

*Pottery*

From layer 76:
    *Argonne:* Chenet 313 (possibly the same vessel as in pit 236).
    *New Forest:* 19.1–3, 43, *52*.*3*; weight, 60 g.; 6·25%.
    *Oxford:* sherds of ?flagon; weight, 30 g.; 3·13%.
    *Hand-made, fabric A:* 123 (2); weight, 460 g.; 47·92%.
    *Black-burnished:* 85, 107, 126; weight, 260 g.; 27·08%.
    *Grey fabrics;* *141*.*2*, 145, 148; weight, 150 g.; 15·63%.
    Total weight: 960 g.

### *Pit 179* (PC 70, trench 99, layers 77, 86 and 87)

Oval shaped pit 4 ft. by 3 ft. 3 in. (1·22 × 0·99 m.), cut to a depth of 1 ft. 8 in. (0·51 m.).
    The lowest filling (layer 87) consisted of typical greenish–grey cesspit filling. It was sealed by a layer (layer 86) of redeposited brickearth above which was a deposit of occupation debris mixed with brown soil (layer 77).

*Pottery*

From layer 77:
    *Hand-made fabric A:* 123 (2); weight, 70 g.
    Total weight: 70 g.

PIT 179

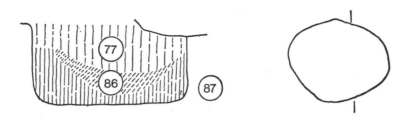

ONE METRE

TWO METRES

THREE FEET          SECTIONS          SIX FEET          PLANS

Fig. 76

*Pit 181* (PC 70, trench 99, layers 79 and 82)

Oval shaped pit 4 ft. (1·22 m.) wide and 1 ft. 9 in. (0·53 m.) deep.

The lowest filling (layer 82) consisted of a layer of brown soil containing charcoal and quantities of pottery. Above (layer 79) the soil was blacker and was mixed with charcoal, pottery and shells.

*Pottery*

From layer 79:
   *New Forest:* 43; weight, 20 g.; 4·40%.
   *Oxford:* 40; weight, 25 g.; 5·49%.
   *Hand-made, fabric A:* weight, 170 g.; 37·36%.

PIT 181

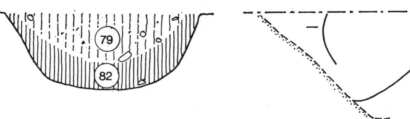

ONE METRE

TWO METRES

THREE FEET          SECTIONS          SIX FEET          PLANS

Fig. 77

11

*Black-burnished:* weight, 70 g.; 15·38%.
*Grey fabrics:* 137.1; weight, 170 g.; 37·36%.
Total weight: 455 g.

*Pit 182* (PC 70, trench 98, layer 60)

Rectangular pit 6 ft. by 4 ft. 6 in. (1·83 × 1·37 m.), cut to a depth of 2 ft. 1 in. (0·63 m.). The filling was uniform, consisting of brown–black soil mixed with flints, oysters, and tiles representing occupation debris.

PIT 182

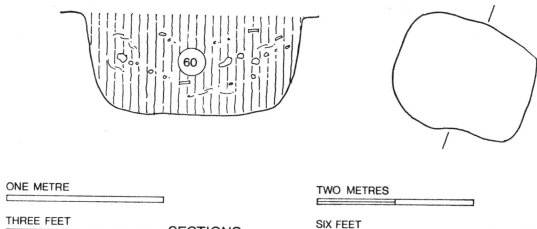

ONE METRE

TWO METRES

THREE FEET          SECTIONS          SIX FEET          PLANS

Fig. 78

*Small Finds*

From layer 60:
   Bronze bracelet          (1930)  twisted rod type, fig. 111, no. 27.

*Pottery*

From layer 60:
   *New Forest:* 2/10.20, *13.6,* 22.1–5, *88.8;* weight, 200 g.; 5·42%.
   *Oxford:* 26, 35·1, 40, 42, 43, 58; weight, 170 g.; 4·61%.
   *Pevensey:* 37.1; weight; 60 g.; 1·63%.
   *Hand-made, fabric A:* 123 (3); weight, 360 g.; 9·76%.
   *Black-burnished:* 85, 107 (2), 126 (2), *175.5;* weight, 190 g.; 5·15%.
   *Grey fabrics:* 85, 129 (2), *131.1,* 149.3 (2), 153.8; weight, 1440 g.; 39·02%.
   *Fabric D:* 137.4–6; weight, 320 g.; 8·67%.
   *Misc.:* 179; weight, 950 g.; 25·75%.
   Total weight: 3690 g.

## Pit 183 (PC 70, trench 98, layer 66)

Rectangular pit 7 ft. 6 in. by 5 ft. (2·29 × 1·52 m.) largely cut away by pit 162, except for the few inches of filling against its west and south sides; dug to a depth of 1 ft. 5 in. (0·43 m.). The pit was also cut by a posthole (layer 67). The relationship between pits 183 and 184 was not defined.

The surviving part of the filling consisted of occupation debris mixed with brown soil.

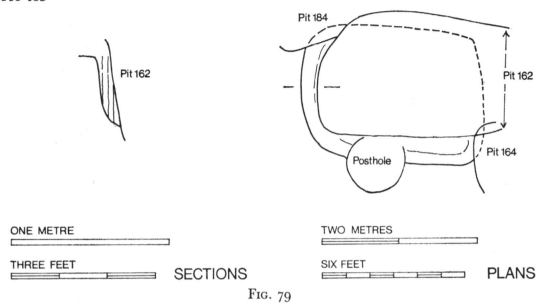

PIT 183

Pit 162

Pit 184

Pit 162

Pit 164

Posthole

ONE METRE

THREE FEET    SECTIONS

TWO METRES

SIX FEET    PLANS

FIG. 79

## Pit 184 (PC 70, trench 99, layers 80 and 81)

Oval shaped pit 6 ft. by 4 ft. (1·83 × 1·22 m.) cut to a depth of 1 ft. 6 in. (0·46 m.).

The lowest layer (layer 81) was typical brown cesspit filling containing bones and shells. Above (layer 80) was a deposit of occupation rubbish, shells and tiles mixed with black soil.

The pit was cut by pit 162; its relationship to pit 183 was not defined.

*Pottery*

From layer 80:
*New Forest:* 22.1–5, 43.9; weight, 50 g.; 5·95%.
*Hand-made, fabric A:* 86, 107; weight, 270 g.; 32·14%.
*Black-burnished;* 107; weight, 90 g.; 10·71%.
*Grey fabrics:* 85, 130, 141; weight, 430 g.; 51·19%.
Total weight: 840 g.
From layer 81:
*Hand-made, fabric A:* weight, 20 g.; 7·41%.
*Grey fabrics:* sherds of storage jar; weight, 250 g.; 92·59%.
Total weight: 270 g.
Weight from both layers; 1110 g.

PIT 184

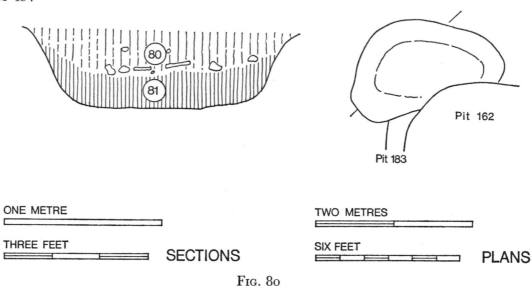

ONE METRE

TWO METRES

THREE FEET                    SECTIONS        SIX FEET                    PLANS

Fig. 80

*Pit 185* (PC 70, trench 99, layer 84)

Rectangular pit 6 ft. by 3 ft. 6 in. (1·83 × 1·07 m.), dug to a depth of 3 ft. 8 in. (1·12 m.). It had been largely removed by the footings of the sixteenth-century storehouse.

The filling consisted of dark brown soil containing flints, and quantities of oysters and tile fragments.

PIT 185

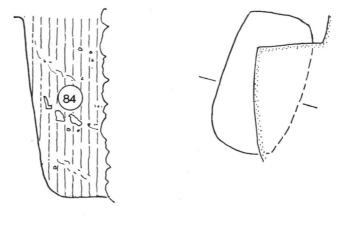

ONE METRE

TWO METRES

THREE FEET                    SECTIONS        SIX FEET                    PLANS

Fig. 81

*Small Finds*

From layer 84:
  Shale bowl                  (1985)  fragment, fig. 122, no. 147.

*Pottery*

From layer 84:
  *Argonne: Chenet* 326.
  *New Forest:* 2/10.5, 66; weight, 100 g.; 6·45%.
  *Hand-made, fabric A:* 86, 107, 123 (5); weight, 850 g.; 54·84%.
  *Black-burnished:* 85, 107, 126 (2); weight, 350 g.; 22·58%.
  *Grey fabrics:* 85, 127, 129; weight, 250 g.; 16·13%.
  Total weight: 1550 g.

### *Pit 186* (PC 70, trench 99, layer 85)

Rectangular pit 5 ft. 6 in. by 4 ft. 9 in. (1·68 × 1·45 m.), cut to a depth of 1 ft. 8 in. (0·51 m.). In the bottom of the pit were found the holes for four stakes each 5 in. (0·13 m.) in diameter and driven into the clay to a depth of 9 in. (0·23 m.). It seems probable that the stakes supported a seat above the cesspit.

The filling was uniform, consisting of black soil mixed with charcoal, and roof tile fragments.

PIT 186

ONE METRE

TWO METRES

THREE FEET          SECTIONS          SIX FEET          PLANS

FIG. 82

*Pottery*

From layer 85:
  *New Forest:* 22.1–5; weight, 90 g.; 8·53%.
  *Oxford:* sherds of fabric 4; weight, 15 g.; 1·42%.
  *Misc.:* 24.3.

*Hand-made, fabric A:* 123 (2); weight, 350 g.; 33·18%.
*Black-burnished:* 85 (2), 107, 126; weight, 250 g.; 23·70%.
*Grey fabrics:* 85, 107, 127; weight, 350 g.; 33·18%.
Total weight: 1055 g.

*Pit 187* (PC 70, trench 99, layers 83, 98 and 99; PC 72, trench 109, layers 16, 17 and 67)

Pit of unknown size but exceeding 15 ft. (4·57 m.) across.

The lowest layer (99 layer 99 and 109 layer 67) consisted of a light brown, slightly clayey soil containing occasional large flints, together with bones, tiles and oyster shells. It was sealed by a discontinuous lens of redeposited natural clay and marl (99 layer 98 and 109 layer 17), above which was a thick deposit of occupation debris (99 layer 83 and 109 layer 16), incorporating charcoal, pockets of marl, oyster shells, bone, pottery and fragments of roof tile. Fragments of daub were recovered from 109 layer 16.

*Small Finds*

From trench 99, layer 83:
    Bronze coin            (1982)   Carausius (A.D. 286–93)
    Bronze coin            (1983)   Constantine I (A.D. 319–22).
    Bronze bracelet       (1984)   *cf.* nos. 40–2 not illustrated.
From trench 99, layer 99:
    Bronze sheet           (1991)   fragment; not illustrated.

*Pottery*

From trench 99, layer 83:
    *New Forest:* 22.1–5, 49, *55.11*; weight, 170 g.; 8·06%.
    *Oxford:* 58; weight, 60 g.; 2·84%.
    *Hand-made, fabric A:* 86, 123; weight, 470 g.; 22·27%.
    *Black-burnished:* 85, 107 (3), 126; weight, 580 g.; 27·49%.
    *Grey fabrics:* 85, 106, 127 (2); weight, 310 g.; 14·69%.
    *Misc.:* 179; weight, 520 g.; 24·64%.
    Total weight: 2110 g.
From trench 99, layer 98:
    *Hand-made, fabric A:* weight, 20 g.; 14·29%.
    *Grey fabrics:* 142, 148; weight, 120 g.; 85·71%.
    Total weight: 140 g.
From trench 99, layer 99:
    *Hand-made, fabric A:* 86; weight, 30 g.; 13·04%.
    *Black-burnished:* 85, 126; weight, 80 g.; 34·78%.
    *Grey fabrics:* 127, 129; weight, 120 g.; 52·17%.
    Total weight: 230 g.
From trench 109, layer 16:
    *Oxford:* 42; weight, 5 g.
    *Hand-made, fabric A:* weight, 5 g.
    Total weight: 10 g.

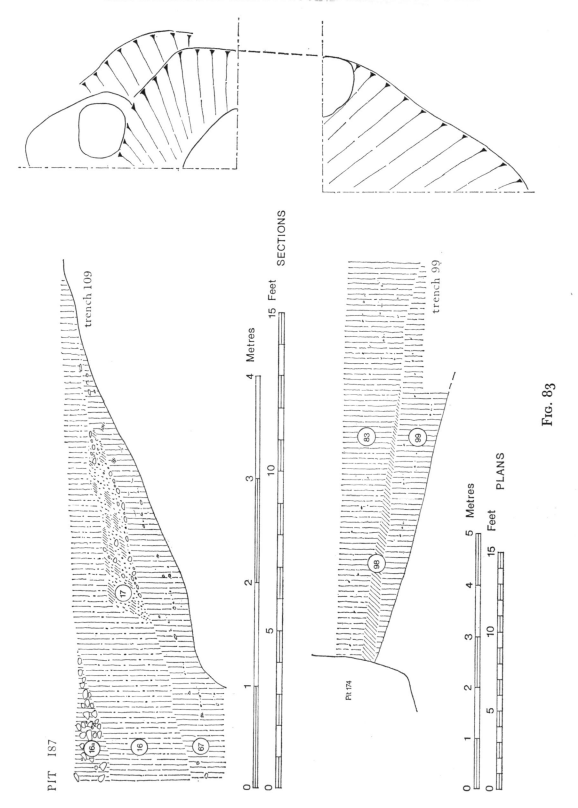

SECTIONS

PLANS

Fig. 83

From trench 109, layer 17:

*New Forest:* 43; weight, 50 g.; 12·35%.
*Oxford:* 63·4; weight, 25 g.; 6·17%.
*Hand-made, fabric A:* 123; weight, 170 g.; 41·98%.
*Black-burnished:* weight, 70 g.; 17·28%.
*Grey fabrics:* 107, 141, 148.2, 157; weight, 90 g.; 22·22%.
Total weight: 405 g.

From trench 109, layer 67:

*New Forest;* 19.1–3, 22.1–5, 43, 55·9; weight, 30 g.; 1·81%.
*Oxford:* 14, 15.1, *17.2;* weight, 30 g.; 1·81%.
*Misc.:* 88.9; weight, 40 g.; 2·41%.
*Hand-made, fabric A:* 86 (2), 123; weight, 630 g.; 37·95%.
*Black-burnished:* 85, 107, 117.1; weight, 250 g.; 15·06%.
*Grey fabrics:* 85, 96, 107, 127 (2), 140 (2), 142; weight, 680 g.; 40·96%.
Total weight: 1660 g.
Weight from all the layers: 4555 g.

## Animal Bones

167 fragments identified (including 60 ribs and 3 skull fragments).
Species represented: ox, 59, sheep, 23; pig, 15; cat, 1; bird, 1; horse, 1.

### *Pit 195* (PC 71, trench 102, layers 79 and 80)

Rectangular pit 4 ft. by 2 ft. 3 in. (1·22 × 0·68 m.), cut to a maximum depth of 2 ft. 3 in. (0·69 m.) below the top of the adjacent clay make-up.

The lowest level of filling (layer 80) was of black soil with quantities of charcoal, oyster shells, bones and tiles. Above (layer 79), the soil was a lighter colour mixed with wads of clay, lumps of plaster, some of which were painted, and a mass of broken tiles.

The pit was cut through layer 66.

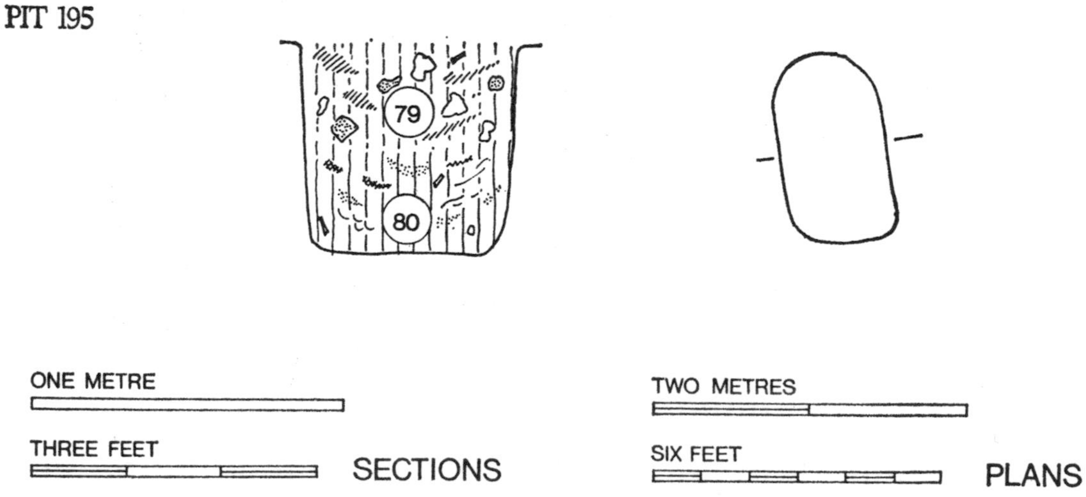

PIT 195

ONE METRE

TWO METRES

THREE FEET      SECTIONS      SIX FEET      PLANS

Fig. 84

*Small Finds*

From layer 79:

Bronze binding       (2137)   U-shaped binding 3 mm. wide in much corroded fragments; not illustrated.

Bone pin       (2136)   fig. 116, no. 94.

*Pottery*

From layer 79:

*New Forest:* 19.1–3, 32, 43 (2), 66; weight, 300 g.; 14·08%.

*Oxford:* 14, *18.10,* 43; weight, 170 g.; 7·98%.

*Misc.:* 31.2, probably Oxford, but rather orange fabric; weight, 10 g.; 0·47%.

*Hand-made fabric A:* 123 (2); weight, 520 g.; 24·41%.

*Black-burnished:* 85, 126; weight, 570 g.; 26·76%.

*Grey fabrics:* 85( 2), 98, 107 (2); weight, 540 g.; 25·35%.

*Fabric D:* weight, 20 g.; 0·94%.

Total weight: 2130 g.

From layer 80:

*New Forest:* sherd of fabric 3; weight, 5 g.; 2·86%.

*Hand-made, fabric A:* 107; weight, 170 g.; 97·14%.

Total weight: 175 g.

Weight from both layers: 2305 g.

*Pit 200* (PC 71, trench 101, layer 70)

Rectangular pit 4 ft. by 2 ft. 3 in. (1·22 × 0·69 m.) and 8 in. (0·20 m.) deep. Filled with black soil containing some fragments of tile and bones.

PIT 200

ONE METRE

THREE FEET      SECTIONS

TWO METRES

SIX FEET      PLANS

Fig. 85

*Pottery*

From layer 70:
   *New Forest:* sherds of fabric 2; weight, 20 g.; 22·22%.
   *Hand-made, fabric A:* 123; weight, 20 g.; 22·22%.
   *Grey fabrics:* 107; weight, 50 g.; 55·56%.
   Total weight: 90 g.

*Animal Bones*

   2 fragments identified.
   Species represented: ox.

### *Pit 201* (PC 71, trench 100, layers 83 and 84)

Square pit 4 ft. 6 in. (1·37 m.) across and 3 ft. 6 in. (1·07 m.) deep.

The lowest filling (layer 84) was a complex deposit of grey clayey soil becoming darker towards the top and mixed with ash and large flints. Above this (layer 83) was a series of tips of grey soil, oyster shells, bones, ash and flints.

The pit was cut by pit 200.

*Small Finds*

From layer 84:
   Bone pin          (2202)  fig. 116, no. 93.

*Pottery*

From layer 83:
   *New Forest:* 19.1–3; weight, 50 g.; 8·93%.
   *Oxford:* weight, 50 g.; 8·93%.

**PIT 201**

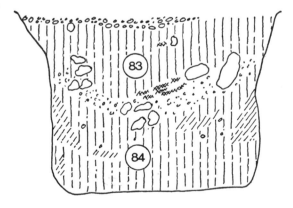

ONE METRE

THREE FEET   SECTIONS

TWO METRES

SIX FEET   PLANS

Fɪɢ. 86

*Hand-made, fabric A:* 86, 123; weight, 150 g.; 26·79%.
*Black-burnished:* 85, 126; weight, 50 g.; 8·93%.
*Grey fabrics:* 107, 127, 136.1; weight, 260 g.
Total weight: 560 g.
From layer 84:
*New Forest:* 19.1–3; weight, 20 g.; 5·41%.
*Oxford:* sherds of fabric 4; weight, 50 g.; 13·51%.
*Hand-made, fabric A:* 86, 123 (2); weight, 100 g.; 27·03%.
*Black-burnished:* 85 (2), 126 (2); weight, 140 g.; 37·84%.
*Grey fabrics;* 109.9, 107; weight, 60 g.; 16·22%.
Total weight: 370 g.
Weight from both layers: 930 g.

## Animal Bones

44 fragments identified (including 8 ribs and 2 skull fragments).
Species represented: ox, pig, red deer.

### *Pit 205* (PC 71, trench 101, layer 99)

Rectangular pit 4 ft. by 3 ft. (1·22 × 0·91 m.), cut to a depth of 8 in. (0·20 m.).
The filling consisted of grey soil with flecks of charcoal, bone and tile.

PIT 205

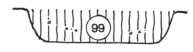 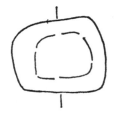

ONE METRE

TWO METRES

THREE FEET SECTIONS SIX FEET PLANS

FIG. 87

## Pottery

From layer 99:
*Black-burnished:* 107; weight, 60 g.
Total weight: 60 g.

## Animal Bones

15 fragments identified (including 10 ribs).
Species represented: ox, sheep, pig, bird.

*Well (pit) 206 (PC 71, trench 102, layers 85, 86, 87 and 88)*

Well shaft oval in plan, 5 ft. 6 in. by 4 ft. (1·7 by 1·2 m.) across. The shaft had originally been lined with timber to revet the packing of clay which filled the space between the well pit and the open shaft. The packing was not excavated. The filling of the shaft was excavated for a depth of 10 ft. (3·05 m.) from the top of the clay bank through which the well had been cut: thereafter excavation was abandoned.

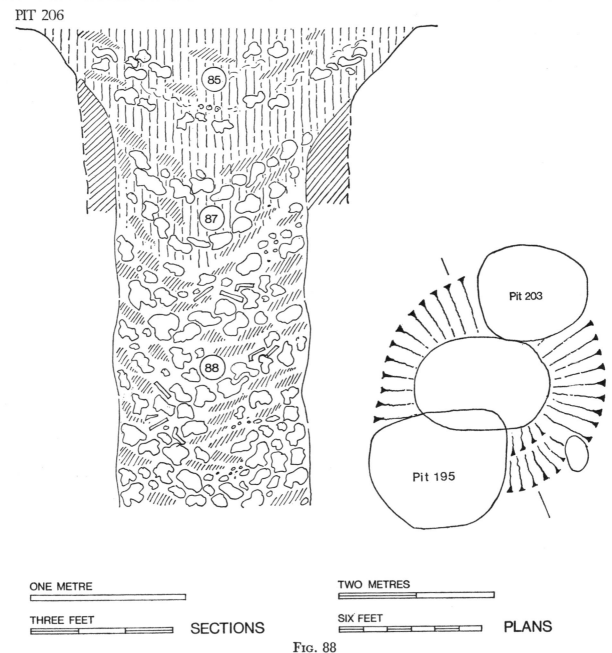

FIG. 88

The lowest level (layer 88) from 10 to 5 ft. (3·1–1·5 m.) consisted of a deliberate fill of tips of clay and gravel mixed with large fragments of brick and tile and bone refuse. Above, from 5 to 2 ft. (1·5–0·6 m.), was a similar deposit (layer 87) but with more soil and fewer flints. The uppermost 2 ft. (0·6 m.) were filled with clayey brown soil (layer 85) containing charcoal and very large numbers of flints together with oyster and winkle shells and fragments of brick and tile. It is evident, therefore, that the well had been deliberately and rapidly filled largely with clay and flints.

The upper part of the shaft had been cut into by two Saxon pits 203 and 195.

## Small Finds

From layer 85:
Shale bracelet     (2228)   D-shaped section, 0·9 mm. wide, 8·4 cm. in external diameter; not illustrated.

From layer 88:
Antler     (2251)   tine sawn and pointed; pl. XXXIII*a*.

## Pottery

From layer 85:
*New Forest:* 29, and sherds of fabric 1; weight, 150 g.; 13·27%.
*Hand-made, fabric A:* 86 (2), 123 (3); weight, 280 g.; 24·78%.
*Black-burnished:* 85 (2), 117, 126 (2); weight, 460 g.; 40·72%.
*Grey fabrics:* 103.1, 107, 129, 140, *177.2*; weight, 210 g.; 18·58%.
*Fabric D:* 137.4–6; weight, 30 g.; 2·65%.
Total weight: 1130 g.
From layer 86:
*Argonne:* Chenet 326; weight, 50 g.; 13·51%.
*New Forest:* sherds of fabrics 1 and 2; weight, 50 g.; 13·51%.
*Hand-made, fabric A:* 123 (2); weight, 80 g.; 21·62%.
*Black-burnished:* 85, 107; weight, 120 g.; 32·43%.
*Grey fabrics:* 85; weight, 70 g.; 18·92%.
Total weight: 370 g.
From layer 87:
*New Forest:* 43, 58; weight, 150 g.; 21·28%.
*Oxford:* 31; weight, 25 g.; 3·55%.
*Hand-made, fabric A:* 107, 123 (2); weight, 150 g.; 21·28%.
*Black-burnished:* 85, 126; weight, 200 g.; 28·37%.
*Grey fabrics:* 77, 107, *109.5*; weight, 180 g.; 25·53%.
Total weight: 705 g.
From layer 88:
*Hand-made, fabric A:* 123; weight, 130 g.
Weight from all the layers: 1335 g.

## Animal Bones

143 fragments identified (including 28 ribs and 2 skull fragments).
Species represented: ox, 58; sheep, 15; pig, 13; dog, 12; horse, 1; red deer, 1.
The pig bones include one fairly complete young animal.

*Pit 209* (PC 71, trench 103, layer 66)

Rectangular pit 4 ft. 6 in. by 2 ft. 3 in. (1·37 × 0·69 m.), dug to a depth of 6 in. (15 cm.) below the top of the clay bank. The pit was cut through the general layers 64 and 65.

The filling was of dark brown soil containing wads of clay and occupation rubbish.

PIT 209

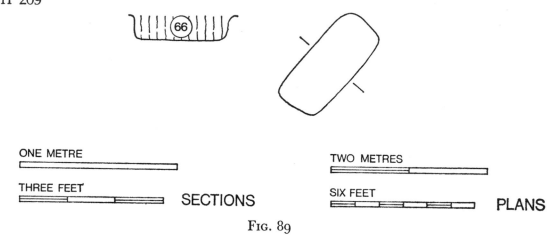

ONE METRE

THREE FEET                           SECTIONS

TWO METRES

SIX FEET                              PLANS

FIG. 89

*Pottery*

From layer 66:
    *Hand-made, fabric A:* 123; weight, 220 g.; 47·83%.
    *Black-burnished:* 85; weight, 90 g.; 19·57%.
    *Grey fabrics:* 76.1, 107, 134, 175; weight, 150 g.; 32·61%.
    Total weight: 460 g.

*Animal Bones*

    18 fragments identified (including 2 ribs and 1 skull fragment).
    Species represented: ox, sheep, bird, pig.

*Pit 210* (PC 71, trench 100, layer 67)

Rectangular pit, more than 5 ft. (1·52 m.) long, largely cut away by the footings of the sixteenth-century building. The pit was excavated to a depth of 1 ft. 10 in. (0·56 m.) but was originally deeper.

The filling was of black occupation soil containing shells and bone.

*Animal Bones*

    22 fragments identified (including 4 ribs and 3 skull fragments).
    Species represented: sheep, ox and horse.

*Pit 221* (PC 72, trench 108, layer 91)

Roughly circular pit 2 ft. 9 in. (0·84 m.) in diameter, dug to a depth of 1 ft. 3 in. (0·38 m.).

The filling was of large flints packed together with wads of clay and some occupation debris.

PIT 210

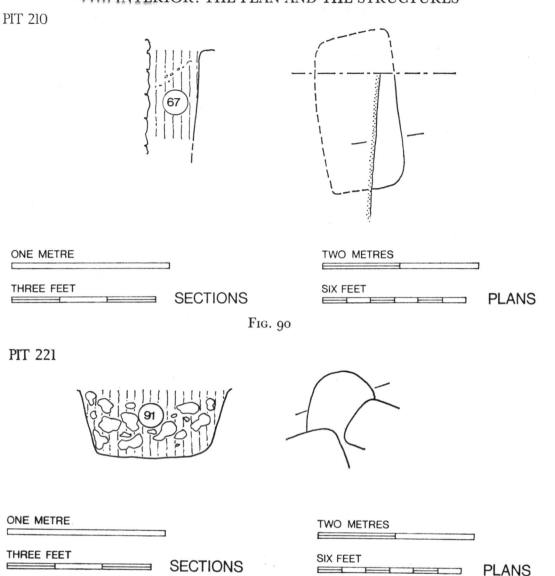

ONE METRE

TWO METRES

THREE FEET          SECTIONS

SIX FEET          PLANS

FIG. 90

PIT 221

ONE METRE

TWO METRES

THREE FEET          SECTIONS

SIX FEET          PLANS

FIG. 91

The pit was cut into by a Saxon posthole, the late Saxon pit 214, and was truncated by the Saxon *Grubenhaus*.

*Pit 222* (PC 72, trench 108, layers 183, 193)

Rectangular pit 4 ft. 3 in. by 5 ft. 2 in. (1·30 × 1·57 m.), dug to a depth of 1 ft. 7 in. (0·48 m.), with sloping sides.

The lower layer (193) was typical cesspit fill containing some fragments of charcoal, oyster shells and occasional pieces of tile. Above this was a uniform packing of wads of brickearth (layer 183), mixed with some occupation material.

PIT 222

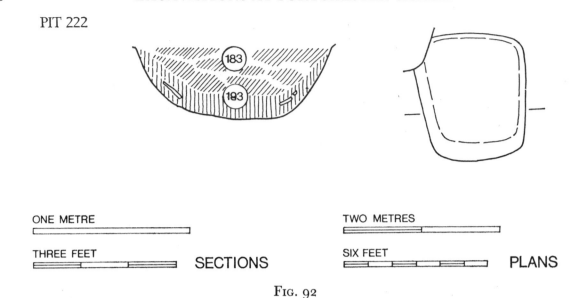

ONE METRE

TWO METRES

THREE FEET    SECTIONS    SIX FEET    PLANS

FIG. 92

The pit was cut through the lower clay bank and is contemporary with the lower occupation. It was also cut through the edge of Roman pit 230 and was cut by late Saxon pit 219.

*Small Finds*

From layer 183:
| | | |
|---|---|---|
| Bronze coin | (2538) | Licinius I (A.D. 310–17). |
| Bronze bracelet | (2537) | fragment, three-strand type; not illustrated. |
| Bronze 'chain' | (2540) | two pairs of two joined loops each made of twisted wire; not illustrated. |

From layer 193:
| | | |
|---|---|---|
| Fragment of lead | (2564) | not illustrated. |

*Pottery*

From layer 183:
*New Forest: 19.4*, 43; weight, 45 g.; 6·57%.
*Hand-made, fabric A:* weight, 120 g.; 17·52%.
*Black-burnished:* 85, 126; weight, 430 g.; 62·77%.
*Grey fabrics:* 129, 134, 140; weight, 90 g.; 13·14%.
Total weight: 685 g.
From layer 193:
*New Forest:* 64, sherd of ?11; weight, 100 g.; 20·83%.
*Oxford:* 15·1.
*Hand-made, fabric A:* 86, *123.10*; weight, 180 g.; 37·50%.
*Black-burnished:* 85, 107; weight, 80 g.; 16·67%.
*Grey fabrics:* 85, 140 (2), 141; weight, 120 g.; 25·0%.
Total weight: 480 g.
Weight from both layers: 1165 g.

*Animal Bones*

251 fragments identified (including 43 ribs and 37 skull fragments).
Species represented: ox, 75; pig, 11; sheep, 9; bird, 2; horse, 2; dog, 1; red deer, 1.

### *Pit 223* (PC 72, trench 108, layers 185, 186, 206, 207)

Rectangular pit 7 ft. 5 in. by 5 ft. (2·26 × 1·52 m.), dug to a depth of 5 ft. (1·52 m.) against the back face of the Roman wall. The sides slope inwards to a bottom measuring 3 ft. 3 in. (0·99 m.) by 1 ft. 8 in. (0·53 m.).

The lower part of the pit (layer 207) was filled with interleaved tips of occupation debris, brickearth and flints, the brickearth deriving from the erosion of the pit sides, while the flints resulted from the gradual collapse of the Roman wall face against which the pit was dug. After the pit had filled up almost to the top, a thick layer of brickearth (layer 206), equivalent to the middle clay, was spread, partly sealing the filling. This was overlaid by two successive tips of occupation rubbish (layer 186 and 185) which are equivalent to middle occupation levels.

The pit was cut through the lower clay bank and was substantially filled during the time when the middle occupation layer was accumulating.

PIT 223

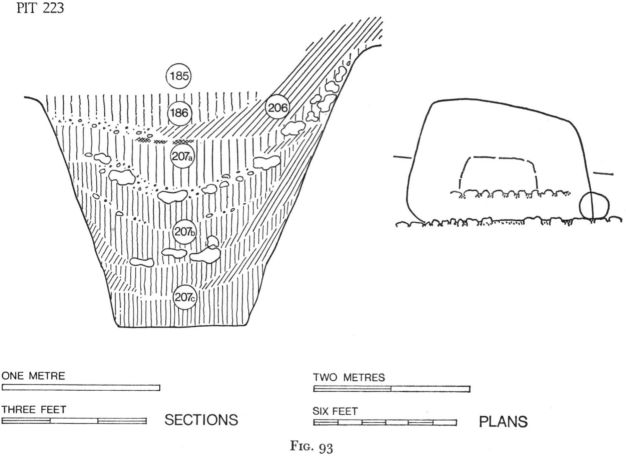

ONE METRE

TWO METRES

THREE FEET    SECTIONS

SIX FEET    PLANS

FIG. 93

*Small Finds*

From layer 185:

| | | |
|---|---|---|
| Bronze fragment | (2541) | not illustrated. |
| Bone pin | (2543) | disc-headed; not illustrated. |

From layer 186:

| | | |
|---|---|---|
| Bronze coin | (2532) | Crispus (A.D. 321–3) |
| Bronze coin | (2534) | Constantine I (A.D. 320–4) |
| Iron object | (2562) | L-shaped clamp 4 cm. long; not illustrated. |

From layer 207:

| | | |
|---|---|---|
| Bronze fibula pin | (2558) | hinged pin; not illustrated. |

*Pottery*

From layer 185:

*TS:* Dr. 18/31 or 31, East Gaul, later second to third century A.D.

*New Forest:* 43, 13, 43; weight, 25 g.; 2·13%.

*Misc.: 31.6*; weight, 10 g.; 0·85%.

*Hand-made, fabric A:* 86, 107 (2), 123; weight, 650 g.; 55·32%.

*Black-burnished:* 85, 126; weight, 150 g.; 12·77%.

*Grey fabrics:* 85 (2), 127 (2), 129·4, 129, 140, 141, 159·4–5, 175; weight; 340 g.; 28·94%.

Total weight: 1175 g.

From layer 186:

*New Forest:* 2/10.20; weight, 5 g.; 0·33%.

*Oxford:* 14, sherds of fabric 4; weight, 30 g.; 1·99%.

*Misc.: 31.7*, joining sherds of same vessel in middle occupation and upper clay; weight, 5 g.; 0·33%.

*Hand-made, fabric A:* 107 (2), ?as in 185, 123; weight, 600 g.; 39·74%.

*Black-burnished:* 107, 126, 175; weight, 580 g.; 38·41%.

*Grey fabrics:* 77, 94, 127, 131.3, 136.2, 137.8, 140; weight, 290 g.; 19·21%.

Total weight: 1510 g.

From layer 206:

*New Forest:* 19.4, 43, 55.8; weight, 200 g.; 50%.

*Hand-made, fabric A:* 86, 123; weight, 120 g.; 30%.

*Black-burnished:* sherds; weight, 20 g.; 5%.

*Grey fabrics:* sherds; weight, 60 g.; 15%.

Total weight: 400 g.

From layer 207:

*New Forest:* 10.2–3, *18.6*, 49, *49.10*, *52.2*; weight, 360 g.; 16·40%.

*Oxford:* 14; weight, 80 g.; 3·64%.

*Misc.: 55.18*, 144.3, sherds of ?same vessel in pit 235, middle occupation and upper occupation; weight, 5 g.; 0·23%.

*Hand-made, fabric A:* 107 (2), 123 (2); weight, 730 g.; 33·26%.

*Black-burnished:* 85, 107, 126 (2); weight, 670 g.; 30·52%.

*Grey fabrics:* 85, 107, 132, 136.2, 137.8, 140; weight, 350 g.; 15·95%.

Total weight: 2195 g.

Weight from all the layers: 5280 g.

*Animal Bones*

701 fragments identified (including 168 ribs and 54 skull fragments).

Species represented: ox, 66; sheep, 15; pig, 12; bird, 4; dog, 1; cat, 1; hare, 1; red deer, 1; roe deer; fox.

*Pit 224* (PC 72, trench 108, layers 188, 189, sealed by 163 and 111)

Rectangular pit 4 ft. 10 in. by 3 ft. (1·47 × 0·91 m.), cut to a depth of 3 ft. (0·91 m.).

The lower filling (layers 188, 189) consisted of typical cesspit filling, containing flecks of charcoal and occasional pockets of brickearth which had eroded in from the side. This was sealed by a general occupation layer (1063) continuous with the middle occupation.

The pit was cut through the middle and lower clay bank and was sealed by the upper clay spread (layer 111). The upper levels of the northern part of the pit were cut away by the early nineteenth-century pit 212.

PIT 224

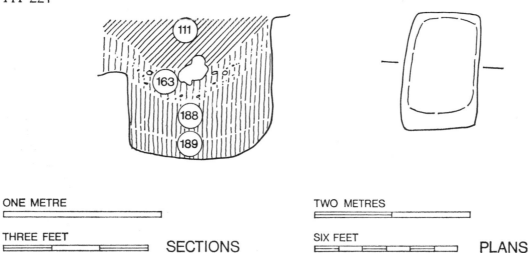

ONE METRE

THREE FEET        SECTIONS

TWO METRES

SIX FEET        PLANS

FIG. 94

*Pottery*

From layer 188:

 *New Forest: 13.1*, sherds of same vessel as in pit 234; weight, 70 g.; 5·38%.
 *Oxford:* sherds of fabric 5; weight, 10 g.; 0·77%.
 *Hand-made, fabric A:* 123 (3); weight, 870 g.; 66·92%.
 *Black-burnished;* 85, 107, 117; weight, 270 g.; 20·77%.
 *Grey fabrics:* 85, 107, 127, 129.4, 140; weight, 80 g.; 6·15%.
 Total weight: 1300 g.

From layer 189:

 *Hand-made, fabric A:* weight, 40 g.; 44·44%.
 *Black-burnished:* weight, 20 g.; 22·22%.
 *Grey fabrics:* weight, 30 g.; 33·33%.
 Total weight: 90 g.
 Weight from both layers: 1390 g.

*Animal Bones*

 85 fragments identified (including 35 ribs and 3 skull fragments).
 Species represented: ox, 62; sheep, 15; pig, 11; bird, 11; red deer, 2.

*Pit 225* (PC 72, trench 108, layers 194, 208, 209, 211)

Rectangular pit 5 ft. 9 in. by 4 ft. 6 in. (1·75 × 1·37 m.), cut to a depth of 2 ft. 6 in. (0·76 m.), with gradually sloping sides.

The lower filling (layer 209) was of grey–brown cesspit filling, mixed with occupation rubbish including quantities of oyster shells and some pottery and bone. Occasional thin lenses of clay represent the erosion of the pit sides. On top of the lower fill was a lens of charcoal (layer 208) which was in turn sealed by a layer of brickearth (layer 211). The upper part of the pit was filled with grey soil (layer 194) containing occupation material. The pit was finally sealed by the upper clay.

The pit was cut by the mid-late Saxon pit.

PIT 225

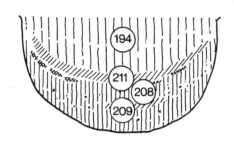
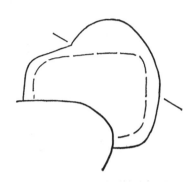

ONE METRE

TWO METRES

THREE FEET          SECTIONS        SIX FEET        PLANS

FIG. 95

*Small Finds*

From layer 194:
  Bone bracelet              (2557)  fig. 117, no. 100.

*Pottery*

From layer 194:
  *New Forest:* 13, 19.1–3, *20.1*, 49; weight, 140 g.; 13·86%.
  *Misc.: 30.7*; weight, 10 g.; 0·99%.
  *Hand-made, fabric A:* 123; weight, 170 g.; 16·83%.
  *Black-burnished:* 85, 126, 175; weight, 300 g.; 29·70%.
  *Grey fabrics: 86.6*, 107, 117, 127 (2), *148.2*, 161; weight, 390 g.; 38·61%.
  Total weight: 1010 g.
From layer 208:
  *New Forest:* 43; weight, 10 g.; 3·33%.
  *Hand-made, fabric A:* 123; weight, 170 g.; 56·67%.
  *Black-burnished:* 175, ?the same as in 194; weight, 70 g.; 23·33%.

*Grey fabrics:* weight, 50 g.; 16·67%.
Total weight: 300 g.
From layer 209:
*New Forest:* 43, as in 208, 49; weight, 265 g.; 34·19%.
*Hand-made, fabric A:* 123; weight, 130 g.; 16·77%.
*Black-burnished:* 175, ?as in 208; weight, 10 g.; 1·29%.
*Grey fabrics:* 107, 127, 136, 137.8; weight, 370 g.; 47·74%.
Total weight: 775 g.
From layer 211:
*Black-burnished:* 126; weight, 10 g.; 40%.
*Grey fabrics:* 98, 107; weight, 15 g.; 60%.
Total weight: 25 g.
Weight from all the layers: 2110 g.

## Animal Bones

188 fragments identified (including 91 ribs and 7 skull fragments).
Species represented: ox, 64; pig, 18; sheep, 14; dog, 2; cat, 1.

### *Pit 227* (PC 72, trench 108, layers 201, 212)

Rectangular pit 5 ft. by 3 ft. (1·52 × 0·91 m.), cut to a depth of 2 ft. (0·61 m.).
The lower layer (layer 212) was cesspit fill sealed with a discontinuous lens of charcoal.
The upper part of the pit (layer 201) was filled with grey soil containing flints, charcoal
and other occupation rubbish.
The pit was cut through the middle clay and was sealed by the upper clay.

## Small Finds

From layer 201:
| | | |
|---|---|---|
| Bronze coin | (2550) | |
| Bone pin | (2560) | type as no. 94; not illustrated. |
| Bone pin | (2561) | type as no. 93; not illustrated. |

PIT 227

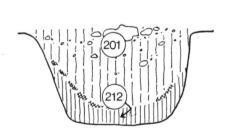

ONE METRE

TWO METRES

THREE FEET    SECTIONS

SIX FEET    PLANS

FIG. 96

From layer 212:
  Bone pin                              (2549)   type 7; fig. 116, no. 96.

*Pottery*

From layer 201:
    *New Forest:* 18.6, sherd joining that in pit 223, 43; weight, 30 g.; 2·91%.
    *Hand-made, fabric A:* weight, 200 g.; 19·42%.
    *Back-burnished:* 85; weight, 240 g.; 23·3%.
    *Grey fabrics:* 77, *175.3*; weight, 560 g.; 54·37%.
    Total weight: 1030 g.
From layer 212:
    *New Forest:* 29, 66.7; weight, 75 g.; 18·99%.
    *Oxford:* 63; weight, 85 g.; 21·52%.
    *Hand-made, fabric A:* 123 (3); weight, 50 g.; 12·66%.
    *Black-burnished:* 85, 107 (2); weight, 180 g.; 45·57%.
    *Grey fabrics:* 175; weight, 5 g.; 1·27%.
    Total weight: 395 g.
    Weight from both layers: 1425 g.

*Animal Bones*

    146 fragments identified (including 54 ribs and 6 skull fragments).
    Species represented: ox, 60; sheep, 20; pig, 14; bird, 4; horse, 1; dog, 1.


*Pit 228* (PC 72, trench 108, layer 213)

    Small rectangular pit: maximum size 4 ft. by 3 ft. (1·22 × 0·91 m.), but with sloping sides; cut to a depth of 1 ft. 1 in. (0·33 m.).

    The uniform filling of this small pit (layer 213) consisted of grey soil mixed with a variety of occupation rubbish.

    The pit was dug after the adjacent scaffold post had been removed or had rotted. It was dug through the middle clay and was sealed by the upper clay (layer 111).

PIT 228

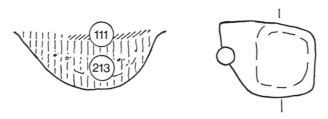

ONE METRE

TWO METRES

THREE FEET                        SECTIONS        SIX FEET                          PLANS

FIG. 97

*Pottery*

From layer 213:
    *New Forest:* 22.1–5, 43; weight, 40 g.; 10·26%.
    *Hand-made, fabric A:* weight, 10 g.; 2·56%.
    *Black-burnished:* 107, 126, weight, 170 g.; 43·59%.
    *Grey fabrics:* 85, 140; weight, 170 g.; 43·59%.
    Total weight: 390 g.

*Animal Bones*

    108 fragments identified (including 25 ribs and 5 skull fragments).
    Species represented: ox, 44; sheep, 23; pig, 18; bird, 3.
    The sheep bones included part of an animal of less than ten months.

### *Pit 229* (PC 72, trench 108, layers 217, 221, 222)

Small rectangular pit 3 ft. by 1 ft. 6 in. (0·91 × 0·46 m.) dug against the back face of the Roman wall to a depth of 1 ft. 3 in. (0·38 m.).

The pit appears to have been left open for a short while, during which time a thin layer of clay washed in from the sides and was mixed with a little cesspit fill (unnumbered on section). Then the pit was sealed by a thick lens of charcoal (layer 222). The lowest filling consolidated rapidly, forcing the charcoal lens to slump violently. A thin deposit of brick-earth was then thrown in (layer 221), after which the pit was filled with grey soil mixed with occupation debris.

The pit had been cut through the middle clay, but was sealed by the upper clay.

*Small Finds*

From layer 217:
    Bronze sheet          (2556)  fragment only; not illustrated.
    Iron hobnails         (2559)  not illustrated.

PIT 229

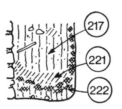 

ONE METRE

TWO METRES

THREE FEET    SECTIONS    SIX FEET    PLANS

FIG. 98

*Pottery*

From layer 217:
    *New Forest: 18.6*, sherd joining in pits 223 and 227; weight, 5 g.; 1·11%.
    *Hand-made, fabric A:* weight, 40 g.; 8·89%.
    *Black-burnished:* weight, 5 g.; 1·11%.
    *Grey fabrics:* 78, joining with sherds in middle occupation, 85, 127 (2), 129; weight, 400 g., 88·89%.
    Total weight: 450 g.
From layer 222:
    *New Forest:* 43; weight, 5 g.; 5·26%.
    *Grey fabrics:* sherds joining 85 in 217; weight, 90 g.; 94·74%.
    Total weight: 95 g.
    Weight from both layers: 545 g.

*Animal Bones*

    105 fragments identified (including 45 ribs and 10 skull fragments).
    Species represented: ox, 50; sheep, 20; pig, 18; dog, 8; bird, 2; red deer, 2.

### *Pit 230* (PC 72, trench 108, layers 184, 224)

Sub-rectangular pit 6 ft. 6 in. by 5 ft. (1·98 × 1·52 m.), cut to a depth of 2 ft. 2 in. (0·66 m.).

The lower filling (layer 224) was of redeposited brickearth with occasional flecks of charcoal, bones and pot sherds. It was sealed by tips of brickearth mixed with rather more occupation material.

The pit had been cut through the lower clay bank and was sealed by the middle clay. Its filling pre-dated the digging of Roman pit 222 and it was also cut by the late Saxon pit 219.

PIT 230

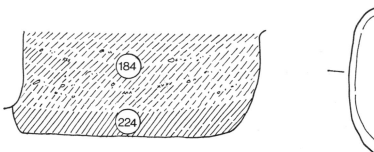

ONE METRE

TWO METRES

THREE FEET     SECTIONS     SIX FEET     PLANS

FIG. 99

*Small Finds*

From layer 184:
| | | |
|---|---|---|
| Bronze coin | (2565) | Constantine I (A.D. 310–17). |
| Whetstone | (2577) | not illustrated, no. 363. |

*Pottery*

From layer 184:
   *New Forest:* 13, 49, 55.*16*; weight, 50 g.; 7·25%.
   *Hand-made, fabric A:* weight, 110 g.; 15·94%.
   *Black-burnished:* 85, 126; weight, 240 g.; 34·78%.
   *Grey fabrics:* 77, 85 (2), 129.4, 140; weight, 290 g.; 42·03%.
   Total weight: 690 g.
From layer 224:
   *Oxford:* 57; weight, 10 g.; 20%.
   *Hand-made, fabric A:* 123; weight, 40 g.; 80%.
   Total weight: 50 g.
   Weight from both layers: 740 g.

*Animal Bones*

   87 fragments identified (including 18 ribs and 4 skull fragments).
   Species represented: ox, 69; pig, 18; sheep, 9; dog, 2; red deer, 2.

### *Pit 231* (PC 72, trench 109, layer 46)

Rectangular pit 3 ft. 6 in. (1·07 m.) wide and of unknown length, cut to a depth of 2 ft. 6 in. (0·76 m.).

The filling (layer 46) was uniform, consisting of grey–brown cesspit filling mixed with lenses of charcoal, oyster shells, and fragments of tile, pottery and bone.

PIT 231

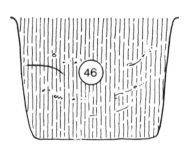
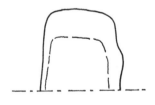

ONE METRE

TWO METRES

THREE FEET      SECTIONS     SIX FEET      PLANS

FIG. 100

*Pottery*

From layer 46:
   *Oxford:* 18.10.
   *Hand-made, fabric A:* weight, 90 g.; 33·96%.
   *Black-burnished:* 126; weight, 80 g.; 30·19%.
   *Grey fabrics:* weight, 95 g.; 35·85%.
   Total weight: 265 g.

*Animal Bones*

   42 fragments identified (including 18 ribs).
   Species represented: ox, sheep, pig, bird.

### *Pit 234* (PC 72, trench 108, layer 214)

Elongated rectangular pit 7 ft. 4 in. by 2 ft. 4 in. (2·24 × 0·71 m.), cut to a depth of 1 ft. 8 in. (0·51 m.).

The filling of the pit was uniform, consisting of a grey–brown clayey soil containing some occupation material. The pit had been filled before the main thickness of middle occupation (layer 163) had accumulated. It was cut through the lower clay bank.

*Pottery*

From layer 214:
   *New Forest: 13.1,* 22.1–5 (2); weight, 420 g.; 20·39%.
   *Oxford:* sherds of fabric 4; weight, 90 g.; 4·37%.
   *Hand-made, fabric A:* 123 (3); weight, 580 g.; 28·16%.
   *Black-burnished:* 126; weight, 230 g. 11·17%.
   *Grey fabrics:* 85, *92.2,* 127 (2), 129.4, 137.8, 140, *177.5;* weight, 740 g.; 35·92%.
   Total weight: 2060 g.

PIT 234

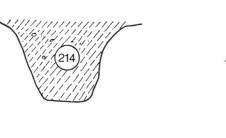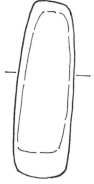

ONE METRE

TWO METRES

THREE FEET      SECTIONS      SIX FEET      PLANS

FIG. 101

*Animal Bones*

205 fragments identified (including 24 ribs and 17 skull fragments).
Species represented: ox, 34; dog, 34; pig, 13; sheep, 12; bird, 5; hare, 1; red deer, 1.
The dog bones recovered from this pit were all from the same animal, aged between 12 and 15 months.

### *Pit 235* (PC 72, trench 108, layers 120, 232)

Irregular hollow measuring overall 7 ft. 2 in. by 3 ft. 6 in. (2·18 m. × 1·07 m.). The depth varied from 4 to 11 in. (10–28 cm.).

Filled uniformly with occupation debris mixed with some redeposited brickearth. Both layers are the same; the different numbering resulted from the order in which the pit was excavated.

PIT 235

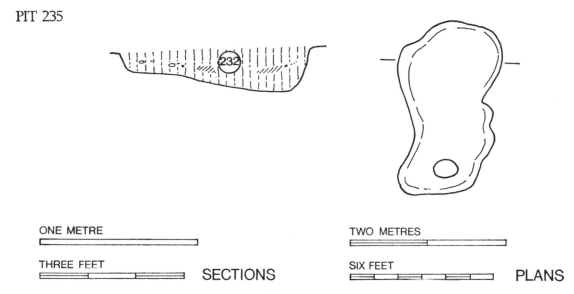

ONE METRE

TWO METRES

THREE FEET      SECTIONS      SIX FEET      PLANS

Fig. 102

*Small Finds*

From layer 120:
  Shale bracelet      (2608)   fragment, plain, external diameter 7·6 cm.; not illustrated.
From layer 232:
  Bone pin      (2612)   shaft fragment only; not illustrated.

*Pottery*

From layer 232:
  *New Forest:* 22.1–5, 43, *105.3*; weight, 200 g.; 24·39%.
  *Misc.:* *15.5*, 144.3; weight, 10 g.; 1·22%.
  *Hand-made, fabric A:* 86; weight, 70 g.; 8·54%.
  *Black-burnished:* 107, 175: weight, 170 g.; 20·73%.
  *Grey fabrics:* 85, 127, 129, 129.4, 139, 140 (2), *142.3*; weight, 370 g.; 45·12%.
  Total weight: 820 g.

*Animal Bones*

    108 fragments identified (including 45 ribs and 5 skull fragments).

    Species represented: ox, 45; sheep, 14; pig, 38; dog, 2; bird, 2; fallow deer, 2.

*Human Bones*

    Infant burial and one tibia of another infant.

### *Well (pit) 236* (PC 72, trench 109, layers 51, 91 and 105–121)

The well was constructed in a circular well pit 6 ft. (1·83 m.) in diameter, the shaft diameter being 3 ft. 9 in. (1·43 m.). Only the shaft of the well was excavated, leaving the packing in position. The bottom was eventually reached at a depth of 19 ft. 2 in. (5·84 m.) from the surface. The shaft was lined with flints, the lining surviving up to a height of 7 ft. (2·13 m.) from the bottom. No attempt was made to draw a half section of the filling, but detailed records were kept of each layer, a summary of which is offered here, with measurements taken from the surface of the natural brickearth.

Layer 121: 17 ft. 10 in. to 19 ft. 2 in. (5·44–5·84 m.)
    Grey chalky silt containing large lumps of chalk and flints.
Layer 120: 16 ft. to 17 ft. 10 in. (4·88–5·44 m.)
    Chalk eroded from the sides of the shaft with a central core of grey-black silt containing organic material.
Layer 119: 12 ft. 8 in. to 16 ft. (3·86–4·88 m.)
    Thick black organic silt containing large flints and fragments of tile, together with quantities of shellfish remains (oysters, cockles, winkles, mussels, and whelks). Much other domestic rubbish including leather, bone and pottery.
Layer 118: 11 ft. 11 in. to 12 ft. 8 in. (3·63–3·86 m.)
    Layer of clay and chalk marl.
Layer 117: 11 ft. 9 in. to 11 ft. 11 in. (3·58–3·63 m.)
    Lens of occupation rubbish.
Layer 116: 11 ft. 5 in. to 11 ft. 9 in. (3·48–3·58 m.)
    Layer of chalk and clay.
Layer 115: 10 ft. 11 in. to 11 ft. 5 in. (3·33–3·48 m.)
    Dark grey soil and occupation rubbish.
Layer 114: 10 ft. 8 in. to 10 ft. 11 in. (3·25–3·33 m.)
    Clay layer with patches of chalk and marl.
Layer 113: 10 ft. 4 in. to 10 ft. 8 in. (3·15–3·25 m.)
    Occupation rubbish.
Layer 112: 9 ft. 10 in. to 10 ft. 4 in. (3·00–3·15 m.)
    Clay layer with patches of chalk and marl.
Layer 111: 9 ft. 8 in. to 9 ft. 10 in. (2·95–3·00 m.)
    Occupation rubbish rich in animal bones.
Layer 110: 9 ft. 2 in. to 9 ft. 8 in. (2·79–2·95 m.)
    Clay layer with patches of chalk and some tile.

Layer 109: 8 ft. 10 in. to 9 ft. 2 in. (2·69–2·79 m.)
Grey–black occupation rubbish containing quantities of shellfish.
Layer 108: 8 ft. 1 in. to 8 ft. 10 in. (2·46–2·69 m.)
Clay layer containing some flints and tile fragments.
Layer 107: 7 ft. 6 in. to 8 ft. 1 in. (2·29–2·46 m.)
Clayey soil mixed with large numbers of flint nodules and blocks of chalk, and quantities of occupation rubbish.
Layer 106: 6 ft. 6 in. to 7 ft. 6 in. (1·98–2·29 m.)
Pinkish-grey ashy layer mixed with charcoal, quantities of flints and tile and occupation debris.
Layer 105: 5 ft. 11 in. to 6 ft. 6 in. (1·80–1·98 m.)
Grey–brown soil with flints and chalk lumps, mixed with occupation debris.
Layers 91 and 51: surface to 5 ft. 11 in. (surface to 1·80 m.)
Black silty soil representing a soil accumulation over a considerable period of time.

From the above summary it will be seen that from the bottom to a depth of 11 ft. 11 in. (3·63 m.) the well was filled with an accumulation of occupation rubbish. Above this, up to 8 ft. 1 in. (2·46 m.), the sides had begun to erode so that lenses of clay were interspersed with the rubbish. Then followed further deliberate tips of rubbish and ash up to 5 ft. 11 in. (1·80 m.) after which the silting seems to have been natural.

*Small Finds*

From layer 91:
| | | |
|---|---|---|
| Bronze coin | (2619) | Constantinopolis (A.D. 330–5). |
| | (2620) | Constantinopolis (A.D. 330–5). |
| | (2618) | Constantine II (A.D. 353–6). |
| Bronze sheet | (2627) | fragment; not illustrated. |
| Iron rod | (2634) | fig. 131, no. 261. |
| Iron chain | (2642) | fig. 131, no. 252. |
| Iron fragment | (2643) | not illustrated. |

From layer 105:
| | | |
|---|---|---|
| Bronze coin | (2617) | Constantine II (A.D. 337–40). |

From layer 108:
| | | |
|---|---|---|
| Bronze bracelet | (2628) | fig. 111, no. 24a. |

From layer 109:
| | | |
|---|---|---|
| Bronze coin | (2616) | House of Constantine (A.D. 322–4). |

From layer 111:
| | | |
|---|---|---|
| Bronze bracelet | (2626) | strip type; not illustrated. |

From layer 113:
| | | |
|---|---|---|
| Iron sheet | (2622) | fragment, not illustrated. |

From layer 115:
| | | |
|---|---|---|
| Bronze coin | (2615) | Carausius (A.D. 286–93). |
| Iron knife | (2636) | fig. 126, no. 198. |
| Tile disc | (2637) | disc c. 2¾ in. (7·5 cm.) diam., perforated; not illustrated. |

From layer 118:
| | | |
|---|---|---|
| Iron bucket handle mount | (2641) | fig. 127, no. 207. |

From layer 119:

| | | |
|---|---|---|
| Bronze fragment | (2647) | not illustrated. |
| Iron shears | (2623) | fig. 127, no. 202. |
| Iron shears | (2644) | fig. 127, no. 203. |
| Iron fragment | (2638) | not illustrated. |
| Iron clamp | (2645) | fig. 128, no. 210. |
| Iron tie | (2646) | fragment of above; not illustrated. |
| Bronze bracelet | (2648) | fragment of twisted wire type; not illustrated. |
| Perforated wooden disc | (2630) | fig. 137, no. 327. |
| Wooden comb | (2631) | fig. 137, no. 323. |
| Leather shoes | (2661–2675) | figs. 132–4, nos. 265–79. |
| | (2679–2713) | figs. 134–5, nos. 283–317. |
| | (2716) | not illustrated, no. 320. |

From layer 120:

| | | |
|---|---|---|
| Iron bucket handle mount | (2640) | fig. 127, no. 205. |
| Wooden peg | (2656) | fig. 137, no. 324. |
| Wooden disc | (2657) | fig. 137, no. 326. |

From layer 121:

| | | |
|---|---|---|
| Stone bead | (2621) | bead, diam. 6 mm. with central perforation. |
| Iron handle | (2633) | fig. 128, no. 209. |
| Leather fragments | (2295–2300) | fig. 136, nos. 382–7. |

*Pottery*

From layer 51:
*New Forest:* 22.7, 43, 64; weight, 200 g.; 32·26%.
*Oxford:* base of fabric 4; weight, 25 g.; 4·03%.
*Hand-made, fabric A:* 86, 107, 123 (3); weight, 300 g.; 48·39%.
*Black-burnished:* weight, 5 g.; 0·81%.
*Grey fabrics:* 141, 142.1–3, 148; weight, 85 g.; 13·71%.
*Fabric D:* weight, 5 g.; 0·81%.
Total weight: 620 g.

From layer 91:
*New Forest:* 2/10.15, 29, 32, 32 (with a spiralling 'rosette' stamp), 43 (2), 55.5; weight, 310 g.; 12·68%.
*Oxford:* 15.1, ?34, 35.1, 42, 63.7; weight, 125 g.; 5·11%.
*Hand-made, fabric A:* 86, 107.5, 123 (6); weight, 1030 g.; 42·13%.
*Black-burnished:* 85 (3), 107, 126; weight, 360 g.; 14·72%.
*Grey fabrics:* 118.1, 129, 131.4, 132, 135, 153.3–4 (the only freshly broken sherd in this fabric); weight, 470 g.; 19·22%.
*Fabric D:* sherds of ?137; weight, 150 g.; 6·13%.
Total weight: 2445 g.

From layer 105:
*New Forest:* 43; weight, 110 g.; 39·29%.
*Hand-made, fabric A:* weight, 80 g.; 28·57%.
*Black-burnished:* weight, 50 g.; 17·86%.

*Grey fabrics:* weight, 40 g.; 14·29%.
Total weight: 280 g.
From layer 106:
  *New Forest:* a joining sherd to 55.5 in 91; weight, 60 g.; 12·77%.
  *Hand-made, fabric A:* 86, 107, 123 (2); weight, 270 g.; 57·45%.
  *Black-burnished:* weight, 40 g.; 8·51%.
  *Grey fabrics:* 127; weight, 100 g.; 21·28%.
  Total weight: 470 g.
From layer 107:
  *New Forest:* 13, 43; weight, 180 g.; 18·95%.
  *Hand-made, fabric A:* 86, 107 (2), 123; weight, 390 g.; 41·05%.
  *Black-burnished:* 85, 126, 175; weight, 270 g.; 28·42%.
  *Grey fabrics:* 92.1, 107, 140.3; weight, 90 g.; 9·47%.
  *Misc.:* 179; weight, 20 g.; 2·11%.
  Total weight: 950 g.
From layer 109:
  *New Forest:* sherds of fabrics 1 and 2; weight, 100 g.; 17·24%.
  *Oxford:* 14, sherd of ?58; weight, 100 g.; 17·24%.
  *Hand-made, fabric A:* 86; weight, 70 g.; 12·07%.
  *Black-burnished:* 85 (3), 117, 126; weight, 310 g.; 53·45%.
  Total weight: 580 g.
From layer 110:
  *Argonne:* Chenet 304 and 313 (probably the same vessel as in pit 178); weight, 60 g.; 13·64%.
  *Hand-made, fabric A:* 123; weight, 320 g.; 72·73%.
  *Grey fabrics:* weight, 60 g.; 13·64%.
  Total weight: 440 g.
From layer 111:
  *New Forest:* sherds of fabrics 1 and 3; weight, 10 g.; 1·94%.
  *Misc.:* 17.3.
  *Hand-made, fabric A:* 86, 123 (4); weight, 430 g.; 83·50%.
  *Black-burnished:* 85; weight, 40 g.; 7·77%.
  *Grey fabrics:* weight, 35 g.; 6·80%.
  Total weight: 515 g.
From layer 112:
  *Hand-made, fabric A:* weight, 5 g.
  *Black-burnished:* 126; weight, 5 g.
  Total weight: 10 g.
From layer 115:
  *Argonne:* Chenet 313 (sherds joining those in 110); weight, 65 g.; 2·16%.
  *New Forest:* 13.2, 43, 66.10, *105.6*; weight, 335 g.; 11·15%.
  *Oxford:* base of 50; weight, 60 g.; 2·0%.
  *Hand-made, fabric A:* 86 (2), 107 (2), 123 (5) weight, 1490 g.; 49·58%.
  *Black-burnished:* 85 (2), 107 (2), 126; weight, 495 g.; 16·47%.
  *Grey fabrics:* 76.1, 107, 129.4, 172.2; weight, 560 g.; 18·64%.
  Total weight: 3005 g.
From layer 117:
  *New Forest:* sherd of fabric 3; weight, 10 g.; 3·13%.

*Oxford:* 40; weight, 5 g.; 1·56%.
*Hand-made, fabric A:* 86; weight, 95 g.; 29·69%.
*Black-burnished:* 85, base of ?117; weight, 140 g.; 43·75%.
*Grey fabrics:* weight, 70 g.; 21·88%.
Total weight: 320 g.
From layer 119:
*New Forest:* sherds of ?19 and 22; 21.6, 29, 43 (2), 48, 49 (2), 64.3; weight, 1475 g.; 12·66%.
*Oxford:* 14, 15 (3), 40, sherds of 57 or 58; weight, 270 g.; 2·32%.
*Misc.:* base (*c.* 100 mm. diameter) of a very large ?flagon in a hard vesicular, brown, sandy fabric, grey to the core. The pot is covered in a black slip and there are two raised bands of rouletting above the base; no other parallel at Portchester.
*Hand-made, fabric A:* 86 (3), 107, 123 (3); weight, 4320 g.; 37·07%.
*Black-burnished:* 85 (4), 107, 117, 126 (5), ?175; weight, 3155 g.; 27·07%.
*Grey fabrics:* 77, 85 (3), 94, 129 (2), 145, 154.4–6; weight, 2335 g.; 20·03%.
*Misc.:* 179 (possibly the same as in 107); weight, 100 g.; 0·86%.
Total weight: 11,655 g.
From layer 120:
*New Forest:* 32, 49; weight, 40 g.; 7·6%.
*Hand-made, fabric A:* weight, 80 g.; 15·24%.
*Black-burnished:* 126; weight, 390 g.; 74·29%.
*Grey fabrics:* weight, 15 g.; 2·86%.
Total weight: 525 g.
From layer 121:
*New Forest:* 43 (2), almost intact, at 650 and 370 g. respectively; weight, 1020 g.
Total weight: 1020 g.
Weight from all the layers: 22,835 g.

*Animal Bones*

2335 fragments identified (including 585 ribs and 169 skull fragments).
Species represented: ox, 54; sheep, 22; pig, 8; bird, 8; dog, 5; red deer, 1; cat, 1; roe deer, horse, mouse, hare, fish, unidentified small mammal.
A large number of nearly complete skulls were recovered from this pit. They are: ox, 13 nearly complete and at least 8 others in a more fragmentary state; sheep, 3 fairly complete, and at least 4 others; pig, approximately half the skull of one animal; horse, part of one skull; bird, one complete skull; dog, 2 complete skulls; red deer, one almost complete skull of a female.
The sheep bones included parts of several young animals, and 27% of the sheep mandibles were from animals of under one year old.
The pig bones also included at least two very young animals, and the ox bones at least one very young animal. The cat bones came from one mature and one immature individual.

*Pit 237* (PC 72, trench 109, layer 82)

Circular pit of uncertain diameter (only partly excavated): depth 3 ft. (0·91 m.).
The filling (layer 82) was a uniform deposit of occupation debris intermixed with grey stony soil.

PIT 237

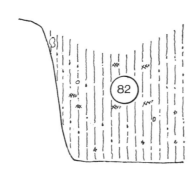
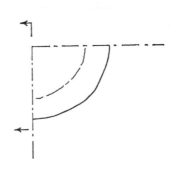

ONE METRE

TWO METRES

THREE FEET　SECTIONS

SIX FEET　PLANS

FIG. 103

*Small Finds*

From layer 82:
　Iron slag; p. 265.

*Pottery*

From layer 82:
　*Oxford:* 43; weight, 10 g.; 5·56%.
　*Hand-made, fabric A:* 86; weight, 10 g.; 5·56%.
　*Black-burnished:* weight, 5 g.; 2·78%.
　*Grey fabrics:* 142.4–5, 145, 175; weight, 150 g.; 83·33%.
　*Fabric D:* 137.4–6; weight, 5 g.; 2·78%.
　Total weight: 180 g.

*Animal Bones*

　10 fragments identified (including 5 ribs).
　Species represented: sheep, ox, pig, bird.

*Pit 238* (PC 72, trench 109, layer 83)

Shallow elongated pit (or gully?), 2 ft. 9 in. (0·84 m.) wide and length exceeding 6 ft. (1·83 m.); maximum depth 5 in. (13 cm.).
Filled with brown earth mixed with some clay, flints and occupation material.

*Pottery*

From layer 83:
　*Hand-made, fabric A:* weight, 5 g.
　*Grey fabrics:* 127; weight, 5 g.
　Total weight: 10 g.

13

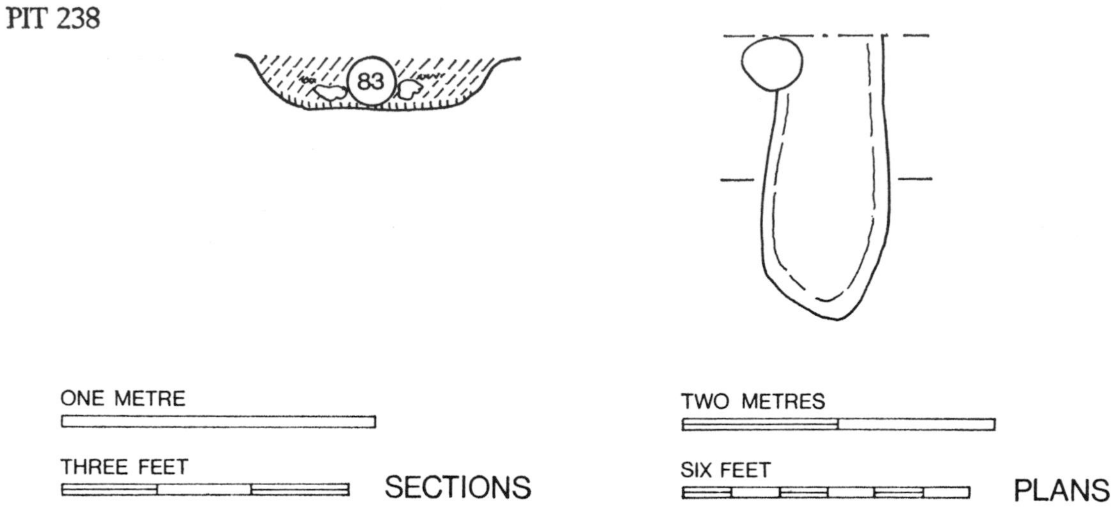

PIT 238

FIG. 104

*Animal Bones*

  1 fragment identified, probably ox.


          *Pit 239* (PC 72, trench 109, layer 84)

  Elongated pit (or gully) 3 ft. wide (0·91 m.) and exceeding 4 ft. 6 in. (1·37 m.) in length; maximum depth 9 in. (23 cm.).

  Filled with brown soil mixed with occupation debris.

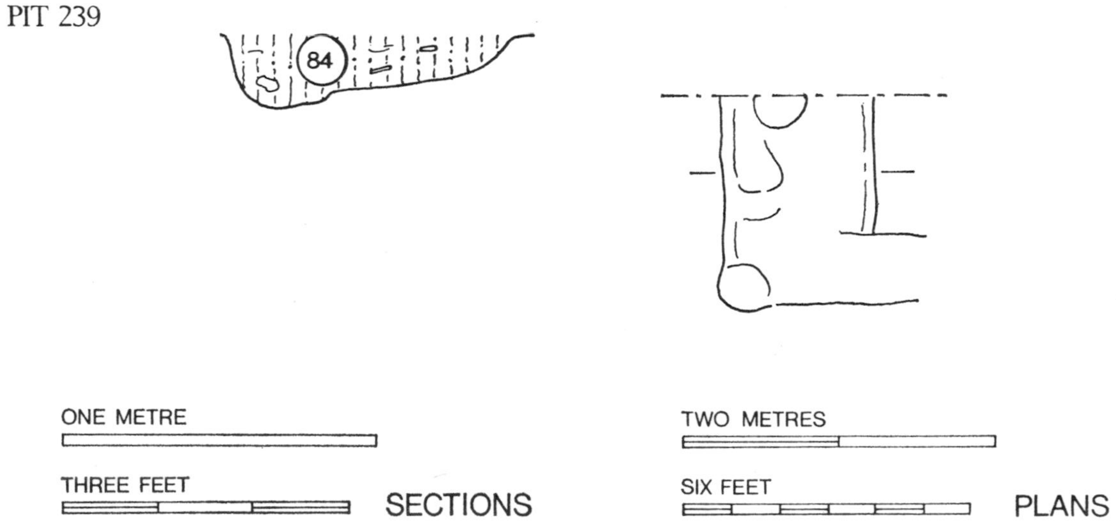

PIT 239

FIG. 105

*Small Finds*

From layer 84:
    Struck flint flake                    (2606)  not illustrated.

*Pottery*

From layer 84:
    *Hand-made, fabric A:* 123; weight, 20 g.; 80%.
    *Black-burnished:* weight, 5 g.; 20%.
    Total weight: 25 g.

*Animal Bones*

    4 fragments identified (including 7 ribs).
    Species represented: sheep, pig.

# V. SUBSIDIARY AREAS

ROMAN levels came to light in several subsidiary excavations within and immediately adjacent to the fort. Area D, against the west wall south of the west gate, covered an area of some 3000 ft.² (280 m.²) and was excavated to the natural subsoil. Elsewhere the areas of the Roman levels exposed were limited in extent and were uncovered as a consequence of excavations designed primarily to examine post-Roman features.

## AREA D (1961)
### (fig. 106)

Area D is situated against the inner face of the west wall of the fort, immediately to the south of the landgate. The area extended for a distance of 30 ft. (9·1 m.) from the surviving, refaced, wall, and overall measured 100 ft. (30·5 m.) in length. The excavation was undertaken because of the impending construction of a public lavatory and changing room — a project which was subsequently abandoned. The area was cleared in five trenches (1–5) with 2 ft. (0·6 m.) baulks between, thus providing continuous sections up to the wall (fig. 218). The baulks were eventually removed.

### The Constitution of the Roman Wall and Gate

All five trenches exposed the back face of the Roman wall which is described above (p. 19). Trench 1 also contained the southern inturn wall of the Roman landgate (above pp. 29–34). At the time of construction a dump of gravelly clay was heaped up on the original ground surface to a maximum depth of 1 ft. 3 in. (0·38 m.) in a single restricted area (trench 3 layer 8). This material presumably derived from the digging of the foundation trench. As construction proceeded a mortar spill, representing the mortar-mixing processes carried out by the Roman masons, accumulated on the original ground surface, spreading up and over the heap of clay. The mortar spill was continuous over all five trenches (1 layer 8, 2 layer 5, 3 layer 4, 4 layer 5, 5 layer 5), but seldom reached a thickness in excess of 1 in. (2·5 cm.). The only finds from within or beneath it were a single sherd of coarse grey pottery and a coin of Saloninus (A.D. 255–8), providing a convenient *terminus post quem* of *c.* 260 for the construction of the fort.

Immediately after the wall had been erected, a layer of gravelly clay (which had probably been piled inside the fort when the foundation trench was dug) was spread out somewhat discontinuously over the area, reaching a thickness of 1 ft. 6 in. (0·45 m.) in trench 4. In the angle between the fort wall and the inturned gate wall the clay was piled up in a low bank to cover the foundation offsets, presumably to protect them from weathering. Once the levelling had been completed the area was left free of buildings.

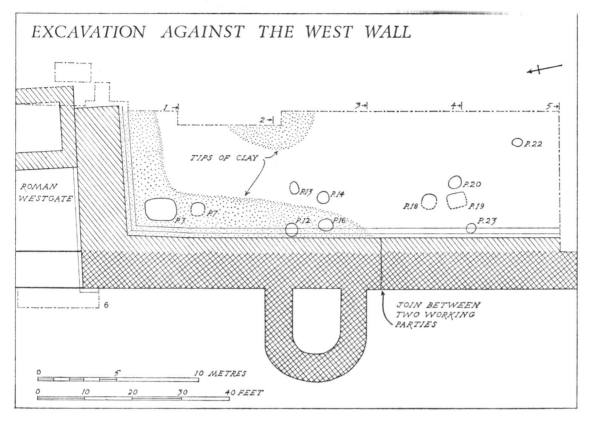

EXCAVATION AGAINST THE WEST WALL

FIG. 106

*Rubbish Tipping behind the Wall*

During the Roman period, the area behind the wall was used for rubbish tipping, which eventually resulted in a 2 ft.- (0·6 m.-) thick layer consisting of grey-brown soil mixed up with quantities of pottery, animal bones and oyster shells. Of the six coins recovered, the four legible examples spanned the period *c.* A.D. 320–70 (below, p. 183), suggesting a date late in the history of the fort for this surprisingly unhygienic practice.

Together with the tipping of rubbish, some individual pits were dug for the disposal of waste. With the exception of pits 3 and 19, which were rectangular, all the others were circular and sometimes as little as 2 ft. (0·6 m.) in diameter. It was impossible to tell from what depth the individual pits had been dug, since they were filled with the same occupation debris as that through which they had been cut; but pit 20, which reached a depth of 2 ft. 6 in. (0·76 m.) below the level of natural, and was only 2 ft. 3 in. (0·69 m.) in diameter, can hardly have been dug from much higher, while conversely pit 12, a mere 6–9 in. (15–23 cm.) deep, is likely to have been cut after the accumulation of some thickness of rubbish. The fact that it produced a coin of Valentinian or Theodosius is a further indication of its late date.

After rubbish tipping had ceased, soil accumulation, accentuated by the erosion of the back face of the wall, gave rise to a thickness of mortary soil which produced a few sherds of early

Saxon pottery (vol. 2). Erosion of an earlier date is also apparent in the section of trench 5 which shows lenses of mortar and flints interlaced with the Roman rubbish deposits. Presumably the wall had started to crumble before the end of the Roman period.

*The Pits* (fig. 106)

A summary of the pits in area D is given below. Since the pits were small and of uniform fill, no half sections are illustrated.

### Pit 3 (PC 61 1 Pit C)

Roughly oblong pit, 6 ft. by 4 ft. 6 in. (1·8 × 1·4 m.), cut through the Roman builders' spread to a depth of 3 ft. 3 in. (0·99 m.) below natural.

The contents were uniform, consisting of grey crumbling soil mixed with animal bones and oyster shells. The pit was cut into by pits 1 and 2.

*Small Finds*

    Iron spearheads           (2658,
                               2659)    fig. 124, nos. 172–3

### Pit 7 (PC 61 2 Pit D)

Small circular pit 2 ft. 3 in. (0·69 m.) in diameter, cut through the builders' spread to a depth of 8 in. (20 cm.).

The filling was uniform, consisting of grey soil mixed with charcoal. The pit was cut by pit 1.

No small finds.

### Pit 12 (PC 61 3 Pit D)

Small circular pit 3 ft. 2 in. (0·97 m.) in diameter, cut through the builders' spread to a maximum depth of 9 in. (0·23 m.) below the top of natural.

The filling was uniform, consisting of grey–brown soil containing quantities of animal bones.

*Small Finds*

    Bronze coin                 (17)      House of Valentinian or of Theodosius

### Pit 13 (PC 61 3 Pit E)

Small oval pit measuring 1 ft. 9 in. by 2 ft. (0·53 × 0·61 m.), cut through the builders' spread to a depth of 1 ft. 3 in. (0·38 m.).

Filled with grey-brown occupation rubbish together with quantities of animal bones.

No small finds.

### Pit 14 (PC 61 3 Pit F)

Small circular pit 2 ft. 3 in. (0·69 m.) in diameter, cut through the builders' spread to a depth of 4 in. (10 cm.) into natural.

The filling consisted of grey-brown occupation rubbish.

No small finds.

## *Pit 16* (PC 61 3 Pit H)

Circular pit 3 ft. 9 in. (1·14 m.) in diameter, largely cut away by pit 9, but remaining to a depth of 4 in. (10·2 cm.) below the bottom of the later pit, i.e. it was originally 2 ft. (0·61 m.) deep below the natural ground surface.

Filled with grey-brown occupation rubbish.

No small finds.

## *Pit 18* (PC 61 4 Pit B)

Small circular pit 2 ft. 8 in. (0·81 m.) in diameter, cut to a depth of 1 ft. 6 in. (0·46 m.) below the top of natural.

Filled with grey-brown occupation soil. Cut by pit 17.

No small finds.

## *Pit 19* (PC 61 4 Pit C)

Small oblong pit 4 ft. (1·22 m.) long but partially cut away by pit 17. Cut to a depth of 1 ft. 5 in. (0·43 m.) below the top of natural.

Filled with grey-brown occupation rubbish.

No small finds.

## *Pit 20* (PC 61 4 Pit D)

Small circular pit 2 ft. 3 in. (0·69 m.) in diameter, cut to a depth of 2 ft. 6 in. (0·76 m.) below the top of natural.

Filled with grey-brown occupation soil.

No small finds.

## *Pit 22* (PC 61 5 Pit B)

Small circular pit 2 ft. 6 in. (0·76 m.) in diameter, dug to a depth of 1 ft. 8 in. (0·51 m.) below the top of natural.

Filled with grey-brown occupation soil.

No small finds.

## *Pit 23* (PC 61 5 Pit C)

Small circular pit 2 ft. (0·61 m.) in diameter, dug to a depth of 5 in. (13 cm.) into natural.

Filled with grey-brown occupation soil. Cut by pit 17.

No small finds.

### *Small Finds from Area D*

*From occupation deposits against back face of Roman wall*

| Bronze coins | | | |
|---|---|---|---|
| | (5) | Crispus (A.D. 317–26) | (1 layer 5) |
| | (4) | Constantine II (A.D. 317–40) | (1 layer 5) |
| | (13) | Constantius II (A.D. 324–61) | (3 layer 3) |
| | (21) | Valentinian I (A.D. 364–75) | (4 layer 3) |
| | (20) | Radiate; late third century | (4 layer 3) |
| | (12) | illegible; fourth century | (2 layer 3) |

| Bronze bracelet | (28) | as no. 26; not illustrated | (1 layer 5) |
| Bronze bracelet | (10) | as no. 26; not illustrated | (2 layer 3) |
| Bronze spoon | (2) | fig. 113, no. 58 | (3 layer 3) |
| Bronze disc | (24) | fig. 115, no. 80 | (5 layer 3) |
| Bronze plaque | (26) | fig. 110, no. 16 | (5 layer 3) |
| Bone pin | (1) | as nos. 81–5; not illustrated | (3 layer 3) |
| Shale bracelet | (14) | 7·0 cm. diam., D-section; not illustrated | (3 layer 3) |
| Shale bracelet | (15) | 6·0 cm. diam., D-section; not illustrated | (3 layer 3) |
| Shale bracelet | (11) | 6·0 cm. diam., D-section; not illustrated | (2 layer 3) |

*From Pit 3*

Iron spearheads    (2658, 2659)    fig. 124, nos. 172–3

*From Pit 21*

Bronze coin    (17)    House of Theodosius

*From builders' spread contemporary with construction of wall*

Bronze coin    (16)    Saloninus (A.D. 255–8)    (2 layer 5)

## TRIAL TRENCHES IN THE CENTRE OF THE FORT
### (fig. 107)

In 1966 four narrow trial trenches (trenches 59, 61, 64, 67) were cut in the centre of the fort close to the churchyard gate, in advance of a road widening scheme which was never implemented.

The features discovered are summarized in fig. 107. Trench 59 was largely disturbed in the post-Roman period, particularly by late eighteenth-century features. Where they survive, the lowest pre-eighteenth-century occupation levels lying above natural contained Saxon and medieval pottery mixed up with Roman sherds. Nine postholes were found but none need be Roman.

Trench 61 sectioned a series of recut gullies probably dug to drain the main east–west road in its various periods. The earliest gully contained only Roman sherds. It was filled with brownish clayey silt, and was dug to a depth of about 1 ft. (0·3 m.) below the surface of natural clay.

Trenches 64 and 67 produced evidence of a continuous spread of tightly packed cobbles, trampled into the natural clay 3 ft. (0·9 m.) below the present ground surface. Two shallow slots each containing postholes ran across the area in a N–S direction: they were cut through the gravel. Since the only finds from within were a few Roman sherds it is possible, but by no means certain, that they represent Roman features.

Interpretation of so small an area is impossible. It is however certain that no substantial masonry structures occurred here. The probability is that the road between the two main gates continued straight across the area.

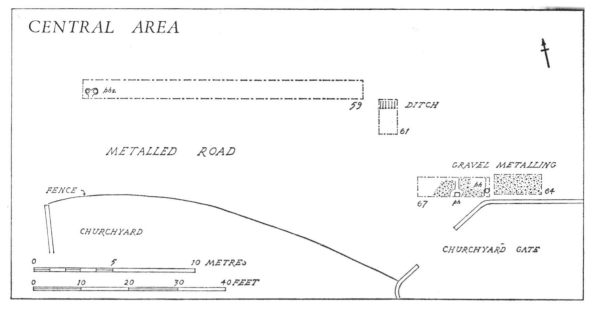

FIG. 107

# EXCAVATION WITHIN THE INNER BAILEY

A number of trenches were dug within the inner bailey to examine details of the medieval structure. Since the work is still in progress and the areas of the Roman ground surface examined are small, description is best left for a later volume. It is sufficient here to say that where the Roman levels survive they consist of between 1 and 2 ft. (0·3–0·6 m.) of black occupation rubbish lying on the surface of the natural clay. A trench (trench 83) cut across the berm between the south wall of the inner bailey and the medieval ditch sectioned an undisturbed Roman occupation layer 2 ft. (0·6 m.) thick.

# EXCAVATIONS WITHIN THE PRIORY

The south-east quarter of the Roman fort was once occupied by an Augustinian Priory of which the church, less its south transept, still survives surrounded by a cemetery. A programme of limited excavation was undertaken by Mr D. Baker in 1968–9, to elucidate the structural history of the Priory. This work, which will be reported in detail in volume 3 of the Portchester reports, incidentally discovered traces of Roman occupation material usually restricted to black occupation rubbish extensively cut away by medieval and later disturbances. Several features, however, deserve discussion.

## The Roman Watergate

Trench P10 which lay against the south face of the Saxon Watergate exposed part of the Roman south inturned wall immediately below the post-medieval levels. The details are incorporated in fig. 17.

### The Roman Fort Wall

Trenches P2 and P8 were dug against the south wall of the Roman fort. In trench P2 a large medieval pit had cut into the wall exposing details of the internal timbering described on pp. 14–15 and illustrated in fig. 9. Trench P8 provided a section through the levels against the back face of the wall. Layer 24 represented the back filling of the foundation trench. It was sealed by a builders' mortar spread, layer 27, and a tip of clay, layer 25, above which lay a thick spread of Roman occupation material, layer 23.

### Cobbled Surface

In trench P5, dug against the south face of the church against the north-west pier of the south transept a layer of hard packed flint cobbles (layer 13), 5 in. (12·7 cm.) thick was found to overly the natural brickearth at a depth of 3 ft. 6 in. (1·07 m.). Above this was a black occupation layer (layer 12) 1 ft. 5 in. (0·4 m.) thick.

## EXCAVATIONS OUTSIDE THE ROMAN DEFENCES

On four separate occasions, trenches were cut through the area outside the Roman wall. Three were sections through the outer rampart: trenches 44 and 48 (1964), trench 81 (1968) and trench 106 (1972); one was an area excavation on the site now occupied by the public lavatory, trench 51 (1965).

All four excavations exposed a layer of black turfy soil up to 1 ft. (0·3 m.) thick, lying on the natural clay, containing quantities of Roman pottery and a few sherds of late Saxon wares. When the layer was removed in trench 81, clear traces of ploughing could be seen in the surface of the natural subsoil. The slightly abraded state of the pottery and the nature of the soil layer were consistent with the area having been ploughed some time between the third and fourteenth century, the upper limit being given by the construction date of the sealing rampart. Greater precision in dating is impossible.

The amount of Roman material recovered suggests that quantities of rubbish were tipped outside the walls during the use of the fort. Little sign of Roman structural activity was found, with the exception of a gully beneath the medieval rampart in trench 106, sealed by the black turfy soil. The gully was flat bottomed, 4 ft. (1·2 m.) wide and 3 ft. 6 in. (1·07 m.) deep, and was filled with a uniform grey silty soil (layer 36). Two coins were recovered from the upper part of the filling (layer 35): one (2303) was illegible, the other (2302) was of Constans (A.D. 348–50).

### Roman Small Finds from Trenches outside the Fort Wall

Trench 44 layer 6:
　　Bronze pin　　　　　　　　(44)　　fragment only; not illustrated.
Trench 51 layers 6 and 7:
　　None.
Trench 81 layer 11:
　　Bronze bracelet　　　　　(858)　　not illustrated, as no. 26.
　　Bronze twisted wire　　　(881)　　fragment, not illustrated, as no. 26.

| Bronze ring | (878) | not illustrated. |
| Bronze coin | (870) | Constantine II (A.D. 335–7) |
| | (888) | Constantius II (A.D. 330–5). |

Trench 106, post-Roman, layers 4, 20, 21:

| Bronze coins | (2316) | Constantine I (A.D. 321–4). |
| | (2307) | Constantine I (A.D. 330–5). |
| | (2308) | Constantinopolis (A.D. 330–45). |
| | (2309) | Magnentius (A.D. 350–3). |

Roman soil, layers 10, 34:

| Bronze coins | (2310) | Constantine I (A.D. 324–6). |
| | (2305) | Constantine II (A.D. 324–30). |
| | (2306) | Constantine I (A.D. 326–30). |
| | (2311) | Urbs Roma (A.D. 330–45). |
| | (2300) | House of Constantine (A.D. 330–45). |
| | (2315) | Constantine I (A.D. 335–7). |
| | (2313) | House of Constantine (A.D. 335–45). |
| | (2301) | Constantius II (A.D. 337–41). |
| | (2298) | Helena (A.D. 337–41). |
| | (2312) | House of Constantine (A.D. 350–60). |
| | (2299) | Illegible, third to fourth century A.D. |

Gully, layer 35:

| Bronze coins | (2302) | Constans (A.D. 348–50). |
| | (2303) | Illegible, fourth century A.D. |
| Bronze pin | (2304) | not illustrated. |

# VI. THE COINS

## by RICHARD REECE

## INTRODUCTION

THE coin list comprises all the coins found in the current excavations together with those found in the Ministry of Works excavations in the 1930s, some of which are now in the Portsmouth City Museum (though others have unfortunately disappeared), and a few coins found on the site and now in private possession. The coins of the earlier excavations were listed by the late B. H. St J. O'Neil, and the coins from the current excavations up to 1966 were identified by D. W. Phillipson; A. S. Esmonde Cleary helped in the identification of the coins from the last two seasons.

References in the list are to the relevant volumes of the standard corpus, *Roman Imperial Coinage*, ed. Mattingly, Sydenham, Sutherland and Carson, or to the two parts of *Late Roman Bronze Coinage*, Carson, Hill and Kent, in which HK refers to part I and CK to part II. Where the coin could not be assigned without doubt to a single reference number the word 'as' has been used, e.g. as RIC 67, meaning that all that can be seen on the coin suggests RIC 67 but other references would be possible. Where reference is made to a mint it should be understood that 'as London 54' means that the mint is not known, but the type is the same as that of London number 54, whereas 'London as 54' means that the mint is certainly London though the precise reference number is in doubt. Similarly, coins which have been copied from regular coins may be quoted as 'copy as HK 48', meaning that the coin copies the type shown on HK 48 but nothing else, e.g. the mint-mark, whereas 'copy of HK 105' means that all the features expected on HK 105 can be seen in the copy. All coins from sealed deposits have been quoted in the appropriate part of the text by the same reference as is used here; the remainder are from mixed deposits.

## COIN LIST

| 1 | Claudius I | As RIC 66 |
|---|---|---|
| 1 | Saloninus | 9 |
| 1 | Gallienus | (Joint reign) 169 |
| 11 | Gallienus | (Sole reign) 176, 179, 193, 207, 256, 267, 325, rev. illeg. (4) |
| 7 | Claudius II | 10, 18, 105, 261, (2) rev. illeg. (2) |
| 1 | Quintillus | 33 |
| 1 | Aurelian | Rev. illeg. (1) |
| 3 | Victorinus | 116, as 116, 118 |
| 14 | Tetricus I | As 80, 100, 126, 136, as 145, rev. illeg. (9) |
| 6 | Tetricus II | 260, 264, 270, as 270, 273, rev. illeg. |

| | | |
|---|---|---|
| 50 | Carausius | As 34, 56, 81, 91, as 91, 98, as 98 but IM CM CARAVSIVS ..., 101 (3), as 101 (3), copy of 101 with * to left, as 110, 118, 121, 155, 295, 320, 324, as 330 but mm. XX, as 353, 478, 484, 487, 604, 791, as 878 (8), as 880, 893, as 893, 927, as 1037, 1038, Pax type overstruck on Gallienus obv. on obv., rev. illeg. (6) |
| 2 | Allectus | As 55, 86 |
| 15 | Radiates | Regular but illegible (4); barbarous obv. of Victorinus (1), reverse Invictus (2), Pax (2), Securitas (1), rev. illeg. (5) |
| 2 | Diocletian | RIC 5. Lyon 26, 28 |
| 10 | | RIC 6 Lon 6a, as 6a but PFAG, as Lon 6a (2), Lon 10, Lon 77a; Trier 151a, 170a; Alex as 14a; rev. illeg. (1) |
| 4 | Maximianus Herc. | RIC Lon 77b; Tr 676b; Ro 100b; Cart as 27b |
| 2 | Constantius I | RIC 6 Lon 20; Tr 527a but not cuirassed |
| 6 | Galerius | RIC 6 Tr 213b, 532, 536b (2), 594b; Lyon 164b |
| 4 | Maximinus II | RIC 6 Lon 209b (2); Tr 667b; Lyon 194a |
| 1 | Divo Claudio | RIC 7 Tr 203 |
| 5 | Licinius I | RIC 6 Lon 209c, 249: 7 Lon 3; Tr 58, as 210 |
| 31 | Constantine I | RIC 6 Lon 121a (3), 153 (2), 234, as Lon 234, as 263 but bust 1gR of p. 134, 280 (3), 281; Tr 870, 872, 873 (3), 890, 893, 897, 899 (3); Lyon 291, 307 (3), 310; rev. illeg. (3) |
| 53 | | RIC 7 Lon 10 (3), 27 (2), 73, 90, 91, 92, 93, 154, as Lon 154, Lon as 154 but AG, 185, as Lon 222, 240, 271, as Lon 289; Tr as 40, 45, 130, 159, 209 (2), 213 (3), copy as 213 (2), 221 (2), 303 (2), 341 (2), as Tr 341, 368 (2), 389, 429 (2), Tr as 430 probably irregular, 449, 475, 504, 509; Lyon 4, 32, 107; Tic 140; Sis 93; Thess 153; Con 22 |
| 18 | | HK 60, 61, 62 (3), 72, as 87, 106, as 106, 180 (2), 202, 207 (2), 367, 398, 537 (2) |
| 10 | Crispus | RIC 7 Lon 230, 291, as Lon 291; Tr 308, 347 (2), 348; Tic 156, 159; Thess 125 |
| 8 | Helena | RIC 7 Tr 481; HK 112 (3), 128 (3), 1046 |
| 8 | Theodora | HK 113 (6), as 113 (2) |
| 10 | Constantine II | RIC 7 Lon 145, 181, 255 (2), 292; Tr 415; Lyon 148, 211, 221, 231 |
| 19 | | HK as 49 (3), 68, 88 (2), as 88 (2), 93 (4), 107, 187 (3), 226, 229, 379 |
| 25 | Urbs Roma | HK 51, as 51 (4), copies as 51 (5), 58 (3), 65 (4), copy of 65, 85, copy of 190, 200, 205, 382, 389, 546 |
| 27 | Constantinopolis | HK 52 (3), as 52 (4), copy of 52 (2), copies as 52 (6), 59 (3), 66 (3), copy of 66, 86 (2), copy as 185, 191, 196 |
| 30 | Constans | HK 84 (2), 90 (2), as 90 (2), 95, as 102, 133 (3), copy of 133, 138 (2), as 138 (5), 140, 148, 150 (2), 155, 160 (2), as 227, as 419, 557, 711 |
| 7 | | CK 33 (2), as 33, 41, 178, 607, 888 |
| 2 | Constantius II | RIC 7 Tr 490; Ar 316 |
| 18 | | HK 50, 89 (2), 108 (3), 126, 132, 139, 182, 210, 242, 354 (2), 400, 441 (2) |
| 2 | | CK 254, 256 |
| 3 | House of Constantine | RIC 7 as Lon 158, as Lon 208a, as Lon 291 |
| 28 | | HK as 48, copies as 48 (5), copies as 49 (3), as 87 (3), copies as 87 (10), copy as 102, as 137 (2), copy of 181, copy as 187, hybrid with obv. as 51 and rev. as 52 |

| 22 | | CK copies as 25 (9), copy as 202, copy as 253, illegible copies (11) |
| 6 | Magnentius | Copies as CK 8 (2), 23, 55, 212, 439 |
| 1 | Decentius | CK 6 |
| 2 | Julian | Silver rev. VOTIS V MVLTIS X mm. illegible; bronze reverse illegible |
| 26 | Valentinian I | CK as 96 (5), as 275 (2), 286, 290, as 296, 330, 479, as 479, 481 (2), 485, 527 (2), 984, 1003, 1020, 1350 (2), 1393, as 1414 |
| 30 | Valens | As 97 (7), 276, as 280 (2), as 301, 309, 315, 348, 352, 480, 483, 507, 510, 520, 526 (2), 528, 722, as 967, 1029, as 1303, 1417 (2), 2335 |
| 17 | Gratian | 297, as 320, 371 (4), 378, 511 (2), 517, 529 (3), 531, 540, 1013, 1421 |
| 10 | House of Valentinian | As 96 (6), as 275 (2), rev. illegible (2) |
| 2 | Valentinian II | 389, 1105 |
| 1 | Magnus Maximus | Silver RIC 9 Trier 84b |
| 1 | Theodosius I | 565 |
| 5 | Arcadius | 167, 392 (2), 1107 (2) |
| 1 | Honorius | As 806 |
| 5 | House of Theodosius | As 162 (2), as 796 (2), reverse illegible (1) |
| 28 | Fourth century | Worn, corroded or illegible |

603

# METHOD OF STUDY

There are two main ways in which coin lists may yield information; through the dates when the coins were minted and supplied, or through the dates when the coins were lost. Only a small proportion of the coins from Portchester were found in sealed deposits so we have little knowledge of when most of the coins were lost. We are therefore left with an assemblage of mass-produced artifacts which reached the site more or less in a known sequence, and all information we can hope to gain must come from a study of the rate of supply rather than anything else. Unfortunately, we have no knowledge at all of the production of coins so far as absolute numbers per year, or even relative numbers or volumes at different times, are concerned. Such knowledge may one day be available, but until the study of Roman imperial coinage in the fourth century is very much further advanced, the only way forward in interpreting site finds lies in the comparison of one chosen site with other sites. First, we can compare Portchester with other sites in Britain, then, as a first and woefully incomplete essay, we can compare Portchester with a few military and civil sites in Italy, the Rhine, and France.

Comparative material in Britain lies to hand in a survey of the coinage found on 14 varied, if not random, sites, recently published.[1] No doubt some of the sites have numismatic defects such as the presence of scattered hoards, the insertion of collectors' material, or the selection of coins for display. Thus Richborough is said to owe its large numbers of coins to hoards which were scattered at some unspecified date uniformly throughout the fort; in the totals published all known hoards have been excluded — a point true for all other sites — and the spectre of unknown hoards has been ignored since no serious answers have yet been advanced

[1] R. Reece, 'A Short Survey of the Roman Coins found on Fourteen Sites in Britain', *Britannia*, iii (1972), 269–76.

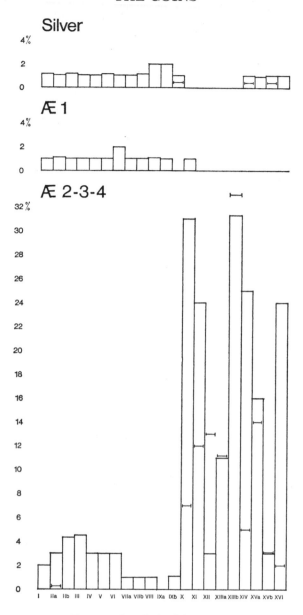

FIG. 108.   Coin histogram

to my exorcism in the fifth Richborough report.[1] Individual sites have individual numismatic quirks at isolated dates, but these can be spotted satisfactorily, and give no reason to avoid using the coins for comparative studies.

The coins found on the 14 British sites (which include Portchester) can be reduced to a single diagram such as fig. 108. This has been constructed by dividing the total coins from

[1] R. Reece, 'Summary of the Roman Coins from Richborough', in B. W. Cunliffe (ed.), *Fifth Report on the Excavations of the Roman Fort at Richborough, Kent* (1968), 200–16.

each site into three categories of silver, large, and small bronze coins — each of which is given a separate bar diagram — and 20 periods, which provide the horizontal axis. The periods are roughly 20-year spans which reflect, in the early empire, reigns such as Hadrian (period V) or Marcus Aurelius (period VIIa), and, in the later Empire, coherent issues of coins of similar weight, size and metal. The dates of these periods are: I, up to A.D. 41; IIa, 41 to 54; IIb, 54 to 69; III, 69 to 96; IV, 96 to 117; V, 117 to 138; VI, 138 to 161; VIIa, 161 to 180; VIIb, 180 to 193; VIII, 193 to 222; IXa, 222 to 238; IXb, 238 to 259; X, 259 to 275; XI, 275 to 294; XII, 294 to 317; XIIIa, 317 to 330; XIIIb, 330 to 348; XIV, 348 to 364; XVa, 364 to 378; XVb, 378 to 388; XVI, 388 to 402.

Each value, e.g. silver coins of Hadrian at Canterbury, could be plotted as a percentage of the total coins at the site which would produce a diagram with a scatter of points. Instead, fig. 108 shows for each period a solid bar which shows the spread of values taken over all sites. Single, abnormal figures have been ignored in drawing the bar so that it represents the 'normal' spread of values over the 14 sites. Thus most values of sestertii of Antoninus Pius (AE1 in period VI) lie between 0 and 2%, and the bar therefore runs from 0 to 2%. Small bronze coins of 317 to 330 (AE 2-3-4 of period XIIIa) form from 0 to 11% of the coins on any site, and this bar therefore runs from 0 to 11%. Against this background of vertical bars the values for Portchester can be shown as horizontal lines. Fig. 108 therefore shows the coins found at Portchester in relation to the coins found on a selection of other sites in Britain.

Any comparative study ought to extend beyond the borders of one individual province or diocese, for Portchester might be a particular type of site rather than a particular British site, and the type of site to which it belongs may have more influence on its coin list than may its geographical position. Ideally we should compare Portchester with the groups of coins collected together for the N. of France and the Rhine,[1] S. France[2] and N. Italy.[3] At present there are two good reasons for postponing such comparisons; the groups are not yet studied in enough detail to allow any fundamental comparisons, and most of the groups come from sites of little known historical background. Any resulting comparison would therefore be lacking in detail, and historically uninstructive. As a temporary measure, for the detailed comparison is now under active consideration, we may select three military sites — Speyer (Rhine), Mainz (Rhine), and Vindonissa (Fundmünzen, published by T. Pekary, 1972), and three civil sites which have produced good coin lists, but are otherwise disparate, Pachten (Rhine), Dijon ('S.' France), and Aquileia (N. Italy). To these European sites can be added a military site in Britain, Richborough, and the towns nearest to Portchester and Richborough, Winchester and Canterbury. If we restrict our enquiry to the period when Portchester actually has numbers of coins, the later third and fourth centuries, the result is shown in Table I.

Little progress can be made by the comparison of crude numbers, as the presence of Richborough in the group amply demonstrates, so Table II shows the same values expressed as percentages of the totals in Table I.

[1] R. Reece, 'Roman Coins in N. France and the Rhine Valley', *Num. Chron.* (1972), 159–65.
[2] R. Reece, 'Roman Coinage in Southern France', *Num. Chron.* (1967), 91–105.
[3] R. Reece, 'Roman Coinage in Northern Italy', *Num. Chron.* (1971), 167–79.

## TABLE I

*Numbers of Coins A.D. 259 to 402*

|  | Win. | Port. | Cant. | Richb. | Speyer | Pachten | Mainz | Vindon. | Dijon | Aquil. |
|---|---|---|---|---|---|---|---|---|---|---|
| X | 186 | 43 | 514 | 4759 | 64 | 52 | 201 | 190 | 787 | 1404 |
| XI | 188 | 69 | 265 | 4099 | 13 | 8 | 38 | 70 | 296 | 933 |
| XII | 13 | 75 | 31 | 351 | 47 | 15 | 68 | 94 | 167 | 976 |
| XIIIa | 24 | 67 | 30 | 855 | 68 | 35 | 107 | 142 | 130 | 1201 |
| XIIIb | 160 | 188 | 377 | 10127 | 80 | 71 | 114 | 381 | 80 | 1357 |
| XIV | 51 | 31 | 317 | 3156 | 25 | 11 | 65 | 167 | 39 | 932 |
| XVa | 55 | 78 | 84 | 2821 | 59 | 28 | 36 | 283 | 33 | 590 |
| XVb | 5 | 5 | 1 | 1084 | 19 | 7 | 14 | 106 | 20 | 412 |
| XVI | 61 | 14 | 92 | 22750 | 2 | 3 | 4 | 83 | 3 | 323 |

## TABLE II

*Percentages of Coins A.D. 259 to 402*

|  | Win. | Port. | Cant. | Richb. | Speyer | Pachten | Mainz | Vindon. | Dijon | Aquil. |
|---|---|---|---|---|---|---|---|---|---|---|
| X | 25 | 7·3 | 29 | 9·5 | 18 | 24 | 32 | 12 | 49 | 17 |
| XI | 25 | 12 | 15 | 8·2 | 3·5 | 3·8 | 5·8 | 4·5 | 25 | 11 |
| XII | 1·7 | 13 | 1·8 | 0·7 | 13 | 7·2 | 11 | 6·2 | 11 | 12 |
| XIIIa | 3·0 | 11 | 1·7 | 1·7 | 19 | 17 | 17 | 9·4 | 8 | 14 |
| XIIIb | 21 | 32 | 21 | 20 | 21 | 34 | 18 | 24 | 5·1 | 15 |
| XIV | 6·8 | 5·3 | 18 | 6·3 | 6·7 | 5·2 | 10 | 11 | 3·1 | 12 |
| XVa | 7·4 | 14 | 5·0 | 5·6 | 15 | 13 | 5·5 | 19 | 2·1 | 7·3 |
| XVb | 0·7 | 0·8 | 0·1 | 2·2 | 5·0 | 3·3 | 2·1 | 7·0 | 1·3 | 5·1 |
| XVI | 8·2 | 2·4 | 5·4 | 45 | 0·6 | 1·4 | 0·6 | 5·4 | 0·2 | 4·0 |
| Dev. | 75 | — | 82 | 93 | 47 | 43 | 69 | 44 | 103 | 51 |

The last line in Table II gives the total difference of each site from Portchester, i.e. the arithmetic sum of the variations from the Portchester value for each site. This helps to show which sites have values near to the Portchester values, and which are further away. The other English sites quoted have values more often further away than the continental sites, particularly Pachten and Vindonissa, though Speyer and Aquileia follow fairly close. The ideal site with which to compare Portchester in greater detail would seem to be Pachten, but unfortunately that site has only produced a total of 230 coins of the relevant period. Fortunately the second choice, Vindonissa, has the great advantage not only of a total of 1516 of the relevant coins, but the recent publication, in excellent detail, and most usable form.

If only a few arbitrary judgements are made it is possible to make out a list in which most of the coins found on the two sites are assigned to a reasonably short period of minting. This list is shown in Table III.

It might be thought that the best way to present the information in Table III would be in a diagram of coins lost per year. I have avoided this *because* I accept the superior impact which

## TABLE III

| Date A.D. | Port. | Vind. | Date A.D. | Port. | Vind. | Date A.D. | Port. | Vind. |
|---|---|---|---|---|---|---|---|---|
| 259–68 | 11 | 61 | 313–17 | 16 | 35 | 348–50 | 7 | 25 |
| 268–70 | 11 | 98 | 317–20 | 20 | 38 | 350–53 | 6 | 20 |
| 270–75 | 21 | 31 | 320–24 | 36 | 76 | 353–60 | 17 | 113 (1AR) |
| 275–86 | 13 | 52 | 324–26 | 6 | 18 | 360–64 | 1 (1AR) | 8 |
| 286–93 | 54 | 15 | 326–30 | 5 | 10 | 364–67 | 15 | 61 |
| 293–96 | 2 | 3 | 330–33 | 46 | 62 | 367–75 | 61 | 216 |
| 296–300 | 5 | 8 | 333–35 | 19 | 43 | 375–78 | 2 | 6 |
| 300–03 | 13 | 6 | 335–37 | 19 | 41 | 378–83 | 5 | 78 |
| 303–05 | 1 | 2 | 337–40 | 31 | 41 | 383–88 | — (1AR) | 27 (1AV) |
| 305–07 | 5 | 5 | 340–41 | 7 | 36 | 388–95 | 12 | 82 |
| 307–10 | 9 | 8 (1AR) | 341–45 | 48 | 19 | 395–402 | 2 | 1 |
| 310–13 | 26 | 29 | 345–48 | 18 | 139 | | | |

diagrammatic presentation holds. The impression left on a viewer by such a diagram would be a statement of the periods of the fourth century in which coins were small, low in face value, and commonly lost; this, though valuable in itself, is not the object of the present exercise. On any coin diagram devoted to 'number' the period 330 to 333 (46 coins) would far outshadow the period 300 to 303 (13 coins), yet the latter is considerably more noteworthy, important, and deserving of comment. Coins of the earlier period are probably more than four times the face value and intrinsic value of the later coins, so that the *value* of coinage lost in the two periods is contradicted by sheer statement of numbers. Whatever the relative monetary significance of the two types of coin, the earlier coins are far less commonly found on sites than the later, and a figure of 13 is remarkably high. As no diagram can at present be drawn which would accommodate these points I prefer not to mislead readers by providing a diagram which will inevitably be misused by many as a quick summary of pages of turgid prose.

The comparative machinery has been assembled; it is now time to see if it can be used.


## DISCUSSION

Fig. 108 makes the first clear and obvious point that, although coinage before the later third century is to be expected on 'normal' sites in Britain, at Portchester it is absent. The only exception is a single coin of Claudius I which fits well with a small scatter of early pottery found (pp. 8–10).

The archaeological evidence makes it quite clear that apart from a slight Claudian occupation there was no activity on the site before the building of the stone walls, so the coin evidence merely adds confirmation. The values in periods X and XIV are low, but well within the 'normal' range; in periods XIIIa, XIIIb, and XVa they are high, but again within the normal range. In period XII (294–317) however, Portchester is highly abnormal, and certainly holds the record for England, if not for archaeological sites in N.W. Europe.

## The Late Third Century A.D.

The coins from Portchester, minted before the reign of Carausius, are comparatively few in number, and worn in condition. The irregular copies of such coins, known as Barbarous Radiates, are similarly poorly represented, but the coins of Carausius are abundant, and often in freshly minted condition. The majority of Carausius' coins seem to belong to the early part of the reign, with few of the fully developed later mint-marks, and, following on from this, there are only two coins of Allectus. While Allectus is less common, in general, than Carausius (Winchester 25 to 4, Canterbury 66 to 13, Richborough 1324 to 292), the ratio of 54 Carausius to 2 Allectus is the lowest such ratio known to me at present.

The best interpretation of the evidence at present seems to be as follows: there is not enough evidence to suggest that any coins reached the site before the reign of Carausius; the worn, earlier, radiate coins enter the site with new Carausian coinage from about 286 to 290, after which very few coins reached the site for perhaps ten years. The low numbers of barbarous radiates, which I would date from 273 to 285, strongly supports this line of reasoning, for if there were continuous provision of coin to the site from c. 265 onwards, reaching a peak under Carausius, then the irregular coinage should be far better represented.

## The Period of the Follis, A.D. 294–303

In the four short periods from 305 to 313, there is astonishingly close agreement in the numbers of coins from Portchester and Vindonissa. Whatever this may mean in terms of supply and activity, it at least gives reason to hope that the discrepancy in the numbers from 296 to 300 and 300 to 303 may represent a real difference between the sites. Portchester, as compared with Vindonissa, is low on coins from 296 to 300 and high in the next group. This suggests that the gap noticed under Allectus continued until about 300, that there was then a sudden influx of new coinage, and that some coins already in circulation came in at the same time.

The whole period of 294 to 317 is one in which Portchester is highly abnormal when judged against all other sites in Britain (see fig. 108). At Vindonissa there seems little doubt that this is a period of garrison by regular troops. The convergence of Vindonissa and Portchester, tied in with the complete divergence of Portchester from Britain, might argue for a garrison at Portchester. It may be noted from Table II that this burst of activity is markedly absent at Richborough, which seems to follow what might be called the 'civilian British pattern'.

## The House of Constantine, A.D. 313–64

From about 313 to about 345 Portchester follows Vindonissa in fluctuations from period to period, but usually with about half the actual number of coins. The variations apparent from 340 onwards are partly artificial in that the copies of coins of the House of Constantine which are far more common in Britain than the continent, have been grouped in the table in between the issues of 337 to 341 and the new issues (with the legend VICTORIAE DD AVGG Q NN) which probably belong to 345 to 348. The great change comes around 345 with the new issues just mentioned, which are few in number at Portchester. In the rest of Britain they are common, and at Vindonissa they form a definite peak of activity, so the small numbers at Portchester may mean a drop in coin supply. This suggestion is enhanced by the comparative rarity of the 'Fel Temp Reparatio' coinage of 348 to 356, and its attendant copies. These coins often form a high proportion of the total coinage of the fourth century on any site in England, so their absence at Portchester is almost certainly not accidental. A tentative explanation could be that the intensive coin-using occupation of the site finished in about 345 and only began again around 364. Alternatively, the period 345 to 364 could have been one of comparative cleanliness and organization in which less coins were lost and less rubbish left lying about the interior of the fort.

### The Later Fourth Century, A.D. 364 to 402

From 364 to 378 there is a definite intensification of coin loss, compared to the preceding decades. The relative numbers in the three subdivisions of this period are satisfyingly similar at Portchester and Vindonissa, suggesting that the variations are in general coin supply rather than specific instances of coin loss. The English variation from continental uniformity from 378 to 388 comes through very clearly, and reference to fig. 108 will show that this occurs on every site in England. In this context the silver coin of Magnus Maximus provides an intriguing contrast.

The last phase of coin use in Britain is represented at Portchester, though many British sites show more substantial activity. If the coinage of the House of Theodosius (378–88 +) really represents a drop from the House of Valentinian (364–78) the virtual gap around 380 makes it very difficult to fix on any date for a sudden change, or even to decide between sudden change or gradual decline. My feeling is that the coins of Gratian of 378 to 383, which are distinctly rare on English sites, represent a similar level of activity to that of 364 to 378; the silver of Maximus seems to indicate some official sort of activity: I would therefore look for a break in occupation in the decade 387 to 397.

This forms a complete contrast with the coinage at Richborough which reaches an all-time peak of supply between 388 and 402 and even has a few silver coins of Constantine III (c. 407) to extend its activity into the fifth century. As there seems to have been an almost complete cessation of the large-scale minting of copper coins in the West around 402, it is pointless to hope for much help on the subject of fifth-century occupation from coin evidence. To this warning must be added a second, that the peak in coinage at Richborough in the last years of the fourth century is abnormal by both British, and European standards. The typical picture at this time is one of decline in coin loss, coin supply, or coin use, in military and some civil sites which contrasts strangely with the documentation on late fourth- or early fifth-century military dispositions provided by the *Notitia Dignitatum*. If the contrast is true at this one period when we have literary evidence to compare with the coin evidence, the dangers of distributing military presences by means of coin lists at earlier dates will be apparent. What is obviously needed is a critical survey of the coin lists of undoubted military sites to determine any particular features which there happen to be of military coin use. Whatever future research might produce on this subject it would seem most unsafe now to accept the decline in coinage at Portchester after 378 as an index of military abandonment. Before 378 there does not even seem to be an arguable decline.

## SUMMARY

When compared with other sites in Britain and the continent the coins from Portchester suggest an initial occupation in the decade 280–90, a period of abandonment from 290 to 300, and a period of intensive occupation from about 300 to 345. From 345 to about 360 there are surprisingly few coins, but, from 360 onwards the site shows a coin list which compares well with other sites occupied until the end of the fourth century. The coins demonstrate no positive occupation continuing into the fifth century, so that if the pottery shows an absence of the latest types round about 400, there would seem to be some possibility of a gap in occupation in the early fifth century.

# VII. THE FINDS

THE manufactured objects, other than coins, glass vessels, building materials or pottery vessels are listed and described below by a number of writers. Janet Webster has kindly contributed the descriptions of the objects of bronze, silver, bone, antler, shale, lead and iron; Timothy Ambrose describes the leather; David Peacock, the whetstones; Margaret Guido, the glass beads; and Martin Henig, the gemstone. A consolidated bibliography is offered at the end (pp. 268–9).

In the case of each object, the trench and layer number is given, together with a brief description of its stratigraphical position. Lists of objects from each situation will be found in the relevant parts of sections II to V. In the case of objects listed as coming from 'general layers' we refer to unsealed Roman soil accumulations which in some areas were disturbed by post-Roman ploughing and other activities. Each object described is given a unique publication number, but the original 'small finds' number is also published in brackets after the trench location. Dates are A.D. unless otherwise stated.

The objects are listed according to material, in the following order:

Bronze and silver
Bone and antler
Shale
Glass (excluding vessels, for which see section IX)
Gemstone
Lead
Iron
Leather
Wood
Pottery, clay and chalk
Metal working activity
Whetstones
Quernstones

## OBJECTS OF BRONZE AND SILVER

### by JANET WEBSTER

*Brooches* (all the brooches are of bronze)

1. Nauheim derivative. The bow is sturdy and of round cross-section; it kicks forward sharply from the head and contracts suddenly at its lower end to form a knife-edge foot; the bow is very straight in profile and the angle of the foot is reversed; the catch-plate is solid. At the head of the brooch, the wire of the bow is flattened into a broad ribbon which forms the three coil spring with internal chord. Cf. *Richborough V*, pl. XXVI, 6. For the type in general cf. *Camulodunum*, 312ff. Type VII; *Richborough V*, 77ff. First century.

   Trench 108 layer 16 (2354): general layer.

2. Nauheim derivative? The bow is flat and tapers gradually from the sharp kick near the head to a knife-edge foot. The upper half of the bow is ornamented with two longitudinal incised lines running approximately down the centre, while the lower half of the bow, above the knife-edge foot, is decorated with horizontal incised lines. The small catch-plate is solid but now damaged and the angle of the foot breaks the curve of the bow profile. At the head of the brooch the bronze tapers into a narrow strand to form the now lost spring and pin.

Trench 63 layer 5 (165): general layer.

3. Enamelled plate brooch of common type. The central circle of the brooch has lost its enamel setting; it is separated from a further band of enamel, now of yellowish-green colour, by a broad raised band of bronze. The star-pattern is defined by bronze walls, each pair terminating, at its inner point, in a raised dot of bronze. The colour of the triangular cells of enamel is now lost. Cf. *Richborough IV*, pl. XXIX, 45; *Newstead*, pl. LXXXIX, 10; *Nor'nour*, fig. 21, 191 and 192. Second century.

Trench 90 layer 52 (1266): general layer.

4. Part of a cross-bow brooch. The head and cross-bar are missing. The upper part of the bow presents a narrow edge to the front but is broad in profile. The foot has a slight transverse moulding at its lower edge. The pin-slot does not extend down the full length **of** the tubular catch-plate; although the latter is hollow throughout, the bronze forms a continuous casing at its lower edge. Third to fourth century.

Trench 96 layer 18 (1732): general layer.

5. The lower part of a cross-bow brooch comprising the lower bow incorporating the tubular catch-plate and foot. The front of the bow is faceted and there is a projecting foot. As in the previous example the pin-slot does not extend all the way down the tubular catch-plate but in this instance the lower portion of the catch-plate is solid. Third to fourth century.

Trench 62 layer 24 (216): general layer.

6. Penannular brooch with milled knob terminals and a slight ridged collar moulding below each terminal. The ring of the penannular is of circular cross-section. The broad ribbon strip of the pin remains coiled round the ring but the narrow lower portion of the pin is lost. The brooch belongs to Fowler's Type A2, first to fourth century in date, but has the additional collar mouldings. Cf. Fowler 1960, 152 and 174.

Trench 88 layer 6 (1000): layer above make-up.

7. A small penannular brooch of circular cross-section with the terminals flattened into broader ribbon strips and coiled round to form spirals at right angles to the plain of the ring. The pin is straight. The brooch belongs to Fowler's Type C; it is current from the first century B.C. and occurs in Anglo-Saxon graves. Cf. Fowler 1960, 152 and 175.

Trench 88 layer 5 (977): layer above make-up.

8. Penannular brooch. The ring is of circular cross-section flattened above and below. The terminals are folded back at right angles to the plane of the ring. Each terminal is notched in the centre of its fold line. On the right-hand terminal the line of this notch is continued to cross, a fraction below its centre, the incised saltire decoration and terminates at the transverse grooving which precedes slight irregular markings at the end of the terminal. On the left-hand terminal the line of the notch is continued a shorter distance and terminates before the incised saltire; there is no transverse moulding here but two incised lines form a sideways V-ornament at the end of the terminal. The ring of the brooch is ornamented on the upper side only with irregular groups of incised lines, sometimes slanted and occasionally formed into a cross by a reverse slant line; groups are separated by plain panels. The narrow straight pin is extant. The brooch seems to be an aberrant form of Fowler's Type D3 of possibly second to fourth century date. Cf. Fowler, 1960, 152 and 176.

Trench 72 layer 6 (364): general layer.

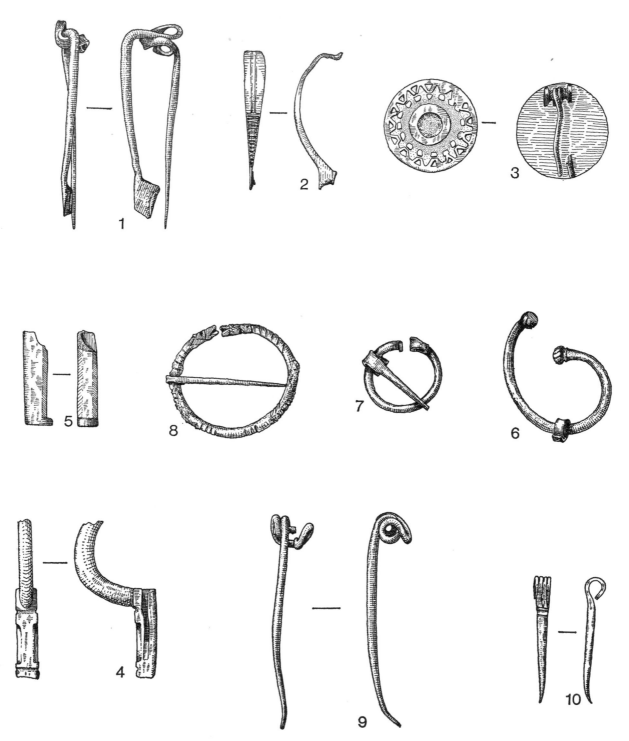

FIG. 109.   Bronze brooches (pp. 198–201). Scale $\frac{2}{3}$

9. Spring and pin from a brooch. The spring has an internal chord. An axial bar of bronze passes through the spring. This combination of spring, pin and internal chord is likely to have come from a one-piece first century brooch such as a La Tène or Nauheim derivative.
Trench 94 unstratified (1867).

10. The pin of a penannular brooch. The flattened strip which was looped round the ring has traces of indented line ornament.
Trench 96 layer 23 (1722): general layer.

*Military Equipment*

11. Gilded bronze acorn terminal. The back is hollow. The lower part of the acorn is ornamented with raised curvilinear triangles, a few of which have additional striated line decoration. Cf. *Trans. Birmingham Arch. Soc.* lxxviii (1962), 36 and fig. 5, 4.
Trench 80 layer 8 (824): general layer.

12. Leaf-shaped bronze fitting with four rivet holes; perhaps a decorative fitting from a scabbard. Cf. for instance *Germania*, xlvii (1969), 112, pls. 19 and 25.
Trench 98 layer 19 (1831); general layer.

13. Buckle of sub-ovoid shape with a straight hinge-bar cast in one piece with the loop. The back surface of the buckle is flat, the front is curved. The buckle is ornamented with two confronted stylized dolphin heads. The buckle belongs to Hawkes and Dunning Type I A. Buckles of this type are thought to have begun to be made only towards the end of the fourth century and to have still been in use in the mid-fifth century. Cf. Hawkes and Dunning, 1961, in particular pp. 21–34 and 41–5.
Trench 99 layer 56 (1935): general layer.

14. Buckle fragment.
Trench 100 layer 18 (2070): general layer.

15. Buckle. This type with loops at right angles to the plane of the buckle to secure the hinge-bar of the belt-plate is common from the Conquest period onwards (cf. *Hod Hill I*, fig. 4, A81, A91, A93 for example) and continues in use into the late Roman period, being copied in barbaric military belt fittings (cf. Hawkes and Dunning, 1961, pp. 53–4, figs. 17, 18). Whether early or late, however, the terminals are usually curved back more or less elaborately and the Portchester buckle is noteworthy for the abrupt finishing of its terminals.
Trench 88 layer 14 (1036): layer below upper make-up.

16. Rectangular strip of sheet bronze with two rivet holes. The ornament consists of a panel of incised wavy line decoration running down the centre, with similar decoration, composed of two rows of short semi-circular lines, running down the sides of the strip and one such similar row running across the top above the rivet holes. At the bottom of the plate the metal shows the faint trace of a curve and the rectangular cut to accommodate the hinge of the buckle-tongue can be seen at the bottom of the central wavy line panel. The ornament has been so deeply pressed into the front of the metal that it is revealed in slight raised lines on the back. The strip is a belt-plate of the type associated with buckles of Hawkes and Dunning Types I A and B. Cf. Hawkes and Dunning, 1961, in particular 21–34 and 41–60.
Trench 5 layer 3 (26): occupation against west wall of fort.

Nos. 17–19 are similar fragments of sheet bronze but without assured military connections.

17. Fragments of a narrow strip of very thin sheet bronze with repoussé ornament consisting of a row of small dots down each edge with two rows of outward pointing 'horse-shoes' in the field with some interspersal of dots. An ornamental attachment.
Trench 95 layer 37 (1585): general layer.

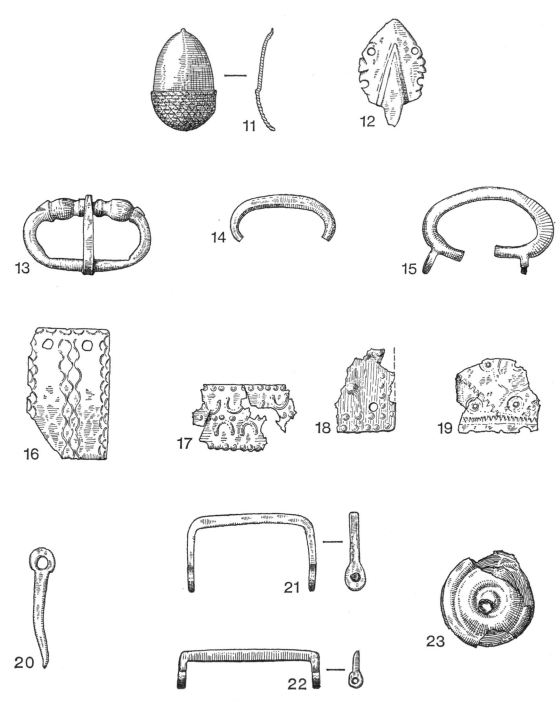

FIG. 110.   Bronze military equipment (pp. 201–3). Scale ⅔

18. Similar fragment of very thin sheet bronze with repoussé ornament. One rivet hole remains and there is a trace of another. The decoration consists of two rows of repoussé dots flanking the two remaining original edges with one large dot in the field. An ornamental attachment.

Trench 89 layer 38 (1168): layer above make-up.

The two decorated strips 17 and 18, while similar in size, ornament and, in the latter case, in the position of the rivet holes, to the belt plates of Hawkes and Dunning Type I A and B, are of sheet bronze too thin to have served such a purpose.

19. Fragment of thin sheet bronze. The fragment is decorated with zig-zag line ornament and with one large and three smaller pierced ring-and-dot motifs. An ornamental attachment.

Trench 54 layer 6 (58): general layer.

Nos. 20–23: harness fittings.

20. A pendant; cf. *Hod Hill II*, fig. 56, 6.
Trench 95 layer 32 (1588): general layer.
21. Square buckle, perhaps from a girth strap; cf. *Hofheim*, pl. XIV, 21, 23 and 26, also p. 176, note 16.
Trench 102 layer 48 (2106): upper occupation.
22. Square buckle in silver, similar to no. 21 above.
Trench 101 layer 36 (2163): general layer.
23. Two circular discs of bronze, attached to each other by means of a ribbon strip of bronze twisted through a central opening in the upper disc. The upper disc is moulded. Probably a piece of horse-harness.
Trench 108 layer 99 (2505): upper occupation.

*Bracelets*

(a) Bracelets of bronze wire. Four examples, other than of twisted bronze wire, were found:

24. A single strip of bronze wire, one end of which terminates in a hook for a simple fastening, the other end of which is lost. There is no decoration.
Trench 91 layer 56 (1305): layer above upper road.
24A. Bracelet of thin bronze wire with each terminal coiled twice round the body of the bracelet forming an expanding fastening. The bracelet can only have been worn by a child. Cf. *Camerton*, fig. 57, 4B.
Trench 109 layer 108 (2628): pit 236.
25. A single strand of bronze wire of square cross-section into which a slight twist has been put at regular intervals. The fastening is simple; at the remaining terminal the wire is drawn out into a thinner strand and turned back on itself to form a hook.
Trench 70 layer 14 (306): pit 63.
26. Twisted bronze wires (not illustrated).
Only fragments have been found. The type is always composed of two strands of wire twisted together with simple ring and hook terminals. The wire varies in gauge.
Twenty-six have been found: (245) pit 61; (1651) pit 144; (10), (28) from 1961 occupation layers; (2526), (2531) from middle occupation, (2214) upper occupation; (1140), (1150), (1253) from layers above upper make-up; (1062), (1296), (1289) from layers above upper road.

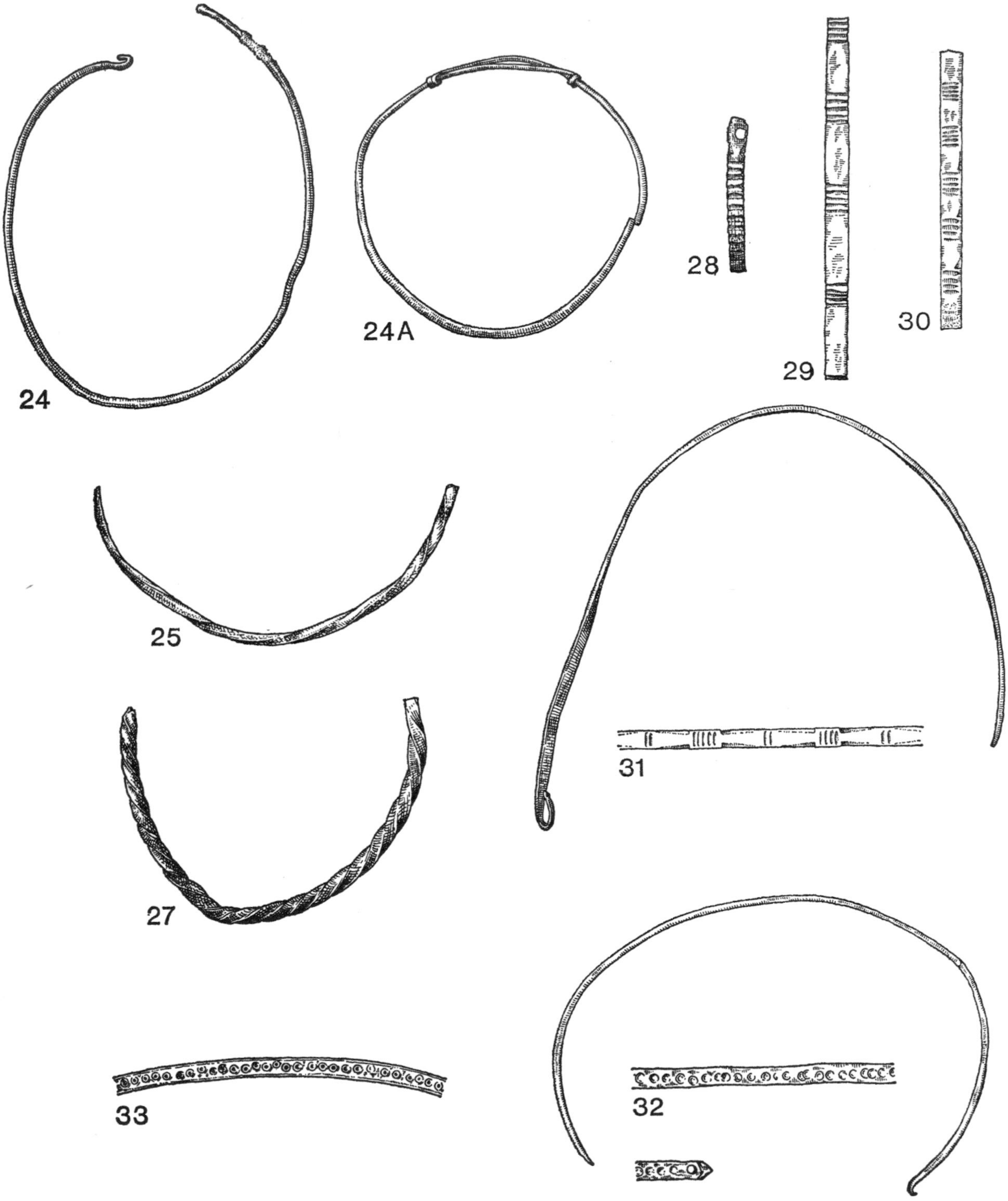

FIG. III. Bronze bracelets (pp. 203–6). Scale $\frac{2}{3}$

In addition to those listed from pits and closely stratified levels, fragments have also been recovered from general layers (134, 188, 258, 261, 288, 347, 422, 858, 887, 1230, 1420, 1625, 2219).

27. Bracelet of solid bronze, of square cross-section at its remaining terminal, twisted tightly to produce an appearance similar to that of a bracelet composed of several strands of bronze wire twisted together.
Trench 98 layer 60 (1930): pit 182.

## (b) Ribbon strip bracelets:

These bracelets are of flat rectangular or of flattened D-shaped cross-section and will have been worn with the flat face resting on the wearer's arm. All the bracelets are ornamented only on the side that showed in use. Altogether some 28 examples have been recovered of which 12 are described and illustrated below. The remaining 16 are from the following provenances: (411) pit 63; (850) pit 95; (1716) pit 144; (1156), (1194), (1204) from above upper make-up; (2438) from the upper clay; (2077), (2115), (2483) from upper occupation; (264), (298), (379), (1222), (1884), (2035) from general layers.

## (i) Ribbon-strip bracelets with transverse line ornament:

28. Only a small fragment remains. It is of flat rectangular cross-section. At one end is a circular hole for fastening. The ornament consists of transverse mouldings separated by deep wide grooves. The final transverse moulding is defined on the side of the fastening, not by a deep transverse groove, but by two notches on each side of the bracelet, which taper away laterally to form two indented elongated triangles; an incised line runs from the fastening hole to cross the first transverse moulding.
Trench 76 layer 29 (829): general layer.

29. Bracelet of rounded D-section. The ornament comprises groups of five indented transverse lines, separated by four transverse mouldings, each such panel being separated from the next by a longer plain panel.
Trench 88 layer 6 (1012): layer above upper make-up.

30. This is of rounded rectilinear cross-section. The ornament comprises groups of four or five indented transverse lines, each such panel being separated from the next by a shorter plain panel. It is very similar to no. 29 above; the ornament is more degenerate, now only indented lines instead of indented lines and transverse mouldings.
Trench 63 layer 5 (213): general layer.

31. This is of flat rectangular cross-section. As in the previous examples the decoration is based on groupings of indented transverse lines. Here groups of four or five such lines are separated from each other by long plain panels, each interrupted at its centre by a small group of two or three similar lines. An attempt has been made to create the impression of an oval form for each of the intervening plain panels with central line ornament; this has been done by cutting shallow elongated triangular notches at each corner of the plain panel ornaments.
The ornament of this bracelet suggests that it may have been decorated to imitate a bead bracelet with long ovoid beads with central ribbing, alternating with closely ribbed beads. The end of the bracelet narrows and is hooked inwards for the fastening.
Trench 99 layer 76 (1970): pit 178.

For bracelets nos. 29–31 cf. *Lydney*, fig. 17, P and S (although as noted above, no. 31 has the notched elaboration). The Lydney bracelets are assigned a date in the later part of the fourth century.

### (ii) Ribbon-strip bracelets with dot decoration:

32. Bracelet of flat rectangular cross-section; at one end the bronze strip narrows and is bent back to form a hook, at the other terminal is a circular hole for the fastening. The bracelet is ornamented with a hollowed dot decoration along its length. Close to the hook terminal the dot decoration gives way to an indented transverse line decoration; at the other end the dot decoration terminates closer to the hole and there is only one transverse line; this terminal has a pointed end with an irregular incised cross between the hole and the point. Cf. *Lydney*, fig. 17E, latter part of fourth century.
    Trench 89 layer 37 (1154): general layer.

33. Gilt bronze bracelet of flat rectangular cross-section. An incised line defines a narrow margin along each edge of the bracelet; the central field is then ornamented with closely placed ring-and-dot decoration. Cf. *Lydney*, fig. 17E, latter part of fourth century.
    Trench 88 layer 5 (969): above upper make-up.

### (iii) Ribbon-strip bracelet with panels of ring-and-dot decoration:

34. Flat rectangular cross-section. The decoration consists of larger panels with a central ring-and-dot motif alternating with narrower panels each of which has two ring-and-dot ornaments. The corners of the panels are cut away in notches, to throw each panel into relief.
    Trench 107 layer 42 (2402): general layer.

### (iv) Ribbon-strip bracelet with ring-and-dot and zig-zag ornament:

35. This is of flat rectangular cross-section and tapers to form a simple hook at one end. The ornament consists of an incised zig-zag line interspersed with ring-and-dot decoration. The strokes of the zig-zag have been individually formed and there is some overlapping of lines. To either side of each ring-and-dot is an elongated triangular hollowing, which throws the ring-and-dot into greater prominence (cf. no. 31 above for the notched hollowing technique). The bracelet has some affinities with *Lydney*, fig. 17F (latter part of fourth century).
    Trench 91 layer 46 (1272): above upper road surface.

### (v) Ribbon-strip bracelets with ring-and-dot and linear ornament:

36. This is of flat rectangular cross-section. Only a small portion of the bracelet remains and the full decorative element may not be represented. On the extant fragment a panel of linear ornament is flanked on one side by a single panel containing ring-and-dot decoration and on the other side by two such ring-and-dot panels; each panel of the design is separated from its neighbour by a group of three indented transverse lines. The linear ornament consists of a deep groove running along the centre of the bracelet parallel to the sides and flanked by notches on the edges of the bracelet. The ring-and-dot decoration is placed centrally within its panel and triangular notches in each corner of the panel throw the ornament into greater prominence; cf. nos. 31 and 35 above. Cf. *Lydney*, fig. 17D and H for linear groove and notches used with ring-and-dot ornament and *Lydney*, 17D for transverse grooving (latter part of fourth century); also *Richborough II*, pl. XXI, 51; *Shakenoak I*, fig. 30, 20 (of late fourth century date). Note that the cutaway section of the Shakenoak example emphasizes the fact that unless the complete bracelet is extant, the design element as a whole cannot be assured.
    Trench 54 layer 9 (69): general layer.

37. Again only a portion of the bracelet survives and the full design of the ornament may not be represented. The linear decoration is similar to that of no. 36, consisting of a central groove running parallel to the sides of the bracelet and flanked by notches on the edges of the bracelet; three transverse grooves separated by slight mouldings lie between the linear ornament and a plain panel which precedes a panel decorated with two rows of five ring-and-dot motifs; this panel is defined on one side by an indented transverse line and on the other by a wide shallow groove and a transverse moulding beyond which is a further plain panel. The bracelet has been gilded and is of flat rectangular cross-section. Cf. *Lydney*, fig. 17D and H for the linear groove and notch ornament and H for the use of a panel comprising two rows of ring-and-dot (latter part of fourth century); also *Richborough II*, pl. XXI, 51.

Trench 89 layer 21 (1147): above upper make-up.

## Two further ribbon-strip bracelets

38. This is of round D-section. It tapers towards the end and is bent back to form a hook. There are two panels of line ornament separated by a pair of indented transverse lines. Close to the hook are indented transverse lines; behind these an indented groove runs down the centre of the bracelet parallel to the sides and flanked along about half its length by notched edges; this line fades before the transverse division is reached but there are faint traces of resumed notchings close to the transverse division. The second panel of line ornament comprises a similar groove, a little off-centre; on one side only this is flanked on the edge of the bracelet by broad notches with forked 'tails' alternating with tiny incised dots.

Trench 63 layer 5 (140): general layer.

39. This is of rounded D-section. The terminal is in the form of an animal head with short snout and partly open mouth; the eye is represented on one side by an indented circle, on the other by a small circle set in an oblong hollow; on the latter side there are further hollowings, perhaps denoting ears. The bracelet widens behind the animal head terminal and is ornamented with a central indented groove running parallel to the sides, flanked by diagonal incised lines, the whole giving a stylized mane effect. This ornament terminates at two transverse grooves which occur a short way from the break.

Trench 72 layer 59 (424): general layer.

(c) Bracelets of oblong cross-section with narrow ornament and wear facets:

A total of 13 examples have been found of which three are illustrated and described. The remainder come from the following contexts: (1984) pit 187; (1288) above upper road; (2438) upper clay; (156), (189), (361), (368), (595), (1425), (2263), (2561) general layers.

40. Only the outer, narrow facet is ornamented. The decoration consists of simple notches evenly spaced. Cf. *Caerleon: Myrtle Cottage Orchard*, fig. 8, 34 (of similar general type and fourth century date); *Leicester: Jewry Wall*, fig. 83, 2.

Trench 69 layer 3 (251): general layer.

41. Again only the outer narrow facet is ornamented. The decoration consists of rounded-square notches cut alternately from each side leaving a raised wavy line. The notching is irregular in some parts and the alternating pattern is lost. Cf. *Caerleon: Myrtle Cottage Orchard*, fig. 8, 34 (similar in general type and fourth century in date); *Shakenoak II*, fig. 48, 73 and 77 (later third century).

Trench 62 layer 5 (127): general layer.

42. Once more only the narrow outer facet is ornamented. The decoration consists of raised plain panels each separated from the next by four indented and three lightly ridged transverse mouldings.

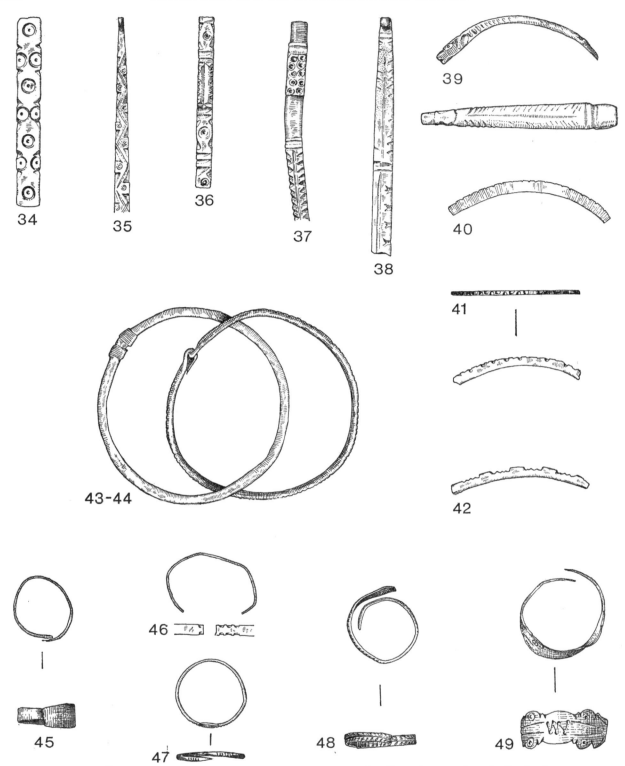

FIG. 112.   Bronze bracelets and rings: no. 49 is silver (pp. 206–10). Scale ⅔

Cf. *Leicester: Jewry Wall*, fig. 83, 3; *Lydney*, fig. 17, 58 (latter part of fourth century); *Shakenoak II*, fig. 49, 104 appears to be a fragment of a similar bracelet and is dated to the later third century; *Verulamium* 1934, fig. 2, 4 (late fourth century).

Trench 76 layer 30 (595): general layer.

Bracelets nos. 40–2 are similar to those illustrated in *Richborough II*, pl. XXII, 61–2, and may originally have been annular.

## (d) Other bracelets:

43–44. A pair of interlocked bracelets, probably for a child because of their small size. One bracelet is plain with narrow wear and exterior facets; at the fastening two ribbon-strips of thin bronze are folded around the bracelet. The second bracelet is of circular cross-section; it is ornamented on the outer side only with panels of transverse indented line decoration separated by plain panels; each panel of transverse lines comprises between 8 and 12 indentations with rounded mouldings between; the alternating plain panels are also rounded and the whole once again gives a bead-like impression, as though rows of small beads with larger beads interspersed had been threaded together. One terminal of this bracelet is bent inwards to form an enclosed hook with a circular hole, the other terminal is hooked to pass through this hole.

Trench 90 layer 30 (1265): general layer.

*General comments on the bracelets*

The simple hook and eye fasteners of the Portchester bracelets can be paralleled in bracelets of a similar late date (cf. *Lydney*, fig. 17, 56 and 58; *Shakenoak I*, fig. 30, 32; all of late fourth century date).

On the ribbon-strip bracelets motifs seem to be largely interchangeable with linear groove and notch, ring-and-dot, and transverse indented line motifs being used in a variety of combinations. Where only a fragment of a bracelet remains it cannot be assumed that the extant decorative motif is repeated in the same form throughout; examples of bracelets similar to the Portchester ones, from Shakenoak (*Shakenoak I*, fig. 30, 20) and Richborough (*Richborough V*, no. 158) show that a focal panel of different design was sometimes incorporated and the Richborough example also shows that the ribbon-strip bracelets with transverse line ornament sometimes had further more elaborate enrichments, as was probably the case with some of the Portchester examples.

Bracelets were clearly a popular form of ornament from the late third century onwards and particularly in the later part of the fourth century, as the hoard (*Richborough IV*, pl. XLIX, 177), the Lydney finds (*Lydney*, fig. 17, 82–3), and the Portchester examples indicate.

Imitations of other forms of jewellery seem to be a feature in the decoration of bracelets and imitation of threaded beads seems particularly popular. Similarly, the use of notching in order to highlight specific panels of ornament is predominant in this late period.

*Finger Rings*

45. Finger ring of flat ribbon-strip of bronze with overlapping terminals. The ring broadens gradually from the narrow underlying terminal to the broad overlapping end.

Trench 78 layer 45 (935): general layer.

15

46. A flat ribbon-strip of bronze. The central ornamental panel of the ring is lost but a little of the flanking decoration remains. This decoration consists of rectangular hollowings at the edges of the ring which throw into relief the narrow plain panels left in between the hollowings.
    Trench 91 layer 46 (1313): layer immediately above upper Roman road surface.
47. Thin bronze wire with overlapping terminals. Each terminal is flattened to a point and close to each the ring is decorated with light transverse ridging.
    Trench 107 layer 41 (2407): upper occupation.
48. A flat bronze strip with the ends overlapping. The ring is decorated with a central groove flanked by diagonal indentations. At the underlying terminal, however, the central groove fades and transverse indented lines supersede the diagonal line ornament.
    Trench 39 layer 3 (41): general layer.
49. Silver finger ring. The bezel is ovoid in shape and is inscribed with a zig-zag line each point of which is further embellished with an indented dot. The zig-zag line seems to form the letters AM with the letter A lacking its cross-bar; the letters are presumably an abbreviation for the words *Anima Mea* (drawing inverted). The bezel is flanked on either side by a panel of ornament with incised line and ring-and-dot decoration. The ring has plain overlapping terminals to be worn at the back of the finger. Cf. for example, *Lydney*, fig. 16, 53, for similar ornament flanking the bezel and a ring of similar general style; *Verulamium 1934*, fig. 47, 75 for a ring with a similar inscribed zig-zag line.
    Trench 87 layer 48 (1270): layer immediately below upper Roman road surface.

## *Pins and Toilet Articles*

50. Pin with faceted knob. The head is in the form of a cube with the corners cut off to leave four main lozenge-shaped facets with four triangular facets above and below. One of the lozengic facets has split and reveals that the pin and knob were made separately and the knob threaded on to the pin at a secondary stage of manufacture. The pin itself tapers towards the knob and towards the point. Cf. *Maiden Castle*, fig. 96, 8; *Richborough IV*, pl. LIII, 199.
    Trench 100 layer 29 (2066): general layer.
51. Similar pin with faceted knob.
    Trench 87 layer 9 (1005): layer immediately above or cutting into upper Roman road surface.

Five similar pins have been recovered in addition to the two illustrated: (815) from pit 121, (1207), (1338), (2083), (2206) from general layers.

52. Spatula-probe/cosmetic spoon, probably the latter, with spiral ornament.
    Trench 101 layer 86 (2235): general layer.
53. Silver scoop.
    Trench 90 layer 26 (1254): general layer.
54. Tweezers. There is no decoration. Cf. *Fishbourne II*, fig. 42, 61–6.
    Trench 103 layer 54 (2276): general layer.
55. A small pair of tweezers, without decoration.
    Trench 63 layer 5 (164): general layer.

Four other pairs of tweezers have been found: (289), (1934) from general layers; (1209) above the upper road; (2482) upper occupation.

56. Nail cleaner with a hole in the head indicating that it was part of a toilet set. At the narrowing below the head is an impressed cross; below this three lines are scored across the object, with an

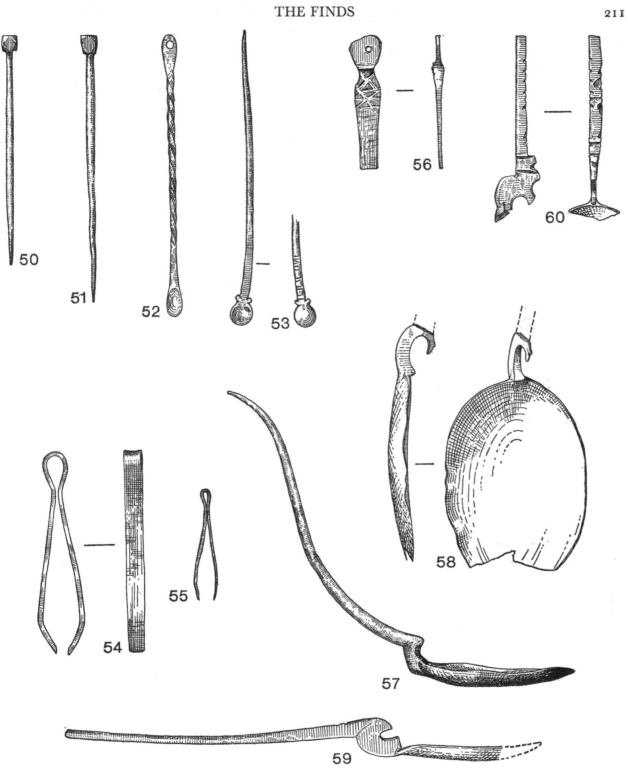

FIG. 113.   Bronze objects (pp. 210–12). Scale ⅔

incised cross superimposed on them. The functional tip of the object is lost. The loop is in the same plane as the blade. Cf. *Richborough V*, pl. XLIII, no. 176.

Trench 70 layer 14 (311): pit 63.

## Spoons

57. Simple bronze spoon with a silvered bowl. The bowl is oval and the greater wear appears to be at the end and suggests a shovelling action on the part of a right-handed user. There is a roughly incised X on the back of the bowl.

Trench 73 layer 10 (505): general layer.

58. The oval bowl of a bronze spoon.

Trench 3 layer 3 (2): general layer behind west wall.

59. Bronze spoon with the bowl in a fragmentary state. The handle is decorated with transverse mouldings.

Trench 63 layer 6 (162): general layer.

60. Fragment of a bronze spoon, comprising the lower part of the handle and a small part of the bowl. The handle is ornamented with transverse and lozengic mouldings.

Trench 107 layer 15 (2343): pit 213 (post-Roman).

For spoons with oval bowls cf. *Fishbourne II*, fig. 47, 122–3; *Lydney*, fig. 19, 89; *Shakenoak I*, fig. 39, 39 (late fourth/early fifth century); for an example in silver, see British Museum *Guide to the Antiquities of Roman Britain*, 1964, fig. 18, 8.

In addition to the four illustrated examples, eight others have been recovered: (2450) upper clay; (2203) general layer; (421) general layer; (1337) layer immediately above or cutting upper Roman road surface; (700) general layer; (269) general layer; (2575) general layer.

## Miscellaneous Objects

61. Bronze bucket mount in the form of an ox-head. Above the head extends a large bronze ring to secure the handle, while behind it is a heavy flange of bronze to fit over the bucket rim; below the snout is a smaller bronze ring whereby the mount was riveted to the bucket. The ox-head itself is somewhat stylized. The unknobbed horns project forward from the brow and are curved upwards almost at right angles to stand straight up. A fillet or band around the animal's head just below the horns is represented by a light ridge of bronze defined by incised lines. Immediately below this fillet are the oval raised eyes, each with a pierced hole representing the pupil. The slender snout widens slightly at the nose and two pairs of diagonal indented lines represent the nostrils. An ox-head bucket mount from Shakenoak was found in association with late fourth-century material (*Shakenoak I*, p. 83, fig. 27, 1). For a general discussion of ox-head bucket mounts see Hawkes, 1951 and Toynbee, 1964, 21–2.

Trench 89 layer 8 (1117): general layer.

62. Cross-bar and suspension handle of a small weighing scales. One end of the cross-bar is lost and the whole is bent badly out of shape. Cf. *Richborough II*, pl. XXI, fig. 2, 56.

Trench 99 layer 18 (1885): general layer.

63. Fish hook. Cf. *Wroxeter III*, pl. XXI, fig. 2, 5.

Trench 91 layer 52 (1293): layer above upper road.

64. Stylus with the point and scraper lost. The panel of ornament consists of a longitudinal groove

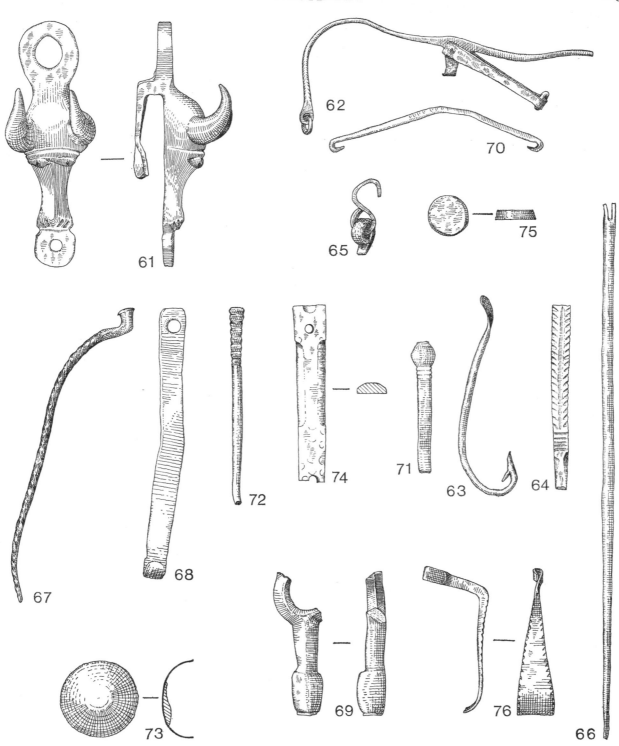

FIG. 114.   Bronze objects (pp. 212–15). Scale $\frac{2}{3}$

flanked by diagonal indented lines down the edges of the stylus. The panel terminates in a series of transverse indented grooves.

Trench 63 layer 9 (168): pit 47.

65. Two links from a bronze chain; each link is beaten into a flat strip and formed into an S-shape. Cf. *Richborough IV*, pl. XXXV, 91, although the Portchester chain links are more substantial than the Richborough necklace and may have served a functional purpose.

Trench 79 layer 60 (893): pit 121.

66. A needle of stout construction and considerable length; the eye now comprises two prongs and may always have been so. Cf. *Leicester: Jewry Wall*, fig. 89, 18 which, it is suggested, was probably a netting needle; also *Fishbourne II*, fig. 52, 177.

Trench 63 layer 5 (144): general layer.

67. A handle of cast bronze, worked in imitation of twisted strands of bronze and having a knobbed terminal.

Trench 99 layer 64 (1940): general layer.

68. A bronze fitting, a narrow strip of cast bronze with a rivet hole at one end, the other folded.

Trench 66 layer 5 (221): general layer.

69. A bronze fitting broken at both ends, perhaps originally a key.

Trench 69 layer 7 (417): general layer.

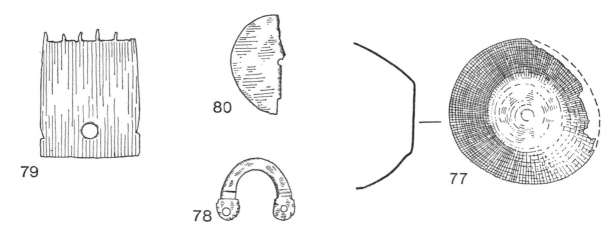

FIG. 115.   Bronze objects (p. 215). Scale $\frac{2}{3}$

70. A bronze strip ornamented in the centre with transverse grooving and with each end turned back to form a hook. It is perhaps a staple.

Trench 71 layer 6 (400): general layer.

71. A pin or nail with flattened ovoid cross-section. The head is knobbed and there are traces of triple-ridged mouldings at the collar. The pin/nail is crude and was perhaps more functional than decorative. Cf. for example, *Leicester: Jewry Wall*, fig. 89, 6.

Trench 103 layer 23 (2279): upper occupation.

72. Pin? with a shaft of rounded rectilinear cross-section, flattened at the head, which is ornamented with transverse ridged mouldings.

Trench 76 layer 4 (484): general layer.

73. Hollow boss.

Trench 99 layer 44 (1924): general layer.

74. Bronze fitting.
    Trench 100 layer 28 (2081): general layer.
75. Bronze disc.
    Trench 108 layer 138 (2504): general layer.
76. Bronze fitting decorated with notched ornament along the external edges.
    Trench 74 layer 4 (609): general layer.
77. Hollow boss of thin bronze.
    Trench 101 layer 94 (2244): general layer.
78. Bronze link.
    Trench 108 + (2597): unstratified.
79. Rectangular panel of bronze with the remains of five teeth projecting from one of the two shorter sides; the plate is pierced with a circular hole close to the centre of the opposite shorter side and level with this piercing on each of the two longer sides is a notch. A hoard of similar objects was found at Chalton, Hants, in a pot of fourth century date. It is possible that they represent the end of either a specialized form of weaving comb or a leather pricker.
    Trench 87 layer 9 (1027): layer above upper Roman road surface.
80. Half a bronze disc with a central piercing.
    Trench 5 layer 3 (24): occupation against the west wall of the fort.

# OBJECTS OF BONE AND ANTLER

## by Janet Webster

*The Pins*

(a) Pin with a plain cone-shaped head:

81. The knobbed head of the pin is drawn up to a pointed tip. The pin has irregular facets and a shank swelling. The shaft is abruptly cut away to form the pin. Cf. for example: *York: The Mount*, p. 306, fig. 14, 90 h, j; *Shakenoak IV*, p. 143, fig. 72, 122.
    Trench 32 layer 12 (37) in guard chamber of east gate. Similar example: (104) general layer.

(b) Pins with a plain cone-shaped head and single collar moulding:

82. The bulbous head is shaped up to a pointed tip and is separated from the pin itself by a flanged collar. The knob has no detailed ornamentation. The body of the pin is faceted irregularly and there is a swelling in the shank.
    Trench 91 layer 46 (1321): above upper road.
83. Similar to the last. The pin lacks a shank swelling.
    Trench 33 layer 9 (38): occupation layer associated with west gate.
84. Similar to nos. 82–3 but the head is longer and thinner. There is no swelling in the shank of the pin and the whole has been fashioned from a curved bone.
    Trench 79 layer 68 (936): pit 121.
85. Similar to nos. 82–4 but the collar moulding is wider and is ornamented with diagonal cuts. Cf. *Shakenoak II*, p. 125, fig. 53, 24, 25.
    Trench 99 layer 64 (1943): general layer.

This is by far the most prolific type of bone pin from Portchester. Altogether 27 are recorded including the four listed above: (639) pit 86; (894), (900), (905), (910), (938), (940) from pit 121; (2294), (2552), (2585) lower occupation; (2439), (2443), (2455), (2551), (2598) middle occupation; (2410) upper occupation; (1345) below upper road; (1246) above upper road; (1294) above upper make-up; (1) occupation behind west wall; (267), (1961), (2207), (2275) general layers. The head may vary from the very bulbous form rising only to a slight tip, as in no. 82 above, to the much more elegant, elongated form of no. 84. At Richborough the type is noted as common (see *Richborough II*, pl. XIX, 23) and further parallels can be quoted from Gatcombe, Somerset (*Gatcombe* 1965–6, fig. 41, 13) with a fourth-century date and from Leicester (*Leicester: Jewry Wall*, fig. 90, 11). See also *Shakenoak I*, p. 111, fig. 37, 7–10 and *Shakenoak II*, p. 125, fig. 53, 20–5, for pins of the same general type but with collar mouldings less pronounced than the Portchester examples. From the numbers in which this type of pin occurs at Portchester it seems likely to have been of local manufacture and indeed pit 121 seems to include the deposited remnant of such activities.

Bone pins frequently have shanks which swell out in profile centrally or in their upper or lower portions; it seems curious that this 'hipping' of pin shanks which presumably derives naturally from the technique of manufacture of bone pins (as well as jet ones) and which is common in late Roman Britain, should not appear in other materials such as bronze, for example, until the seventh century.

### (c) Pins with a cone-shaped head and multiple collar mouldings:

86. This is similar to the pins with plain cone-shaped head and single collar moulding, but the pin has two transverse mouldings at the collar. The grooves separating the cone and the mouldings from each other have not been cut to an equal depth all round and at one point there is no division between the moulding and the cone. Cf. *Leicester: Jewry Wall*, p. 265, 1; *Shakenoak I*, p. 111, 10 (third century) and 9 (fourth century).
   Trench 67 layer 4 (225): general layer.
87. A somewhat debased form of the type. The cone is small and rounded and below it are three large transverse mouldings. The cone and mouldings are not circular, as in the other examples, but the mouldings in particular are drawn out and have an oblong cross-section. Cf. *Leicester: Jewry Wall*, p. 265, 3.
   Trench 100 layer 39 (2089): general layer.

One other example is recorded: (2456) middle occupation.

### (d) Pins with a cuboid faceted-knob head:

88. The knob of the pin takes the form of a rough cube from which the corners have been cut away to leave four lozenge-shaped facets interspersed above and below by triangular facets.
   Trench 88 layer 6 (1011): above upper make-up.
89. Similar to the last. The knob is broader in one direction than the other and as a result two of the lozenge-shaped facets are broad, while the other two are narrow. The pin is faceted.
   Trench 34 layer 18 (39): in guard chamber of east gate.
90. Similar to nos. 88–9.
   Trench 70 layer 37 (323): pit 65.

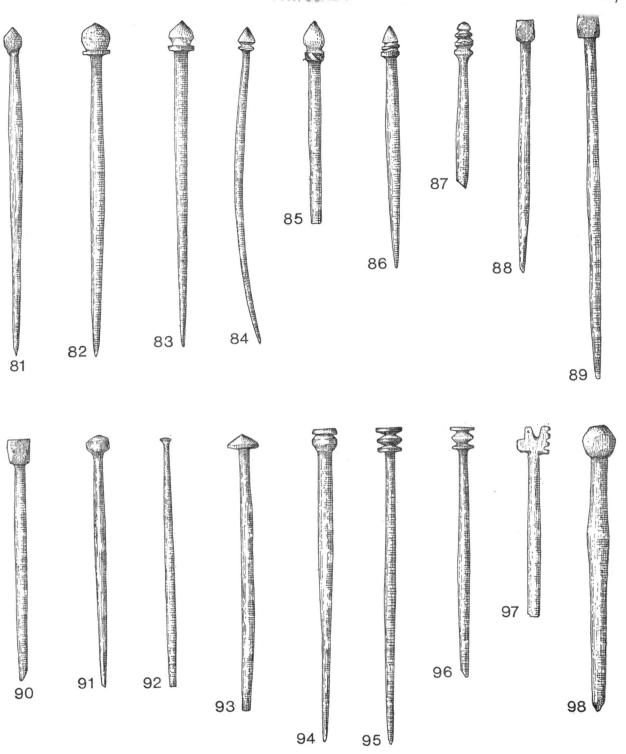

FIG. 116. Bone pins (pp. 215–18). Scale 2/3

Pins similar to nos. 88–90 occur on other sites, e.g. *Lydney*, p. 85, fig. 18, 70–4 (jet, shale and bone parallels); *Richborough IV*, pl. LIII, nos. 199 and 201 (in bronze); *Eboracum*, pl. 69, 11 and 16 (in jet).

Three similar pins are not illustrated: (132), (1361), (2166) from general layers.

91.  Pin with a knobbed head, not dissimilar from those with cuboid faceted knobs.
      Trench 88 layer 74 (1101): general layer.

## (e) Nail-headed pins:

92.  The pin has a tiny, flat head. Cf. *Shakenoak I*, p. 111, fig. 37, 12.
      Trench 65 layer 5 (193): general layer.
93.  Similar to the last but the broad head rises to a point.
      Trench 100 layer 84 (2202): pit 201.
Two other examples are recorded: (2543) pit 223; (2561) pit 227.

## (f) Pins with heads comprising transverse mouldings:

94.  The head comprises a bulbous moulding surmounted by a narrow flat moulding.
      Trench 102 layer 79 (2136): pit 195.
95.  The head comprises three narrow transverse mouldings of graduated size.
      Trench 108 layer 163 (2553): middle occupation.
96.  Two narrow transverse mouldings are separated by a broader similar moulding to form the head of this pin. Cf. *Shakenoak I*, p. 111, 13.
      Trench 108 layer 212 (2549): pit 227.

Two other examples are recorded: (2544) middle occupation; (2560) pit 227.

## Other pins:

97.  Bone pin with flat carved head. Cf. *Leicester: Jewry Wall*, p. 265, 15 and 17.
      Trench 71 layer 8 (362): general layer.
98.  Pin with a large rounded knob, with some faint traces of faceting and with a marked shank swelling. The pointed lower tip of the pin is cut away very sharply on one side, with very minor shaping on the other faces.
      Trench 98 layer 34 (1969): pit 163.

### *Bracelets*

99.  Curved strip of bone. Each end of the fragment is pierced by a hole, one hole occurring in the midst of the decoration, the other in a plain panel, the latter coloured green from contact with corroding bronze. The cross-section of the bone is of round D-form and the rounded face is ornamented with two rows of indented line notches alternating one with the other from the outer edges. The fragment may be part of a fairly large bracelet; this was perhaps made up in sections with at least one bronze link or perhaps the bracelet broke in wear and was repaired by means of a fastening secured through the holes in the ornamented section.
      Trench 102 layer 63 (2147): middle occupation.

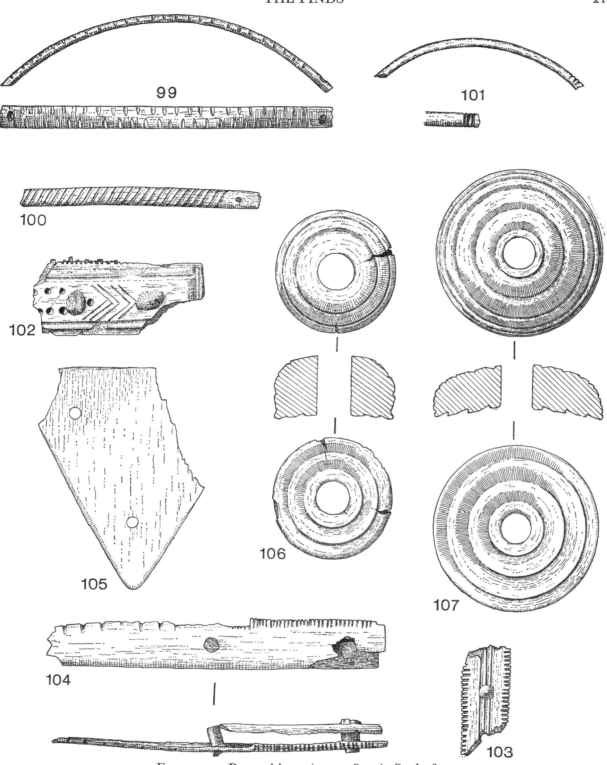

FIG. 117. Bone objects (pp. 218–20). Scale ⅔

100. Fragment of a bone bracelet of rounded D cross-section. The curved outer face is ornamented with diagonal incised lines throwing into relief diagonal ridges. The whole gives an effect similar to a spirally twisted bronze wire bracelet. One end of the fragment terminates in a plain oblong panel pierced by a hole by means of which a bronze fastening was secured to the terminal; part of this bronze clasp remains extant.

   Trench 108 layer 194 (2557): pit 225.

101. Fragment of bone bracelet, plain except for two transverse ridged mouldings with flanking and intervening indentations.

   Trench 63 layer 14 (183): pit 48.

Fragments of three others are recorded: (305) pit 63; (1158) layer above upper make-up; (1314) pit 130a.

### Combs

102. The remaining part of the comb comprises part of an outer decorated strip of bone pierced by two iron rivets which secure the only two remaining bone tooth panels. The corresponding outer rectangular strip to secure the tooth panels from the other side is lost and the teeth are missing. Each of the tooth panels afforded teeth to either side of the medial panel. The decoration on the remaining outer strip comprises drilled dot and incised diagonal line ornament on the central panel between the rivets while the edges have carved linear margins. Cf. *Richborough III*, pl. XIII, 42; *Richborough IV*, pl. LIV, 216 (*c.* A.D. 400 and described as 'a normal late Roman type').

   Trench 71 layer 32 (353): pit 77.

103. Similar in construction to the last. Only one tooth panel remains and again only one decorative outer strip. The lines of the teeth were continued on to the medial panel in the form of cuts along its edges, presumably implying that the comb was assembled before the teeth were cut (cf. *Dinas Powys*, p. 154). The centre of the panel was decorated with line ornament.

   Trench 101 layer 46 (2218): general layer.

104. A similar comb to those above but in several fragments. The two outer panels remain, the tooth panels are lost. One of the outer panels has along one edge only the cut marks made when the teeth were cut out. These cut marks seem to show that in this instance a panel of widely spaced teeth and a panel of closely spaced teeth lay adjacent to each other on the same side of the comb.

   Trench 73 layer 10 (503): general layer.

### Objects connected with Spinning and Weaving

105. Part of a triangular bone plate pierced with a hole in each of the remaining two angles. Used for the tablet weaving of braids. Cf. *Verulamium I*, p. 153, fig. 55, 204 (an example dated A.D. 360–70); *Richborough IV*, pl. LVI, 267; Wild, 1970, 73ff. and figs. 63 and 66.

   Trench 88 layer 35 (1055): pit 125b.

106. Spindlewhorl with concentric incised line ornament on the domed surface and sides and with further similar decoration on its flat face. Cf. Wild, 1970, pl. IIIb and pp. 32ff. for a discussion of spindlewhorls.

   Trench 107 layer 41 (2405): upper occupation.

107. Spindlewhorl decorated with concentric incised lines, widely spaced on its domed surface and closely spaced on the sides. Similar rings on the concave under-surface of the whorl throw into high relief intervening strips of bone.

   Trench 89 layer 21 (1141): layer above make-up.

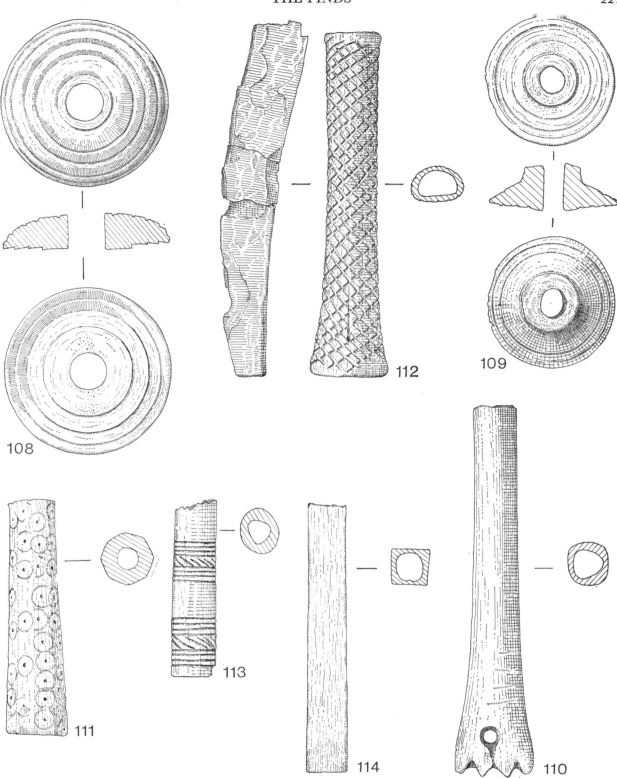

FIG. 118. Bone objects (p. 222). Scale ⅔

108. Similar to the above but the lower surface is flat with projecting circular panels of bone.
    Trench 89 layer 21 (1163): layer above make-up.

109. Spindlewhorl. It is flat underneath and rises to a central cone above. Incised circular line decoration.
    Trench 63 layer 9 (195): pit 47.

110. Metapodial of a sheep or goat, hollowed longitudinally at the proximal end to receive some sort of implement, and pierced transversely at the other end with a circular hole. The object seems closely related to bone bobbins of Iron Age type. Cf. *Glastonbury II*, pp. 421ff.; *Maiden Castle*, pl. XXXV A, pp. 306–7. For the interpretation of such an object as a bobbin used to carry thread between spinning and warping see Wild, 1970, 34. Such an interpretation would require the insertion of a pin into the longitudinal hollowing of the bone, the circular piercing serving to secure the end of the thread. For a closely similar example of unidentified use see *Bourton-on-the-Water*, p. 118, fig. 10, 7.
    Trench 71 layer 8 (345): general layer.

## Handles

111. Tapering handle of approximately circular cross-section. The handle is faceted lengthwise and each facet bears ring-and-dot decoration.
    Trench 92 layer 20 (1398): general layer.

112. The handle is decorated by means of intersecting diagonal lines which throw lozenge shapes into relief. It was found in contact with fragments of considerably corroded bronze and the whole is perhaps the fragmentary remains of a clasp knife. Cf. *Richborough V*, pl. XLIX, 235–6 for bone handles similarly decorated.
    Trench 87 layer 27 (1111): above upper road surface.

113. The decoration on this handle comprises panels of straight transverse and diagonal incised lines, the panels being separated from each other by plain areas. Cf. *Richborough V*, pl. XLIX, 237, for a bone handle with similar ornament.
    Trench 62 layer 9 (151): general layer.

114. Handle of square external and circular internal cross-section tapering slightly.
    Trench 71 layer 7 (354): general layer.

115. Half a handle. The decoration consists of bands of incised lines.
    Trench 69 layer 8 (276): general layer.

116. Part of a handle. Fragments of iron adhere to the inside of the handle. The bone is grooved close to the end and fragments of a band of metal remain in the groove. Adjacent to this groove on one side is a raised panel of bone with deep diagonal incisions widely spaced; a wide shallow groove separates this panel from a slight marginal ridge at the end of the handle. Adjacent to the filled groove on the opposite side from the raised panel is slight indented line ornament.
    Trench 94 layer 93 (1643): general layer.

117. Probably part of a handle. The decoration consists of panels widely spaced between double ring-and-dot decoration, separated by lengthwise bands ornamented by short diagonal lines in the form of inverted Vs; one such lengthwise band has an additional incised line dividing it longitudinally.
    Trench 91 layer 32 (1669): general layer.

118. Probably a fragment of a handle. The decoration consists of evenly spaced shallow transverse grooves separated by light ridges.
    Trench 63 layer 14 (177): pit 48.

119. Very similar to the last.
    Trench 62 layer 5 (153): general layer.

120. Half a handle with incised line ornament at one end.
    Trench 91 layer 46 (1475): above upper road surface.

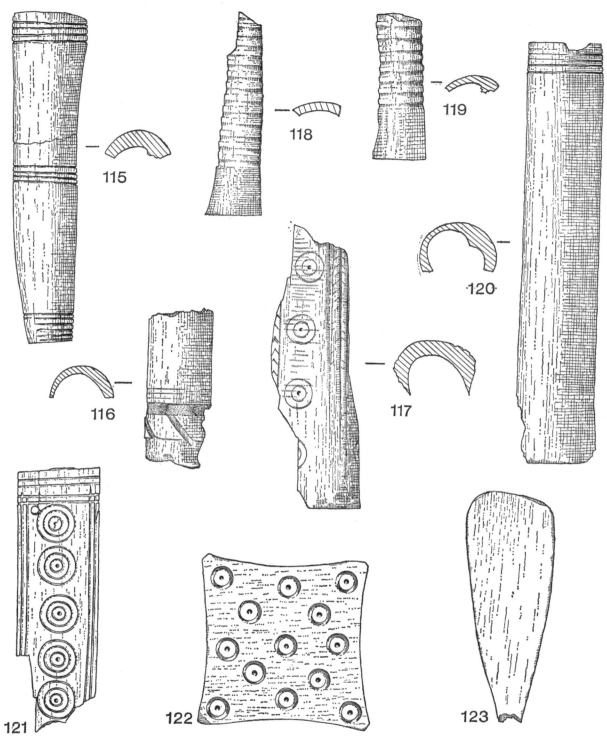

FIG. 119.   Bone objects (pp. 222–4). Scale ⅔

*Miscellaneous Bone Objects*

121. A rectangular strip of thin bone, ornamented with a row of triple ring-and-dot decoration in the centre and with narrow double margins along the long edges defined by incised lines; the extant short end has further margins similarly defined. A hole is pierced through the strip close to the beginning of the ring-and-dot decoration and this will have housed a small bone peg for attachment. It is part of the inlay of a box or casket. Cf. *Richborough IV*, pl. LVII, 276; *Richborough V*, pls. LXI–LXII, 225.

  Trench 88 layer 5 (998): above upper road surface.

122. Plaque of lozenge shape ornamented with incised ring-and-dot arranged with one motif in each corner, one in the centre and the rest grouped to form a rough square around the central ring and dot. There is no means of attaching this piece of rather thick bone to any other object. It may have been a gaming counter.

  Trench 79 layer 60 (898): pit 121.

123. Fragment of shaped bone.

  Trench 87 layer 9 (1003): above upper road surface.

*Objects of Antler*

124. A large curved handle which presumably once supported a substantial iron knife blade. A slot was cut into the antler to accommodate the tang of the knife blade and this tang was secured to the handle by means of rivets. The handle is broken close to the innermost point of the tang, at the rivet hole, and beyond this point only half of the handle remains, the other half and the implement it secured being lost.

  Trench 79 layer 33 (2290): pit 103.

125. Fragment of deerhorn, faceted and polished. A similarly shaped piece of solid bone occurs at Richborough (*Richborough IV*, pl. LVI, 273) but it is ornamented with ring-and-dot decoration and fitted with rings for suspension. It has been suggested that the Richborough object may have served as a talisman in the form of a pendant and that it may be akin to the crescentic ornaments formed of boars' tusks united by bronze mountings which were a feature of the horse trappings of the late Romano-barbarian cavalry. If the Portchester example is another instance of the Richborough pendant-type it must be thought of as unfinished. Cf. *Richborough IV*, 151; Hawkes and Dunning, 1961, 29–30.

  Trench 95 layer 148 (1989): general layer.

126. Ring cut from an antler tine: roughly whittled.

  Trench 95 layer 151 (2649): pit 144.

Other objects of antler not drawn but shown in pl. XXXIII include:

(a) Pair of tines cut from the skull below the burr. The burr end has been perforated. Both tines show signs of wear.

  Trench 98 layer 75: general layer.

(b) Tine sawn from shaft and cut roughly to a square section. Possibly it was intended to be a pick-like tool.

  Trench 102 layer 88 (2251): pit 206.

(c) Tine sawn from a shaft. The shaft stub is perforated obliquely. The tine partly squared, its tip showing signs of wear.

  Trench 107 layer 52 (2460): middle occupation.

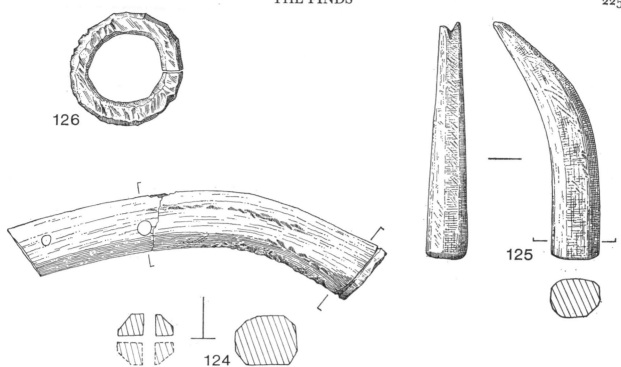

FIG. 120.   Antler objects (p. 224). Scale $\frac{2}{3}$

(d)    Strip cut from an antler.
          Trench 91 layer 67 (1366): layer below upper road surface.
(e)    End of a tine smoothed by use.
          Trench 91 layer 46: layer immediately above road surface.
(f)    End of a tine showing some signs of wear.
          Trench 107 layer 53 (2436): middle clay.
(g)    End of a tine whittled and notched at the end.
          Trench 88 layer 103: pit 135.
(h–k) Fragments of tines showing signs of sawing and whittling.
          Trench 102 layer 46: upper occupation.
          Trench 107 layer 31: upper occupation.
          Trench 98 layer 74: general layer.
          Trench 88 layer 100: general layer.

Not illustrated are fragments of antler showing marks of sawing and cutting from:

          Trench 108 layer 163: middle occupation.
          Trench 89 layer 38: layer above make-up.
          Trench 78 layer 15: pit 103.
          Trench 108 layer 72: upper occupation.
          Trench 88 layer 103: pit 135.
          Trench 91 layer 46: layer immediately above road surface.
          Trench 108 layer 90: upper occupation.
          Trench 108 layer 99: upper occupation.

# OBJECTS OF SHALE

## by Janet Webster

*Spindlewhorls*

127. An undecorated example.
Trench 88 layer 10 (1030): above upper make-up.
128. An incised line describes a circle concentric with and a short way from the central drilled hole on each face.
Trench 74 layer 69 (679): pit 94.
129. A circle similar to that described above (see no. 128) occurs on both faces of this spindlewhorl and each face is slightly concave within the area thus defined. The point of maximum girth is ornamented with two incised lines encircling the object. Cf. *Maiden Castle*, p. 320, fig. 111, 21 for no. 129 and nos. 130–2 below.
Trench 89 layer 82 (1229): pit 130a.
130. The whorl has similar incised circles as those described above (nos. 128–9) with dished areas within those circles. Again two incised lines encircle the whorl at the point of maximum girth. See no. 129 above.
Trench 91 layer 63 (1344): general layer.
131. Similar to no. 130 but without the concavity about the central piercing and without lines at the maximum girth point. The whorl is in poor condition. Traces of cutting radiate out from the drill hole on one face. It has been in contact with fire. See no. 129 above.
Trench 79 layer 68 (929): general layer.
132. The spindlewhorl has only one face extant; the other has been severely damaged. A lightly incised line describes a circle on the one remaining face; within this line is a lightly ridged margin with a central depression. See no. 129 above.
Trench 62 layer 5 (163): general layer.

In addition to the six examples illustrated a further six have been recovered: (35) occupation near landgate; (412) from pit 63; (337), (582), (1415), (1972) general layers.

*Bracelets*

133. Plain bracelet, probably for a child, or perhaps a hair-ring. Cf. *Maiden Castle*, p. 320, fig. 111, 17–19 (late Roman); *Verulamium I*, p. 155, fig. 57, 225 (early fourth century). For a selection of shale bracelets of late third- to early fifth-century date see ibid., pp. 153–5.
Trench 98 layer 70 (1992): pit 164.
134. Plain bracelet.
Trench 99 layer 59 (1923): general layer.
135. Plain, heavy bracelet.
Trench 88 layer 10 (1037): general layer.
136. Bracelet with central grooving and corresponding faceting.
Trench 88 layer 10 (1031): general layer.
137. The ornament here comprises two markedly ridged mouldings defined and separated from each other by incised lines.
Trench 89 layer 21 (1388): above upper make-up.

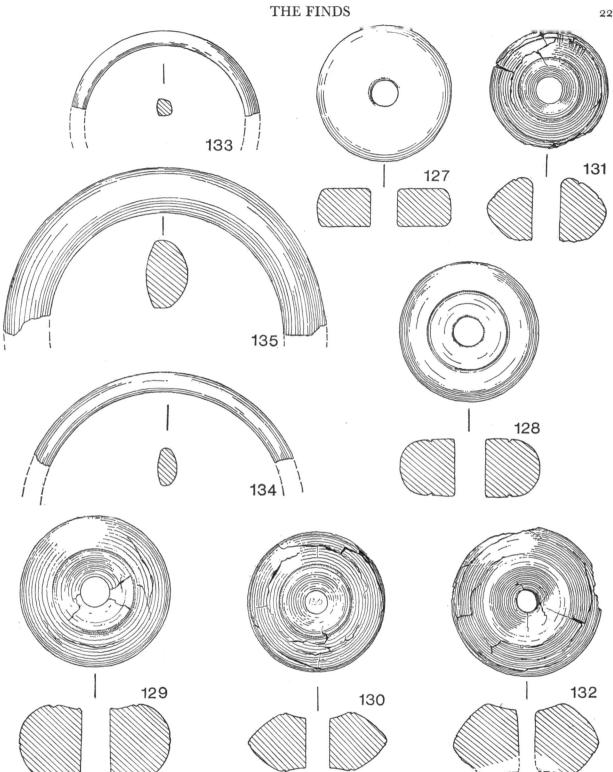

FIG. 121.   Shale objects (p. 226). Scale ⅔

138. The underside and side surfaces of the bracelet are faceted. The upper side is rounded and has a lightly incised groove running along its centre. From each edge, pairs of short, diagonal, incised lines form corresponding chevron patterns on each side of the central line.

Trench 87 layer 9 (1022): above upper road surface.

139. Heavy, curved, ornamented fragment of shale. The object would be readily interpreted as a bracelet but for the smooth flat facet curiously placed so as not to correspond with that facet of a bracelet which would be worn next to the skin. It is in fact placed so that it would be exposed on the side of the bracelet when in use. The flat facet would be more appropriate if the fragment were of sufficiently large curvature to have been part of a necklet. It is possible that the object may have been a handle. The ornament comprises two sets of diagonal incised lines extending from the flat facet over the rounded part of the object but not meeting in the centre. Between each pair of diagonal lines a broad ridge of shale remains which widens into a lozenge between the tips of the diagonal cuts; the rounded profile of the object is flattened along these lozenges.

Trench 11 layer 3 (33): occupation layer near landgate.

Shale bracelets are particularly common at Portchester: altogether fragments of 37 examples have been found. With the exception of the illustrated specimens all were plain and of circular or D-shaped cross-section. Where it was possible to assess diameter they varied from 5 to 8 cm. internally.

(244) pit 61; (302) pit 64; (618) pit 83; (1962), (1968) pit 178; (2228) pit 206; (2608) pit 235; (11), (14), (15) layers against the west wall; (2120) middle occupation; (1304) below upper make-up; (2518) upper occupation; (2459) upper clay; (1026) above upper road; (142), (157), (277), (380), (501), (519), (928), (1308), (1358), (1855), (2079), (2284), (2519), (2546), (2578) general layers.

## Beads

140. Shale bead.

Trench 69 layer 8 (274): general layer.

141. Bead pierced with two holes, flat underneath and with a circular incised line ornament on the front face separating the rounded outer margin from the central domed area. Cf. *Lydney*, fig. 18, 77 and p. 84.

Trench 108 layer 93 (2496): general layer.

## Vessels

142. A fragment of a bowl with a footring. There is a small hollowed circle in the base close to the footring; this hole will be one of the several whereby the bowl was fixed to the lathe by means of a pronged chuck (cf. *Cranborne Chase I*, p. 139). On the inside of the bowl there are rough widely spaced grooves encircling the base. The bowl will have had a total diameter of approximately 17 cm. with a base of 8 cm. diameter.

Trench 77 layer 5 (743): general layer.

143. Wide mouthed jar or bowl. Diameter 16 cm.

Trench 88 layer 10 (1390): above upper make-up.

144. Bowl or wide-mouthed jar. Diameter 20 cm.

Trench 69 layer 28 (308): general layer.

145. Part of the circular base with abraded footring of a shale vessel. The outer side of the footring is grooved. The diameter of the base is about 8 cm.

Trench 71 layer 8 (338): general layer.

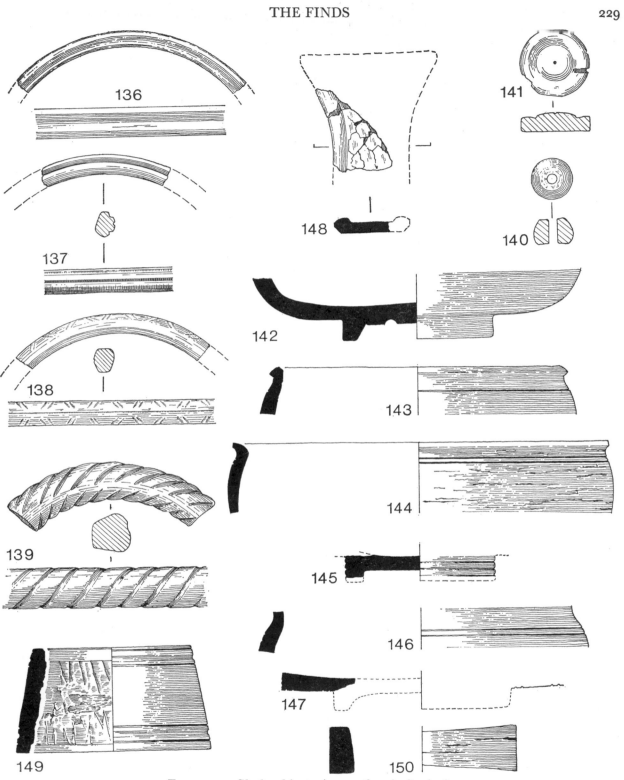

FIG. 122.   Shale objects (pp. 226–30). Scale ⅔

146. Fragments of shale from the shoulder of a vessel.
     Trench 58 layer 8 (222): general layer.
147. **Base** of a shale vessel. The underneath surface is decorated with encircling incised lines. The rough surface adjacent to the innermost set of incised lines seems likely to represent the position of a footring of *c.* 9 cm. diameter.
     Trench 99 layer 84 (1985): pit 185.
148. **Fragment** of a patera/skillet handle. The radius of the curve is *c.* 6·5 cm. Cf. *Cranborne Chase I*, pl. XLVIII, 5–6.
     Trench 62 layer 9 (141): general layer.

## Other Objects of Shale

149. Fragment of a circular band of shale. The object seems likely to have served as a slightly conical collar or binding, perhaps on a piece of furniture. The external surface is smooth and polished and close to the outer edge is a panel of ornament comprising a groove flanked by incised lines encircling the object. The radii of the two rims differ to the extent of 1 cm., being 4 and 5 cm. respectively. The interior of the object has a smooth upper and lower margin (each 0·50 cm. wide) at the rim but for the rest is very roughly cut, leaving a jagged uneven surface which can never have been intended to be seen, and has the appearance of being left rough deliberately to provide adhesion.
     Trench 63 layer 6 (161): general layer.
150. Curved fragment of shale broad at one end and tapering to a point.
     Trench 63 layer 7 (198): pit 46.

# OBJECTS OF GLASS (EXCLUDING VESSELS)

## by Margaret Guido

### Glass counters

151. Counter of green glass.
     Trench 45 layer 3 (51): general layer.
152. Half counter of blue glass.
     Trench 65 layer 5 (192): general layer.

### Glass Beads

The beads are all characteristic late Roman types well known from other sites in the country.

153. Bluish-green segment of a small round segmented bead.
     Trench 87 layer 44 (1133): above upper road surface.
154. Three segments, now in three parts, of a similar bead.
     Trench 91 layer 52 (1298): above upper road surface.
155. As above but darker green and one segment only.
     Trench 95 layer 151 (2650): pit 144.
156. As above; two segments of another, originally green.
     Trench 89 layer 48 (1413): general layer.

157. Bead of three irregular segments; greenish-blue.
   Trench 101 layer 46 (2171): general layer.
158. Two irregular segments; green.
   Trench 86 layer 11 (939): general layer.

These are all parts of small segmented beads of common late Roman type. The hill top site on Cold Kitchen Hill, Brixton Deverill, Wilts, produced several hundred of these and they are widely represented on late Roman sites.

159, 160. Both bluish-green, originally perhaps translucent cylinder beads. 159: length 11 mm., dia. 2 mm.; 160: somewhat larger. This again is a common Roman form.
   Trench 101 layer 86 (2240): general layer.
   Trench 91 layer 46 (1277): above upper road surface.
161. Almost opaque cobalt blue. This small bead has a diamond shaped section and appears still to retain a piece of wire.
   Trench 70 layer 4 (292): general layer.
162. Long biconical bead c. 10 mm. long in dull, almost opaque, blue glass. A common late Roman type.
   Trench 71 layer 8 (346): general layer.
163. As above.
   Trench 70 layer 14 (414): pit 63.
164. Small annular blue bead: diameter 10 mm., height 3 mm., perforation diameter 5 mm. A long-lasting type.
   Trench 75 layer 7 (691): general layer.

## GEMSTONE

### by MARTIN HENIG

165. (pl. XXXIIb) Red jasper intaglio, in good condition apart from chipping on left side of upper surface and around sides. The stone retains a high polish and cannot have sustained heavy wear. Flat, oval. 16·5 by 2 mm. The subject is Mercury standing towards the front and facing left.[1] He is nude apart from a drape over his left forearm. In his left hand he holds a caduceus and in his right a money-bag. The type is a very common one on intaglios.[2] The gem is boldly cut, although the workmanship is rather coarse. One is reminded of the products of the later Aquileian 'Officinae', notably the *Officina del Diaspri Rossi* and the *Officina delle Linee Grosse*.[3] The 'patterned' texture of the god's hair and the stylized musculature of the chest are characteristic of intaglios cut at the end of the second century and in the third century A.D.[4] Certainly the stone is not likely to date much later than the foundation of the Saxon Shore fort and it may, indeed, be earlier. The late Saxon

[1] Cast described.
[2] Cf. Henig in Cunliffe, *Fishbourne II*, 85, Type C; also *Archæol. Ael.* 4th ser., xlviii (1970), 147 and pl. XVI, no. 2. Note the Mercury facing right on a gem from Richborough; *Richborough I*, 46 and pl. XIV, no. 24.
[3] G. Sena Chiesa, *Gemme del Museo Nazionale di Aquileia* (Aquileia, 1966), 60–3 and pls. xci–xciii. As the name of the first 'Officina' suggests, red jasper was especially common in late Antonine and Severan times.
[4] Henig in *Archæol. Ael.* 4th ser., xlix (1971), 223–6. Note the Mercury from Richborough cited above.

plough soil in which it was found contained much redeposited Roman material, and there is
nothing to suggest that the gem was re-used at this period.[1]

Trench 90 layer 26 (1186): general layer.

# OBJECTS OF LEAD

## by JANET WEBSTER

166. Steelyard weight of lead with an iron attachment at the top for suspension. The weight is pear-
shaped and shows considerable signs of damage and frequent use. It now weighs approximately
1 lb. 13 oz. and will have originally represented 2½ Roman pounds.

Trench 65 layer 5 (182): general layer.

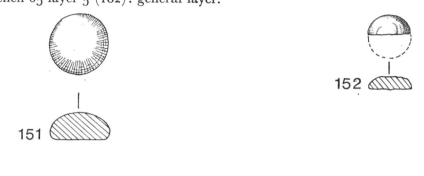

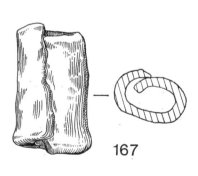

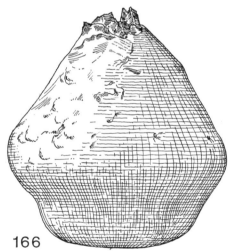

FIG. 123.   Objects of glass and lead (pp. 230–3). Scale ⅔

[1] For Roman gems in Saxon settings, cf. *Report of the
Proceedings of the Annual Meeting of the Trustees and Guardians of
Shakespeare's Birthplace* (24th April 1935): square-headed
brooch from Alveston set with a cornelian intaglio depicting
a cupid milking a goat; *Arch. Cant.* lxix; (1955), 24 and
pl. ix, 3: kidney-shaped attachment plate from Lyminge
with a red jasper intaglio showing Ceres (not Athene [*sic*] as
stated); *Archaeometry* ix (1966), 104–5 and fig. 1, no. L, 9:
gold pendant found at Canterbury set with a cornelian cut
with the figure of Minerva; *Archaeologia* l (1887), 404:
nicolo intaglio from Anglo-Saxon cemetery at Sleaford,
showing Minerva. This gem was found in the grave of an
adult and was *not* set.

167. Net weight made from a folded sheet of lead.
     Trench 63 layer 14 (2655): pit 48.

# OBJECTS OF IRON

## by JANET WEBSTER[1]

*Swords*

168. Sword tip.
     Trench 91 layer 52 (1299): gully 10 (cut through upper road).
169. Sword tip.
     Trench 90 layer 52 (1271): general layer.

*Ballista-bolt, Spear- and Arrow-heads*

170. Ballista bolt.
     Trench 79 layer 18 (768): general layer.
171. Spearhead with midrib and cleft socket. Cf. *Richborough I*, pl. XVI, no. 36.
     Trench 75 layer 22 (844): pit 95.
172–3. Spearheads.
     Trench 1: pit C (2658), (2659): pit 3.
174. Spearhead. For small spearheads in general see *Richborough IV*, pl. LVIII and LIX, pp. 152–4.
     Trench 101 layer 126 (2266): general layer.
175. Lightweight spearhead.
     Trench 62 layer 5 (150): general layer.
176. (Not illustrated.) Lightweight spearhead.
     Trench 103 layer 21 (2211): general layer.
177. Small spearhead. Cf. *Richborough IV*, pl. LIX, no. 290.
     Trench 70 layer 19 (299): pit 64.
178. Small spearhead or ballista arrow-head. Cf. *Richborough IV*, pl. LIX, nos. 297 and 299; *Maiden Castle*, p. 282, fig. 93, no. 3.
     Trench 69 layer 8 (270): general layer.
179. Small spear- or arrow-head.
     Trench 102 layer 48 (2104): upper occupation.

*Spurs*

180. Rivet spur. Enlarged plates at the ends of the arms each house two rivets to secure the spur to leather straps. The prick is long; it swells out half-way along its length, adopting a lozengic cross-section, and runs in four triangular facets to a sharp point. There is no heel-hook, usually a feature of the Roman rivet-spur (see Shortt, 1959). The spur was found in a Roman occupation level and although there is a possibility of later contamination, it is probable that the spur is of Roman date. Cf. a portion of a spur from Fishbourne (*Fishbourne II*, p. 135, fig. 60, no. 52; from the third period, A.D. 100–280). There is also a close parallel to the Portchester spur from Lydney Park, Gloucs., unpublished but displayed in the museum among the ironwork from the Roman

[1] I should like to thank Dr W. H. Manning for his help in the preparation of the iron report and for reading through the draft and making many helpful suggestions.

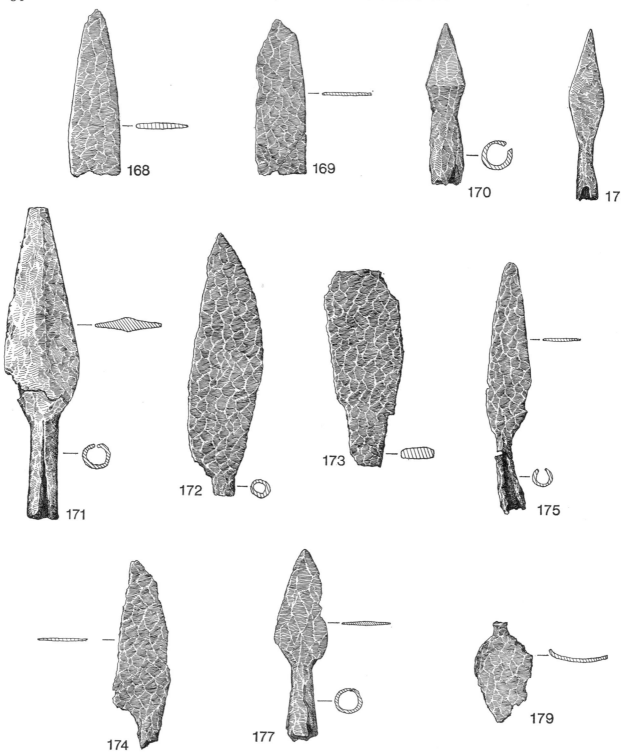

FIG. 124. Iron objects (p. 233). Scale $\frac{2}{3}$ except 168, 169 and 177, $\frac{1}{3}$

site. If the Lydney example is from the Roman site it would probably have a late fourth- to early fifth-century date, although there is always a possibility that it may be a stray from the medieval castle on the adjacent hill.

Trench 88 layer 5 (990): layer above make-up.

181. Rivet spur. Again secured to leather straps by two rivets at the end of each arm. The arms are curved. There is a long prick, similar in shape to no. 180 above but with a shorter tip. Again there is no heel-hook. From a Roman context but with the possibility of being a later intrusion.

Trench 73 layer 10 (531): general layer.

## Horseshoes

182. Complete horseshoe with regular curved outline. The ends are bent back to form calkins and there are three oblong nail holes on each side of the shoe, three with fragments of nails remaining in them. The shoe is from a Roman occupation level, possibly contaminated by later material, but a Roman date is acceptable for the shoe. Cf. late fourth- to early fifth-century stratified horseshoes from Maiden Castle (*Maiden Castle*, p. 290, pl. XXX, B).

Trench 68 layer 4 (260): general layer.

183. Complete horseshoe. The outline of the shoe expands slightly opposite each nail hole, to give a wavy outline. Cf. *Maiden Castle*, pl. XXX, B, no. 12 and p. 290. There are very slight calkins.

Trench 88 layer 5 (991): layer above make-up.

Another example, unillustrated, from trench 89 layer 58 (1320): below upper make-up; see also no. 241.

## Knives

184. Narrow-bladed knife with a solid handle.

Trench 87 layer 41 (1132): layer above upper road surface.

185. Knife with the blade and handle made in one piece. The end of the handle is curved round to form a loop. The cutting edge of the blade is curved but the line of the curve is not continued as far as the handle; the blade terminates at the handle in a diagonal line. The knife probably served as a small chopper.

Trench 63 layer 5 (210): general layer.

186. Knife with large tang. The cutting edge and the back of the blade are both straight.

Trench 87 layer 47 (1351): layer above upper road.

187. The tip of the blade is missing. There is a long tang. The cutting edge of the blade is straight.

Trench 90 layer 30 (1210): layer above make-up.

188. (Not illustrated.) Knife with straight cutting edge.

Trench 79 layer 60 (920a): pit 121.

189. Knife with straight cutting edge, curved back, and tang.

Trench 63 layer 5 (143): general layer.

190. Knife blade with a short portion of the tang missing.

Trench 68 layer 12 (272): pit 61.

191. Narrow knife blade with a straight cutting edge curving sharply upwards at the tip.

Trench 101 layer 41 (2234): general layer.

192. Small knife with a portion of the tang. The cutting edge describes a full curve from the tip of the blade to the tang. It is presumably a chopper.

Trench 88 layer 95 (1419): general layer.

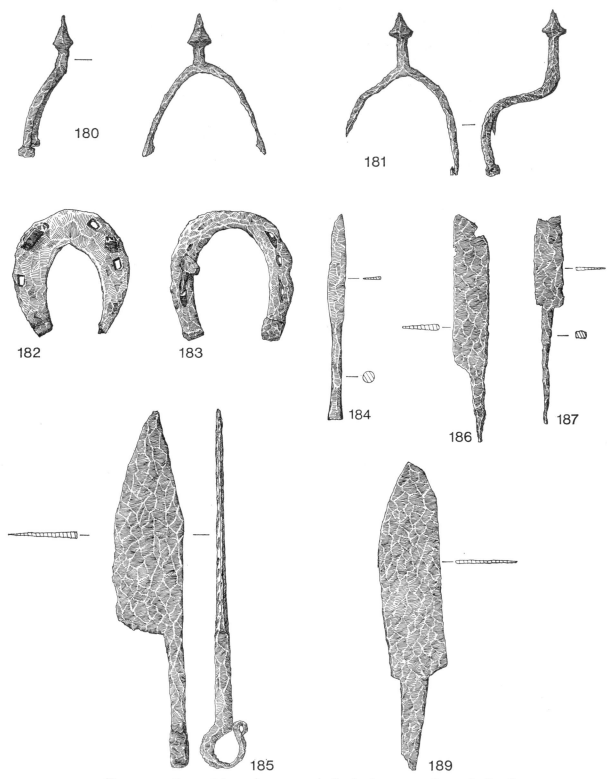

FIG. 125.   Iron objects (pp. 233–5). Scale ⅓ except 185 and 189, ⅔

193. Small knife with the tip of the blade missing.
     Trench 72 layer 35 (405): general layer.
194. The blade has a straight cutting edge with the back of the blade curved sharply to the tip. A
     considerable section of the tang remains. This may possibly be part of a pair of shears.
     Trench 79 layer 68 (932): pit 121.
195. Small knife.
     Trench 96 layer 37 (1771): general layer.
196. Knife, perhaps of a similar type to nos. 186 and 187 above, although it could also be a dagger.
     Trench 103 layer 87 (2295): lower occupation.
197. Perhaps a small chopper.
     Trench 91 layer 52 (1292): layer above upper make-up.
198. Knife.
     Trench 109 layer 115 (2636): pit 236.

## Cleaver

199. Socketed cleaver with the blade missing. Cf. Wheeler, 1946, pl. XXXIV, nos. 1 and 2.
     Trench 101 layer 94 (2245): general layer.

## Shears

For a brief discussion of Roman shears see *Verulamium I*, p. 176, nos. 44–5, fig. 65.

200. Fragment of shears, consisting of one blade and part of the spring.
     Trench 89 layer 38 (1177): layer above make-up.
201. Half a pair of shears comprising one blade and part of the spring. The length of the cutting blade
     is some 13 cm. and it is, therefore, not inconceivable that these were a sheep-shearing tool. Cf.
     Wild, 1970, 22–3.
     Trench 101 layer 94 (2212): general layer.
202. Fragment of shears comprising part of the shaft, the upper part of the blade and the lower pointed
     tip of the blade.
     Trench 109 layer 119 (2623): pit 236.
203. Further fragments of the same shears as no. 202, comprising the U-shaped spring and the upper
     part of the other blade.
     Trench 109 layer 119 (2644): pit 236.
204. The blade, shaft and beginning of the spring of half a pair of shears.
     Trench 71 layer 7 (325): general layer.

## Bucket Fittings

205. Bucket-handle mount, rounded and thickened at the top and tapering to a sharp point at the
     bottom where the tip bends inward at a right-angle to the plate itself, and served to secure the
     lower end of the mount to the bucket instead of the more normal nail. The top of the plate is
     pierced by a hole for the bucket handle, and a short way below this hole a substantial nail pierces
     the plate to bend upwards, on the inner side of the mount, at a right angle. The nail had in fact
     been partially withdrawn, hence the head is no longer flat against the outer side of the mount. The
     withdrawal of the nail was not successfully accomplished, however, and the fitting, although it
     must have been extracted from the abandoned bucket, was thrown away down the well. Cf.
     *Verulamium I*, p. 179, fig. 66, nos. 53–4; *Newstead*, pl. LXIX, no. 4.
     Trench 109 layer 120 (2640): pit 236.

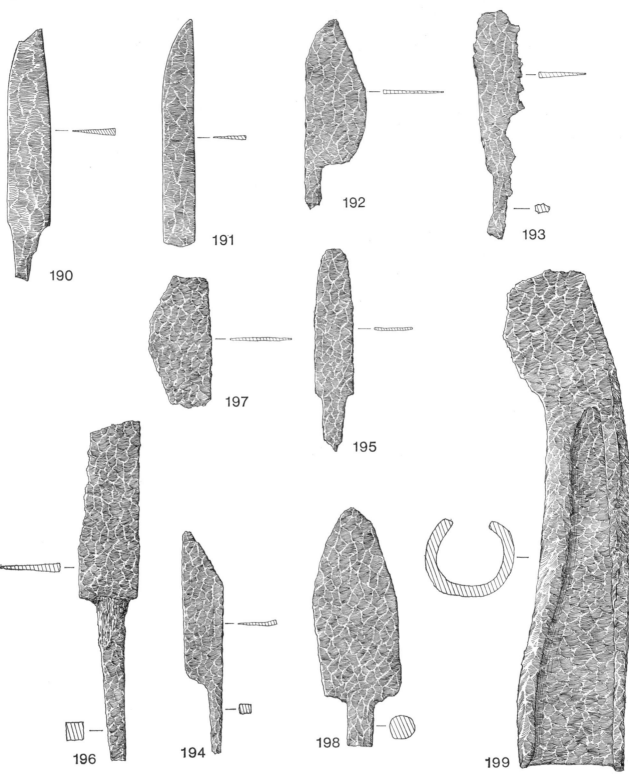

FIG. 126.   Iron objects (pp. 235–7). Scale $\frac{2}{3}$

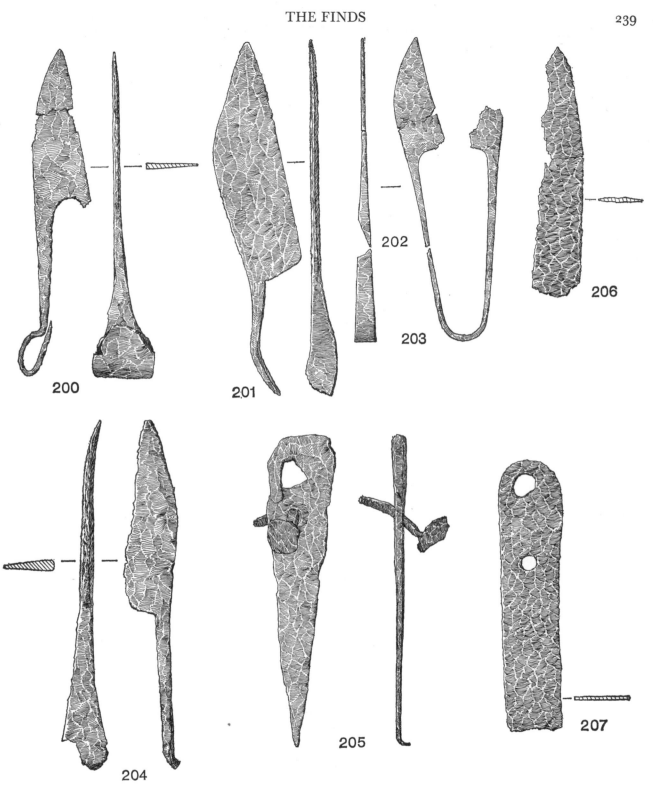

FIG. 127. Iron objects (pp. 237–40). Scale ⅔ except 200, ⅓

206. Bucket-handle mount.
     Trench 91 layer 44 (1260): general layer.
207. Bucket-handle mount.
     Trench 109 layer 118 (2641): pit 236.
208. Rim of a bucket with a loop for the handle. It is probably from a leather bucket.
     Trench 74 layer 24 (646): pit 85.
209. Bucket handle with a hook at the lower end for attachment to the bucket. It widens out towards the top centre of the handle to provide a grip.
     Trench 109 layer 121 (2633): pit 236.
210. Iron tie for use in carpentry. Two plates, of rectangular form with rounded ends, were pierced by two nails, each driven in from the opposite side and close to the ends of the plates. Only one plate now remains intact with a fragment of the other extant. It seems likely that this was a device used for securing a joint between two pieces of wood; cf. the method suggested for securing the joint of a wheel (*Newstead*, pl. LXIX, fig. 2 and 2*b*) although the Portchester tie suggests the use of a plate to front and back of the joint, not merely on one face as the Newstead diagram suggests. The size of the Portchester tie suggests that it was for use on a small object although the thickness of the wood must have been in the vicinity of 1·8 cm. It is not inconceivable that this object may too be associated with the construction or repair of a bucket.
     Trench 109 layer 119 (2645): pit 236.

## Tools

211. Paring chisel.
     Trench 79 layer 60 (919): pit 121.
212. Awl, with the point intact. The other end will have been set into a handle.
     Trench 100 layer 66 (2134): general layer.
213. Awl.
     Trench 102 layer 60 (2122): middle occupation.
214. Draw knife.
     Trench 80 layer 7 (834): general layer.
215. Iron bar with a wide head. The upper part of the shaft is of rectangular cross-section while, at the lower end, the shaft flattens and widens slightly. It is probably a chisel. Cf. *Newstead*, pl. LIX, no. 4.
     Trench 95 layer 92 (1736): pit 144.
216. Drill. Cf. *Cranborne Chase I*, pl. XXIX, no. 9 and p. 89.
     Trench 100 layer 33 (2067): pit 138.
217. Leaf hook.
     Trench 108 layer 111 (2520): upper clay.

## Locks and Keys

218. The mechanism of a barb-spring padlock. The three teeth are extant and spring barbs remain on two of the teeth and will have been attached to the third also. The hasp has been squashed down. For the workings of this type of lock see *Verulamium I*, p. 181 and the British Museum *Guide to the Antiquities of Roman Britain*, 1964, fig. 41, lower. The barb-spring padlock is common. Compare, for instance, five examples from Shakenoak: *Shakenoak I*, p. 103, fig. 34, nos. 1 and 2; *Shakenoak II*, p. 121, fig. 51, no. 93; *Shakenoak IV*, p. 119, fig. 56, nos. 354–5.
     Trench 71 layer 8 (340): general layer.

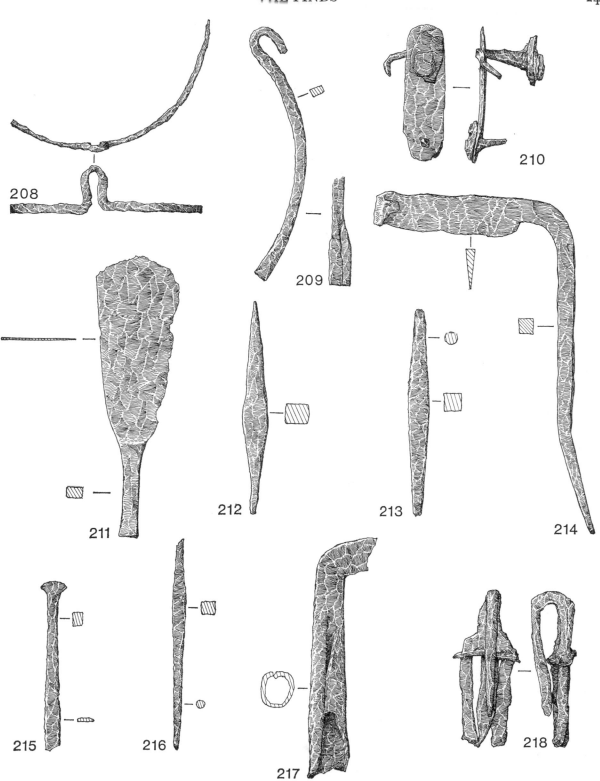

FIG. 128.   Iron objects (p. 240). Scale ⅔ except 208, 211 and 215, ⅓

219.  L-shaped tumbler-lock lift key. The bit has three teeth. The shaft has a marked swelling below the loop at the top. For the workings of this type of key, see *Verulamium I*, p. 181 and the British Museum *Guide to Greek and Roman Life*, 1920, pp. 149–50 and fig. 184.
      Trench 79 layer 68 (917): pit 121.
220.  L-shaped tumbler-lock lift key, similar to the last. The bit has the remains of two teeth. The shaft has an enlarged rectangular section below the looped top.
      Trench 70 layer 19 (320): pit 64.
221.  Another L-shaped tumbler-lock lift key. The bit is damaged and only one tooth remains, although there were originally three. The top is looped.
      Trench 65 layer 18 (181): pit 54.

For other tumbler-lock lift keys see *Shakenoak IV*, p. 119, fig. 56, nos. 356 and 358.

222.  Lever lock rotary key. The bit has three teeth to the front and two to the back. The shaft, of circular cross-section, terminates level with the three forward teeth. The ring at the end of the key is separated from the shaft by a ridged collar.
      Trench 79 layer 60 (899): pit 121.

*Structural Fittings*

223.  Split-spike loop with arms bent outwards. Cf. *Verulamium I*, p. 185, fig. 68, no. 90, for a parallel to this example and a general discussion of the type and its uses.
      Trench 89 layer 21 (1127): layer above make-up.
224.  Split-spike loop with straight arms. Cf. for example, *Verulamium I*, p. 185, fig. 68, no. 91.
      Trench 79 layer 68 (912): pit 121.
225.  Eyelet spike. Cf. for example, *Cranborne Chase I*, p. 88, pl. XXIX, no. 16.
      Trench 79 layer 68 (920b): pit 121.
226.  Eyelet spike with a ring passing through it.
      Trench 108 layer 62 (2499): upper occupation.
227.  Another ring and tie (drawn from an X-ray photograph).
      Trench 79 layer 68 (922): pit 121.
228.  Iron tie. The tie consists of a shaft with a circular head at one end and a lozenge shaped plate at the other. It was probably used in carpentry. Cf. *Fishbourne II*, p. 127, fig. 55, nos. 6–7.
      Trench 87 layer 9 (1033): layer above upper road surface.
229.  Cleat or staple. Cf. *Shakenoak IV*, p. 128, fig. 62, no. 450.
      Trench 73 layer 14 (513): pit 79.
230.  Joiner's dog. Cf. *Verulamium I*, p. 185, fig. 68, nos. 84ff.
      Trench 98 layer 50 (1981): pit 164.
231.  Hook with a ring for suspension.
      Trench 89 layer 55 (1184): general layer.
232.  Hook.
      Trench 79 layer 27 (797): pit 103.
233.  Hook or bracket.
      Trench 74 layer 24 (647): pit 85.
234.  Hook.
      Trench 70 layer 19 (397): pit 64.

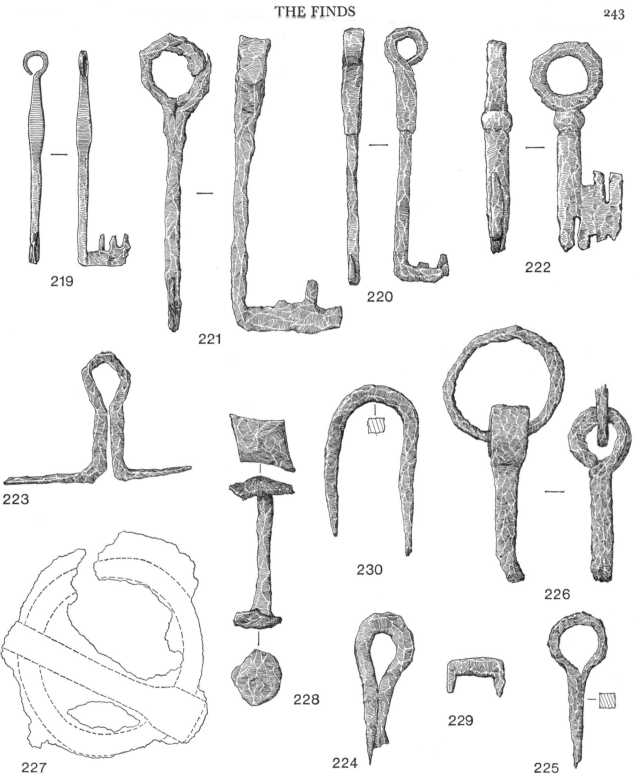

FIG. 129. Iron objects (p. 242). Scale ⅔ except 219, ⅓

235. Hinge.
     Trench 88 layer 42 (1120): general layer.
236. ? Nail head.
     Trench 69 layer 7 (262): general layer.


*Boot Fittings*

237. A collection of hob-nails from a leather boot.
     Trench 89 layer 58 (1319):                    .
     Also another group from trench 108 layer 217 (2559): pit 229.
238. Staple for the toe of a boot or shoe.
     Trench 101 layer 46 (2231): general layer.


*Bindings*

For a discussion of iron bindings in general, see *Verulamium I*, p. 188, 190.

239. Piece of iron binding with rounded end and pierced by two rivet holes.
     Trench 88 layer 10 (1605): general layer.
240. Binding pierced with one rivet hole.
     Trench 79 layer 68 (918): pit 121.
241. Flat ring binding with three rivet holes, possibly part of a horseshoe. Cf. a much larger but similar
     object, *Verulamium I*, p. 192, fig. 71, no. 148.
     Trench 87 layer 9 (1032): layer above upper road.
242. Iron binding rod with a flattened end pierced by a rivet, the other end describing a sharp bend
     before the break. The whole binding is slightly curved over its length.
     Trench 90 layer 30 (1205): layer above make-up.


*Styli*

For styli in general see, for example: *Verulamium I*, p. 176, fig. 65, no. 49; *Newstead*,
pl. LXXX; *Richborough IV*, pl. LIX, nos. 304–16; *Shakenoak IV*, p. 122, fig. 58, nos. 401–03.

243. The pointed tip is lost.
     Trench 68 layer 8 (273): pit 60a.
244. A complete but bent stylus.
     Trench 70 layer 14 (296): pit 63.
245. The pointed tip is missing.
     Trench 101 layer 22 (2157): general layer.
246. The pointed tip is lost. It is stepped. Cf. *Cranborne Chase III*, pl. CLXXXIII, nos. 13–14 for
     stepped styli.
     Trench 100 layer 66 (2135): general layer.
247. (Not illustrated.) A bent stylus.
     Trench 108 layer 109 (2506): general layer.
248. Stylus with a square-shaped eraser and a long pointed tip, separated from the shank by a marked
     step.
     Trench 66 layer 5 (214): general layer.

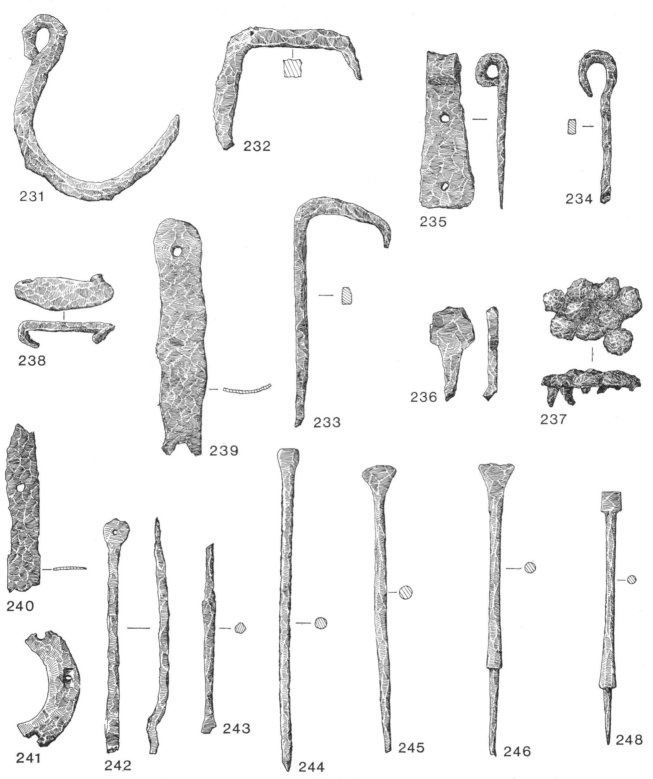

FIG. 130. Iron objects (pp. 242–4). Scale ⅔ except 235, 240, 241 and 242, ⅓

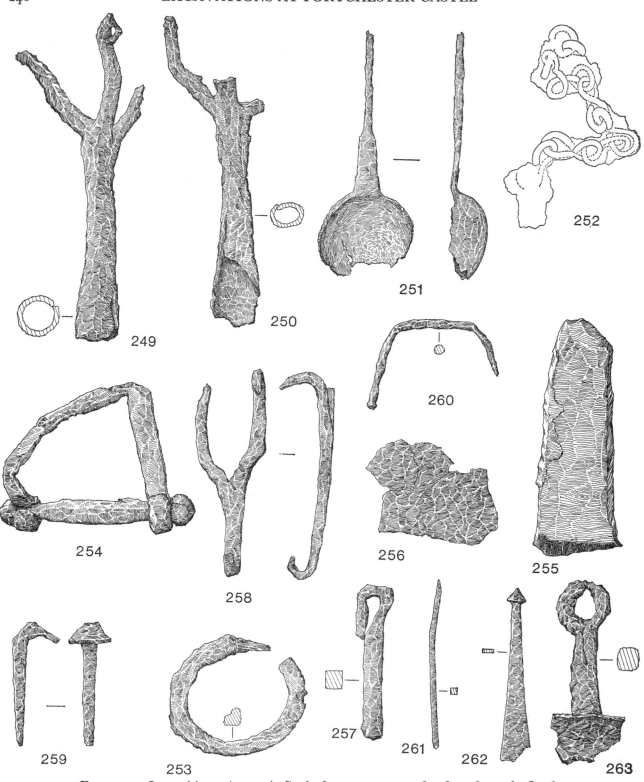

FIG. 131.   Iron objects (p. 247). Scale $\frac{2}{3}$ except 251, 256, 260, 261 and 262, $\frac{1}{3}$

*Candlesticks*

249. Tripod candlestick. Two of the legs are extant and have turned out feet, the third leg is broken (drawing inverted). Cf. *Verulamium I*, p. 177, fig. 65, no. 51.
      Trench 74 layer 27 (652): pit 86.
250. Tripod candlestick (drawing inverted).
      Trench 90 layer 30 (1218): layer above make-up.

*Miscellaneous*

251. Iron ladle. The bowl is almost complete. Behind the bowl the handle is broad and flat and tapers into a tang of rectangular cross-section. Cf. *Shakenoak I*, p. 105, no. 23.
      Trench 91 layer 46 (1278): layer above upper road.
252. A much corroded length of iron chain (drawn from an X-ray photograph). Cf. for example, *Cranborne Chase I*, p. 97, pl. XXXI, no. 1.
      Trench 109 layer 91 (2642): pit 236.
253. Ring of ovoid form. Cf. *Shakenoak IV*, p. 131, fig. 64, no. 503.
      Trench 87 layer 33 (1057): above upper road.
254. Large buckle. There are unpublished examples of this type in the Newport Museum, Monmouthshire, from Roman Caerwent.
      Trench 71 layer 5 (398): general layer.
255. Piece of iron stock bar.
      Trench 89 layer 55 (1174): general layer.
256. Piece of iron plate, apparently with two parallel sides and one rounded end.
      Trench 89 layer 21 (1139): layer above make-up.
257. Looped terminal.
      Trench 91 layer 46 (1275): layer above upper road.
258. Fork or two-pronged hook; the single prong was probably bent accidentally and represents the tang.
      Trench 95 layer 64 (1646): general layer.
259. A tang?
      Trench 88 layer 10 (1028): layer above make-up.
260. Handle of squarish form. One knobbed terminal remains.
      Trench 88 layer 62 (1095): layer above make-up.
261. Iron rod of square cross-section and unknown purpose.
      Trench 109 layer 91 (2634): pit 236.
262. A tapering piece of flat iron broken at the broad end and terminating in a knob at the narrow end. Perhaps a very thin paring chisel.
      Trench 107 layer 44 (2412): upper occupation.
263. Part of a two-link snaffle bit.
      Trench 101 layer 94 (2250): general layer.

# THE LEATHER

## by TIMOTHY AMBROSE

264. Left foot shoe — bottom unit, quarters and heel quarters. Overall length 20·4 cm., width at waist 5 cm., width at ball 6 cm., width at heel, 4·5 cm. Insole complete except for some deterioration along edges, thonged to middle-sole filling section (thong, 4–5 mm. wide; filler, length 18 cm.,

width 3·5–2·5 cm., thickness 2 mm.). Indentations of bracing threads across filler indicate that the upper has been string lasted. Fragment of middle sole with indentations of central line thonging and bracing threads. Parallel indentations either side of the central line thonging indicate further thonging along bottom unit. Heel quarters, deteriorated around lasting margin and right hand top edge. Round gimped decoration on top edges, rising to a central peak on heel quarters. Peak: height 8 mm., width 1·2 cm. Top edge of quarters folded over and stitched inside. Inside stiffener complete although slightly laminated, with skived upper edge. The stud arrangement is standard with a row running along the centre line, and a row running around both edges. Estimated number of studs: centre line row 8, heel end 2, left hand row 10, right hand row 11.

Trench 95 layer 150 (2660): pit 144.

265. Right foot shoe — bottom unit, upper lasting margins and stiffener. Bottom unit much deteriorated. Overall length 28 cm. (estimated original length *c.* 31 cm.), width at waist 7 cm., width at ball 10 cm. Insole much deteriorated at heel end and along edges. Middle sole filler with thonging holes, terminated at waist by a diagonal cut. There is no indication of further filling towards heel. Middle sole layer below filler much deteriorated, showing stud holes and side-thonging holes along edges. Sections of upper lasting margins run along the left hand edge and right forward edge, showing stud holes. The upper has been lasted between the bottom middle sole layer and the insole, although there is a possibility that an upper middle sole layer was placed below the insole. Sole, greatly deteriorated, with some studs in position (1 cm. diameter). The studs are rather worn. Inside stiffener, deteriorated slightly, with lasting margins showing stud holes (see also no. 284).

Trench 109 layer 119 (2661): pit 236.

266. Right foot shoe — part of bottom unit, upper and heel quarters, and upper toe piece (pl. XXXVI). Overall length 21 cm., width at waist 5·5 cm., width at ball 6·5 cm., width at heel 4·5 cm. Upper is whole cut. Insole complete except for some deterioration at heel end. Middle sole filling section thonged to insole along central line: the thonging is still in position (thong 4–5 mm. wide). The sole and middle sole layers survive only at the front of the shoe. Twelve studs are in position along the central line and the right hand edge of the sole. The studs show a certain amount of wear. Upper lasting margin *in situ* along the edges of the forepart, with indications of string lasting. The upper toe piece is decorated.

A plain margin, 7–8 mm. wide, running down its centre line divides the toe piece into two roughly triangular panels. Each of these panels is decorated with seven short lines of impressed wave pattern motif, 5–6 mm. apart, running at right angles from the central margin. They increase in length from 1 to 3 cm. as they move up the toe piece, emphasizing the curve of the sides of the toe. These lines of wave pattern are alternated with parallel lines of light scoring, also at 5–6 mm. intervals, which run from the central margin to the extreme edges of the toe. The uppermost line of scoring has a short line of wave pattern, wrongly aligned by the craftsman, cutting across it. It may be that these scored lines were applied first to provide guidelines for the lines of wave pattern. The upper edge of the toe piece has a row of incised three-quarter circles along it, broken at the central margin.

Both the right hand upper lasting margin and the torn end of the central margin indicate the presence of a vamp, but how this was decorated and what form it took can only be guessed at. The top edges are in good condition and are decorated with round gimping, which runs from the back tie-loop to the peak on the heel quarters. Parallel with the top edges and some 4 mm. below them are two parallel lines of shallow grooving 4 mm. apart, which run around the heel between the tie loops. Below the lines of grooving, on both sides of the quarters, is a panel of square lattice cut-out decoration. The cut-outs are some 4 × 4 mm. and the overcuts at their corners show that a sharp, narrow-bladed chisel, *c.* 3 mm. in width, has been used to create them. The bottom edge of the

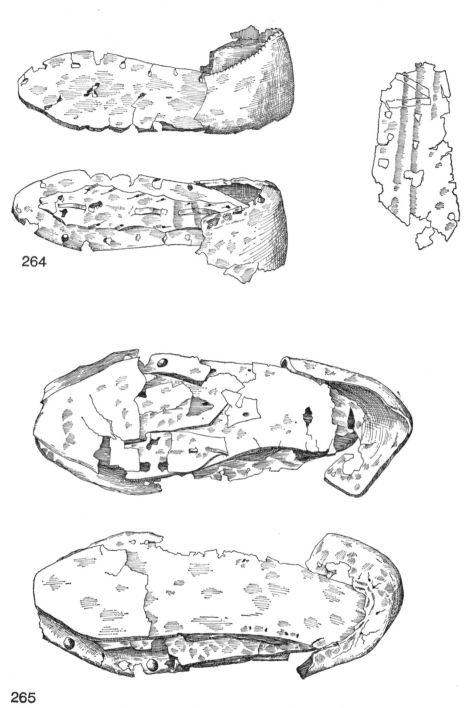

264

265

FIG. 132. Shoes (pp. 247–8). Scale $\frac{2}{3}$

panel curves upwards with the line of the heel, forming as it does a lower row of triangular cut-outs. Along the strips of leather left between the rows of cut-outs are shallow grooved lines, running both horizontally and vertically. The horizontal grooves terminate at the line of the triangular cut-outs on the one hand, and a vertical groove running down the centre of the back tie-strap on the other. The vertical groove stops at the lower horizontal channel below the top edge. As with the scored lines on the toe pieces, this network of grooved lines may represent a system of guidelines for the craftsman.

In front of the panel of cut-out work, on both sides of the shoe, is an instep tie-strap (the back tie-strap) which forms the forward edge of the panels. The back tie-straps have curved tie-loops with crescent-shaped tongues. Around the inside of the top edge is a length of horizontal lacing (lacing holes at *c*. 9 mm. apart). The lacing may have originally come through the tie-loops from the inside to tighten the top edges around the ankle. In front of the back tie-strap is a second instep tie-strap, separated from it by a vertical gap cut in the upper. The forward edge has round gimped decoration similar to that of the top edges, while the back edge is plain. Two lines of light scoring run up the sides of the forward tie-strap to meet at a point at the top end. The ends of both forward tie-straps are torn and their tie-loops are missing. Running from the sides of the toe piece around the lower sides of the shoe are two parallel lines of light scoring. These join a third at the heel quarters below the panels of cut-out work, and all three lines curve upwards to the peak on the heel. The inside stiffener is complete and cut much lower than usual so as not to block the inside of the cut-out work. Both the size and the decoration suggest that this is a woman's shoe. The decoration and the fact that it is whole cut (with a side seam) indicate that it is a high-grade example (Charlesworth and Thornton, 1973).

Trench 109 layer 119 (2662): pit 236.

267. Left foot shoe — upper complete except for some deterioration around the top edge and quarters of the right-hand side, insole, ? filling and sole intact (pl. XXXV). Overall length 19 cm. (modern child's size 11), width at waist 5 cm., width at ball 7 cm., width at heel 5 cm. Upper is whole cut (see no. 266) with a cross-laced vamp seam. The lower 4 cm. of the seam are stitched. The vamp seam has been turned inside and the lacing holes are on average 1·2 cm. apart. There are lacing marks running along each line of lacing holes. The shoe has an inside side seam with part of the lacing arrangement still *in situ*, the lacing actually being cut from the upper and then stranded. The lacing holes along the side seam are *c*. 5 mm. apart. The top edges of the quarters are plain and have been folded over inside the shoe and stitched down *c*. 5 mm. below the edge. The sole is complete and except for one missing stud the nailing pattern is intact. The centre row has nine studs along it, the two side rows eight (diam. 6–14 mm.). The shoe shows little sign of wear (see below p. 260).

Trench 109 layer 119 (2663): pit 236.

268. Left foot shoe — incomplete bottom unit, insole, ? filler, sole, upper fragments heavily deteriorated. Present length 20 cm., estimated original length 25–26 cm., width at waist 6 cm., width at ball 8 cm. Insole (or perhaps upper middle sole layer) complete except for the heel end. Upper lasting margins *in situ* along most of the edges, with part of the forepart vamp surviving. Part of the vamp seam has survived on this last fragment. The stitching holes are at 4 mm. intervals. The sole is much deteriorated, and the heel end is not preserved. It has some 16 studs intact (diam. 6–14 mm.) and the original pattern would appear to have been five parallel rows, at least from the waist to the toe.

Trench 109 layer 119 (2664): pit 236.

269. Right upper shoe — bottom unit much deteriorated, with fragment of upper lasting margin at toe end. Overall length 18 cm., width at ball 7 cm., width at waist 5 cm. Insole deteriorated along both edges, thonged to middle sole filling sections, thong *c*. 4 mm. wide. Lower filling layer below filling sections greatly deteriorated. Sole, much deteriorated along right edge and across forepart. Two

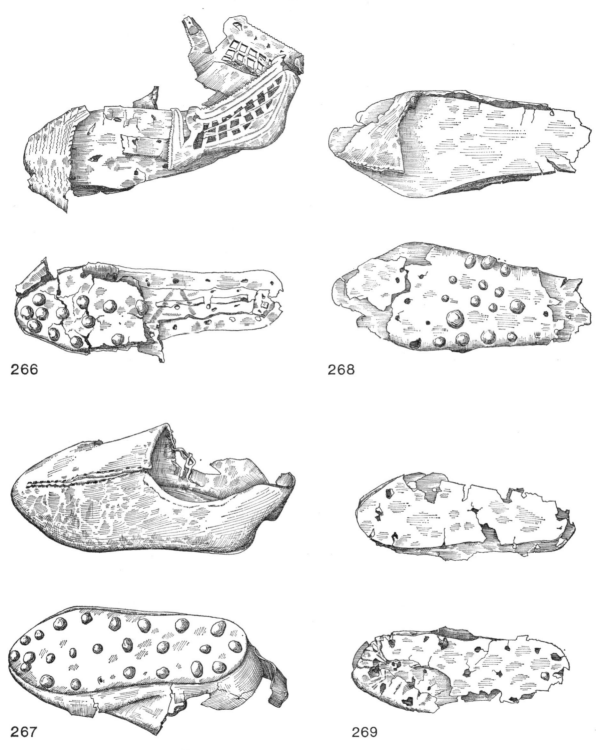

266

268

267

269

FIG. 133.   Shoes (pp. 248–50). Scale ⅔

studs remain *in situ*, diam. *c.* 1 cm. Fragment of upper lasting margin around toe end has traces of the grooves worn by string lasting. The upper lasting margin is *in situ* along the left-hand edge of the sole to the waist, and there are slight traces of a lacing arrangement for a side seam at this point.

Trench 109 layer 119 (2665): pit 236.

270.  ? Right foot shoe, part of bottom unit; insole, middle sole filling section and fragments of ? lower middle sole layer or sole. Length at present 21–22 cm., width at waist 6 cm., width at heel 5 cm. Insole complete at heel and waist, but forepart missing. Middle sole filling section runs the whole length of the insole and has the customary diagonal cut at the toe end. A row of thonging holes runs along the central line of the filler section, *c.* 3 cm. apart.

Trench 109 layer 119 (2666): pit 236.

271.  Right foot shoe — fragment of bottom unit deteriorated. Length at present 13 cm., width at waist 8 cm. Fragment of middle sole layer, filler and fragment of upper lasting margin. The filling section has a straight cut at the waist and is thonged along the central line (thong, 6 cm. wide). The filling section is unusual in that it is thonged to the upper lasting margin (thongs, 3–4 mm. wide). The lasting margin is very narrow. The middle sole layer has a row of stud holes around its outer edges and indications of a central line. (Compare with no. 267 and see below.)

Trench 109 layer 119 (2667): pit 236.

272.  (Not illustrated.) Left foot shoe — bottom unit, much deteriorated. Length 26 cm., width at ball *c.* 9 cm., width at waist *c.* 7 cm. Middle sole layers and middle sole filling section. The middle sole layers have stud holes showing along their central lines and around their edges and toe ends; the heel end is deteriorated. The middle sole filling section (3–4 cm. wide) runs the whole length of the middle sole and is slightly curved along its right hand edge, with a small nick out of the centre of its left hand edge. It has a thong still *in situ c.* 3–4 mm. wide. Above the filler is a second middle sole layer much deteriorated along its edges and heel end.

Trench 109 layer 119 (2668): pit 236.

273.  (Not illustrated.) ? Right foot shoe, greatly deteriorated fragments of bottom unit. Middle sole fragments showing torn stud holes (3–4 layers). One fragment has a short length of thong *in situ* (thong 3–4 mm. wide).

Trench 109 layer 119 (2669): pit 236.

274.  (Not illustrated.) Heel quarters and right-hand quarters, fragment of sole and upper lasting margin and stiffener (greatly deteriorated). Fragment of sole with thin strip of upper lasting margin held in position by one stud (diam. *c.* 9 mm.). Fragment of leather from ? quarters. The heel quarters, right-hand quarters and stiffener are badly deteriorated, and distorted. The quarters have a plain top edge and a finished, vertical forward edge (7 cm. high) with a line of stitch holes running down it and some 2 cm. behind it (stitch-holes at 5–6 mm. intervals, stitching *c.* 2 mm. wide). A fragment of upper lasting margin is stitched along the outside of this line. This construction differs from the previous examples. It would appear that the heel quarters and quarters have been stitched to the forepart of the shoe along a vertical instep side seam.

Trench 109 layer 119 (2670): pit 236.

275.  (Not illustrated.) Much deteriorated forepart of bottom unit — sole, middle sole and insole fragments. The edges of these pieces are very torn and deteriorated, making accurate measurement impossible.

Trench 109 layer 119 (2671): pit 236.

276.  (Not illustrated.) Description as above.

Trench 109 layer 119 (2672): pit 236.

277.  (Not illustrated.) Description as above.

Trench 109 layer 119 (2673): pit 236.

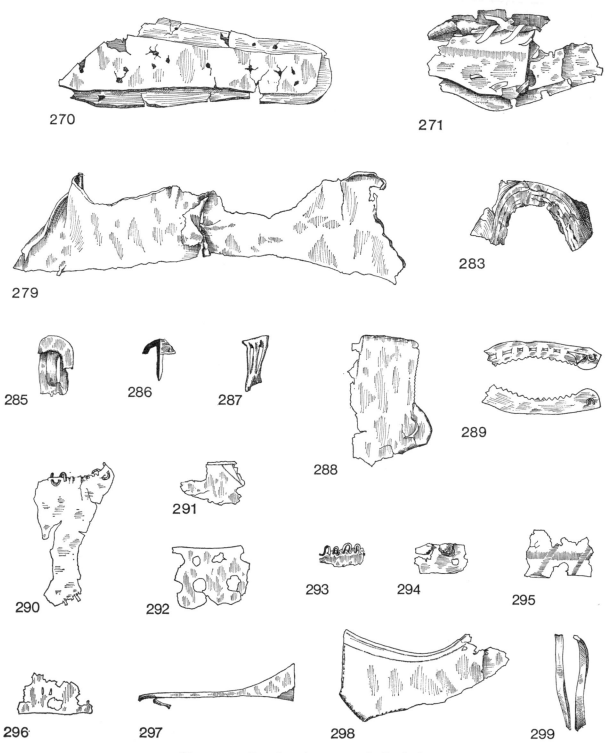

FIG. 134. Leather (pp. 252–5). Scale ⅔

278. (Not illustrated.) Much deteriorated forepart section of bottom unit — sole, middle sole fragments. Width at ball, 9 cm.
Trench 109 layer 119 (2674): pit 236.

279. Heel quarters and quarters. Top edges, lasting margins and heel much deteriorated. Top edges appear to have been folded over and stitched down, and ? undecorated. Traces of a tie loop on left quarters.
Trench 109 layer 119 (2675): pit 236.

280. (Not illustrated.) Fragment of inside stiffener, much deteriorated, with stud holes showing on bottom lasting edge.
Trench 95 layer 150 (2676): pit 144.

281. (Not illustrated.) Piece of soft leather, 8 cm. in length, 2·4 cm. wide, narrowing to a point. Perhaps an offcut as there are no stitching holes along the margins and the edges are clean cut.
Trench 95 layer 150 (2678): pit 144.

283. Leather fragment, semi-circular shape. Possibly the toe piece of a moccasin type shoe. Large stitch holes/thong holes at 6 mm. intervals along the upper edge. Lower edge, although much deteriorated, also has traces of stitching.
Trench 109 layer 119 (2679): pit 236.

284. (Not illustrated.) Heel-stiffener, much deteriorated. Found inside a larger stiffener (see no. 265). Lasting margin shows stud holes. It is possible that this is a secondary inner stiffener for 265, although the size suggests that this is unlikely.
Trench 109 layer 119 (2680): pit 236.

285. Tie loop with torn bottom edge. Possibly from no. 268. Formed by cutting a double slot through the end of the tie strap leaving a central rectangular tongue 9 mm. wide. Upper edge curved and folded over.
Trench 109 layer 119 (2681): pit 236.

286. Sole stud. Iron sole stud, included to illustrate how the point of the stud has been turned on a shoe-maker's last.
Trench 109 layer 119 (2682): pit 236.

287. Tie loop with torn bottom edge. A more delicate example than no. 285, but fashioned in the same way. The central continuous tongue is 4 mm. wide. Probably from a woman's shoe.
Trench 109 layer 119 (2683): pit 236.

288. Fragment of right-hand quarters. Deteriorated along line of lasting margin and forepart. Round gimped decoration on top edge. Tie loop attached to quarters, round tongued with slightly curved upper edge.
Trench 109 layer 119 (2684): pit 236.

289. Left tie strap, 9·5 cm. long. Forward edge has round gimped decoration, back edge is plain. The strap terminates in a tongued tie loop and is torn at the bottom end. Running along the centre line on the inside of the strap is a narrow thong (c. 2 mm. wide). The end has been cut in a rough triangle to prevent the thong from being pulled out (see no. 266 for similar gimped decoration on a tie strap).
Trench 109 layer 119 (2685): pit 236.

290. Fragment of left ? quarters, much deteriorated (drawing shows reverse side). Upper edge deteriorated. Three parallel impressed lines 4 mm. apart run below the upper edge. A side seam runs down the back edge with two short lengths of lacing still in position (lacing 2 mm. wide — lacing holes at 4 mm. intervals). On the forward edge are the remains of a tie piece, with narrow thongs alternating with round gimps (thongs 2 mm. wide). Running from the top of the back edge seam to the centre of the lower edge is a raised stitched seam c. 3 mm. wide (stitching holes 3–4 mm. apart). (See no. 274 for similar side seam.)
Trench 109 layer 119 (2686): pit 236.

291. Fragment of leather deteriorated around the edges, although upper edges suggest a top edge. An impressed line runs parallel with the upper edge and some 2 mm. below it. Hanging from this line is an impressed triangle.
    Trench 109 layer 119 (2687): pit 236.

292. Fragment of sole showing stud holes and thonging.
    Trench 109 layer 119 (2688): pit 236.

293. Fragment of seam. Lacing *in situ* (lacing 2–3 mm. wide; lacing holes at 5–6 mm. intervals).
    Trench 109 layer 119 (2689): pit 236.

294. Fragment of sole with stud in position. Stud 1·2 cm. diameter.
    Trench 109 layer 119 (2690): pit 236.

295. Fragment of upper lasting margin showing indentations of middle sole thonging and string lasting.
    Trench 109 layer 119 (2691): pit 236.

296. Fragment of middle sole showing thonging holes and stud holes.
    Trench 109 layer 119 (2692): pit 236.

297. Thong/? offcut. As with no. 289, the thong has been cut with a triangular shaped end to prevent the thong from being pulled out. It seems too large to belong to a shoe.
    Trench 109 layer 119 (2693): pit 236.

298. Piece of leather, 5 mm. thick. Upper edge has two parallel lightly impressed lines below it, 6–8 mm. apart. There are indications of a thong hole on the right-hand edge. Around the left-hand edge and part of the bottom edge are stitching holes 3–4 mm. apart. The rest of the bottom edge is deteriorated. Function uncertain.
    Trench 109 layer 119 (2694): pit 236.

299. Two strips of leather, length 7·5 cm., width 6–7 mm., thickness 2 mm. (fig. 135).
    Trench 109 layer 119 (2695): pit 236.

300. Fragment of heavy leather (2–3 mm. thick). The fragment has a raised, stitched seam (stitch holes at 4–5 mm. intervals). The seam divides into two, but there is deterioration at this point. Function uncertain.
    Trench 109 layer 119 (2696): pit 236.

301. Two pieces of leather joined by a heavy inside turned seam. Stitch holes at 5–6 mm. intervals.
    Trench 109 layer 119 (2697): pit 236.

302. Fragment of left quarters. Two parallel lightly impressed lines 5–6 mm. apart run below the deteriorated top edge. Edges much deteriorated (compare with no. 279).
    Trench 109 layer 119 (2698): pit 236.

303. Fragment with folded upper edge. ? Part of shoe upper.
    Trench 109 layer 119 (2699): pit 236.

304. Fragment, slightly laminated. Perhaps an offcut.
    Trench 109 layer 119 (2700): pit 236.

305. Fragment. Slightly distorted in centre. Saw tooth decoration along upper edge. Decoration is impressed and consists of two narrow triangles hanging from an upper horizontal line. There is a semi-circular cut-out between the bases of the triangles (diam. 8 mm.).
    Trench 109 layer 119 (2701): pit 236.

306. (Not illustrated.) Thong, length 17 cm., width 2 mm.
    Trench 109 layer 119 (2702): pit 236.

307. Fragment 9·5 by 4–5 cm. Thonging hole with short length of thong in position (thong 2 mm. wide). Perhaps part of middle sole filling section.
    Trench 109 layer 119 (2703): pit 236.

308. Fragment of right upper quarters. Round gimped decoration on top edge. Three parallel bands of decoration 5 mm. apart below the top edge. Upper band — two parallel grooves 6 mm. apart

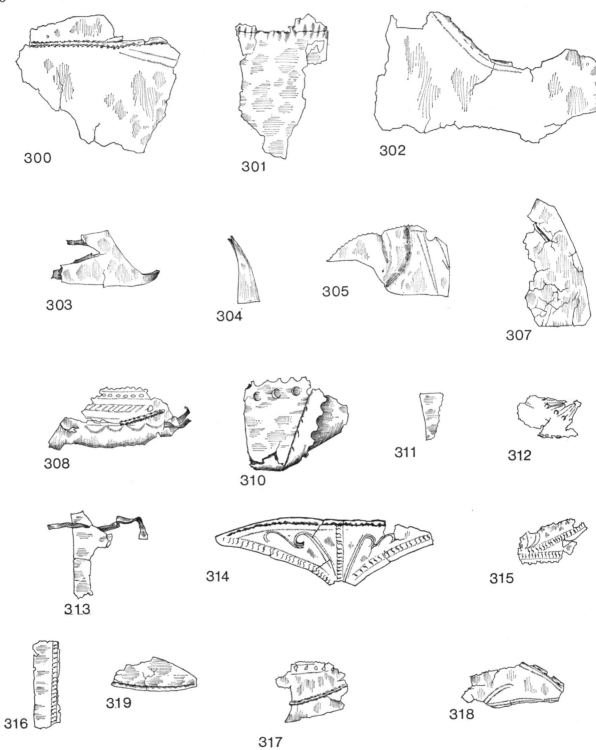

FIG. 135.   Leather (pp. 255–8). Scale ⅔

containing a row of elliptical cut-outs at 6 mm. intervals. Middle band — two parallel grooves 5 mm. apart containing a row of diagonal hatches at 4 mm. intervals, terminated by a ? lacing hole (diam. 4 mm.). Lower band — two parallel grooves 5 mm. apart containing a raised stitched seam (stitching holes at 5 mm. intervals). Hanging from this band are four grooved double loops. On the right hand edge, under the lower band, are traces of a lacing arrangement. The bottom edge is stitched (stitching holes at 5 mm. intervals).
Trench 109 layer 119 (2704): pit 236.

309. (Not illustrated.) Fragment of left quarters. Round gimped decoration on top edge. Three parallel grooves 5–6 mm. apart below the top edge. The upper and middle grooves contain a row of cut-out holes 7 mm. apart. The middle and lower grooves contain a row of wide triangles. Below these three grooves and curving upwards towards the top of the heel run two parallel channelled lines containing a raised stitched seam some 3 mm. wide.
Trench 109 layer 119 (2705): pit 236.

310. Rectangular fragment 7 by 8 cm. Semi-circular cut-outs along top edge. Below this is a line of three-quarter circular tongued cut-outs at 1·5 cm. intervals (diam. 6 mm.). Repeated on bottom edge. The fragment is folded along the lower line of cut-outs and along the left edge. Function uncertain.
Trench 109 layer 119 (2706): pit 236.

311. Fragment. Saw tooth decoration along right hand edge.
Trench 109 layer 119 (2707): pit 236.

312. Decorated fragment. Four incised lines radiate from a common point and terminate at three-quarter circular cut-outs. Between these lines are lightly impressed parallel lines of the same length. There are indications of a stitching seam along the lower edge.
Trench 109 layer 119 (2708): pit 236.

313. Fragment with 4 mm. wide thong running through it.
Trench 109 layer 119 (2709): pit 236.

314. Decorated panel. Upper edge and right-hand corner slightly deteriorated. The upper edge is folded over and stitched (stitching holes at 1·1 cm. intervals). There are no stitching holes on the lower edge. Two parallel impressed lines (4 mm. apart) containing S stamp decoration divide the panel in half. The lower edges of the panel have similar lines of impressed and stamped decoration. The S stamp decoration has not been very accurately applied. The spacing of the S stamps is not constant and at times the stamps cut across the guide lines. The open areas either side of the central division are decorated with double cresting wave motifs springing from the middle point of the lower edge. The wave motifs are formed from two lightly scored parallel lines with a central line of heavier scoring. The heavier scoring allows greater flexibility in the panel. The middle point of the lower edge is torn and suggests that the panel is but one part of a larger unit. Panels of similar shape and decoration come from saddles found at Valkenburg (Groenman–van Waateringe, 1967, p. 111). (See also nos. 315 and 316.)
Trench 109 layer 120 (2710): pit 236.

315. Decorated fragment. Decoration as no. 314. Lower edge torn along seam. Probably from same unit as no. 314.
Trench 109 layer 120 (2711): pit 236.

316. Rectangular fragment 7 by 2 cm. Decoration as nos. 314 and 315.
Trench 109 layer 119 (2712): pit 236.

317. Fragment 4 by 4 cm. Two parallel impressed lines 6 mm. apart contain a row of small holes (2 mm. diam.). Traces of gimping along the upper edge. Raised stitched seam runs across the middle of the fragment (stitching holes at 5–6 mm. intervals). (See nos. 308 and 309 for similar decoration.)
Trench 109 layer 119 (2713): pit 236.

18

318. Fragment 7 by 3 cm. Stitching along right hand edge (stitching holes at *c*. 6 mm. intervals). Impressed parallel lines 3 mm. apart run along lower and right-hand edges. Function uncertain.
      Trench 95 layer 150 (2714): pit 144.
319. Fragment 6 by 3 cm. Upper edge folded over and stitched (stitching holes at 5 mm. intervals). Right-hand edge deteriorated. Left-hand edge clean cut. Function uncertain.
      Trench 95 layer 150 (2715): pit 144.
320. (Not illustrated). Other fragments of shoes, showing no diagnostic features.
      Trench 109 layer 119: pit 236 and trench 95 layer 150: pit 144 (2716).

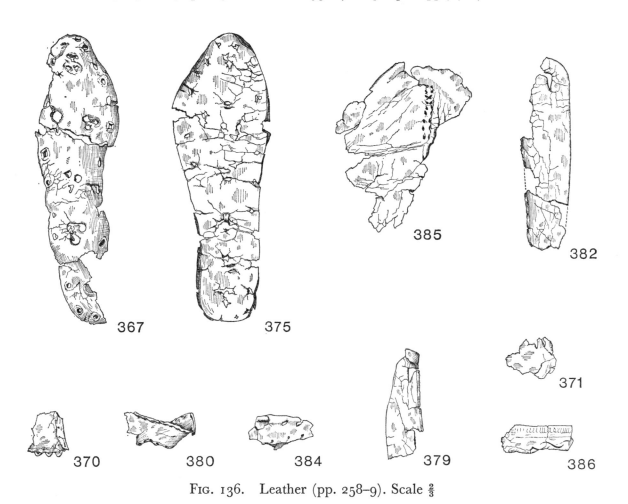

Fig. 136.   Leather (pp. 258–9). Scale ⅔

321. (Pl. XXXIV*b*). Fragments of dried, shaped skin, perhaps a skin vessel.
      Trench 63 layer 7 (200).
367. Left foot shoe — sole. Edges and heel end deteriorated. Overall length 22 cm., width at ball 7·5 cm., width at waist 5 cm. A row of stud holes runs around both edges, but instead of the normal central row, four clusters of three stud holes run along the centre line with two further clusters on the ball. Estimated number of studs: right hand row 13, left hand row 13.
      Trench 95 layer 142 (2280): pit 144.

368. (Not illustrated.) Fragment of insole. Broken across ball. Width at ball 6·5 cm., width at heel 4 cm. Three pairs of thonging holes survive at 4·5 cm. intervals. Fragment of thonging *in situ* (6 mm. wide). Perhaps originally attached to no. 369.
     Trench 95 layer 142 (2281): pit 144.

369. (Not illustrated.) Middle sole filling section. Width at ball 5 cm., width at waist 3·5 cm., overall length 17 cm. Central row of *c.* 12 stud holes, with further stud holes around toe end, much deteriorated. Short strips of thonging in position at waist and toe end (5–6 mm. wide). (See no. 368.)
     Trench 95 layer 142 (2282): pit 144.

370. Fragment of seamed leather. Lacing *in situ* (lacing 2–3 mm. wide; lacing holes at 5 mm. intervals). Top edge of fragment has been folded over inside and stitched down 5 mm. below the edge. Possibly part of a side seam (see no. 293).
     Trench 95 layer 142 (2283): pit 144.

371. Fragment of tie loop. Much deteriorated, with torn edges.
     Trench 95 layer 142 (2284): pit 144.

372. (Not illustrated.) Fragment of heel quarters. Central peak along upper edge. The piece has been folded and is heavily deteriorated.
     Trench 95 layer 142 (2285): pit 144.

373. (Not illustrated.) Eight fragments, greatly deteriorated and torn. All have stud holes, and are either pieces of torn lasting margin or middle sole filler.
     Trench 95 layer 142 (2286): pit 144.

374. (Not illustrated.) Fragment of leather, length 12 cm., width 8 cm. Edges much deteriorated. A row of 9 lacing holes, at 5 mm. intervals, runs along one edge. Function uncertain.
     Pit 95 layer 142 (2287): pit 144.

375. Left foot shoe — sole. Deteriorated along both edges. Length 23 cm., width at ball 7·5 cm., width at waist 6 cm., width at heel 5 cm. The stud arrangement is similar to that of no. 367. There are 12–13 stud holes along either edge and four clusters of 2–3 stud holes along the centre line, with two more clusters on the ball. A single thong also runs along the centre line, with thonging holes at 3–5 cm. intervals.
     Trench 95 layer 151 (2288): pit 144.

376. (Not illustrated.) Fragment of middle sole, heavily deteriorated. Indentations of bracing threads and centre line thonging present. A short strip of bracing thread is *in situ*. Stud holes at 12 mm. intervals.
     Trench 95 layer 151 (2289): pit 144.

377. (Not illustrated.) Fragment of heel quarters and inside stiffener. Both heavily deteriorated and distorted. Inside stiffener shows traces of a lasting margin.
     Trench 95 layer 151 (2290): pit 144.

378. (Not illustrated.) 12 fragments of middle sole filler sections, showing stud holes and thonging indentations. Heavily deteriorated.
     Trench 95 layer 151 (2291): pit 144.

379. Tie strap. Torn along side and bottom edge. Length 8 cm.
     Trench 95 layer 151 (2292): pit 144.

380. Fragment. Width 5 cm., length 7 cm. Right hand edge stitch at 3 mm. intervals. Left hand edge and lower edge have lacing holes at 4–5 mm. intervals. Top edge torn. Possibly part of a tie strap.
     Trench 95 layer 151 (2293): pit 144.

381. (Not illustrated.) Two pieces of leather. 11 cm. × 3 cm. and 9 cm. × 2 cm. Edges torn and deteriorated.
     Trench 95 layer 151 (2294): pit 144.

382.  Tie strap? Length 15 cm., width 5 cm. The bottom and left hand edges are torn. (Compare with
      no. 379).
        Trench 109 layer 121 (2295): pit 236.
383.  (Not illustrated.) Two fragments of middle sole. Heavily deteriorated.
        Trench 109 layer 121 (2296): pit 236.
384.  Piece of folded leather. Three stitching holes run along the bottom edge at 12 mm. intervals.
      Along the top edge are three lacing holes at 1 cm. intervals. Function uncertain.
        Trench 109 layer 121 (2297): pit 236.
385.  Fragment of leather, heavily deteriorated and torn along edges. The fragment has a raised
      stitched seam, which terminated before reaching the forward edge. (Stitch holes at 4–5 mm.
      intervals.) Possibly part of an upper with a vamp seam. One of the edges is turned over and
      appears to show torn stud holes (see nos. 300 and 267).
        Trench 109 layer 121 (2298): pit 236.
386.  Strip of leather. Length 5·5 cm., width 2·5 cm. Bottom and side edges torn. Decorated along
      upper edge with a row of vertical reverse S stamp decoration, c. 3 mm. in height. Below this is a
      shallow channelled line. Under this line occurs a band of larger horizontal S stamps. The motifs
      are formed with a single incised line (see nos. 314–316, 318).
        Trench 109 layer 121 (2299): pit 236.
387.  (Not illustrated.) Piece of leather, c. 25 cm. × 28 cm. Much deteriorated and distorted. Two
      edges are cut at right angles. There are no stitching or lacing holes. The folding on the piece
      suggests that the leather has been stretched over some form of framework. It is possible that the
      piece is part of a tent, although the absence of stitching holes along the edges seems to make this
      unlikely. It is perhaps best viewed as either part of a garment or part of military equipment.
        Trench 109 layer 121 (2300): pit 236.


*Discussion*

   The leather finds from the excavations at Portchester Castle are not indicative of on-site
leather working. Except for one or two examples, the shoes are all badly deteriorated and
worn, and are best interpreted as cast-offs. The associated finds are mostly of domestic refuse
(see pits 144 and 236 — contents). Three points, however, are worthy of note.
   Except for three examples (nos. 268, 367, and 375), the shoes from Portchester have a
simple three-row stud arrangement. The nailing pattern was one of the criteria used on the
large deposit of Roman shoes from Saalburg for differentiating men's shoes from women's and
children's shoes (Busch, 1965, p. 175). The sample from Portchester is too small and in too
fragmentary a condition for this criterion to be used effectively. However, both its size and
decoration suggest that no. 266 is a woman's shoe. Nos. 264, 267 and 269 are of very similar
size to no. 266, and may also have belonged to women or children. Size alone suggests that
nos. 265 and 272 are men's shoes. The presence of women and children within the fort is
further attested by the large number of personal finds recovered (see p. 427).
   Secondly, no. 267 is of especial interest in the context of a Saxon shore fort. It seems to
show something of a marriage between Roman and Germanic shoemaking traditions. The
stud arrangement is of normal Roman type, whereas the upper illustrates features later to
become common on Anglo-Saxon shoes. The vamp seam is cross-laced for most of its length
and the right hand side seam has a lacing arrangement cut from the upper. There are no tie
straps. One other fragment (no. 271) has similar features. The upper lasting margin is thonged

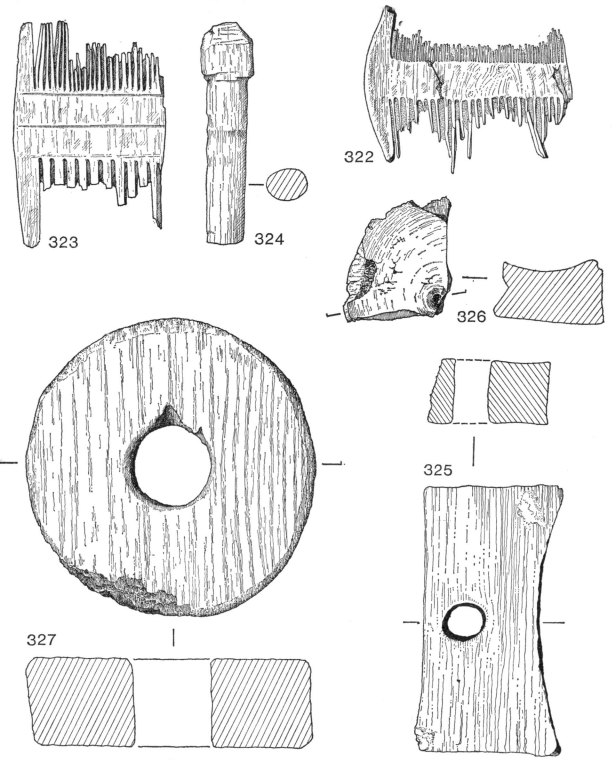

FIG. 137. Wooden objects (p. 262). Scale ⅔

to the middle sole filling section along its edge in much the same way as on a Saxon shoe in Winchester Museum.[1] Further finds from Portchester may provide more positive evidence for this merging of shoemaking traditions.[2]

Thirdly, certain fragments do not appear to come from shoes. It has been tentatively suggested that nos. 314 and 315 are part of an appliqué panel from a saddle. The identification of nos. 281, 291, 300 and 310 remains uncertain, but it is not impossible that they are parts of clothing.

## OBJECTS OF WOOD

322. Comb; undecorated, with teeth of two different sizes.
    Trench 95 layer 151 (2651): well 144.
323. Comb: the stem is decorated with three shallow grooves. The teeth are of two different sizes.
    Trench 109 layer 119 (2631): well 236.
324. Peg: oval in section with roughly cut head.
    Trench 109 layer 120 (2656): well 236.
325. Block with perforation showing signs of wear as if by cord.
    Trench 95 layer 151 (2654): well 144.
326. Part of a disc with central depression. Signs of wheel turning suggest that it may be from the base of a container.
    Trench 109 layer 120 (2657): well 236.
327. Disc with central perforation.
    Trench 109 layer 119 (2630): well 236.
328. Bung with an expanded head.
    Trench 95 layer 151 (2653): well 144.
329. Peg with an expanded head: the shank is sawn half across and perforated.
    Trench 95 layer 151 (2652): well 144.

## OBJECTS MADE FROM POTTERY, BAKED CLAY, AND CHALK

330. Spindlewhorl of baked clay, undecorated.
    Trench 73 layer 10 (606): general layer.
331. Spindlewhorl cut from a pottery vessel of black-burnished ware.
    Trench 100 layer 81 (2182): general layer.
332. Spindle whorl cut from a sherd of coarse pottery.
    Trench 63 layer 14 (176): pit 48.
333. Domed spindlewhorl of chalk.
    Trench 80 layer 7 (819): general layer.
334. Pottery counter, grey on the external grooved surface, orange–buff on the internal flat surface.
    Trench 63 layer 14 (175): pit 48.
335. Sherd from a black-burnished dish with a scratched symbol on the exterior. It is presumably an owner's mark. I should like to thank Mr R. P. Wright for commenting on this piece.
    Trench 90 layer 71 (1327): general layer.

[1] Winchester City Museum Accession No. EUB/59.
[2] I am indebted to Miss J. M. Swann and Mr J. H. Thornton for bringing this point to my notice and for their kind attention during the preliminary stages of this report.

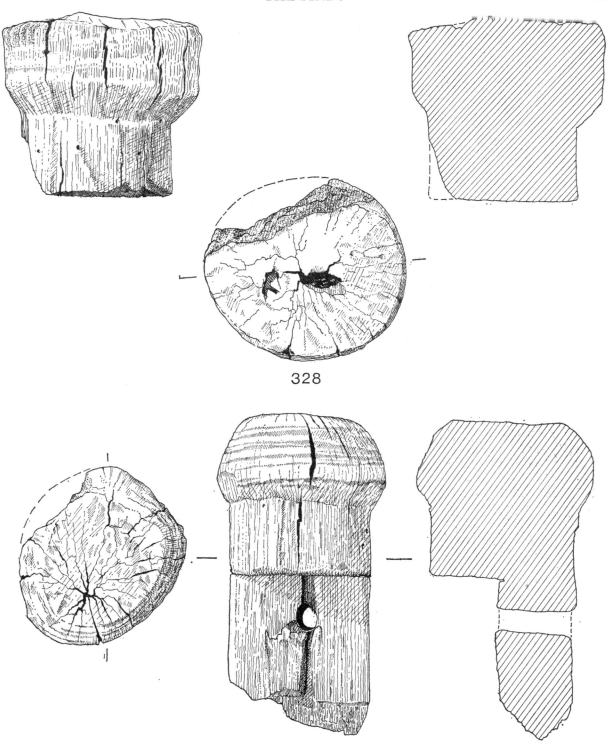

328

329

FIG. 138.   Wooden objects (p. 262). Scale $\frac{2}{3}$

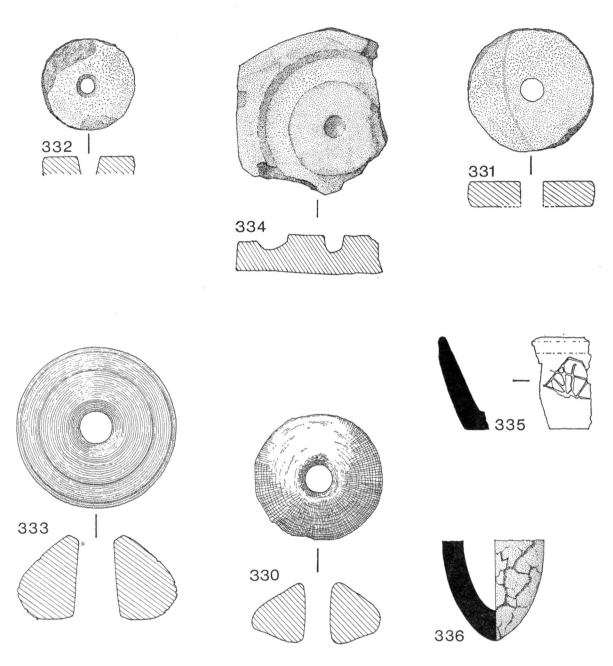

FIG. 139. Objects of stone and clay (pp. 262, 265). Scale $\frac{2}{3}$

## METAL WORKING ACTIVITY

Evidence for the working of bronze, lead and iron, has been found in various phases of the Roman occupation.

*Bronze*

336. Fragment of a crucible. A small piece of bronze survives in an internal crack.
    Trench 63 layer 7 (199): pit 46.
Not illustrated. Small angular fragment of copper ore about 40 mm. across. Identified by Dr Peacock as bornite/chalcocite, probably from Devon or Cornwall.
    Trench 5 layer 3 (25): general layer.

*Lead*

Samples of lead which have been melted and not re-formed have been found in pits 47, 48 and in trench 62 layer 5 and 63 layer 14 in general layers.

*Iron*

Iron slag has been recovered from the following contexts: well 135; pits 79, 95, 237; from upper occupation layers and layers above the make-up in trenches 89 layer 21, 91 layer 53 and 108 layer 99, and from Roman general layers, trench 72 layer 7 and 66 layer 5.

## WHETSTONES

### by DAVID PEACOCK

The whetstones recovered from Roman levels are described in the schedule below. Of these, 17 have a distinct rectangular shape, modified to varying degrees by usage, and none is complete, suggesting that they were discarded after breakage. The remaining ten whetstones appear to be utilized pebbles.

The source of raw materials is difficult to determine without more work, but it is reasonable to assume that the pebble whetstones would have a distinctly local origin. However, the possibility of specific gravel beds being deliberately worked for usable pebbles must not be ignored, and under such circumstances trade might be envisaged. The shaped whetstones may have come from further afield, and eleven rock types are present, perhaps implying as many sources. Nos. 337–41 are very similar, in the hand specimen, to certain third-century whetstones from Fishbourne, ascribed to the Hythe beds of Kent (*Fishbourne II*, 155): they may well come from this source. Nos. 347–50 appear to be Palaeozoic rocks, perhaps from western Britain or Brittany.

*Shaped Whetstones* (not illustrated)

337. Grey sandy limestone (140 × 60 × 8 mm.).
    Trench 69 layer 8 (268): general layer.

338. Grey sandy limestone (45 × 15 × 11 mm.).
   Trench 76 layer 30 (840): general layer.
339. Grey sandy limestone: groove on two faces (80 × 20 × 15 mm.).
   Trench 79 layer 60 (908): pit 121.
340. Grey sandy limestone (50 × 13 × 13 mm.).
   Trench 88 layer 5 (1009): above upper make-up.
341. Grey sandy limestone: groove on one face (100 × 20 × 20 mm.).
   Trench 100 layer 36 (2084): general layer.
342. Fine grey laminated sandy limestone: rhomb shaped (90 × 50 × 12 mm.).
   Trench 95 layer 151 (1995): pit 144.
343. Fine grey laminated sandy limestone: broad depression on one face (70 × 20 × 14 mm.).
   Trench 95 layer 148 (1988): pit 144.
344. Blue limestone with some shell (70 × 20 × 40 mm.).
   Trench 79 layer 28 (831): pit 103.
345. Grey argillaceous limestone; groove down one side (44 × 30 × 17 mm.).
   Trench 89 layer 21 (1152): above upper make-up.
346. Reddish-brown laminated shelly limestone: little used (100 × 17 × 17 mm.).
   Trench 91 layer 73 (1367): above upper road surface.
347. Greywacke sandstone (80 × 60 × 15 mm.).
   Trench 89 layer 38 (1189): above upper make-up.
348. Greywacke sandstone (55 × 44 × 25 mm.).
   Trench 108 layer 225 (2609): lower occupation.
349. Hard indurated black mudstone (90 × 18 × 13 mm.).
   Trench 102 layer 48 (2097): upper occupation.
350. Hard buff indurated mudstone; good polish on surfaces (65 × 27 × 15 mm.).
   Trench 107 layer 52 (2458): middle occupation.
351. Greenish-grey micaceous sandstone (75 × 45 × 17 mm.).
   Trench 71 layer 8 (363): general layer.
352. Buff–grey micaceous sandstone; U-shaped indentation on one side (56 × 50 × 10 mm.).
   Trench 103 layer 74 (2293).
353. Grey–buff laminated micaceous sandstone (50 × 40 × 20 mm.).
   Trench 89 layer 23 (1148): above upper make-up.

*Pebble Whetstones* (not illustrated)

354. Quartz mica granulite; fragment (40 mm. long).
   Trench 57 layer 9 (96): general layer.
355. Bluish–grey indurated mudstone; used as end rubber; circular scratch marks on unabraded surfaces (pl. XXXIV*a*); broken (85 mm. long).
   Trench 60 layer 5 (115): general layer.
356. Grey argillaceous limestone; fragment (45 mm. long).
   Trench 70 layer 28 (295): pit 63.
357. Blue–grey sandy limestone (85 mm. long).
   Trench 79 layer 60 (908): pit 121.
358. Fine grey–black micaceous sandstone; small chip.
   Trench 89 layer 35 (1187): above upper make-up.
359. Grey micaceous sandstone (80 mm. long).
   Trench 107 layer 44 (2431): upper occupation.

360. Compact grey siltstone, weathering purplish-brown (150 mm. long).
    Trench 91 layer 65 (1339): below upper make-up.
361. Compact grey siltstone, weathering purplish-brown (135 mm. long).
    Trench 107 layer 52 (2454): middle occupation.
362. Dark grey micaceous sandstone; fragment (85 mm. long).
    Trench 103 layer 23 (2283): upper occupation.
363. Grey micaceous metamorphosed sandstone (100 mm. long).
    Trench 108 layer 184 (2577): pit 230.

# QUERNSTONES

## (fig. 140)

Quernstones are surprisingly rare in the Roman levels of Portchester. Altogether only 11 fragments of stone similar to that used for quernstones were recovered; one from the middle occupation level, two from layers above the make-up, the rest from general occupation levels. Three examples are illustrated.

364. Lower stone of quern with rectangular central perforation; greensand.
    Trench 63 layer 6: general layer.
365. Fragment of lower stone of quern, probably re-used as a sharpening stone; greensand.
    Trench 89 layer 55: general layer.
366. Segment of stone of circular shape. Possibly a quern but since no working surface survives it could have been part of a column drum constructed of segments; ferruginous sandstone.
    Trench 74 layer 4 (624): general layer.

All the other fragments were of greensand with the exception of one from trench 108 layer 124, which was of a coarse sandy conglomerate.

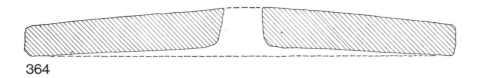

364

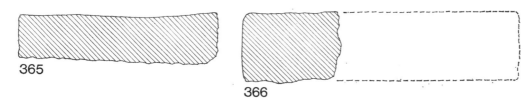

365       366

FIG. 140.   Querns (p. 267). Scale ¼

# BIBLIOGRAPHY: FINDS

(a) *Quoted Sources*

BUSCH, A. L. 1965. 'Die römerzeitlichen Schuh- und Lederfunde der Kastelle Saalburg, Zugmantel und Kleiner Feldberg'. *Saalburg-Jahrbuch* xxii, 158–210.

CHARLESWORTH, D. and THORNTON, J. H. 1973. 'Leather found in Mediobogdum, the Roman fort of Hardknott'. *Britannia*, iv, 141–52.

FOWLER, E. 1960. 'The origin and development of the penannular brooch in Europe'. *Proc. Prehist. Soc.* xxvi, 149–77.

GROENMAN-VAN WAATERINGE, W. *Romeins Lederwerk uit Valkenburg Z.M. Groningen.* (Nederlands Oudheden ii).

HAWKES, C. F. C. 1951. 'Bronze-workers, cauldrons and bucket-animals in Iron Age and Roman Britain'. In *Aspects of Archaeology in Britain and Beyond: Essays Presented to O. G. S. Crawford* (ed. W. F. Grimes), 172–99. London.

HAWKES, S. C. and DUNNING, G. C. 1961. 'Soldiers and settlers in Britain, fourth to fifth century'. *Med. Archaeol.* v, 1–70.

PESCHECK, C. 1969. 'Ein germanisches Gräberfeld in Oberfranken'. *Germania* xlvii, 129–45.

SHORTT, H. DE S. 1959. 'A provincial Roman spur from Longstock, Hants, and other spurs from Roman Britain'. *Antiq. J.* xxxix, 61–76.

TOYNBEE, J. M. C. 1964. *Art in Britain Under the Romans.* Oxford.

WEBSTER, G. 1962. 'The defences of Viroconium (Wroxeter)'. *Trans. Birmingham Archaeol. Soc.* lxxviii, 27–39.

WHEELER, R. E. M. 1946. *London in Roman Times.* London Museum Catalogue No. 3.

WILD, J. P. 1970. *Textile Manufacture in the Northern Roman Provinces.* Cambridge.

(b) *Quoted Sites*

*Bourton on the Water:* H. Donovan, 'Excavation of a Romano-British building at Bourton on the Water, 1934'. *Trans. Bristol & Gloucs. Archaeol. Soc.* lvi (1934), 99–128.

*Caerleon: Myrtle Cottage:* A. Fox, 'The legionary fortress at Caerleon, Monmouthshire: excavations in Myrtle Cottage Orchard, 1939'. *Archaeol. Cambrensis* xcv (1940), 101–52.

*Camerton:* W. J. Wedlake, *Excavations at Camerton, Somerset.* Camerton Excavation Club, 1958.

*Camulodunum:* C. F. C. Hawkes and M. R. Hull, *Camulodunum: First Report on Excavations at Colchester 1930–39.* London, 1947.

*Chalton:* S. S. Frere, 'Late Roman objects from Chalton, Hants.'. *Antiq. J.* xxxvii (1957), 218–20.

*Cranborne Chase:* Lt.-Gen. Pitt-Rivers, *Excavations in Cranborne Chase*, vols. i (1887), ii (1888), iii (1892), iv (1898). Printed privately.

*Dinas Powys:* L. Alcock, *Dinas Powys.* Cardiff, 1963.

*Eboracum: Eboracum: Roman York.* Royal Commission on Historical Monuments, 1962.

*Fishbourne II:* B. Cunliffe, *Excavations at Fishbourne 1961–9: Vol. 2, The Finds.* London, 1971.

*Gatcombe 1965–6:* B. Cunliffe, 'Excavations at Gatcombe, Somerset, in 1965 and 1966'. *Proc. Univ. of Bristol Speleological Soc.*, vol. 2, no. 2 (1967), 126–60.

*Glastonbury Lake Village:* A. Bulleid and H. St. George Gray, *Glastonbury Lake Village*, vol. i (1911), ii (1917).

*Hod Hill I:* J. Brailsford, *Hod Hill*, Vol. i. British Museum, 1962.

*Hod Hill II:* I. A. Richmond, *Hod Hill*, Vol. ii. British Museum, 1968.

*Höfheim:* E. Ritterling, 'Das frührömische Lager bei Hofheim im Taunus'. *Annalen des Vereins für Nassauische Altertumskunde und Geschichtsforschung*, xl (1912).

*Leicester: Jewry Wall:* K. M. Kenyon, *Excavations at the Jewry Wall Site, Leicester.* London, 1948.

*Lydney:* R. E. M. and T. V. Wheeler, *Excavation of the Prehistoric, Roman and Post-Roman site in Lydney Park, Gloucestershire.* London, 1932.

*Maiden Castle:* R. E. M. Wheeler, *Maiden Castle, Dorset.* London, 1943.

*Newstead:* J. Curle, *A Roman Frontier Post and its People. The Fort of Newstead in the Parish of Melrose.* Glasgow, 1911.

*Nor'nour:* D. Dudley, 'Excavations on Nor'nour in the Isles of Scilly, 1962–6'. *Arch. J.* cxxiv (1967), 1–64.

*Richborough I:* J. P. Bushe-Fox, *First Report on the Excavation of the Roman Fort at Richborough, Kent.* London, 1926.

*Richborough II:* J. P. Bushe-Fox, *Second Report on the Excavation of the Roman Fort at Richborough, Kent.* London, 1928.

*Richborough III:* J. P. Bushe-Fox, *Third Report on the Excavation of the Roman Fort at Richborough, Kent.* London, 1932.

*Richborough IV:* J. P. Bushe-Fox, *Fourth Report on the Excavation of the Roman Fort at Richborough, Kent.* London, 1949.

*Richborough V:* B. Cunliffe, *Fifth Report on the Excavation of the Roman Fort at Richborough, Kent.* London, 1968.

*Shakenoak I, II* and *IV:* A. C. C. Brodribb, A. R. Hands and D. R. Walker, *Excavations at Shakenoak Farm, near Wilcote, Oxfordshire,* Pt. I (1968), Pt. II (1971), Pt. IV (1973). Printed privately, Oxford.

*Verulamium I:* S. S. Frere, *Verulamium, Excavations,* Vol. I. London, 1972.

*Verulamium 1936:* R. E. M. Wheeler and T. V. Wheeler, *Verulamium: A Belgic and Two Roman Cities.* London, 1936.

*Wroxeter III:* J. P. Bushe-Fox, *Third Report on the Excavations on the site of the Roman town of Wroxeter, Shropshire, 1914.* London, 1916.

*York: The Mount:* C. Dickinson and P. Wenham, 'Discoveries in the Roman cemetery on the Mount, York'. *Yorks. Arch. J.* xxxix (1958), 283–323.

# VIII. THE POTTERY

## by MICHAEL FULFORD

## INTRODUCTION

MORE than 350 kg. of Roman pottery were recovered from pits and stratified layers at Portchester. Most of the pottery dates within the bracket, c. A.D. 280–c. 400, and, with the exception of a few residual sherds, like the samian, presumably brought in when the fort was built, and some first/second-century material (pp. 8–10), it can, in the broadest terms, be seen as a late third/fourth-century group. For this reason unstratified types have been incorporated in the type series. However, pit and stratified groups make it possible to divide the pottery into four main periods:[1]

1. A small group belonging to the construction phase, c. 280–90.
2. Some rubbish layers and pits dating from c. 280–90 to c. 325.
3. More rubbish layers and most of the pits, dating c. 325 to c. 345.
4. More rubbish layers dating from c. 345.

The layers above the Roman road surface (p. 50) probably reflect the latest Roman pottery brought into the fort.

It is very difficult to date the end of the 'Roman' occupation in terms of pottery, because of a lack of large, distinctive groups within the post-345 material, which might pinpoint ceramic trends within that group as a whole. The latest layers have suffered most from subsequent activity on the site and what is left accounts for only about 20% of the total stratified material from the fort. If drastic changes are to be expected in the latest Roman period, there is no evidence of this in the latest Portchester groups. The Oxfordshire colour-coated fabrics increase, and there is no sign of significant fall-off in the black-burnished fabrics from Dorset. If the phasing out of black-burnished in the north after 367 is reflected in the south (Gillam, 1957; Farrar, 1969), then the Portchester group shows little indication of it. The only changes are a decline in the wheel-thrown grey wares, but this is more a mirror of the growth of the Oxfordshire colour-coated industry than of increase in more local, 'crude', hand-made pottery. New Forest fine wares were possibly beginning to decline after 350. If any conclusions can be drawn from these threads of evidence, then they are that the latest groups at Portchester consist largely of pottery dating pre-c. 380. Occupation after that, which the coin evidence attests, is perhaps not great enough to influence the trends already present. The latest group from the fort was deposited after 378 (pit 63). This does not mean that pottery dating later than c. 380 is not present in the latest layers, but it is not distinguishable as such.

---

[1] Details of the types and quantities found in each stratified layer are given above in the relevant sections of parts III and IV.

The importance of the Portchester groups lies in their size. For the first time on a fourth-century site it is possible to make comparisons within the various groups and to detect significant trends in both fabrics generally and types in particular. Not only is the presence of a type important, but so also its absence from a layer, or group of layers. Comparison of large groups also allows for more precise dating of types. Fabric weight has been added as a further quantifiable variable, to balance somewhat inaccurate estimations based only on the possible minimum number of vessels represented by rims or sherds.

Detecting trends in types and fabrics is dogged by the vital, but unknown, 'residual factor'—that is the rate at which vessels will continue to be used and discarded after their production has ceased. In plotting the number of occurrences of any type against time, there is no formula which can predict at what point on the resulting curve that type ceased to be manufactured. Without other sites in the south to compare with Portchester, dating assessments must be treated with caution. Lack of groups to cover the first decades of the fourth and the last of the third century means that the starting dates for many types are probably put too late. Similarly, where doubt exists concerning the end date of a type, more well-stratified groups from the end of the fourth century would provide a narrower range. Equally the residual problem becomes greatest with the latest groups.

Whatever deductions can be made about trends in the pottery must be qualified, not only with provisos about the residual element, but also with some cautions expressed about the nature of the occupation and how far it is unique or comparable with other fourth-century sites in southern Britain. The possibility that the pottery merely reflects the consumption of an army unit cannot be ruled out until more comparative material is available. But there is yet no evidence from the south for the existence of a contract situation between the army and the production centres at this period, as there is likely to have been in the first and second centuries. The ratios in terms of fabrics and types from Portchester is closely comparable with those from Winchester, Clausentum and Dorchester (Dorset). In certain respects trends detectable at Portchester (particularly the growth of the Oxfordshire industry) can be paralleled at Leicester, London, Verulamium (see p. 285) and at Richborough. By the fourth century it is unlikely that considerable differences existed between the requirements of civilian and military populations in terms of pottery: fashion or social habits would be the main regulator.

If, however, the possibility of different kinds of occupation at Portchester is envisaged, with perhaps civilian settlement following on after an initial military phase, then it is instructive that over 70% of the stratified pottery probably lies in a bracket of c. 325–45, which may be a period of civil occupation. If this is the case, then the military contract problem is irrelevant. Indeed the possibility that during military occupation all rubbish was scrupulously cleared out of the fort cannot be discounted. Certainly there is very little stratified pottery for the period c. 280–c. 325.

Despite all qualifications, Portchester remains important to our understanding of the development of both the New Forest and Oxfordshire colour-coated industries, as well as in elucidating the relationship between these and non-colour-coated fabrics, of both hand-made and wheel-made types.

# THE POTTERY FROM THE PITS AND WELLS

The pottery from the pits and wells accounts for over 55% of the total pottery assemblage at Portchester which has been considered in this report as having a stratified context. Only 18 pits have coins in them to provide *termini post quos* for the layers in which they occur and for those layers above. The problem with the rest is whether or not they can be grouped together as part of one phase of occupation, or whether their filling can straggle over the whole period of Roman occupation, *c.* 280–*c.* 400. Whatever conclusion is reached in this respect influences the value that may be placed on each, or all, of the pits, and on the presence or absence of types and fabrics in the fills, particularly with regard to the dating of individual types.

There are three ways of examining the date ranges possible for the pits: by looking at the coin evidence for individual pits; by looking at the pottery types present or absent when compared with the other groups within the fort; or by taking account of a set of variables (in this case the ratios of the main fabrics present) and determining whether they can be sorted meaningfully.

1. *Coins*
   (a) Pits with coins pre-*c.* 325: pits 46, 60, 62, 86, 121, 178, 222, 223, 227 and 230 (which stratigraphically must be pre-*c.* 325).
   (b) Pits with coins *c.* 325–*c.* 340: pits 63, 92, 138, 144 and 236.
   (c) Pits with coins later than *c.* 340: pits 63, 66 and 236 (upper layers only).

In all these cases the coins need not strictly define the date of fill, rather a lower limit. With the well pits, in particular, it is possible that deliberate back-filling may confuse the issue with the likelihood of both coins and the pottery being earlier than the real date of filling.

2. *Pottery Types and Fabrics*

The pottery itself can only be of limited value if comparisons are made with the other large groups against the wall up to the upper clay seal (accounting for only about 22% of the pottery from the fort) or with those in the interior which accumulated before *c.* 345. The presence or absence of different types and fabrics between these and the pits may serve as an indication of the upper limit of the filling of the pits. Several colour-coated types, particularly red-slipped bowls, in both Oxfordshire and New Forest fabrics tend to occur only in pits and later non-pit groups, e.g. types 2/10.7–12, 6, 18, 30, 33, 34, 35 (with one exception), 36, 37, 52 and 55 (some fabrics). Some other types occur commonly in pits, e.g. 2/10.4–5, 31 (two exceptions), 38, etc. Among the coarse wares, fabric D types are more common in pit groups and later, with only a few occurring in layers below the upper clay seal. These differences may be only a reflection of the greater size of the total pit assemblage compared with the other layers which allows the possibility of a wider range of types to be present in the pits. However, it is equally possible that some of the pits were being filled (and the pits with the late coins are excepted here) after *c.* 345/50, depending on when one places the date of the upper clay seal.

This comparative argument cannot be pursued in the period before 325/30 because of the lack of good, non-pit groups. Absence of a type in any one pit cannot be used as an indicator, since, compared with the large non-pit groups, too little material is available to make a valid reference.

### 3. *Single-link Cluster Analysis: Program and Application to Portchester by N. G. Gummer*

A third approach to the problem of dating the pits was made using a single link cluster program (Hodson, 1970) to determine whether the ratios of the main, individual fabric groups, both between separate pits and layers within pits, might produce any distinct clusters of pits that could then be related back to the coins and other external evidence. The computer program used for the Portchester data employs the single-link method of clustering, based on similarities derived from Euclidean distance. It produces a hierarchical division of the set of items into groups, sub-groups, sub-sub-groups, and so on, and presents the results in the form of a dendrogram. This can be regarded as a family tree of the relationships between the groups. For each layer at Portchester, the program was provided with the weights of each of seven types of pottery (New Forest; Oxfordshire; miscellaneous colour-coated; hand-made, fabric A; black-burnished; grey fabrics; and fabric D) expressed as a percentage of the total weight of pottery found in the layer or pit. A total of 129 pits and or layers was included in the analysis.

Most of the pits tended to cluster together and it was only a very few (many of which were layers within well pits) which were grouped apart. However, the analysis has probably not found all the useful groupings that exist because the results appear to suffer to some extent from a shortcoming of the single-link method, namely chaining. The shortcoming is noticed when there are some items that are intermediate in type between two groups. One of the groups can then appear on the dendrogram as a chain of single items rather than as a group. At any given level on the dendogram the items can best be divided into a main group plus a number of ungrouped single items. It is hoped to reprocess the data using a program, now in the course of preparation, that implements the method that Hodson calls k-means, which does not suffer from the tendency towards chaining. Although the formation of chains does result in some loss of information, the fact that many of the items may be of intermediate type could well be of archaeological significance. It is not necessary to reproduce the dendrogram, because of the lack of good clusters, but those pits and layers that did not fit in to the main 'family' group are as follows:

Group 1: Pit 125, layer 35; large percentage of colour-coated fabrics against coarse wares. Among the types are some which do not otherwise appear pre-*c.* 330–40.

Group 2: Pit 79; a small total amount with high percentage of colour-coated fabrics.
Pit 236, layers 120 and 121 combined; lowest layer of the well pit, likely to be pre-330; a very high percentage of colour-coated fabrics.
Pit 182; high percentage of miscellaneous, mostly due to the large part of one pot (type 179).
Pit 164, layers 54 and 69 combined; small sample of colour-coated and miscellaneous fine fabrics in large amount (well pit).

Group 3: Pit 206, layer 86; well pit; no Oxfordshire, but high percentage of New Forest and Argonne fabrics.
Pit 144, layer 142; well pit; high percentage of miscellaneous, probably one example of type 179; low colour-coated fabrics.
Pit 187; layer 83; again distortion due to large amount of one type 179.

These exceptions can be explained firstly by the small amounts of pottery in each case, and

19

hence by the possibility of distortion due to the presence of one or two vessels which, if almost complete when discarded, will drastically alter the ratios of the fabrics. It is interesting that several well pits have atypical layers in this respect. The dating, however, of all these 'rogues' need not be affected or considered separate from the rest of the pits which belong together in one 'family'.

Group 4: The remaining pits; these will not be listed although there are one or two clusters within this family.

Single-link analysis has not been able to divide the pits in any meaningful way, in terms of dates suggested by coins. Within the main group (4) both early and late pits (on coin evidence) and upper and lower well pit fills are clustered together. Although the results are not spectacular, they do suggest that the pits were not being filled over such a length of time as to produce distinct clusters for different periods. Perhaps a new analysis using a seriation program and taking into account more variables, such as the types in the pits, the shape and volume of the latter, animal bones, etc. may produce improved results.

### Conclusions

Any conclusions about the range of date of the pit fills must be tentative. It is likely that some pits were dug and filled after the deposition of the middle occupation and upper clay seal layers against the wall, although only a very few (those pit layers with late coins) appear not to have been completely filled by c. 350–60 at the latest. Although pits 222, 223 and 230 were all dug before c. 325, on stratigraphical grounds, it is difficult to be certain about others even when the coin evidence is suggestive. While only four pits have coins that can be no later than 319, it is still possible for all the cesspits to have been dug and sealed by c. 325, with later rubbish gradually accumulating on their sagging clay seals.

In no case was enough material gathered from beneath the clay cess seal of any pit to help determine a pre-325 date for the use of the pit for cess. However, if the middle and upper clay layers against the wall represent spoil from the pit digging this would imply that most pits were not dug until c. 325. The evidence, therefore, for the beginning of cesspit use within the fort is ambiguous. As for establishing the date of currency of any particular pottery type, the evidence of the pits cannot be used without great caution, and it is best to use only those pits with coins to provide *termini post quos*. More generally, on the basis of comparisons with the larger non-pit groups of pottery, a tentative suggestion might be that the pits belong to the phase c. 325–c. 345, with respect to both their digging and filling.

### Well Pits

It was hoped that some significant differences might be established between the upper and lower layers of well pits, but on the whole all the fills cluster with the rest of the pits. Clearly the layer sequence within the wells is likely to represent a chronological sequence, although the possibility of deliberately dumping residual material to stabilize a disused and dangerous well shaft, interleaved with the gradual accumulation of day to day rubbish, must always be borne in mind. On the evidence of pottery and coins there is no reason why all the wells, except pit 135, were not out of use by 340–50, and that in most cases they had completely filled with rubbish by 350–60. It is also possible that the pits had ceased to function as wells much earlier, say *c.* 330, e.g. pits 121 or 164, and had filled up with rubbish largely in the period *c.* 330–50. However, if the pits were an integral part of the *c.* 325–45 phase, then it is unlikely that the wells had all ceased to function before *c.* 345. If one considers the possibility of gradual settlement of the well fills after primary filling, then it is likely that the uppermost feet of fill may not have been deposed until very much later than the bulk of the fill. Pit 236, with a coin of 353–6 in the upper fill, corroborates this point, and that is the latest coin from any well. The pottery also from the upper layers tends to contain types which are rare in the other pits or in layers below the upper clay layer.

## METHODS OF STUDY

The pottery from Portchester is presented not only typologically, with a quantitative assessment of how much is represented in terms of rim or distinctive body sherds, but also by the main fabric constituents and their relative weights. In addition all the stratified groups are presented in terms of the type series, but not with drawings. The quantity of vessels militated

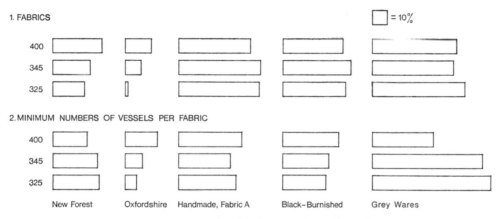

Fig. 141. The main fabric trends at Portchester

against visual presentation by group; moreover, such a work would have involved an enormous amount of wasteful repetition. Nevertheless, all the stratified groups can be reconstructed in terms of the type series; similarly the associations of each type and variant are recorded.

The division into fabrics is an attempt to see whether the ceramic trends can be more objectively defined, disregarding individual types (fig. 141). This approach also tends to highlight the progress of the kiln centres themselves. Each fabric type was weighed in each stratified group. This method of quantification will be of enormous importance in cross-comparing groups both within Portchester and outside. It appears that there is an interesting lack of correlation between fabrics and minimum numbers of types as a percentage of the total assemblage concerned (cf. fig. 141). Essentially the pottery falls into five main groups:

New Forest, Oxfordshire, hand-made, fabric A (grog-tempered), black-burnished (BB 1), and grey wares. These are described separately below.

Heavy mineral analysis (Peacock, 1967) was used to help define the grog-tempered fabric in terms of possible manufacturing centres. Visual identification of the black-burnished fabric was similarly backed up by analysis. Characterization of the grey fabrics, however, presented a much greater problem. Since a number of fabrics and sources seemed likely, a selection was analysed to try and define groups, and, if possible, sources. Unfortunately, too few results were obtained to allow generalization (but see p. 293 under grey wares).

Attempts at dating individual types have been made in the type series, but these are to a certain extent dependent on variations in percentage of the type in question from one group of stratified layers to the next. Two standards are employed, one slightly more refined than the other. First, as a fine measure, the rubbish layers against the wall have been used,[1] i.e.

LO/M. Clay      (*c.* 300–*c.* 325)
MO/Up. Clay     (*c.* 325–345)
UO              (*c.* 345 +)

Secondly, as a coarser guide three more general groups were assembled, i.e.

1. All layers pre-325, incorporating the same layers as above.
2. All layers pre-345, which incorporates layers BMU and BURRS as well as MO/Up. Clay.
3. All layers post-345, which incorporates AMU and AURRS, as well as UO.

Alongside these trends in individual types can be set the trend in basic fabric types, which is represented in figs. 141, 151–2, 158. No explanation can yet be offered for the lack of correlation between type and fabric as a percentage of the groups indicated above.

# THE SAMIAN

## by Joanna Morris

*Potters' Stamps* (fig. 142)

T(?): on Dr. 31; Central Gaul, Hadrianic–Antonine; u/s.
Fig. 142*a*: on Dr. 33; Priscus of Lezoux, *c.* 130–160; u/s.
Fig. 142*b*: wheel stamp on Dr. 31; East Gaul, later C2–mid C3; u/s.

[1] The abbreviations used here and in the following pages are:
L. Clay Bank, lower clay bank
LO, lower occupation
MO, middle occupation
UO, upper occupation
M. Clay, middle clay
Up. Clay, upper clay
BMU, below upper make-up
BURRS, below upper Roman road surface
AMU, above upper make-up
AURRS, above upper Roman road surface
u/s, not from a closed group.

 A     B

FIG. 142.   The samian stamps. Scale $\frac{1}{1}$

*Decorated Ware*

Dr. 37 in the style of Cinnamus of Lezoux; his ovolo 1 with border of ovoid beads (cf. Stanfield and Simpson, 1958, pl. 162, 60), *c.* A.D. 150–180; u/s.

*Plain Wares*

Flavian: Dr. 18; South Gaul, very worn; u/s.
Hadrianic–early Antonine: Dr. 18/31; Central Gaul; u/s (4).
　　　　　　　Dr. 31; Central Gaul; UO (1); u/s (1).
　　　　　　　Dr. 33; Central Gaul; u/s (2), one of which is probably that stamped by Priscus.
Antonine: Dr. 31; Central Gaul; pits 52 and 144; u/s (4).
　　Dr. 33; Central Gaul; MO (1); u/s (1).
　　Dr. 45; Central Gaul; u/s (1).
Second century: Dr. 18/31 or 31; either Central or East Gaul; u/s (1).
　　　　Dr. 18/31; Central Gaul; u/s (1); East Gaul; u/s (1); either Central or East Gaul; u/s (1).
　　　　Dr. 36; Central Gaul; pit 121; u/s (1); either Central or East Gaul; u/s (1).

Later second to mid-third century:

|  | East Gaul | Either Central or East Gaul |
|---|---|---|
| Dr. 18/31 or 31 | Pit 223 |  |
| Dr. 31 | AMU (1); u/s (2) | u/s (1) |
| Dr. 31R |  | Pit 41; u/s (1) |
| Dr. 33 | Pit 144 |  |
| Dr. 37 | u/s (1) |  |
| Dr. 38 | u/s (3) |  |
| Dr. 43 or 45 | u/s (1) | u/s (1) |
| Dr. 45 | AURRS (1) |  |
| Curle 15 | u/s (2) |  |
| Curle 21 | u/s (1) |  |

Altogether 1200 g. of samian, both stratified and unstratified, were recovered. This amounts to about 0·3% of all the pottery from the site. It is unlikely that this represents evidence of occupation in the late second or third centuries, although the Flavian sherd may be connected with the first- to second-century coarse pottery, which occurred in a small quantity (pp. 8–10).

More probable is the explanation that these sherds represent old pottery (cf. type 74) brought to the site by the first occupants, possibly as treasured heirlooms or antiques! In fact it would be strange if there were no remnants at all of such a large, fine-pottery industry in the later third or fourth centuries. Such an explanation will surely account for those late sites where a little samian occurs without supporting coarse wares.

## THE ARGONNE WARE

### (fig. 143)

Altogether 1025 g. of Argonne ware, representing between about 15 and 30 vessels, were recovered from Portchester. Only 385 g. were stratified. The types and different varieties are listed according to Chenet (1941):

Type 304: pit 236.
Type 313: pits 178 and 236 (possibly sherds of the same vessel); (cf. Chenet, fig. 18, no. 9).
Type 320: with stamp no. 8 or 191; u/s; fig. 143a.
Type 320: with stamp no. 65; u/s (cf. type 320e); fig. 143b.
Type 320: with stamp no. 303; AMU (not illustrated).
Type 320: with stamp no. 304; u/s (2); fig. 143c.
Type 320: rims only from; BURRS (1); AURRS (2); u/s (2).
Type 324: AMU (1).
Type 326: pits 185 and 206; UO (1); u/s (6).
Type 328: pit 138; AURRS (1); UO (1); u/s (3).
Type 329: AMU (1).
Summary: pits (6); BURRS (1); AURRS (3); AMU (3); UO (2); u/s (15).

The Argonne ware forms a very small proportion of the pottery at Portchester (0·27%) and it is difficult to interpret its presence as either through trade or the casual import of belongings by individuals. Argonne ware is rare in Britain, although one would not perhaps expect much importation of fine pottery in the face of competition from the Oxfordshire and similar potteries. On the basis of the distribution of Argonne ware in Britain, Portchester represents part of the extreme westward drift. Eastwards, at Richborough, there are decorated sherds which represent four or five times the amount at Portchester, while at Pevensey there is perhaps twice the amount. However, as in neither of these cases do we know the original size of the excavated sample, these sites can only be used as a very rough guide. On the grounds of the distribution which shows a bias towards south-east Britain, both in numbers of sites and the amount at each, it is reasonable to see the Argonne ware at Portchester as the result of trade. In view of the location of the major British fine-pottery producing factories, the south-east concentration would be an expected pattern.

While there are no sealed contexts with roller-stamped pieces, the plain forms appear to have a wide date range, being present both in the pits and later contexts, which give a wide bracket from c. A.D. 320 onwards. This does not conflict with Hübener's (1968) dating for Argonne ware. The roller stamped pieces belong to his categories 2, 3 and 5, which have, in the first two cases, a range from *c.* 330 to *c.* 360, while group 5 ranges from *c.* 360 to 390. None of these dates are incompatible with the evidence from Portchester.

It is noteworthy that the bulk of the Portchester types are plain forms, in contrast to a general absence of plain forms among the published Argonne ware from many other sites. It will not be possible to understand the development of the Argonne industry until all the products of the kilns have been considered together.

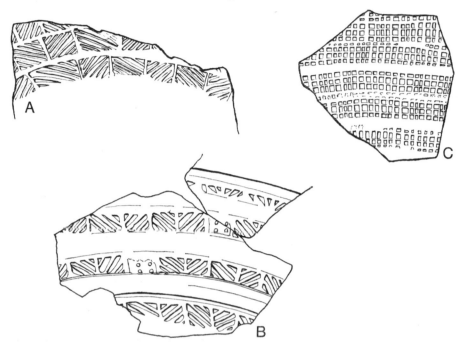

FIG. 143.   The Argonne ware. Scale ⅟₁

## OTHER IMPORTS

In addition to the samian and Argonne ware, there are several other sherds which are recognizable as imports to Portchester from outside the British Isles:

(a) Two sherds of beaker from either the Rhineland or Lezoux (Type 27).
(b) Four sherds of Spanish globular amphorae (Type 74).
(c) Two sherds of 'Mayen' ware (Type 151).[1]
(d) Two sherds in a sandy fabric with a Rhineland origin (Types 99.1 and 161.4).[1]

## COLOUR-COATED FABRICS

To save undue repetition, the common colour-coated fabrics have been numbered according to source and these will be used in the general descriptions in the type series.

[1] Fulford and Bird, forthcoming.

*New Forest, Fabric 1*

The fabric is a fine paste with a range of hardness up to a stone-ware. Inclusions are usually absent except in the form of haematite/limonite grains, up to 0·5 mm. diameter. When oxidized, which is rare, the fabric is medium hard and pale yellow or brown, sometimes with a grey core. Usually it is reduced and light grey, perhaps brown towards the surface. The stone-ware examples are dark grey all through.

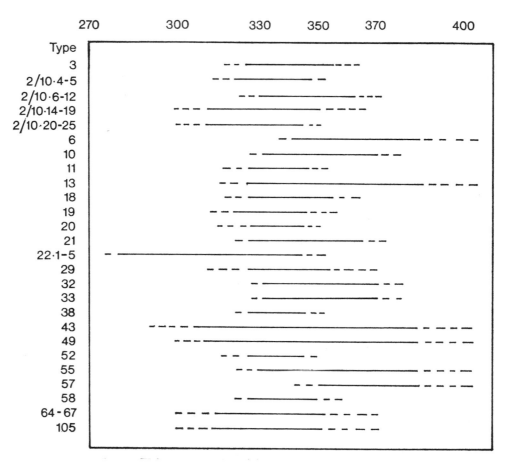

FIG. 144.　Date ranges of New Forest types at Portchester

The slip corresponds with the different degree of firing temperature and the oxygen content of the kiln. It may vary (and sometimes a whole range of colour is present on the same vessel) from a light, reddish-yellow, through light and dark reddish-browns to a dusky red or purple, which often has a metallic sheen to it. It does not seem sensible to record the range of slip and fabric of each type, whenever it occurs, for the reasons above: thus a reference to fabric 1 includes both fabric and slip descriptions as above, since the two are so closely related.

Types in this fabric and slip are: 2, 3, 5, 6, 10, 13, 18, 19, 20, 21, 22, 23, 39, 52, 55, 56.

*New Forest, Fabric 2*

This fabric is very similar to fabric 1, but is always oxidized and never high-fired to a stone-ware. If the fabric is not fine and cream in colour, with occasional haematite/limonite grains, then it is more granular and rough with a reddish-yellow colour. In the latter instance, it is difficult to distinguish between an Oxfordshire and New Forest product. Fortunately this problem does not arise very often. The colour-coat varies from a reddish-yellow to a reddish-brown, although the former is most common.

Types with this fabric and slip are: 29, 30, 32, 33, 34, 38, 40, 41, 43, 44, 47, 57, 58, 61, 88, 95, 175.

*New Forest, Fabric 3*

This fabric is the New Forest fabric known as 'parchment ware': it is white and heavily sanded. Although the majority of types are unslipped, certain types do possess a brown to purple slip, but these will be listed in the type series. Mortaria types invariably have crushed flint trituration grits.

Types in this fabric are: 10, 11, 12, 48, 49, 53, 54, 55, 56, 64, 65, 66, 67, 105.

*New Forest, Fabric 3a*

This fabric is like fabric 3, but it is fine and sand free. Kiln 3 in Amberwood Inclosure (Fulford, 1973(a)) produced type 49 in this fabric. Occasionally, when a slightly iron-rich clay was used, then an overall white slip was necessary to achieve the 'parchment' effect.

Types in this fabric are: 48, 49, 50, 64.

*Oxfordshire, Fabric 1*

This fabric has a granular or laminated appearance in fracture. The colour is a reddish-brown, often with a grey core, and the fabric is usually very micaceous. In general this ware is higher fired than its New Forest equivalent. The slip is usually a bright red, sometimes a little pale, and contrasts noticeably with that of the New Forest fabric 2.

Types in this fabric and slip are: 28, 30, 31, 33, 34, 35, 36, 40, 41, 42, 43, 53, 54, 57, 58, 59.

*Oxfordshire, Fabric 2*

This fabric comprises most of the beaker wares, and in many cases, because of the lack of certainty as to whether the type is Oxfordshire or not, individual variants are separately described in the type series. Generally the fabric is light brown, somewhat granular in appearance and very micaceous. Occasionally it occurs as a fine, hard brown ware with a grey core. Unlike New Forest beakers, high firing temperatures were seldom used with the Oxfordshire types. The colours of the slips range widely from a matt, dirty yellow or red–brown, to a muddy blue–black. Semi-glossy surfaces are rare.

Types with this fabric and slip range are: 1, 3, 7, 14, 15, 16, 17, 18, 24, 25.

*Oxfordshire, Fabric 3*

This is the Oxfordshire equivalent to the New Forest 'parchment' fabric, but is much finer, although still sandy. However, it is never finer than the New Forest, fabric 3a ware. The colour is off-white or very pale yellow and sometimes there may be a covering of a thin yellow–brown wash or a white slip. Inclusions of rounded, translucent quartz do occur (up to 1–1·5 mm. diameter), particularly in mortaria types where they are the standard type of trituration grit.

Types in this fabric are: 48, 50, ? 55, 63.

### Pevensey Ware

This fabric is extremely hard and laminated in fracture, with visible inclusions of haematite or limonite. There is a tendency for the fabric to flake apart. It is reddish-brown in colour, usually with a grey core, while the slip is a bright red or reddish-brown and is pimply and uneven on the surface. The fineness, hardness and finish make this fabric readily distinguishable from the New Forest, fabric 2, or Oxfordshire, fabric 1, equivalents. No exact source is known for this ware, but the name of 'Pevensey' ware has been suggested (Fulford, 1973(b)), as the highest percentage of this fabric in any assemblage occurs there.

Types in this fabric are: 35, 37, 42, 43.

### New Forest Wares: Discussion

Prior to this report the evidence for the development of the New Forest pottery industry and the dating of individual types or kiln groups was limited (summarized in Fulford, 1973(c)). The pottery from Portchester can, however, provide the skeleton of a new framework. Briefly, it would appear that a distinctive range of colour-coated bottles, beakers, flagons and parchment ware types was in production by A.D. 320/30. This was then augmented by red slipped bowls and more beaker and jug types as the first group gradually went out of production (see fig. 144 and the detailed evidence in the type series). The latest phase of the industry is attested in Amberwood Inclosure (kiln 3) with a range of colour-coated types and 'parchment' bowls generally without further decoration (Fulford, 1973(a)).

In terms of the kiln groups within the Forest, it would seem that the earliest production of colour-coated wares was at Sloden (Wilson, 1968, and information from the excavator, Mrs V. G. Swan) and Crock Hill (Akerman, 1853; Bartlett, 1873; Sumner, 1927, 110–12), with subsequent shift of emphasis to Ashley Rails and Pitts Wood (Sumner, 1927, 17–41 and 114–15), Islands Thorns (Sumner, 1927, 101–8 and 112–13) and Amberwood (Fulford, 1973(a)). There is probably a considerable overlap from one main group to another. Coarse ware kilns are more difficult to date, but if the decline in grey wares at Portchester in the second half of the fourth century claims more support from other sites, then it is likely that the Linwood, Sloden (Sumner, 1927, 45–101; Cunliffe, 1965), Crock Hill (Cunliffe, 1965) and Amberwood (Fulford, 1973(a)) kilns, which produced *only* coarse wares, date to the first half of the fourth century. The coin evidence, flimsy as it is, does not contradict this hypothesis (Sumner, 1927, 81).

### Oxfordshire Wares: Discussion

The evidence for the production of colour-coated and 'parchment' fabrics in the Oxfordshire is summarized in May (1922), Harden (1936), Atkinson (1941), Case and Kirk (1953), and Young (1973). Portchester is clearly very important to the dating of many of the

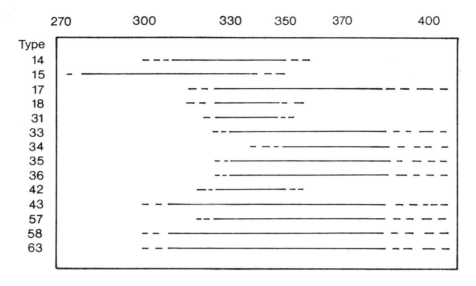

FIG. 145.   Date ranges of Oxfordshire types at Portchester

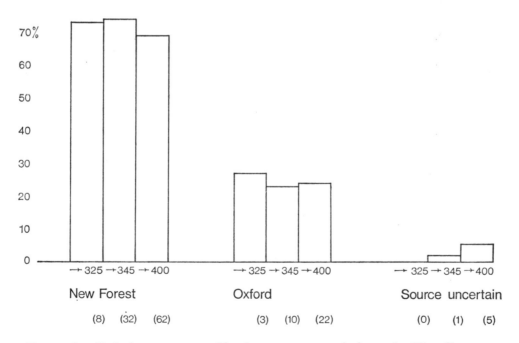

FIG. 146.   Relative amounts of beakers, types 13–26, from the New Forest,
Oxfordshire, etc. at Portchester

Oxfordshire types, whatever reservations may be made about the nature of the occupation and the distance of Portchester from the production centre. With the exception of those forms which closely imitate plain samian forms, like Dr. 31, 36, 38 and 45, it seems that the bulk of the red-slipped bowl forms are not being produced until *c.* A.D. 330 (cf. fig. 145). Decoration of finely executed rouletting, or combinations of both paint and rouletting, probably precede the use of stamps, which may not come in until *c.* 350. The sherd impressed with a coin of *c.* 300 seems to be a freak, and by itself is no evidence for the use of rosette stamping, etc., early in the century (Webster, 1968). Cordoned and handled bowls are likewise late. The beakers, on the other hand, like those from the New Forest, date from the late third century (if the diagnosis of an Oxfordshire source is right), but fade out in the second half of the fourth century. However, this situation may only be a reflection of a regional marketing trend, due to a pre-ference for new Forest beakers. Portchester has no contribution to make to the dating of the 'parchment' fabrics. Like the New Forest equivalents, they probably have a long life and, in

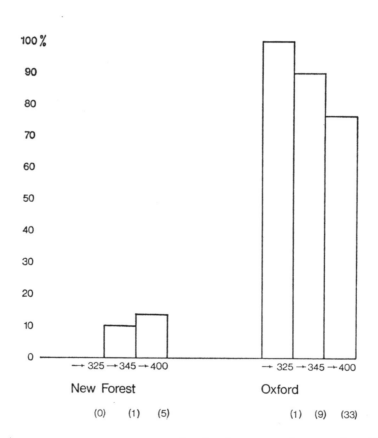

FIG. 147.   Relative amounts of red colour-coated mortaria, types 57–61, from the New Forest and Oxfordshire at Portchester

the case of mortaria, production is attested in the second century (Frere, 1962, 145–6). On a wider level, it is interesting that the date of the increase in red-slipped Oxfordshire bowls is close to that of the start of roller-stamped Argonne ware (Hübener, 1968). If the industries reflect the availability of consumer capital, then it is interesting that this is more or less contemporary on both sides of the Channel in the fourth century. To complement Portchester large groups are needed for the first two decades and the second half of the fourth century. But it is reassuring that the Portchester evidence for the dating of Oxfordshire types and the development of the industry supports the slight evidence that we have from other sites, e.g. Leicester (Kenyon, 1948, 209–10) and Verulamium (Wilson, 1972, 348–63), for expansion after the first third of the fourth century.

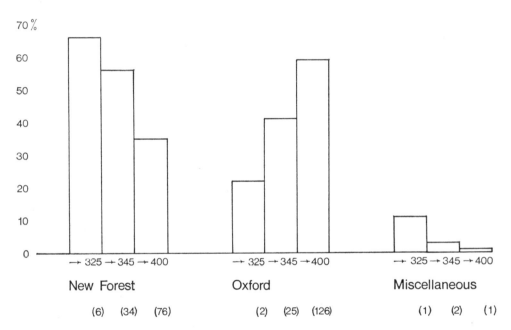

FIG. 148.   Relative amounts of red colour-coated bowls and mortaria, types 28–61, from the New Forest, Oxfordshire, etc. at Portchester

*New Forest and Oxfordshire Competition*

The relationship between the New Forest and Oxfordshire colour-coated types is illustrated in figs. 146–152, where the predominance of each centre in different types over time can be clearly seen. It would seem that the New Forest industry was rather overwhelmed by the Oxfordshire kilns in the second half of the fourth century, except with respect to some beaker, jug, jar and 'parchment' types. While the Oxfordshire kilns were still in the ascendant, in the latest Portchester groups, the New Forest types had begun to decline. The difference between the representation of the two centres in the later fourth century may be better explained if many of the New Forest types went out of production by *c.* 370–80, leaving only Oxfordshire types on the market. More groups dating towards the end of the century may resolve this problem. It seems unlikely, however, that the New Forest kilns would have survived much beyond the end of the fourth century.

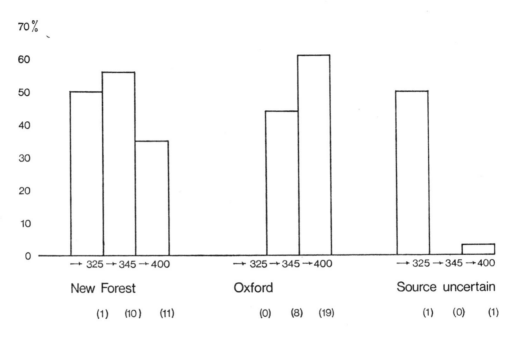

Fig. 149. Relative amounts of 'parchment' ware mortaria, types 63–67, from the New Forest, Oxfordshire, etc. at Portchester

# GROG-TEMPERED FABRIC, HAND-MADE (FABRIC A)

This fabric, first described by Cunliffe (1970, 67–8), is a medium hard, black or dark brown, grog-tempered ware. Inclusions of grog are either red or black and spherical (*c.* 1 mm. diameter) in shape. Occasionally crushed flint or shell appear as temper, but this is not common. The fabric is used in three main types; the flanged bowl type 86, the dish type 107 and the everted rim jar type 123, although it is used for others as well, e.g. types 88, 93, 100, 106, 111, 114 and 158 (cf. figs. 163–8). Altogether the fabric accounts for about one-third of non-colour-coated wares in all phases. Like black-burnished vessels, grog-tempered types are made without the wheel, but the latter are much more roughly finished. Outside surfaces are

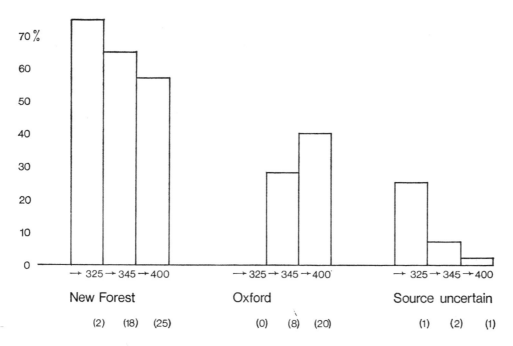

FIG. 150.   Relative amounts of all 'parchment' ware vessels, types 48–67, from the New Forest, Oxfordshire, etc. at Portchester

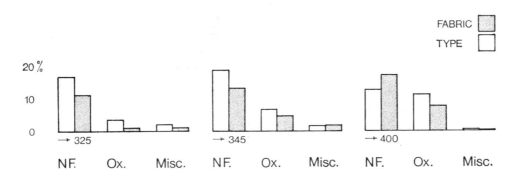

FIG. 151.   Relative amounts of New Forest, Oxfordshire and other colour-coated types by rim count and fabrics by weight as percentages of the main groups at Portchester

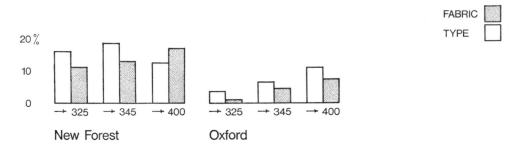

FIG. 152.   Comparison of the relative amounts of New Forest and Oxfordshire types by rim count and fabrics by weight as percentages of the main groups at Portchester

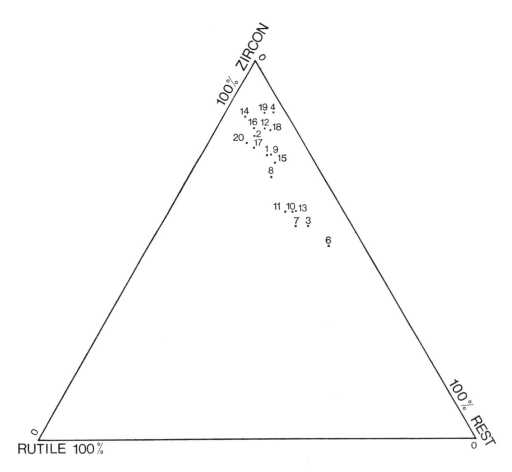

FIG. 153.   Grog-tempered ware, fabric A; heavy mineral analysis: zircon, rutile and the rest

generally smooth burnished, usually with zones of diagonal or lattice pattern burnishing, according to the type of vessel. The similarity in form and decoration between the black-burnished types and the grog-tempered is striking. The currency of the fabric is from the late third century, where it is present in the construction layers of the fort, until some time in the fifth. As a basic constituent of the ceramic assemblage it alters proportionally very little, although it becomes slightly more important among the non-colour-coated wares after A.D. 345 (fig. 158).

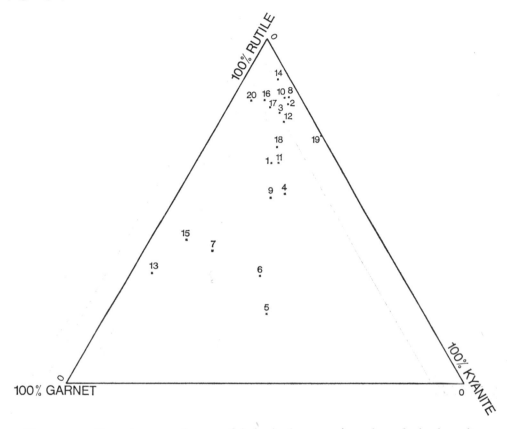

FIG. 154.  Grog-tempered ware, fabric A; heavy mineral analysis: kyanite, rutile and garnet

As it is a crudely made product compared with the other grey wares, it seemed worthwhile to try to determine whether it was of diverse local manufacture or from one 'factory' source. To effect this a programme of heavy mineral analysis was carried out with samples not only from Portchester, but also from all over Hampshire, where grog tempering occurs widely in the fourth century. Visually the fabric of sherds from different sites appears homogeneous, with only subtle differences in colour and texture. The results of the analysis are listed below and on ternary charts (figs. 153–5), which show sets of individual minerals compared against one another.

In interpreting the results it should be stressed that minerals apart from zircon, tourmaline and rutile are only represented in very small quantities. Consequently the pattern of results, on figs. 154 and 155 in particular, tends to exaggerate small numerical differences in the actual number of the less important minerals.

Until wasters are found and analysed it is not possible to determine the level at which the results may be best grouped in order to reflect the real kiln centres. But if we take those results

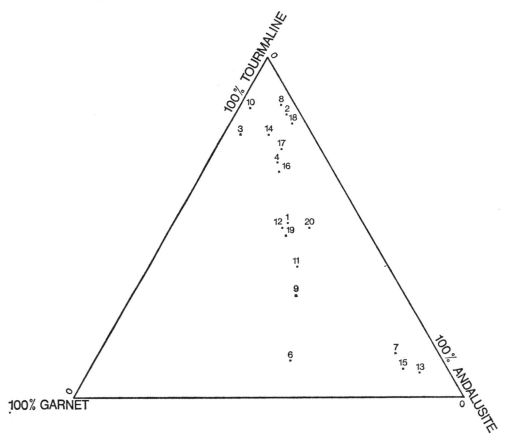

FIG. 155.   Grog-tempered ware, fabric A; heavy mineral analysis:
tourmaline, andalusite and garnet

which recur together in two of the three charts, or in isolation, the following groups emerge (number of analyses per site in brackets):

1. Botley, Downton, East Anton, New Forest, Portchester (4), and Winchester (3).
2. Holbury, Sparsholt (3).
3. Winchester (3).
4. Tournerbury.

Although the Winchester group 3 and the group 1 figures tend to merge, there does seem enough evidence (cf. fig. 153) to make a division. The results imply one large concern marketing to the whole Hampshire basin area with secondary centres producing for the immediately local market. The lesser groups may indicate the possibility of itinerant potters, although the large coarse ware producing centres like Alice Holt and the New Forest appear, in a similar way, to have been competed against by a series of very local concerns (see under grey wares).

As fig. 156 shows, the main area using this fabric is narrowly defined by the triangle of Winchester, Portchester and Bitterne (Clausentum) and on locational grounds one might expect one large centre to serve all of these major sites. It may turn out, therefore, that all the anomalies present in the minor groups are feasible within the total range of mineral variations from one kiln centre (cf. the results of the New Forest kiln analysis). However, until wasters are found, it seems safer to over-estimate the possible number of sources rather than minimize them.

Elsewhere grog tempering of this kind is not found although hand-made pottery in these forms does occur widely; that from Richborough or Pevensey, for example, is very different. It is this restricted distribution which suggests a limited number of production centres.

The occurrence of 'crude' hand-made pottery at Portchester alongside fine wheel-made wares throughout the fourth century, apparently acting as a local competitor to the black-burnished fabrics, must stand as a warning to those who tend to generalize about hand-made pottery representing the degenerate continuation of Roman forms after the breakdown of the wheel-made pottery industry. The Hampshire fabric is very likely the product of specialist potters and stands in the tradition of hand-made pottery which is present throughout the Roman period in one area or another (cf. Alcock, 1971, 182–183).

*The Heavy Mineral Analyses*[1]

| | Zircon | Tourmaline | Rutile | Kyanite | Garnet | Staurolite | Andalusite | Epidote | Zoisite | Anatase | Apatite | Brookite | Total number of grains counted |
|---|---|---|---|---|---|---|---|---|---|---|---|---|---|
| 1. Winchester | 75·3 | 4·2 | 9·8 | 2·9 | 2·4 | — | 1·6 | 1·0 | | | 1·0 | 2·1 | 377 |
| 2. Portchester | 80·1 | 3·7 | 10·5 | 1·9 | | | | | | | | | 674 |
| 3. Winchester | 56·2 | 20·0 | 10·5 | 2·0 | 1·0 | — | 4·8 | 2·0 | | 2·7 | 1·0 | | 105 |
| 4. New Forest | 86·5 | 4·6 | 2·7 | 1·4 | | — | 1·2 | | | 1·2 | | | 740 |
| 5. Sparsholt | 59·0 | 6·7 | 3·3 | 6·6 | 6·6 | — | 4·9 | 3·3 | | 8·2 | | | 61 |
| 6. Tournerbury | 51·2 | 2·0 | 7·9 | 8·4 | 9·2 | — | 7·1 | 1·0 | | 4·3 | 7·9 | | 393 |
| 7. Sparsholt | 55·6 | 2·6 | 13·0 | 5·9 | 14·6 | — | 1·9 | 1·0 | 1·0 | | 3·5 | | 575 |
| 8. Winchester | 69·0 | 10·3 | 12·0 | 2·0 | — | — | 1·3 | | 1·0 | 1·0 | | | 543 |
| 9. Winchester | 75·2 | 7·6 | 9·1 | 1·5 | — | — | 1·0 | | | 1·6 | | | 552 |
| 10. Winchester | 60·6 | 3·3 | 11·9 | 5·3 | 4·5 | 1·6 | 2·9 | 1·6 | 3·7 | | 2·1 | | 244 |
| 11. Winchester | 60·3 | 3·1 | 13·6 | 4·5 | 3·1 | — | 1·8 | 1·6 | 2·5 | | 3·5 | | 551 |
| 12. East Anton | 81·8 | 1·2 | 6·7 | 1·5 | — | 2·0 | — | | | 2·0 | 1·8 | | 611 |
| 13. Sparsholt | 59·8 | 1·9 | 11·0 | 1·9 | 21·1 | — | 1·9 | | | | 1·6 | | 318 |
| 14. Botley | 85·3 | 2·4 | 10·2 | 1·0 | — | — | | | | | | | 586 |
| 15. Holbury | 73·9 | 1·2 | 9·0 | 2·0 | 10·5 | | 1·6 | | | | | | 190 |
| 16. Portchester | 82·1 | 3·5 | 9·5 | 1·0 | 1·0 | 1·0 | — | | | | | | 402 |
| 17. Portchester | 77·3 | 5·2 | 11·7 | 1·5 | 1·2 | | | | | | | | 427 |
| 18. Downton | 81·5 | 6·2 | 6·5 | 1·8 | 1·2 | | — | | | | | | 341 |
| 19. Portchester | 86·1 | 3·3 | 5·4 | | 2·1 | | 1·5 | | | | | | 331 |
| 20. New Forest | 77·9 | 2·9 | 13·4 | — | 2·1 | | | | | | | | 484 |

[1] The dash — indicates the presence of a mineral in quantities less than 1%.

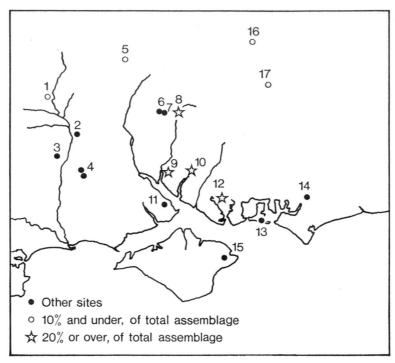

Fig. 156. Distribution map of grog-tempered ware, fabric A. 1, Durrington Walls, Wilts.; 2, Downton, Wilts.; 3, Rockbourne, Hants (Down site and Villa); 4, New Forest kiln sites, Hants; 5, East Anton, Hants; 6, Ashley Camp, Hants; 7, Sparsholt villa, Hants; 8, Winchester, Hants; 9, Bitterne, Hants; 10, Botley, Hants.; 11, Holbury Manor Farm, Hants.; 12, Fort Wallington, Hants; 13, Tournerbury, Hants; 14, Chichester, Sussex; 15, Brading villa, I.O.W.; 16, North Warnborough, 17, Neatham, Hants.

## BLACK-BURNISHED WARE (FABRIC B)

This is a black, coarse sandy fabric which was used at Portchester for types 85, 107, 117 and 126, in particular, as well as types 88, 102, 115, 116, 119, 120, 154 and 175 (figs. 163–8). All types are made without the wheel. Macroscopic characterization of this fabric was first usefully undertaken by Gillam (1961), who named it BB 1, to distinguish it from a second, similar fabric (BB 2). Heavy mineral analysis of BB 1 from west Midland sites by Peacock (1967) suggested the possibility of a south-western origin for the fabric. Publication of wasters from the Poole Harbour area in Dorset indicated one centre of manufacture (Farrar, 1969), and heavy mineral analysis of the local sands agreed with the sherd analysis (Peacock, 1973). It is to this Dorset source that the Portchester black-burnished can be assigned. Sherds of types 85 and 126 were analysed for their heavy mineral content with the following results for the main constituents:

| Zircon | Tourmaline | Rutile | Garnet | Andalusite | Epidote | Apatite | Total number of grains counted |
|---|---|---|---|---|---|---|---|
| 38·4 | 32·7 | 4·4 | 10·1 | 2·5 | 1·7 | 3·1 | 159 |
| 36·1 | 33·3 | 5·9 | 8·8 | 3·9 | 1·6 | 2·3 | 143 |

No other analyses of pottery of other classes from Portchester gave remotely similar results and it seems likely that the visual sorting was satisfactory.

There is no close relationship between the percentage of black-burnished, in terms of the minimum number of types from group to group, and the percentage of the fabric alone in the same assemblages. Presumably the latter is a more accurate reflection of the amount per period, or perhaps an average of the two factors would be better. Taking either the fabric or the average as a measure (fig. 158), there is some evidence of decline in quantity in the post-345 groups. However, there can be no certainty as to when black-burnished ceased to come in to Portchester. If intensive occupation ended after c. 370–80, it is not likely that any change would be apparent. The Portchester curve may be reflecting the decline that presumably took place before the factories finally closed. On the other hand, the situation on Hadrian's Wall, where the fabric does not appear in post-367 levels (Gillam, 1957, Types 146–8, 228, 329) may not be relevant in the south with sites much nearer the production centre. In this case if there was considerable occupation at Portchester after 370–80, no decline need necessarily be apparent. More evidence is needed from late fourth-century levels in the south, particularly from Dorchester (Dorset), to complement our flimsy knowledge at present, before we can plot the decline of the industry in the south more accurately.

## THE GREY WARES (FABRIC C)

This is the third and largest non-colour-coated fabric group from Portchester and, unlike the others, it probably represents more than one or two kiln sources. Both fine and coarse sandy fabrics are present; slipped and unslipped. Some are lighter, some darker than others, some more brown than grey; yet amongst these visually distinctive variations it is doubtful if any have significance with regard to the kiln centre that produced them, or which, if any, of all the apparent variables are significant in attribution to source. In order to try to define some groups which might be meaningful in terms of kilns and kiln groups, a programme of heavy mineral analysis (Peacock, 1967) was carried out and the results compared with others obtained from the analysis of waste material from known kiln sites. The possibility of defining groups is hampered by the difficulty of defining significant variations in the tertiary clays in the Hampshire basin area. Each group of results was clustered according to the programme described on pp. 273–4 and the dendrograms are presented as a 'family tree' in figs. 159 and 160.

Any conclusions that can be drawn from these analyses must be qualified by reservations about the size of sample (39), as large only as time would allow. 75% of the results belong to the same 'family', although there are clusters within it. These can be divided into two main groups, which broadly agree with a visual characterization of the sherds sampled. Slides 24–32 and 9–10 form a group which has fine grey fabrics and, where visible, a grey or silvery grey slip. In terms of form and decoration, these can be closely matched with both Alice Holt and New Forest products since both industries produce very similar types. However, when the results are compared with sherds known to come from the New Forest and Alice Holt kilns, few differences are apparent, the results being surprisingly homogeneous. Since the kilns of each group cover several square miles, it need not be surprising if the variations in the mineral assemblages from one group coincide with those from another, although the bulk of each may be seen to be slightly different overall. In this case, the Portchester group could belong to either industry. If time had allowed, further Alice Holt analyses might have produced clearer differentiation. On the other hand, even with a small number of samples, the Rowlands Castle and Shedfield kilns seem to have separated from the New Forest and Alice Holt results. Subjectively a New Forest source might be preferred on the grounds that the latter is closer to Portchester and access by river or road is easier than the cross-country route from Alice Holt.

With the other clusters (slides 41–33 and 29–4) there again seems to be some correspondence between the heavy minerals and visual characterization of the sherds. The bulk of these slides belong to the non-slipped, coarser grey to black sandy fabrics (except 2, 13, 19, 27) which are not unlike those from the Rowlands Castle kiln site. Generally speaking, the coarser non-slipped fabrics only appear to be used for flanged bowls (type 85), simple dishes (type 107) and jars (types 139–141), whereas the finer, white slipped grey fabrics are used for these types as well as other jars, bowls, mugs, jugs, etc. If the analyses are of any value, then it is to support the hypothesis that the fine, slipped, grey fabrics are probably from the New Forest and Alice Holt kilns, while the rest are from local sources, perhaps in the Rowlands Castle or Botley area, if not closer to Portchester itself. Both Chichester, Botley and Portchester are likely to have had coarse ware kilns closer to hand than the New Forest and Alice Holt centres, and there is no reason for pottery production attested in the first/second centuries at Shedfield, near Botley (Cunliffe, 1961) or in the second/third centuries at Rowlands Castle (Cunliffe, 1971, 253–4) not to have continued in those areas into the fourth century. It may be suggested that about 75% of the grey wares comes within a five to ten mile radius, or even less, of Portchester, while only some 25% comes from further afield, say 20–30 miles, and most of that is from either the New Forest or Alice Holt centres.

As far as dating can be established with the grey wares, there is a decline in the percentage in groups later than c. 345, if the average amount between fabric (by weight) and minimum number of types (by rim) is considered. This does not mean that grey wares were no longer being produced in the later fourth century, rather that white or grey slipped types were gradually being replaced by more colour-coated varieties, while the range of day to day types (flanged bowl, dish and jar) were still being produced locally.

To refine the definition of grey wares further would require more analysis of both Portchester and original kiln data, taking into consideration not only all the visible features of form and decoration, but also more variables within the heavy mineral assemblages, such as shape and size of mineral types. A comparison using grain size analysis (Peacock, 1971) might also produce useful results.

## Heavy Mineral Analysis Results

| No. | Zircon | Tourmaline | Rutile | Garnet | Kyanite | Staurolite | Andalusite | Sillimanite | Epidote | Zoisite | Anatase | Apatite | Biotite | Collophane | Barite | Total number of grains counted |
|---|---|---|---|---|---|---|---|---|---|---|---|---|---|---|---|---|
| 1 | 84.7 | | 9.4 | | 1.5 | | | | 1.5 | | | | | | | 543 |
| 2 | 74.5 | | 16.1 | 4.1 | 1.1 | | 1.5 | | 1.3 | | | | | | | 459 |
| 3 | 46.7 | 16.1 | 7.3 | | 15.8 | 7.3 | 8.8 | | | | 1.0 | | 1.5 | | | 95 |
| 4 | 83.2 | | 10.2 | 1.0 | 1.0 | | | | | | 2.0 | | | | | 463 |
| 5 | 63.4 | 3.4 | 14.6 | 2.2 | 2.2 | | 4.9 | 1.0 | 1.2 | | 7.0 | | | | | 410 |
| 6 | 59.4 | 1.9 | 16.9 | | 5.0 | | 8.1 | 2.5 | | | 3.1 | | | | | 160 |
| 7 | 65.9 | 1.4 | 9.7 | 1.4 | 1.7 | | 2.6 | | 2.0 | 8.6 | 2.3 | 2.6 | | | | 349 |
| 8 | 35.7 | | 17.4 | 4.1 | 16.3 | 1.0 | 2.0 | 1.0 | 6.1 | 2.0 | 1.0 | 13.3 | | | | 98 |
| 9 | 66.5 | 2.7 | 9.6 | | 13.0 | | 2.0 | | 4.0 | | | | | | | 301 |
| 10 | 67.2 | 2.9 | 8.6 | | 12.1 | | 1.7 | 1.7 | 4.0 | | | | | | | 174 |
| 11 | 70.6 | 4.4 | 20.5 | | 3.0 | | | | | | | | | | | 439 |
| 12 | 80.3 | | 9.3 | | | | 3.1 | | 1.7 | | | 3.5 | | | | 290 |
| 13 | 69.8 | | 8.3 | 1.2 | | | 4.9 | | | | | 7.5 | | | | 348 |
| 14 | 85.7 | | 11.4 | | | | | | | | | | | | | 525 |
| 15 | 73.9 | 3.0 | 7.2 | 2.1 | | | 8.4 | | 1.2 | | | 2.5 | | | | 866 |
| 16 | 38.4 | 32.7 | 4.4 | 10.1 | | | 2.5 | | 1.9 | 4.4 | 1.3 | 3.1 | | | | 159 |
| 17 | 66.9 | 9.3 | 6.1 | | 6.1 | 4.8 | 3.4 | | 1.7 | | | | | | | 643 |
| 18 | 80.7 | 4.7 | 9.1 | 1.0 | 2.4 | | 1.0 | | | | | | | | | 384 |
| 19 | 69.2 | | 10.5 | 1.3 | 1.0 | | 16.8 | | | | | | | | | 477 |
| 20 | | | | | | | | | | | | | | | | |
| 21 | 79.5 | | 8.0 | | | | 8.0 | | | 1.5 | | | | | | 400 |
| 22 | 65.9 | 9.1 | 11.4 | 1.1 | 4.6 | 3.4 | 2.3 | | | | 1.1 | 1.1 | | | | 88 |
| 23 | 84.4 | 3.3 | 7.8 | | | | 2.5 | | | | | | | | | 397 |
| 24 | 81.0 | | 7.1 | 4.3 | 1.0 | | 3.8 | | | | | 2.8 | | | | 211 |
| 25 | 87.4 | 4.7 | 4.7 | 1.0 | 1.0 | 1.0 | | | | | | | | | | 452 |
| 26 | 79.0 | | 6.1 | 4.4 | 2.2 | | 1.8 | | 1.0 | 1.8 | | | | | 1.8 | 228 |
| 27 | 73.9 | | 14.3 | 2.5 | 3.9 | | | | 2.5 | | | | | | | 203 |
| 28 | 88.5 | 1.8 | 6.2 | 1.8 | | | | | | | | | | | | 339 |
| 29 | 76.1 | 6.9 | 5.4 | 3.0 | 2.7 | | | | 2.7 | | 1.5 | | | | | 335 |
| 30 | 84.7 | 2.8 | 8.4 | 1.1 | | | | | | | | | | | | 537 |
| 31 | | | | | | | | | | | | | | | | |
| 32 | 82.2 | 1.4 | 11.0 | | | | 2.5 | | | | | 1.0 | | | | 365 |
| 33 | 69.4 | | 11.3 | 9.7 | | | 4.5 | | | 3.2 | | | | | | 62 |
| 34 | 85.3 | | 8.3 | 4.6 | 1.0 | | 1.0 | | | | | | | | | 545 |
| 35 | 69.2 | 3.1 | 15.4 | 4.6 | 3.9 | | 3.1 | | 1.0 | | | | | | | 130 |
| 36 | 74.7 | 2.5 | 10.5 | | 6.4 | 2.4 | 1.5 | | | | 1.1 | | | | | 545 |
| 37 | 78.2 | 6.3 | 4.7 | | 4.5 | 4.1 | 1.3 | | | | | | | | | 556 |
| 38 | | | | | | | | | | | | | | | | |
| 39 | 71.7 | 12.3 | 10.4 | | | 3.8 | | | | | | | | | | 106 |
| 40 | 74.1 | | 18.1 | | 4.4 | | | | 1.6 | | | | | | 1.0 | 320 |
| 41 | 70.9 | 1.0 | 7.0 | 14.1 | 2.9 | 1.0 | | | 1.0 | | | 1.0 | | | | 388 |
| 42 | 29.3 | | 2.3 | 16.9 | | | | | | | | | | 50.7 | | 444 |

## Analysis of kiln waste

| No. | Zircon | Tourmaline | Rutile | Garnet | Kyanite | Staurolite | Andalusite | Sillimanite | Epidote | Zoisite | Anatase | Apatite | Biotite | Collophane | Barite | Total number of grains counted |
|---|---|---|---|---|---|---|---|---|---|---|---|---|---|---|---|---|
| | | | | | | | Alice Holt | | | | | | | | | |
| 1 | 81·3 | | 6·4 | 1·6 | 2·2 | | 2·9 | | 1·6 | | | 3·1 | | | | 453 |
| 2 | 74·7 | | 10·8 | 7·6 | 2·2 | | | | | | | | | | | 462 |
| 3 | 70·0 | 5·4 | 10·4 | | 5·5 | | 5·4 | | | | | | 1·5 | | | 653 |
| 4 | 84·1 | | 7·9 | | 1·9 | | 2·2 | | | | | 1·6 | | | | 315 |
| | | | | | | | New Forest | | | | | | | | | |
| 5 | 75·4 | 1·0 | 14·1 | | 2·3 | | 2·8 | | 1·0 | | | 1·3 | | | | 398 |
| 6 | 64·2 | | 21·1 | 2·7 | 4·0 | | 1·7 | | 1·7 | | 2·2 | | | | | 402 |
| 7 | 83·3 | | 8·0 | 1·4 | 1·4 | | 2·6 | | | | 1·0 | | | | | 498 |
| 8 | 63·7 | | 23·8 | 6·5 | 1·1 | | | | | | | 2·8 | | | | 465 |
| 9 | 60·2 | 3·7 | 18·3 | | 3·2 | | 2·6 | | 2·6 | | | | | | | 433 |
| 10 | 74·2 | | 8·4 | 1·9 | 4·5 | | 1·9 | | 1·9 | | 1·3 | 1·3 | | | | 155 |
| 11 | 81·5 | 6·6 | 10·4 | | | | | | | | | | | | | 595 |
| 12 | 79·1 | 9·6 | 7·3 | | 1·0 | | | | | | | | | | | 480 |
| 13 | 87·5 | | 7·1 | | 2·1 | 2·1 | | | | | | | | | | 240 |
| 14 | 75·4 | 10·7 | 9·8 | | | | 2·1 | | | | | | | | | 479 |
| 15 | 73·6 | 3·8 | 19·1 | 1·9 | | | | | | | | | | | | 523 |
| 16 | 77·8 | 5·9 | 13·5 | | | | | | | | | | | | | 392 |
| 17 | 86·7 | | 12·0 | | | | | | | | | | | | | 548 |
| 18 | 84·4 | | 13·0 | | 1·3 | | | | 1·3 | | | | | | | 77 |
| 19 | 86·6 | | 10·2 | 1·8 | | | | | | | | | | | | 508 |
| 20 | 86·0 | 1·9 | 8·7 | | 1·0 | | | | | | | | | | | 378 |
| 21 | 82·1 | | 15·5 | | | | | | | | | | | | | 335 |
| 22 | 74·5 | 10·6 | 9·2 | | 2·1 | | | | | | | | | | | 141 |
| | | | | | | | Rowlands Castle | | | | | | | | | |
| 23 | 80·5 | | 6·8 | 7·5 | 1·5 | | 1·5 | | 1·5 | | | | | | | 133 |
| 24 | 67·7 | 2·2 | 5·4 | 5·4 | 3·2 | | 7·5 | 1·0 | | 1·0 | 6·5 | | | | | 93 |
| 25 | 83·3 | 4·9 | 2·9 | 3·0 | 1·5 | 1·0 | | | 1·0 | | 1·0 | 1·0 | | | | 204 |
| | | | | | | | Shedfield | | | | | | | | | |
| 26 | 76·3 | | 12·3 | | 6·1 | | | | | | | | 3·5 | | | 570 |
| 27 | 90·9 | | 2·3 | 2·3 | | | | | | | 2·3 | | 2·3 | | | 44 |
| 28 | 75·5 | | 10·8 | 1·4 | | | 3·6 | | | | | | 4·3 | | | 139 |
| 29 | 64·6 | 2·0 | 11·5 | 2·0 | 5·2 | | 1·0 | | 3·1 | | 1·0 | | 8·3 | | | 96 |

Nos. 5–10: Amberwood Inclosure; 11, 12, 15, 17, 20: Sloden Inclosure; 14, 21: Linwood; 13: Ashley Rails; 18: Pitts Wood; 16: Islands Thorns; 19, 22: Crock Hill.

*The Portchester Samples*

Slide No.  1. Type 132
          2. Type 133
          3. Type 98?
          4. Type 140
          5. Type 149
          6. Type 140
          7. Type 77
          8. Type 88.9
          9. Type 153.6
         10. Type 153.6
         11. Base ? type 127
         12. Type 141
         13. Type 159.5
         14. Type 129
         15. Type 172
         16. Type 85 (BB 1)
         17. Type 177/179
         18. Type 85
         19. Type 153.8
         20. Type 137.4–6 (fabric D, no results)
         21. Type 77 or 92 (pedestal base only)
         22. Type 141

Slide No. 23. Type 77
         24. Type 129
         25. Type 107
         26. Type 141
         27. ? Type 29, red slipped, body sherd
              only
         28. Type 136
         29. Type 140
         30. Type 85
         31. Type 137.4–6 (fabric D),
              no results
         32. Body sherd ? types 127–133
         33. Type 85
         34. ? Type 127–133, body sherd only
         35. Type 85/87
         36. Base ? type 107
         37. Type 85
         38. Sherd of hard, micaceous, light
              brown fabric, no results
         39. Type 94
         40. Sherd of jar ? type 140/141
         41. Base of jar ? type 140/141
         42. Type 140

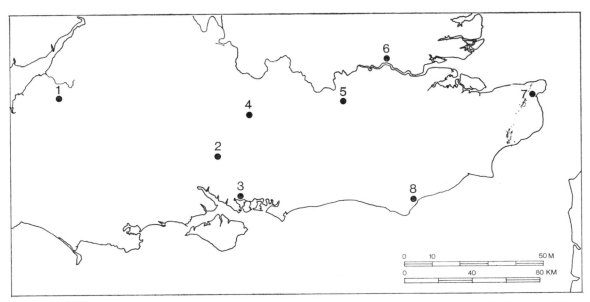

FIG. 157. Distribution map of fabric D wares. 1, Chew Valley, Somerset; 2, Winchester, Hants; 3, Portchester, Hants; 4, North Warnborough, Hants; 5, Cobham, Surrey; 6, London; 7, Richborough, Kent; 8, Pevensey, Sussex

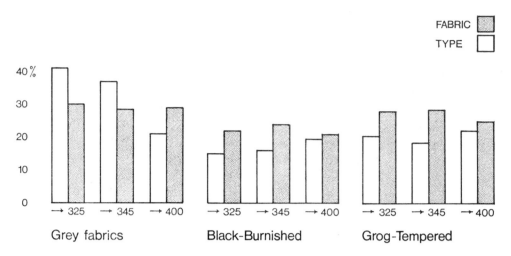

FIG. 158. Relative amounts of the main non-colour-coated ware types by rim count and fabrics by weight as percentages of the main groups at Portchester

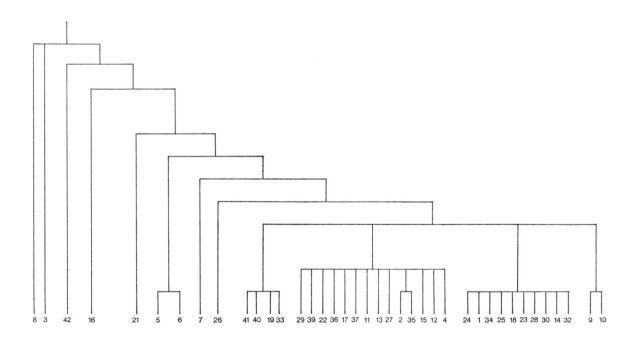

FIG. 159. Cluster analysis: heavy mineral analyses of Portchester grey wares

## CREAMY SANDY WARES (FABRIC D)

This is a very distinctive fabric, the source of which is not yet recognized. It is very hard and granular, coloured dirty yellow, sometimes with a grey core. The surface ranges from a dirty yellow to a reddish-yellow and is fairly rough with translucent quartz grits (no more than 0·5 mm.) showing through at random all over. It is instantly distinguishable from the other non-colour-coated wares. Preliminary results of heavy mineral analysis have not been helpful in characterizing the fabric. The types represented in it are nos. 87, 89, 97, 109, 137, 155, 173.

The fabric has a wide distribution (from visual inspection) in south-east England, occurring at London (unpublished material in the Guildhall Museum), Richborough (Bushe-Fox, 1932, pl. 40, nos. 336–8; 1949, pl. 93, nos. 470 and 472), Cobham, Surrey (Frere, 1947, fig. 7, no. 2), Pevensey (unpublished material in Lewes Museum) and elsewhere (fig. 157).

At Portchester this fabric does not appear before c. A.D. 325 and very few types are present in the middle occupation and upper clay layers against the wall, although all varieties occur in later groups. There is a slight conflict between the minimum number of types and the fabric weights as representing the development of the ware, but neither suggests any decline after 350.

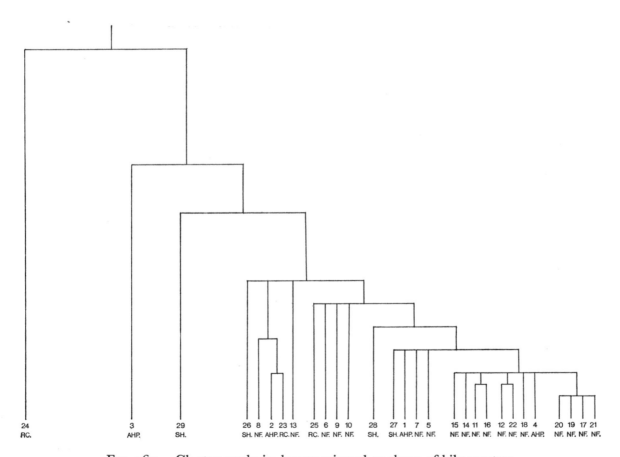

FIG. 160. Cluster analysis: heavy mineral analyses of kiln wasters

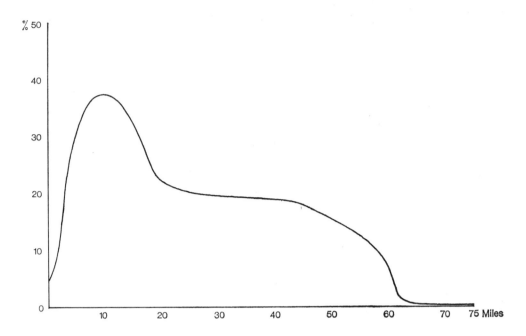

FIG. 161. Amounts of pottery compared with distance from the suggested source

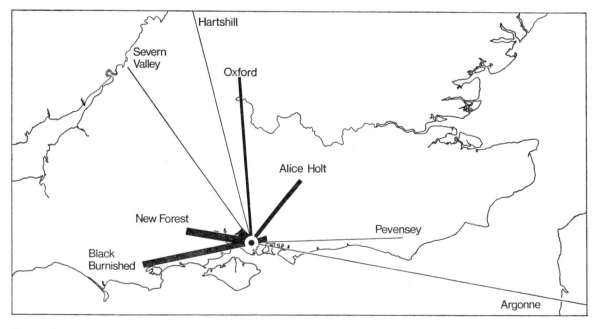

FIG. 162. Map showing the relative proportions of pottery originating from known sources

Minimum number of types as a percentage of group:
  All groups pre-350, 0·16%.
  All groups post-350, 1·88%.
Fabric weight as percentage of group:
  All groups pre-350, 0·80%.
  All groups post-350, 0·92%.


## THE SOURCES OF THE POTTERY

An attempt has been made on figs. 161 and 162 to show what amounts of pottery came from what distances and sources during the period *c.* 325–*c.* 345. The thickness of the bars on fig. 162 is proportional to the amount supplied from that source. Clearly, as has been discussed already, not all the sources of the pottery are known, but for the grog-tempered and the bulk of the grey wares, a source or sources near Portchester (5–15 miles) have been suggested. The problem of the Alice Holt and New Forest contributions to the grey wares has been resolved by dividing the amount equally (25% of the grey wares) between the two. For the colour-coated and black-burnished fabrics, we can be certain, in most cases, of the source within a mile or so.


## THE TYPE SERIES

### *The Closed Forms*

*Bottles*

Type 1:   with a closed nozzle mouth and no handle:
          1.1, a fine, hard red fabric with a matt black slip; possibly Oxfordshire; MO (1).
          1.2, a hard, red–brown fabric with a matt red–brown slip; possibly Oxfordshire; u/s (1).
Type 2:   with an open mouth and no handle; New Forest, fabric 1.
          2.1, u/s (1).
          2.2, pit 121, u/s (1).
          2.3, u/s (1).

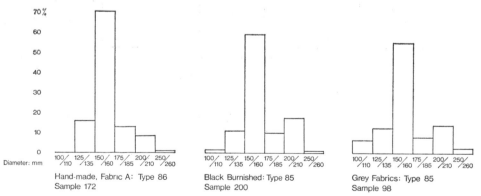

FIG. 163.   Rim diameter variation of flanged bowls, types 85 and 86 (pp. 335–8)

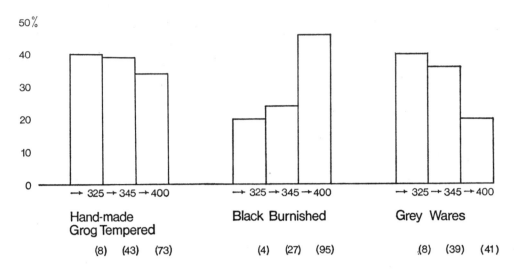

FIG. 164.   Relative amounts of flanged bowls, types 85–87, in the three main
non-colour-coated fabric groups (pp. 335–9)

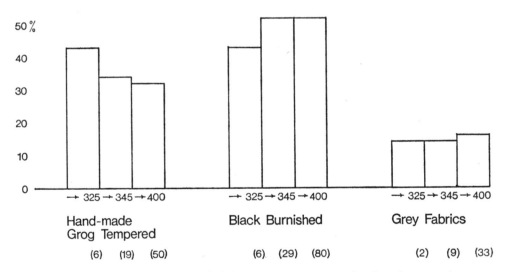

FIG. 165.   Relative amounts of dishes, types 107–109, in the three main non-
colour-coated fabric groups (pp. 342–5)

*Flagons*

Type 3: globular body with a closed nozzle and handle attached to a flange on the neck; New Forest, fabric 1, except 3.3, which has a fabric like 1.2.
Pits (6), (51, 103 (2), 121 (2), 144); BURRS (1); AURRS (2); BMU (1); MO (3); u/s (3); total 16. While those in pit 121 may have been deposited before 320, most of the rest belong to pre-345 contexts. Those AURRS are probably residual.
Bases that could belong to this type, or types 2 and 10, occurred in pits (3), (48, 121 (2)); AURRS (1).

Type 4: a collared neck with a handle attached to the neck.
A pale red, sandy fabric, with a burnished slip, mottled, pale red in colour; cf. Gose (1950), forms 270–1; MO (1).

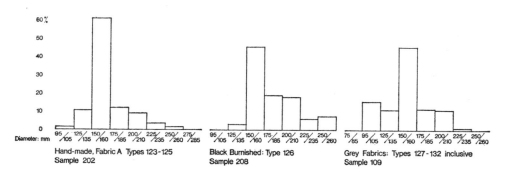

FIG. 166. Rim diameter variation of jars, types 123–132 (pp. 347–52)

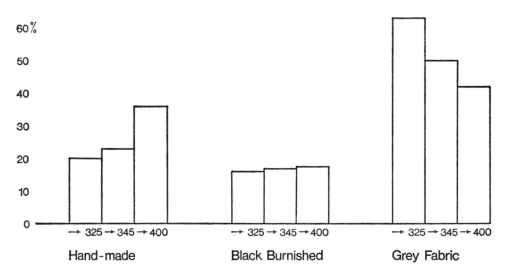

FIG. 167. Relative amounts of jar types 127–149 in the three main non-colour-coated fabrics (p. 357)

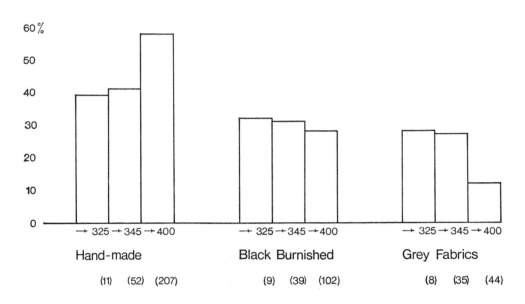

FIG. 168. Types 123–7: black-burnished, fabric B, jars and their close
imitations in grog-tempered and grey fabrics (pp. 348–50)

Type 5:      with an open and cupped rim, to which the handle is attached; New Forest, fabric 1;
all variants u/s (4).

Type 2/10: body sherds with distinctive decoration, which could belong to all or any of types 2, 3, 5 and
10. Occasionally it is not always possible to distinguish body sherds of beakers from the
closed forms, since both type ranges were made in the same kilns and share the same range of
decorative motifs. All are New Forest, fabric 1, except 2/10.3.
2/10.1–2, Cylindrical body, with horizontal grooves.
2/10.1, possibly belonging to type 2; pit 144; AURRS (1); Up. Clay (1).
2/10.2, similar to above and also perhaps of type 2; UO (1).
A date after c. 330 seems likely for this pair; probably residual in AURRS or by ? c. 370.
2/10.3, body of either type 1 or 2; laminated, light-brown fabric with a dull brown slip;
source uncertain; u/s (1).
With 'rouletted' decoration:
2/10.4, pit 69.
2/10.5, similar; pits (6), (47, 63, 77, 103, 144, 185). The date range could be either c. 300–
c. 350, or possibly c. 315–c. 345.
With incised and stab decoration:
2/10.6, u/s (1).
2/10.7, pit 144.
2/10.8, pit 144.
2/10.9, UO (1); u/s (1).

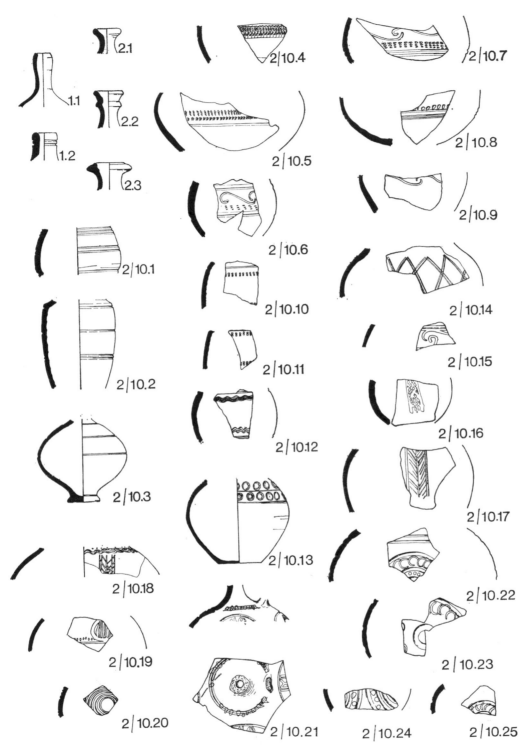

FIG. 169.    Pottery types 1–2 (pp. 301–6). Scale ¼

2/10.10 and 11, possibly sherds of the same vessel; both from pit 41; others from AURRS (1); u/s (4).

2/10.12, u/s (1).

A date range *c.* 325–*c.* 360/70 seems likely for this type of decoration. None of the pits with this type would seem to have been filled pre-325, and comparison with the sherds of the beaker type 21 would support this.

With 'rosette' impressions:

2/10.13, pit 63; this is associated with coins dating 367–78.

With varieties of white painted decoration:

2/10.14, lattice pattern; u/s (1).

2/10.15, scroll pattern; pits 92, 147, 168 and 236; u/s (1).

2/10.16, lattice pattern; pit 103; MO (1).

2/10.17, herring-bone pattern; pits 92, 103 and 130; AMU (1); Up. Clay (1); UO (1); u/s (6); total 12.

2/10.18, painted lattice and incised wavy motif; LO (1).

2/10.19, UO (1).

With incised concentric circles and, usually, painted decoration:

2/10.20, no paint; pits (5), (103, 130, 164, 182, 223); MO (1); Up. Clay (1); UO (1); u/s (1); total 9.

2/10.21, circles enclosing painted lattices; pits 46, 103 and 125; AMU (1).

2/10.22–25, similar, but painted dots and crescents within the circles; pits 48 and 103; BURRS (3); AMU (1); LO (2); M. Clay (2); MO (2); UO (2); u/s (8); total 22. This type appears to be common in layers pre-325 and rare after 345. It is possible that there is a devolution in decoration from large circles and white painted patterns as in 2/10.21 to the plain style, like 2/10.20. The first is much closer to the cut glass parallels which were presumably copied at the outset. The date range is supported by the evidence for the beaker, type 20.

Type 6:  with an open mouth and handle attached to a double beaded rim; New Forest, fabric 1; pits 144 and 168; AMU (2); u/s (3); a base probably belonging to this type from AMU. A date after *c.* 340/50 is compatible with the filling of the pits. This type seems to be current at the end of the century as it is the commonest pottery grave offering in the latest Lankhills graves, dated to the end of the fourth or early fifth century (Fulford, forthcoming).

Type 7:  with a flared out and cupped mouth; the handle is attached to the rim:
7.1, a light red fabric with haematite/limonite grains and a polished red-brown slip; pit 69 (cf. fabrics of 8.2 and 9.3).
7.2, a fine, light red fabric with a grey core and a dark grey to brown slip; possibly Oxfordshire; MO (1).

Type 8:  similar to the last, but a squared profile to the rim:
8.1, a fine reddish-yellow fabric with a grey core and a dull red–brown slip; u/s (2).
8.2, a light brown fabric with a grey core and haematite/limonite inclusions and covered by a dull brown slip; u/s (1); cf. 7.1 and 9.3.
8.3, a fine, slightly sandy light red fabric with a reddish-brown burnished slip; u/s (1).

Type 9:  with an everted profile and handle attached to a flange on the rim; sources unknown:
9.1, fine, sandy yellow–red with a burnished brown slip; pit 164.
9.2, fabric as above, but a light red slip; u/s (1).
9.3, fabric as 7.1 and 8.2, but light brown slip; u/s (1).

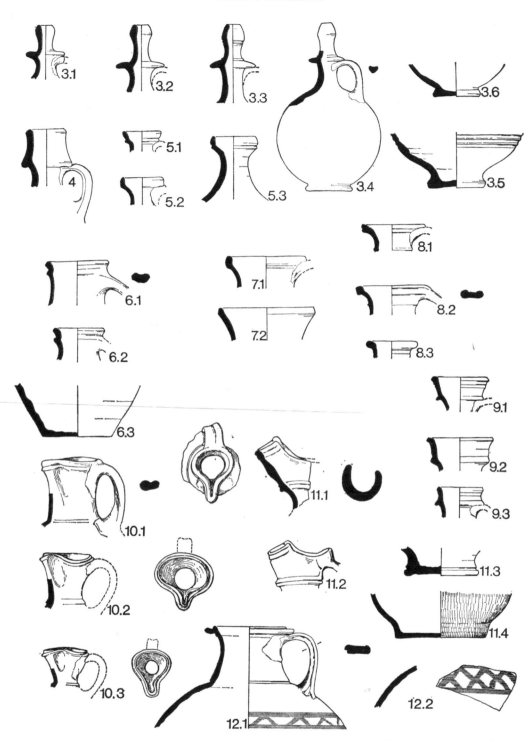

FIG. 170.   Pottery types 3–12 (pp. 303–8). Scale ¼

Type 10:    with a pinched out spout and slightly flanged rim:
            10.1, New Forest, fabric 3, no slip; pit 63; BURRS (1).
            10.2 and 3, New Forest, fabric 1, purple slip; pits 144 and 223; BURRS (2); AURRS (1);
            AMU (1); UO (1); u/s (4); total 12.
            Possible date range of *c*. 325–*c*. 370/80.

Type 11:    jug with 'U' profile pourer; thumb stop on the handle; New Forest, fabric 3, purple slip;
            spouts from; MO (2); AURRS (1); u/s (1); sherd only from the neck in pit 48. Bases that
            probably belong to this type from AMU (1); MO (1).
            Possible date range of *c*. 325–*c*. 345.
            11.4, base in a white sandy fabric with haematite/limonite grains visible and 'roulette'
            decoration; pit 144.

Type 12:    large jug with a flanged rim.
            New Forest, fabric 3, brown paint on the body; u/s (1).

*Beakers*

Type 13:    bulbous-bodied beakers with tall necks and plain bodies.
            New Forest, fabric 1. It is likely that some of the body sherds of indented beakers belong to
            this type as well as to type 22. Included here are all occurrences of rim sherds giving no
            indication of the decoration of the body, although it is certain that many will belong to
            decorated types. As for other New Forest fabric 1 types it does not seem worthwhile to
            record the exact colour and hardness of each; it must be accepted that there is a range.
            Generally the slip covers all the outer surfaces, as well as 3 or 4 cm. below the inside of the rim.
            The only complete example occurred in pit 234, with sherds of the same vessel in pit 224.
            The rest occurred in pits (11), (46 (2), 65, 121, 144 (2), 182, 225, 230, 236 (2)); BURRS (1);
            AURRS (5); AMU (4); MO (4); UO (7); u/s (26); total 58. Of these it may be observed
            that 13.3 and 13.5 and 6 with shallow grooves on the neck occurred in pits 46 and 182;
            AURRS (4); AMU (1); UO (1); u/s (3).
            This is one of the few New Forest types that seems to increase as a percentage of the group
            concerned after 340/50. It rises from 0·79% of groups pre-340/50 to 1·07% of later assemblages.

Type 14:    this type accounts for all the non-New Forest beakers of the type described above. The fabric
            is generally a fine, somewhat granular, light brown, micaceous clay, with a brown to black
            slip. It is likely that many are from the Oxfordshire kilns. Stone-wares occasionally occur, e.g.
            type 14.2. The rim form also includes varieties like 13.1 and 2, although the most common
            range is as type 15.1–3. Again, as for type 13, all occurrence of plain rims, giving no
            indication of body decoration are included, but, unlike type 13, no complete, plain beaker in
            non-New Forest fabrics was recovered. Therefore the occurrences of the rim must also be
            compared with those of types 15, 17 and 18, from which presumably they are derived.
            Pits (9), (61, 121, 144, 187, 195, 223 (2), 236 (2)); BURRS (1); AURRS (5); AMU (3);
            LO (1); MO (3); u/s (17); total 39.
            The currency of this type would seem to be from *c*. 300–*c*. 325/45.

Type 15:    as type 13 and 14, but the body is decorated with two zones of 'roulette' or 'glass mark'
            impressions. There were very few occasions when rim and body survived as one, so the
            incidence of all the body sherds that would seem to belong to this type are listed.
            15.1, fine, brown, micaceous and granular fabric with a brown to black slip; Oxfordshire
            kilns; pit 144.
            Other body sherds in a similar fabric and also probably from the Oxfordshire kilns occurred
            in pits (17), (48, 60, 63, 85, 86, 92, 95, 121, 130, 144 (2), 187, 222, 236 (4)); BURRS (1);

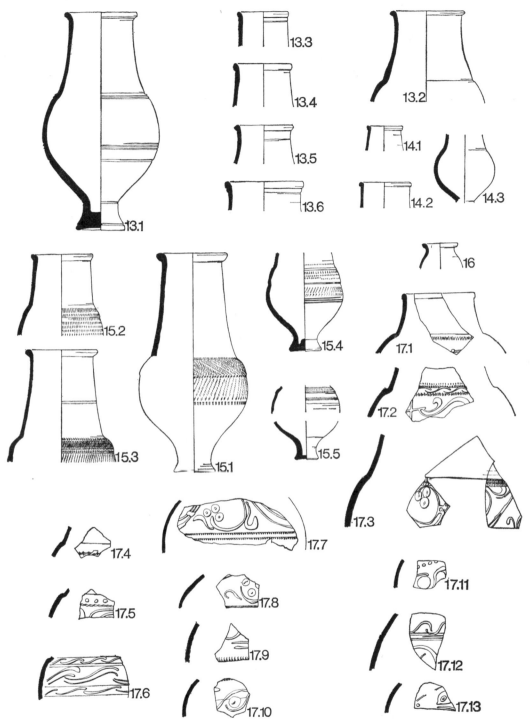

FIG. 171. Pottery types 13–17 (pp. 308–10). Scale ¼

AURRS (2); BMU (1); AMU (2); L. Clay Bank (1); M. Clay (1); Up. Clay (2); u/s (5); total 33.

15.2, soft, rough, reddish–brown fabric, with an uneven surface, roughened inside, and covered in a dark brown slip; source unknown; pit 130; others in AURRS (1); u/s (1).

15.3, a fine, somewhat granular, reddish-yellow fabric with a grey core and a dark brown slip; source unknown; pit 144; u/s (1).

15.4, a fine, dirty yellow fabric with a matt brown slip; the 'rouletting' is very faint; source unknown; pit 41; similar in pit 86; u/s (1).

15.5, a hard grey fabric with a thin black slip; source unknown; pit 235.

The date range suggested by the contexts of this type would appear to be from c. 280–c. 345.

Type 16:   small, bulbous bodied beaker with a fine, very hard red fabric and a light brown, polished slip with a slightly roughened finish; source unknown; MO (1).

Type 17:   as for types 13 and 14, except for the decoration which is of abstract motifs 'en barbotine'. Besides 17.1, all examples are body sherds, and it is possible that some belong to flagons and bottles, rather than beakers. The source of the majority is likely to be the Oxfordshire kilns. Each variant is described separately.

17.1, a fine, hard, grey fabric with a matt, deep reddish-brown slip; source uncertain; u/s (1).

17.2, a hard, brown, granular fabric with a grey core and a glossy, dusky red slip; pit 187; u/s (4); probably Oxfordshire.

17.3, a fine, hard, yellow to brown fabric with a grey core and a matt red–brown slip; pits 144 and ? 236; probably Oxfordshire.

17.4, a yellow to brown, fine fabric with a glossy reddish-brown slip; pit 41; source uncertain.

17.5, a laminated reddish-yellow, fine fabric with a grey core and a glossy dark red slip; pit 125; u/s (2); probably Oxfordshire.

17.6, a hard brown fabric with a grey core and a dirty, yellow slip; UO (1); probably Oxfordshire.

17.7 (this and the following sherds described for this type could belong to bottles and flagons, rather than beakers), a hard grey fabric with a glossy brown slip; this sherd u/s, but others similar in pit 103; AURRS (3); AMU (1); u/s (3); probably Oxfordshire.

17.8, similar to 17.7, but a glossy, reddish-brown slip; probably Oxfordshire; AURRS (1).

17.9, a hard, light brown, granular fabric with a grey core and a matt black slip; source uncertain; u/s (2).

17.10, reddish-yellow fabric with a grey core and a matt dark, red–brown slip; pit 92; MO (2); u/s (4); probably Oxfordshire.

17.11, similar to 17.7; pits 46, 63 and 121; AURRS (1); u/s (1); probably Oxfordshire.

17.12, a hard, reddish-yellow fabric with a grey core and a dull, dark reddish-brown slip; AMU (1); probably Oxfordshire.

17.13, reddish-yellow fabric with a brown slip; ? animal head figured; u/s (1); similar sherd but no animal in pit 69; source uncertain.

Other sherds with barbotine decoration too small to illustrate occurred in pits 92, 144 and 178; AURRS (1); AMU (1); u/s (3).

Summary of contexts:

Pits (14); AURRS (6); AMU (3); MO (2); UO (1); u/s (18). The pit evidence does not suggest a date pre-c. 325 for the start of the type, while the end may lie between c. 370 and c. 400.

Type 18:   as types 13 and 14, but the decoration consists of white paint, sometimes in relief, and commonly as scroll patterns. Except for 18.1, all specimens are body sherds. Like type 17, some sherds may belong to non-beaker forms.

18.1, a hard reddish-brown granular fabric with white paint trailed on a matt black slip; slight indentations on the body; pit 121, with a similar in pit 157; probably Oxfordshire.

18.2, fabric 1, New Forest; indented body; very worn slip; UO (1).

18.3, a granular reddish-brown fabric with a bronze–black slip and white paint, slightly in relief; pit 125; probably Oxfordshire.

18.4, New Forest, fabric 1; pit 103; u/s (2).

18.5, a hard reddish-brown fabric with a bright red slip; u/s (1).

18.6, New Forest, fabric 1; joining sherds in pits 223, 227 and 229.

18.7, New Forest, fabric 1; UO (1); u/s (1).

18.8, a light red fabric with occasional chalk inclusions and a dark, red–brown slip; AURRS (1); probably Oxfordshire.

18.9, a hard red fabric with a dusky bronze slip and trailed white paint; pit 46; u/s (2); probably Oxfordshire.

18.10, reddish-yellow fabric with a dull brown slip and trailed white paint decoration; pit 195; probably Oxfordshire; similar in pit 231.

18.11, a hard reddish-yellow fabric with a dull light brown slip; u/s (1); probably Oxfordshire.

Other body sherds in a thin, very hard red fabric with a brown to black, glossy slip (cf. fabric of 1.1) and trailed white paint decoration from: pit 164; AMU (1); u/s (4). Fabric parallels in this form in Essex and Kent suggest an origin in that area.

Summary of contexts:

New Forest: pits (2); UO (2); u/s (3); total 7.

Oxfordshire: pits (6); AURRS (1); u/s (4); total 11.

Misc.: pits (1); AMU (1); u/s (4); total 6.

If the contexts for the painted 2/10 variants are compared with those for type 18, then it would seem likely that the date range for this style and type lay from c. 325–c. 345. It is possible that the New Forest varieties were current a little later than the other fabrics, although again the emphasis seems to lie within the given bracket.

Type 19:   New Forest, fabric 1; tall necked with an ovoid body; white painted 'fir tree' patterns between the indentations. Most recorded examples are body sherds only. Besides 19.4 in pits 222 and 223; AMU (2); u/s (1); and 19.5 (u/s), the rest belong to type 19.1–3 and occur in pits (8), (46, 60, 178, 187, 195, 201 (2), 225); BURRS (1); BMU (3); AMU (2); M. Clay (1); MO (2); UO (2); u/s (11); total 30. Pit 222 confirms a pre-325 date for the type. It is probably residual by 350/60 as it falls from being 0·95% of the 325–45 assemblage to 0·40% of the later group.

Type 20:   New Forest, fabric 1; form as type 13, but decoration consists of incised concentric circles with painted motifs, either between or within each circle; all examples are of body sherds only:

20.1, pits 144 and 225; MO (1).

20.2, pit 46.

20.3, BURRS (1); u/s (1).

All examples belong to contexts c. 325–c. 345, but a wider date bracket may be indicated by the contexts of the 2/10 variants, with this form of decoration, and an earlier starting date is possible.

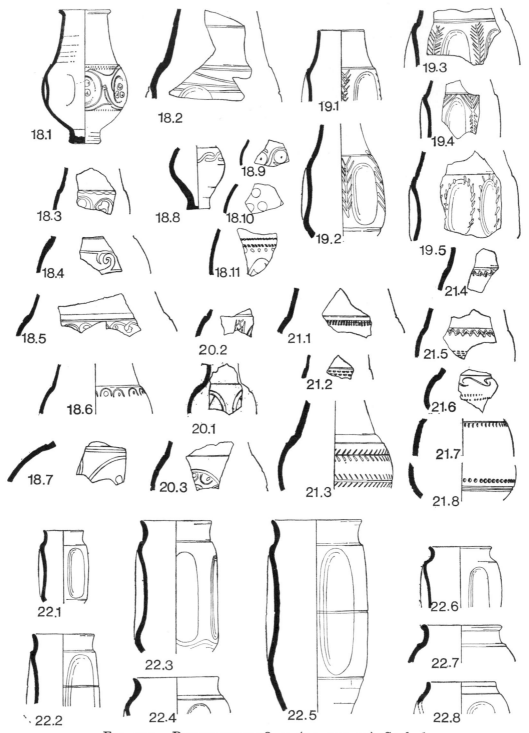

FIG. 172.   Pottery types 18–22 (pp. 311–13). Scale ¼

Type 21: New Forest, fabric 1; form as type 13, but decoration consists of either 'stab', furrowed, or incised motifs, or combinations in pairs. Both single and multiple pointed instruments appear to have been used, and it is probable that the same point could be employed for both static and running motifs. Only body sherds of this type are recorded.

21.1, AURRS (2); MO (1); UO (2).

21.2, u/s (1).

21.3, MO (1).

21.4 and 5, pit 69; AURRS (2); AMU (2); u/s (2).

21.6, pit 236; u/s (2).

21.7, Up. Clay (1); possibly belonging to a bottle or flagon.

21.8, MO (1); possibly belonging to a bottle or a flagon.

While 21.6 was probably deposited before 330, the rest belong to the period c. 325–360/70. As a percentage of each group, c. 325–345 and 345–c. 400, this type is 0·64% and 0·54% respectively. The date range is in agreement for the 2/10 variants.

Type 22: New Forest, fabric 1; unlike type 13, this beaker is characterized by a short neck and a mouth, which is as wide as its body. The rim is usually simple and pointed.

22.1–5, pits (33), (41 (2), 46 (2), 47 (2), 48, 49, 65, 77, 83, 95 (3), 103 (6), 121 (2), 130 (2), 144, 182, 184, 186, 187, 228, 234 (2), 235); BURRS (4); AURRS (7); AMU (7); L. Clay Bank (1); LO (6); MO (7); Up. Clay (3); UO (8); u/s (39); total 115.

22.6 and 7, the rim is slightly thickened and bent out, and the shape more globular; pit 236; AURRS (3); AMU (2); u/s (6); total 12.

22.8, inward sloping rim, still pointed; pit 92; AMU (1); UO (1); u/s (1); total 4.

Total of all variants: 131.

This type is definitely one of the earliest to be produced in the New Forest kilns. As a percentage of the assemblage, variants 1–5 range from 5·56% in contexts pre-325, to 2·23% in the group of 325–345 and to 1·48% in the latest groups. The difference between the pre- and post-325 groups suggest that these variants were not being produced much after 325, if not earlier. However, if the small typological differences are significant in the variants 22.6–8, then a continued development of the type may be accepted after 345, though clearly it is not as important as at the beginning of the century. On the other hand, since this type is the most common from the New Forest, then large amounts of residual are to be expected.

Type 23: New Forest, fabric 1; bag-bodied form.

23.1 and 2, pit 164 (2); AURRS (1); MO (1); u/s (1).

23.3, with 'stab' and furrowed decoration; u/s (1).

Although the sample is small, it would be expected that this type was one of the earliest New Forest types, but none of it appears to have been deposited before c. 325. 23.3 and its decoration equally does not suggest an early date.

Type 24: globular beakers with rustication; body sherds only.

24.1, a hard, light brown fabric with a grey core and a rich, brown slip; applied rustication; pit 103; MO (1); u/s (3); source uncertain.

24.2, fabric as above; matt brown slip; rustication between indentations; u/s (1); source uncertain.

24.3, reddish-yellow fabric, grey to the core, with a light reddish-brown slip; pit 186; similar in pit 92; AURRS (1); u/s (1).

24.4, a hard grey and slightly sandy fabric with a black slip; BURRS (1); u/s (1).

This is not a common enough variety at Portchester to make definite conclusions about date, except that there is only one post-345 context, which is probably residual. The fabrics suggest a variety of unrecognized sources.

Type 25:  a hard, slightly sandy, creamy fabric with brown paint and 'rosette' impressions on the body; pit 92; possibly New Forest.

Type 26:  a fine, hard, brown fabric with a grey core and a dark brown slip. Decoration of 'cog' impressions in vertical zones; body sherds only; pits 103 and 182; AURRS (1); u/s (4); probably Oxfordshire.

Type 27:  a very hard, fine, pale red fabric, grey at the core and covered with a glossy black slip; u/s (1); similar sherd MO (1); either Rhenish or Lezoux.

*Bowls*

Type 28:  (not illustrated), Oxford, fabric 1; base only with very worn, illiterate stamp, as in samian; u/s (2).

Type 29:  New Forest, fabric 2; hemispherical bowl. Excepting the imitation Drag. 38, this is the commonest red slipped bowl from the New Forest at Portchester.
29.1, 2 and 4–6, pits (16), (47, 52, 60, 61, 63 (3), 66 (2), 85, 144, 171, 206, 227, 236 (2)); AURRS (9); AMU (6); MO (9); Up. Clay (1); UO (6); u/s (33); total 80.
29.3, with white painted decoration; Up. Clay (1); UO (1); u/s (2).
As percentage of group:

|  |  |  |  |
|---|---|---|---|
| MO/Up. Clay | 2·1% | All groups pre-345 | 1·59% |
| UO | 1·64% | All groups post-345 | 1·41% |

The evidence of the pits implies that some were deposited pre-325, and the absence of this type in LO may not be significant. The relatively slight difference between the earlier and later groups can either be regarded as the result of survivals (cf. the MO/UO contrast) or currency perhaps up to 360–70.

Type 30:  similar in form to type 29, but tending to a slightly everted, straight-sided profile.
(a) undecorated:
30.1, New Forest, fabric 2; u/s (1).
(b) 'rouletted' decoration:
30.2, a reddish-yellow, somewhat sandy fabric with a red–brown slip; similar to Oxford, fabric 1, but seems finer (cf. Atkinson, 1942, fig. 46, D1); pit 144; AMU (1); LO (1); UO (2); u/s (5).
30.3, Oxford, fabric 1; u/s (1).
30.4, Oxford, fabric 1, worn slip in pit 41; also u/s (2).
30.5, Oxford, fabric 1; u/s (1).
(c) white paint decoration, with and without 'rouletting':
30.6, Oxford, fabric 1; UO (1); u/s (4).
30.7, very sandy, 'coarse', red–brown fabric with matt red, burnished, slip; source unknown; pit 225 (no paint/rouletting); Up. Clay (1).
30.8, Oxford, fabric 1; UO (1).
(d) uncertain form:
30.9, Oxford, fabric 1; grooves on the body; pit 144; AMU (1); u/s (1).
Besides 30.2 which was deposited before 325, in one instance, none of the others of this type would appear to have been lost before 325, although there is, necessarily, doubt over the date of the fills of pits 41 and 225. It is also interesting that 30.2 is the only decorated red slipped type, which appears in contexts definitely pre-325.

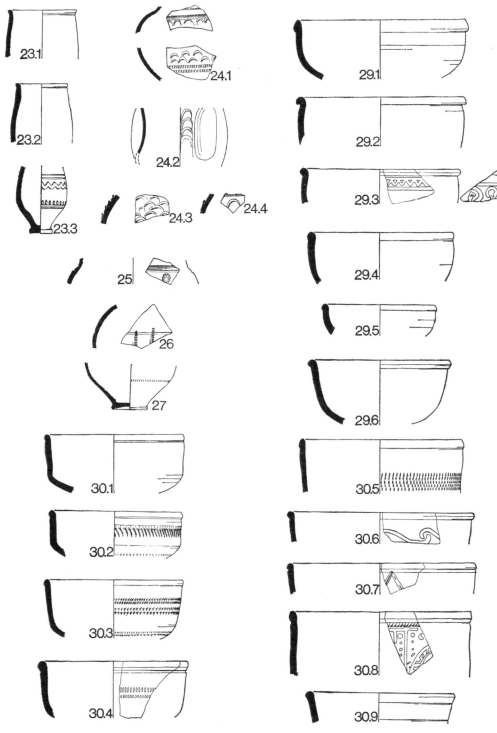

FIG. 173.  Pottery types 23–30 (pp. 313–14). Scale ¼

Type 31 :    carinated bowls with double beaded rims:
Oxford, fabric 1, except 31.6, which has a red–brown sandy fabric with a burnished red slip, AMU (1), and 31.7, which has a red–yellow sandy fabric with a burnished orange slip, of which joining sherds occurred in pit 223, MO and Up. Clay. The source of both of these is uncertain. The rest occurred in:
Pits (6), (41, ?47, 52 (sherd probably from same vessel in pit 54), 85, 122, 195, 206); BURRS (1); AURRS (1); u/s (2); total 10.
While it is clear that this type does not date later than c. 345/50, a starting date is more obscure and rests with the pits and the possibly significant absence in layers pre-325. If c. 330 is too late because it implies too short a life, then c. 320 may be reasonable.

Type 32 :    New Forest, fabric 2; similar in form to type 31, but no double-beading on the rim:
Pits (11), (46, 63 (2), 121 (2), 144 (2), 195, 236 (3) — one of the latter had traces of a rosette stamp, cf. type 33.10); AURRS (1); UO (1); u/s (4); total 17.
None of the pits suggests a pre-325 date, as it is likely that the pits 144 and 236 examples were not deposited until after 340/50, while pit 63 is definitely filled post-370. On this slender evidence it seems possible that this type is slightly later than (c. 330/40–c. 370) and imitating type 31, which is basically an Oxford type.

Type 33 :    form similar to type 30 and 32, but a slightly inverted profile.
(a) undecorated:
33.1, Oxford, fabric 1; u/s (1).
33.2, New Forest, fabric 2; pit 144; u/s (1).
(b) 'rouletted' decoration:
33.3, Oxford, fabric 1; pit 125.
33.4, Oxford, fabric 1; u/s (1).
(c) painted decoration:
33.5, New Forest, fabric 2; pit 103.
33.6, with 'rouletted' decoration; Oxford, fabric 1; AMU (1).
(d) with 'rouletted' and impressed decoration:
33.7, Oxford, fabric 1; u/s (2).
33.8, Oxford, fabric 1; u/s (1).
(e) stamp impressions only:
33.9, New Forest; fabric 2; AURRS (1).
33.10, New Forest, fabric 2; u/s (1).
33.11, Oxford, fabric 1; AMU (1).
33.12, Oxford, fabric 1; with vertical rows of 'cog' impressions; pit 103 (1).
None of the variants date pre-330, but, within them, a possible division between the plain, painted and 'rouletted' examples and the stamped, or stamped and 'rouletted', may be significant. The former cluster c. 325–c. 345, while the latter are later than c. 350, if the curious 33.12 is excepted.

Type 34 :    carinated bowls with a central cordon dividing two panels of stamped decoration:
34.1, New Forest, fabric 2; AURRS (1).
34.2, Oxford, fabric 1; UO (1); u/s (2).
34.3, Oxford, fabric 1; AURRS (1).
34.4, Oxford, fabric 1; pit 236 (similar); AURRS (1); u/s (1).
34.5, Oxford, fabric 1; AURRS (1); u/s (2).
34.6, Oxford, fabric 1; pit 63; others similar, but only half the profile, in pits 46 and 103.
34.7, Oxford, fabric 1; AURRS (2); AMU (1).

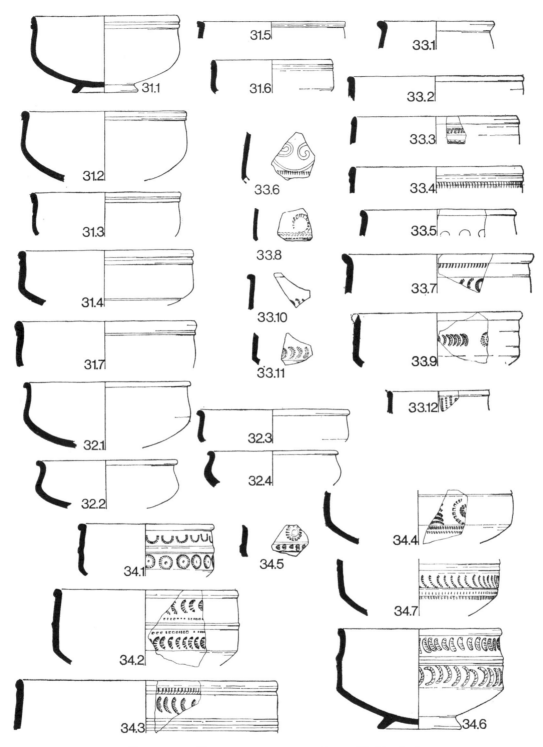

FIG. 174.   Pottery types 31–34 (p. 316). Scale ¼

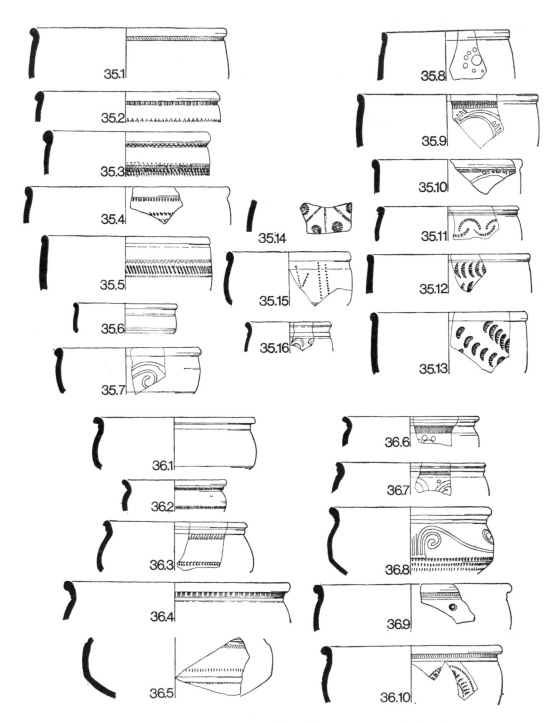

FIG. 175. Pottery types 35–36 (pp. 319–20). Scale ¼

Where the full profile of this type is present, there is no evidence for a pre-345 date. Though stamped, the pits 46 and 103 pieces are likely to be earlier, *c*. 325/45, but they may not belong to this type, because the sherds are too small for one to be certain.

Type 35: bowls with rounded and slightly swelling profiles:
(a) 'rouletted' decoration:
35.1, Oxford, fabric 1; pits 103, 125, 182, 236; AMU (1); u/s (2).
35.2, Pevensey ware; AMU (2).
35.3, Pevensey ware; u/s (1).
35.4, Oxford, fabric 1; pits 46 and 168; u/s (2).
35.5, Oxford, fabric 1 (cf. type 30.2–5); u/s (1).
35.6, Oxford, fabric 1; AMU (1); UO (1); u/s (3).
(b) painted decoration:
35.7, Pevensey ware; u/s (3).
35.8, Oxford, fabric 1; UO (1).
(c) 'rouletted' and painted decoration:
35.9, Oxford, fabric 1; MO (1); UO (1); u/s (1).
35.10, Oxford, fabric 1; AMU (2).
(d) stamped impressions:
35.11, brown, fairly sandy fabric with dull brown slip; source uncertain; u/s (1).
35.12, Oxford, fabric 1; pit 168; u/s (1).
35.13, Oxford, fabric 1; AMU (2); u/s (3).
35.14, Oxford, fabric 1; joining sherds from AURRS and AMU.
35.15, Pevensey ware; pit 147; AURRS (1); UO (1); similar, but with demi-rosettes in AURRS (1).
35.16, fine, hard, light brown fabric with a black slip; u/s (1); source uncertain, but possibly New Forest.
Although all the variants seem to occur before *c*. 345, it does seem that the plain, painted and 'rouletted' examples are more common before *c*. 345 than after, while the opposite seems true of the stamped variants. None of those from pits are likely to be pre-*c*. 325.

Type 36: this type is characterized by its reverse 'S' profile and a pronounced drawing-in below the rim; in the list of variants that follows there is a bias towards 36.1 because of the number of instances of rim sherds without enough determinant body detail. All are of Oxford, fabric 1.
(a) undecorated:
36.1, AURRS (2); AMU (1); UO (1); u/s (9); total 13.
(b) 'rouletted' decoration:
36.2, UO (1); u/s (4).
36.3, pit 63; AMU (1).
36.4, u/s (1).
36.5, pit 147; UO (1).
(c) 'rouletted' and painted decoration:
36.6, u/s (1).
36.7, pit 69; AURRS (1).
36.8, pit 46.
(d) 'rouletted' and stamped decoration:
36.9 and 10, possibly sherds of the same vessel, despite apparent unrelated decoration; AMU (1).
36.11, u/s (1)

36.12, AMU (1); u/s (1).

36.13, u/s (1).

36.14 and 15, u/s (2).

36.16, UO (1).

36.17, UO (1).

Although none of the stamped examples can date pre-345, the sherds in the pits (apart from pit 63 with the late coins) suggest an earlier date for those with painted and 'rouletted' decoration, although they need not be much earlier. None of the pits in question will have been filled before 325.

Type 37:  Pevensey ware; form similar to type 36, but the walls are thicker and there is often a slight shoulder below the rim; white paint decoration; pits 66, 130, 147 and 182; AURRS (1); AMU (1); u/s (1).

This type is unlikely to date before 325/45.

Type 38:  New Forest, fabric 2; the form suggests a reverse 'S' profile with a pointed rim; pits 48 and 79.

Type 39:  New Forest, fabric 2; simple, hemi-spherical bowls with plain rim; this type may be a development from a failed bottle or flagon type.

39.1, white paint on black slip; u/s (1).

39.2, white paint; UO (1).

39.3, this is probably a base sherd of this type, with faint traces of 'rosette' impressions; pit 121 (scale: ½).

Type 40:  wide mouth bowl imitating Drag. 31 or Ludowici Type Sh:

40.2, New Forest, fabric 2; BURRS (1); u/s (5).

The rest are Oxford, fabric 1, from pits (13), (46, 65, 69, 83, 103 (2), 138, 144 (2), 181, 182, 236 (2)); BURRS (1); AURRS (5); BMU (1); AMU (7); MO (3, of which sherds of one occurred in the Up. Clay and UO, 40.4); UO (4); u/s (23); total 57.

The absence of this type from definite pre-325 layers is probably not significant, and it is likely that some of the pit contexts, e.g. 65, 83, 181 are pre-325.

As percentage of group:

| | | | |
|---|---|---|---|
| MO/Up. Clay | 0·63% | All groups pre-345 | 0·80% |
| UO | 1·09% | All groups post-345 | 0·81% |

This suggests that the type had a long life, perhaps in to the fifth century, and that it had not reached the peak of its popularity until after A.D. 340/50.

Type 41:  shallow bowl imitating Drag. 35/36:

41.1 and 2, Oxford, fabric 1; white paint on the rim; AURRS (1); u/s (4).

41.3, New Forest, fabric 2; pits 63 and 144; AMU (1); u/s (1).

On the coin evidence for the pit fills, this type does not date pre-340/50. If the type is a conscious samian imitation, then it is surprising that it is so late, although it would not be unreasonable for the New Forest examples to be a little later than the Oxford ones.

Type 42:  shallow bowl imitating Drag. 36:

42.1 and 2, with white paint and/or 'rouletting' on the rim; Oxford, fabric 1; pits 129, 182, 187 and 236; BURRS (1); AMU (1); Up. Clay (1); UO (1); u/s (8); total 16.

Pevensey ware (not illustrated); AMU (1); UO (1).

This type, at least in the Oxford fabric, dates before 340/50, although none of the pit contexts can necessarily push it pre-325. The closer resemblance with the samian counterpart would make an earlier date than type 41 more sensible.

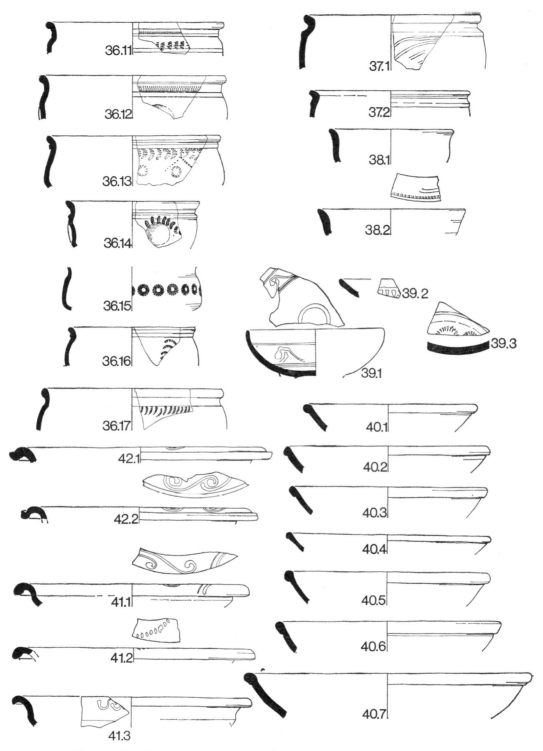

FIG. 176. Pottery types 36–42 (p. 320). Scale ¼ (except 39.3, ½)

# EXCAVATIONS AT PORTCHESTER CASTLE

Type 43 : bowl imitating Drag. 38; this is the commonest colour-coated type at Portchester. The decorated types are listed first:

43.8, with a pronounced flange and a mottled orange slip, very like 'marbled' ware but New Forest, fabric 2 (cf. type 47); pits 46 and 144.

43.9, New Forest, fabric 2; half the average size of the majority; pits 144 and 184; AURRS (1); UO (1).

43.10–12, Oxford, fabric 1; with white paint; pits 65 (43.12) and 103; AMU (3); UO (2); u/s (4); total 11.

43.13, New Forest, fabric 2; pit 223; u/s (1).

The rest are plain and occurred:

(a) New Forest, fabric 2; pits (57), (41 (2), 46, 48, 51, 52, 60 (2), 63 (2), 65, 66, 77, 103 (3), 121 (2), 125, 130 (3), 144 (7), 163, 164, 168, 178, 181, 187 (2), 195 (2), 206, 222, 223 (2), 225, 227, 228, 229, 235, 236 (10)).

(b) Oxford, fabric 1; pits (16), (46, 51, 52, 61, 63 (2), 69, 138, 144 (2), 147, 164 (2), 182, 195, 237).

The contexts of the other plain types can best be illustrated by a table:

|  | New Forest (43.1, 2, 4, 5, 6) | Oxford (43.3) | Pevensey (43.7) | Total |
|---|---|---|---|---|
| Pits | 57 | 16 | 0 | 73 |
| BURRS | 5 | 3 | 0 | 8 |
| AURRS | 9 | 11 | 0 | 20 |
| BMU | 2 | 2 | 0 | 4 |
| AMU | 15 | 12 | 2 | 29 |
| LO | 4 | 1 | 0 | 5 |
| M. Clay | 1 | 0 | 0 | 1 |
| MO | 12 | 0 | 0 | 12 |
| Up. Clay | 3 | 1 | 0 | 4 |
| UO | 16 | 6 | 0 | 22 |
| u/s | 83 | 35 | 1 | 119 |
| Total | 207 | 87 | 3 | 297 |

Type 43 as a percentage of each group:

|  | New Forest | Oxford |  | New Forest | Oxford |
|---|---|---|---|---|---|
| LO/M. Clay | 4.76% | 0.79% | All groups pre-325 | 4.76% | 0.79% |
| MO/Up. Clay | 2.95% | 0.21% | All groups pre-345 | 3.34% | 0.95% |
| UO | 4.37% | 2.19% | All groups post-345 | 2.75% | 2.28% |

Although both types had a life span of the entire fourth century, the percentages above illustrate the dramatic difference in importance of the Oxford types after 350. The percentage of type 43 in any assemblage does not seem to alter much, though it is possible that the drop in the 325–345 group may be significant. Whether Oxford types were not readily available before 345, or whether the Portchester picture reflects different sorts of purchaser in the general groups is debatable.

Type 44 : New Forest, fabric 2; moulded rim and body:

44.1, u/s (1).

44.2, UO (1).

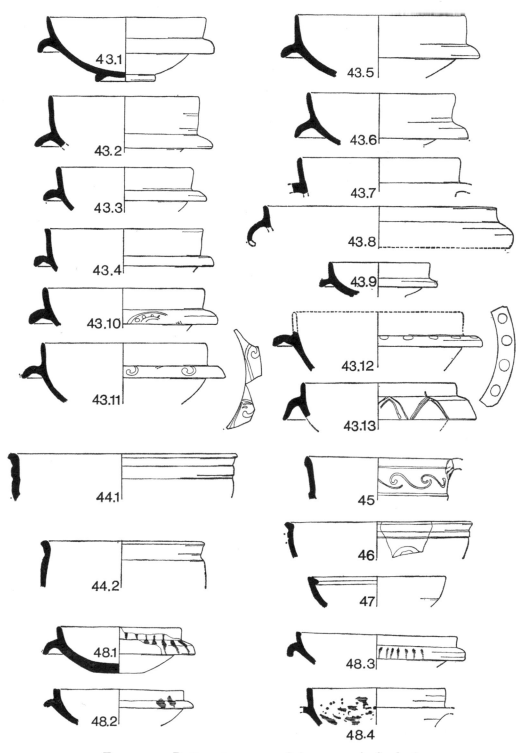

FIG. 177.   Pottery types 43–48 (pp. 322–4). Scale ¼

**Type 45:** hard, fine, creamy fabric, grey towards the core, covered in a black slip; bowl with cordon and handle; AMU (2); UO (1); u/s (1); either New Forest or Oxford.

**Type 46:** hard, red–brown sandy fabric with a thick grey core and an orange–red, burnished slip; LO (1); source uncertain.

**Type 47:** New Forest, fabric 2; with a glossy orange slip (cf. type 43.8); UO (1).

*Bowls (painted)*

**Type 48:** flanged bowls, generally with brown paint splashed on the flange:
48.1 and 2, New Forest, fabric 3; pit 236; AMU (1); MO (1); u/s (1).
48.3, New Forest, fabric 3a (cf. type 49.8); u/s (1).
48.4, Oxford, fabric 3, but an unusual form; brown paint on the inside only, to give a mottled effect (cf. 56.2); u/s (1).

**Type 49:** New Forest, fabric 3, except 49.8, which is fabric 3a, like type 48.3; bowls with an internal flange and red–brown paint either on the flange, or in zones beneath it, or in combinations of both. There is no paint externally; pits (14), (48, 63, 77, 79, 95, 187, 223 (2), 225 (2), 230, 236 (3); AURRS (4); AMU (3); LO (1); MO (5); UO (1); u/s (19); total 47.
Type 49 as a percentage of each group:

| | | | | |
|---|---|---|---|---|
| LO/M. Clay | 0·79% | | All groups pre-325 | 0·79% |
| MO/Up. Clay | 1·05% | | All groups pre-345 | 0·79% |
| UO | 0·27% | | All groups post-345 | 0·54% |

The date range of this type is long — from pre-325 to post 370–80. The less sandy fabrics, as in Amberwood kiln 3, may be typical of the late examples of this type.

**Type 50:** carinated bowl with moulding on the rim and at the carination; painted decoration can occur in horizontal zones on both the inside and outer surfaces:
50.1, a pale red, sandy fabric with red paint; Oxford; pits 85 and 86 (sherds of the same vessel); u/s (1).
50.2 and 3, fairly fine creamy fabric, grey towards the core, with red–brown paint on a white all-over slip; Oxford, fabric 3; base in pit 236; AURRS (1); u/s (1).
50.4, fine, pale yellow to dirty cream fabric, ? New Forest, fabric 3a; brown paint on an all-over white slip; UO (1). It seems likely that this variant is a New Forest imitation of the basic Oxford type, but the fine parchment fabric is unusual.

**Type 51:** hard, white sandy fabric; brown paint in wave pattern outside; either New Forest or Oxford, unusual form; u/s (1).

*Cups*

**Type 52:** New Forest, fabric 1:
(a) plain:
52.1 and 2, pits 157 and 223; u/s (1).
(b) furrowed or impressed decoration:
52.3 and 4, pits 85, 92 and 178; u/s (2).
52.5, UO (1).

*Dishes*

**Type 53:** with a slightly convex profile and a plain rim:
53.1, New Forest, fabric 3; with a thin, glossy black slip; sherds of the same vessel occurred in AMU, MO and UO.
53.2, Oxford, fabric 1, a dull red slip; AMU (1); u/s (1).

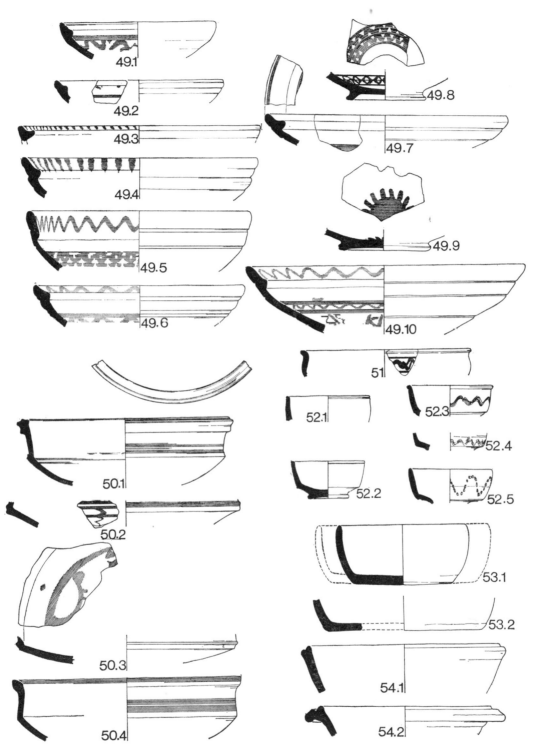

FIG. 178.   Pottery types 49–54 (pp. 324–6). Scale ¼

Type 54:    dishes or bowls with an everted profile and a slight flange:
54.1, New Forest, fabric 3; with a black slip; pit 64.
54.2, hard, fine, brown–yellow fabric, grey at the core, covered with a purple slip; either New Forest or Oxford; u/s (1).

*Jars*

Type 55:    everted rim jars or bowls; in all cases the slip covers the outside surfaces as well as the upper surface of the rim:
55.1, fine, light brown fabric with a brown slip; source uncertain; u/s (1).
55.2, fabric similar to 55.1, but slightly vesicular and slightly glossy finish to the slip; AURRS (1); Up. Clay (1); UO (1); u/s (3).
55.3, as 55.2.
55.4, New Forest, fabric 3; with a purple slip; AURRS (1).
55.5–7, New Forest, fabric 1; slip usually purple, but occasionally brown or red–brown; pit 236; AURRS (1); AMU (1); u/s (2).
55.8–9, New Forest, fabric 3; with brown or purple slip; pits 103, 187 and 223; BURRS (2); AURRS (1); u/s (2).
55.10 and 11, New Forest, fabric 1; pit 187; AURRS (1); MO (1); u/s (1).
55.12, New Forest, fabric 1; red–yellow slip with a blob of white paint outside; UO (1).
55.13, New Forest, fabric 1; hard-fired with white paint on a purple slip; AURRS (1).
55.14, fine, cream, sandy fabric with zones of red–brown paint outside; source uncertain; u/s (1).
55.15, New Forest; fabric 1; yellow–brown slip; u/s (1).
55.16, New Forest, fabric 3; with a black slip; pit 230.
55.17, light brown fabric with a grey core and a streaky slip of brown paint below the rim; the uneven surface of the fabric is very reminiscent of Pevensey ware; MO (1); u/s (1).
55.18, creamy, slightly sandy fabric with a pink core; bands of brown paint; source uncertain; pit 223.
55.19, hard, white sandy fabric; with circular patterns of brown paint; either New Forest or Oxford; u/s (1).
55.20, New Forest, fabric 1; swelling on the neck; UO (1).
55.21, New Forest, fabric 1; purple slip; possibly a jar, but exact type uncertain; AURRS (1).
Type 55 as a percentage of each group:

| LO/M. Clay | 0 | All groups pre-325 | 0 |
|---|---|---|---|
| MO/Up. Clay | 0·63% | All groups pre-345 | 0·79% |
| UO | 0·82% | All groups post-345 | 0·79% |

The New Forest variants divide in to two fabrics, of which the fabric 3 group is clearly the earlier:

| Fabric 1 | | Fabric 3 | |
|---|---|---|---|
| MO/Up. Clay | 0·16% | MO, etc. | 0·32% |
| UO, etc. | 0·47% | UO, etc. | 0·13% |

In general terms, while a pre-*c.* 325 starting date is not ruled out for the colour-coated jars, it is clear that the type, whatever the fabric, was current from *c.* 325–*c.* 400. The variety of fabrics is interesting.

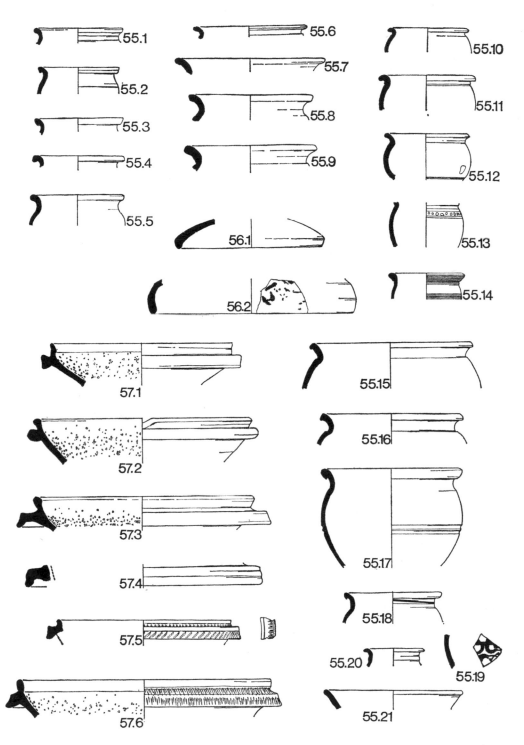

Fig. 179. Pottery types 55–57 (pp. 326–8). Scale ¼

*Lids*

Type 56:　56.1, New Forest, fabric 3; possibly a lid for type 49; yellow surface, but no trace of paint; u/s (1).

56.2, similar to Oxford, fabric 3; mottled red–brown paint outside; BURRS (1); LO (1); MO (1); UO (1).

*Mortaria*

Type 57:　flanged, the flange usually being turned down:

57.1, Oxford, fabric 1; with translucent, rounded quartz grits; corresponding red slip; pits (6), (52, 129, 144, 157, 147, 230); BURRS (1); AURRS (2); AMU (6); MO (1); UO (2); u/s (13); total 31.

57.2–4, New Forest, fabric 2; with crushed flint gritting; corresponding reddish-yellow to brown slips; each variant AMU (1); the rest u/s (3).

57.5 and 6, Oxford, fabric 1; with fine 'rouletted' decoration; AMU (1); u/s (1).

Type 57 as a percentage of each group:

| | | | |
|---|---|---|---|
| MO/Up. Clay | 0·21% (Oxford only) | All groups pre-345 | 0·32% |
| UO | 0·55% (Oxford only) | All groups post-345 | 0·94% |

Although one or two of the Oxford variants from pits may date pre-*c.* 325, it seems clear that this type had not become fully popular until after *c.* 345. None of the New Forest examples date earlier than this.

Type 58:　wall-sided mortaria imitating Drag. 45:

58.1, New Forest, fabric 2, with flint gritting; pits 103, 144 (2) and 206; u/s (1).

58.2 and 3, Oxford, fabric 1, with translucent, rounded quartz grits; pits (21), (46, 63 (2), 65 (2), 86, 92, 103 (2), 119, 121, 125, 130 (2), 144 (4), 147, 182, 187); BURRS (1); AURRS (5); AMU (10); LO (1); MO (4); Up. Clay (2); UO (6); u/s (47); total 97.

58.4, New Forest, fabric 2; crushed flint gritting; UO (1).

58.5, Oxford, fabric 1; painted decoration; pits 61 and 164.

58.6, Oxford, fabric 1; 'rouletted' decoration; AMU (1); u/s (1).

Type 58 as a percentage of each group:

| | | | |
|---|---|---|---|
| LO/M. Clay | 0·79% | All groups pre-325 | 0·79% |
| MO/Up. Clay | 1·27% | All groups pre-345 | 1·11% |
| UO | 1·91% (New Forest and Oxford) | | |
| | | All groups post-345 | 1·55% |
| | | (New Forest and Oxford) | |

The length of popularity of this type is great and it spans all the fourth century. The possibility of comparative decline post-345 may merely reflect the growing numbers of type 57. At the moment there is no indication as to when this type became residual.

Type 59:　Oxford, fabric 1; imitating Drag. 45, as type 58, but unusually large:

59.1, sherds of same vessel in pits 87 and 94.

59.2, u/s (1).

Type 60:　New Forest, fabric 3a; traces of a yellow wash; no grits visible; AMU (1).

Type 61:　New Forest, fabric 2; imitating Drag. 44; MO (1).

Type 62:　New Forest, fabric 3a; with traces of a reddish-brown slip; furrowed, wavy line decoration with stab (pointed) impressions; u/s (1).

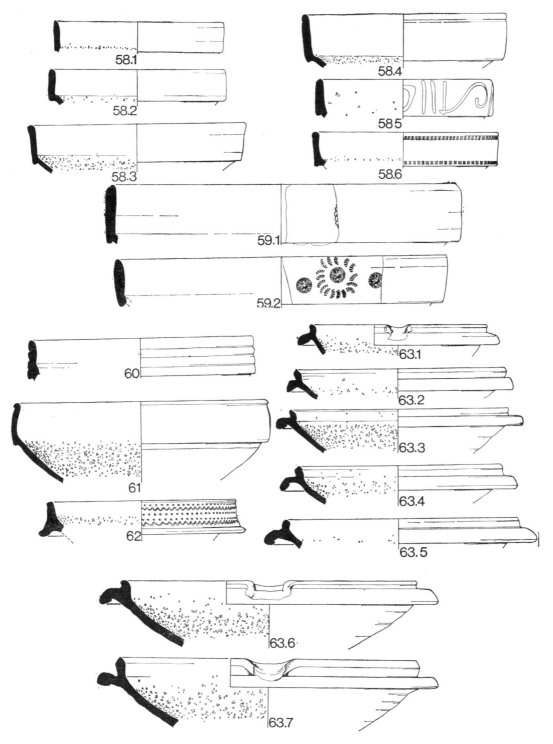

FIG. 180.   Pottery types 58–63 (pp. 328–30). Scale ¼

*Mortaria — plain*

Type 63:  Oxford, fabric 3, except 63.4, which is like fabric 1 — a fine, hard red ware with a grey core, but a white rather than a red slip. Among the others a thin orange or red–brown wash is common. As with the other Oxford mortaria, they all have translucent, rounded, quartz grits. Pits (12), (40, 46 (2), 54, 61, 103, 121, 130, 147, 226, 227, 236); BURRS (2); AURRS (5); AMU (4); MO (5); UO (4); u/s (15); total 47.
63.4, pits 103, 129 and 187; AMU (3); MO (1); UO (3); u/s (4); total 14.
Type 63 as a percentage of each group:

| MO/Up. Clay | 1·27% | All groups pre-345 | 1·27% |
| UO | 1·91% | All groups post-345 | 1·28% |

The pit evidence as well as rimless sherds in layers against the wall suggests that this type was occurring from the beginning of occupation at Portchester, and at the moment there is not enough evidence to try to look for subtle variation with time, within the type.

Type 64:  New Forest, fabric 3, except 64.4, which is fabric 3a, with a yellow–brown surface. Decoration of horizontal rilling on the flange. The grits of this and all the following New Forest types are of crushed flint. Pits (6), (86, 95, 130, 222, 236 (2)); AURRS (2); AMU (1); MO (2); UO (2); u/s (6); total 19.

Type 65:  New Forest, fabric 3; these are classed together as they have horizontal or near horizontal flanges. BURRS (1); AMU (2); MO (2) (one of these with a join in UO); UO (1); u/s (3); total 9.

Type 66:  New Forest, fabric 3; these are classed together as they have angled flanges with two possible facets for decoration. The latter can consist of either furrowed, wavy lines made by a single or multiple pointed instrument, or of stab marks similarly caused, or of combinations of both varieties. Pits (8), (63, 121, 130, 144, 185, 195, 227, 236); AURRS (1); AMU (1); LO (1), (with a joining sherd in MO); MO (4); UO (1); u/s (12); total 28.

Type 67:  New Forest, fabric 3; distinguished by size from the others; pit 85; MO (1).
Types 64–67 as a percentage of each group:

| LO/M. Clay | 0·79% | All groups pre-325 | 0·79% |
| MO/Up. Clay | 1·9% | All groups 325–345 | 1·6% |
| UO | 1·09% | All groups post-345 | 0·74% |

Types 64–67 have been taken together because in terms of fabric and basic form they can be considered as one, with minor variation in decoration between each type. While some at least were being deposited before 325, the peak of popularity seems to lie *c.* 325–*c.* 345. Pressure from the Oxford kilns seems to have an effect after 345, and it is possible that production ceased by *c.* 370. This type is not present in the late kilns at Amberwood (Fulford, 1973a).

Type 68:  very sandy brown fabric, grey on the surface of 68.2; rounded quartz grits; source unknown.
68.1, furrowed, wavy decoration; LO (1).
68.2, stab/slash marks; u/s (1).

Type 69:  fabric D; pale red, vesicular with a grey core and a yellow surface; rounded quartz grits; pit 47.

Type 70:  hard, fine, white fabric with brown paint outside; large, black, angular grits; Hartshill/ Mancetter; u/s (1).

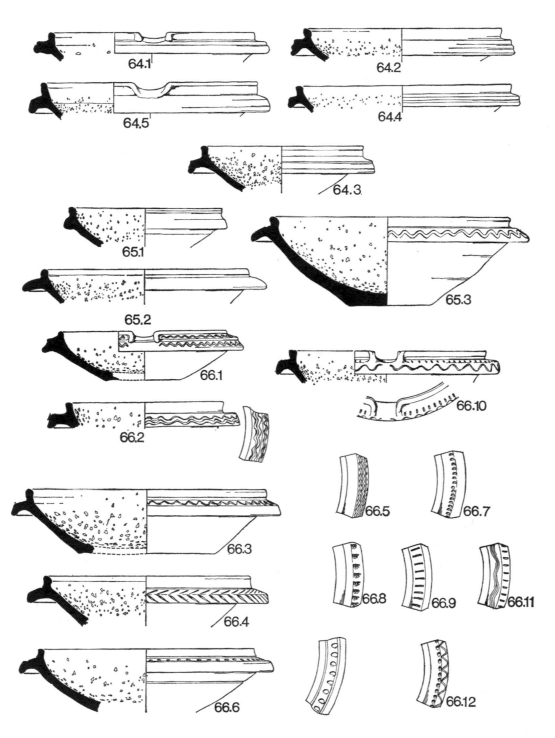

FIG. 181. Pottery types 64–66 (p. 330). Scale ¼

Type 71 : hard, dirty cream, slightly vesicular fabric with a grey core and a cream–yellow surface; flint grits; u/s (1). K. Hartley kindly supplied the following note: 'the fabric and form can be matched fairly closely with Fishbourne Type 294 (Cunliffe, 1971); a source in southern England is likely. There is a fragmentary impression of an ansate stamp on the collar. Ansate stamps are rare. Probable date of manufacture *c*. 160–*c*. 200.'

Type 72 : hard, brown, sandy fabric with a grey core and a brown surface; small, rounded quartz grits; second/third century type; u/s (1).

Type 73 : bright red, sandy fabric with a burnished red-brown slip and large quartz grits; AURRS (1). Of all the mortaria, there are only 6 whose source is uncertain.

## The Grey Wares and Miscellaneous

*Amphorae*

Type 74 : hard, pale red fabric with a cream to brown surface, micaceous; Spanish type; two rim sherds, possibly of the same vessel, AURRS (1); u/s (1). Two body sherds in similar fabric to the others from pit 70; u/s (1). Dr D. P. S. Peacock suggests a date no later than 250/60 for this type, and so the amphora (all the sherds could have come from the same vessel) was probably enjoying a use secondary to that for which it was intended when it came to Portchester. Total weight of these sherds: 850 g.

*Beakers*

Type 75 : narrow mouthed beaker with globular body:
75.1, hard grey, granulated fabric; hand-made; burnished outside and inside the rim; pit 90.
75.2, fine, grey sandy fabric; stroke-scored decoration on the body; silvery grey slip outside and traces inside, below the rim; pit 103.
75.3, fine, grey sandy fabric; a silvery grey slip, burnished on the rim outside; u/s (2).
75.4, fine, grey sandy fabric; all over white slip; burnished; u/s (1).

Type 76 : with tall neck and globular body:
76.1, fine, grey sandy fabric; a silvery grey slip outside and on the rim, with light vertical burnishing on the neck; pits (5), (40, 63, 144, 209, 236); AURRS (1); AMU (1); u/s (3); total 10.
76.2, fine, grey sandy fabric; traces of a grey slip outside and on the rim; pit 121; MO (1); Up. Clay (2); u/s (2).
76.3, a hard, light grey, somewhat granular fabric; no slip, but burnished outside and on the upper surface of the rim; AURRS (1).
76.4, a red–brown, sandy fabric with a grey core and haematite/limonite inclusions; a black, well-burnished slip outside; hand-made, with traces of luting inside; MO (1); UO (1).
76.5, hard grey sandy; traces of burnishing outside; UO (1).
76.6, fabric B; burnished surface with vertical strokes on the neck and horizontal zones on the body; the body and neck joint clearly visible inside; M. Clay (1).
Summary (see type 77):
Pits (6); AURRS (2); AMU (1); M. Clay (1); MO (2); Up. Clay (2); UO (2); u/s (5).

Type 77: as type 76, but the body is decorated with panels of incised patterns, scored with a blunt-nosed instrument; opposed diagonals between pairs of verticals is the commonest variety; apart from 77.1, only body sherds are known of this type. It is quite probable that the rims of type 76.1 and 2 belong to these sherds, (cf. types 80 and 92). Fine, grey sandy fabric with

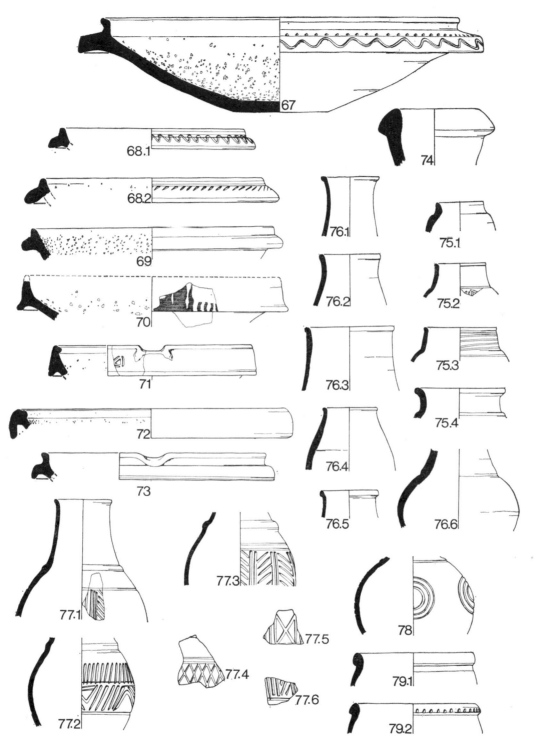

FIG. 182. Pottery types 67–79 (pp. 330–4). Scale ¼

either a white or black slip. Probably New Forest, although not known yet from kilns there. The technique of the decoration compares with that used on New Forest bottles, beakers, mortaria (see this report) and the distribution of known examples circumscribes the New Forest area (e.g. at Rockbourne, Sparsholt (type 92), Winchester).

77.1, burnished body and neck, where decoration is absent. This seems to be typical of all the sherds, when enough survives.

Apart from 77.3; pit 164; and 77.4; MO (1); and 77.5; pit 121, all the illustrated examples were unstratified; similar pieces occurred in: pits (7), (60, 63, 206, 223, 227, 230, 236); AURRS (2); AMU (3); LO (1); MO (1); u/s (10); total 24.

Type 78:    dark grey sandy fabric; probably from a beaker; incised circular decoration; horizontal wheel burnishing; cf. types 2/10.20–25 and 20. Probably a New Forest type. Joining sherds from pit 229 and MO.

Types 76–78: Comparison of the frequency of occurrence of each type and then of all the beakers together:

|  | Type 76 | Type 77 | Type 78 | Types 76–8 |
|---|---|---|---|---|
| LO/M. Clay | 0·79% | 0·79% | 0 | 1·58% |
| MO/Up. Clay | 0·84% | 0·42% | 0·21% | 1·47% |
| UO | 0·55% | 0 | 0 | 0·55% |

As a percentage of all groups:

|  | Type 76 | Type 77 | Type 78 | Types 76–8 |
|---|---|---|---|---|
| (a) pre-325 | 0·79% | 0·79% | 0 | 1·58% |
| (b) *c.* 325–*c.* 345 | 0·64% | 0·32% | 0·16% | 1·12% |
| (c) post-345 | 0·34% | 0·34% | 0 | 0·68% |

From both the pit evidence and the layers against the wall, it seems that grey ware beakers were current before *c.* 325–45 and that they were probably out of production before *c.* 370. Even the decorated types seem to be at the peak of popularity before *c.* 345 (cf. type 92), and can, perhaps, be paralleled with the colour-coated New Forest equivalents using this decorative technique, both in terms of style and date.

*Bowls*

Type 79:    bowl with bead rim:
79.1, a grey, granular fabric with a burnished outer surface; AMU (1).
79.2, fine, grey sandy fabric; silvery grey slip outside and inside the rim; 'notch' or finger-nail decoration; u/s (1).

Type 80:    bowl with bead rim:
80.1, fine, grey sandy fabric; black slip outside and inside the rim; burnished and scored decoration (cf. types 77 and 92); UO (1).
80.2, fine, grey sandy fabric; white slip with traces of lightly scored burnish strokes on the body; pit 144.

Type 81:    bowl with simple rim:
hard, orange–brown, sandy fabric with a grey core; deeply scored cross on a burnished orange outer surface; AURRS (1).

Type 82:    bowl with everted rim:
orange sandy fabric with a burnished orange surface (cf. type 81); pit 164

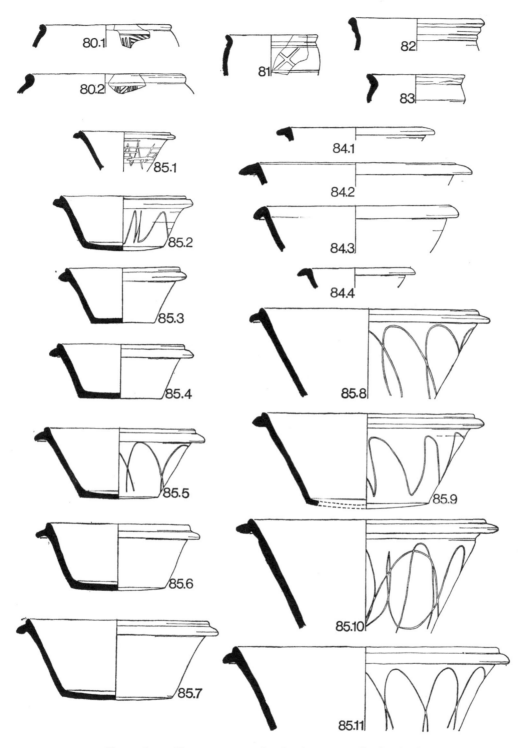

FIG. 183. Pottery types 80–85 (pp. 334–6). Scale ¼

Type 83: carinated bowl:
grey to brown sandy fabric with a black surface and traces of a white slip; u/s (2). Possibly a first/second-century type.

Type 84: bowl with flange at the rim:
84.1, fine, grey sandy fabric; grey slip, burnished outside; pit 61.
84.2, pale grey to white sandy fabric with upper surface of the flange burnished; u/s (1).
84.3, hand-made, fabric A; very micaceous; burnished on all surfaces; AMU (1).
84.4, fine, grey sandy fabric with an orange surface; no traces of a slip; cf. 88.6; pit 138.

Type 85: bowl with flange and bead; pie-dish:
In form it is impossible to distinguish between those bowls hand-made in the black-burnished fabric (B) and those wheel-made in grey, sandy fabrics. Thus, though from at least two — and very probably many more — sources, they will all be considered as one type. Bowls in fabric B are type 85.4, 6–8 and 11. Generally the inside, and sometimes some of the outside, is covered in a black, or, very rarely, a white slip; the inside is burnished smooth as well as the top surface of the flange, while outside are burnished running loops and arcades, where they have not been rubbed away; these can occur on the base also. The grey-ware bowls have a fine, sandy fabric, sometimes with a grey core, and are invariably covered in a black or a silvery grey slip. As with the black-burnished vessels, the slip is generally on the flange and inside, but not commonly over the whole bowl, and it is similarly well burnished inside and on the flange, while only arcading decorates the outer wall surfaces. Sometimes on the inside of the base there are traces of slightly deeper scored burnishing in parallel lines. Type 85.1–3, 5 and 9–10 are in this fabric.
Fabric B bowls occurred as follows:
Pits (119), (40, 41, 46 (7), 47 (2), 48 (4), 49 (2), 52 (2), 54 (4), 60 (2), 62, 63 (5), 66, 79, 83, 85 (3), 86, 95 (5), 103 (5), 119, 121 (9), 125, 129, 130 (3), 142, 144 (8), 155, 157, 163, 164 (3), 178, 182, 185, 186 (2), 187 (3), 195, 201 (3), 206 (4), 209, 222 (2), 223 (2), 224, 225, 227 (2), 230, 236 (15)); BURRS (6); AURRS (34); BMU (2); AMU (41); LO (4); MO (13); Up. Clay (6); UO (20); u/s (116); total 361.
Grey fabrics occurred as follows:
Pits (61), (46, 47 (2), 48 (2), 52 (2), 54, 60, 63 (3), 64 (2), 79, 86 (3), 103 (5), 121 (2), 125, 138, 142, 144 (2), 157 (2), 163, 168, 182, 184, 185, 186, 187 (6), 195 (2), 206, 222, 223 (3), 224, 228, 229, 230 (2), 234, 235, 236 (3)); BURRS (4); AURRS (10); AMU (10); LO (6); M. Clay (2); MO (26); Up. Clay (8); UO (9); u/s (104); total 240.
The frequency of rims to diameter is shown in fig. 163. Although no account can be taken of possible different depths of a bowl for any one diameter, it is felt that the measurement of rim diameters does give some idea of standardization and what the potters were aiming at. Fig. 164 also shows how the three main fabric groups relate and compare with one another through time. Rim sherd count shows how close fabrics A (type 86) and B are in terms of possible numbers of this form of vessel, although the weight comparison, ignoring type variation, tends towards greater amounts of fabric A (cf. fig. 158). This is not surprising in view of the thick and clumsy shape of the grog-tempered vessels.

Type 86: flange-bowl, as type 85:
The main distinguishing feature of this type is the crudeness with which it was made. Like fabric B bowls they are hand-made, but there is no attempt to produce an even thickness in the vessel wall or a standard profile. Some have straight sides, while others have rounded, sagging profiles; the flange varies enormously in length and thickness. In each group, whether early or late, there is a variety in finish and it is not possible, at the moment, to

distinguish between early and late examples. A small selection is offered to illustrate the range.

The fabric is a fairly soft, slightly granular, heavily 'grog'-tempered ware. Occasionally shell and flint occur, but the red and grey round (0·5–1 mm.) 'grog' inclusions are ubiquitous in a dark brown to black matrix.

Decoration consists of stroke-burnish lattice, vertical and zig-zag patterns on a totally burnished surface. Presumably this is trying to imitate the true 'black-burnished' finish, but, owing to the general uneven surface, patterns of arcading, for example, are not easily executed.

86.6 does not belong to this fabric group. Although it is hand-made, the fabric is a coarse sanded ware, black on the surface. Except the outer wall all parts are burnished regularly. On the outer wall there are diagonal strokes under a broad, burnished zone. Occurred LO (1). Hand-made, fabric A occurred in: pits (89), (40 (5), 41 (2), 46 (3), 47 (2), 48 (3) 54, 60 (2), 62 (2), 63 (3), 64, 65 (2), 66, 69, 77, 79, 92, 95 (2), 103 (7), 121 (3), 122, 125 (2), 129, 130 (4), 144 (7), 147, 164 (2), 166, 168, 184, 185, 187 (2), 201 (2), 206 (2), 222, 223 (2), 234, 235, 236 (12), 237); BURRS (8); AURRS (28); BMU (1); AMU (30); LO (7); M. Clay (1); MO (30); Up. Clay (4); UO (15); u/s (98); total 311.

It is interesting to notice that this figure, which is a purely hypothetical reflection of the original number of bowls, because it is based on a count of rim sherds, suggests that there were less than the 'black-burnished' type 85 (fig. 164). Weight analysis suggested that the opposite might be the case, but it probably reflects the greater weight per vessel in the 'grog'-tempered fabric (cf. fig. 158).

On fig. 163, there are histograms to show the frequency of the varying rim diameters. It is interesting to see how well they fall in to the pattern of other bowls of this type and how, in particular, the preferred size is 150/160 mm. This suggests that, far from being a rough and ready peasant type, the potters were making them to a demand which fits in to the pattern of the conventional material, i.e. black-burnished and the grey fabrics.

Type 87:  flanged bowl; as type 85:
Besides the main fabrics in this type, already listed, there were a considerable number of flanged bowls in different fabrics and with slight differences in form.

87.1, fine, grey sandy fabric, covered all over in a silvery grey slip; inside, the surfaces have been stroke-burnished in a random fashion below a zone of total burnishing; outside, the flange is burnished and there is intermittent burnishing on the body. This is similar to the grey ware type 85, but the difference in slip and the squat flange have taken it out of type 85. Pit 129; others in AURRS (2); AMU (3); UO (2); u/s (8); total 16.

87.2, fabric D; pits 52, 54 and 170; BURRS (1); AURRS (1); AMU (1); UO (1); u/s (6); total 13. This type probably dates from c. 325–c. 400.

87.3, with a low under-cut flange; fabric fine, grey sandy with an all-over white slip; inside and the upper surface of the flange are burnished; pit 60; u/s (1).

87.4, a very coarse, grey sandy fabric; burnished inside and on the flange; u/s (1).

87.5, a pale grey, coarse sandy fabric, burnished inside and on the flange; no slip; UO (1); u/s (2).

87.6, fabric as for 87.5; no slip and wheel-burnishing marks inside and on the flange, and intermittently outside; pit 147; others u/s (3).

87.7, a micaceous, fine, grey sandy fabric with a grey slip inside; the distinctive characteristic of this type is the reeding on the top of the rim. This example from pit 94; others from AURRS (1); u/s (2). Fig. 164 shows the differing proportions of each of the main fabric

23

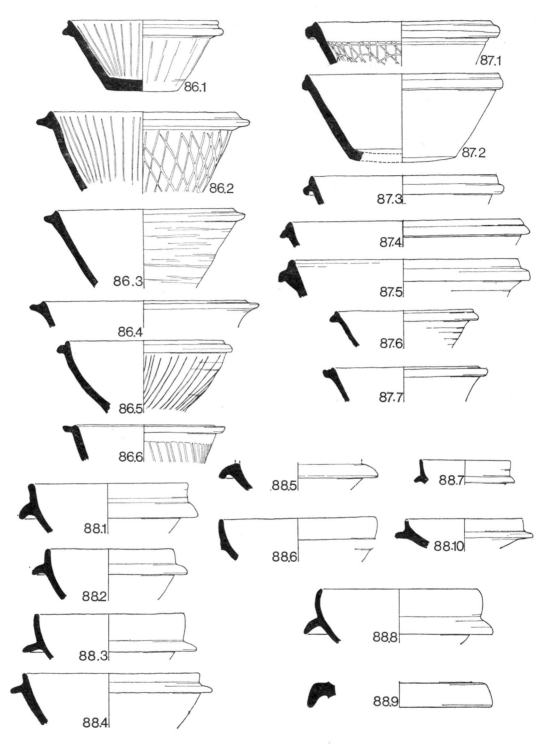

Fig. 184. Pottery types 86–88 (pp. 336–9). Scale ¼

groups in this type. The apparent displacement of the grey fabrics by the black-burnished is interesting especially as, in terms of fabric weight, the latter seems to decline in importance after *c.* 345 (cf. fig. 158).

Flange bowls as a proportion of the assemblage remain fairly constant throughout:

     pre-325    15·9%          *c.* 325-345    17·3%          post-345    14·0%

**Type 88:**    bowl with large flange projecting from the middle of the wall:

88.1, coarse, grey, sandy, burnished inside and above the flange outside; u/s (2).

88.2, black-burnished(fabric B); AMU (1).

88.3, medium coarse, pale grey sandy fabric with an all-over black slip, burnished inside and above the flange outside; u/s (1).

88.4, hand-made, fabric A; yellow–brown surface; probably an extreme variant of type 86; LO (1); UO (1).

88.5, fine red–brown fabric on a grey core, with traces of a burnished surface all over (cf. type 84.4); u/s (1).

88.6, very coarse grey sandy with a brick red, worn surface; traces of burnishing; u/s (1).

88.7, soft, yellow–brown, slightly sandy fabric with traces of a burnished, brown slip on all surfaces; u/s (1).

88.8, New Forest, fabric 2; no slip, but a burnished yellow–red surface; pit 182; AURRS (1); u/s (2).

88.9, hard, granular, reddish-orange sandy fabric with a dark red burnished slip; possibly a mortarium, but no trace of grits; AURRS (ill.); AMU (1); similar in pit 187.

88.10, New Forest, fabric 2; no slip, but burnished pale yellow surface; pit 69.

**Type 89:**    bowl with inturned rim:

89.1, fine, grey sandy with traces of a white slip on the flange and possibly burnishing also; u/s (2); probably New Forest.

89.2, brown to grey sandy fabric with a black slip all over; u/s (1).

89.3, fabric D; u/s (1).

89.4, fine, grey sandy fabric with a black slip, burnished outside; AURRS (1).

**Type 90:**    bowl with thickened and moulded rim:

90.1, coarse, grey sandy fabric with a thick, black slip; u/s (1).

90.2, dark grey, micaceous sandy fabric; u/s (3). Probably New Forest types, cf. Amberwood, kiln 1 (Fulford, 1973.)

**Type 91:**    ? small bowl with reeded outer surfaces:

coarse, grey sandy fabric with a white slip inside, probably burnished; AMU (1).

**Type 92:**    two-handled bowl, probably with a pedestal foot:

fine, grey sandy fabric with a silvery grey slip outside and inside the rim; decoration consists of scored lattices, or zones of diagonal patterns over the outside. A round-nosed instrument has been used, possibly the same as the general burnishing tool (cf. types 77 and 80); pits (5), (47, 48, 61, 234, 236); AURRS (1); AMU (1); UO (1); u/s (9); total 16; both rims and distinctive body sherds were recorded. Although there were no examples stratified against the wall before *c.* 345, all the pits, except 236 were filled by then, if not much earlier. So the date range is likely to be the same as for type 77 (see under type 78), *c.* 325/30–70.

**Type 93:**    bowls with turned out rim:

93.1, hand-made, fabric A, grey surface; burnished inside and on the upper surface of the rim; AURRS (3).

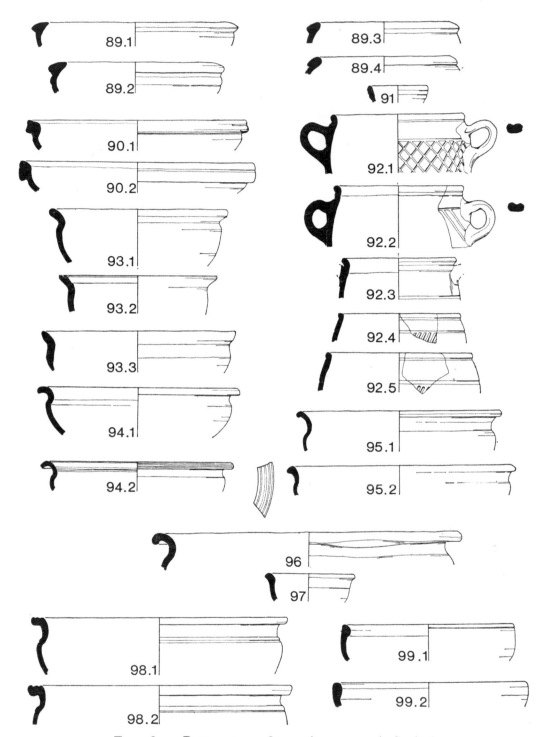

FIG. 185.    Pottery types 89–99 (pp. 339–41). Scale ¼

93.2, pale, red–brown sandy fabric with a pink to white slip all over, grooving on the rim; u/s (1).

93.3, coarse, grey sandy; probably hand-made, or finished on a slow wheel; burnished upper surface of the rim; u/s (1).

Type 94: bowls with rolled out rims; the complete form may be a colander, but there was no firm evidence:
dark grey, sandy fabric, slightly micaceous, occasionally with haematite/limonite grains visible:
94.1, with a black slip, which is burnished in bands outside and all over the upper surface of the rim.
94.2, apparently no slip, but has clearly been burnished on the upper surface of the body; these and similar occurred in: pits (5), (47, 121, 125, 223, 236); AURRS (1); AMU (1); MO (2); Up. Clay (1, with a join in UO), UO (1); u/s (4); total 15.

Type 95: wide-mouthed bowl or jar, turned out rim:
95.1, hard, pale yellow–brown, slightly micaceous fabric; similar coloured surface (cf. type 144); Severn Valley; u/s (1).
95.2, New Forest, fabric 2; no trace of slip; pit 94.

Type 96: hard, dark grey, coarse sandy fabric; no slip; pit 187.

Type 97: small bowl with thickened, out-bent rim:
hard, granular, grey sandy fabric with a pale cream slip outside and on the upper surface of the rim; possibly fabric D; pits 51 and 69.

Type 98: large bowl with out-bent and reeded rim;
fine, dark grey sandy fabric:
98.1, with an all over white slip; pit 103.
98.2, apparently no slip, but quite worn; traces of burnishing on the body and rim; pits 83, 130, 195, 225; AMU (1); MO (2); u/s (6); total 13.

Type 99: bowl with a thickened rim internally:
99.1, hard, yellow sandy fabric; Gose (1950), form 489; u/s (1) (Fulford and Bird, forthcoming).
99.2, reddish-brown, sandy fabric with traces of burnishing outside; u/s (1).

Type 100: bowl with thickened rim, slightly out-bent:
100.1, hand-made, fabric A; burnished on all surfaces; AMU (1).
100.2, fine, hard grey sandy fabric with a black slip outside (upper half only) and inside the rim; MO (1).
100.3, coarse, grey sandy fabric with a brown surface; hand-made; white slip outside and on the inside of the rim; AMU (1).

Type 101: bowl with folded out rim:
coarse, grey sandy fabric; hand-made; traces of stroke-burnishing inside; BURRS (1); AMU (2); possibly all one vessel.

Type 102: bowl, base only; black-burnished fabric B; stab decoration on the carination with triple pointed instrument; u/s (1).

Type 103: wide-mouthed bowl with thick, out-bent rim:
103.1, fine, grey sandy, somewhat micaceous; burnished slip inside; pits 144 (2), 164, 206; BURRS (1); AMU (4); LO (1); u/s (3); total 13.
103.2, pale grey sandy with a light grey surface; UO (1).

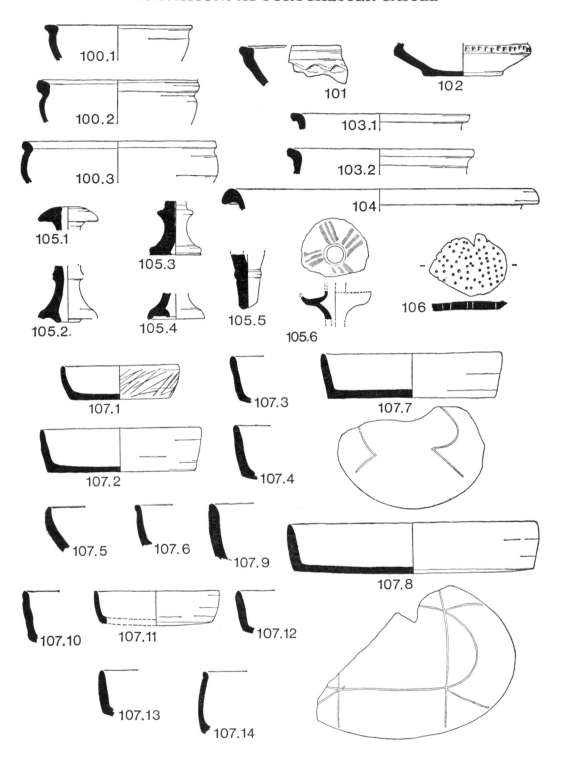

FIG. 186.   Pottery types 100–107 (pp. 341–4). Scale ¼

Type 104: wide-mouthed bowl with thick, out-bent and rounded rim; coarse grey sandy with a white slip all over; u/s (1).

*Candlesticks*

Type 105: New Forest, fabric 3; off-white to cream surface; pits 235(.3) and 236(.6); AURRS(.5); AMU(.1); LO (1); UO (1) (.4); u/s (1) (.2); total 7.

*Colanders*

Type 106: form possibly as type 94:
(a) grey sandy fabric with a black slip; pit 187; AMU (1); Up. Clay (1); u/s (3); total 6.
(b) hand-made, fabric A; pit 121.

*Dishes*

Type 107: plain dish:
107.1–6, hand-made, fabric A; usually burnished all over, sometimes with zig-zag scribble outside. As so many were recovered of this type only a small selection of variants are drawn to show the basic range. There appears to be no discernible development from one group to another in this type.
107.1 and 2 and similar, pits (55), (46 (2), 47, 48, 52, 63 (2), 64 (2), 66 (2), 85, 86 (3), 103 (4), 119, 121, 125 (3), 130 (2), 140, 144 (3), 163 (3), 164 (2), 170, 184, 185, 195, 206, 223 (6), 226, 236 (8)); BURRS (6); AURRS (17); AMU (12); LO (4); M. Clay (2); MO (11); Up. Clay (2); UO (11); u/s (57).
107.3, AMU (2); u/s (2).
107.4, AURRS (1); AMU (2).
107.5, pits 46, 60, 63, 83 and 121; AURRS (3); AMU (2); total 9.
107.6, pit 85.
107.7–10, black-burnished, fabric B; either a white (rare) or a black slip is used. The inside surfaces are invariably smooth-burnished with superimposed designs on the inside base, as in 107.7 and 8. It is quite possible that many of the recorded rims will, in fact, belong to type 117, but, without evidence of handles, accurate typing of the sherds is not possible.
107.7, pit 103; 107.8, pit 54; 107.9, u/s (2); 107.10, pit 119; others similar in pits (88), (40, 41 (2), 46 (6), 47 (2), 48 (2), 51, 54, 60 (2), 61, 63 (2), 64, 66, 70, 79, 83, 85, 92 (2), 95, 103 (7), 121 (7), 125 (2), 130 (3), 144 (6), 163 (2), 164 (3), 166, 168, 178, 182 (2), 184, 185, 186, 187 (4), 205, 206, 222, 223 (2), 224, 227 (2), 228, 235, 236 (4)); BURRS (9); AURRS (32); BMU (3); AMU (33); LO (5); M. Clay (1); MO (15); Up. Clay (2); UO (15); u/s (90); total 298.
107.11–14, fine, grey sandy fabrics, except 107.12, which has a white, sandy fabric. The inside surfaces of the type are usually covered in a white or black slip, which spreads over the upper part of the rim outside. The slip is usually burnished. On form alone there is no means of distinguishing those in this fabric from the black-burnished equivalents in this type.
107.11, pit 103; 107.12, AURRS; 107.13, AURRS; 107.14, with a beaded rim and a slightly convex profile; AURRS (1); u/s (1); others similar from: pits (42), (65, 66, 70, 77, 85 (2), 86, 103 (4), 119, 121 (2), 125, 130, 144 (4), 157, 163, 166, 168, 186, 187 (2), 195 (2), 200, 201 (2), 206 (2), 209, 223, 224, 225 (3), 236 (2)); AURRS (6); AMU (5); LO(2); MO (7); Up. Clay (1); UO (10); u/s (39); total 117. Fig. 165 shows the relative quantities of this type through time in each of the main fabric groups. Like type 85, the black-burnished

fabric shows little sign of the expected decrease after 350. The proportion of dishes in the various groups shows little variation:

pre-*c.* 325     11·1%          *c.* 325–345     8·9%          post-345     10·34%

Type 108: probably a plain dish, but might be the rim for a wall-sided mortarium:
hard, orange–brown, sandy fabric with a yellow to orange burnished, surface all over (fabric compares with that of type 82); pit 168.

Type 109: dishes with beading or grooving on the rim:
109.1–3, dark grey, fairly fine sandy fabric with a slip all-over inside and over the rim outside; usually white to dirty cream; stroke-burnished patterns inside on both base and wall; probably Alice Holt.
109.1 and 2, pit 51; 109.3, pit 69; others similar in BURRS (1); UO (2); total 6.
109.4, light grey, coarse sandy fabric; stroke-burnishing outside (cf. fabric of type 76.3); horizontal burnishing inside; pit 147.
109.5, coarse, grey sandy, burnished all over inside; pit 206; others similar AURRS (2); u/s (1); total 4.
109.6, dark grey sandy with an all-over black slip; lattice burnishing inside and horizontal burnishing outside; AMU (1); others similar in pit 41; AURRS (1); AMU (2).
109.7, fine, grey sandy with a white slip inside and over the rim; AMU (1); u/s (1).
109.8, fabric D; pit 51; others similar in pits 69, 144 and 182; AMU (1); u/s (7); total 12.
109.9 and 10, hard grey sandy; no slip, but burnished inside and out; pit 201(.9); u/s (4); total 6.
109.11, coarse, grey sandy with a black slip all over; burnished all over inside and stroke-burnished outside; AMU (1).

Type 110: dish with notch decoration on the rim:
fine, grey sandy fabric with a white to grey slip inside and on the rim; u/s (1).

Type 111: dish with a slight, protruding rim:
111.1, fine, grey sandy with a white slip inside and on the rim; all over burnishing; u/s (1).
111.2, hand-made, fabric A, black surface; burnished inside and on the rim; u/s (1).
111.3, brown, sandy fabric with an all over black slip, burnished outside; MO (1).

Type 112: dish; coarse, grey sandy fabric; no slip; groove on the upper surface of the rim; u/s (2).

Type 113: dish with a pair of knob handles at opposite ends:
red–brown, sandy fabric with a pale red to white slip all over; pit 121; u/s (1).

Type 114: dish with simple rim and knob on the middle of the vessel wall; hand-made, fabric A, dark surface; burnished all over; BURRS (1); AURRS (2); AMU (3); u/s (4); total 10.

Type 115: dish with flanged rim:
black-burnished, fabric B; inside surface is burnished and the flange; no means of distinguishing this type from type 85, unless large enough sherds survive; only one certain find; u/s (1).

Type 116: two-handled dish with a protruding ledge rim; black-burnished, fabric B; burnishing on the upper surface of rim; MO (1). Probably a second-century survival.

Type 117: two-handled dish with simple rim:
117.1, black-burnished, fabric B; occasional use of a white slip; there is a basic problem of distinguishing between this type and type 107, when rim sherds survive with no trace of the handle. No example illustrated, but sizes like 117.2 were probably present. Pits (14), (41, 46, 60, 86, 121 (2), 144 (3), 187, 206, 224, 236 (2)); AURRS (2); AMU (4); MO (3); Up. Clay (1); UO (2); u/s (11); total 37.

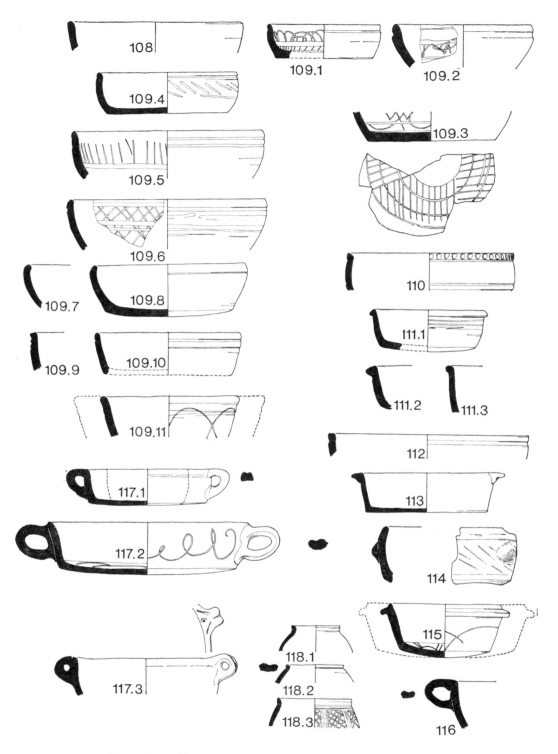

FIG. 187.   Pottery types 108–118 (pp. 344–6). Scale ¼

117.2, fine, grey sandy fabric with a black slip all-over; burnishing all-over inside and stroke-burnishing outside; as with 117.1, there is the possibility of confusing this type with 107. Pits (5), (65, 86, 164, 225, 226); AURRS (2); AMU (10); LO (3); MO (4); UO (5); u/s (14); total 43.

117.3, grey sandy with a black slip; burnished on the handle; deeply scored grooves on the handle; u/s (1).

Type 117 as a percentage of each group:

|            | B-B   | Grey  |                      | B-B   | Grey  |
|------------|-------|-------|----------------------|-------|-------|
| LO/M. Clay |       | 1·1%  | All groups pre-325   |       | 1·1%  |
| MO/Up. Clay| 0·8%  | 0·8%  | All groups 325–345   | 0·6%  | 0·6%  |
| UO         | 0·6%  | 1·4%  | All groups post-345  | 0·5%  | 1·1%  |

The figures do not reveal any significant trends, but suggest that the type spans the fourth century, with the same importance at all times.

## Jars

Type 118: jar with bead rim; possibly belonging to type 175:
dark grey, fine, sandy fabric, usually with a black slip outside and over the rim; 118.3 has fine, burnished lattices between vertical strokes; AURRS (1); the rest from pits 103(.1), 119 and 236; AURRS (1); AMU (2); MO (1); UO (1); u/s (3); total 12.

Type 119: jar with bead rim; unlikely that many will belong to type 175:
119.1–4, fine, grey sandy fabric with either a white or a black slip over the upper half of the vessel and over the rim; pits 40, 47(.1, with sherds of same vessel in pit 48), 60, 61, 164; AURRS (1); AMU (2); LO (1); MO (3); UO (1); u/s (3); total 16.

119.5, black-burnished, fabric B; lattice pattern burnished all over smoothed surface; u/s (1). This and type 118 seem to occur fairly evenly throughout the century.

Types 118 and 119 as a percentage of each group:

|             |        |                      |        |
|-------------|--------|----------------------|--------|
| LO/M. Clay  | 0·79%  | All groups pre-325   | 0·79%  |
| MO/Up. Clay | 0·84%  | All groups pre-345   | 0·64%  |
| UO          | 0·55%  | All groups post-345  | 0·61%  |

Type 120: as type 119, but with more pronounced rim and a cordon below on the join of neck and body:
120.1, black-burnished, fabric B; burnished outside and the upper surface of the rim; u/s (1).
120.2 and 3, fine, grey sandy fabric with an all over white or black slip; pit 61; AURRS (1); MO (1).

Type 121: jar with bead rim:
a fine, hard white fabric with a silvery grey slip all over; (cf. type 169); AMU (1).

Type 122: jar with carinated body:
122.1, grey to brown sandy fabric; no slip; u/s (1).
122.2, fabric as last; AMU (4); u/s (1).
Possibly a first/second-century type.

Type 123: jar with everted rim:
hand-made, fabric A; diagonal, criss-cross or lattice burnishing on the body; horizontal burnishing between that and the base and smooth burnishing over the zone below the rim and above the main, decorated area; smooth burnishing on the upper surface of the rim. Probably imitating type 126. No significant changes can be detected in this type throughout the fourth century, but a large selection is drawn to show the range in minor variation. See

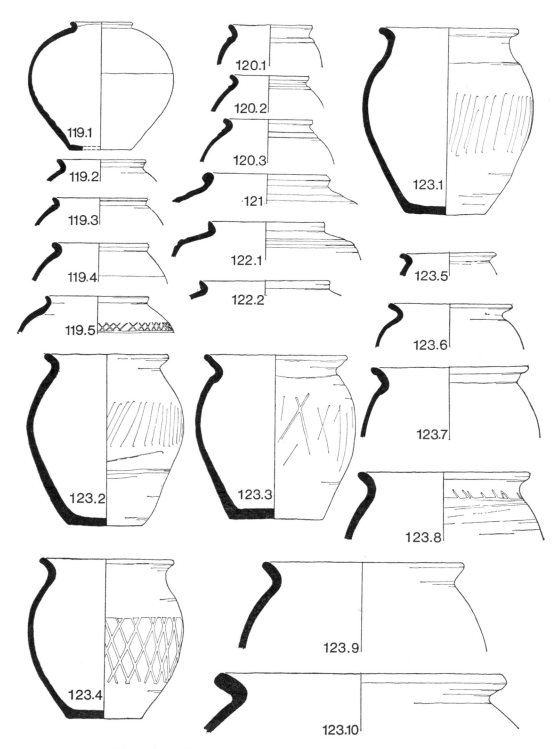

FIG. 188.   Pottery types 119–123 (pp. 346–8). Scale ¼

fig. 166 for the frequency of different diameters and fig. 168 for the relationship with the grey and black-burnished equivalents.

123.1, 2 and 3, pit 121; 123.4, pit 52; 123.5, AURRS; 123.6, pit 103; 123.7, pit 144; 123.8, pit 46; 123.9, pit 121; 123.10, AURRS; similar in pit 222.

Others similar from: pits (258); (40 (5), 41, 46 (8), 47, 48 (11), 49 (2), 51, 52 (4), 54 (3), 60 (6), 61, 62, 63 (10), 64 (3), 65, 66 (5), 69, 77 (4), 79, 83 (2), 85 (5), 86 (3), 90, 92 (5), 95 (6), 103 (14), 119 (2), 121 (19), 122 (2), 125 (3), 129, 130 (4), 138 (2), 144 (16), 147 (3), 157 (2), 163 (4), 164 (6), 166, 168, 171, 178 (2), 179 (2), 182 (3), 185 (5), 186 (2), 187 (3), 195 (2), 200, 201 (3), 206 (8), 209, 222, 223 (5), 224 (3), 225 (3), 226, 227 (3), 230, 234 (3), 236 (25), 239); BURRS (13); AURRS (81); BMU (2); AMU (79); L. Clay Bank (2); LO (8); M. Clay (1); MO (24); Up. Clay (14); UO (44); u/s (223); total 717.

Type 124: as type 123, but grey to brown very sandy hand-made fabric; horizontal burnishing:
124.1; grey surface, very micaceous, rough finish; pit 63 (3); u/s (1).
124.2; dark brown to black coloured fabric; UO (1).

Type 125: as type 123, but distinctive 'cavetto' appearance at join of rim and body; fabric and appearance as type 123:
125.1; AMU (1).
125.2; light grey, slightly sandy; u/s (1).

Type 126: jar with everted rim:
black-burnished, fabric B; smooth burnishing on the upper surface of the rim and on the body above the zone of lattice decoration; wipe marks below the latter.
126.1: pit 85; 126.2, pit 65; 126.3, pit 46; 126.4, pit 85.
Others similar from: pits (145); (40 (3), 41 (2), 46 (10), 47, 48 (5), 49 (2), 52 (2), 54 (4), 60 (3), 61 (2), 63 (2), 64 (3), 65, 66 (3), 69, 77, 83 (2), 85 (5), 86 (4), 90, 92 (3), 95 (2), 103 (6), 119, 121 (14), 125, 130 (3), 144 (12), 153, 163, 164 (6), 168, 178, 182 (2), 185 (2), 186, 187 (2), 195, 201 (3), 206 (3), 222, 223 (4), 225 (2), 228, 230, 231, 234, 236 (11)); BURRS (10); AURRS (36); BMU (1); AMU (44); LO (8); M. Clay (1); MO (18); Up. Clay (9); UO (22); u/s (97); total 393.
See fig. 166 for the frequency of different diameters and fig. 168 for the relationship with the 'grog' tempered and grey ware equivalents.

Type 127: as type 126, but fine, grey sandy fabrics; the upper half of the body and the upper surface of the rim are covered in a light grey to black slip, sometimes smooth burnished. Like type 126, there is a panel of scored lattice decoration in the middle of the body.
127.1; the fabric is much sandier than the others, although not like the black-burnished fabric; pit 103.
127.2; pit 144; 127.3, pit 54; 127.4, pit 121.
Others similar to the last three came from: pits (78); (46 (2), 47, 48 (6), 52, 54 (2), 60, 61 (2), 63 (4), 65, 85, 103 (14), 119, 121 (4), 130, 144 (5), 147, 157 (2), 163 (4), 164, 166, 185, 186, 187 (5), 201, 206, 223 (3), 224, 225 (3), 229 (2), 235, 236, 238); BURRS (4); AURRS (9); BMU (3); AMU (18); LO (7); M. Clay (1); MO (22); Up. Clay (6); UO (17); u/s (106); total 275.
This type seems to have lost ground after c. 345, although popular from at least the beginning of the century.
Type 127 as a percentage of:

| | |
|---|---|
| All groups pre-325 | 6·35% |
| All groups pre-345 | 5·56% |
| All groups post-345 | 2·95% |

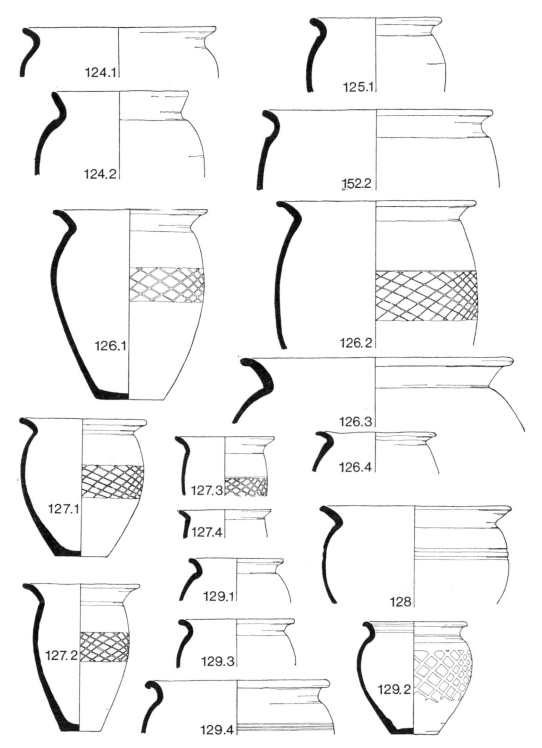

FIG. 189.   Pottery types 124–129 (pp. 348–50). Scale ¼

Fig. 168 shows the relationship of this type with the black-burnished and hand-made equivalents.

Type 128: as type 127, but no lattice decoration on the body and diameter usually over 20 cm. Fabric and position of slip as type 127, except the illustrated example which has a coarse, sandy fabric and a plain, burnished surface only (pit 85). Others from: pit 121; AURRS (1); AMU (3); LO (2); MO (2); UO (2); u/s (15); total 27.
This type seems to have a similar life-span to type 127.

Type 129: jar with everted rim, less flared than type 127, and beaded at the end; like type 127, the upper surface is usually covered in a silvery grey slip with a zone of lightly scored lattice burnishing on the body; sometimes the slip on the rim and upper part of the body is smooth burnished; fabric, fine, grey sandy; pits (68); (41 (2), 46, 48, 49, 54 (2), 60, 63 (7), 65 (2), 66, 69 (3), 77 (2), 79 (2), 83 (2), 85 (2), 86 (2), 92 (2), 95 (2), 103 (3), 121 (4), 130 (3), 138, 144 (5), 164 (5), 168, 182 (2), 185, 187, 206, 222, 229, 235, 236 (3)); BURRS (5); AURRS (6); AMU (5); LO (7); MO (4); UP. Clay (1); UO (5); u/s (42); total 143.
There were also other examples in this form, but in slightly different fabrics:
(a) pale yellow, sandy fabric, very like fabric D; plain surface; UO (1); u/s (3).
(b) a very coarse grey sandy fabric, with a white slip on the rim and upper half of the body; pits 63, 144 and 223; BURRS (2); AURRS (1); AMU (3); Up. Clay (1); total 10.
129.4; as type 129, but no lattice decoration and diameter usually over 20 cm. Like type 128 a pair of grooves on the body limit both slip and burnishing (when it occurs) on the upper half of the vessel. Pits (13); (48 (3), 63 (2), 64, 65, 223, 224, 230, 234, 235, 236); AURRS (4); BMU (1); AMU (7); LO (1); MO (9); Up. Clay (2); UO (2); u/s (17); total 56.
Like types 127 and 128, this type seems to span most of the fourth century, although there are signs of a fall off after 350.
Type 129 as a percentage of:

| | |
|---|---|
| All groups pre-325 | 6·35% |
| All groups pre-345 | 3·97% |
| All groups post-345 | 2·28% |

It may be that production ceased before 345, but, with a common type, the amounts of residual material will be great and confusing.

Type 130: coarse grey sandy fabric; burnished on the rim and lattice burnished on the body; no slip; pit 184.

Type 131: jar with slightly everted rim and beading or under-cutting at the end; a variety of fabrics:
131.1; pale grey sandy fabric with a pale grey surface; no slip, no burnishing; pit 182; AMU (1); u/s (4).
131.2; coarse grey sandy fabric with an all over black slip, burnished outside and on the rim; pit 54.
131.3; light grey sandy fabric; light grey surface, no slip, no burnishing; pits 46 and 223; AURRS (1); AMU (2); LO (1); u/s (5); total 11.
131.4; coarse grey sandy fabric; dark grey surface; no slip, no burnishing; pits 95 and 236; AURRS (2); MO (1); UO (3); total 8.
131.5; coarse brown sandy fabric; hand-made; black slip outside (? upper half only) and over the rim; pit 60.
131.6; light grey sandy fabric with a white, streaky slip all over; AURRS (1); MO (1); u/s (2).

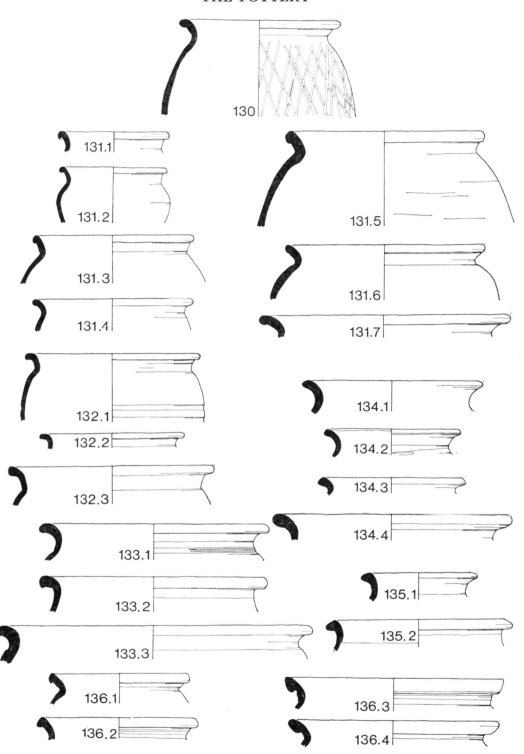

FIG. 190.    Pottery types 130–136 (pp. 350–3). Scale ¼

131.7; brown sandy fabric with a grey core and a red–brown surface; burnished all over; u/s (1).

Summary: pits; (7) AURRS (4); AMU (3); LO (1); MO (2); UO (3); u/s (12); total 32. This type is probably best considered as an amalgamation of a few vessels differing from one another in fabric, but unified by the form.

Type 132: jar with out-bent and flat-topped rim:

132.1 and 2; fabric with grey to white slip over the upper half of the body and on the rim, like types 127–129. Like 128 and 129.4, grooves limit the spread of slip on the body; pits 47, 49, 63 (2), 92, 130 (2), 144 (2), 147, 223, 236); BURRS (4); AURRS (3); LO (1); UO (2); u/s (16); total 38.

132.3; red–brown, sandy fabric with a grey core and a burnished, red–brown surface outside and on the rim; AURRS (1).

Although there are fewer examples of this type than types 127–129, their contexts do not contradict the pattern of decline in importance after 345, seen with the other types.

Type 133: as type 132, but diameter invariably over 20 cm. and the rim is much heavier.

133.1 and 2, fine, grey sandy fabric with a white slip outside and on the rim, often smooth burnished; pits 40 (2) and 226; AURRS (5); BMU (1); AMU (5); LO (2); MO (5); UO (2); u/s (18); total 41.

133.3; coarse, grey sandy fabric, no slip but burnished surfaces; AURRS (1); AMU (1); u/s (1).

As a percentage of each group:

|  |  |
|---|---|
| All groups pre-325 | 1·59% |
| All groups pre-345 | 0·95% |
| All groups post-345 | 0·94% |

While on their own the figures are inconclusive, when considered with types 127–129 and 132, then a fall-off after 345, if not earlier, seems indicated.

Type 134: jar with slightly out-bent rim:

134.1–3; fine, grey sandy fabric with a white to grey slip outside and over the rim; upper surface of the rim often polished; pits 52, 144, 209, 222; BURRS (1); AURRS (8); AMU (12); MO (1); UO (1); u/s (8); total 35.

134.4; coarse, very sandy fabric; no slip, but rough, though burnished surface; UO (1); u/s (5).

Although this type appears before 330 (pit 222), the bulk of the contexts are post-345. Type 134 as a percentage of:

|  |  |
|---|---|
| All groups pre-325 | 0 |
| All groups pre-345 | 0·32% |
| All groups post-345 | 1·48% |

Type 135: as type 134, but 'L' shaped rim:

fine, grey sandy fabric with a white slip outside and on the rim; the upper surface of the latter is usually burnished; pit 236; AMU (3); u/s (1).

This type does not date pre-340–50.

Type 136: jar with 'triangular', under-cut terminal to the rim; slight cupping internally on the inside of the rim:

dark grey sandy, or brown sandy fabric with a grey core; except 136.2, which has a white to grey slip outside and on the rim, the rest have no slip and are not burnished.

136.2; occurred in pit 223; u/s (1); while the rest occurred in pits (9), (62 (2), 63 (4), 66, 225, 226); BURRS (2); AURRS (6); AMU (6); MO (4); UO (2); u/s (18); total 47. This type seems to spread out sporadically, but evenly, throughout the century.

Type 137:  as type 136, but smaller rim terminals, less sharply under-cut, and no cupping inside the rim:
137.1; grey to brown sandy fabric, with similar coloured surface; rilling on the body; no slip; pits 144 and 181; AMU (1); MO (1); Up. Clay (1); u/s (2); total 7.
137.2; as 137.1, but plain surface the same colour as the grey/grey–brown fabric; pits 103 (2), 121, 129, 130, 144 (2), 223; AURRS (2); AMU (7); LO (1); M. Clay (1); MO (1); UO (1); u/s (16); total 37.
137.3; fine grey sandy with a grey surface; light grey slip all over; faint rilling on the body; AMU (1).
137.4–6; fabric D; rilling on the body; pits (17); (48, 63, 69 (2), 77, 83 (2), 103 (2), 119, 125, 129, 138, 170, 182, 206, 237); AURRS (8); AMU (9); UO (4); u/s (29); total 67.
Absence of this distinctive type from MO, BMU and BURRS suggests a late starting date. However, as it is common in the pits, then the dating must go back to c. 325, but it would be strange if it went earlier, because of its absence from the large layers that are contemporary with the pits.
137.7; red–brown, sandy fabric with a red–brown surface, burnished outside and on the rim; AMU (2); MO (1); UO (1).
137.8; coarse, grey sandy fabric; no slip; pits 147, 223 (2), 225, 234; AMU (6); total 11.
Type 137, as a whole, as a percentage of each group:

| | |
|---|---|
| All groups pre-325 | 1·59% |
| All groups pre-345 | 0·64% |
| All groups post-345 | 1·41% + 1·41% (fabric D) = 2·82% |

Because there are a variety of different fabrics involved, it is very difficult to draw any conclusions about the type. The renewed popularity after 345 is due to fabric D and perhaps, too, to the tendency to unslipped vessels in the second half of the fourth century.

Type 138:  wide-mouthed jar with internally cupped rim:
fine, light grey sandy fabric, darker to the surface; polished surfaces, no slip; pit 226; MO (1); Up. Clay (1, sherds of same vessel in UO); UO (1); u/s (1); total 5.

Type 139:  jar with simple, pointed rim:
light to dark grey coarse sandy fabric; note batch marks on 139.2 and 3; cf. Fishbourne, type 313 (Cunliffe, 1971), which may be from the Rowlands Castle kiln site. The type does not appear significantly after 350, but there are many similarities with types 140–142, which may imply some continuity, either at Rowlands Castle, or at a workshop derived from there, throughout the fourth century.
Pits (7), (103, 130 (2), 144, 164 (2), 235); BMU (1); AMU (3); LO (1); M. Clay (1); MO (1); Up. Clay (2); u/s (6); total 22.

Type 140:  jar with simple, pointed rim, sometimes, slightly cupped:
coarse grey sandy fabric with black grains; no slip; no burnish; 140.2 has burnished lines on the body; cf. types 139 and 141; probably of very local manufacture; pits (36), (40, 47 (2), 54, 61, 63 (4), 64, 65 (2), 66 (2), 69, 85, 87, 103 (2), 157, 187 (2), 206, 223 (3), 224, 228, 230, 234, 235 (2), 236); BURRS (6); AURRS (12); AMU (7); LO (2); M. Clay (1); MO (11); Up. Clay (5); UO (8); u/s (50); total 138.

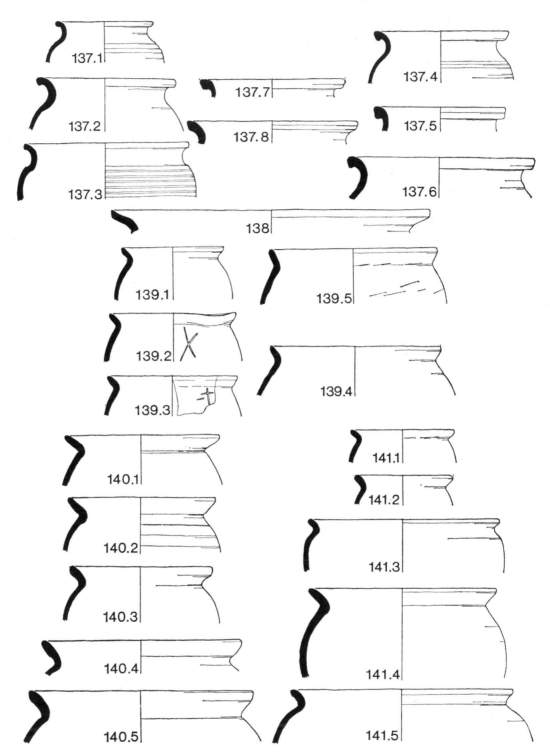

FIG. 191. Pottery types 137–141 (pp. 353–5). Scale ¼

Type 140 as a percentage of each group:

| All groups pre-325 | 2·38% |
|---|---|
| All groups pre-345 | 3·5% |
| All groups post-345 | 1·81% |

Although there is a decline after 345, this is not significant in the light of the general decline of grey fabrics in jar types after 345.

Type 141: jar with simple, stubby rim:
light grey, coarse sandy fabric, sometimes with large black grains and/or occasional burnt flint or chert; no slip, no burnishing; cf. types 139, 140 and 142; pits (11), (48 (2), 60, 144 (2), 155, 178, 184, 187, 222, 236); BMU (1); AMU (2); UO (1); u/s (11); total 26.

Type 142: jar with simple, stubby rim; cf. types 139–141:
light to dark grey coarse sandy with diagonal burnished strokes on the body; 142.1–3, pits (8), (46, 52, 92, 95, 164, 187 (2), 222); BURRS (3); AURRS (6); BMU (1); AMU (4); MO (6); Up. Clay (2); UO (8); u/s (24); total 62.
142.4 and 5 (plain), pits 144, 235, 237; AMU (3); Up. Clay (1); UO (1); total 8.
This type is fairly constant in all the groups, throughout the century.

Type 143: hard, coarse grey sandy fabric, burnished on the rim and scored chevron pattern decoration on the body; no slip:
BURRS (1); AURRS (1); u/s (3); total 5.

Type 144: miscellaneous non-grey ware everted rim jars:
144.1, a hard orange fabric, brown to the core, with a yellow–brown surface; Severn Valley fabric; u/s (1).
144.2, a very hard fabric with a yellow–brown surface (almost golden) on a dark grey core; sherds of same vessel from MO and Up. Clay; Severn Valley fabric; similar jar, but a reddish-brown fabric with similar coloured burnished slip; pit 79.
144.3, hard, reddish-brown, fine fabric with a red, burnished slip all over outside and on the rim; sherds of same vessel in MO and UO; very similar sherds, possibly of the same vessel; pit 223 and 235.
144.4, fabric as 144.2, but the surface is a pale yellow to brown and very micaceous; Severn Valley; MO (1).

Type 145: small jar:
fine, light to dark grey, sandy fabric with a white slip on the top half of the body and on the rim; easily confused with type 129.
Pits (7): (54, 87, 92, 121, 178, 236, 237); BURRS (3); AURRS (2); AMU (3); LO (1); M. Clay (1); MO (5); Up. Clay (1); UO (3); u/s (5); total 31.
This type, in fabric and style, belongs to the group, 127–129.

Type 146: small jar:
brown to grey, fine sandy with red grains; there are traces of burnishing on the upper half of the body and the rim; pit 138; AMU (1); u/s (5).

Type 147: small jar with pedestal foot:
red–brown sandy; similar coloured surface; burnished on the rim and on the body; u/s (1).

Type 148: small jar:
148.1, fine brown sandy fabric with an all over black slip burnished on the rim and all over outside; pits (8), (40, 63, 144, 164 (2), 178, 187, 236); M. Clay (1); u/s (2); total 11.

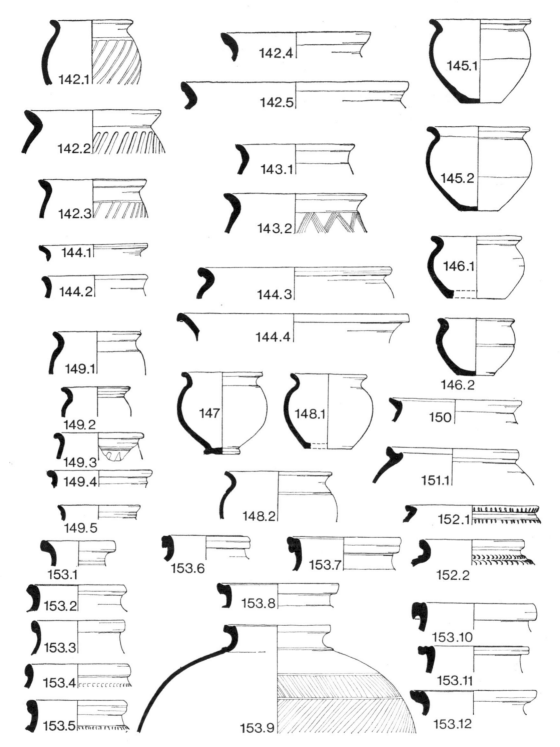

FIG. 192.   Pottery types 142–153 (pp. 355–8). Scale ¼

148.2, a micaceous, brown sandy fabric, somewhat flaky; all over black slip, burnished on the body and upper surface of the rim; pits 61, 187, 225; AMU (1).

Type 149: small jars; miscellaneous:

149.1, micaceous, grey–brown, sandy fabric; similar coloured surface, burnished on the rim and on the body; pits 103 and 125; BURRS (1); u/s (1).

149.2, hard, vesicular, slightly sanded and micaceous; burnished outside and on the rim; AMU (2); u/s (1).

149.3, dark grey sandy fabric with a burnished pattern on the body; black surface; pit 182 (2); AURRS (1); AMU (1); u/s (1).

149.4, coarse, black sandy with a black surface; pit 163.

149.5, brown sandy micaceous fabric; white or black slip outside and on the rim; pit 170.

Types 127–149: A summary:

Leaving aside types with very few examples and types with many slight variants, the everted rim jars break in to three major grey fabric groups:

(a) fine grey fabrics with white slips; types 127, 128, 129, 122, 133, 145;
(b) rather coarser grey fabrics, seldom with a slip, rarely burnished; types 139, 140, 141 and 142;
(c) similar fabrics to (b) and no slip; includes fabric D and jars with a 'triangular' terminal; types 136, 137 and 138.

Each group of types as a percentage of each assemblage:

|  | Groups pre-325 | Groups pre-345 | Groups post-345 |
|---|---|---|---|
| Type Group (a) | 18·26% | 12·87% | 7·51% |
| Type Group (b) | 5·56% | 6·05% | 3·69% |
| Type Group (c) | 2·38% | 1·75% | 3·83% |
| All grey ware jars | 27·78% | 21·62% | 16·44% |
| All jars, types 123–149 | 43·65% | 36·09% | 38·59% |

While all the figures could be explained by the changing popularity of any one type, without implying the end of production, the drop in the percentage of grey jars after 345 seems significant. More hand-made jars are coming in at the expense of group (a) in particular, although, apart from group (c) and types like 134, all the other types suffer as well. It seems likely that group (a) jars went out of production after 345 or just before, at a time when colour-coated vessels are becoming more popular. Other grey ware groups probably continued to be made and these, except fabric D, are likely to have been from the nearest kilns to Portchester, whereas group (a) must be either from the New Forest or Alice Holt kilns.

Fig. 167 shows the relation between the three main fabric groups in the jar types.

Type 150: lid-seated jar:
fine, grey sandy fabric; no slip; u/s (1).

Type 151: lid-seated jar:
a very hard, almost stone-ware fabric, dirty yellow in colour; surface as the fabric, but also rough and 'warty' to feel; Gose (1950), form 547.
In thin section: augite, brown hornblende, sanidine, andesine, leucite and quartz in a light brown isotropic matrix (cf. Frechen, 1948); Mayen ware; pit 62; u/s (1) (Fulford and Bird, forthcoming).

Type 152: jar with neck and out-bent rim:
>152.1, fine, grey sandy with a black slip outside and over the rim; finger-nail impressions; u/s (1).
>152.2, hard, coarse, grey sandy with traces of burnishing; finger-nail decoration; joining sherds in MO and Up. Clay.

Type 153: jar with narrow mouth, neck and heavy, square rim:
>153.1, fine, grey sandy; traces of a white slip; u/s (1).
>153.2, fine, grey sandy fabric; white slip outside and on the rim; pit 48; AURRS (1); u/s (2); total 4.
>153.3, hard, dark grey sandy; white slip outside and on the rim; pit 236; u/s (1).
>153.4, fine, grey sandy fabric with a black slip, burnished outside; shallow, ? finger tip indentations on shoulder; MO (1).
>153.5, fine, grey sandy fabric; white slip outside; AMU (1).
>153.6, fine, grey sandy fabric; white slip outside; AMU (3); u/s (6).
>153.7, fine, grey sandy fabric; worn, no trace of slip; pit 95.
>153.8, fine, grey sandy fabric; white slip outside, and inside the rim; slight internal cupping; pits 64, 85 and 182; BURRS (2); AURRS (1); AMU (3); MO (1); u/s (3); total 13.
>153.9, like 153.8, but lightly incised chevron decoration on the body, under a white slip; AMU (1).
>153.10, fine, grey sandy fabric; black slip outside; u/s (1).
>153.11, fine, grey sandy fabric; white slip outside and on the rim; u/s (1).
>153.12, dark grey sandy fabric; burnished outside and on the rim; u/s (1).
>Summary: pits (6); BURRS (2); AURRS (2); AMU (8); MO (2); u/s (16); total 36.
>The dating of this type is difficult to establish, both because there is no difference in the percentage of the type in pre- and post-345 groups (0·64, pre-345; 0·60, post-345) and because each vessel is likely to have had a long life as a storage, rather than an everyday cooking vessel. This factor is likely to affect the residual element more than usual. Other evidence (flanged bowls and everted rim jars) suggests that slipped fine grey ware pots become scarce after 345. Type 153 will fit in to this pattern (the fine fabrics are very comparable) if the possibility of a long life for the individual jar is acceptable. With the pits the span of the type becomes *c.* 320/30–*c.* 350/60. The long life argument can be applied in reverse, and it might be expected that this type was current from much earlier than *c.* 320–30. The same sort of reasoning surely applies to types 176–178.

Type 154: jar with flange on the rim:
>154.1–3, black-burnished, fabric B; burnished on the rim/neck, both inside and out; grey-white slip on 154.2 and 3; AMU (2); u/s (1).
>154.4, fine, grey sandy fabric; all over white slip; u/s (2).
>154.5, as above; pit 47; u/s (1).
>154.6, as above; pits 103 and 236; AURRS (1); AMU (1); MO (1); Up. Clay (1); u/s (2); total 8.
>For dating arguments, etc. see above, type 153.

Type 155: deep, straight-sided jar:
>fabric D; pink to yellow surface; faintly scribed bands of wave decoration outside; AURRS (1).

Type 156: ? as type 155:
>156.1, reddish-brown sandy fabric with a grey core and a burnished red slip; pits 51 and 69; probably sherds of the same vessel.

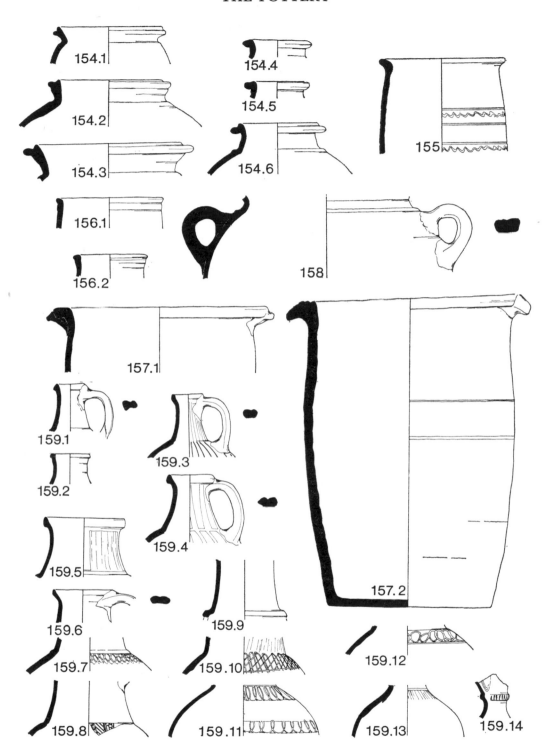

FIG. 193.   Pottery types 154–159 (pp. 358–60). Scale ¼

156.2, hard grey sandy fabric; white, silvery grey slip outside and over the rim; u/s (1).

Type 157: deep jar or churn with a pair of opposing, knob handles; hard grey sandy fabric; no slip; pit 187; AMU (1); MO (1); UO (1); u/s (1); total 5. This type was being produced in Amberwood, kiln 1; but manufacture in another centre is also possible (Fulford, 1973.

Type 158: jar with two handles; rim missing:
hand-made, fabric A, light brown surface; MO (1).

*Jugs*

Type 159: jugs with simple collar rims:
fine to coarse, grey sandy fabric; white to grey slip outside, or, very rarely, no slip (159.2 and 5); vertical burnishing on the neck, diagonal on the shoulder; probably a New Forest type:
159.1 and 2, small jugs; pit 41; AURRS (1); MO (1); u/s (6).
159.3, pits 40 and 121; UO (1); u/s (2).
159.4 and 5 and others similar occurred in pits (6), (86, 95, 103, 144, 164, 223); BURRS (2); AURRS (5); AMU (1); MO (5); Up. Clay (1); UO (1); u/s (11); total 32.
159.6, slightly outbent rim; pit 144; u/s (5).
Summary: pits (10); BURRS (2); AURRS (6); AMU (1); MO (6); Up. Clay (1); UO (2); u/s (24); total 52.
body sherds only; fine, grey sandy fabrics covered in a white or black slip with vertical burnishing on the neck and diagonal or loop decoration on the shoulder; presumably these sherds belong to the preceding rims:
159.7–9, pit 46; 159.10, MO; 159.11, UO; 159.12, AURRS; 159.13, pit 121; others similar from pits 60, 63 and 83; AURRS (2); MO (1); UO (1); u/s (3); total 17.
159.14, hard, brown to grey fabric with white to brown slip; AURRS (1).
159.15 (not illustrated), neck sherd only; hard orange fabric with a grey core; no slip, but surface burnished with vertical strokes; pit 83.
Besides 159.14 and 15, summary: pits (7); AURRS (3); MO (2); UO (2); u/s (3).
Type 159 as a percentage of each group:

| MO/Up. Clay | 1·9% | All groups pre-345 | 1·8% |
| UO | 1·1% | All groups post-345 | 0·9% |

It is unfortunate that no examples occurred pre-325 in secure contexts. The pit evidence implies that the type was current before. The trend after 345 is not necessarily significant, although it is interesting that colour-coated jugs become more common after 345 (e.g. type 6). At Amberwood in the New Forest, jugs of type 159 were not being made in the later of the three kilns, although colour-coated types were present.

Type 160: as type 159, but squared rim:
fine, grey sandy fabric; the upper two-thirds covered in a silvery grey slip, burnished diagonally on the shoulder and in a broad zone below; pit 119; others similar in pit 164; UO (1); u/s (1); Alice Holt type.

Type 161: as above, but triple reeded handle and rounded rim profile:
161.1, fine, grey sandy fabric with a black slip; pit 225; AURRS (1).
161.2, brown to grey sandy fabric with a thick white to brown slip, except on the handle; u/s (1).
161.3, fine, grey sandy fabric with a black slip; probably of this type, though not enough rim for indication of handle; pit 103; u/s (1).
161.4 (not illustrated), hard, grey sandy fabric, handle only; u/s (1); Rhenish (Fulford and Bird, forthcoming).

Type 162: jug with flanged rim:

fine, grey sandy fabric with a white or black slip all over; no trace of burnishing; pits 60 and 63; AURRS (2); u/s (2).

Type 163: jug with flared-out rim:

fine, grey sandy fabric with a black slip; AURRS (1).

Type 164: jug with narrow mouth:

fine, grey sandy with a white slip; u/s (1).

Type 165: jug with everted mouth:

fine, grey sandy fabric with a white slip outside, and inside the rim; u/s (1).

Type 166: ? jug or ? jar, with sharp, undercut rim:

166.1, grey sandy fabric; no slip; UO (1).

166.2, brown to grey sandy fabric; no slip, but burnished on upper surface of the rim; u/s (1).

Type 167: jug with flange on the neck:

fine, grey sandy fabric with a grey slip; u/s (1).

Type 168: ? jug or ? jar, reeding below the rim:

fine, grey sandy fabric with a grey slip; u/s (1).

Type 169: jug with pinch mouth and thumb stop on handle:

very light grey, granular fabric with a grey slip (cf. type 121); MO (1).

Type 170: ? jug with cupped mouth:

a hard yellow–brown fabric with smoothed, but not burnished self-coloured surface; pit 130.

Type 171: jug:

hard white, granular fabric, yellow–brown to the core; white surface; u/s (1); possibly first/second century.

*Lids*

Type 172: with a V-shaped rim, fabric varies from brown to grey sandy; no slip.

172.1–6, pits 60, 83, 121, 164, 236; AURRS (3); AMU (1); MO (2); UO (2); u/s (10).

172.7, New Forest, fabric 2; no trace of slip; AURRS (1).

Type 173: with a turned down rim:

173.1, fabric D; AURRS (1); AMU (1), u/s (2).

173.2, grey sandy fabric, dark grey surface; u/s (1).

173.3, hand-made, fabric A, grey to yellow surface; AMU (1).

Type 174: with simple rim;

174.1, grey sandy fabric; no slip; AMU (1).

174.2, light grey sandy fabric; no slip; pit 144.

174.3, hand-made, fabric A; burnished all over; AURRS (1); AMU (1).

Dating of types 172–174 indeterminate.

*Mugs*

Type 175: mug with two handles:

175.1–3, fine grey sandy fabric with a white slip outside and over the rim; pits (12), (48(.2), 62, 92, 121(.1) (2), 144, 164, 209, 223, 227 (2), (.3), 237); AURRS (2); AMU (2); MO (2); u/s (5); total 23.

175.4 black-burnished, fabric B; all-over burnishing outside and stroke burnishing around the handles; pits (8), (65, 182, 223, 225 (2), 235, 236 (2)); AURRS (4); MO (1); UO (1); u/s (4).

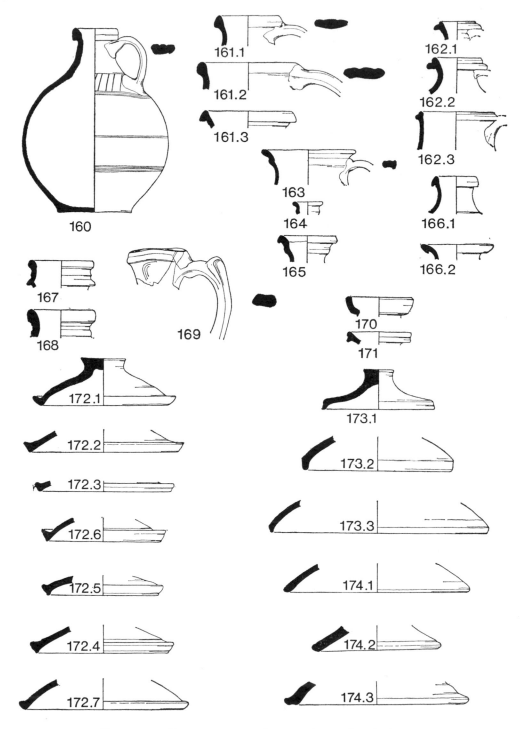

FIG. 194.   Pottery types 160–174 (pp. 360–1). Scale ¼

The date range of this type in both fabrics must be from before 325 on the evidence of the pits to, perhaps, *c.* 370. There is no evidence of a fall-off trend after 345.

*Storage Jars*

Type 176: with simple folded-out bead rim:
176.1, fine grey sandy fabric with a silvery grey slip outside and over the rim; AMU (1); UO (1).
176.2, very coarse, grey sandy; hand-made; pit 54; AURRS (1).
176.3, as above, but finger impressions on the rim; UO (1).

Type 177: pronounced and everted rim:
177.1, fine, grey sandy fabric with a silvery grey slip; AURRS (1); AMU (1); UO (1); u/s (3).
177.2, hard grey sandy fabric, burnished on the rim and body, but not the neck; no slip; pit 206; u/s (1).
177.3, hard grey, sandy fabric; hand-made; u/s (2).
177.4, fine, grey sandy fabric with a white slip outside and over the rim; AURRS (1); AMU (1); u/s (1).
177.5, hard grey sandy with a white slip outside; pit 234.
177.6, grey sandy with a white to grey slip outside; hand-made; AMU with sherds of the same vessel from UO; u/s (2).

Type 178: hard grey sandy; no trace of slip; 'pie crust' finger impression on the rim; pit 46; MO (1); AURRS (2); AMU (2); u/s (2).

Types 176–178: body sherds that could belong to any of the preceding storage jar types:
176–8.1, hard grey sandy with two zones of white slip either side of a chevron pattern of slash marks; executed with a five pointed instrument; u/s.
176–8.2, grey sandy fabric with a silvery grey to black slip below a zone of comb decoration in a chevron pattern; u/s.
176–8.3, grey sandy with a zone of white slip with lattice burnished decoration below a zone of wavy comb decoration; u/s; similar in pit 164.
176–8.4, light grey sandy fabric with incised circles and wavy line stroke burnishing; AMU (1); u/s (1).
176–8.5, fine, grey sandy fabric; with a white slip and regular incised wave patterned zone between shallow, incised lines; u/s.
Summary of grey ware storage jar types 176–178: pits (5); AURRS (6); AMU (8); MO (1); UO (5).
Although there appears to be an increase in storage jars after 345 (0·16, pre-345 and 1·0, post-345), this may merely be a reflection of their individual long life. In this respect many jars were very worn. If the increase is significant, it must be seen against an overall decline in grey ware types, particularly slipped ones, post-345.

Type 179: storage jar:
brittle red, flaky clay with some grog and flint temper; sometimes a grey core; red–brown surface; nail and slash marks on the rim and finger impressions on the body:
179.1, pit 85; others from pits 182, 187 and 236 (? 2); AURRS (1); UO (1); u/s (1).
179.2, pit 147.
179.3, u/s (1).
179.4, pit 69.

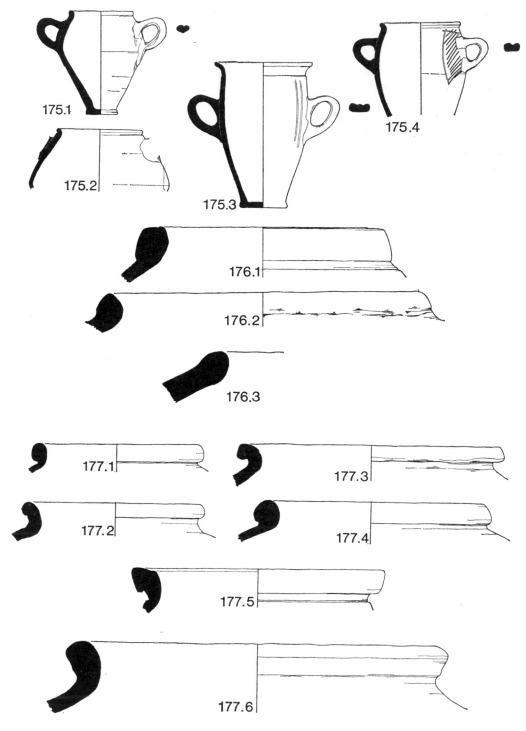

FIG. 195. Pottery types 175–177 (pp. 361–3). Scale ¼

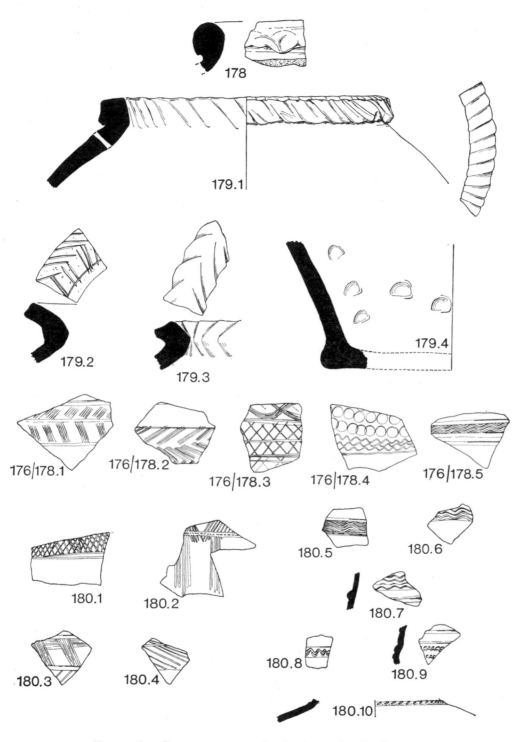

FIG. 196.   Pottery types 178–180 (pp. 363–6). Scale $\frac{1}{4}$

This type seems to be particularly associated with the pits and perhaps has a limited date range *c.* 325–45. Perhaps it fills a gap in the supply of more durable large jars. Owing to the fragility of the fabric its manufacture must be very local, if not at Portchester itself.

Type 180: body sherds only from grey ware jars and bowls:

    180.1, stroke-burnishing on a thick, black, burnished slip; MO (1).
    180.2, coarse, grey sandy fabric; no slip, but stroke-burnishing; MO (1).
    180.3, as above; u/s.
    180.4, fine grey sandy; stroke-burnishing on a white slip; u/s.
    180.5, grey sandy; no slip; comb decoration; u/s.
    180.6, as above; u/s.
    180.7, fine, grey sandy with a silvery grey slip; comb decoration; u/s.
    180.8, wavy decoration on a grey sandy fabric.
    180.9, grey sandy with a white slip; stab decoration; u/s.
    180.10, grey sandy with a white slip; stab decoration at the join of neck and body; possibly from a jug.

# BIBLIOGRAPHY: POTTERY

AKERMAN, J. Y. 1853. 'An account of excavations on the site of some ancient potteries in the western district of the New Forest'. *Archaeologia*, xxxv, 91–9.

ALCOCK, L. 1971. *Arthur's Britain*. London.

ATKINSON, D. 1942. *Report on Excavations at Wroxeter, 1923–7*. Oxford.

ATKINSON, R. J. C. 1941. 'A Romano-British potter's field at Cowley, Oxon.'. *Oxoniensia*, vi, 9–21.

BARTLETT, J. P. 1873. 'The ancient potteries of the New Forest, Hampshire'. *Arch. J.* xxx, 319–24.

BUSHE-FOX, J. P. 1932. *Third Report on the Excavations at Richborough, Kent*. London.

BUSHE-FOX, J. P. 1949. *Fourth Report on the Excavations at Richborough, Kent*. London.

CASE, H. and KIRK, J. R. 1953. 'Notes and News'. *Oxoniensia*, xvii/xviii, 224–5.

CHENET, M. G. 1941. *La Céramique gallo-romaine du IVe siècle*. Mâcon.

CLARKE, G. (forthcoming). *The Lankhills Roman Cemetery*.

CUNLIFFE, B. W. 1961. 'Report on the Roman pottery kiln at Hallcourt Wood, Shedfield, Hants.'. *Proc. Hants Field Club*, xxii, 8–21.

CUNLIFFE, B. W. 1965. 'Report on the excavation of three pottery kilns in the New Forest, 1955'. *Proc. Hants Field Club*, xxiii, 29–45.

CUNLIFFE, B. W. 1970. 'The Saxon culture-sequence at Portchester Castle'. *Antiq. J.* l, 67–85.

CUNLIFFE, B. W. 1971. *Excavations at Fishbourne*, Vol. II. London.

DETSICAS, A. (ed.) 1973. *Current Research in Romano-British Coarse Pottery*. C.B.A. Research Report 10.

FARRAR, R. A. H. 1969. 'A late Roman black-burnished pottery industry in Dorset and its affinities'. *Proc. Dorset Nat. Hist. Archaeol. Soc.* xc, 174–80.

FRECHEN, J. 1948. 'Ergebnisse der mineralogischen Untersuchung'. *Bonner Jahrbücher* cxlviii, 296–8.

FRERE, S. S. 1949. 'The late Roman bath-house at Cobham'. *Surrey Arch. Coll.* l, 73–98.

FRERE, S. S. 1962. 'Excavations at Dorchester on Thames'. *Arch. J.* cxix, 114–49.

FRERE, S. S. 1972. *Verulamium Excavations*, Vol. I. London.

FULFORD, M. G. 1973(a). 'Excavation of three Romano-British kilns in Amberwood Inclosure, near Fritham, New Forest'. *Proc. Hants Field Club*, xxviii (1971), 5–28.

FULFORD, M. G. 1973(b). 'A fourth-century colour-coated fabric and its types in south-east England'. *Sussex Arch. Coll.* cxi, 41–4.

FULFORD, M. G. 1973(c). 'The distribution and dating of New Forest pottery'. *Britannia*, iv, 160 78.

FULFORD, M. G. (forthcoming). 'The Roman Pottery', in Clarke, (forthcoming).

FULFORD, M. G. and BIRD, J. (forthcoming). 'Imported Pottery from Germany in Late Roman Britain'. *Britannia* (forthcoming).

GILLAM, J. P. 1963. 'The coarse pottery', in Steer (1963), 113–29.

GILLAM, J. P. 1968. *Types of Roman Coarse Pottery Vessels in Northern Britain*. Newcastle-on-Tyne.

GOSE, E. 1950. *Gefässtypen der römischen Keramik im Rheinland*. Beiheft der *Bonner Jahrbücher*.

HARDEN, D. B. 1936. 'Two Romano-British potters' fields near Oxford'. *Oxoniensia*, i, 81–102.

HODSON, F. R. 1970. 'Cluster analysis and archaeology: some new developments and applications'. *World Archaeology*, i, 299–320.

HÜBENER, W. 1968. 'Eine Studie zur spätrömischen Rädchen-sigillata (Argonnensigillata).' *Bonner Jahrbücher* clxviii, 241–98.

KENYON, K. M. 1948. *Excavations at the Jewry Wall Site, Leicester*. London.

MAY, T. 1922. 'On the pottery from the waste heap of the Roman potters' kilns discovered at Sandford near Littlemore, Oxford, in 1879'. *Archaeologia*, lxxii, 225–42.

PEACOCK, D. P. S. 1967. 'The heavy mineral analysis of pottery: a preliminary report'. *Archaeometry*, x, 97–100.

PEACOCK, D. P. S. 1971. 'The petrography of certain coarse pottery', in Cunliffe (1971), 255–9.

PEACOCK, D. P. S. 1973. 'The black-burnished pottery industry in Dorset', in Detsicas (ed.) (1973), 63–5.

STANFIELD, J. A. and SIMPSON, G. 1958. *Central Gaulish Potters*. London.

STEER, K. 1963. 'Excavations at Mumrills Roman fort 1958–60'. *Proc. Soc. Antiq. Scotland* xciv, 86–132.

SUMNER, H. 1927. *Excavations in New Forest Roman Pottery Sites*. London.

WEBSTER, G. 1968. 'A sherd of pottery from Cirencester'. *Antiq. J.* xlviii, 102–3.

WILSON, D. R. (ed.) 1968. 'Roman Britain in 1967: sites explored'. *J. Roman Studies* lviii, 212.

WILSON, M. G. 1972. 'The other pottery', in Frere (1972), 263–370.

YOUNG, C. J. 1973. 'The pottery industry of the Oxford region', in Detsicas (ed.), 1973, 105–15.

# IX.  THE GLASS

## by D. B. HARDEN

## INTRODUCTION

THE glass falls into two stratigraphical categories:
(a) Roman glass from Roman contexts: nos. 1–25.
(b) Roman glass from post-Roman levels: nos. 26–34.

Apart from the solitary fragment of a matt/glossy window-pane of the earlier Roman period, the Roman material, whether vessel or window, presents a very uniform fourth-century aspect. Most of the fragments can be readily recognized as belonging to one or other of the fourth-century forms discussed by Clasina Isings (her nos. 105–34).[1] A number of the types are also to be seen among the late third- and fourth-century fragments from site C at Shakenoak, Oxon.[2] Indeed the fragments are all very diagnostic and there can be no doubt that they belonged to the inhabitants of the fourth-century Saxon shore fort.

The majority are small and not particularly significant, apart from their value as dating material. A few, however, deserve some comment. Nos. 3 and 4 are fragments of bowls with geometric facet and linear cutting; cut ware was never prolific in Roman Britain and any fragments that occur are worth attention. No. 5 is peculiar. It belongs, I think, to a mould-blown head-vase, and represents part of the hair at the back of the head or neck. Roman head-vases are usually janiform, but this is a 'one-face' type; two examples of the type I have in mind are illustrated by R. W. Smith.[3] The most prolific late Roman types at Portchester are cups and cone-beakers of colourless or yellowish-green glass with knocked-off, everted rims, some of the beakers being decorated with blue blobs (nos. 9–14). These types existed throughout the empire at this period, and it is satisfactory to find them in such comparative quantity at Portchester. It is also satisfactory to find that, with one exception (the matt/glossy fragment, no. 22, which is probably a stray from some earlier habitation on or near the site), all the Roman window-glass is of the double-glossy variety, now recognized as the normal window-glass of the fourth century (if not also of the third century) in Roman Britain.[4] However much dispute there may be about whether the early matt/glossy window-glass was cast or blown, all agree that the later double-glossy type is cylinder-blown, i.e. 'muff' glass.

---

[1] Clasina Isings, *Roman Glass from Dated Finds*, Groningen/Djakarta, 1957, pp. 126–62.

[2] A. C. C. Brodribb *et al.*, *Excavations at Shakenoak IV*, (1973), 102 ff., nos. 208 ff.

[3] *Glass from the Ancient World*, Corning, 1957, pp. 141, 145, nos. 279 and 288.

[4] Cf. Harden in *Glastechnische Berichte*, 32K (1959), Heft VIII, 8–16; *id.* in E. M. Jope ed., *Studies in Building History*, London, 1961, pp. 44–9; and G. C. Boon in *J. Glass Studies*, viii (1966), 41–7.

# INVENTORY (figs. 197–9)

## A. *Glass from Roman Contexts*

Unless otherwise stated the fragments come from Roman general layers.

*Vessels*

1. Fragment of rim of shallow bowl; greenish-colourless. Blown. Rim outbent, lip finely ground. Irregular band of wheel-incisions below lip. Whitish to black weathering film, mostly flaked off and leaving iridescent surface. D. *c.* 18 cm. Late third to fourth century.
   Trench 101 layer 86: layer above make-up.
   Similar fragment: Trench 88 layer 10. From a smaller and thinner bowl. D. *c.* 14 cm.

2. Fragment of rim of shallow bowl; greenish-colourless. Blown. Rim incurved, lip finely ground. Irregular band of wheel-incisions below lip. Weathering as no. 1. D. 24 cm. Late third to fourth century.
   Trench 101 layer 86.

3. Fragment of rim and side of bowl; greenish-colourless. Blown. Rim outbent, lip finely ground. Irregular band of wheel-incisions near rim and, lower down, part of geometric design of thick and thin horizontal and sloping facets. Weathering as no. 1. D. *c.* 19 cm. Late third to fourth century.
   Trench 101 layer 86.

4. Fragment of side of deep bowl; greyish-colourless. Blown. Convex side. Part of geometric design of horizontal wheel-cuts and vertical and sloping thick and thin facets. Surface pitted and iridescent in parts. D. *c.* 9 cm. Late third to fourth century.
   Trench 70 layer 4.

5. Fragment of head-vase showing hair on back of head or neck; clear dark blue. Mould-blown. Milky film and iridescence. 3 by 3·5 cm. Third century.
   Trench 71 layer 8.

6. Fragment of rim and side of cylindrical cup; colourless. Blown. Almost vertical side, curving in slightly at top, plain horizontal lip, knocked off and finished by grinding. Shallow wheel-cut below rim. Poor, streaky and bubbly glass; advanced flaking weathering with iridescence. D. 7·5 cm. Late third to fourth century.
   Trench 74 layer 46: pit 86.
   Similar fragments: trench 79 layer 60, pit 121. Colourless. No decoration. Dulled but not flaking.
       Trench 87 layer 27: layer above upper road. Greenish-colourless. No decoration.

7. Fragment of rim of bowl or jar; bluish-green. Blown. Rim outsplayed with solid thickened lip formed by outward folding. Rest of shape uncertain. Incipient iridescence; many small bubbles. D. *c.* 9 cm. Late third to fourth century.
   Trench 72 layer 7.

8. Fragment of rim of bowl; yellow. Blown. Rim vertical, with a hollow tubular lip formed by folding outwards. Sides slope inwards from underneath lip; shape of rest of bowl uncertain. Milky weathering film, flaking away and leaving iridescent pits. D. *c.* 15 cm. Probably fourth century.
   Trench 87 layer 5.

25

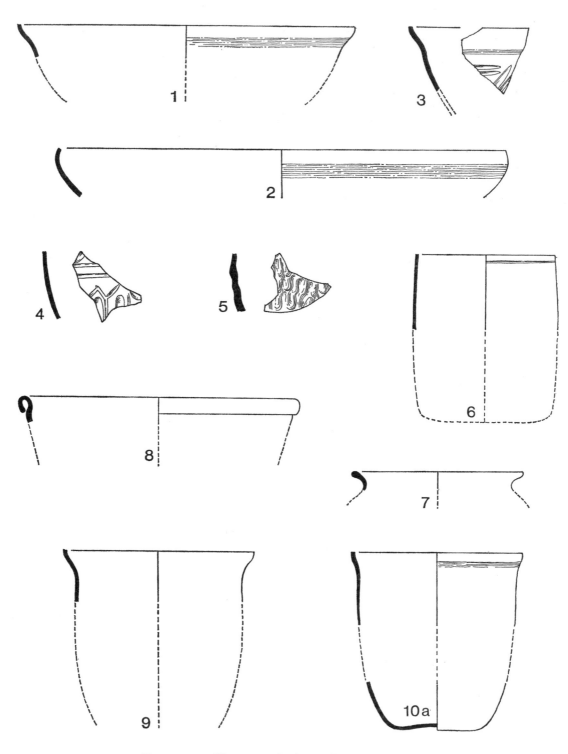

FIG. 197.   Glass vessels (pp. 369, 371). Scale ½

9. Fragment of rim of cup; yellowish-green. Blown. Rim outsplayed with lip knocked off and slightly smoothed; walls convex with downward taper. Incipient weathering. D. *c.* 10 cm. Fourth century.

    Trench 88 layer 6: layer above make-up.
    Similar rim-fragments: Trench 91 layer 47: layer above upper road.
                    Trench 62 layer 4. D. *c.* 9 cm.
                    Trench 103 layer 23: upper occupation. Thinner walls, greener glass. D. *c.* 9 cm.
                    Trench 69 layer 8. Walls and colour as previous example. D. *c.* 7·5 cm.

10. Group of fragments from a gully, all from cups of the same general type and date as no. 9:
    (a) Ten fragments, not contiguous, but probably giving full profile of cup; dark yellowish-green. Blown. Rim slightly outsplayed, lip knocked off and smoothed. Walls cylindrical at top, but taper lower down to curved junction with concave bottom. Broad group of wheel-incisions near rim. Poor, bubbly glass; incipient iridescence. D. 9 cm. H. *c.* 9 cm.
        There are also two rim fragments, similar in shape and colour, but *c.* 10 cm. diameter.
    (b) Nine fragments, not contiguous, and not providing complete profile of cup; greenish-yellow. Shape and dimensions similar to (a). Group of wheel-incisions at rim, and another 2 cm. lower down body.
    (c) Fragment of rim and side of cup; yellowish-green. Side tapers in towards bottom. At greatest diameter of body a band of blue blobs (only two extant). Bubbly and iridescent. D. *c.* 9·5 cm.
    (d) Three small fragments, two of which bear the greater part of one blob each, the third having parts of two, from one or more other cups, greenish-yellow, and a fragment of body, green with large bluish-green blob.
        Trench 63 layer 6: Saxon (?) gully.

11. Two contiguous fragments of rim and side of cone-beaker; colourless. Blown. Rim out-turned with lip knocked-off and smoothed; sides taper downwards. Bubbly; no weathering. D. 6·5 cm. Fourth century.
    Trench 79 layer 68: pit 121.

12. Fragment of body of cone-beaker; yellowish-green. Blown. Bubbly and streaky; thick film of black weathering, mostly flaked off and leaving an iridescent surface. D. *c.* 6 cm. Fourth century.
    Trench 63 layer 9: pit 47.

13. Fragment of body of cone-beaker, colourless. Blown. Raised trail of similar glass, vertically, with drop-on at the lower end. Thin horizontal band of wheel-incisions near bottom of fragment. Bubbly and streaky; weathering as no. 12. D. *c.* 6 cm. Third to fourth century.
    Trench 74 layer 44: pit 85.

14. Fragment of bottom of cone-beaker; green. Sides taper slightly to rounded basal angle; bottom concave with rounded kick. Very bubbly; no visible weathering. D. bottom 3 cm. Fourth century.
    Trench 65 layer 11: pit 51.
    Similar fragment: Trench 74 layer 19: pit 83. Much flaking and iridescence.

15. Rim of flask; light green. Rim widely splayed, lip thickened and rounded. Surface flaking off, leaving iridescence. D. 7·5 cm. Late third to fourth century.
    Trench 102 layer 38.

16. Rim of flask; dull green. Shape as no. 15, but with self-coloured trail below lip, outside. D. *c.* 5 cm. Late third to fourth century.
    Trench 54 layer 6.

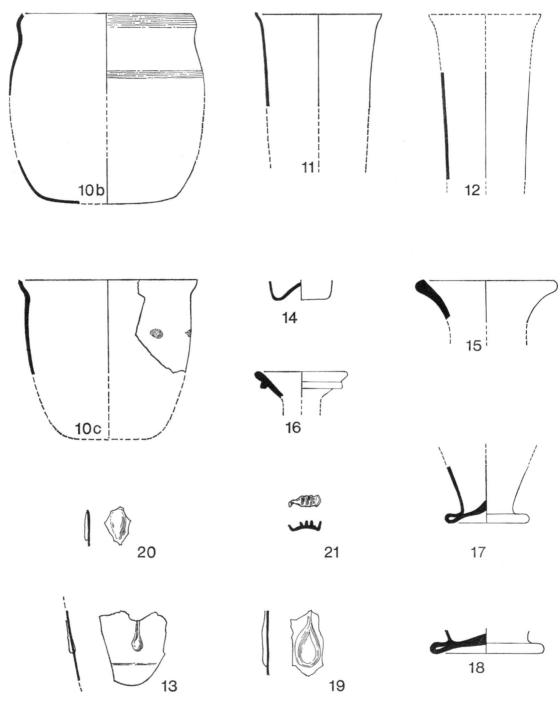

FIG. 198. Glass vessels (pp. 371, 373). Scale ½

17. Base-ring and part of lower body of jug; greenish-colourless. Sides taper to base-ring, which is pushed-in and hollow, with concavity and low, pointed kick below. Streaky and bubbly; surface dull and rough through weathering. D. base-ring 4·5 cm. Fourth century.

> Trench 79 layer 68: pit 121.
> Similar fragments: Trench 103 layer 51 (2277). D. base-ring 4·4 cm.
> > Trench 98 layer 75: pit 164. Half of base-ring only. D. 4·2 cm.

18. Quarter of base-ring of bowl or cup; dark bluish-green. Shape as no. 17. Recognizable trace of pontil-mark. Bubbly and streaky; incipient iridescence. D. base-ring *c.* 6 cm. Fourth century.

> Trench 62 layer 5.
> Similar fragments: Trench 89 layer 48.
> > Trench 88 layer 10: layer above make-up.

19. Fragment of body bearing end-loop of vertical trail; colourless with greenish tinge. Shape uncertain. Bubbly; no weathering. Late third to fourth century.

> Trench 98 layer 73: pit 164.

20. Fragment of body bearing an oval prunt or flattened knop; green. Shape uncertain. Bubbly; flaking film and iridescence. Late third to fourth century.

> Trench 91 layer 52 (1301): layer above upper road.

## *Tag-end of trailing*

21. Tag-end of open-work trailing from a vessel(?); dark green. Iridescent. Trail flattened and then pincered out four times at right angles. Length 1·5 cm., width 0·6 cm. Late third to fourth century.

> Trench 64 layer 7.

## *Window-glass*

22. Fragment of matt/glossy window glass showing part of rounded edge; bluish-green. Thick pane, rounded but not thickened at edge. Bubbly; whitish film flaked away, leaving iridescent, pitted surface. First to second century.

> Trench 71 layer 8.

23. Fragment of double-glossy window-glass with part of rounded edge; bluish-green. Pane thick in parts, with thin edge. Bubbly and streaky, flaking and iridescent. Fourth century.

> Trench 103 layer 23: upper occupation.
> Similar fragments, but no thinning at edge of pane: Trench 77 layer 5.
> > Trench 62 layer 20.

24. Two fragments of double-glossy window-glass, one showing part of the rounded edge; bluish-green. Thin pane with thickened edge. Bubbly and streaky; dulled, no iridescence. Fourth century.

> Trench 79 layer 68: pit 121.
> Similar: Trench 70 layer 23: pit 66.
> > Trench 87 layer 50 (1362): layer below upper road.
> > Trench 88 layer 55: layer above make-up.

25. Two fragments of double-glossy window-glass, each showing part of the rounded edge; bluish-green. Thin pane with thin edge. Bubbly and streaky; flaking and iridescent. Fourth century.

> Trench 88 layer 10: layer above make-up.
> Similar: Trench 78 layer 14: pit 103.
> > Trench 62 layer 20.

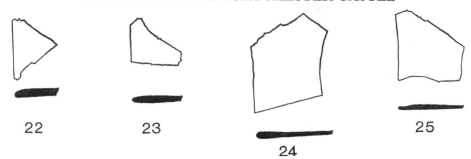

FIG. 199.   Window-glass (p. 373). Scale ½

## *B. Roman Glass from Post-Roman Levels*

26.  (Not illustrated.) Fragment of pane of double-glossy window-glass; no part of edge extant; bluish-green.

Trench 87 layer 33: *Grubenhaus.*

27.  (Not illustrated.) Fragment of three-ribbed handle of small jug; greenish-colourless.

Trench 88 layer 9: pit 135.

28.  (Not illustrated.) Fragment of bottom of body of drop-shaped unguent-bottle; green.

Trench 88 layer 9: pit 135.

29.  (Not illustrated.) Fragment of slightly incurved rim of bowl; dark green.

Trench 88 layer 11: pit 135.

30.  (Not illustrated.) Two fragments of double-glossy window-glass; bluish-green.

Trench 88 layer 33: pit 135.

31.  (Not illustrated.) Fragment of double-glossy window-glass with part of one grozed edge; bluish-green.

Trench 88 layer 80: pit 135.

32.  (Not illustrated.) As no. 31, with parts of a diamond-cut (?) edge and a grozed (?) edge; yellowish-colourless.

Trench 88 layer 81: pit 135.

33.  (Not illustrated.) Fragment of rim of bowl; greenish. Splayed rim, knocked off and smoothed at lip. For shape cf. no. 1 above.

Trench 85 layer 21: Saxon slot.

34.  (Not illustrated.) Fragment of cylindrical neck of bottle; green. From a tall-necked cylindrical bottle with two 'dolphin' handles at base of neck. For shape cf. example from Shakenoak, *op. cit.* in p. 368, note 2, p. 104, no. 232, fig. 52, and refs. *ad loc.* Late third or fourth century.

Trench 76 layer 4: medieval layer.

# X.   THE HUMAN BONES

## by BARI HOOPER

## DISCUSSION

WITH one exception all of the human remains recovered from the Roman levels at Port-chester are of infants. The exception is an adult over the age of 23 years, represented by only a few fragments of pelvis. Not enough remained to establish the sex of this individual. It is quite possible that these pieces are not Roman but are intrusive from the Saxon level.

A number of problems arose in studying the infant remains, not the least being the small number of bones surviving in most burials. Only in four instances were anything like complete skeletons recovered. Unlike mature bones which will frequently yield much valuable informa-tion about disease and congenital anomaly, immature specimens by their very nature are less than informative. Suffice it to say in this instance that no evidence of disease or congenital change could be found. Beyond cataloguing them and attempting to assess their chronological age little else can be said. To assess the age at death the bones were compared with those of modern infants of known age. It must however be understood that direct comparison of size between bones of different periods for the purpose of establishing the chronological age of one group is a crude method of study. The different environmental, genetic and ethnic back-grounds of the two groups will have influenced the size to age ratio. But until a more scientific method of ageing immature bones is developed the direct comparison method remains as a guide. Another difficulty encountered was in trying to decide whether the bones of a full-term infant were immediate ante- or post-natal. Neither case can be proved with the present material, although some bones are several weeks old. It was therefore decided, with the above reservations, to divide the burials into two groups according to age: Group A being ante neo-natal; Group B being from neo-natal up to about 18 weeks. The obvious problem of the overlap between the upper range of Group A and the lower range of Group B cannot be overcome, but the classification should be seen as a tentative attempt to find out at which end of the scale most deaths occurred. And from it, it appears that most of the infants survived the actual birth but succumbed within the first few weeks of life. The rate of infant mortality in Roman Britain has not yet been established, but it is reasonable to assume that it was high. The low life expectancy of infants in the Graeco-Roman period is referred to by Aristotle in Book vii of the *Historia Animalium,* where, speaking of babies he says '*Most* are carried off before the seventh day; that is why they give the child its name then, as they have more confidence by that time in its survival' (author's italics). Aristotle was writing in the fourth century B.C., but there is no documentary evidence in the Empire period of Rome to suggest any improvement in life expectancy for the new-born. Indeed even in Britain as late as the eighteenth century the chances of a child reaching adulthood were poor. The London Bills of Mortality for 1762–71 show that two-thirds of the children died before the age of five years, and 75% of these deaths occurred below the age of two years (Still, 1931).

This brings us to the question of the location and method of burial. The ancient Roman law of the Twelve Tables expressly forbade the burying or burning of a corpse within a city (*hominem mortuum in urbe ne sepelito neve urito*). It appears however that newly born babies were not affected by this law and it is not surprising to find the Portchester inhumations within the confines of the fort. There are many other examples from Britain, the most notable being at the villa of Hambleden, Bucks., which yielded no fewer than 97 infant burials (Cocks, 1921). Similarly the scarcity of infant burials in the large Romano-British cemetery at Trentholme Drive, York, favours the hypothesis that the inhumation of infants in the communal burial ground was not a general custom (Warwick, 1968). At Portchester, 13 of the 27 infants were interred in pits along with a selection of animal, bird and fish bones. The classes represented were ox, pig, sheep, dog, cat, horse, red deer, roe deer, fallow deer, hare, birds and fish. The deposition of animal remains with the dead is occasionally noted in Romano-British contexts. At Trentholme Drive 105 specimens of animal remains were found in the cemetery and 12 of these were associated with particular skeletons. The classes represented were horse, ox, sheep, pig, cat, red deer, roe deer and birds. Eight of the Portchester pit assemblages and one from a well had among the mammalian remains a neo-natal or very young pig. A full analysis of these pit groups is contained in the section on animal bones in this report. It will be seen that some types of animal consistently occur with the infant burials which might suggest that their deposition was part of funeral ritual. Pits full of the normal detritus of the Roman household do sometimes contain the skeletons of infants, as at Radwinter, Essex, where six infants were found in a rubbish pit (Hooper, forthcoming).

As at Hambleden a few double burials were noted; these occurred in one pit and in the upper and middle occupation and middle clay layers. It is impossible to determine whether the second infant in each pit or grave was buried contemporaneously with the first or later.

## INVENTORY OF HUMAN REMAINS FROM PORTCHESTER

| Location | Inventory | Age group |
|---|---|---|
| Pit 46 | Humeri, right scapula, left radius, vertebrae and ribs | B |
| Pit 47 | Right tibia | B |
| Pit 60b | Left humerus | A |
| Pit 63 upper | Skull and jaw fragments, vertebrae and ribs, scapulae, right radius, left femur and left tibia | B |
| Pit 63 lower | Fragment of left ulna | B |
| Pit 64 | Skull and jaw fragments, vertebrae and ribs, right scapula, left clavicle, right humerus and ulnae | A |
| Pit 86 | Right radius | B |
| Pit 92 | Skull and jaw fragments, vertebrae, scapulae, clavicles, pelvis, left humerus, femora and tibiae | B |
| Pit 119 | Right clavicle | A |
| Pit 129 | Jaw fragment, left scapula and right ulna | A |

| Location | Inventory | Age group |
|---|---|---|
| Pit 235 | Skull fragments, vertebrae and ribs, scapulae, pelvis fragments, humeri, radii, left ulna, left femur and tibiae | B |
| Pit 164 (well) | Humeri and tibiae | B |
| 107 layer 52 mid occupation | Left ulna | B |
| 108 layer 163 mid occupation | Left femur | A |
| 107 layer 50 upper clay | Skull fragments, right scapula, pelvis fragment, ribs, tibiae | A |
| 108 layer 111 upper clay | Skull and jaw fragments, humeri, right radius, right ulna, right femur, tibiae | A |
| 108 layer 111a upper clay | Right humerus, right femur and right tibia | A |
| 107 layer 53 mid clay | Right femur | B |
| 107 layer 53a mid clay | Fragment of left humerus and right femur | B |
| 107 layer 61 lower occupation | Fragment of left humerus | B |
| 108 layer 202 lower occupation | Right ulna | B |
| 107 layer 44 upper occupation | Left ulna, left radius, right femur and right tibia | B |
| 107 layer 44a upper occupation | Right femur and right tibia | B |
| 108 layer 62 upper occupation | Right femur | A |
| 108 layer 99 upper occupation | Right femur | B |
| 87 layer 9 above road | Right humerus | B |
| 91 layer 43 above road | Fragment of pelvis | Adult |

# BIBLIOGRAPHY

COCKS, A. H. 1921. 'A Romano-British homestead, in the Hambleden Valley, Bucks.'. *Archaeologia*, lxxi, 150.

STILL, G. F. 1931. *The History of Paediatrics; the Progress of the Study of Diseases in Children up to the End of the XVIIIth Century*. London, pp. 454–5.

WARWICK, R. 1968. 'The skeletal remains', in Wenham, L. P., *The Romano-British Cemetery at Trentholme Drive, York*. London, pp. 113–71.

# XI.  THE ANIMAL BONES

## by ANNIE GRANT

## INTRODUCTION

SOME 36,000 bone fragments were examined by the writer, of which 28,908 were identified. The remaining 7000 were generally too small to allow positive identification. The bones were those recovered from the Roman pits, wells and well-stratified layers against the Roman wall. Because of the obvious dangers of analysis of bone material from multi-period sites, the bones from those layers where there was risk of contamination from later levels were not examined. It is hoped that this minimized the chance that Saxon and medieval bones were included amongst the Roman material, although this possibility cannot entirely be excluded.

It has been demonstrated by Payne (1972) that, in excavations where sieving is not common practice, the recovery of animal bones is very heavily biased against small animals in favour of larger species. Payne's findings have been backed up by the writer's own experience of controlled sieving experiments. Excavation at Portchester was often in the hands of volunteers who were required to work quickly and no sieving was carried out. Inevitably, the recovery of animal bones will have been biased and this fact must be borne in mind when reading this report.

For the purposes of some analyses the bones were divided into five main and one subsidiary group. These are shown in Table I, with their contexts and approximate dates. They will be referred to as group 1, group 2, etc., during the report. When no groups are individually referred to, the discussion can be assumed to apply to the Roman bones as a whole.

## TABLE I

| Group | Archaeological context | Approximate date A.D. |
|---|---|---|
| 1 | Pits (excluding wells and the upper layers of pits 63 and 66) | 290–325 |
| 2 | Lower occupation and middle clay | 290–325 |
| 3 | Middle occupation and upper clay | 325–345 |
| 4 | Upper occupation, above road surface and make-up and the upper layers of pits 63 and 66 | 345 onwards |
| 5 | Wells | 290–360 |
| a | Below road and upper make-up | 290–345 |

# THE ANIMALS REPRESENTED

## (fig. 200)

Bones were recovered of cattle, sheep, pigs, birds, dogs, cats, red deer, horses, roe deer, hare, foxes, badgers, fallow deer, fish, voles and mice. Five bones were recovered of a small mammal that was not positively identified. It was rarely possible to distinguish sheep from goat and so 'sheep' is used throughout to mean 'sheep and/or goat'.

Several methods of determining relative proportions of different animals are in common use and much has been written about their various merits (e.g. Chaplin, 1971; Clason, 1972). The writer has already discussed the possible advantages of counting only those bones which have at least part of an epiphysis present (Grant, 1970), over the method of counting all bone fragments identified. For some analyses, the 'minimum number of animals' method is to be preferred. It does give some idea, however vague, of how many animals we are actually dealing with, but it does not distinguish between animals represented by one or two bone fragments and those represented by complete or nearly complete skeletons. This might be important on sites where some animals are represented by joints rather than carcasses, or where some parts of an animal were specially collected for an industrial use, such as bone tool manufacture or glue making. It is the author's opinion that, ideally, as many different methods should be used for calculating the proportions of animals as possible. The results can then be compared, with allowances made for the possible biases of each. Three main methods have been used for this report.

'Epiphyses only' includes only those bones with part of an epiphysis or fusion surface present and mandibles with at least one tooth present. Mandibles without teeth, skull fragments including upper jaws and horn cores, and vertebrae are excluded. Adjustments are made where an animal has two bones in the place of a single bone in the more commonly represented animals. For example, the numbers of pig metapodia have been divided by two. Carpals, tarsals (except calcanea and astragali) and other small bones are not counted because they are so rarely recovered for small animals. Whole bones are counted twice, once for each epiphysis, except in the case of phalanges, which are rarely broken, and far more frequently recovered from cattle than from any smaller animals.

'Total fragments' includes all bone and tooth fragments identified and assigned to a species, except for skull fragments without teeth or horn cores. These are excluded because the very brittle nature of much of the bone of the skull means that the number of skull fragments can double during the transportation of the bones from the excavation to the place of analysis. Ribs are also excluded because of the difficulty of precise species identification.

'Minimum numbers of individuals' have only been calculated for the better represented animals. No attempt has been made to try to match pairs of bones to determine whether or not they could have come from the same animal. This would have presented enormous practical problems in a sample of this size, and is anyway of dubious validity. Minimum numbers have been calculated by the rough and ready method of dividing by two the number of the most commonly represented bone for each animal in each group.

The results are shown in Table II and fig. 200, where the percentages of the more common animals in each group have been presented in histogram form. Tables II(a) and II(b) give

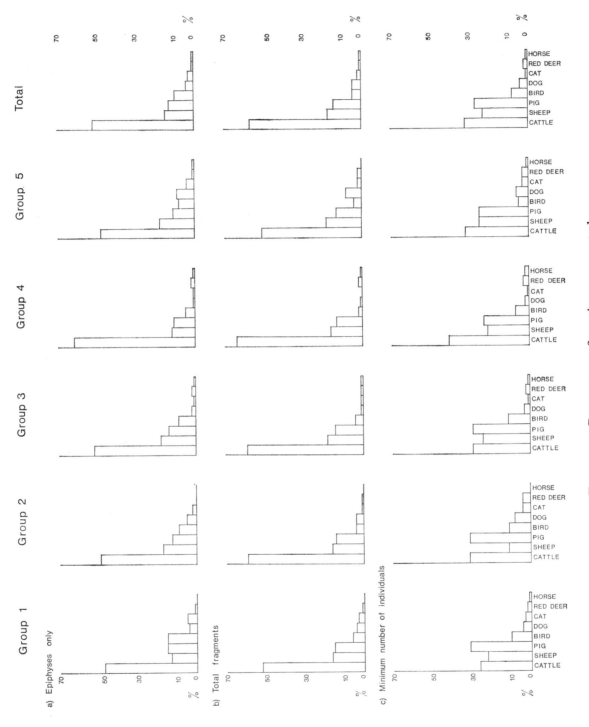

Fɪɢ. 200.    Percentage of species represented

broadly similar results, except that the 'total fragments' method gives slightly higher percent ages for cattle and slightly lower percentages for small animals, especially birds, than does the 'epiphyses only' method. This is precisely what was expected, as the 'epiphyses only' method was designed to help combat the bias against the smaller animals. The main disadvantage of this method is that where animals are represented only by bone fragments without epiphyses, they will not appear at all. The 'total fragments' method might be expected to give better results for very poorly represented animals. However, since these are generally very small animals with poor chance of recovery on unsieved sites, the results, however calculated, will not be very significant.

Using for the moment the results of table II(a), it would seem as if approximately half the animals found at Portchester were cattle. The numbers of sheep and pig seem fairly equal and together they represent just over a quarter of the bones recovered. Next in importance are birds, then dogs and cats. Red deer, horses, roe deer, hares, foxes, badgers, voles, fallow deer, fish and mice together only form approximately 3% of the total. Between the groups small changes are seen. The percentage of cattle bones increases slightly over the time span represented, from 47% in groups 1 and 2 to 62% in group 4. The proportions of pig and sheep bones vary slightly from group to group, but only become significantly different in group 5, where sheep bones form 18% of the total compared to 11% pig bones. Bird is most common in group 1, where it forms 15% of the total. In group 4, bird forms only 5%. Dogs are found most commonly in group 5, and least frequently in group 4. Cats, too, are most common in group 5 and group 1, and least common in groups 3 and 4. Changes in the percentages of the other animals represented are not significant because of the small number of animals involved, although it should be mentioned that some deer bones, especially when they are fragmented, can be confused with cattle and sheep bones. It is therefore possible that the percentages given might slightly under-represent the deer.

Although, because of the size of the sample, most of the percentage differences between the species are statistically significant when tested to 95% confidence limits using Rosenbaum's (1959) method, because of the recovery biases and because only a part of the interior of the fort was excavated, the percentages calculated should only be used as a general guide. This is very much reinforced when we examine the results of the 'minimum numbers of individuals' calculations, given in Table II(c). Here a very different picture is obtained, with pig more important or as important as cattle in groups 1, 2 and 3. In fact only in group 4 are cattle significantly more important than pigs. Sheep seem to be slightly less important than pigs in the first three groups, although they equal pigs in the last two groups.

Other differences between the groups are similar to those noted above, although bird is most common in groups 1, 2 and 3. Small differences are not statistically significant using this method, because the sample is fairly small. The figures given for group 2 should be treated with special caution.

Some of the reasons for the wide discrepancy between the results calculated by the 'epiphyses only' method and the 'minimum numbers of individuals' method are discussed in detail in the next section. It certainly serves as a warning to those trying to interpret the results of animal bone analysis. It is also worth noting that although the sample, nearly 30,000 bones, is by many standards quite large, we may in fact be dealing with the remains of only relatively few animals — a minimum of 216 cattle, 151 sheep, 180 pigs, 25 dogs, 7 horses,

# TABLE II

| | Group 1 | | Group 2 | | Groups 1 and 2 | | Group 3 | | Groups 1, 2, 3 and 4 | | Group 4 | | Group 5 | | Total | |
|---|---|---|---|---|---|---|---|---|---|---|---|---|---|---|---|---|
| | no. | % | no. | % | no. | % | no. | % | no. | % | no. | % | no. | % | no. | % |
| **(a) Epiphyses only** | | | | | | | | | | | | | | | | |
| Cattle | 1602 | 47 | 126 | 49 | 1728 | 47 | 790 | 52 | 2564 | 49 | 1662 | 62 | 1106 | 48 | 5332 | 52 |
| Sheep | 455 | 13 | 45 | 17 | 500 | 14 | 268 | 18 | 779 | 15 | 367 | 14 | 405 | 18 | 1551 | 15 |
| Pig | 500 | 15 | 39 | 15 | 539 | 15 | 216 | 14 | 761 | 14 | 354 | 13 | 246 | 11 | 1361 | 13 |
| Bird | 505 | 15 | 23 | 9 | 528 | 14 | 142 | 9 | 670 | 13 | 145 | 5 | 177 | 8 | 992 | 10 |
| Dog | 138 | 4 | 14 | 5 | 152 | 4 | 31 | 2 | 183 | 3 | 31 | 1 | 204 | 9 | 418 | 4 |
| Cat | 155 | 5 | 5 | 2 | 160 | 4 | 15 | 1 | 176 | 3 | 14 | 1 | 91 | 4 | 281 | 3 |
| Red deer | 32 | 1 | 1 | | 33 | 1 | 24 | 2 | 61 | 1 | 54 | 2 | 33 | 1 | 148 | 1 |
| Horse | 12 | | — | | 12 | | 8 | 1 | 22 | | 23 | 1 | 15 | 1 | 60 | 1 |
| Roe deer | 1 | | — | | 1 | | 3 | | 4 | | 11 | | 5 | | 20 | |
| Hare | 7 | | 2 | 1 | 9 | | 2 | | 11 | | 5 | | 1 | | 17 | |
| Fox | 2 | | — | | 2 | | 15 | 1 | 17 | | 5 | | — | | 22 | |
| Badger | 4 | | 2 | 1 | 6 | | 7 | | 13 | | — | | — | | 13 | |
| Vole | 3 | | — | | 3 | | — | | 3 | | 3 | | — | | 6 | |
| Fallow deer | 3 | | 1 | | 4 | | 4 | | 8 | | — | | — | | 8 | |
| Fish | — | | — | | — | | — | | — | | — | | — | | — | |
| Mouse | — | | — | | — | | — | | — | | — | | 2 | | 2 | |
| Small mammal | — | | — | | — | | 2 | | 2 | | — | | 6 | | 8 | |
| Total | 3419 | | 258 | | 3677 | | 1527 | | 5274 | | 2674 | | 2291 | | 10,239 | |
| **(b) Total fragments** | | | | | | | | | | | | | | | | |
| Cattle | 3143 | 53 | 331 | 59 | 3474 | 53 | 1813 | 59 | 5383 | 55 | 3457 | 64 | 1934 | 51 | 10,774 | 57 |
| Sheep | 978 | 16 | 89 | 16 | 1067 | 16 | 551 | 18 | 1638 | 17 | 878 | 16 | 696 | 18 | 3212 | 17 |
| Pig | 919 | 15 | 79 | 14 | 998 | 15 | 426 | 14 | 1444 | 16 | 700 | 13 | 510 | 13 | 2654 | 14 |
| Bird | 386 | 6 | 21 | 4 | 407 | 6 | 120 | 4 | 528 | 5 | 107 | | 163 | 4 | 798 | 4 |
| Dog | 259 | 4 | 23 | 4 | 282 | 4 | 39 | 1 | 321 | 3 | 48 | 1 | 311 | 8 | 680 | 4 |
| Cat | 168 | 3 | 7 | 1 | 175 | 3 | 18 | 1 | 194 | 2 | 15 | | 87 | 2 | 296 | 2 |
| Red deer | 52 | 1 | 7 | 1 | 59 | 1 | 28 | 1 | 90 | 1 | 106 | 2 | 66 | 2 | 262 | 1 |
| Horse | 27 | | — | | 27 | | 17 | 1 | 46 | | 59 | 1 | 14 | | 119 | 1 |
| Roe deer | 4 | | 2 | | 6 | | 6 | | 12 | | 20 | | 6 | | 38 | |
| Hare | 5 | | 2 | | 7 | | 9 | | 16 | | 5 | | 1 | | 22 | |
| Fox | 4 | | — | | 4 | | 15 | | 19 | | 3 | | — | | 22 | |
| Badger | 4 | | 1 | | 5 | | 5 | | 10 | | 1 | | 2 | | 13 | |
| Vole | 2 | | — | | 2 | | — | | 2 | | 1 | | — | | 3 | |
| Fallow deer | 3 | | 1 | | 4 | | 6 | | 10 | | 1 | | — | | 11 | |
| Fish | 3 | | — | | 3 | | 3 | | 6 | | 4 | | 1 | | 11 | |
| Mouse | — | | — | | — | | — | | — | | — | | 3 | | 3 | |
| Small mammal | — | | — | | — | | 1 | | 1 | | — | | 4 | | 5 | |
| Total | 5957 | | 563 | | 6520 | | 3057 | | 9720 | | 5405 | | 3798 | | 18,923 | |
| **(c) Minimum nos. individuals** | | | | | | | | | | | | | | | | |
| Cattle | 51 | 26 | 8 | 31 | 59 | 27 | 30 | 29 | 91 | 27 | 78 | 41 | 47 | 32 | 216 | 32 |
| Sheep | 43 | 22 | 3 | 11 | 46 | 21 | 25 | 24 | 73 | 22 | 40 | 21 | 38 | 25 | 151 | 23 |
| Pig | 60 | 31 | 8 | 31 | 68 | 31 | 30 | 29 | 99 | 30 | 43 | 23 | 38 | 25 | 180 | 27 |
| Bird | 20 | 10 | 3 | 11 | 23 | 11 | 11 | 11 | 35 | 11 | 13 | 7 | 8 | 5 | 56 | 8 |
| Dog | 8 | 4 | 2 | 8 | 10 | 5 | 3 | 3 | 13 | 4 | 3 | 2 | 9 | 6 | 25 | 4 |
| Cat | 6 | 3 | 1 | 4 | 7 | 3 | 1 | 1 | 9 | 3 | 2 | 1 | 4 | 3 | 15 | 2 |
| Red deer | 4 | 2 | 1 | 4 | 5 | 1 | 2 | 2 | 8 | 2 | 6 | 3 | 4 | 3 | 18 | 3 |
| Horse | 1 | 1 | — | | 1 | | 1 | 1 | 3 | 1 | 3 | 2 | 1 | 1 | 7 | 1 |
| Total | 193 | | 26 | | 219 | | 103 | | 331 | | 188 | | 149 | | 668 | |

18 deer, 15 cats and 56 birds. Even taking into account the fact that only an eighth of the fort has been excavated to date, this is a very small number of animals for a fairly long occupation, and unless the population was very small, probably represents only a fraction of the animals kept, eaten, or hunted by the inhabitants. Domestic refuse might well have been thrown in places other than the pits and wells and occupation layers inside the fort.

It is impossible to make any estimation of the amount of cereal and vegetable crops grown and eaten, so we do not know what proportion of the diet was made up of meat. Davies (1971) has discussed the importance of meat in the Roman military diet, although it is not clear how much of the occupation here was in fact military. Because of the location of the site, sea foods are likely to have been of some considerable importance. Large numbers of oyster shells were recovered during the excavation. The very small quantity of fish bones recovered is far more likely to reflect poor survival and recovery than a distaste for fish.

Again the small numbers of horse bones may not truly reflect their position in the economy. Any military occupation is likely to have involved some use of horses, but they would not generally have formed a part of the diet. Horses in Roman times were sometimes buried separately, outside the area of occupation, and so their rarity amongst what on the whole appears to be domestic refuse is not necessarily surprising.

The large number of birds found at the site is interesting and unusual and they are discussed in detail by Anne Eastham below (pp. 409–15).

The vast majority of the meat must have been provided by the cattle, sheep and pigs, for 56 birds would have provided very little in the way of food. Wild animals seem to have been of very little importance at the site, and deer might have been hunted as much as a source of raw materials as a source of food. This is discussed again later. Table III gives the figures for the main food animals, calculated by the 'minimum number of individuals' method, adjusted to show the relationships of each in terms of meat yield. The weights used are those given by Carter et al. (1965).

Cattle 900 lb.
Sheep 125 lb.
Pigs    200 lb.

## TABLE III

| | Group 1 | | | Group 2 | | | Group 3 | | | Group 4 | | | Group 5 | | | Total | | |
|---|---|---|---|---|---|---|---|---|---|---|---|---|---|---|---|---|---|---|
| | No. | % | Meat yield (%) | No. | % | Meat yield (%) | No. | % | Meat yield (%) | No. | % | Meat yield (%) | No. | % | Meat yield (%) | No. | % | Meat yield (%) |
| Ox | 51 | 33 | 73 | 8 | 42 | 78 | 30 | 35 | 75 | 78 | 48 | 84 | 47 | 38 | 77 | 216 | 39 | 78 |
| Sheep | 43 | 28 | 8 | 3 | 16 | 4 | 25 | 29 | 9 | 40 | 25 | 6 | 38 | 31 | 9 | 151 | 28 | 8 |
| Pig | 60 | 39 | 19 | 8 | 42 | 17 | 30 | 35 | 17 | 43 | 27 | 10 | 38 | 31 | 14 | 180 | 33 | 14 |

The weight of an animal does, of course, depend on many factors including breed, sex, age at death and plane of nutrition. The figures given in the table above can only be used as a very rough guide.

Cattle would certainly appear to be the most important source of meat, on whatever basis the percentages of animals are calculated. The 'minimum numbers of individuals' method used for this analysis gives cattle the lowest importance of all the methods used and yet the table shows that the amount of beef consumed far exceeds the amount of pork and lamb. This is interesting in the light of much of the evidence of Roman writers. In Italy, cattle were kept mainly for traction and sometimes milk, and pork seems to have been the most common meat eaten, especially judging by the recipe books. Sheep were kept mainly for wool, and only secondarily for milk and meat. The uses of the domestic animals in Roman Italy are discussed in detail by White (1970). The environmental as well as cultural differences between Roman Italy and Roman Britain will have had an enormous effect on the type of animal husbandry practised. One of the problems of keeping cattle for milk in Italy lay in the shortage of good grass. This is unlikely to have been such a problem in Hampshire. The results of the bone analysis of Fishbourne Roman villa (Grant, 1971) show a far higher percentage of pig at this site. There is obviously a time and a cultural difference involved, but the environmental differences are not so great. When analysis of the Saxon and medieval bones from Portchester has been completed, it might be possible to attempt some distinction between environmental and cultural factors.

The last group of animals is the domestic, probably non-food animals, the dog and the cat. The numbers of these animals recovered at Portchester are very high in comparison to many sites of all periods, especially the numbers of cats. They may have been kept as household pets or working animals or, the cats especially, could have been strays living and breeding around the fort.

## BUTCHERY AND ANALYSIS OF BONES REPRESENTED

We now turn to a more detailed analysis of the bones recovered from the three main food animals. Table IV and fig. 201 give a breakdown of the bones recovered for each animal. Fig. 201 does not include an analysis of group 2 because of the small numbers of bones involved. Table V shows the number of rib and skull fragments found for all species in each group. Where percentages are given in Table IV they are percentages of the greatest number. The figures have been adjusted to allow for accurate comparison between each bone. Thus, the number of phalanges have been divided by two, and assigned to front and back legs in the same ratio as that of the distal end of the metacarpal to the distal end of the metatarsal. The numbers of atlases and axes have been multiplied by two. Where no percentage is given, it has not been thought possible to give a realistic comparison with the other bones. Two figures have been given for the skull. The first of these includes all large and fairly diagnostic fragments (excluding horn cores and jaws); the second includes small fragments, mainly broken frontal bone, and other thin areas of the skull.

The work of Brain (1969) and Isaac (1967) has clearly shown that some parts of the skeleton have a far lower chance of survival than some others. Brain, who did his work on goat bones, related this in part to the specific gravity of the bone and in part to the age of fusion of the bone. Bones with a low specific gravity are those with a spongy internal structure and thin walls. These have less chance of survival than parts of bones with a dense compact structure. Bones with low specific gravity are proximal ends of humeri, proximal ends of tibiae,

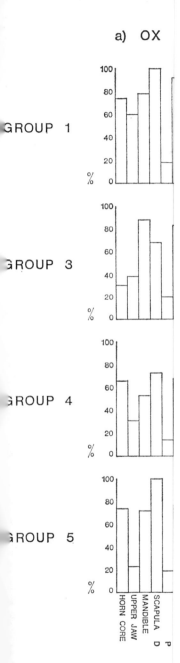

a)  OX

GROUP 1

GROUP 3

GROUP 4

GROUP 5

vertebrae and skull fragments. Because immature bone is less resistant to decay and fragmentation than mature fused bone, those bones that fuse late also have a poorer chance of survival than those which fuse early. In fact, the two sources of bias operate together in some cases, and bones which fuse early are generally far more dense than those which fuse later in the animal's life. The bones that will be affected in this way are again the proximal end of the humerus, the proximal end of the tibia and the distal end of the femur.

Recovery is also another possible source of bias in these figures. Large bones will be recovered far more frequently than small bones such as phalanges, carpals and tarsals.

The other factor which will affect the survival of bones is the activity of dogs and other gnawing animals. Teeth marks, apparently those of dogs, are found frequently on the Portchester bones. The cattle bones most commonly affected are calcanea, distal ends of humeri, metapodia, femora, and less frequently distal ends of scapulae, pelves, phalanges, and proximal ends of tibiae and vertebrae. Pig bones that were commonly gnawed include distal humeri, scapulae, ulnae, calcanea and vertebrae, and sheep bones gnawed include distal humeri, proximal radii, metapodia, and proximal ends of tibiae and calcanea.

In some cases of dog gnawing, the whole epiphysis and part of the shaft appear to have been completely destroyed, although in most of the cases noted only part of the bone has been destroyed. The smaller the animal, the greater chance of complete destruction of bones by dogs. Some bones may well have been completely removed from the site by dogs or other flesh-eating animals. Pl. XXXIXc shows the distal end of a cattle humerus which has been gnawed and partly destroyed by a dog or similar animal.

There might in fact be further scope for a more careful analysis of tooth marks on bones than has been carried out at the time of writing this report. The incidence of gnawing could be correlated with the numbers of dogs found in any group. Incidence of gnawing might also reflect methods of rubbish disposal. Animal bones left lying on the ground surface might be expected to be gnawed more frequently than those thrown into pits or wells shortly after they were discarded. Similarly, it might be possible to make a distinction between groups or sites where a deliberate policy of feeding dogs was practised and those where dogs were left to scavenge as they might.

To return to table IV, with all the possible sources of bias just discussed operating, it becomes extremely difficult to draw too many firm conclusions from the percentages of the various skeletal parts. In the case of the cattle bones shown in table IV(a), many of the discrepancies between the various bones can be explained in terms of the possible sources of bias discussed above. Brain and Isaac have shown that, even when whole skeletons are initially represented, after fairly short amounts of time have elapsed, there will be several parts missing. We should not expect every bone to be evenly represented even where whole animals are involved. We should certainly not be too rash in our interpretation of butchery practices from this sort of analysis. Even changes such as are seen from group to group may be the result of natural occurrences rather than deliberate policies. Use of bone as a raw material might explain some anomalies, and if the tools manufactured were traded away from the site, there might be no evidence of this left in the archaeological record. The relatively low occurrence of horn core in groups 2 and 3 may be the result of some form of industrial activity connected with horn cores. The patterns of survival from group to group are in fact fairly similar, although there are some differences, such as the high percentage of calcanea found in

26

group 1. Table IV(b) gives the analysis for sheep bones. There is far less bone from the skulls of these animals in relation to the number of jaws than was found among the cattle bones. The skulls of sheep will tend to fragment into fewer pieces than the much larger cattle skulls, and this might be the explanation. The percentage of horn cores is also fairly low (excluding group 2 where the small sample makes the figure unreliable). The low numbers of both skull fragments and horn cores may together be related to some sort of industrial use, especially if the horns were cut from the heads with a large amount of skull attached. The discrepancy between the numbers of upper and lower jaws in all animals is probably due to the greater fragility of the maxillary bone. There are few significant differences between the groups, apart from the small number of distal radii in group 4. Some differences between groups are to be expected since the bones from groups 1 and 5 were probably better protected than those from groups 2, 3 and 4, which might have been exposed for some time on the ground surface.

Analysis of the pig bones given in table IV(c) shows a quite considerable discrepancy between the numbers of jaws, especially mandibles, and the numbers of all other bones. This is true to a lesser degree also in the case of sheep. It is this fact that has caused such a wide difference between the results of the various methods of calculating percentages. At Fishbourne, pig mandibles were the most common pig bones too. It is very difficult to explain the large numbers of pig jaws except in terms of survival and recovery. It is well known that pig bones do not survive as well as those of cattle and sheep. Mandibles are made from fairly dense bone and the teeth themselves must add to their strength and durability. Mandibles, too, tend to have a good recovery rate because they are conspicuous and easily identified by the untrained volunteer. Other interpretations are of course possible. In his analysis of fourth-century animal bones from Lefevre Road, Rixson (1969) also found a high proportion of jaws for sheep and pigs, which he interpreted as the unsaleable debris left near a butcher's shop. One well, no. 121, had a particularly large number of jaws in it, especially pig jaws.

If the reason for large numbers of pig jaws is one of poorer survival of the other bones, this argues in favour of using the 'minimum numbers of individuals' method of species analysis. However, if they have either been deliberately collected or left behind as unsaleable butchers' debris the 'epiphyses only' method would provide a more valid analysis of the eating habits of the inhabitants of the area. It would certainly seem to argue for the use of both methods together.

On the whole the writer believes that the indications are that whole animals were brought into the fort, either dead or alive. There is no clear evidence of any preliminary butchery of the animals away from the area of occupation or outside the fort on any major scale.

Many of the bones have cuts or chops on them that seem to result from butchering the animals. These butchery marks were examined in some detail, but there is only space in the present report to discuss them briefly. The majority of cuts were found on the bones of cattle. This of course reflects both the larger numbers of cattle bones recovered and the smaller size of sheep and pig carcasses.

For cattle we even have evidence of the method of killing the animal. Where skulls were complete enough, the majority showed evidence of pole-axing, that is, hitting the animal with a heavy instrument or pole-axe in the centre of the frontal bone, just above the eyes. This method of killing is still used today, although in a modern slaughterhouse a gun with a fixed bolt is used instead of a pole-axe (Hammett and Nevell, 1929). Two variations of pole-axing

# TABLE IV

|  |  | Group 1 | | Group 2 | | Group 3 | | Group 4 | | Group 5 | |
|---|---|---|---|---|---|---|---|---|---|---|---|
|  |  | No. | % | No. | % | No. | % | No. | % | No. | % |
| (a) *Cattle* |  |  |  |  |  |  |  |  |  |  |  |
| Horn core |  | 75 | 74 | 6 | 38 | 18 | 30 | 103 | 66 | 69 | 74 |
| Skull |  | 69 |  | 18 |  | 99 |  | 171 |  | 124 |  |
|  |  | (264) |  | (10) |  | (120) |  | (230) |  | (204) |  |
| Upper jaw |  | 61 | 60 | 6 | 38 | 23 | 38 | 48 | 31 | 21 | 23 |
| Mandible |  | 80 | 78 | 16 | 100 | 53 | 88 | 82 | 53 | 67 | 72 |
| Scapula | D | 102 | 100 | 6 | 38 | 41 | 68 | 113 | 73 | 93 | 100 |
| Humerus | P | 18 | 18 | 1 | 6 | 12 | 20 | 21 | 14 | 18 | 19 |
|  | D | 94 | 92 | 6 | 38 | 50 | 83 | 106 | 68 | 72 | 77 |
| Radius | P | 83 | 81 | 5 | 31 | 38 | 63 | 67 | 43 | 72 | 77 |
|  | D | 73 | 72 | 6 | 38 | 41 | 70 | 58 | 37 | 53 | 57 |
| Ulna | P | 61 | 60 | 5 | 31 | 32 | 53 | 80 | 52 | 49 | 53 |
| Metacarpal | P | 98 | 96 | 6 | 38 | 49 | 82 | 135 | 87 | 61 | 66 |
|  | D | 76 | 75 | 6 | 38 | 49 | 82 | 81 | 52 | 51 | 55 |
| 1st phalange |  | 75 | 37 | 8 | 25 | 35 | 30 | 51 | 17 | 36 | 19 |
| 2nd phalange |  | 25 | 13 | 2 | 6 | 11 | 10 | 14 | 5 | 10 | 5 |
| 3rd phalange |  | 27 | 14 | 1 | 6 | 11 | 10 | 18 | 6 | 10 | 5 |
| Pelvis with acetabulum |  | 82 | 80 | 9 | 56 | 44 | 73 | 86 | 55 | 37 | 40 |
| Femur | P | 64 | 63 | 1 | 6 | 25 | 42 | 49 | 32 | 37 | 40 |
|  | D | 44 | 43 | 4 | 25 | 14 | 25 | 21 | 14 | 31 | 33 |
| Tibia | P | 45 | 44 | 3 | 19 | 20 | 33 | 46 | 30 | 35 | 38 |
|  | D | 69 | 68 | 4 | 25 | 24 | 40 | 72 | 46 | 61 | 66 |
| Calcaneum |  | 76 | 75 | 8 | 50 | 29 | 48 | 68 | 44 | 52 | 56 |
| Astragalus |  | 64 | 63 | 2 | 13 | 19 | 32 | 54 | 35 | 38 | 41 |
| Metatarsal | P | 86 | 84 | 4 | 25 | 60 | 100 | 155 | 100 | 66 | 71 |
|  | D | 63 | 61 | 7 | 44 | 40 | 66 | 98 | 63 | 52 | 56 |
| 1st phalange |  | 69 | 34 | 9 | 28 | 29 | 25 | 62 | 20 | 37 | 20 |
| 2nd phalange |  | 23 | 12 | 3 | 13 | 9 | 8 | 18 | 6 | 11 | 6 |
| 3rd phalange |  | 24 | 12 | 2 | 6 | 9 | 8 | 21 | 7 | 11 | 6 |
| Atlas |  | 22 | 43 | 3 | 38 | 18 | 60 | 22 | 28 | 18 | 39 |
| Axis |  | 18 | 35 | 1 | 13 | 19 | 63 | 28 | 36 | 15 | 32 |
| Cervical vertebrae |  | 44 |  | 13 |  | 45 |  | 46 |  | 33 |  |
| Thoracic vertebrae |  | 58 |  | 13 |  | 64 |  | 67 |  | 37 |  |
| Lumbar vertebrae |  | 25 |  | 8 |  | 21 |  | 20 |  | 19 |  |
| Sacrum |  | 12 |  | 6 |  | 17 |  | 19 |  | 5 |  |
| Caudal vertebrae |  | 8 |  | — |  | 6 |  | 4 |  | 1 |  |
| Vertebra fragments |  | 434 |  | 35 |  | 236 |  | 287 |  | 202 |  |
| Loose teeth |  | 183 |  | 22 |  | 98 |  | 403 |  | 51 |  |
| (b) *Sheep* |  |  |  |  |  |  |  |  |  |  |  |
| Horn core |  | 15 | 17 | 4 | 80 | 4 | 8 | 13 | 16 | 18 | 24 |
| Skull |  | 26 |  | 1 |  | 20 |  | 9 |  | 24 |  |
|  |  | (31) |  |  |  | (19) |  | (7) |  | (25) |  |
| Upper jaw |  | 27 | 31 | 1 | 20 | 21 | 42 | 13 | 16 | 38 | 48 |
| Mandible |  | 86 | 100 | 2 | 40 | 50 | 100 | 79 | 100 | 75 | 100 |
| Scapula | D | 20 | 23 | 2 | 40 | 11 | 22 | 20 | 25 | 21 | 28 |
| Humerus | P | 10 | 12 | 2 | 40 | 7 | 14 | 9 | 11 | 10 | 13 |
|  | D | 32 | 37 | 1 | 20 | 15 | 30 | 18 | 23 | 22 | 29 |

## Table IV—*continued*

|  |  | *Group 1* | | *Group 2* | | *Group 3* | | *Group 4* | | *Group 5* | |
|---|---|---|---|---|---|---|---|---|---|---|---|
|  |  | *No.* | % | *No.* | % | *No.* | % | *No.* | % | *No.* | % |
| Radius | P | 27 | 31 | 2 | 40 | 16 | 32 | 28 | 35 | 29 | 39 |
|  | D | 11 | 41 | 1 | 20 | 10 | 20 | 6 | 6 | 16 | 21 |
| Ulna | P | 18 | 21 | — |  | 6 | 12 | 5 | 6 | 18 | 24 |
| Metacarpal | P | 34 | 39 | 4 | 80 | 18 | 36 | 43 | 54 | 30 | 40 |
|  | D | 15 | 17 | 2 | 40 | 8 | 16 | 13 | 16 | 18 | 24 |
| 1st phalange |  | 8 | 5 | 1 | 10 | 4 | 4 | 2 | 1 | 2 | 1 |
| 2nd phalange |  | — |  | — |  | — |  | — |  | — |  |
| 3rd phalange |  | 1 | 1 | — |  | — |  | — |  | — |  |
| Pelvis |  | 45 | 52 | — |  | 15 | 30 | 16 | 20 | 15 | 20 |
| Femur | P | 14 | 16 | 5 | 100 | 9 | 18 | 8 | 10 | 20 | 27 |
|  | D | 11 | 13 | 4 | 80 | 8 | 16 | 9 | 11 | 11 | 15 |
| Tibia | P | 6 | 7 | 2 | 40 | 6 | 12 | 9 | 11 | 12 | 16 |
|  | D | 36 | 42 | 5 | 100 | 22 | 44 | 37 | 47 | 22 | 29 |
| Calcaneum |  | 13 | 15 | — |  | 5 | 10 | 4 | 5 | 7 | 9 |
| Astragalus |  | 4 | 5 | 1 | 20 | 4 | 8 | 4 | 5 | 1 | 1 |
| Metatarsal | P | 27 | 31 | 5 | 100 | 25 | 50 | 33 | 42 | 29 | 38 |
|  | D | 14 | 16 | 2 | 40 | 7 | 14 | 12 | 15 | 19 | 25 |
| 1st phalange |  | 6 | 3 | — |  | 5 | 5 | 2 | 1 | 2 | 1 |
| 2nd phalange |  | — |  | — |  | — |  | — |  | — |  |
| 3rd phalange |  | — |  | — |  | — |  | — |  | — |  |
| Atlas |  | 6 | 14 | — |  | 1 | 4 | 7 | 18 | 4 | 11 |
| Axis |  | 3 | 7 | — |  | 3 | 12 | 3 | 8 | 4 | 11 |
| Cervical vertebrae |  | 6 |  | — |  | 7 |  | 1 |  | 6 |  |
| Thoracic vertebrae |  | 22 |  | — |  | 2 |  | 4 |  | 8 |  |
| Lumbar vertebrae |  | 8 |  | 2 |  | 5 |  | 7 |  | 5 |  |
| Sacrum |  | — |  | 1 |  | 1 |  | 1 |  | — |  |
| Caudal vertebrae |  | 3 |  | — |  | 2 |  | — |  | — |  |
| Vertebra fragments |  | 65 |  | 7 |  | 22 |  | 15 |  | 20 |  |
| Loose teeth |  | 78 |  | 8 |  | 38 |  | 94 |  | 36 |  |
| **(c) *Pig*** |  |  |  |  |  |  |  |  |  |  |  |
| Skull |  | 44 (70) |  | 3 (3) |  | 17 (19) |  | 25 (22) |  | 14 (41) |  |
| Upper jaw |  | 58 | 48 | 5 | 33 | 27 | 46 | 55 | 65 | 54 | 71 |
| Mandible |  | 120 | 100 | 15 | 100 | 59 | 100 | 85 | 100 | 76 | 100 |
| Scapula | D | 29 | 24 | 3 | 20 | 8 | 14 | 42 | 49 | 14 | 18 |
| Humerus | P | 12 | 10 | 1 | 6 | 4 | 7 | 1 | 1 | 4 | 5 |
|  | D | 20 | 17 | 2 | 13 | 13 | 22 | 22 | 26 | 20 | 26 |
| Radius | P | 28 | 23 | — |  | 7 | 12 | 18 | 21 | 11 | 14 |
|  | D | 14 | 12 | — |  | 6 | 10 | 7 | 8 | 5 | 7 |
| Ulna |  | 33 | 28 | 4 | 27 | 17 | 29 | 40 | 47 | 19 | 25 |
| Metacarpal | P | 16 | 13 | 2 | 13 | 9 | 15 | 11 | 13 | 7 | 9 |
|  | D | 15 | 13 | 2 | 13 | 8 | 14 | 10 | 12 | 5 | 7 |
| 1st phalange |  | 2 | 2 | — |  | 2 | 3 | 2 | 2 | 1 | 1 |
| 2nd phalange |  | 1 | 1 | — |  | 1 | 2 | 1 | 1 | — |  |
| 3rd phalange |  | 1 | 1 | — |  | — |  | 1 |  | — |  |
| Pelvis |  | 24 | 20 | 2 | 13 | 14 | 24 | 19 | 22 | 10 | 13 |
| Femur | P | 18 | 15 | — |  | — |  | 8 | 9 | 7 | 9 |
|  | D | 10 | 8 | 1 | 6 | 7 | 12 | 3 | 4 | 11 | 14 |

Table IV—*continued*

|  |  | Group 1 No. | Group 1 % | Group 2 No. | Group 2 % | Group 3 No. | Group 3 % | Group 4 No. | Group 4 % | Group 5 No. | Group 5 % |
|---|---|---|---|---|---|---|---|---|---|---|---|
| Tibia | P | 15 | 13 | — |  | 4 | 7 | 8 | 9 | 8 | 11 |
|  | D | 49 | 41 | — |  | 12 | 20 | 28 | 33 | 15 | 20 |
| Calcaneum |  | 18 | 15 | 1 | 6 | 7 | 12 | 8 | 9 | 3 | 4 |
| Astragalus |  | 5 | 4 | — |  | 3 | 5 | 6 | 7 | 3 | 4 |
| Metatarsal | P | 16 | 13 | 2 | 13 | 9 | 15 | 12 | 14 | 7 | 9 |
|  | D | 15 | 13 | 1 | 6 | 9 | 15 | 10 | 12 | 6 | 8 |
| 1st phalange |  | 1 | 1 | — |  | 2 | 3 | 1 | 1 | — |  |
| 2nd phalange |  | — |  | — |  | 1 | 2 | — |  | — |  |
| 3rd phalange |  | — |  | — |  | — |  | — |  | — |  |
| Atlas |  | 4 | 7 | — |  | 2 | 7 | 2 | 5 | 5 | 13 |
| Axis |  | 1 | 2 | — |  | 1 | 3 | 2 | 5 | 4 | 11 |
| Cervical vertebrae |  | 3 |  | — |  | 1 |  | 3 |  | 1 |  |
| Thoracic vertebrae |  | 13 |  | — |  | 8 |  | 10 |  | 7 |  |
| Lumbar vertebrae |  | 7 |  | 1 |  | 2 |  | 11 |  | 6 |  |
| Sacrum |  | 2 |  | — |  | 1 |  | — |  | — |  |
| Vertebra fragments |  | 40 |  | 4 |  | 30 |  | 22 |  | 33 |  |
| Loose teeth |  | 65 |  | 3 |  | 43 |  | 93 |  | 31 |  |

P = Proximal; D = Distal.

are used in modern times, and both seem to have been practised at Portchester. In one method, the skull is pierced and a rod is introduced into the opening to destroy the medulla oblongata and brain. In the second method the animal is merely stunned by the blow, and is then hoisted and bled. There is no evidence for the bleeding, but pl. XXXVIII*e* shows a skull which has been struck with a blow that merely fractured but did not penetrate the skull, whereas pl. XXXVIII*a* shows a skull where a large area of the frontal bone has been destroyed by the blow. The numbers of pole-axed skulls found indicated that both the killing and the subsequent butchery of the animal were performed on the site.

The actual butchery of the animals seems to have been carried out with the aid of at least three different kinds of tool, a sharp heavy tool, such as an axe or chopper, a knife and a saw. The results of the use of each of these tools can be seen in pls. XXXVIII*d*, XXXIX*f*, and XXXVIII*f* respectively.

Horn cores were frequently cut from the skull; generally the cuts were made to include part of the skull, but in some cases the horn itself must have been damaged in the process of removing it. Pl. XXXVIII*g* shows a skull with a cut that for some reason has not quite severed the horn core from the skull. Pl. XXXVIII*d* gives an example of a case where the horn itself must have been damaged when it was removed. It is not clear whether the horns were cut off for use as raw material, for glue, or whether they were just discarded as waste.

Cuts on the head and jaws seem to be the result of boning out the head and cheek meat, and removing the lower jaw and perhaps the tongue from the head. Where whole skulls were found the frontals were not normally split or smashed sufficiently to allow the removal of the brain. This does not mean that this did not happen in every case. Most skulls were so

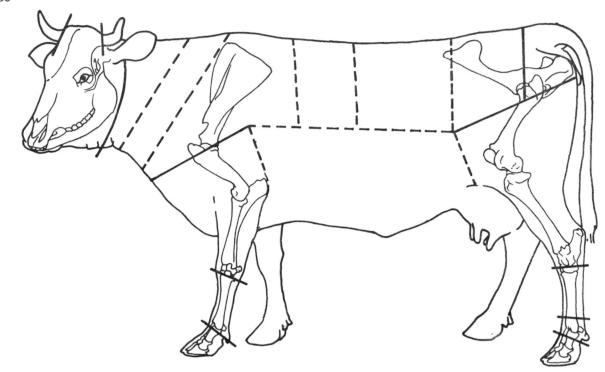

FIG. 202.    Diagram of a cow with the main butchery points indicated

fragmented that it was impossible to deduce anything about butchery from them, and some of the fragmentation could have occurred when the brain was removed.

The skull seems generally to have been severed from the rest of the body between the occipital condyles and the atlas. This is seen clearly in pl. XXXVIII*b*. The vertebrae themselves are found chopped, either longitudinally or at right angles to the backbone, or occasionally in both directions. Even today, butchery techniques are remarkably conservative, and regional differences in the technique are fairly rigidly adhered to. However, since vertebrae with each kind of cut are found in every group, the differences between splitting vertebrae and not splitting vertebrae may not in this instance be cultural ones. There may

## TABLE V

|  | Group 1 | | Group 2 | | Group 3 | | Group 4 | | Group 5 | | Total | |
|---|---|---|---|---|---|---|---|---|---|---|---|---|
|  | *No.* | *%* | *No.* | *%* | *No.* | *%* | *No.* | *%* | *No.* | *%* | *No.* | *%* |
| Ribs | 2854 | 30 | 379 | 39 | 1465 | 30 | 1902 | 24 | 1448 | 25 | 8090 | 28 |
| Skull fragments | 615 | 7 | 35 | 3 | 295 | 6 | 502 | 6 | 436 | 8 | 1895 | 7 |
| Other bone fragments | 5957 | 63 | 563 | 58 | 3057 | 63 | 5405 | 69 | 3798 | 67 | 18,923 | 65 |
| Total | 9426 | | 977 | | 4817 | | 7809 | | 5682 | | 28,908 | |

# TABLE VI

|  | Group 1 | | | Group 2 | | | Group 3 | | | Group 4 | | | Group 5 | | |
|---|---|---|---|---|---|---|---|---|---|---|---|---|---|---|---|
|  | B | C | %C | B | C | %C | B | C | %C | B | C | %C | B | C | %C |
| **(a) Cattle** | | | | | | | | | | | | | | | |
| Humerus | 92 | 2 | 2 | 6 | — | 0 | 50 | — | 0 | 105 | 1 | 1 | 68 | 4 | 6 |
| Radius | 61 | 12 | 16 | 6 | — | 0 | 39 | 3 | 7 | 59 | 8 | 12 | 57 | 15 | 21 |
| Metacarpal | 54 | 44 | 45 | 4 | 2 | 33 | 29 | 20 | 41 | 96 | 39 | 29 | 30 | 31 | 51 |
| Femur | 61 | 3 | 5 | 4 | — | 0 | 24 | 1 | 4 | 49 | — | 0 | 31 | 6 | 16 |
| Tibia | 65 | 4 | 6 | 4 | — | 0 | 22 | 2 | 8 | 67 | 5 | 7 | 35 | 6 | 15 |
| Metatarsal | 51 | 35 | 41 | 7 | — | 0 | 43 | 17 | 28 | 113 | 42 | 27 | 32 | 34 | 52 |
| Total | 384 | 100 | 21 | 31 | 2 | 6 | 207 | 43 | 17 | 489 | 95 | 16 | 253 | 96 | 28 |
| **(b) Sheep** | | | | | | | | | | | | | | | |
| Humerus | 26 | 6 | 19 | 1 | 1 | 50 | 12 | 3 | 20 | 15 | 3 | 17 | 13 | 9 | 41 |
| Radius | 20 | 7 | 26 | 1 | 1 | 50 | 14 | 2 | 13 | 28 | — | 0 | 16 | 13 | 45 |
| Metacarpal | 24 | 10 | 29 | 3 | 1 | 25 | 12 | 6 | 33 | 33 | 10 | 23 | 14 | 16 | 53 |
| Femur | 10 | 4 | 29 | 4 | 1 | 20 | 9 | — | 0 | 6 | 3 | 33 | 10 | 10 | 50 |
| Tibia | 32 | 4 | 11 | 4 | 1 | 20 | 21 | 1 | 5 | 33 | 4 | 11 | 12 | 10 | 33 |
| Metatarsal | 16 | 11 | 41 | 3 | 2 | 40 | 18 | 7 | 28 | 23 | 10 | 43 | 12 | 17 | 59 |
| Total | 128 | 42 | 25 | 16 | 7 | 30 | 86 | 19 | 18 | 138 | 30 | 18 | 77 | 75 | 49 |
| **(c) Pig** | | | | | | | | | | | | | | | |
| Humerus | 12 | 8 | 44 | 2 | — | 0 | 13 | — | 0 | 21 | 1 | 5 | 16 | 4 | 20 |
| Radius | 25 | 3 | 11 | — | — | — | 5 | 2 | 29 | 14 | 4 | 22 | 7 | 4 | 36 |
| Femur | 12 | 6 | 33 | 1 | — | 0 | 7 | — | 7 | 0 | 1 | 13 | 7 | 4 | 36 |
| Tibia | 44 | 5 | 10 | — | — | — | 12 | — | 0 | 24 | 4 | 14 | 9 | 6 | 40 |
| Metapodia | 16 | 47 | 75 | 2 | 6 | 75 | 3 | 32 | 91 | 8 | 38 | 83 | 8 | 19 | 70 |
| Total | 109 | 69 | 43 | 5 | 6 | 54 | 40 | 34 | 46 | 74 | 48 | 39 | 47 | 37 | 44 |
| **(d) Dog** | | | | | | | | | | | | | | | |
| Humerus | 7 | 8 | 53 | 1 | — | 0 | 3 | 3 | 50 | 2 | 2 | 50 | — | 15 | 100 |
| Radius | 4 | 10 | 71 | 1 | — | 0 | 5 | — | 0 | 2 | 2 | 50 | 3 | 13 | 81 |
| Femur | 1 | 9 | 90 | — | — | — | 1 | 1 | 50 | — | 1 | 100 | 3 | 15 | 83 |
| Tibia | 5 | 6 | 55 | 2 | 1 | 33 | — | 1 | 100 | 3 | 1 | 25 | 2 | 12 | 86 |
| Metapodia | 1 | 6 | 86 | — | 1 | 100 | — | 4 | 100 | 2 | 3 | 60 | — | 36 | 100 |
| Total | 18 | 39 | 68 | 4 | 1 | 20 | 9 | 9 | 50 | 9 | 9 | 50 | 8 | 91 | 92 |
| **(e) Cat** | | | | | | | | | | | | | | | |
| Humerus | 3 | 9 | 75 | — | — | — | 1 | 1 | 50 | 1 | 1 | 50 | 1 | 6 | 86 |
| Radius | 2 | 6 | 75 | — | — | — | 2 | — | 0 | — | — | — | 2 | 3 | 60 |
| Femur | 2 | 6 | 75 | — | 1 | 100 | — | 1 | 100 | 3 | — | 0 | 1 | 4 | 80 |
| Tibia | 2 | 10 | 83 | — | — | — | — | — | — | 2 | — | 0 | — | 8 | 100 |
| Metapodia | 2 | 38 | 95 | — | — | — | — | 2 | 100 | — | 1 | 100 | — | 3 | 100 |
| Total | 11 | 169 | 86 | — | 1 | 100 | 3 | 4 | 57 | 6 | 2 | 25 | 4 | 24 | 86 |

B = Broken. The figure represents the number of either proximal or distal ends of the bone, whichever is greater.

C = Complete.

%C = Percentage of complete bones.

have been different butchery techniques used on animals required for immediate consumption and those intended for salting or smoking and preserving. None of the vertebrae from the Lefevre road site had been split, but many had been chopped across. Some of the Portchester vertebrae had been chopped twice as if chops were being cut.

Ribs had cuts generally made from the inside, but sometimes made from the outside of the animal. They were located both near the articulation with the vertebrae and nearer the belly.

The forelimb seems to have been cut from the carcass at the shoulder joint. Cuts into the distal end of the scapula, and the head of the humerus, where these survive, are very commonly found. The nature of this butchery will of course have had an effect on the survival of any particular part of the body.

The elbow joint is another very common site for cuts, although it is not certain that the cuts in this region resulted in the severance of the bones. They do in fact appear to have been made while the meat was being cut from the bone in this area. The limb might have been severed again between the distal end of the radius and the proximal end of the metacarpus. The majority of the meat on the forelimb lies above this joint, and most of the cuts are found on the bones of the upper part of the limb. Many bones also show the marks of the removal of the flesh from the bone shafts. The spine of the scapula has frequently been cut off, probably when the shoulder meat was removed from the blade of the scapula.

The hind limb seems to have been severed from the body at the hip joint, by cutting off the head of the femur. Detached femur heads are fairly frequently found, and corresponding marks are found in the border of the acetabulum. The pelvis itself is frequently cut in half through the acetabulum.

The cuts on the distal end of the femur and the proximal end of the tibia are similar to those found at the elbow joint, in that they seem to result from cutting off the meat from the bones rather than from severing the leg at this point.

The leg is cut again between the metatarsus and tibia, sometimes between the scapho-cuboid and the astragalus. Because it is difficult to distinguish between front and back phalanges we can only assume that the treatment of each was the same, though occasionally the whole foot has been cut off just above the distal end of the metatarsus. Cuts are rare on first phalanges and very rare on second and third phalanges. When cuts are found they seem either to result from severing the toes from the metapodia, or to be knife marks such as might have resulted from cutting through the ligaments. Such knife marks are also found at the distal ends of the metapodia, and around other joints; knives seem to have been used mainly for severing ligaments and larger tools for cutting up bones.

The toes themselves may have been boiled for glue or stew, or the hoofs cut off and used. Flesh-removing cuts were also found on the bones of the hind limb(pl. XXXIX*b*).

Not enough information was available to build up a picture of the butchery of sheep and pigs, although some evidence of the butchery techniques was found. Evidence of the splitting of the skull through the line of the frontal suture was found for both animals (pl. XXXIX*i, j*), and in the case of the pig, the mandibles were frequently split apart, between the two central incisors. The forelimb of the pig had, on some animals at least, been cut through at the elbow joint.

Pl. XXXIX illustrates a selection of bones with cut marks, mainly from cattle, and fig. 202 is a drawing of a cow with the main butchery points indicated.

Most of this analysis of butchery is based on the cuts seen on the articular facets of the bones. Butchery is likely also to have involved cutting through the shafts of bones, but it is frequently very difficult to be certain whether breaks in the shafts of bones are deliberate or accidental. Table VI shows the percentage of bones found whole for each period and each animal, including dog and cat. It can be seen that the percentage of whole bones is far higher amongst the animals presumed to have been kept as pets and not for food, the cats and dogs. There is also a far higher percentage of whole bones of sheep and pig than of cattle. As has already been mentioned, this must reflect carcass size. A modern shoulder of lamb will include a complete scapula, humerus and most of the radius. The marrow content of the bones might also be reflected in this table — humeri, tibiae and femora are rich in marrow and might have been smashed to remove it. There is no evidence of the Saxon and medieval method of splitting bones longitudinally for marrow in the Roman period. The higher numbers of whole bones from pits and especially wells will reflect the better preservation of bones from these protected contexts.

## AGE STRUCTURE

The aging of the animal bones was attempted by two main methods — epiphyseal fusion and tooth eruption and wear. The dangers of applying modern data on fusion and eruption are understood, but it is less likely that the sequences of eruption and wear will have changed, than the actual ages of these events.

## TABLE VII

| Approximate age at fusion | Bone | | Group 1 | | | Group 2 | | | Group 3 | | | Group 4 | | | Group 5 | | |
|---|---|---|---|---|---|---|---|---|---|---|---|---|---|---|---|---|---|
| | | | UF | F | %F | UF | F | %F | UF | F | %F | UF | F | %F | UF | F | %F |
| (a) *Cattle* 10 months | Pelvis | | 2 | 50 | 96 | — | 7 | 100 | 4 | 39 | 95 | 9 | 66 | 88 | 2 | 33 | 94 |
| 18 months | Humerus Radius 1st phalange 2nd phalange | D P | 18 | 353 | 95 | 1 | 33 | 97 | 1 | 166 | 99 | 10 | 310 | 97 | 4 | 224 | 98 |
| 2–2½ years | Metacarpal Tibia Metatarsal | D D D | 27 | 185 | 87 | 3 | 16 | 84 | 10 | 104 | 91 | 37 | 219 | 85 | 14 | 160 | 92 |
| 3½ years | Calcaneum Femur | P | 32 | 84 | 72 | 0 | 4 | 100 | 14 | 27 | 66 | 23 | 64 | 74 | 23 | 49 | 68 |
| 3½–4 years | Humerus Radius Ulna Femur Tibia | P D P D P | 75 | 130 | 63 | 8 | 8 | 50 | 38 | 62 | 62 | 56 | 100 | 64 | 59 | 95 | 62 |

## Table VII—continued

| Approximate age at fusion | Bone | | Group 1 | | | Group 2 | | | Group 3 | | | Group 4 | | | Group 5 | | |
|---|---|---|---|---|---|---|---|---|---|---|---|---|---|---|---|---|---|
| | | | UF | F | %F | UF | F | %F | UF | F | %F | UF | F | %F | UF | F | %F |
| (b) *Sheep* 10 months | Scapula Humerus Radius Pelvis | D D P | 25 | 101 | 80 | 5 | 1 | 17 | 6 | 53 | 90 | 9 | 69 | 88 | 55 | 33 | 38 |
| 1½–2 years | Metacarpal Tibia Metatarsal | D D D | 22 | 41 | 65 | 4 | 6 | 60 | 8 | 29 | 78 | 25 | 43 | 63 | 38 | 27 | 41 |
| 2½ years | Ulna | | 8 | 6 | 43 | — | — | — | 2 | 1 | 33 | 1 | 1 | 50 | 6 | 1 | 14 |
| 2½–3 years | Femur Calcaneum Radius | P D | 28 | 10 | 26 | 7 | — | 0 | 16 | 10 | 38 | 12 | 8 | 40 | 32 | 11 | 26 |
| 3–3½ years | Humerus Femur Tibia | P D P | 26 | 4 | 13 | 5 | 3 | 38 | 18 | 7 | 28 | 24 | 14 | 37 | 30 | 3 | 9 |
| (c) *Pig* 1 year | Humerus Radius 2nd phalange Pelvis | D P | 18 | 60 | 77 | — | 7 | 100 | 5 | 29 | 85 | 13 | 48 | 79 | 13 | 31 | 70 |
| 2–2¼ years | Metapodia 1st phalange Tibia Calcaneum | D D | 81 | 45 | 36 | 5 | 2 | 28 | 42 | 15 | 26 | 58 | 20 | 26 | 22 | 18 | 45 |
| 3½ years | Humerus Radius Ulna Femur Femur Tibia | P D P D P | 74 | 11 | 13 | 4 | — | 0 | 24 | 3 | 11 | 31 | 2 | 6 | 36 | 4 | 10 |

F = Fused; UF = Unfused; P = Proximal; D = Distal.

Table VII analyses the bones from the main meat animals where evidence of the state of fusion of the bone is present. Each bone has been analysed separately, and then groups have been made of bones that, on modern evidence at least, fuse at more or less the same time. This, it is hoped, will have the effect of ironing out some of the inconsistencies due to poor survival and recovery. The ages used are those given by Silver (1969), but they are intended to be used as a general guide only. It is likely that unfused bones, especially those from animals in their first year, will be under-represented. Higher percentages of young animals than are given in this table might be expected.

The figures reveal a strikingly different age structure in the three animals, with approximately 60 % of the cattle bones coming from animals at least four years old, and only 6–12 % of pig bones and 9–37 % of sheep bones coming from animals of 3½ years or more.

The age structure of the bones found does not necessarily reveal the age structure of the herds and flocks from which the animals were taken. If we are dealing with a society which is self-supporting in terms of its meat supply, then the age structure of the animal bones from the

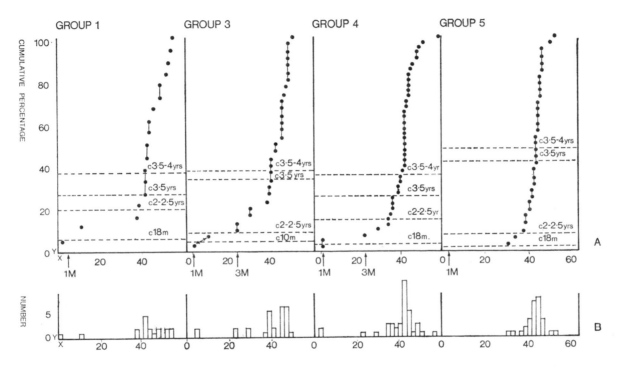

FIG. 203.   Age structure of cattle mandibles (x axis : tooth wear stage)

domestic refuse should closely resemble that of the herd. However, many other situations could exist where the age structure of the food refuse bears little relationship to that of the herd. The meat might be bought entirely from markets or local farms, or the inhabitants of the fort could have kept animals that they used partly for their own meat supply and partly for sale to markets. The animals eaten could be those that were killed because they were not required for traction, milk or wool production. In which case, especially if the non-meat animals were killed or sold elsewhere when they had outlived their usefulness, the age of the food animals might provide a negative picture of the structure of the live herd. The incidence of illness and accidents is also reflected in the age at death of the animals.

The main disadvantage of the epiphyseal fusion method of determining the age of the animals is that it only allows the bone material to be divided into very broad groups, and gives no further information about the ages of animals beyond the date of fusion of the last bone. The writer has been working on tooth wear as a more precise guide to the age of the animals than epiphyseal fusion. Details of this method are laid out in Appendix B, where full details of the wear stages of the Portchester animals are given. The numerical equivalents of these wear stages are plotted against cumulative percentages and as histograms in figs. 203–6 for each animal in each group (excepting group 2 where the sample was again too small for useful analysis). In order to combine the results of both methods of assessing age, the age structure revealed by epiphyseal fusion is also plotted on the graph. Group 1 excludes all pits up to pit 103 and group 5 excludes pit 121. The identification of the bones from these pits was made before the method of analysing tooth wear was fully evolved. The corresponding epiphyseal fusion tables have been adjusted accordingly. It is of course assumed that the bones and teeth come from the same population of animals. This has already been discussed in the previous section. There is a difference in sample size, especially in the case of the pig, where there are far more mandibles than any single long bone. This might be expected to lead to some anomalies in the correlations of the two methods, so they are to be used with an expected margin of error that is greater for pig than for cattle. Of course, if the long bones and mandibles are not from the same animals the correlation will be invalid.

The analysis of cattle jaws is shown in fig. 203. There seems to be a fair degree of consistency in the age at death from period to period as shown by the slope of the curve, although there are small differences revealed on closer examination. The most common age at death of the animals is about $3\frac{1}{2}$–4 years in group 1, slightly later in group 4 and perhaps nearer $4\frac{1}{2}$ or 5 years in groups 3 and 5, where the peak occurs at stages 45 to 48. The interval of time between stages will be far greater between the higher numbers than between the lower numbers representing wear stages. This is discussed in the appendix. Very few animals were eaten which were older than those at the peak killing age in each group. Group 4 has the largest number of old animals, while group 3 has the smallest. The oldest animal found at the site is represented by the mandible in group 4 which has a wear stage of 57+. This animal must have been very old. It is unfortunate that it is not possible at the moment to correlate sex with age as this would aid greatly an interpretation of the animal husbandry. It is unusual to keep bulls to a very great age because they present a major management problem, so this animal is perhaps a very old cow.

Very few young animals are found amongst the Portchester cattle bones. Group 5 has the lowest percentage and groups 1 and 3 the highest. We might have expected generally higher percentages of young animals which had either been killed for the purposes of herd management or had died from natural causes. The animals could have been kept primarily for traction or milk, with the young animals that were surplus to these requirements sold off elsewhere. Roman writers quoted by White (1970) discuss the practice of not allowing a cow to conceive until she was at least two or even four years old. Milk animals would thus be relatively old animals. Oxen used for traction would also be fairly old before they were killed off to ensure sufficient return for the trouble of training them.

Fig. 204 shows the analysis of sheep mandibles. It is a great disadvantage not to be able to distinguish between sheep and goat for the purpose of this analysis, since the management of these animals may well have been entirely different. On the whole, the climate of England is more favourable to sheep than to goats, since these latter animals are very sensitive to changes of temperature. We might expect that more sheep than goats were kept, but the presence of horn cores from both species indicates that some goats were kept as well. It would be dangerous to calculate their relative proportions merely on the basis of the horn cores since these bones might reflect a difference in industrial use; however, the majority of goat horn cores were found in group 4.

There is a similar pattern in the age structure of the first three groups, but group 5 shows a far higher proportion of young animals. In groups 1 and 3, the peak killing age is between 1½

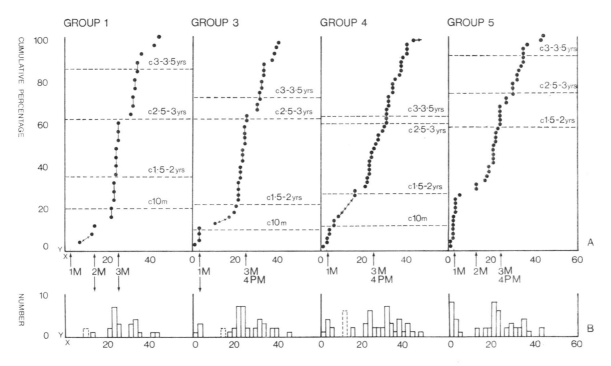

FIG. 204.    Age structure of sheep/goat mandibles (x axis : tooth wear stage)

and 2½ years, probably in the early part of the period at wear stages 21 to 24. In group 4 there is also a peak at this stage, but another at wear stages 31 and 32, possibly representing animals of about 3–3½ years. The first two groups have a slightly smaller peak at this stage. Groups 3 and 4 have younger animals represented than group 1, but this might only reflect the small size of the sample in group 1. The distribution of tooth wear stages is not continuous and there appear to have been ages when animals were not killed. This is represented in groups 1 and 3 by the gaps between stages 25 and 30. It raises the vexed question of autumn killing. We might be seeing, especially in groups 3 and 4, peaks at six months, 1½ years and then 3½ years, which could possibly reflect an autumn killing policy. There is evidence discussed in the section on disease that the plane of nutrition was relatively low. If this is so, winter feeding might have presented difficulties.

The mandibles of group 5 reflect a slightly different picture, in the very high percentage of young animals found. However, the date of this group overlaps that of groups 1, 2, 3 and part of 4, so we are probably not seeing the results of any changes in animal husbandry or of sudden illness affecting new-born animals, but a deliberate disposal of the carcasses of young animals in the wells. If we examine the pit summaries given in the main text, it is clear that some pits and especially wells contain animal bones which do not seem to be the result of

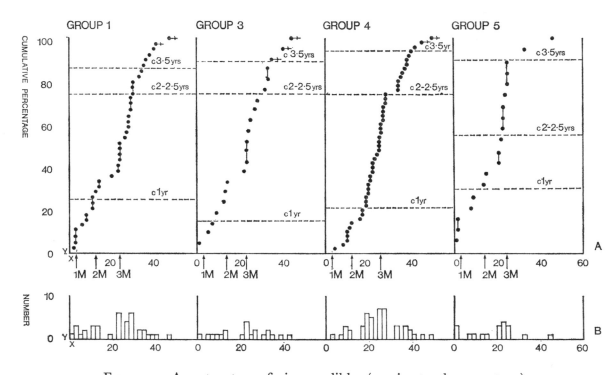

FIG. 205.   Age structure of pig mandibles (x axis : tooth wear stage)

haphazard rubbish disposal. These are the pits with young animal carcasses, whole ox skulls, complete dog and cat skeletons and human infant bones. It would appear that some significance was attached to the deposits thrown into wells and the high percentage of young sheep found there might reflect this.

Some animals were evidently kept for some time after the second peak at stages 30 to 34, although after this time most groups show a more gradual kill-off of animals. The oldest animals are those represented by stages 45 and 47+. These might be from animals of seven or eight years.

Fig. 205 gives the analysis of pig mandibles. The pattern is similar from group to group, with the peak stage for killing falling between 21 and 26. This might occur at the end of the second year. The eruption of the third molar occurs at this time, and this would agree with Silver's date of 17 to 23 months for the eruption of this tooth. Even if the actual ages are not accurate for ancient animals, it would imply that the sequence was correct.

In group 4 it would appear that animals were killed fairly evenly throughout the period represented, including during the first year. Young animals also seem to have been killed off throughout the first year in the other periods, with the highest number of young animals found in groups 1 and 5. This reflects the higher percentages of young sheep in these groups, but contrasts with the small numbers of young cattle, especially in group 5. In groups 1 and 3 we find only a few animals between two and three years, although more were killed at this time in groups 4 and 5.

It would appear to have been uncommon practice to keep very old pigs at the site. The oldest animals are represented by those with wear stages of 45 to 50 +. The age structure of the pig mandibles reveals the sort of pattern one might expect where pigs are kept as part of the household or social group and killed off as they are needed. White (1970) quotes Tremulus Scrofa as saying that 'in our fathers' day the man who went to the butcher to buy the flitch that hangs in his larder was called a lazy spendthrift'. Pigs are some of the easiest of animals to keep as they will more or less feed themselves by foraging and eating scraps. This is discussed in the appendix: the pig's omnivorous feeding habits have an effect on the amount of tooth wear.

Throughout this section, the writer has used the ages of epiphyseal fusion given by Silver to facilitate discussion of the age structure. The age at which bones fuse and teeth erupt depends on many factors such as breed, sex, age of castration, and planes of nutrition. Modern breeds have been 'improved' to obtain more rapid maturity. It is likely that, before selective breeding, maturity was reached slightly later. This means that the fusion ages and eruption dates used are probably slightly too young. This should not however affect the relative age structure of the group.

## METRICAL ANALYSIS

Measurements were taken of bones when their condition made it possible. It is always hoped that measurements taken on bones will reveal the sex structure of the bones as well as indicate size and possibly breed of animals. However, determining the sex structure of a group of animal bones is by no means easy, especially when there are males, females and also castrates present in the sample. We would certainly expect to find castrates here, as in most samples of animal bones that were closely related to human populations. Analysis of the cattle metapodia using the method proposed by Howard (1963) was undertaken. The indices

$$\frac{\text{Distal breadth}}{\text{Length}} \times 100 \text{ and } \frac{\text{Minimum transverse diaphyseal breadth}}{\text{Length}} \times 100$$

were calculated for each complete metapodial. The second index calculated is slightly different to that used by Howard. She used the transverse breadth at the mid-point of the overall length of the bone. However, since the minimum diaphyseal breadth almost always occurs at or near the mid-point of the bone, there is not likely to be very much difference in the results. The results of the calculations on the metatarsals did not give satisfactory results. It is known that there is generally less sexual dimorphism in this bone than in the corresponding bone of the front leg. The indices calculated for the metacarpals are given in table VIII, and plotted as a histogram in fig. 206. The upper and lower extremes of the range can be taken fairly confidently as respectively males and females. Where the females/castrates and castrates/males

## TABLE VIII

| Distal index | Possible sex | Shaft index | Possible sex | Distal index | Possible sex | Shaft index | Possible sex | Distal index | Possible sex | Shaft index | Possible sex |
|---|---|---|---|---|---|---|---|---|---|---|---|
| *Group 1* | | | | *Group 3* | | | | *Group 4* | | | |
| 33·5 | C | 16·3 | F | 32 | C | 17·3 | C | 28·0 | F | 15·3 | F |
| 31·3 | C | 17·6 | C | 31·9 | C | 19·3 | M | 29·1 | F | 15·2 | F |
| 30 | C | 15·7 | F | 26·8 | F | 15·8 | F | 27·8 | F | 15·4 | F |
| 35·4 | M | 18·7 | C/M | 31·9 | C | 18·5 | C | 34 | M | 18·6 | C/M |
| 29·4 | F | 15·8 | F | 28·7 | F | 16 | F | 27·8 | F | 15·9 | F |
| 28·5 | F | 15·0 | F | 28·3 | F | 14·9 | F | 23·6 | F | 12 | F |
| 31·4 | C | 18·6 | C | 26·3 | F | 13·2 | F | 29·4 | F | 15·7 | F |
| 34·2 | M | 18·1 | C | 27 | F | 14·8 | F | 27·7 | F | 13·4 | F |
| 33·4 | C | 20 | M | 29 | F | 15·5 | F | 32·4 | C | 18 | C |
| 30·5 | F/C | 15·9 | F | 31·7 | C | 18·1 | C | 28·3 | F | 15·4 | F |
| 27·5 | F | 15·5 | F | 29·4 | F | 15·7 | F | 34·8 | M | 20 | M |
| 29·9 | F | 16·0 | F | 27·2 | F | 14·7 | F | | | | |
| 33·3 | C | 19·2 | C/M | — | — | 15·6 | F | *Group 5* | | | |
| 26·4 | F | 13·7 | F | 28·7 | F | 16·5 | F | 28·5 | F | 16 | F |
| 30·3 | C | 15·9 | F | 30·3 | C | 17 | F/C | 31 | C | 15·8 | F |
| 29·2 | F | 15·7 | F | 33 | C | 18·7 | C | 32·9 | C | 18·6 | C |
| 33·2 | C | 17·6 | C | | | | | 28·7 | F | 15·4 | F |
| 32·6 | C | 17·0 | C | | | | | 29·4 | F | 15·3 | F |
| 28·2 | F | 14·3 | F | *Group 4* | | | | 31·9 | C | 18 | C |
| 35·6 | M | 19·8 | M | 29 | F | 13·2 | F | 29·3 | F | 15·8 | F |
| 27·6 | F | 14·0 | F | 27·6 | F | 14·9 | F | 32·9 | C | 17·4 | C |
| 35 | M | 19·1 | M | 29·1 | F | 15·8 | F | 33·2 | C | 18 | C |
| 31·6 | C | 17·1 | C | 27·3 | F | 14 | F | 26·9 | F | 14 | F |
| 28·9 | F | 15·1 | F | 28·5 | F | — | — | 35·2 | M | 19·7 | M |
| 31·5 | C | 17·2 | C | 31·1 | C | 18·0 | C | 28·2 | F | 14·5 | F |
| 33·3 | C | 17·5 | C | 29·1 | F | 16·4 | F | 27 | F | 16·8 | F |
| 31·4 | C | 18·2 | C | 34·5 | M | 18·3 | C | 29 | F | 15·7 | F |
| 26·8 | F | 14·8 | F | 32·1 | C | 18·1 | C | 34·9 | M | 19·8 | M |
| 35·1 | M | 19·3 | M | 31·9 | C | 17·7 | C | 29·8 | F | — | — |
| 28·9 | F | 15·5 | F | 29·1 | F | 17 | F/C | 30·9 | F/C | 15·9 | F |
| 27·5 | F | 15·7 | F | 30·5 | F/C | 16·9 | F | 31·5 | C | 18·2 | C |
| 27·8 | F | 14·9 | F | 28·2 | F | 15 | F | 27·2 | F | 15·9 | F |
| 28·6 | F | 15·4 | F | 28·5 | F | 16 | F | 34·2 | M | 18·5 | C/M |
| 28·7 | F | 15·3 | F | 22·9 | F | 15·4 | F | 27 | F | 14·4 | F |
| 29·5 | F | 16 | F | 29·5 | F | 17 | C/F | 26·7 | F | 14·6 | F |
| 31·1 | C | 16·3 | F | 28·7 | F | 15·7 | F | 26·4 | F | 13·4 | F |
| 29 | F | 16 | F | 27·6 | F | 15·1 | F | 27·3 | F | 15·9 | F |
| 27·5 | F | 13·3 | F | | | | | 33·5 | C/M | 19·5 | M |
| *Group 2* | | | | | | | | 27·6 | F | 15·9 | F |
| 28·1 | F | 15·4 | F | F = Female; C = Castrate; | | | | 26·6 | F | 14·7 | F |
| 31·9 | C | 17·5 | C | M = Male. | | | | 28·2 | F | — | — |

## TABLE IX

| Group | ♀ No. | ♀ % | ♀ or ♂ No. | ♀ or ♂ % | ♂̊ No. | ♂̊ % | ♀ or ♂ No. | ♀ or ♂ % | ♂ No. | ♂ % |
|---|---|---|---|---|---|---|---|---|---|---|
| 1 and 2 | 22 | 51 | 6 | 13 | 9 | 21 | 2 | 5 | 4 | 9 |
| 3 | 10 | 63 | 1 | 6 | 4 | 25 | 1 | 6 | — | — |
| 4 | 33 | 83 | — | — | 4 | 10 | 2 | 5 | 1 | 2 |
| 5 | 19 | 63 | 2 | 7 | 5 | 17 | 1 | 3 | 3 | 10 |
| Total | 84 | 65 | 9 | 7 | 22 | 17 | 6 | 5 | 8 | 6 |

borders lie is not so clear. There is likely to have been some degree of overlap between the groups that makes interpretation difficult. The dotted lines on the figure indicate the possible sexual groupings, but these are extremely tentative. The problem was further complicated when the two indices calculated for the same bone gave differing results. Plotting the indices against the length of the bone did nothing to clarify the position. However, if we accept the sexual divisions given in table VIII and fig. 206 the results shown in table IX are obtained. This of course will only reflect the sex structure of the animals of 2–2½ years and more. This is the age at which the metacarpals fuse. No measurements were taken of immature bones.

The indications are that the majority of the cattle bones are from females, with very small numbers of bulls and a few castrates. Varro (White, 1970) gives a ratio of one bull to every 60 cows, while Columella gives a ratio of 1 to 15 cows. The writer has already discussed the possibility that the cattle were being kept primarily for milk.

One of the problems of trying to define sexual dimorphism is that the proportions of the bones are affected not only by the sex of the animal but also by the breed, the age that castration is carried out, the plane of nutrition and the age of the animal at death (*vide* Hammond *et al.*, 1971). If the animal bones are from a mixed population, fed at different levels, there will be considerable difficulty in reliably determining the sex of the bones.

Measurements of the distal ends of the tibia and length and distal breadth of the metatarsal used by Jewell (1962) in his analysis of size changes in cattle indicate that as at Corstopitum, the Roman site in his analysis, both small cattle and much larger animals are present at Portchester. Table X gives the range and number of these measurements and those from Corstopitum.

## TABLE X

(a) *Distal width of tibia*

| | | |
|---|---|---|
| Portchester | 50–69 mm. | No. = 143 |
| Corstopitum | 45–68 mm. | No. = 78 |

(b) *Length and distal width of metatarsal*

| | Distal width | | Length | |
|---|---|---|---|---|
| Portchester | 43–70 mm. | No. = 172 | 183–240 mm. | No. = 108 |
| Corstopitum | 42–65 mm. | No. = 127 | 181–244 mm. | No. = 67 |

27

This shows animals as small as the Iron Age cattle and as large as modern shorthorns. The Romans are supposed to have introduced larger breeds of cattle into Britain. These measurements support this view.

No further analysis of the measurements of the animals has been attempted at this moment. However, full details of the measurements of all the Portchester animals can be obtained from the writer.

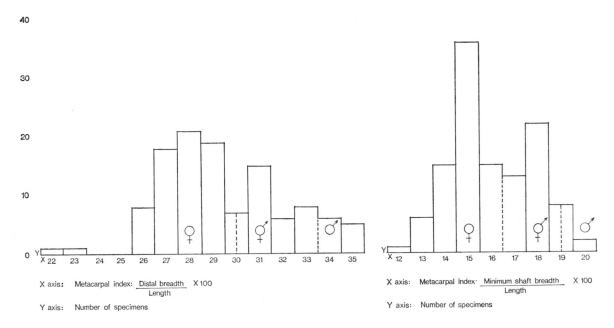

FIG. 206.   Ox metacarpals

# DISEASE AND INJURY

The bones of the animals were examined for evidence of disease. The majority of the bones came from apparently healthy animals, but of course many of the animals probably in fact suffered from diseases and parasites that did not affect the bone. Only a few diseases commonly affect the bone, although the advanced stages of other diseases which in their early stages affect the tissue may also affect the bony substances. The diseases and injuries of the bones that were seen fall into three main groups: these are, arthritis and allied conditions, dental diseases and anomalies, fractures and trauma.

*Arthritis and Allied Conditions*

Evidence of disease was found at some of the joints of cattle bones that may have been caused by arthritis or other similar conditions. The joints most commonly affected were the hip joints and the ankle joints. These conditions are rarely found in sheep or pig bones, but this might be because old animals occur so rarely amongst the sheep and pigs. Where deposition of bone has occurred within the joint, eburnation or polishing of the joint surface occurs.

Pl. XXXVII*i* shows two tarsals fused together and proliferation of bone at the margin and pl. XXXVII*h* shows a metatarsal fairly severely affected by a disease resulting in erosion and deposition of the bone. In some cases, the degree of severity of the condition would have made the animal quite lame.

## Dental Diseases and Anomalies

The jaws of sheep are most commonly affected by disease. Sheep are very prone to periodontal disease — this remains a problem even today where premature incisor loss in sheep is a problem without a clear-cut solution. The problem is discussed in detail by Duckworth *et al.* (1962) who believe that one of the causes might be dietary deficiency. Certainly the main result is inability to feed properly and consequent starvation. The periodontal disease in the Portchester animals is generally recognized by a reduction of the bone just below the teeth causing the teeth to become very loose in their sockets. Although the incisors are rarely found and the front part of the jaw is almost invariably damaged, it is likely that the incisors would have been affected as well. In some severe cases abscesses are found as well. Pl. XXXVII*a* and *b* show a mandible and a maxilla with fairly severe periodontal disease. It is surprising that the farmer did not kill these animals sooner, as their ability to feed is likely to have been badly affected. Periodontal disease is not by any means a rare occurrence amongst the Portchester mandibles, which might indicate that they were feeding at a low nutritional level. The older the animal is, the more likely it is to become diseased, and so the age structure of the herds might reflect the difficulty of keeping healthy animals beyond three or four years. The animal husbandry will reflect a compromise between what is desired in terms of marketable commodities and meat supply, and what the food availability and the health of the animals will allow.

Sheep mandibles are also very prone to overcrowding, especially when the deciduous molars are replaced by the permanent premolars. It is a rare occurrence to find a sheep mandible that does not exhibit some degree of overcrowding of the teeth. Overcrowding is also seen in pig jaws where it may cause rotation of the teeth, especially the premolars. It is far rarer in cattle jaws. The congenital absence of the second premolar was found in cattle jaws as was the absence of the third pillar on some third molars. These anomalies have been noted on other prehistoric material (Jackson, 1948). It is not known whether they are linked to inheritance or are random mutations.

## Fractures and Trauma

Several bones of various species were found with signs of rehealed fractures. These fractures were found in the limbs of smaller animals and only in the ribs of cattle. It is not usually possible to do anything with a cow or horse that has broken its leg; the only economic course of action is slaughter. Smaller animals are well able to get around on three legs and so a broken limb would not be too great an inconvenience, especially to a dog or a cat. Pl. XXXVII*c–f* and *k* shows a selection of bones with rehealed fractures. The dog radius and ulna have a large amount of irregular bony growth around the site of the fracture which indicates that it was hanging loose and unsupported for some time, before the bones began to fuse together. In fact the radius was not completely fused at death. This would argue against the use of splints to aid rehealing, although the pig tibia and sheep metatarsal, *c* and *d*, have healed fairly neatly and so might have been splinted. The bird femur, *f*, shows how little a fracture would affect a small animal — the distal part of the bone is severely displaced and yet the bird evidently survived some time after the fracture. A piece of cattle humerus showed a fairly unusual feature. A fragment of the shaft of the bone seemed to have been detached from the main part of the bone and had moved from its original position before fusing with the bone again. The limb itself presumably would not have been completely broken, hence the survival of the animal for some time after the fracture.

Other examples of trauma were seen that would have had very little effect on the animal at all, like the blow to the horn cores of a sheep, shown in pl. XXXVII*m*, which merely caused a restriction of the bone at the point of the blow, and was then followed by normal growth.

In a few cases the extent of the injury or disease was so great that the animal affected would have been seriously incapacitated. Pl. XXXVII*b* shows an ox tibia with very severe destruction of the proximal end, possibly due to an infected abscess. The amount of ossification would indicate that some time had elapsed since the abscess burst. Pl. XXXVII*g* shows the second and third phalanges of a cow fused together. This must have been the result of a very severe infection of the foot.

Both of these animals would have been made lame by their conditions and would probably not have been able to feed themselves effectively in open pasture. This raises the possibility that there were stalling facilities in or near the fort for injured animals that it was not thought expedient to kill, and perhaps for pregnant and nursing animals.

The value of an examination of diseased bones lies not just in the evidence it provides for the incidence of disease in ancient animal populations, but on the information it might give on the nature of the animal husbandry, the feeding levels, veterinary practices and possible use of stalls even where there is no direct archaeological evidence for them.

# CONCLUSIONS

*Cattle*

Although much was written by Romans about the animals of Italy and the neighbouring areas, we have little documentary evidence about areas as far afield as Britain and so must rely almost exclusively on archaeological evidence. The Roman writers paid little attention to breed, even in their own country, and so we can only give the most general discussion of this question, especially when colour and type of hair are important in the diagnosis of particular breeds. Where they were whole, most of the skulls recovered were of the same general type, although there was some variation in the form of the horn core. This is seen in pl. XXXVIII*a* and *g*. Pl. XXXVII*c* shows the only example recognized of a different type of skull — one with a prominent frontal eminence.

The evidence of the measurements of the bones indicates a wide range of sizes of animals, although it is not certain that these necessarily reflect breed differences. We have discussed the possibility that the cattle may be predominantly female, and kept for milk rather than meat, although there is no doubt that they were eaten in the end, from the frequency with which butchery cuts are found.

Cattle probably provided all sorts of by-products that would leave no trace in the archaeological record, from hides to paint brushes to glue and blood. Most peoples will exploit all the possibilities of an animal carcass, and cattle certainly provide many, as well as a large amount of meat.

### Sheep and Goats

The evidence of the horn cores certainly implies that both species were present although in what proportions it is impossible to say. There is also evidence of a hornless breed of sheep, illustrated in pl. XXXIX*j*. The bones of many of the animals are small and slender, although larger and more robust bones are also found. It is not clear whether the animals were intended mainly for meat, milk or wool, although in any case all three products would undoubtedly have been utilized. Lamb — or occasionally mutton — provided a fairly small though not insignificant proportion of the meat diet. The animals seem to have been troubled by diseases of the mouth and in fact the location of Portchester was probably more suitable for cattle than for sheep rearing. It is possible that they were killed off in peaks before the winter. This, and the incidence of dental and periodontal disease may imply a lack of suitable food for the winter, making the keeping of too many store animals through this season uneconomical.

### Pigs

Again there is possible evidence of two breeds of pigs — one with a shallow sloping forehead and one with a more raised and prominent nuchal crest, although the evidence is rather fragmentary.

Pigs can only be kept for meat, as they give neither milk nor wool, and are certainly not suitable for traction. They may have been left to forage in or around the fort, and killed when there was a need for meat.

### Birds

These are the subject of a separate report (pp. 409–15).

### Dogs

A selection of dog bones was sent to Mr R. Harcourt whose report is appended (pp. 406–8). The writer is in agreement with the conclusions reached by Mr Harcourt.

### Cats

The most significant feature of the cats is their presence in such large numbers. They can only be presumed to have been pets and strays living in and around the fort. The fact that several whole carcasses were put in wells and pits might imply that some at least were kept as pets.

### Horses

These animals are represented in very small numbers at the site. This may be a result of special treatment of the dead animals, or it may mean a lack of importance of the horse to the economy.

*Deer*

Red, roe and fallow deer were all found, although red deer were by far the most common at the site. The majority of the bone fragments identified as red deer were from antlers. This indicates their importance as a source of raw material rather than food. The report on the bone small finds shows that both antlers and metapodia were commonly used for tool manufacture. Antlers could be picked up in the forested areas at some times of the year, although they are not as common as might be expected since the deer themselves eat them as sources of minerals.

Fallow deer are supposed to have been introduced into Britain by the Romans, so it is interesting to find them at the site, even if only in very small numbers.

*Hare, Fox, Badger, Vole, Fish and Mouse*

The small numbers of the remains of wild animals apart from deer indicate that they did not form a significant part of the economy, although the Romans are known to have had a very catholic taste in food. Fish, despite its poor representation, should be expected to have provided a reasonable proportion of the food. The representation of all these small animals is probably very much underestimated because they have a very small chance of recovery.

We have at Portchester a picture of an economy based on beef as the main source of meat. It seems more likely that the inhabitants were self-supporting than that they brought in meat from the markets, especially in the light of the lack of major industrial activity so far discovered at the site. The level of the economy is impossible to assess, although analysis of the bones from the later periods might help to isolate the factors determined by environment from those determined by choice and deliberate policy on the part of the inhabitants.

The division of the bone material into different groups has not revealed any startling differences. In fact many of the differences may be due to the different type of location from which the bones were recovered. Other differences may be more significant, but it does not seem as if there were any major economic changes made during the Roman occupation of the fort.

# ACKNOWLEDGEMENTS

I would like to thank Mr E. S. Higgs, Mrs H. Jarman and Mr D. Allen for their help on some points of identification. Messrs. Peter Robins and Bari Hooper gave valuable advice on the diseased bones. I would also like to thank Mr Harcourt for looking at the dog bones, and Professor Cunliffe for his encouragement and discussions.

# THE DOG BONES

## by R. Harcourt

A minimum of 14 animals was represented and they showed the wide variation in size characteristics of dogs in the Romano-British period. The shoulder heights ranged from an estimated 25 cm. (10 in.), similar to that of a modern toy poodle, to 63 cm. (25 in.), which is as tall as an Alsatian. Height apart, no other resemblance to such modern breeds is implied by these comparisons.

As is nearly always the case the shortest bones were relatively the stoutest, but in no instance did any of the long bones show any appreciable bowing, a feature quite common among Roman dogs, but not yet seen by the writer in those of any other period.

## TABLE XI

*Measurements of Long Bones*

|          | No. | Range (mm.) | msd Index[1] (%) | Ht.[2] (cm.) |
|----------|-----|-------------|-------------------|--------------|
| Humerus  | 12  | 85–191      | 6·7–10·6          | 28–60        |
| Radius   | 9   | 76–202      | 6·4–11·8          | 25–65        |
| Ulna     | 7   | 88–235      | —                 | 24–63        |
| Femur    | 9   | 86–208      | 6·5–10·5          | 26–63        |
| Tibia    | 6   | 99–213      | 6·6–10            | 29–62        |

[1] msd Index = midshaft diameter expressed as a percentage of the total length.

[2] Ht. = shoulder height. The total length in millimetres of the humerus is multiplied by 3·37, radius by 3·22, ulna by 2·67, femur by 3·01 and tibia by 2·92 to give the height in centimetres. The result is an estimate only.

There were three complete skulls of which the measurements are shown in table XII. The dimensions of these varied but their overall shape and relative proportions were very similar, a fact best shown by the small variation in the values of the cranial, snout and snout width indices. These give, respectively, a measure of the breadth of the skull, the length of the snout and the breadth of the muzzle, allowing a comparison to be made between skulls of widely differing sizes.

One bone showed a pathological abnormality. This was a right tibia from trench 95 layer 150. The upper 3 cm. of the shaft were tilted sideways which had had the effect of tilting the

## TABLE XII

*Measurements of Skulls from Well (Pit) 144*

| Feature no. | Layer 150 | Layer 151 | |
|-------------|-----------|-----------|---|
| I. Occipital protuberance to anterior margin of incisors | 161 | 193 | 216 |
| II. Occipital protuberance to posterior junction of nasal bones | 92 | 107 | 121 |
| III. Posterior junction of nasal bones to anterior margin of incisors | 78 | 95 | 105 |
| IV. Bizygomatic breadth | 91 | 105 | 111 |
| IX. Palatal length | 74 | 93 | 97 |
| X. Palatal breadth PM$^4$/M$^1$ | 53 | 60 | 64 |
| XI. Length of maxillary tooth row | 53 | 66 | 69 |
| XII. Width of snout across canine alveoli | 31 | 39 | 40 |
| XV. Length of mandibular cheek tooth row | — | 73 | 76 |
| Length of lower first molar (M$^1$) | — | 21·5 | 22·1 |
| Cranial index IV/I . 1000 | 56·5 | 54·5 | 51·5 |
| Snout index III/I . 100 | 48·5 | 49 | 48·5 |
| Snout width index XII/III . 100 | 39·7 | 41 | 38 |

articular surface sideways and slightly backwards. In addition, the upper half of the outer margin of the shaft was less rounded than normal. Such a distortion could have occurred only when the animal was young and the bone still plastic and may have been brought about by an interference with the blood supply to the uppermost part of the bone.

It should not be assumed that early and prehistoric dogs were necessarily used for any particular purpose and it is quite possible that those of medium size, at any rate, were nothing more than scavengers living by their wits, performing a very useful function none the less. Furthermore, size alone is an unreliable guide to the ability of a dog to perform a given task; at the present day the spectrum of dogs used for 'hunting' of one sort or another extends from small terriers to large hounds. It seems, however, highly probable that the smallest dogs found at this site, and others even smaller found at other Roman sites, must have been house dogs kept as pets. It is hard to imagine how else they could have survived. The largest of those present here could have been guard dogs.

# BIBLIOGRAPHY

BRAIN, C. 1969. 'The contribution of Namib Desert Hottentots to an understanding of Australopithecine bone accumulations'. *Scientific Papers of the Namib Desert Research Station*, xxxix, 13–22.

CARTER, P. L. and PHILLIPSON, D. and HIGGS, E. S. 1965. 'The animal bones', in Hastings, Cunliffe *et al.*, 'The excavation of an Iron Age farmstead at Hawks Hill, Leatherhead'. *Surrey Archaeol. Coll.* lxii.

CHAPLIN, R. E. 1971. *The Study of Animal Bones from Archaeological Sites*. London.

CLASON, A. T. 1972. 'Some remarks on the use and presentation of archaeozoological data'. *Helinium*, xii, 139–53.

DAVIES, R. W. 1971. 'The Roman military diet'. *Britannia*, ii, 122–42.

DUCKWORTH, J., HILL, R., BENZIE, D. and DALGARNO, A. C. with ROBINSON, J. F. 1962. 'Studies in the dentition of sheep: I. Clinical observations into the shedding of permanent incisor teeth by hill sheep'. *Res. Vet. Sci.* iii.

GRANT, A. 1971. 'The animal bones', in Cunliffe, B. W., *Excavations at Fishbourne 1961–69*, II. London, pp. 377–88.

HAMMETT, A. C. and NEVELL, W. H. 1929. *A Handbook on Meat and Textbook for Butchers*. London.

HAMMOND, J., MASON, I. L. and ROBINSON, T. J. 1971. *Hammond's Farm Animals*. London.

HOWARD, M. 1963. *The metrical determination of the metapodials and skulls of cattle*. Royal Anth. Institute Occ. Papers.

ISAAC, G. L. 1967. 'Towards the interpretation of occupational debris: some experiments and observations'. *Kroeber Anth. Soc. Papers*, xxxvii, 31–57.

JACKSON, W. 1948. 'The animal remains from Little Woodbury'. *Proc. Prehist. Soc.* xiv, 19–23.

JEWELL, P. A. 1962. 'Changes in size and type of cattle from prehistoric to medieval times in Britain'. *Zeits. f. Tierz. u. Zuchtungsb.* lxxviii, 159–67.

PAYNE, S. 1972. 'On the interpretation of bone samples from archaeological sites', in Higgs, E. S., *Papers in Economic Prehistory*. Cambridge.

RIXSON, D. 1971. 'The animal bones', in Sheldon, H., 'Excavations at Lefevre Road, Old Ford, E.3'. *Trans. Lond. Middx. Arch. Soc.* xxiii, 42–77.

ROSENBAUM, S. 1959. 'A Significant Chart for Percentages'. *Applied Statistics*, viii, 45–52.

SILVER, I. A. 1969. 'The ageing of domestic animals', in Brothwell, D. and Higgs, E. S., *Science in Archaeology*. London.

WHITE, K. D. 1970. *Roman Farming*. London.

# XII. THE BIRD BONES

## by ANNE EASTHAM

AT Portchester Castle bird bones were found in many of the very numerous rubbish pits scattered around the site. We can assume that all the skeletal remains were deliberately disposed of in these pits, that probably none of the species arrived there by accident and that most of them were eaten. The list given below shows that, while the number of species is small, certain of them are surprising and unusual and apart from raven and jackdaw no passerines were found on the site.

*List of species*

| | |
|---|---|
| *Gallus gallus* | Domestic fowl. |
| *Pavo cristatus* | Peacock. |
| *Gavia immer* | Great Northern Diver. |
| *Anser anser* | Grey lag goose. |
| *Tadorna tadorna* | Shelduck. |
| *Anas platyrrhyncos* | Mallard. |
| *Anas crecca* | Teal. |
| *Anas querquedula* | Garganey. |
| *Anas penelope* | Wigeon. |
| *Falco tinnunculus* | Kestrel. |
| *Perdix perdix* | Common partridge. |
| *? Scolopax rusticola* | Woodcock. |
| *Sterna hirundo* | Common tern. |
| *Columba livia* | Rock dove. |
| *Corvus corax* | Raven. |
| *Corvus monedula* | Jackdaw. |

As the accompanying table shows (table XIII), out of a total of 378 bones 234 belonged to domesticated fowl and peacock, 95 were waterfowl, and 9 were bones of gamebird and pigeon, all of which could have been consumed, though the flesh of the diver is extremely unpalatable. The remainder, 29 raven bones, 7 jackdaw, 3 tern and 1 kestrel died or were killed for perhaps a variety of reasons other than for the table.

The most common species is, as might be expected, the farmyard fowl, with a total of 230 bones. Out of the thirty-two pits in which bird remains were found, chickens appeared in all but one of them. Seven pits and gullies 3 and 9 contained only chicken. In pits 12, 62, 107, 121 and 223 fowl bones were accompanied by those of Mallard or domesticated duck. However, the total number of individuals does not appear on the basis of comparative size and the number of bones to have been large. The chart below suggests a total of between 48 and 60 individuals from the whole site. The greatest concentration of bones was 90 in pit 92

## TABLE XIII

*Numbers of Bird Bones Discovered*

Cell values are given as **L / R** (left / right). A single value with no slash partner is shown on its side.

| Bone | P/D | Gallus gallus | Pavo cristatus | Gavia immer | Anser anser | Tadorna tadorna | Anas platyrrhyncos | Anas crecca | Anas penelope | Anas querquedula | Falco tinnunculus | Perdix perdix | ?Scolopax rusticola | Sterna | ? hirundo | Columba livia | Corvus corax | Corvus. monedula |
|---|---|---|---|---|---|---|---|---|---|---|---|---|---|---|---|---|---|---|
| Skull | | | | 1 / | | | | | | | | | | | | | 1 / | |
| Mandible – upper | | | | 1 / 1 | | | | | | 1 / | | | | | | | | |
|       – lower | | | | 1 / 1 | | | | | | | | | | | | | 1 / | 1 / |
| Coracoid | | 7 / 7 | | 1 / 1 | | | 4 / 2 | | | 1 / | | | | | | 2 / 1 | | |
| Sternum | | 1 / 1 | | | | | 4 / | | | | | | | | | | | |
| Furcula | | 9 / | | 1 / | | | 3 / | | / 1 | | | | | | | | | |
| Scapula | | 5 / 3 | | 1 / | | | 2 / | | | | | | | | | | | |
| Vertebrae | | 3 / | | / 3 | | | 3 / | | | | | | | | | | | |
| Ribs | | | | | | | | | | | | | | | | | | |
| Pelvis | | 1 / 3 | | | | | | | | | | | | | | | | |
| Humerus | P | 12 / 16 | 2 / | 1 / 1 | / 1 | | 3 / 1 | | | | | | | 1 / | | 1 / 1 | 4 / 3 | |
| | D | | | | | | | | | | | | | | | | | |
| Radius | P | 13 / 8 | | 1 / | | / 1 | 2 / 5 | 1 / | | | | | 1 / | | | | | |
| | D | | | | | | | | | | | | | | | | | |
| Ulna | P | 13 / 11 | | 1 / 1 | | 1 / | 10 / 4 | | | | | | | 1 / | | 2 / | 6 / 4 | |
| | D | | | | | | | | | | / 1 | | | | | | | |
| Carpo-Metacarpus | P | 7 / 5 | | 1 / | | | 7 / 2 | 1 / | | | | | | | 1 / | | | 1 / 1 |
| | D | | | | | | | | | | | | | | | | | |
| Digits | | | | | | | | | | | | | | | | | | |
| Femur | P | 14 / 13 | | 1 / | | | 2 / | | | | | 1 / | | | | | 2 / 3 | 3 / 2 |
| | D | | | / 1 | | | | | | | | | | | | | | |
| Tibio-Tarsus | P | 12 / 15 | | | | | 1 / | | | 2 / 1 | | | | | | | 1 / 2 | |
| | D | | | | | / 1 | | | | | | | | | | | | |
| Fibula | | | | 1 / | | | | | | | | | | | | | | |
| Tarsus-Metatarsus | P | 15 / 12 | 2 / | 1 / 1 | 1 / | | 1 / | | | | | | | 1 / | | | 1 / | |
| | D | | | | | | | | | | | | | | | | | |
| Phalanges | | 6 / | | | | / 1 | | | | | | | | | | | | |
| **Total** | | 230 | 4 | 23 | 3 | 3 | 58 | 2 | 1 | 5 | 1 | 2 | 1 | 3 | 6 | | 29 | 7 |

and these included bones from all parts of the body, with ribs and many sections of axial skeleton, representing probably a minimum of 6–8 individuals, whereas in other pits mainly limb bones were found.

    There was very little variation in the size of the domestic fowl at Portchester. Any variation there is, is easily explained as a factor of sex and age and there is no sign of differential breeding. Even the three tarsi-metatarsi with spurs and the detached spur found in pit 92 are not

# TABLE XIV

*Minimum Numbers of Individuals from Chicken Bones in Each Pit*

| Pit | Quantities of bone | Minimum numbers of individuals |
|---|---|---|
| 12 | 4 | 2 |
| 18, 19, 49 | 9 | 2 |
| 40 | 3 | 1 |
| 47 | 5 | 1 |
| 62 | 1 | 1 |
| 63 | 15 | 4 |
| 64 | 2 | 1 |
| 71 | 8 | 3 |
| 73 | 2 | 1 |
| 74 | 17 | 2–3 |
| 79 | 14 | 2–3 |
| 89–90 | 2 | 1 |
| 91 | 2 | 1–2 |
| 92 | 90 | 6–8 |
| 107 | 5 | 1–2 |
| 108 | 6 | 1–2 |
| 109 | 2 | 1 |
| 121 | 15 | 4–5 |
| 187 | 1 | 1 |
| 223 | 6 | 1–2 |
| 236 | 5 | 2 |
| Gully 3 | 1 | 1 |
| Gully 7 | 1 | 1 |
| Gully 9 | 7 | 2–3 |
| Miscellaneous | 10 | 2–3 |
| Totals | 230 | 48–60 |

overlarge for the domestic cock bird and would be on the small side for a game or fighting cock. In any case the total number of chickens is not sufficient to suggest that they were kept or farmed to any real extent on the site. There can be no comparison here, therefore, with the domestic fowls at Fishbourne (Eastham, 1971, pp. 391–3), where there was a strong suggestion based on comparative measurements that the occupants might have had a certain interest in keeping a variety of different breeds of chicken.

The other domesticated member of the *Gallus* family to be found on the site is the Peacock. There were only four bones found, two tarsi-metatarsi in pit 47 and two humeri in a miscellaneous sample of bones, so that probably only two or three individual birds are represented. This would seem to be a rather surprising species to find in southern Britain at this period, although they are commonly quoted as dishes for feast days during the middle ages and large numbers of them occurred in the medieval rubbish pits at Winchester. There does not appear to have been sufficient systematic study of bird fauna of Roman sites to assess just how infrequent a species in Britain the Peacock was.

The Peacock is a native of the Indian peninsula and of Ceylon. The fact that it was the favourite bird of Hera, who in mythology had bestowed on its plumage the hundred eyes of Argus after he had been killed by Zeus for spying on him for Hera, suggests that the Greeks knew of it from a fairly early period, but were probably not very familiar with the species until after the conquests of Alexander. In Roman mythology the Peacock was sacred to Juno in her capacity of Regina. In so far as Juno, as protectress of the city of Rome, had geese as her sacred animals and they were supposed to have warned the city of the approach of the invading Gauls, possibly the Peacock, with its excessively strident voice, may have had a similar function of alarm. In art, the Peacock is most often represented with Hera or Juno. In a military context, the officer's badge of Aurelius Cervianus of the third century A.D., in the Bibliothèque Nationale in Paris, has a low relief of a Peacock occupying the lower third of the medal. Its appearance as a symbol in such a military object raises a number of speculations as to its significance. In the Byzantine church (Matthew, 1963, p. 35), because its flesh was held to be incorruptible, the bird came to be a symbol of everlasting life and later of the Eucharist. One of the earliest representations of it in this context is in the mosaics of St. Costanza in Rome built between A.D. 320–30; another is in Hagios Georgios, Thessaloniki of A.D. 400 and from the fifth century onwards there are many examples, including the pair which confront one another in the carvings on the throne of the Emperor Maximian of A.D. 545.

Waterfowl of various species are fairly common on the site. If one looks at a table estimating the minimum numbers of individuals, these amount to a possible 31 Mallard, 5 Garganey, 2 Teal, a Grey lag goose, a Wigeon and a Shelduck. Of these, some of the Mallard and the Goose might have been domesticated but the bones are consistent in size with the wild breed and very few of them are from immature specimens, a factor which could suggest that they had been reared for the table. In any event the sample is rather small for the determination of any marked domestication features.

The most unusual and unexpected water bird to be found on the site was the almost complete skeleton of *Gavia immer*, the Great Northern Diver, all bones together in pit 236. The skull and mandibles were in numerous pieces which it was possible to reassemble. Of the axial skeleton, there was found both coracoids, a scapula, part of the furcula and some vertebrae. The limb bones were very nearly complete, except that both femora were missing and no phalanges or wing digits were recovered.

The Great Northern Diver is a very shy bird which, at the present day, breeds in Iceland and occasionally in the Hebrides and Northern islands (Vaurie, 1965, p. 7). In the winter it migrates southwards along sea coasts and is sometimes seen off Cornwall and even as far south as the coasts of southern Spain. On Roman sites in Britain it seems to be practically unknown. One was found in the Broch of Ayre in Orkney which belongs to the first century A.D., and in a second century culture sequence in a Fife cave bones of a Red-throated Diver were discovered.

The bird at Portchester Castle is a fully mature if not aged specimen and the measurements of each complete bone (given in the table below) fall within the size limits for an adult male of the species. Why or how it came to be thrown away in pit 236 seems unanswerable. It is at best distinctly unpalatable as food. The fact that all the bones were found together might suggest, however, that it might have been accidentally bagged on a wildfowling trip and thrown out into the rubbish pit without more ado.

*Measurements of the complete bones of* Gavia immer

| Bone | Side | Length (mm.) | Proximal width (mm.) | Distal width (mm.) |
|---|---|---|---|---|
| Skull (reconstructed) | | 150·25 | orbit width 46·6 | |
| Bill | | 93·5 | | |
| Mandible (reconstructed) | | 151·5 | | |
| Coracoid | Right | 70·5 | | |
| Humerus | Left | 190·7 | 29·35 | 15·9 |
| | Right | 190·65 | 28·8 | 15·85 |
| Radius | Left | 150·80 | 12·5 | 7·8 |
| Ulna | Left | 159·2 | 15·0 | 21·8 |
| | Right | — | 15·25 | — |
| Carpo-metacarpus | Left | 10·2 | 11·45 | 9·85 |
| Tibio-tarsus | Left | over 155·0 | 19·5 | 16·1 |
| | Right | — | — | 16·1 |
| Tarsus-metatarsus | Left | 95·25 | 17·5 | 13·25 |
| | Right | 95·65 | 17·6 | 13·25 |

# TABLE XV

*Minimum Numbers of Wildfowl in Each Pit, Estimated from the Bones*

| Pit | Anser anser Bones | Individuals | Tadorna tadorna Bones | Individuals | Anas platyrrhyncos Bones | Individuals | Anas crecca Bones | Individuals | Anas querquedula Bones | Individuals | Anas penelope Bones | Individuals |
|---|---|---|---|---|---|---|---|---|---|---|---|---|
| 8 | | | | | 4 | 3 | | | | | | |
| 12 | | | | | 4 | 1 | | | | | | |
| 47 | | | | | 1 | 1 | | | 1 | 1 | | |
| 48 | | | | | 5 | 2 | | | 1 | 1 | | |
| 62 | | | | | 2 | 2 | | | | | | |
| 63 | | | | | 5 | 2 | | | | | | |
| 64 | | | | | 1 | 1 | | | | | | |
| 79 | | | | | 6 | 2 | | | 4 | 1 | | |
| 85 | | | | | | | | | | | 1 | 1 |
| 92 | | | | | 12 | 2 | | | | | | |
| 107 | | | | | 3 | 1 | | | | | | |
| 108 | | | | | 4 | 2 | | | | | | |
| 109 | | | | | 4 | 1 | 1 | 1 | | | | |
| 121 | | | 3 | 1 | 2 | 1 | | | | | | |
| 223 | | | | | 1 | 1 | | | | | | |
| 236 | 3 | 1 | | | 8 | 2 | 1 | 1 | 2 | 2 | | |
| Totals | 3 | 1 | 3 | 1 | 62 | 24 | 2 | 2 | 8 | 5 | 1 | 1 |

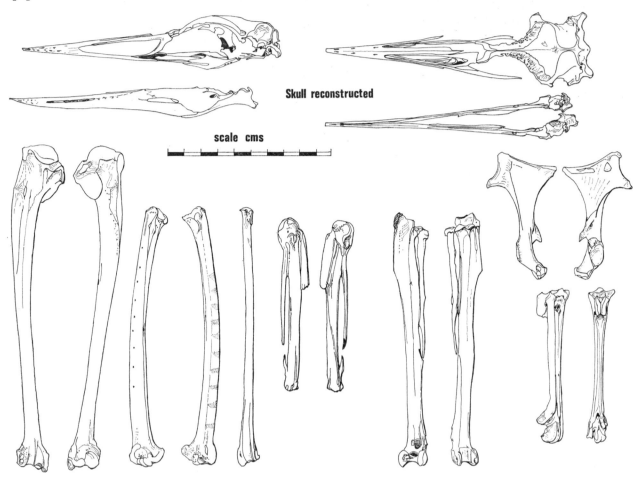

Skull reconstructed

scale cms

FIG. 207.   *Gavia immer* from pit 236

The remaining birds, apart from the crow family, would seem to rank as accidentals. The Tern could be expected on a site as close as this to the sea. The single Partridge and Woodcock and the pair of Doves are only noteworthy because there are so few of them. And the Kestrel, although it could have been one tamed for hunting purposes, is just as likely to have been a chance death.

The Jackdaws will have been residents and there are always deaths in any nesting colony of them. The Ravens are a different matter. The Romans are well known to have tamed them and taught them to talk. Six pits yielded bones of Raven and the total of 30 bones represent a probable minimum of eight individual birds.

The two birds of pit 236 are of very different size but both fully mature. It is not possible to be certain of the sex of crows from the skeleton but the size difference of this pair suggests the possibility of their being kept for breeding at the castle either as pets or mascots.

## TABLE XVI

*The Distribution and Numbers of Raven at Portchester Castle*

|         | Bone number | Individual number |
|---------|:-----------:|:-----------------:|
| Gully 9 | 5           | 1                 |
| Pit 63  | 1           | 1                 |
| 64      | 1           | 1                 |
| 73      | 2           | 1                 |
| 108     | 1           | 1                 |
| 236     | 20          | 2                 |
| Total   | 30          | 7                 |

Any conclusions to be reached about the birds found in the Roman levels at Portchester Castle are very brief. The finds do not show that birds were either kept in captivity or hunted for food to any appreciable degree. Accidental corpses are a minimum and none of the more frequent passerine species like thrushes, blackbirds and sparrows etc., which very often occur in Roman debris, appeared here. Unusual species were, however, brought on to the site, two Peacocks and a Great Northern Diver and explanations for either of these are a matter for speculation.

## BIBLIOGRAPHY

EASTHAM, A. 1971. 'The Bird Bones', in Cunliffe, B. W., *Excavations at Fishbourne 1961–69* (Reports of the Research Committee of the Society of Antiquaries of London nos. XXVI and XXVII).

MATTHEW, G. 1963. *Byzantine Aesthetics.*

PETERSON, MOUNTFORT and HOLLOM 1965. *A Field Guide to the Birds of Britain and Europe.*

VAURIE, C. 1965. *Birds of the Palaearctic Fauna.*

WITHERBY, JOURDAIN, TICEHURST and TUCKER 1943. *The Handbook of British Birds.*

# XIII. THE CARBONIZED CEREALS

## P. MURPHY and J. M. RENFREW

### Department of Archaeology, University of Southampton

SIX samples of carbonized cereals collected in 1966 from Roman layers and pits were received for examination. The samples consist of carbonized caryopses of wheat, barley and a species of oat. In general they are in poor condition, with a rather eroded appearance, and there are unidentifiable fragments of cereal grains mixed with them. A careful inspection detected no weed seeds, and in only one case were any spikelet parts preserved.

## TABLE XVII

*Carbonized Seeds Identified in the Samples*[1]

| Sample no. | Hordeum vulgare | T. spelta or T. dicoccum | Wheat | Avena sp. |
|---|---|---|---|---|
| 63 (5) | — | — | 1 fragment | 1 |
| 63 (6) | 11 | 7 2 glume fragments | 1 | — |
| 65 (5) | 1 | 4 | — | 2 |
| 65 (12) | 3 | 5 | 2 | — |
| 65 (15) | 2 | 6 2 fragments | — | — |
| 65 (18) | — | 2 | — | — |

[1] The sample from trench 65 (12) came from pit 52, that from trench 65 (18) from pit 54. The rest are from Roman occupation levels.

Wheats (*Triticum* sp.)

In the table 'wheat' denotes a grain too poorly preserved to be more closely identified.

The better preserved grains have the appearance of being spelt (*Triticum spelta*) or emmer (*Triticum dicoccum*) and no grains of a bread/club wheat type are present. The detection of spelt and emmer requires either a large sample to enable the inspection of metrical distributions (Morrison, 1959) or the presence of spikelet parts to confirm identifications based on grain morphology (Helbaek, 1952). In sample 63 (6) there are two fragments of glumes, which though badly preserved have the strongly nerved appearance of glumes from spelt. One may suspect that in this sample at least the wheat represented is spelt, though definite identification is not possible with this material.

## TABLE XVIII

*Dimensions of Measurable Wheat Grains (mm)*

|          | Length | Breadth | Thickness |
|----------|--------|---------|-----------|
| 63  (6)  | 5·6    | 3·0     | 2·8       |
|          | 5·3    | 2·7     | 2·7       |
|          | 4·8    | 2·6     | 2·2       |
|          | 4·7    | 2·7     | —         |
| 65 (12)  | 6·3    | 3·5     | 2·9       |
|          | 5·5    | 3·0     | 2·7       |
| 65 (15)  | 5·8    | 2·9     | 2·9       |
|          | 5·0    | 2·6     | 2·2       |

Barley (*Hordeum vulgare*)

One species is represented in the samples: *Hordeum vulgare*, a hulled 6-row barley. In the absence of intermodes the spike type, whether dense or lax, remains unknown. In one specimen from 65 (12) the lemma base is well preserved and it is of the plain (spurium) type. Unfortunately lemma bases are not a reliable indication of spike type (Renfrew, 1973, 78).

None of these samples constitutes a statistically useful population, and comparison with the known ranges of dimensions for carbonized barley grains (see, for example, Van Zeist, 1970, p. 160) would be invalid.

Straight grains from median spikelets are in the majority in these samples. In sample 63 (6) there are six such grains as opposed to three twisted grains from lateral spikelets.

## TABLE XIX

*Dimensions of Measurable Barley Grains (mm)*

|          | Length | Breadth | Thickness |
|----------|--------|---------|-----------|
| 63  (6)  | 5·7    | 3·1     | 2·6       |
|          | 5·4    | 2·8     | 2·5       |
|          | 5·1    | 3·0     | 2·6       |
|          | 5·0    | 2·9     | 2·7       |
|          | 5·2    | 2·7     | 2·3       |
|          | 5·0    | 2·7     | 2·7       |
|          | 4·7    | 2·1     | 2·0       |
|          | 5·2    | 2·9     | 2·6       |
| 65  (5)  | 5·4    | 2·8     | 2·5       |
| 65 (15)  | 5·2    | 2·8     | 2·3       |

Oats (*Avena* sp.)

Three caryopses of oats are present. The two from 65 (5) are badly distorted and unmeasurable whilst the single caryopsis from 63 (5) has: length 4·8 mm.; breadth 1·2 mm.; thickness 1·4 mm. Species determination is not possible in the absence of flower bases, so the grains may represent wild oats (*Avena fatua*) or the cultivated oats (*Avena sativa* and *Avena strigosa*).

One can conclude from the samples that hulled wheat, 6-row barley and possibly oats were being grown near, or at least consumed at, the Saxon shore fort in the middle of the fourth century.

## BIBLIOGRAPHY

HELBAEK, H. 1952. 'Spelt (*Triticum spelta* L.) in Bronze Age Denmark'. *Acta Archaeologica* xxiii, 97–107.

MORRISON, M. E. S. 1959. 'Carbonized cereals from the Roman villa of North Leigh, Oxfordshire'. *Oxoniensia*, xxiv, 13–21.

RENFREW, J. M. 1973. *Palaeoethnobotany: the prehistoric food plants of the Near East and Europe*. Methuen.

VAN ZEIST, W. 1970. 'Prehistoric and Early Historic Food Plants in the Netherlands'. *Palaeohistoria*, xiv, 419.

# XIV. DISCUSSION

HAVING now amassed the basic data upon which the interpretation of the Roman phase of Portchester Castle must at present rest, we may now consider them in relation to the contemporary scene both in Britain and on the continent. One method would be to discuss the Portchester evidence against the background of late third- and fourth-century military history. Such an approach would, however, prejudice the interpretation by the very fact of supposing that a relationship was maintained between Portchester and the army. Instead, it has been thought advisable to discuss separately the elements which constitute the evidence and only by way of conclusion to offer a summary of the more plausible historical interpretations.

## THE DEFENCES: THEIR FORM AND DATE

The walls, bastions, gates and ditch system of Portchester fall within a general category of defensive structures which can be paralleled in Britain and on the continent in late Roman contexts, dating to after the middle of the third century A.D.[1] The thickness of the wall (10 ft. (3 m.) above foundation offset) is comparable to other British sites of this type (e.g. Richborough, Lympne, Dover, Pevensey and Clausentum) and presumably represents the standard width regarded as optimum for free standing masonry walls, as compared with 8 ft. (2·4 m.) for walls of earlier forts backed by ramparts (e.g. Dover (*Classis Britannica* fort), Reculver, Brancaster and Burgh Castle), and the walls of towns, which vary between 4 and 10 ft. (1·2–3·0 m.). A similar standardization can be seen among the European forts of comparable date.

Less is known of contemporary ditch systems, but the pair of V-shaped ditches at Portchester are clearly within the third-century tradition represented at Reculver and Richborough. A single V-shaped ditch also occurs in the fourth-century fort at Pevensey but by the third quarter of the fourth century wide flat bottomed ditches seem to have become the norm.

The development of forward-projecting bastions in Britain can be traced by reference to the architecture of the shore forts and to the late stages of certain town defences. At the beginning of the sequence lies Burgh Castle, where it is evident that the fort began to be constructed in the style of the early third century, with internal corner towers, ramparts and rounded corners[2] comparable to Brancaster and Reculver, but was modified during construction by the addition of external bastions of sub-circular plan and solid form. The date of this change is uncertain, but is likely to lie towards the middle of the third century. There-

---

[1] For a general description of the shore forts, Collingwood and Richmond (1969), 47–57. For a discussion of the sequence, with detailed references, Cunliffe (1968). A summary of the continental evidence is contained in Petrikovits (1971) (with references). Specific British sites: Dover (Philp, 1971); Reculver (Philp, 1969); Carisbrooke (Rigold, 1966); Pevensey (Peers, 1953); Richborough (Cunliffe, 1968; Johnson, 1970); Brancaster (St Joseph, 1936); Lympne (Roach Smith, 1850, 1852); Clausentum (Cotton and Gathercole, 1958); Bradwell (*V.C.H. Essex*, iii, 52–5); Burgh Castle (Morris, 1949); Cardiff (Nash-Williams, 1954); Caer Gybi (Wheeler, 1924).

[2] Information from the late Mr Charles Green.

after, bastions of various forms were commonly adopted in fort architecture: Richborough, Portchester and possibly Lympne dating to the late third century, Pevensey to the early fourth, with less certainty attaching to the dates of Bradwell, Walton Castle, Cardiff and Caer Gybi. In the second half of the fourth century, bastions were added to the existing walls of a number of towns, and several small settlements, defended for the first time in this period, were provided with bastioned walls (e.g. Clausentum, Gatcombe (Cunliffe, 1967), Mildenhall,[1] etc.).

On the continent the development of forward-projecting towers can be seen to begin somewhat earlier than in Britain, starting in the last quarter of the second century. By the time that many of the Gaulish towns were being provided with new defensive circuits under Probus (after A.D. 276), bastioned walls had become a regular feature of defensive architecture.

Little standardization is apparent in the form of the bastions; the elongated D-shaped, hollow type at Portchester is one of many variants. In Britain the D-shaped variety was more commonly adopted than the circular type set astride the wall (cf. Carisbrooke)[2] or the rectangular type (cf. Richborough). The Portchester bastions, however, differ from those of Lympne and Pevensey in that they are hollow, a characteristic not uncommon in northern Europe.

The two principal gates in the centres of the east and west sides of Portchester are of a somewhat unusual type. In each case, the gatehouse has been set back at the end of a courtyard formed by inturning the walls of the fort. A similar arrangement is apparent at the so far undated fort at Carisbrooke, where, at the east gate, the fort wall was inturned for a distance of 46 ft. (14 m.), leaving a gap of 18 ft. (5·5 m.) to accommodate both road and any guardchamber which might have been built. The early fourth-century fort of Pevensey provides a variation of the same basic idea. Here, at the west gate, the courtyard effect was created not by inturning the fort wall but by placing a bastion on either side of the approach and setting the guard-chambers back wholly behind the wall. Elsewhere in Britain and in northern Europe parallels are difficult to find, the more normal arrangement involving gate towers on the line of, and often projecting in advance of, the fort wall. Only at the Bürgle, near Gundremmingen (Bersu, 1964) has anything approaching a forecourt been recognized, but the site is little more than a pair of defended barrack buildings, and therefore not strictly comparable. Comparison might be made with the gate of Split (Marasović, 1968), where an enclosed forecourt preceded by projecting towers was constructed: the similarity is, however, tenuous. It is best, therefore, to regard the gates of Portchester, Pevensey, and possibly Carisbrooke, as a specialized southern British type.

The two postern gates at Portchester were simple arched openings through the wall, similar to the east gate of Pevensey. They contrast, in their simplicity, with the angled posterns found in the north wall of Pevensey and in the north and south walls of Richborough, where flanking protection was provided by inserting the gates into bastions in the manner also recorded at Caelius Mons (Kellmünz) and Icorigium (Jünkerath).[3]

The British shore forts, in so far as the evidence is available, fall into two size groups; those between 6 and 7½ acres in extent, including Brancaster, Burgh Castle, Reculver and Rich-

[1] No definitive report but notes in *Wilts. Arch. Mag.* lvii (1958–60), 233, 397; lviii (1961–3), 35; lx (1965), 137.
[2] Carisbrooke is anomalous. In spite of internal excava-

tions there is no dating evidence: Rigold (1966) suggests that it was unfinished.
[3] Conveniently summarized in Petrikovits (1971), fig. 30

borough, and those between 8 and 10 acres, to which class Lympne, Pevensey and Port-chester belong. Superficially the groupings would seem to represent two different periods, the smaller forts all belonging to the period before Carausius, the larger forts dating to the Carausian period and later. Whereas the smaller forts correspond to the larger British auxiliary establishments, the later forts are significantly larger and may well reflect a difference in function — a problem returned to in more detail below.

From the discussion so far, it would appear that in constructional detail and plan the shore forts of south-eastern Britain display a variety which at first sight is confusing. It is, however, possible to isolate certain characteristics which allow broad groupings to be defined.[1] The earliest forts in the series are undoubtedly Brancaster and Reculver. With their classic 'playing card' shape, internal turrets and ramparts, the absence of bastions and tile courses, they must be placed at the beginning of the series, probably in the first half of the third century, a dating entirely consistent with the associated finds. Next, typologically, comes Burgh Castle, representing a transitional form, begun in the earlier style, but modified during construction by the addition of solid, sub-circular bastions. Burgh displays two further features, which recur in certain of the other forts, the lack of strict rectangularity and the presence of regular tile courses. One or more of these elements can be seen at Dover, Bradwell, Lympne, and Richborough (earliest stone phase). Precise dating evidence is sadly lacking for all but Richborough, where it has been argued that construction was begun, modified and later completed probably within the 270s and certainly before the appearance of Carausius in A.D. 285 (Johnson, 1970). If the shared characteristics of these forts imply a broad contemporaneity (and the coin evidence does not dispute this) the date range for the group must lie within the third quarter of the third century. There is no need to suppose that all were built at the same time or as a response to the same stimulus — a perfectly acceptable hypothesis being that forts were put up individually, as the threat of pirate raids made itself increasingly felt, culminating in a burst of activity at the instigation of Probus in A.D. 276–7. Where in this sequence the construction of Lympne should be placed is unclear, but its elongated D-shaped bastions, some of which had hollow chambers in their bases, are not unlike those of Port-chester, hinting at the possibility of a late pre-Carausian date.

Portchester is the only fort for which a Carausian construction date may now reasonably be argued. Briefly summarized, the evidence consists of one coin of Saloninus and two of Gallienus, in contexts immediately pre-dating construction levels, together with a coin of Tetricus I and one of Carausius in primary layers against the fort wall. These significantly stratified coins, taken in conjunction with Dr Reece's carefully argued assessment of the full coin list, strongly suggest that the defences of Portchester were erected early in the reign of Carausius, probably between A.D. 286 and 290.

The contrast between Portchester and the forts previously discussed is striking. Although elements are shared in common, the overall impression given is that Portchester represents the imposition of a rigorous order not previously apparent. Such an order would agree with the view that the wall was built by military engineers employed in the early years of the Carausian campaigns, regularizing the techniques and concepts which had gradually been developed in the preceding decades. The only comparable structure in Britain is the largely undated fort at

[1] The dating evidence is summarized in Cunliffe (1968, 260–8), but see Johnson (1970) for new thoughts on the dating of Richborough.

Cardiff, but here the presence of an apparently contemporary rampart seems to distinguish it from Portchester. On the continent, regular square planning is a feature shared by several of the fourth-century forts, including Március, Budapest (late third-century), Oudenberg (pre-Crispus), Köln-Deutz and Haus Bürgel (Constantinian) and Alzey (Valentinian I).[1]

In Britain the preference for square planning was shorter-lived, since the builders of the fort at Pevensey, which probably dates to the 340s, or later, blatantly rejected any semblance of rectangularity, choosing instead to follow the contour of the hillock upon which the enclosure was sited. The same underlying concept is apparent in the defence of Clausentum, constructed after 367, although there is no reason to consider Clausentum to be military rather than civilian.

Sufficient will have been said to show that the fort at Portchester, probably built by Carausius, lay within the broad tradition of military engineering which spanned the north-west provinces of the late Roman empire. Its construction followed a period of intensive fortification around the shores of the North Sea, which began in the first half of the third century and culminated in the strengthening of the Channel crossing by the reconstruction of the earlier military works of Richborough, Dover and Lympne, some time probably in the 270s, perhaps by Probus following his restoration of Gaul in A.D. 277. Why, in the next decade, Carausius should have chosen to build an isolated fort in the centre of the south coast is a problem which will be further explored in the final paragraphs (pp. 428–31).

# THE HISTORY OF THE SITE

The reconstruction of an historical framework against which to assess the military, social and economic functions of the settlement depends upon a general consideration of the coin sequence (pp. 188–97) together with an assessment of the phases represented in the detailed stratigraphy preserved against the south wall of the fort (pp. 38–61). The coin series itself is of dubious value. Although the numbers are large enough to be representative of the coins *lost* on the site, there is no sure way of interpreting the meaning of a period of intensive loss or, conversely, a period represented by only a few coins. One view would be that intensive loss represents intensive occupation, but an equally plausible alternative is that coins were only lost in quantity when site conditions became squalid and rubbish was allowed to pile up in the fort; at other times, when rubbish was removed, the coin loss would be thin. Until it is possible to excavate large areas outside the fort, in the regions in which the rubbish was at certain times tipped, in order to recover a sufficiently large sample of coins to compare with those found inside the walls, there seems to be no easy way out of the dilemma.

At best the coin evidence suggests a short initial period of coin loss in the decade A.D. 280–90, followed by a period of ten years represented by remarkably few coins. From 300–45 sufficiently large numbers were lost to suggest continuous interior occupation. Few coins of the period 345–60 were found but from 360 to the end of the century a moderate number points to continued occupation at least until about 400.

Turning now to the dating evidence from the stratified layers against the south wall (summarized pp. 59–61) it is possible to recognize certain periods of constructional activity which it might be possible to correlate with changes in the main coin sequences. Following the

---

[1] Dating briefly summarized in Petrikovits (1971). For Oudenburg see Mertens (1962).

construction in *c*. 285–90, occupation rubbish accumulated in piles against the wall until about 325, at which time the filth was sealed by a deposit of freshly quarried brickearth. The principal question to be raised of this occupation phase (period 2) by the coin series is, was occupation continuous throughout the 40 years or was it interrupted? That coins occur in reasonable numbers after 300, but are very rare from 290–300, could well be seen to imply a period of abandonment very soon after construction, followed by re-occupation of a rather untidy nature after 300. The alternative, of course, is that the site was under military control until 300 and was kept clean but was turned over to civilian use after this. Certain aspects of the structural evidence have a bearing on the problem. The lack of any buildings of a permanent nature belonging to the initial period might imply that the interior arrangements were never completed. Streets were only lightly metalled and do not appear to have been properly edged or drained while the only evidence of buildings consists of the rectangularly arranged gullies on site A (fig. 22), which could well represent drainage gullies around tents, or other light structures. The discontinuous patches of gravel trampled into the natural clay would suggest the haphazard filling of puddles between temporary structures of this kind. Similarly, the scattered ovens, some of which might belong to this early period, would be in place in a phase of short-lived occupation.

Taken together, the evidence points to the initial occupation of *c*. 285–90 being of a slight character. It is possible that the fort was intended to be occupied in this manner, but the alternative, that the work was never completed, only temporary accommodation for the builders being erected, is equally acceptable as a hypothesis, which must be considered in an historical context later.

If the phase of temporary initial occupation was short-lived, it might account for the surprising lack of coins in the decade 290–300 to which Dr Reece has drawn attention. The appearance of coins in plenty after 300 could then be seen to represent a new phase of occupation to which the rubbish tips against the wall belong. Thus, in terms of the sequence summarized on p. 61, period 2 may tentatively be divided into 2a, a phase of abandonment lasting *c*. 290 to 300, and 2b, a phase of occupation spanning the years 300 to 325.

The deposition of the middle clay in period 3, dated to about 325, represents a time of tidying up when the rubbish deposits against the wall were sealed. The origin of the clay itself presents an interesting problem. It could, of course, have been brought in from outside but the distinct possibility remains that it was derived from the two large quarry pits (pits 103 and 187) close to the centre of the fort, augmented perhaps by clay produced during the digging of the cesspits.

Next follows a period of intensive occupation, period 4, spanning the two decades from approximately 325 to 345 (p. 60). Only one structure can be shown to have been in use during this time, the 'guard house', built of upright timbers on the west side of the south postern gate. Elsewhere in the fort, while no conclusive evidence of buildings survives, it seems likely that light timber structures were laid out along the north–south road, the spaces between them being reserved for the digging of cesspits (p. 77), of which several clearly defined groups can be recognized. The dating evidence for the use of the cesspits assigns the bulk of them to period 4 (pp. 77–8).

If, as suggested above, pits 103 and 187 were quarry pits dating to *c*. 325, it is interesting to remember that pit 103 was largely filled with the rubbish from the careful dismantling of at

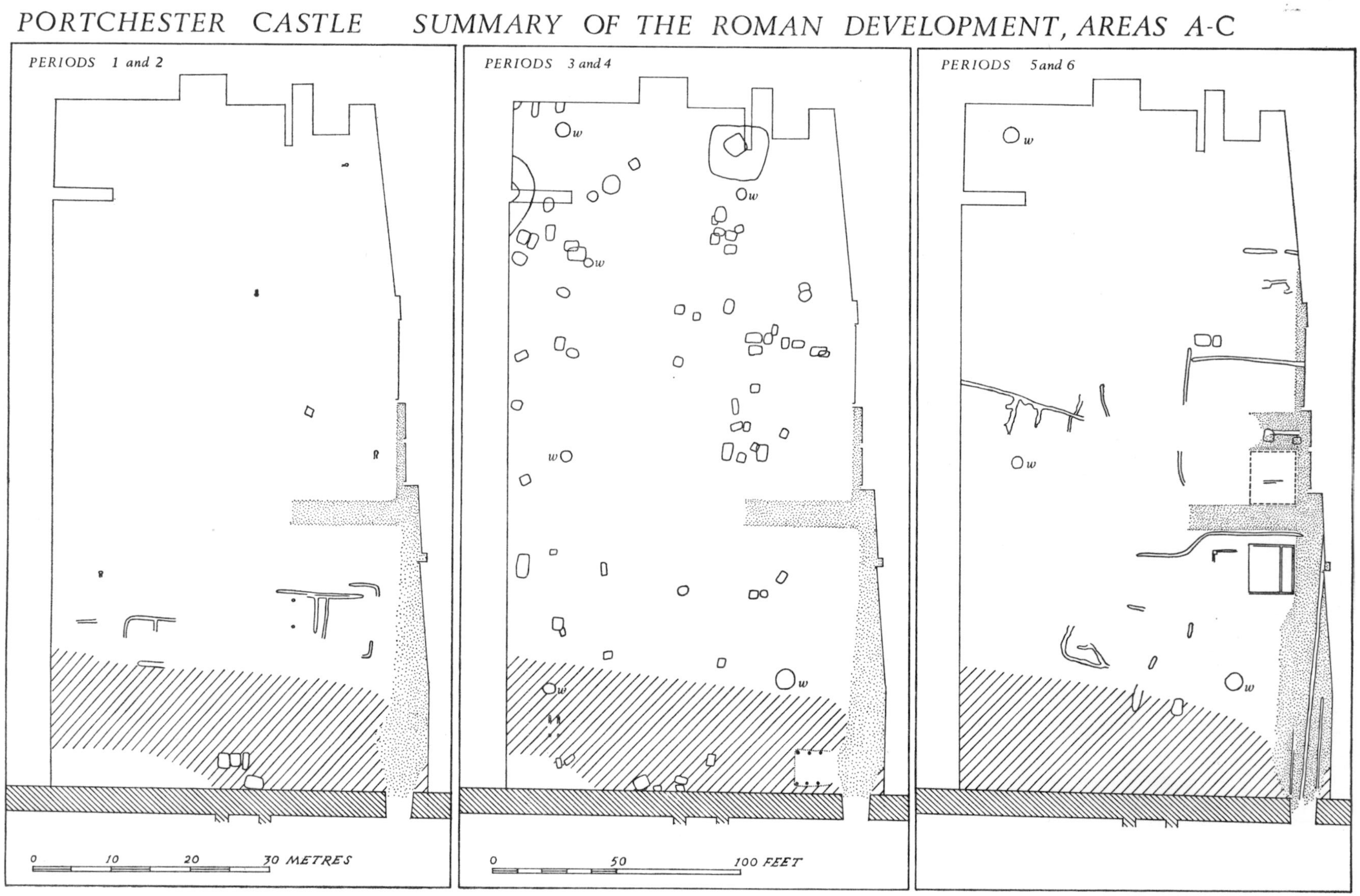

PORTCHESTER CASTLE    SUMMARY OF THE ROMAN DEVELOPMENT, AREAS A-C

PERIODS 1 and 2

PERIODS 3 and 4

PERIODS 5 and 6

0    10    20    30 METRES

0    50    100 FEET

FIG. 208

least one timber building, the re-usable materials such as roof tiles having been removed, such an act of deliberate demolition would fit well with the tidying up and replanning of c. 325.

The number of coins lost during the period 325–45 in general reflects the fluctuations in coin supply in the province as a whole in such a way as to suggest that occupation at Portchester was continuous. The presence of no less than five contemporary wells is indicative of settled occupation.

Early in the 340s, perhaps as late as 345, a new phase of building activity is discernible, represented by the further sealing of the rubbish tip against the fort wall and the remetalling of the major roads, together with the construction of timber gutters. To this period belong timber buildings R4 and R5, which were apparently constructed on sill beams at the time when the roads were re-surfaced. Most of the cesspits and some of the wells were by this stage filled; wells 164 and 206 were deliberately packed with clay, the others became choked with refuse, with the exception of 135 which was kept in use. It was also at this time that large expanses of cobbles were spread out over the western part of the excavated area.

The activity speaks of an attempt to impose an order. How long into period 6 this phase lasted it is impossible to say. Dr Reece has drawn attention to the relative scarcity of coins at Portchester from 345–64, but again the explanation could as well be cleanliness as lack of activity. On the evidence of the coins, however, period 6 may be divided into three phases: phase (a) represents the dearth of coinage, 345–64; phase (b) covers the intensification of coin loss from 364–78, while phase (c) reflects a sharp decrease in the number of coins belonging to the period 378 to 400 + in contrast to other sites in Britain where issues of this period are relatively common. How these phases are to be interpreted in terms of site history is less certain. Archaeologically, one can define a period of activity represented by irregular drainage gullies cutting through the cobbled metalling and associated with further tips of rubbish which spread out over the roads. Clearly, occupation continued but no longer of the ordered kind represented by the reconstruction of period 5, and presumably the first phase of occupation following it (period 6a). It is not unreasonable, therefore, to assign the new squalor to the phase of intensive coin loss from c. 364–78 (period 6b) after which occupation continued, but possibly not on the same scale as before, until coins ceased to be issued.

The tentative historical framework outlined above may now be summarized:

| Period 1 | (285–90) | Construction phase and temporary internal structures. |
| Period 2a | (290–300) | Abandoned. |
| Period 2b | (300–25) | Occupation. |
| Period 3 | (325) | Middle clay seal, quarry pits, guard house. |
| Period 4 | (325–45) | Occupation, cesspits, wells. |
| Period 5 | (345) | Upper clay seal, remetalling of roads, rebuilding, cobbling, filling of wells. |
| Period 6a | (345–64) | Ordered occupation. |
| Period 6b | (364–78) | Intensive disordered occupation, drainage gullies. |
| Period 6c | (378–400 +) | Continued disordered occupation. |

## SOCIAL AND ECONOMIC IMPLICATIONS

The life style and activities practised by those living at Portchester can to some extent be reconstructed from the material remains recovered from the excavation.

A military presence is indicated by a small group of 13 bronze fittings (nos. 11–23), certainly or probably of military character, some of them comparable to those used by detachments of the late Roman army (Hawkes and Dunning, 1961). One buckle (no. 15) occurred in a layer below the make-up and therefore belongs to period 4 or earlier (pre-345); the remainder cannot be assigned to any particular phase of the Roman occupation. Further evidence suggestive of an army presence is provided by two fragments of swords, a ballista bolt, and seven or eight spearheads, together with two spurs and two complete horseshoes, all of which came from either general layers or occupation layers of period 6. Although the presence of each object could be explained individually in terms of retired veterans or the iron work being of non-military purpose, taken together the collection is strongly suggestive of a military presence both before and after A.D. 345. There is, however, no necessity to suppose continuous army occupation, or even an army majority among the inhabitants, during their period of residence. It is as well to emphasize these points, if only to counter the widely held assumption that all shore forts were purely military institutions.

A wide range of activities were carried on by the occupants of the fort. Metal working is represented by iron slag, a crucible, copper ore and lead trimmings (p. 265). Antler working is implied by the quantity of sawn and cut antler, while the unusually large number of bone pins, particularly from well 121, might suggest local production. Similarly, the way in which some of the horn cores were cut would indicate the careful removal of horn (p. 389) although this need not have taken place in the fort. Other activities of a manufacturing nature include spinning and weaving, as evidenced by spindlewhorls of shale, bone, clay and stone, and a triangular bone tablet for braid making. While the majority of these pursuits would not be out of place in a military establishment, weaving would surely indicate the presence of women.

The community was amply provided with meat, beef clearly being the most favoured. Mrs Grant's discussion of the animal bones strongly suggests that cattle were slaughtered on the site. The alternative explanation, that entire carcasses were transported from the slaughter-house, would seem less likely when transport on the hoof was so much more economic. The question is thus raised, were animals quartered for any period in the fort? To this there can be no answer except that the large open area, consolidated on more than one occasion with metalling, would have been admirably suited to coralling should it have been necessary. The fact that several wells were close to hand was an additional advantage. Sheep, too, seem to have been important. In gross numbers, they represented some 23% of the total animal sample. The existence of at least one pair of shears large enough to have been used for sheep shearing raises the possibility of shearing on the spot.

Evidence for baking was far from plentiful. Ovens are few and seem to be restricted to the early period, while milling (and probably baking) must have surely been centralized either within the fort or somewhere outside, since even quernstones are surprisingly rare.

Hunting and gathering do not seem to have played a major part in the economy, with the exception of oysters, which may, anyway, have been provided by specialists and sold to the inhabitants. A few marsh birds such as mallard, may have been caught locally, as presumably were fish. A lead net weight, a netting needle, and a fish hook may be taken as reasonable evidence for this.

That the range of activities outlined above are entirely appropriate to an essentially civilian population deserves further consideration. The discussion as to the relative significance of the civilian and military element must hinge on the presence or absence of women living in the fort in a permanent capacity. Here the evidence of the infant burials is decisive (pp. 375–7): altogether the bones of some 27 infants were discovered, of whom 13 were found in pits. The distribution in time is interesting: two belong to period 2b (lower occupation), two to period 3 (middle clay), 15 to period 4 (middle occupation and pits), three to period 5 (upper clay) and five to period 6 (upper occupation, etc.). In short, infants were being interred at Portchester from about A.D. 300 onwards at all periods (although not necessarily throughout each period), with a particular preponderance between 325 and 345. Unless it is supposed that some abnormal ritual was practised requiring infant burial, the simplest explanation is that the community living in Portchester included resident women from about A.D. 300, who adopted the accepted expedient of disposing of dead infants with little ceremony in convenient places around the living site. That many of the pits containing infants also produced unusual animal bone assemblages might however imply that the body of the child was accompanied with an offering (p. 376).

Other evidence may be quoted to support the suggestion of the presence of women. We have already mentioned the extensive collection of spinning and weaving equipment; to this should be added personal jewellery, including finger rings, bracelets of bronze and shale, toilet equipment, and beads, all more appropriate to the dress of womenfolk than to soldiers. Finally we should draw attention to women's shoes, preserved in the collection of leather work from the wells (p. 260). Altogether the evidence for resident females is persuasive.

As to the general quality of life, the small finds offer some indications. The silver ring and the gemstone were evidently of some value; locks and keys imply personal privacy, while the number of styli represent a high level of literacy. Beyond this it is difficult to go, except to say that buildings were insubstantial, living conditions were sometimes squalid, and the site was infested with cats.

There are three ways of viewing the evidence summarized in the preceding paragraphs. It could be supposed that (a) civilians occupied the site in the intervals between military residence; or (b) that the fort was occupied throughout by the military who gradually allowed wives and children to move into the defended area; or (c) that it housed a basically civilian community, among whom was billeted a small militia. That the three explanations are historically possible is a reflection partly of the complexity of relations between soldier and civilian in the later Roman empire[1] and partly of the general lack of knowledge about late fort sites. The most reasonable compromise, based on all the available internal evidence including both sequence and material finds, is that the fort was established by Carausius in or soon after A.D. 285 but was abandoned not long after. Following the re-establishment of central government rule in Britain by Constantius, a largely civilian community took over the abandoned installations either as the result of a gradual process of drift or, more likely, as part of a deliberate policy for the settlement of peasant militias in key positions, not unlike the establishment of *laeti* in northern Gaul. While it is evident that the civilian character of the

[1] The complex and changing situation is well summarized in MacMullen (1967).

occupation remained strong, the periodic attempts to create some semblance of internal order in and following 325 and 345 could be seen as the assertion of some form of control, occasioned perhaps by the billeting of new contingents in times of potential trouble. In this way the style of occupation of the fourth century would have passed imperceptibly into that of the fifth.

## HISTORICAL CONTEXT

If the above interpretation of the internal evidence can be accepted, it remains only to see how, if at all, such a development relates to the broader historical and social picture.[1] It is now clear that the so-called 'shore fort' system did not originate as a unified defensive measure, but rather grew piecemeal as the threat of pirate attack gradually increased. Until the 280s it is highly unlikely that the south coast of Britain was defended further west than the cluster of strong points guarding the Channel crossing.

The concentration of forts at this point, including Boulogne, Richborough, Dover and possibly Lympne, would have been sufficient to prevent the pirates who infested the North Sea from penetrating into the English Channel. That the situation soon deteriorated is shown by the appointment of a new naval commander in 285, M. Aurelius Carausius, whose specific task was to 'rid the seas of Belgica and Armorica of pirates',[2] implying that the raiders had finally penetrated the Dover–Boulogne defences and were now roaming the Channel coasts. Within a year Carausius had usurped his power and taken control of the province, whilst still retaining his hold on the north Gaulish coast. It was in these troubled times that Portchester was built.

Two explanations are possible: either the fort was erected to serve as the centre of the Channel-based arm of the fleet engaged in mopping up the pirates, or it was constructed after the break with Rome as a defence against threat of Roman re-conquest. The latter suggestion seems highly unlikely in spite of arguments put forward in its favour (White, 1961). An isolated coastal garrison was no adequate defence against an organized invasion, as the events of 296 were soon to show, nor could it be thought to constitute part of a chain of strong points serving as refuges from which the defenders of the island could sally forth, since the fort was more than 100 miles from its nearest contemporary neighbour at Lympne.[3] Moreover, at just the time when the argument would have required the fort to have been most heavily inhabited, i.e. c. 290–96, the evidence strongly suggests not only a dearth of activity but possibly even abandonment.

If, however, Portchester is seen as an early Carausian construction designed specially as the home base of a naval detachment patrolling the Channel, the logistics of the situation make more sense. Assuming, as the panegyric implies, that pirates had broken through the Dover–Boulogne block, then a new defensive axis would have been required to hinder their further passage west. In such a scheme Portchester could well have served as the British base with a counterpart on the north French coast, for which *Grannona*, probably sited near Bayeux

---

[1] The most convenient survey of these events is to be found in Frere (1967). For the life of Carausius, see White (1961).

[2] Eutropius ix, 21.

[3] This is always supposing that no fort has been lost by coastal erosion along the intervening coast.

(Grenier, 1931, 393–3) is the most likely contender.[1] A 50-mile range from each would have allowed a fleet so based to have effectively sealed the Channel, thus bottling up would-be attackers and driving them back on the already strongly defended straits of Dover. In short, Portchester makes some strategic sense as part of a cross-Channel 'frontier' against a naval enemy instead of as an element in a British coastal *limes* designed to combat the potential invasions of a land-based army.

Once the immediate threat of piracy had been overcome, a base at Portchester would have decreased in significance, and when, soon afterwards, Carausius lost his hold on Gaul altogether, the value of the now-isolated garrison would have been still further reduced. Such an interpretation provides a reasonable context for the brief period of occupation which, on purely archaeological grounds, has been suggested for period 1. The apparent abandonment in period 2a (290–300) would, then, represent a time when efforts were concentrated more on watching the Dover Straits and the Rhine mouth, where Maximian was concentrating his fleet, than on guarding the southern shores. The ease with which Asclepiodotus managed his landing on the southern coast in the autumn of 296 may be a reflection of the lack of preparedness in this region. The landing succeeded by surprise.

In the period which followed the re-establishment of central government control, the area within the fortifications at Portchester came back into regular use, occupied, it would seem, by a community in which women and children were present. Throughout the first half of the fourth century (periods 2b to 4) little change can be detected, rubbish piled up within the walls, buildings of wattle and daub with tiled roofs and glazed windows continued to be rebuilt, while cesspits and wells were dug when required. The only recognizable 'event' during this time was the sealing of the rubbish against the south wall and the construction of the 'guard-house' adjacent to the south postern gate. The overall impression gained from the surviving structures and the material evidence is that the community was substantially, if not wholly, civilian. In the relative peace of the early fourth century there may have been little need to maintain a garrison on this part of the south coast. The pirates, if at all active, were presumably once more restricted to the North Sea.

Early in the 340s a change can be detected at Portchester: the interior was tidied up, the rubbish tips and the pits were sealed, and the roads were roughly remetalled. At the same time there is evidence of levelling and rebuilding. While it could be argued that these changes were merely of local significance, contemporary events elsewhere imply more widespread change. It was probably at this time that the fort of Pevensey was built, while the coin evidence from Richborough suggests major activity after several decades of virtual abandonment (or more precisely a phase of extensive coin loss following one of sparse loss). It is tempting to relate these changes to the visit made by the newly appointed emperor Constans in the winter of 342, presumably for the purpose of initiating improvements in the defences of the province.

Constans may well have established the command of the *Comes Litoris Saxonici*, later recorded in the *Notitia Dignitatum*. Restricted territorial commissions held by Counts were unknown under Constantine the Great, but the rank of *Comes Maritimi Tractus* was in existence in Britain by 367. If Constans was the creator of the new command, what prompted the choice of the phrase *Saxon Shore*? Either it refers to a shore attacked by Saxons or a shore defended by them.

---

[1] The significance and date of the fortlet on Alderney still need defining. If contemporary with the Carausian scheme it could have served as a valuable rearward base in the new arrangement.

The debate is a long-established one,[1] and this is not the place to rehearse the relevant arguments; suffice it to say that the generally accepted view is that the Count's command was named after its attackers. There is, however, much that could now be said in favour of the alternative. In particular, Myres' recent study of Anglo-Saxon pottery (Myres, 1969, 65–83) points conclusively to the settlement of German *laeti* in eastern England, possibly even as early as the late third century. In fulfilling such a policy, the governors of Britain were simply following the well-established traditions common at the time in the continental provinces. Although the ceramic record for the south coast is less demonstrative (and the 'Romano-Saxon' pottery unknown) there is no need to suppose that this region was excluded from the general policy. If then we can accept that Germanic *laeti* were extensively employed as paramilitary mercenaries in coastal regions by the middle of the fourth century, there would seem to be no good reason for opposing the view that *Litus Saxonicum* meant 'coasts settled by Saxons'. Such an hypothesis would open the way for the further suggestion that it was Constans who formalized the coastal command by appointing a *Comes* to organize it, possibly even introducing additional drafts of *laeti* from the continent to add strength.

If major reorganization was undertaken by Constans, some signs might be expected in the excavation at Portchester. We have already referred to the structural changes in period 5 (*c.* A.D. 345). To these may be added the appearance of a woman's or child's shoe made in a distinctively Germanic manner found in the rubbish tipped into well 236 (p. 261). Neither observation proves anything, but they are wholly consistent with an increased Germanic presence after the mid-340s. Comparable evidence from elsewhere would go some way towards supporting the 'coast settled by . . .' hypothesis.

It is now evident (*contra* Cunliffe, 1968, 268–71) that the occupation of Portchester continued into the fifth century without a major break in 369 at the time of the restoration of the province by Theodosius. There may indeed have been shifts of emphasis in the deployment of troops but the fortification of Clausentum after 367 is best seen as the creation of an additional safe refuge rather than as a replacement to Portchester. The community occupying the fort continued much as before, the families living in close proximity to their refuse tips. That the Germanic element was maintained is demonstrated by the group of characteristic military fittings belonging to the *Laetenhorizont* dated, in the German frontier region, to the last third of the fourth century and the early fifth. The discovery of a silver coin of Maximus is a hint that official pay was still being handed out as late as the 380s.

The last indication we have of the organization of the Saxon Shore is provided by chapter XXVIII of the *Notitia Dignitatum*, which provides a list of nine coastal sites and their garrisons under the command of the *Comes Litoris Saxonici*.[2] The date of the final compilation of the chapter is still very much a matter of debate. It is generally assumed to represent the situation in the third quarter of the fourth century, although the most recently stated view supports an early fifth-century date (Ward, 1973). Whatever the outcome of the discussion, the document clearly indicates a measure of established order.

Whether or not Portchester featured on the list is debatable. The first eight names listed can all be assigned to known forts between Pevensey and Brancaster, but the ninth, *Portus Adurni*, where the *Numerus Exploratorum* was based, is without certain location. Some writers

---

[1] Usefully summarized in White (1961).

[2] *Not. Dig. Occ.* xxviii: discussed in detail by Stevens (1941) and summarized by Frere (1967), 228–38.

have suggested that it was Portchester by virtue of its position on the list following Povensey, but since the other forts are not listed in strict geographical order, the argument lacks conviction: it could equally well be the other unnamed fort of Walton Castle. Short of new epigraphic evidence the Roman name of Portchester will remain unknown.

In any event, Portchester continued in use into the fifth century. In the last years of the Roman occupation its massive defences, enclosing $8\frac{1}{4}$ acres, would, together with the neighbouring defended sites of Chichester and Clausentum, have formed a welcome refuge for the rural population in moments of crisis. It is at this point that the first volume of these reports ends and the second volume will begin.

# APPENDIX A: THE SECTIONS

THIRTY-ONE sections have been selected for illustration here (figs. 209–18) in addition to the sections of the individual pits and wells published above (figs. 26–105). They cover all major areas of complex stratigraphy, and include examples of areas where Roman layers are sparse. Sections 1–3 illustrate the landgate, 4–6 the watergate, 7–25 the main interior area, and 26–30 the area against the west wall.

A brief commentary on the Roman layers shown on each section follows. Comment on the post-Roman layers will be reserved for later volumes.[1]

## Section 1 (Trenches 1, 8, 110)

The Roman wall and Roman gate-tower platforms were primary. To the south of the wall, the offset of the Roman wall was sealed by a heap of stony clay (trench 1, layer 6) above which occupation rubbish accumulated (trench 1, layer 4). Within the gate-tower successive make-up layers are represented by trench 8, layers 5 and 9. Above this was an accumulation of soil containing some occupation material (trench 8, layer 4). Between the gate-towers builders' debris (trench 110, layers 33, 12 and 11) underlay the flint metalling of the road (trench 110, layer 10). Part of the walls of the Roman gatehouse collapsed (trench 8, layer 3) and were subsequently robbed (trench 8, layers 6 and 7, and trench 110, layer 26).

## Section 2 (Trenches 10 and 11)

The foundations for the Roman gate-tower were primary. Building spreads of construction period butted up to the surviving greensand foundation (trench 10, layers 12 and 13). Above this a layer of soil and mortar (trench 10, layer 11) accumulated. The Roman superstructure was extremely robbed.

## Section 3 (Trench 110)

The builders' mortar spread and subsequent make-up levels are represented by layers 30, 31, 32 and 34. Occupation material accumulating on this surface and in the drainage gully includes layers 8 and 33. Above this, soil mixed with mortary rubble represents the weathering and collapse of the superstructure of the guard-chamber.

## Section 4 (Trenches 32 and 34)

The Roman wall and the foundation platform for the gate-towers are primary. Make-up layers within the north gate-tower include trench 32, layers 20 and 19. Layer 18 represents the relaying of a hearth which is sealed by occupation debris (layer 17), mortary gravel make-up (layer 16) and more occupation rubbish (layer 15). The road surface of flints (trench 34, layer 21) is bedded on clayey gravel (trench 34, layer 22) and is cut by a drainage gully filled by soil and flints (trench 34, layer 24). The whole road is sealed by occupation material (trench 34, layer 14).

Layers representing different phases in the robbing of the Roman gatehouse superstructure include trench 32, layer 9, and trench 34, layer 13.

---

[1] In the main area excavation most of the latest Roman layers have been disturbed by Saxon and medieval ploughings. This matter will be discussed in detail in volume 2.

*Section 5 (Trenches 33, 34 and 38)*

Builders' debris of construction date includes trench 34, layers 40 and 41 and trench 35, layers 10 and 11. Trench 33, layer 10, represents clay piled up around the inturned Roman gate wall. Eroded mortar rubble from the weathering of the gate-tower includes trench 33, layer 14 and trench 34, layer 39. A later soil accumulation containing only Roman material is represented by trench 33, layers 7, 8, 9; trench 34, layer 38, and trench 38, layer 8.

*Section 6 (Trench 34)*

The foundation platform for the north gate-tower was cut into the natural brickearth.

Builders' debris of construction date (layer 20) is overlaid by clay hearths interleaved with soil (layers 18 and 17) which is sealed by gravelly mortar (layer 16), sealed in turn by soil (layer 15).

Outside the gate tower, builders' debris is represented by layer 40. This is sealed by mortary rubble (layer 39) derived from the weathering of the gate-tower superstructure. The robber trench for the gate-tower wall is filled by layers 38 and 37.

*Section 7 (Trenches 87 and 91)*

The primary clay bank was piled against the back face of the Roman wall (trench 91, layer 69).

Late metalling of the road surface was represented by trench 91, layer 70, and can be seen in the bottom of trench 87. Occupation accumulation was represented by trench 91, layer 46 and trench 87, layer 48.

*Section 8 (Trenches 87, 91 and 107)*

Foundation trench fill against back face of the Roman wall (trench 107, layers 81 and 82).
Primary clay bank (trench 107, layer 74).
Lower occupation (trench 107, layer 61).
Middle clay (trench 107, layers 44, 53).
Middle occupation (trench 107, layer 52).
Upper clay (trench 107, layer 50).
Make-up (trench 91, layer 77; trench 87, layers 20 and 41).
Layers below make-up (trench 91, layer 78).
Occupation above make-up (trench 87, layer 10; trench 91, layer 46 and trench 107, layers 41 and 31).

*Section 9 (Trenches 100, 101, 103)*

Primary clay bank, unexcavated and unnumbered.
Lower and middle occupation (trench 103, layers 47 and 77).
Upper clay (trench 103, layers 46 and 74).
Upper occupation and general occupation layers (trench 100, layer 66; trench 101, layers 103 and 117; trench 103, layers 23, 69 and 72).
Cobbles equivalent to make-up layers and make-up (trench 100, layer 99; trench 101, layer 94).
Occupation beneath (trench 100, layers 107, 118, 124).
Builders' mortar spread (trench 101, layers 123 and 135).
Gullies (trench 101, layer 122).

*Section 10 (Trench 102)*

Primary clay bank; unexcavated and unnumbered.
Lower occupation (layer 66).

29

Middle clay (layer 65).
Middle occupation (layers 60 and 63).
Upper clay (layer 62).
Upper occupation and general occupation (layers 44, 46, 47, 48).

### Section 11 (Trench 91)

Section shows the foundation trench for the Norman blocking wall of the south postern gate cutting through the Saxon and Roman layers. Layers 16, 17 and 18 are Roman occupation layers, 17 representing a layer of eroded mortar. Layer 10 consists of more eroded mortar and rubble of late Roman or early Saxon period.

### Section 12 (Trench 108)

Primary clay bank (unnumbered) separated by a thin lens of occupation material, layer 231, from a further levelling of clay, layer 225, belonging to the construction period.
Lower occupation (layer 205).
Middle clay (layer 204).
Middle occupation (layer 163).
Upper clay (layers 75 and 111).

### Section 13 (Trenches 100, 101, 102)

Foundation trench filling behind the Roman wall (trench 102, layer 30).
Primary clay bank (trench 102, layer 34 and trench 101, layer 63).
Lower occupation (trench 102, layer 32).
Middle clay (trench 102, layer 28).
Middle occupation (trench 102, layers 24, 25, 26, 27).
Upper clay (trench 102, layer 22).
Upper occupation and general occupation levels (trench 102, layers 21 and 33a; trench 101, layer 49; and trench 100, layers 24, 29, 32).

### Section 14 (Trench 88)

Early quarry pit (layer 34).
Early drainage gully (layer 46).
Late scoop (layer 40).
Make-up (layer 45).
General occupation (layer 42).

### Section 15 (Trenches 72, 71, 73, 80, 82)

Throughout the area crossed by this section, the Roman occupation material had been reduced to a single layer by post-Roman ploughing. This appears immediately above natural as trench 72, layers 7 and 6; trench 71, layer 6; trench 73, layer 10; trench 80, layer 7; trench 82, layer 9.

In trench 71, layer 23 represents an area of cobbling sealing occupation material (layer 38). In trench 72, a layer of chalky mortar (layer 9) is sealed beneath the Roman general layer.

### Section 16 (Trenches 94, 95, 96, 97, 98, 99, 109)

Section 16 parallel, to Section 15, reflects much the same simple stratigraphy. The Roman general layers include trenches 94, layer 37b; trench 95, layers 61 and ?113; trench 96, layer 25; trench 97,

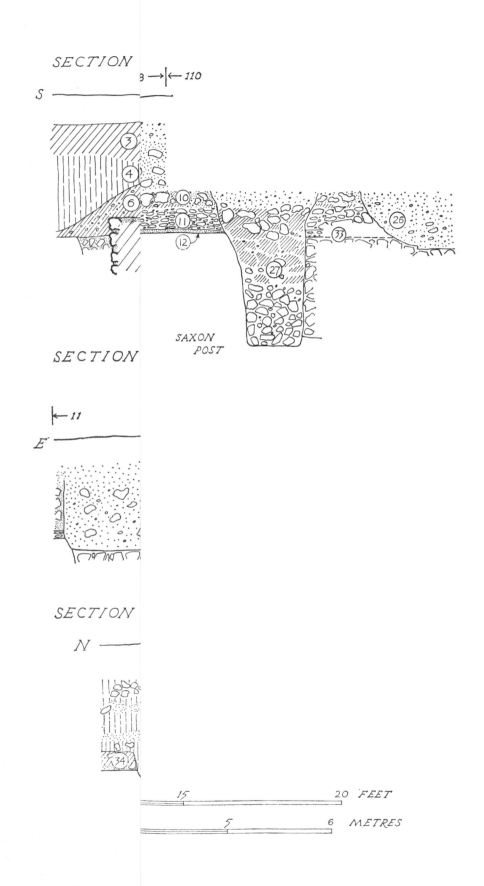

SECTION

3 →|← 110

S

③

④

⑥ ⑩
⑪
⑫

㉖

㉝

㉗

SAXON
POST

SECTION

|← 11

E

SECTION

N

㉞

15                    20 FEET

5              6 METRES

# APPENDIX B: THE USE OF TOOTH WEAR AS A GUIDE TO THE AGE OF DOMESTIC ANIMALS— A BRIEF EXPLANATION

## By ANNIE GRANT

THIS is a brief outline of the method used to record and interpret the wear on the teeth of the Portchester mandibles.

The amount of tooth wear is commonly used by farmers and veterinary surgeons as a guide to the age of farm animals. This assessment of age is generally made from the incisor teeth which are the only teeth readily visible in the live animal. Unfortunately for the archaeologist, mandibles are rarely found with the incisors in place, and on unsieved sites the incisors themselves are rarely recovered. Assessment of age from the wear on molar teeth has been used to some effect for game animals where annual culls and natural deaths of animals of known age have made possible a proper study of the value of the method (*vide* Lowe, 1967). Since mandibles with molar teeth in place are frequently recovered on archaeological sites, a method based on molar wear should be of great practical value to animal bone workers.

When a tooth erupts, its upper surface is completely covered in enamel. As the tooth comes into wear, the enamel of the occlusal or biting surface is gradually worn away revealing the darker coloured dentine below. At first 'islands' of internal enamel are left within the dentine, but as wear proceeds these 'islands' gradually disappear, so that the biting surface of the tooth is formed entirely of dentine with a border of enamel around the edge. In later stages still the tooth wears right down to its roots, and will finally fall out. In sheep and pig mandibles especially, the enamel on the sides of the teeth that touch the next teeth in the row may also wear away. This is due to overcrowding of the teeth in the jaw and has no direct bearing on the following study.

Figures 220–2 give the 'stages' of wear observed on the four last teeth of the mandibular row of cattle, sheep and pigs. In practice it has been found that almost every worn tooth seen can be fairly readily assigned to one of these stages although, since the wear on a tooth is a continual process, occasionally wear patterns will be seen that lie between two stages illustrated. In these cases, the teeth can be assigned to one or other of the stages closest to the wear stage of the tooth in question. The wear on a tooth is normally heaviest on the first cusp of a tooth as this cusp erupts first and consequently comes into wear sooner than the second or third cusp of the tooth. Sometimes teeth are seen that have more severe wear on the second cusp than on the first cusp. This might be caused by unequal pressures from the upper jaw due to the loss of a tooth or some other anomaly. It makes assigning a 'stage' to the wear of the tooth rather difficult. In practice the writer has usually found it best to assign the tooth to the stage that shows approximately the same *amount* of wear as the anomalous tooth, but the anomaly should always be noted. Uneven wear is found fairly frequently on very heavily worn teeth but this does not always affect the pattern of wear. In any case it is recognized that these later stages are somewhat variable.

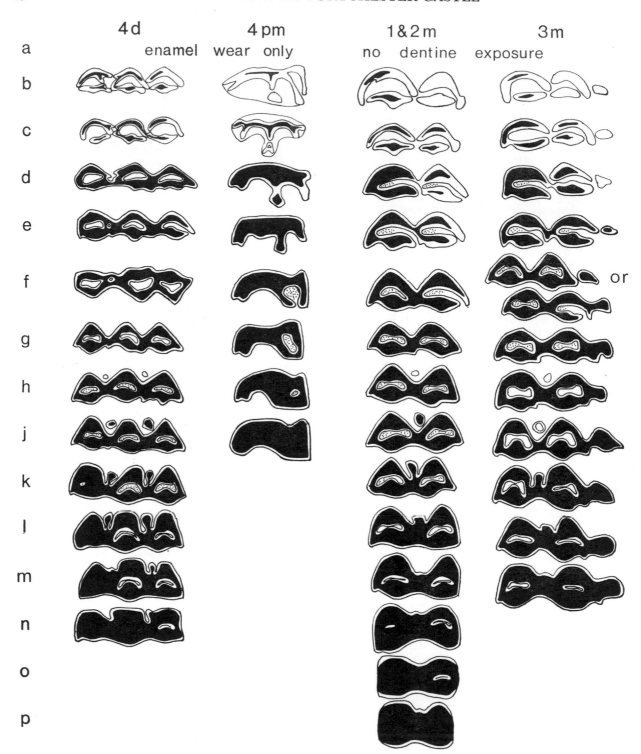

Fig. 220.    The tooth wear stages of cattle

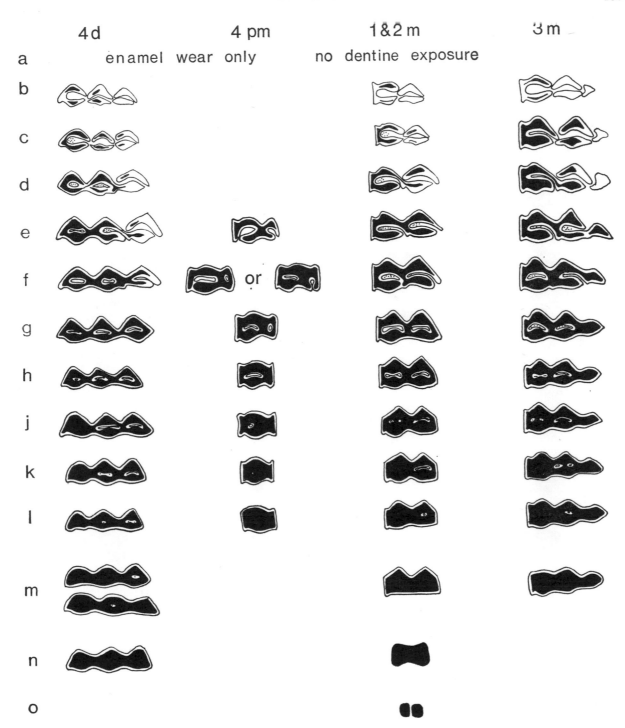

FIG. 221.   The tooth wear stages of sheep

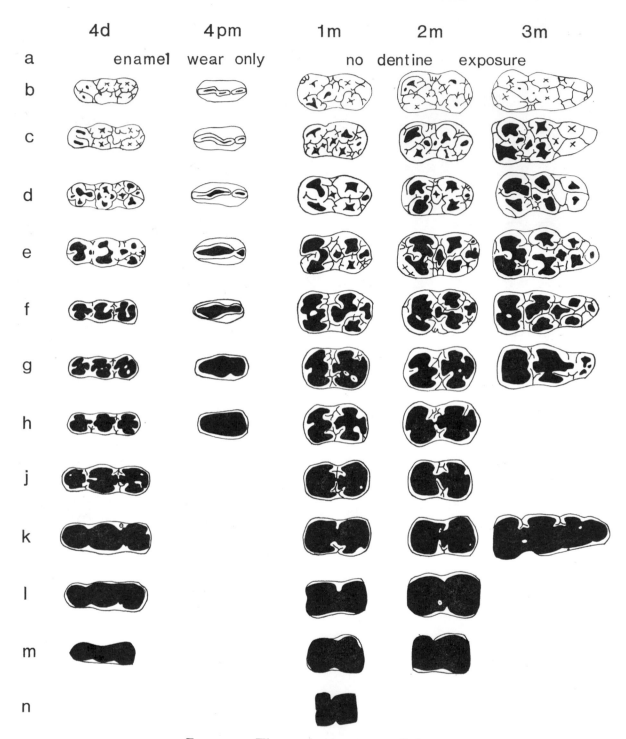

FIG. 222. The tooth wear stages of pig

The wear on the fourth premolar is also variable, especially in sheep jaws. This is mainly because overcrowding of the jaw often causes this tooth to become impacted against the first molar. The rate of eruption and the angle of wear of the tooth will be severely affected by this. It is for this reason also that the early stages of wear of this tooth in sheep are not given.

For the stages of eruption of the teeth, the writer has used the notation proposed by Ewebank *et al.* (1964) although it is generally only necessary to record the eruption of the first cusp of the tooth, unless one has a sample with very large numbers of young jaws. In this case the method proposed by Ewebank could be employed for the very young mandibles. The symbols used are:

C — perforation in crypt visible
V — tooth visible in crypt but below head of bone
E — tooth erupting through bone
½ — tooth half erupted
U — tooth almost at full height but unworn

The next stage will be stage 'a' on the tooth wear charts.

Using Ewebank's scheme and the tooth wear charts, it is possible to record the state of eruption or wear for each of the last four teeth in the mandibular row of cattle, sheep and pig. This can be done very quickly with a small amount of practice, especially by recording the jaws on paper ruled with vertical columns for each tooth. Although the state of wear of the first three (two in the case of cattle and sheep) deciduous molar or premolar teeth is not

## TABLE XX

| Eruption/ Wear stage | Numerical equivalent |
|:---:|:---:|
| C | 1 |
| V | 2 |
| E | 3 |
| ½ | 4 |
| U | 5 |
| a | 6 |
| b | 7 |
| c | 8 |
| d | 9 |
| e | 10 |
| f | 11 |
| g | 12 |
| h | 13 |
| j | 14 |
| k | 15 |
| l | 16 |
| m | 17 |
| n | 18 |
| o | 19 |
| p | 20 |

recorded, their presence and the state of eruption can be noted. Any anomalies, caries, diseases, impacted teeth and post- or ante-mortem tooth loss should also be recorded at the same time. Deciduous teeth can be distinguished from permanent teeth by the use of brackets round a wear stage that refers to a deciduous tooth.

Once all the mandibles from a site or group have been recorded in this way, the results can be analysed. This is begun by using the eruption or wear stages on the first molar to place the mandibles in ascending order of degree of wear. Subdivisions will be made by referring to the stage of wear on the other teeth present.

The wear of the fourth premolar will be the least reliable for this as discussed above. If a jaw does not have the first molar present, or for that matter any other tooth, it can usually be satisfactorily placed into the sequence constructed from the wear on the first molar by reference to those teeth that are present. Where a jaw has only one of the relevant teeth present, it is not generally possible to place it in the sequence very precisely, unless it is a tooth in a stage of eruption or in a very early stage of wear. Some jaws that do not precisely agree with the sequence of wear and tooth replacement of the majority of the mandibles will always be found, but they should be placed in the sequence where they best fit. Tables XXI–XXIII show the mandibles from Portchester placed in 'wear order'. Those that did not have enough teeth present to be thought reliable for this analyses are not included.

The next stage is to assign a numerical value to the tooth wear of the mandibles as a whole. Each eruption and wear stage is given a numerical equivalent as shown in Table XX. The numerical value of the jaw as a whole is found by adding up the value of the three molar teeth only. The deciduous and premolar teeth are not used for this purpose. However, where a jaw has one or more of the molar teeth absent, a decision has to be made as to whether one can reliably predict what the state of wear on the missing teeth would have been. This is done by reference to the state of wear of those teeth that are present including the deciduous molar or fourth premolar. If it is found that for jaws which have teeth in the same stages of eruption and wear as those present in the jaw in question, there is little or no variation in the state of wear of the missing tooth, the stage of wear of that tooth can be fairly confidently predicted. Sometimes, however, a range within which the jaw should fall has to be given. Tables XXI–XXIII include the numerical values of the Portchester mandibles. Where the values have been estimated they are followed by an 'e'.

It should be noted at this stage that the intervals between the tooth wear stages are by no means equal in time. Some stages last for very short amounts of time while others are very long-lasting. Stage 'g' for first, second and third molars of sheep is very long-lasting, while the early stages of wear for all teeth tend to be relatively short. On the whole the early wear stages last a short time and the later stages last slightly longer, but this is a very general rule. In sheep, the stage 'g' is the longest lasting of all.

Some idea of the length of any stage can be gained by looking at the number of stages the other teeth in the row go through while one tooth is in any one stage. For example, while the first molar of sheep is in stage 'g' the second molar stages range from 'b' to 'g'. The wear on the other teeth obviously subdivides the time represented by a very long-lasting stage in one tooth. Given a sheep mandible with only a molar in stage 'g' present, it would be very unwise to try to predict the wear stages of the other teeth.

Once numerical values of the jaws have been calculated for each jaw it then becomes possible to construct histograms and cumulative percentage charts as in figures 209–5. What these graphs and histograms show is a relative time scale. They also demonstrate 'peak' killing stages and allow groups of mandibles from the same environment to be compared. By correlating the analysis of epiphyseal fusion of the long bones, and by using eruption ages of the teeth given by Silver (1969) tentative absolute ages can be fixed. For reasons already mentioned, the time intervals between the numerical wear stages are likely to be short in the early stages and relatively long in the later stages. The teeth possibly wear more slowly in old animals too. It has been shown with human teeth that the length of time it takes any tooth to reach a given stage depends on its position in the tooth row. The first molar will reach the stage the most rapidly with the second and third molars each taking longer than the tooth before (*vide* Miles, 1963; Murphy, 1969).

## TABLE XXI

*Wear Stages in Cattle Mandibles*

| Group One | | | | | Group Three | | | | |
|---|---|---|---|---|---|---|---|---|---|
| 4PM | 1M | 2M | 3M | Numerical value | 4PM | 1M | 2M | 3M | Numerical value |
| (½) | V | | | 2 | (½) | — | | | 4–6e |
| (d) | e | V | | 12 | (b) | — | | | 6e |
| — | h | g | g | 37 | (k) | g | — | E | 24e |
| E | k | j | d | 38 | — | — | d | V/E | 24e |
| e | k | j | g | 41 | — | — | f | b | 30e |
| e | k | j | g | 41 | — | — | g | b | 30e |
| f | k | j | — | 41e | — | k | g | f | 38 |
| f | k | k | g | 42 | e | k | h | f | 39 |
| f | l | h | g | 42 | ½ | k | j | e | 39 |
| — | l | k | — | 43e | c | k | j | f | 40 |
| — | l | k | g | 43 | c | k | j | f | 40 |
| — | — | k | j | 45e | — | k | j | f | 40 |
| k | m | l | k | 48 | — | k | j | f | 40 |
| — | — | l | k | 48e | f | k | k | g | 42 |
| — | m | m | m | 51 | — | — | k | g | 42e |
| h | n | m | m | 52 | f | l | k | j | 45 |
| h | o | m | — | 53 | f | l | k | j | 45 |
| h | o | n | m | 54 | g | l | k | — | 45e |
| | | | | | — | l | k | j | 45 |
| | | | | | — | l | k | — | 45e |
| | | | | | g | m | l | g | 45 |
| | | | | | f | l | k | k | 46 |
| | | | | | — | m | k | k | 47 |
| | | | | | g | m | l | k | 48 |
| | | | | | g | m | l | k | 48 |
| | | | | | — | m | l | k | 48 |
| | | | | | — | m | l | — | 48e |
| | | | | | — | — | l | k | 48e |
| | | | | | h | n | m | h | 48 |
| | | | | | g | m | m | l | 50 |

## Table XXI—*continued*

| | Group Four | | | | | Group Five | | | |
|---|---|---|---|---|---|---|---|---|---|
| *4PM* | *1M* | *2M* | *3M* | *Numerical value* | *4PM* | *1M* | *2M* | *3M* | *Numerical value* |
| (e) | ½ | | | 4 | (l) | h | f | — | 31e |
| (f) | ½ | | | 4 | d | j | g | c | 34 |
| (m) | g | d | EV | 24 | c | k | g | f | 38 |
| — | g | f | b | 30 | — | — | h | f | 39e |
| (o+) | k | g | c | 35 | — | — | g | g | 39e |
| ½ | — | g | c | 35e | — | k | j | g | 41 |
| — | — | g | d | 36e | — | — | j | g | 41e |
| — | h | g | g | 37 | f | k | k | g | 42 |
| k | k | g | f | 37 | — | — | k | g | 42 |
| U | k | g | f | 37 | d | k | k | g | 42 |
| — | k | g | g | 39 | e | l | k | g | 43 |
| — | k | g | g | 39 | — | l | k | g | 43 |
| — | k | j | g | 41 | — | k | k | j | 44 |
| — | k | j | — | 41e | f | l | k | — | 44e |
| f | k | k | g | 42 | f | l | k | — | 44e |
| — | l | k | g | 43 | f | l | k | — | 44e |
| e | l | k | — | 43e | — | l | l | g | 44 |
| — | l | k | — | 43e | g | l | k | j | 45 |
| — | l | k | g | 43 | g | l | k | j | 45 |
| — | l | k | g | 43 | g | l | k | j | 45 |
| — | — | k | g | 43e | — | k | k | j | 45e |
| — | — | k | g | 43e | — | l | k | j | 45 |
| — | l | k | — | 43e | g | l | k | k | 46 |
| f | l | k | — | 43e | — | l | k | k | 46 |
| f | l | k | — | 43e | — | l | k | k | 46 |
| — | l | l | g | 44 | g | m | k | j | 46 |
| — | — | j | j | 44e | g | m | l | j | 47 |
| — | l | k | j | 45 | — | m | l | — | 47e |
| — | l | k | j | 45 | — | m | k | — | 47e |
| g | l | k | j | 45 | h | m | k | k | 47 |
| — | l | k | j | 45 | g | n | m | — | 51e |
| — | — | k | j | 45e | h | o | m | m | 53 |
| — | l | k | k | 46 | | | | | |
| — | l | l | — | 47e | | | | | |
| — | m | l | — | 49e | | | | | |
| — | m | l | k | 49 | | | | | |
| — | m | m | — | 50e | | | | | |
| — | o | m | l | 52 | | | | | |
| — | — | p | m | 57+e | | | | | |

e = estimated
— = tooth lost post-mortem
( ) = deciduous tooth
a-m = lost ante-mortem

# TABLE XXII

*Wear Stages in Pig Mandibles*

| Group One | | | | | Group Three | | | | |
|---|---|---|---|---|---|---|---|---|---|
| 4PM | 1M | 2M | 3M | Numerical value | 4PM | 1M | 2M | 3M | Numerical value |
| (b) | V | | | 2 | (U) | | | | →1 |
| (b) | E | | | 3 | (b) | U | | | 5 |
| (b) | E | | | 3 | (f) | b | | | 7e |
| (c) | E | | | 3 | (j) | c | C | | 9 |
| (k) | a | V | | 6 | — | c | E | C | 12 |
| (k) | b | — | | 8e | (g) | d | E | — | 13 |
| — | b | — | | 8e | — | e | E | — | 14 |
| — | c | V | C | 11 | — | g | b | E | 22 |
| (k) | c | — | — | 11 | — | g | b | ½ | 23 |
| (j) | c | V | — | 11e | b | g | b | — | 23 |
| (j) | c | a | — | 12e | — | g | b | — | 23 |
| — | | ½ | C | 14e | — | g | c | ½ | 24 |
| (k) | d | | — | 15e | c | h | c | — | 25e |
| b | g | a | V | 20 | — | j | c | U | 27 |
| b | g | b | — | 23e | b | k | c | U | 28 |
| — | g | c | E | 23 | d | l | f | U | 32 |
| b | g | c | ½ | 24 | — | k | f | b | 33 |
| a | g | c | — | 24 | e | k | f | — | 33e |
| b | g | c | ½ | 24 | — | — | f | c | 35e |
| — | | c | — | 25e | — | — | k | c | 40e |
| — | j | c | ½ | 26 | — | — | — | f | 44+e |
| b | g | d | a | 27 | | | | | |
| d | g | d | b | 28 | | | | | |
| b | h | e | a | 28 | | | | | |
| c | h | d | — | 28e | | | | | |
| — | g | f | b | 29 | | | | | |
| c | l | d | ½ | 29 | | | | | |
| — | j | c | U | 29 | | | | | |
| b | j | e | a | 30 | | | | | |
| b | j | e | a | 30 | | | | | |
| — | — | e | a | 30e | | | | | |
| d | l | e | b | 33 | | | | | |
| d | l | f | — | 34e | | | | | |
| e | l | g | b | 35 | | | | | |
| e | m | f | c | 36 | | | | | |
| — | m | g | c | 38 | | | | | |
| — | m | g | d | 40 | | | | | |
| f | n | — | — | 41+e | | | | | |
| — | — | m | f | 47+e | | | | | |

## Table XXII—continued

| Group Four | | | | | Group Five | | | | |
|---|---|---|---|---|---|---|---|---|---|
| 4PM | 1M | 2M | 3M | Numerical value | 4PM | 1M | 2M | 3M | Numerical value |
| (c) | ½ | | | 4 | (½) | | | | 1 |
| (b) | a | | | 8 | (b) | V | | | 2 |
| (j) | b | E | | 10 | (b) | V | | | 2 |
| (k) | c | V | | 10 | — | b | C | | 8 |
| — | c | V | — | 10 | — | b | V | | 9 |
| — | c | V | C | 11 | (m) | f | E | | 14 |
| (m) | d | E | — | 12 | — | e | ½ | — | 15e |
| (k) | d | a | — | 16e | — | e | b | — | 22e |
| ½ | d | b | — | 17e | b | e | — | — | 22e |
| (l) | e | U | — | 17e | b | e | c | U | 23 |
| — | e | b | V | 19 | b | f | b | — | 23e |
| — | — | b | V | 19 | b | g | b | V | 21 |
| — | e | b | — | 19e | — | h | b | E | 23 |
| b | e | c | — | 20e | — | — | c | ½ | 24e |
| — | e | c | — | 20 | c | g | c | — | 25e |
| — | — | c | V | 20e | c | h | c | ½ | 25 |
| — | g | b | — | 21e | c | h | d | — | 26e |
| — | g | b | — | 21e | c | l | e | b | 33 |
| c | g | c | V | 22 | f | a–m | — | d | 46e |
| — | g | c | V | 22 | | | | | |
| — | — | c | V | 22e | | | | | |
| c | g | d | — | 23e | | | | | |
| — | h | d | V | 24 | | | | | |
| — | j | c | E | 25 | | | | | |
| c | l | d | E | 25 | | | | | |
| c | l | c | ½ | 25 | | | | | |
| b | h | c | U | 26 | | | | | |
| — | — | c | ½ | 26e | | | | | |
| — | — | — | ½ | 26e | | | | | |
| c | h | g | V | 27 | | | | | |
| c | k | g | E | 27 | | | | | |
| — | k | d | E | 27 | | | | | |
| c | k | d | — | 27 | | | | | |
| — | — | c | a | 28e | | | | | |
| — | k | c | U | 28 | | | | | |
| e | **k** | g | b | 34 | | | | | |
| e | **m** | e | b | 34 | | | | | |
| — | — | e | b | 34e | | | | | |
| f | l | f | c | 35 | | | | | |
| e | m | f | b | 35 | | | | | |
| — | — | g | b | 36e | | | | | |
| f | m | g | c | 37 | | | | | |
| f | n | g | c | 38 | | | | | |
| f | n | g | c | 38 | | | | | |
| f | n | g | d | 39 | | | | | |
| — | — | h | d | 40e | | | | | |
| g | n | l | d | 42 | | | | | |
| — | — | l | e | 45+e | | | | | |
| — | — | — | l | 50+e | | | | | |

e = estimated; — = tooth lost post-mortem; ( ) = deciduous tooth; a-m = lost ante-mortem

# TABLE XXIII

## *Wear Stages in Sheep Mandibles*

| Group One 4PM | 1M | 2M | 3M | Numerical value | Group Three 4PM | 1M | 2M | 3M | Numerical value |
|---|---|---|---|---|---|---|---|---|---|
| (e/f) | — | — |  | →13e | (a) | C |  |  | 1 |
| (g) | e | — |  | →14e | (c) | E |  |  | 3 |
| (h) | f | E |  | 14 | (e) | E |  |  | 3 |
| — | g | c | V | 22 | (d) | — |  |  | 3e |
| V | g | c | — | 22e | (g) | d | — |  | 10–17e |
| (k) | g | d | — | 23e | (h) | d | — |  | 10–17e |
| — | g | d | CV | 23 | (h) | f | b | C | 19 |
| V | g | d | — | 23 | — | f | c | C | 20 |
| (l) | g | e | V | 24 | — | f | c | — | 21e |
| (m) | g | e | — | 24e | — | f | c | — | 21e |
| — | g | d | E | 24 | (g) | f | d | — | 21e |
| V | g | e | — | 24e | (h) | g | c | C | 21 |
| (k) | g | e | E | 25 | — | f | c | E | 22 |
| (l) | g | f | — | 26e | (h) | g | c | V | 22 |
| — | — | — | ½ | 26e | (j) | g | C | — | 22e |
| e | g | g | b | 31 | (h) | g | d | c/V | 23 |
| ½ | h | f | c | 32 | (j) | g | d | c/V | 23 |
| — | h | g | b | 32 | V | g | d | — | 23e |
| — | g | g | d | 33 | E | g | e | — | 24e |
| — | h | g | c | 33 | E | g | e | V | 24 |
| f | g | g | e | 34 | — | g | e | V | 24 |
| — | g | g | e | 34 | ½ | g | e | E | 25 |
| — | h | g | f | 36 | (l) | g | f | E | 26 |
| l | m | h | g | 42 | — | g | e | c | 30 |
| l | m | k | g | 44 | — | g | e | — | 30e |
|  |  |  |  |  | — | g | f | c | 31 |
|  |  |  |  |  | — | g | g | b | 31 |
|  |  |  |  |  | — | g | g | c | 32 |
|  |  |  |  |  | — | g | g | — | 32e |
|  |  |  |  |  | g | g | g | d | 33 |
|  |  |  |  |  | g | g | g | d | 33 |
|  |  |  |  |  | — | — | g | d | 33e |
|  |  |  |  |  | — | — | g | f | 37e |
|  |  |  |  |  | h | j | g | — | 38e |
|  |  |  |  |  | — | k | g | g | 39 |
|  |  |  |  |  | — | l | g | g | 40 |
|  |  |  |  |  | l | l | l | h | 45 |

## Table XXIII—*continued*

| Group Four | | | | | Group Five | | | | |
|---|---|---|---|---|---|---|---|---|---|
| 4PM | 1M | 2M | 3M | Numerical value | 4PM | 1M | 2M | 3M | Numerical value |
| (a) | | | | →1 | (½) | | | | →1 |
| (d) | E | | | 3 | (½) | | | | →1 |
| (d) | E | | | 3 | (½) | V | | | 2 |
| (c) | E | C | | 4 | (c) | V | | | 2 |
| (e) | — | — | | 4e | (c) | V | | | 2 |
| (f) | ½ | — | | 6e | (d) | V | | | 2 |
| (f) | ½ | V | | 6 | — | V | | | 2 |
| (f) | b | — | | 8–15 | (d) | — | | | 2e |
| (f) | — | — | | 8–15 | (d) | E | | | 3 |
| (f) | — | — | | 8–15 | (e) | E | | | 3 |
| (g) | b/c | — | | 8–15 | (e) | — | | | 3e |
| (g) | — | — | | 8–15 | (e) | — | | | 3e |
| (f) | c | — | | 8–15 | (f) | ½ | C | | 5 |
| (g) | f | V | | 15 | (g) | e | E | | 13 |
| (k) | g | c | C | 21 | (g) | e | — | | 13 |
| (g) | f | c | E | 22 | (h) | f | U | C | 17 |
| — | f | d | — | 22e | — | e | b | — | 18e |
| — | g | d | — | 23e | (h) | f | U | C | 19 |
| (h) | g | — | — | 23e | (g) | g | b | — | 19 |
| (k) | g | d | — | 23e | (h) | g | c | — | 21 |
| E | g | d | V | 23 | — | — | c | C | 21 |
| — | g | c | — | 24 | (h) | g | c | C | 21 |
| — | g | c | ½E | 24 | (k) | g | c | — | 21 |
| — | g | e | ½ | 25 | (l) | g | c | — | 21e |
| E | g | e | ½ | 26 | (h) | g | d | — | 22e |
| — | g | e | ½ | 27 | — | g | d | — | 22e |
| — | g | f | b | 27 | (h) | g | e | — | 23 |
| — | g | — | c | 29 | (h) | g | e | V | 23 |
| — | g | e | — | 30 | ½ | g | d | E | 24 |
| f | g | e | b | 31e | — | g | e | E | 25 |
| — | — | g | b | 31e | (l) | g | e | — | 25e |
| — | — | g | b | 31e | — | g | f | C | 24 |
| — | g | f | c | 31 | V | g | e | U | 25 |
| — | g | g | c | 32 | ½ | g | e | — | 27 |
| f | h | g | — | 32 | (m) | g | e | — | 27e |
| — | h | g | b | 32 | f | g | e | c | 30 |
| — | g | g | e | 34 | — | g | f | b | 30 |
| — | g | g | e | 34 | — | g | f | b | 30 |
| j | h | g | d | 34 | — | g | f | d | 32 |
| — | g | g | f | 35 | — | g | g | c | 32 |
| — | h | g | g | 37 | — | g | g | d | 33 |
| j | k | g | f | 38 | — | — | g | e | 34 |
| k | k | g | f | 38 | g | — | g | e | 35 |
| — | — | g | f | 38 | — | g | g | f | 35 |
| h | l | g | — | 39e | g | h | g | e | 35 |
| — | m | g | g | 41 | — | h | g | — | 35e |
| k | m | g | g | 41 | — | j | g | — | 37e |
| k | m | — | — | 41e | l | m | j | g | 43 |
| l | m | k | g | 44 | l | m | k | g | 44 |
| l | n | n | — | 47+e | | | | | |

e = estimated; — = tooth lost post-mortem; ( ) = deciduous tooth; a-m = lost ante-mortem.

It is hoped that with further research, it may be possible to put more precise age values to the wear stages. Possible lines of research are studies of modern aged animals in different environments and feeding conditions and analysis of incremental structures in teeth.

By examining the sequence of mandibles made for each group however, further information can be elicited. It is known and has been stated by Chaplin (1971) that the *rate* of wear will be affected by many variables, especially the amount of mineral or abrasive material in the foodstuff. The age of the eruption of the teeth will also vary according to such factors as breed and state of nutrition. The advantage of using a method that records the wear of each tooth individually, rather than of the mandible as a whole, is that one can more readily assess the possible effects of these variables. This can be done by examining the wear stage of, for example, the first molar in jaws where the second molar is actually erupting. If there is a great deal of wear on the first molar, it could either mean that the rate of wear was very rapid, or that the age of eruption of the second molar was very late. Analysis of the soil type in the area where the animals are expected to have grazed can be carried out. Correlation with the epiphyseal fusion data, which might be expected to be affected by the same factors that cause late eruption of teeth but not by abrasive conditions, might help the bone worker decide which of the possible causes is the most likely to be affecting any group of jaws. By careful appraisal of these factors it might be possible to compare the results of such tooth wear analyses for sites in very different environments.

On the whole the writer has found fairly little variation in the relationships of the wear stages of the teeth in the jaws of sheep and cattle in any single group of bones. The variation tends to be greater for pig mandibles. This must certainly be in part related to the omnivorous feeding habits of the pig. A pig fed on soft foods would be expected to show far less tooth wear than a pig that was left to forage. The individual feeding preferences of different pigs within the same population would also be expected to cause anomalies in the tooth wear. This is seen in the larger number of pig jaws that do not fit precisely into the sequence. A small range of variation is to be expected in any species.

There are obvious dangers in using this method of recording and analysing tooth wear. Some have been mentioned above; others are not so obvious. Cattle and sheep cannot chew on both sides of their mouths at once. Observations in zoos of other animals with similarly constructed jaws have shown that some have a marked preference for one side of the jaw over the other. This will obviously affect enormously the wear on the teeth. It is generally expected that the chewing forces will be equally divided between the two jaws, whereas an animal chewing on one side of the mouth rather than the other will have very unequal wear on the two sides of its jaw. It is to be hoped that very unequal chewing habits are rare. On the few occasions that the writer has examined pairs of jaws that definitely belong to the same animal, the state of wear has been the same on each jaw.

As it stands, this method can only be used to indicate the relative ages of animals within a population. Actual ages can only be guessed at. The method seems to work best for sheep, although in fact there is always the possibility of the presence of goat in the sample. It may be that the teeth of goats wear at the same rate as those of sheep in the same environments but this should be tested by further research. The method is probably least reliable for pig, for the reasons discussed.

The value of this method in comparison to some other methods of ageing animals is that it is quick and easy to use, involves no destruction of the bone, and since jaws are usually very well recovered even on unsieved sites, the sample available for analysis is usually relatively large and represents the complete age range of the animals present. If it were adopted by other animal bone workers it would allow more direct comparisons to be made between bone assemblages analysed by different people. It is only by standardizing and clarifying the methodology, that animal bone workers can produce reports that are of real value. Only then can we lift the level of animal bone reporting from the isolated appendix at the back of a site report to proper and valid research into the relationship of man to his animals and environment.

## ACKNOWLEDGEMENT

I am grateful to Mr Don Brothwell for his advice.

## BIBLIOGRAPHY

CHAPLIN, R. E. 1971. *The Study of Animal Bones from Archaeological Sites*. London.

EWEBANK, J. M., PHILLIPSON, D. W. and WHITEHOUSE, R. D. with HIGGS, E. S. 1964. 'Sheep in the Iron Age: amethod of study'. *P.P.S.* xxx, 423–6

LOWE, P. A. 1967. 'Teeth as indicators of age with special reference to Red Deer (*Cervus elaphus*) of known age from Rhum'. *J. Zool. Lond.* clii, 137–53.

MILES, A. E. W. 1963. 'The dentition in the assessment of individual age', in Brothwell, D., *Dental Anthropology*. London.

MURPHY, T. 1969. 'The changing pattern of dentine exposure in human tooth attrition'. *Amer. J. of Phys. Anth.* 167–78.

SILVER, I. A. 1969. 'The ageing of domestic animals', in Brothwell, D. and Higgs, E. S., *Science in Archaeology*. London.

# INDEX

PLATE I

General view of Portchester Castle from the air
*(photo: Arthur Rule)*

PLATE II

The south wall of the fort from the outside
(*photo: David Baker*)

PLATE III

*a.* The west wall, as exposed in the 1961 excavation, showing the join of two working parties
(*photo: David Baker*)

*b.* The west wall showing the same joining of the working parties from the outside
(*photo: David Baker*)

PLATE IV

*a.* The 1961 excavation facing south, looking along the Roman wall
(*photo: David Baker*)

*b.* The 1961 excavation facing towards the landgate
(*photo: David Baker*)

PLATE V

(a)

a. The inner face of the south wall, with clay bank in position, exposed in trench 108
(*photo: Mike Rouillard*)

(b)

b. The inner face of the south wall exposed to the level of the footings seen between the footings of the sixteenth century storehouse in trenches 102 and 103
(*photo: David Leigh*)

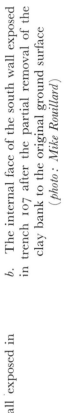

*b.* The internal face of the south wall exposed in trench 107 after the partial removal of the clay bank to the original ground surface
*(photo: Mike Rouillard)*

*a.* The clay bank against the back face of the south wall exposed in trenches 107 and 108
*(photo: Mike Rouillard)*

PLATE VII

*a.* Bastion no. 16
(*photo: David Baker*)

*b.* Bastion no. 20
(*photo: David Baker*)

PLATE VIII

b. Excavation in the top of Bastion 5 showing Roman masonry with an offset probably for a timber platform
(*photo: David Baker*)

a. Bastion no. 5
(*photo: David Baker*)

PLATE IX

*a.* The site of bastion no. 9. The figure stands where the north side of the bastion once was
(*photo: David Baker*)

*b.* The foundation of bastion no. 9 at its junction with the fort wall. The offset of the wall is below the rod
(*photo: David Baker*)

PLATE X

*a.* The site of bastion no. 7. The figure stands at the extremity of the bastion footing exposed in the excavations
(*photo: David Baker*)

*b.* The foundation of bastion no. 7 at its junction with the fort wall
(*photo: David Baker*)

PLATE XI

*a.* Roman pointing surviving on the face of the fort wall with bastion no. 7
(*photo: David Baker*)

*b.* Bastion no. 15 at its junction with the fort wall (wall to the right of the rod) showing stone courses and ironstone used in the base
(*photo: David Baker*)

PLATE XII

*a.* Bastion no. 18 showing the excavation from within the bastion
(*photo : David Baker*)

*b.* Bastion no. 18 showing the inner face of the fort wall behind the bastion
(*photo : David Baker*)

PLATE XIII

*b.* The north postern gate: general view showing Roman footings and the medieval gate partly underpinned

*(photo: David Baker)*

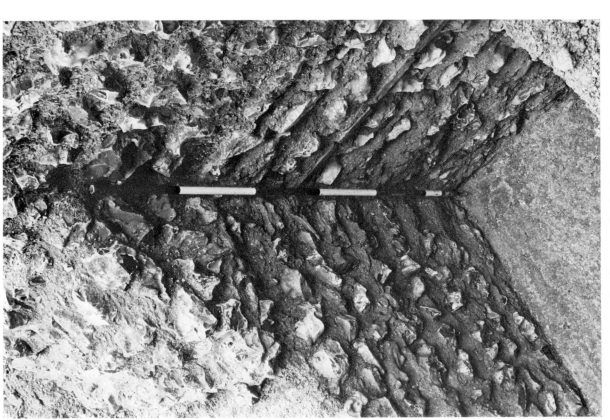

*a.* Bastion no. 18: the inner angle

*(photo: David Baker)*

PLATE XIV

*a.* The north postern gate, west side
(*photo: David Baker*)

*b.* The north postern gate, east side
(*photo: David Baker*)

PLATE XV

*a.* The south postern gate showing the west side with the clay bank in section
(*photo: David Baker*)

*b.* The south postern gate with the clay banks and road surface removed. The Norman blocking wall is
behind the rod
(*photo: David Baker*)

PLATE XVI

The landgate, showing the Norman blocking wall, built with chalk blocks in its core, and the adjacent Roman wall to the right of the rod
(*photo: David Baker*)

PLATE XVII

*b.* The landgate: outside the fort, showing the junction between the Norman blocking wall (extreme left) and the Roman wall. The rod lies at the base of the Roman offset parallel to the edge of the foundation trench

*(photo : David Baker)*

*a.* The landgate: inside the fort showing the junction between the Norman blocking wall (right) and the Roman gate wall. The flints are the foundation of the Norman wall

*(photo: David Baker)*

PLATE XVIII

*a.* The landgate: the south inturned wall at its junction with the fort wall
(*photo: David Baker*)

*b.* The landgate: the south inturned wall
(*photo: David Baker*)

PLATE XIX

*a.* The landgate: the south inturned wall at its point of junction with the gate tower
*(photo: David Baker)*

*b.* The landgate: the north inturned wall beneath the Norman gate
*(photo: David Baker)*

PLATE XX

*a.*   The landgate: the south gate tower looking east
(*photo: Mike Rouillard*)

*b.*   The landgate: the south gate tower looking west
(*photo: Mike Rouillard*)

PLATE XXI

b. The landgate: the foundation of the north gate tower projecting from beneath the Norman landgate
(*photo: David Baker*)

a. The landgate: the footing of the north gate tower inside the Norman landgate
(*photo: David Baker*)

PLATE XXII

*a.* The watergate: general view of the excavation in progress
(*photo: David Baker*)

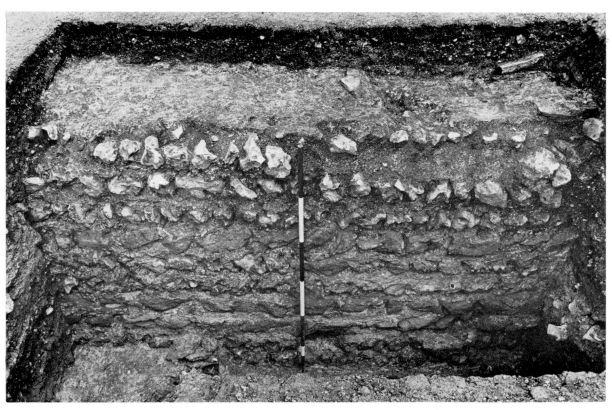

*b.* The watergate: the south face of the north inturned wall
(*photo: David Baker*)

PLATE XXIII

b. The watergate: the face of the north inturned wall.
The late Saxon blocking wall is to the right
*(photo: David Baker)*

a. The watergate: the south inturned wall projecting from
beneath the late Saxon gate house
*(photo: David Baker)*

Plate XXIV

b.  East–west Road 1
(*photo : David Baker*)

a.  The main north–south road facing the blocked south
postern gate
(*photo : David Baker*)

PLATE XXV

*a.* Gravelled area in trench 100
(*photo : David Leigh*)

*b.* Gravelled area in trenches 65 and 66
(*photo : David Baker*)

PLATE XXVI

*a.*   General view of metalling and gullies in trenches 100–103. The wall footings are
sixteenth-century
(*photo: David Leigh*)

*b.*   General view of the clay bank behind the south wall of the fort in trenches 107–8
(*photo: Mike Rouillard*)

PLATE XXVII

*a.* General view of the Roman ground surface in trenches 89 and 90. The stone structure is a fourteenth-century limekiln
(*photo: David Baker*)

*b.* General view of the Roman ground surface in trenches 88 and 89. The quarry hollow is below the rod. To the right is pit 135 in an early stage of excavation
(*photo: David Baker*)

PLATE XXVIII

*a.* Trenches 60, 62, 63 and 65 showing features of all periods, including a group of
Roman cesspits
(*photo: David Baker*)

*b.* General view of trenches 77–82 showing features of all phases
(*photo: David Baker*)

PLATE XXIX

b. Oven 4 and adjacent pit (the rod is in 25 cm. divisions)
(photo : David Leigh)

a. Impression of a sill beam belonging to building R5
(photo : David Baker)

PLATE XXX

*a.*   Pit 103
(*photo: David Baker*)

*b.*   Hearth 4
(*photo: David Baker*)

PLATE **XXXI**

Selection of decorated box tiles (p. 72 ). Scale ⅓
(*photon: R. Wilkins*)

Plate XXXII

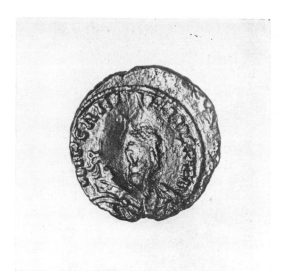

*a.*  Double struck coin of Tetricus I. Scale $\frac{2}{1}$
(*photo: R. Wilkins*)

*b.*  Gemstone (p. 231). Scale $\frac{4}{1}$
(*photo: R. Wilkins*)

PLATE XXXIII

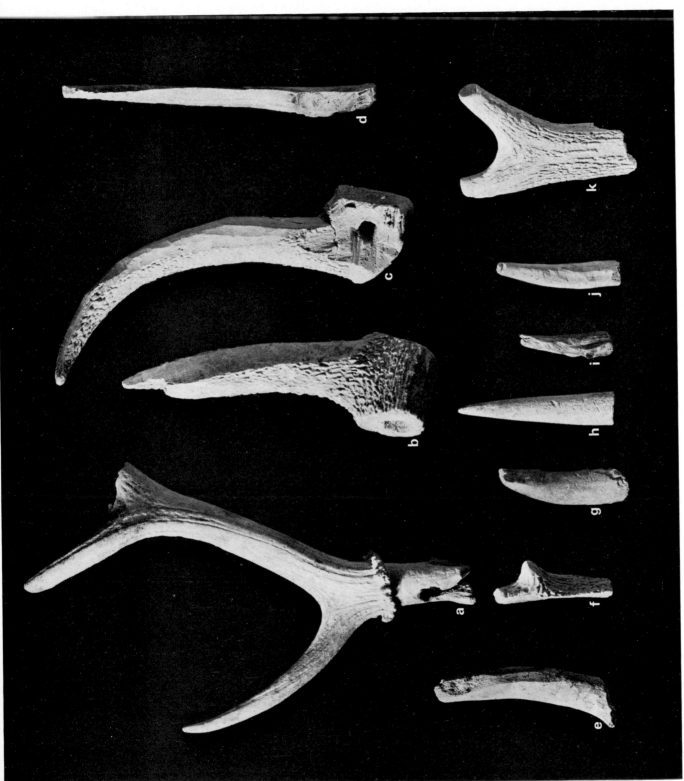

Worked antler (p. 224). Scale $\frac{2}{5}$
(*photo : R. Wilkins*)

Plate XXXIV

*a.* Whetstone, no. 355, decorated with incised lines. Scale $\frac{1}{1}$
(*photo: R. Wilkins*)

*b.* Skin vessel, no. 321. Scale $\frac{1}{1}$
(*photo: R. Wilkins*)

PLATE XXXV

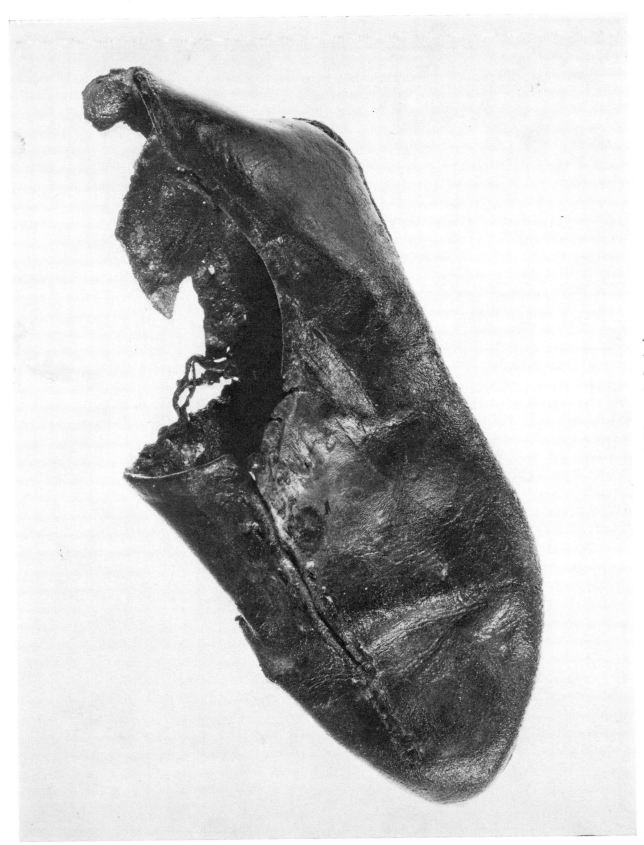

Shoe no. 267 (fig. 133). Scale $\frac{1}{1}$

(*photo: R. Wilkins*)

Plate XXXVI

Shoe no. 266 (fig. 133). Scale $\frac{1}{1}$.
(*photo: R. Wilkins*)

PLATE XXXVII

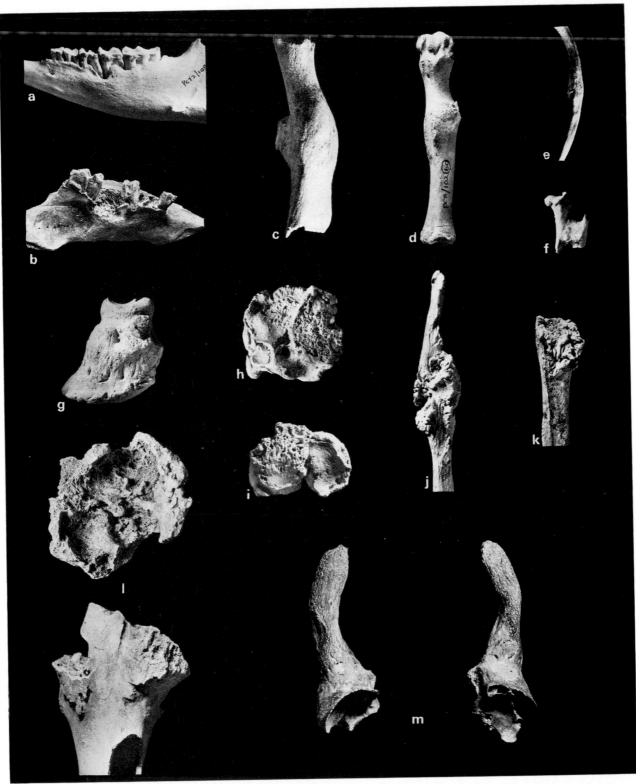

Examples of diseased and injured bones (scale ¼). (a) A sheep mandible with periodontal disease; (b) a sheep maxilla showing the site of a large abscess; (c, d, e) a pig tibia, sheep metatarsal and dog rib with neatly healed fractures; (f) a fractured bird femur: the distal end of the bone was displaced before the two parts of the bone fused together; (g) the fused second and third phalanges of an ox; (h, i) the proximal end of an ox metatarsal and two fused tarsals showing bony proliferation probably due to arthritis; (j, k) the ulna and part of the radius of a dog with a large amount of bony growth around the site of a fracture; (l) the proximal end of an ox tibia showing severe destruction of the bone, probably due to an infected abscess; (m) a pair of sheep horn cores showing restruction of the bone: probably due to an injury early in animal's life

(photo: R. Wilkins)

PLATE XXXVIII

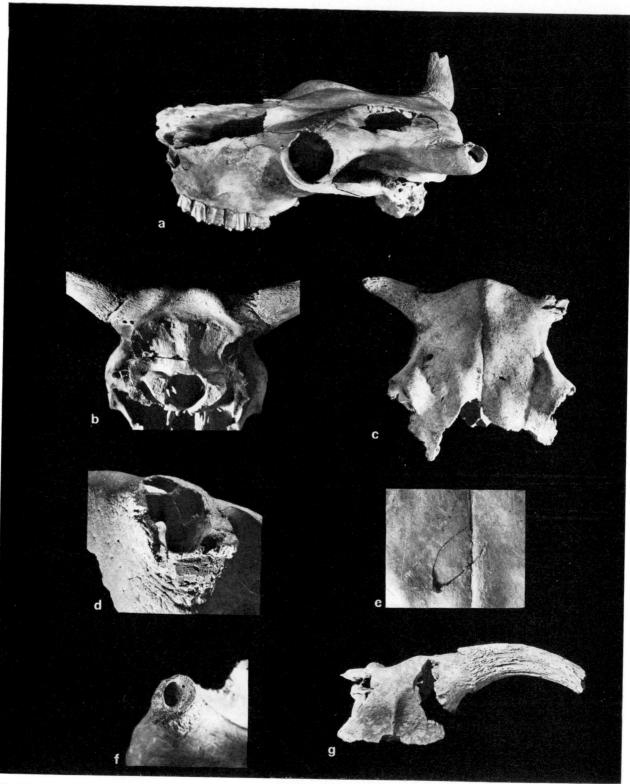

Cattle skulls (scale ¼). (a) An ox skull with part of the frontal bone destroyed through pole-axing; (b) the back of an ox skull showing the marks resulting from the severance of the skull from the atlas; (c) an ox skull with a prominent frontal eminence; (d) chop marks on a horn core; (e) detail of the frontal bone of a skull fractured by a pole-axing blow; (f) saw marks on a horn core tip; (g) a horn core partly severed from the skull
(*photo: R. Wilkins*)

PLATE XXXIX

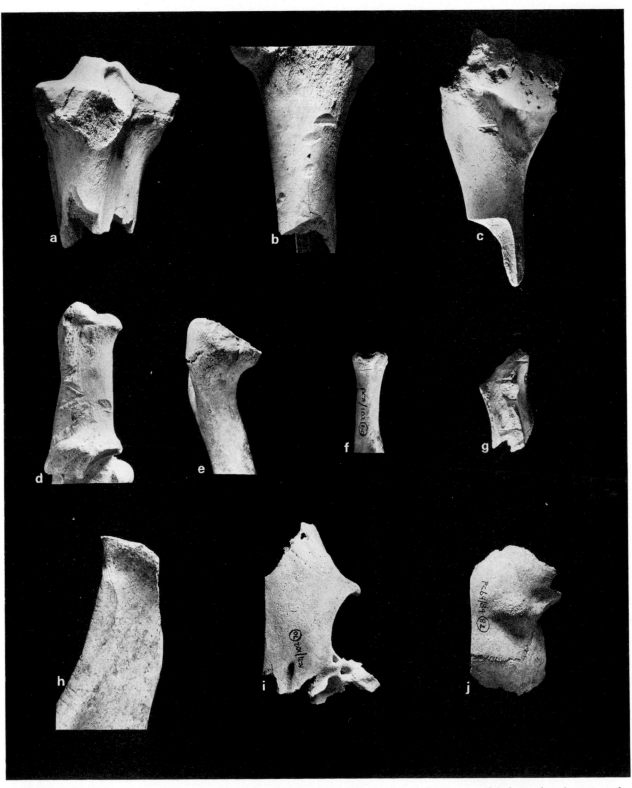

Examples of butchery marks (scale $\frac{1}{2}$). (a) Ox tibia; (b) ox femur; (c) ox humerus; this bone has been partly destroyed by gnawing; (d) ox calcaneum; (e) pig humerus; (f) sheep metatarsal; (g) ox ulna; (h) ox scapula; (i) pig skull; (j) sheep skull; this is an example of a hornless type

(*photo: R. Wilkins*)

PLATE XL

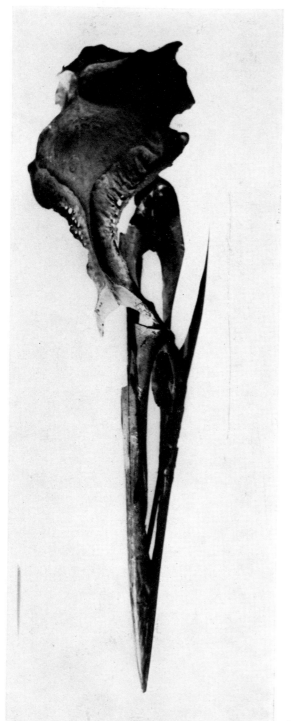

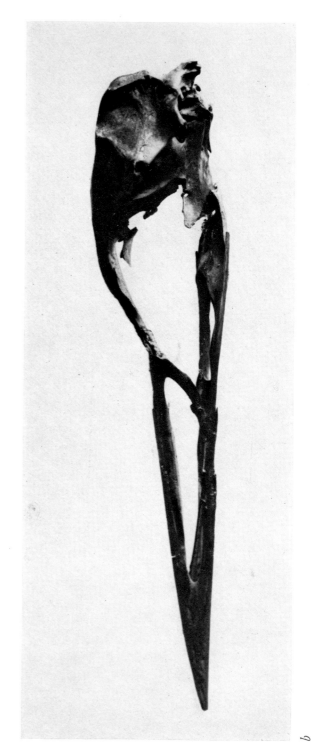

*a, b.* Skull of *Gavia immer* (scale $\frac{1}{1}$)

*a*

*b*

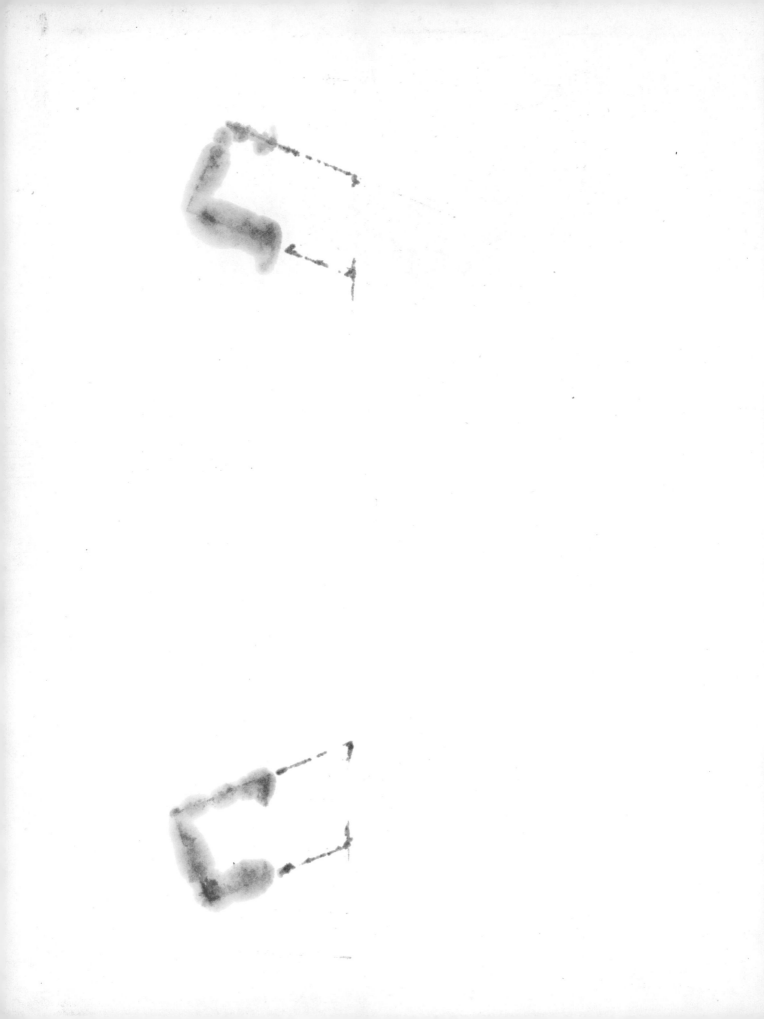

'Unbelievably good. So clever, so haunting and melancholic. A novel about obsession, love and loss; an exploration of trauma and delusion; a meditation on writing and what it means to create, to be trapped in a world of your own making, tormented by your own characters. It's so beautiful, so dark and so vivid'
Jennifer Saint, author of *Ariadne*

'This twisted tale of ghosts and murderers, derailed lives and childhood traumas is a vertical labyrinth that will take you straight down into the heart of darkness. Enthralling and heartbreaking'
M.R. Carey, author of *The Girl With All The Gifts*

'This gripping horror is a masterful exploration of storytelling. It will lure you to the dark side before quietly blowing your mind, time after time. A haunting tale of friendship, creativity and revenge, with prose as deep and sweeping as the cliffs of *Looking Glass Sound* itself'
Janice Hallett, author of *The Appeal*

'Devastatingly beautiful, bone-chilling and enchanting. *Looking Glass Sound* is further proof that no one writes like Catriona Ward. No one conjures such heartbreak from such raw fear. An alchemist of storytelling'
Chris Whitaker, author of *We Begin at the End*

'One of the finest literary craftsmen currently working is writing horror. *Looking Glass Sound* is a masterclass in atmosphere. Nearly every sentence is faultless, gutting and precise. Come for the family secrets but stay for the humanity, tenderness, and empathy that are so central to Ward's storytelling. This book will truly haunt you long after you read'
Olivie Blake, author of *The Atlas Six*

'What a totally stunning book. Such an intricate plot that you just have to sit back and enjoy as there's no point trying to work it out. At its heart a book about the madness of storytelling, possession and grief. I loved it'
**Araminta Hall, author of *Everything and Nothing***

'A marvel of storytelling, sinister as hell, and, at points where I thought I understood where it was going, Catriona drowned me with her signature "oh no, you don't" dark turns'
**L.V. Matthews, author of *The Twins***

'Serial killings, magic, literary theft, love and betrayal ... So clever and original'
**Mark Edwards, author of *Here to Stay***

'Murder, magic and monsters from the deep: Ward weaves her dark magic once again in this atmospheric, horror-drenched coming-of-age tale, with twist after head-spinning twist'
**Ellery Lloyd, author of *People Like Her***

'Stephen King meets *Atonement* meets ... screw it, you've read nothing like it before. This is so much more than a horror novel. Impossibly compelling, brilliantly plotted and incredibly moving all at once. This is Catriona Ward at her most special, most intimate and most ambitious. I think at this point we can all just agree to follow Ward wherever she takes us'
**Virginia Feito, author of *Mrs March***

'I felt like I was on a rollercoaster. Her characters, the way she weaves together all the storylines, the reveals – all of them brilliantly done, and all while my heart was banging out of my chest'
**Lisa Hall, author of *The Perfect Couple***

# Looking Glass Sound

Also by Catriona Ward and from Viper

*The Last House on Needless Street*
*Sundial*

# Looking Glass Sound

## CATRIONA WARD

First published in Great Britain in 2023 by
VIPER, part of Serpent's Tail,
an imprint of Profile Books Ltd
29 Cloth Fair
London
EC1A 7JQ

www.serpentstail.com

Copyright © Catriona Ward, 2023

Designed by Crow Books

1 3 5 7 9 10 8 6 4 2

Printed and bound in Great Britain by
Clays Ltd, Elcograf S.p.A.

A CIP catalogue record for this book is available from the British Library.

Hardback ISBN 978 1 80081 097 6
Trade paperback ISBN 978 1 80081 098 3
eISBN 978 1 80081 100 3

For Edward Christopher McDonald

# The Dagger Man of Whistler Bay

*From the unpublished memoir by Wilder Harlow*
*June, 1989*

I'm looking at myself in the bathroom mirror and thinking about love, because I plan on falling in love this summer. I don't know how or with whom. Outside, the city is a hot tarry mess. There must be someone in New York who . . . I wish I wasn't so weird-looking. I'm not even asking to be loved back, just to know what it feels like. I make a face in the mirror, pulling my lower lip all the way down so the inside shows on the outside. Then I pull my lower eyelids down so they glare red.

'Hello,' I say to the mirror. 'I love you.'

I give a yell as my mom bursts in without knocking. 'Mom! Privacy!' A startled roach breaks from behind the pipes and runs across the cracked tile floor, fast and straight like it's being pulled by fishing line.

'You want privacy, you lock the door.' She grabs me by the arm. 'Come on, monkey. Big news.'

She drags me to the living room where the air con roars like lions.

Dad holds a piece of paper. 'Probate is finished,' he says. 'The cottage is ours.' The paper trembles; I can't tell if it's from the aircon or whether his hands are shaking. He looks exhausted. Good and bad can feel like the same thing, I think, if they're intense enough.

Dad takes off his glasses and rubs his eyes. Uncle Vernon died in April. Dad really loved him. He goes up every summer to visit – well, he did. We never went with him.

'Vernon's crabby,' Dad always said. 'Doesn't much like women or kids.' Uncle Vernon was the last of that side of his family. We Harlows aren't much good at staying alive so Uncle Vernon did better than most; he made it to his seventies.

'We have to list it right away,' Dad says. 'Sell while the summer's still fine. I know that.' We all know that. The envelopes with red on them come through the door all the time.

'Tell you what,' Mom says. 'Let's go up there first, OK? Before we sell.'

'What?' Dad keeps wiping his glasses. His eyes are pink and naked.

'Let's have a vacation,' Mom says. She tucks a strand of imaginary hair behind her ear, which is a sign that she's excited. We haven't had a vacation since that trip to Rehoboth Beach when I was seven. 'What do you say, Wilder?'

'That could be fun,' I say, hesitant. The ocean sounds like a good place to fall in love. Plus, if we take a vacation maybe my mom and dad might stop fighting. They think I don't hear but I do. In the night a certain kind of whisper sounds louder than yelling.

'You deserve a vacation, monkey,' she whispers. 'We're so proud of you.' The phone call came yesterday – Scottsboro Prep are renewing my full-board scholarship. I let her hug me. The truth is that things at Scottsboro got pretty bad by the end of term. I was at breaking point, walking to class as quickly as I could so as not to be caught in the hallway by others, or taking a book to lunch so no one could catch my eye. That way I could at least pretend not to hear what they said about me. My hands got red and sore from wringing out clothes, ties that were soaked wet with toilet water and bleach, sometimes other stuff.

My scholarship makes it possible for me to go to Scottsboro, which is very expensive. All I have to do is hold on for a couple more years. It has to end one day. *Just hold on*, I tell myself over and over, in my head. I'll go to college and from then on, everything will be different. I'm going to write books.

I don't tell my parents about what happens at Scottsboro. It might make things even worse between them.

We leave the city in a warm June dawn that promises another sweltering day, and drive up through the woods. We move backwards through the season, travelling through time, the summer growing younger and cooler as we make our way north.

In the late afternoon we leave the highway. The grass gets tall and green. There are wildflowers I don't know, the sound of crickets. The warm wind is full of salt.

Evening's falling as we pull over at the foot of a green hill marked by a shingle path. The cottage perches above like a gull on the cliff. We walk, sweating, up the green swathe of land, suitcases leaving tracks in the rough grass. The house is surrounded by a white picket fence with a gate. It's white clapboard with blue shutters, and I think – *I've never seen anything so neat, so perfect.* There are rows of seashells on the porch and twisting silver driftwood hangs above the door. The leaves of the sugar maple whisper – under it, there's a high-pitched whine, a long shrill note like bad singing.

This is the first time I hear it, the whistling for which the bay is named. It sounds like all the things you're not supposed to believe in – mermaids, selkies, sirens.

I come to with my mother's hand on my shoulder. 'Come on inside, Wilder,' she says, and I realise I've been just standing there, mouth open.

'What's that sound?' It seems like it's coming from inside me, somehow.

Dad pauses in the act of unlocking the door. 'It's the stones on the beach. High tide has eaten away at them, making little holes – kind of like the finger stops on a flute – and when the wind is in the east, coming over the ocean, it whistles through. Neat, huh?'

'It's spooky,' I say.

'Come to think of it,' Dad says thoughtfully, 'the way Uncle Vernon was found was pretty spooky, too. He was just sitting up on those rocks as they whistled around him, eyes staring. Like he'd been taken before his time, whistled to death by Whistler Bay . . .'

'Dork,' I mutter as I follow him inside. I know Uncle Vernon died in hospital of a heart infarction.

Inside the cottage everything is bare and white and blue, like a shore washed clean by the ocean. My room has a single bed covered in rough wool blankets, and a round window like a porthole.

'Keep the windows closed at night,' my father says. 'There have been some break-ins around here. I'll get locks in the morning.'

'And careful in the water,' my mother adds, anxious. 'There's a drowning almost every year.'

'Yes, mother dearest.'

She slaps my arm. Sometimes she gets mad when I'm what she calls *fresh*, but mostly she likes it.

I open the porthole and fall asleep to the sound of the stones and the sea.

In the morning I wake before my parents. I realise as soon as I put them on that my swimming shorts are way too small. I've grown a lot since last summer. I didn't think of it before we left New York. So I put on some underwear and flip flops, grab a towel and slip out the back door.

The red ball of the morning sun is burning off the last sea mist. I go down the path, gravel skittering from my sandalled feet, towel slung over my shoulder.

On the beach the pebbles are already warm from the sun. I take off my glasses and rest them gently on a rock. On an impulse I slip off my underwear too and go into the sea naked. The water takes me in its glassy grip. For a second I wonder, *riptide?* But the sea is still and cool. It's a homecoming. I think, *I'm a sea person and I never even knew it.* Even underwater I can still hear the wind singing in the rocks. And I hear a voice, too, calling. I break the surface, coughing, water streaming from my head.

A girl and a boy stand on the shore. I think they're about my age. She wears overalls and a big floppy hat. Her hair is a deep, almost unnatural red, like blood. She wears a man's watch on her wrist, gold and clunky. It's way too big and it makes her wrist look very slim. I think, *frick that was fast,* because I am in love with her right away.

I see what she holds: a stick, with my underwear hanging off the pointed end. She wrinkles her nose in an expression of disgust. 'What kind of pervert leaves their underwear lying around on the beach?' Her scorn mingles perfectly with her accent – she's English. Not the sunburned kind who throng round Times Square, but the kind I thought existed only in movies. Classy.

The wind billows in the fabric of my shorts, filling them. For a second it looks like I am still in the shorts – invisible, struggling, impaled.

'Hey,' the boy says. 'He didn't know anyone else was here.' *Heah.* Is he British, too? He's tall with an easy, open look to him. I think, *it's boys like that who get the girls.* As if to confirm this thought, he puts a hand on the girl's back. 'Give 'em, Harper.'

*Harper* – it seems an odd name for a British girl but it suits her. Maybe her parents are big readers.

Reluctantly she swings the stick around at him. He takes off his shirt, plucks the underwear off the end of the stick and wades into the shallows. He doesn't seem to mind his shorts getting wet. 'Stay there,' he calls. 'I'll come out.' He swims out in long slow strokes to where I bob in the centre of the cove.

'Here you go.' *Heah ya go.* Not British. He hands me my shorts. Then he swims back towards the shore. I struggle into the underwear, catching my feet in the fabric. I begin the endless swim back.

The boy is talking to the girl – she's laughing. I think with a bite of fear, *they're laughing at me.* But he puts another gentle hand on Harper's back and turns her away, pointing inland, towards something on the cliff. I realise he's being kind to me again, making sure I can get out of the water in privacy.

I huddle, cold, in my towel. I'd thought there was something special about this place this morning but there isn't. The world's the same everywhere. It's all like school.

'See you around,' I say and make my way back up the path. I feel their eyes on my back and I stumble on the incline. The rocks make their evil whistling and I hurry away from the kids' gaze and the sound, which seem part of each other. I go straight indoors and stay there until long after I hear them come up from the beach and past the cottage, long after their footsteps have faded away down the hill, towards the road.

I wonder what the relationship between them is, if they're dating, if maybe they're doing *it*. I don't know enough about *it* to tell. He

6

touches her with a casual assurance but they didn't behave roman-tically towards one another – not the way the movies have led me to expect.

I had planned to journal each day, here. But I don't want to write down what happened this morning. I wash my face over and over again with cold water before breakfast, so Mom and Dad don't see redness around my eyes or any other traces of tears.

I want to go home so badly I can taste it. I think of my usual seat at the library in the city, near the end of one of those long tables, the lamps with their green glass shades throwing circles of warm light. Everyone helps you understand things, there.

'Come on, sport,' my father says. 'Good for you to get out. You can't sit in your room all vacation.' So I go with him to run errands in Castine. What else am I going to do?

Waiting for him to finish at the post office, I gaze glumly at the sacks of chickenfeed piled outside the general store, wander up the main street. It's lonely being with family sometimes.

A pickup pulls up with a screech on the other side of the street, outside a cheerful white and blue shop. *Fresh Fish*, reads the sign overhead. The truck is battered and rusty with panels beaten out badly where they've been staved in by collisions. Probably a drinker, I say to myself, knowing. A line comes to me. *Living by the sea is tough on paint, and just as hard on the mind.* Maybe I'll write it down later.

A thin man in a vest gets out of the truck. He busies himself with coolers and crates, and a moment later, the rich smell of raw fish reaches me. I watch the man with interest. He's so easy in himself, unloads the truck in quick, decisive movements, every now and then spitting a thin vein of brown juice into the gutter. *A man of the sea,* I think. He's weather-beaten, skin as brown as shoe leather, but his

7

eyes are a warm blue, striking in his worn face. I imagine him living in a board shack, bleached silver by the sun and salt, down by the water, going out in his boat every day before dawn. Some tragedy lies in his past, I'm sure of it. He has a rough, sad look like a cowboy in a western. But he's a sea cowboy, which is even cooler. I back into the shadow of a little alley. I don't want to be seen staring.

A bell jingles, and a young woman comes out of the blue and white store and greets him, friendly. He nods back. Her eyes are swollen, her nose red. She's been crying, I realise, and I feel a spurt of hot sympathy for her. Or maybe she has a cold. She blows her nose heartily and stuffs the Kleenex back in her pocket. She takes the crates into the jingling doorway and brings them back empty, swinging from her hand. The bell announces her exits and her entrances, jaunty. It isn't a cold; she's been crying, for sure. In fact she's still crying. Fresh tears shine on her face. She dabs them dry with tiny movements.

'Sorry,' I hear her say to the fisherman, as if she's offending him somehow. The man nods gently. The world is full of sorrow, his silence seems to say. *Maybe they were lovers*, I think, excited. *Maybe he left her.*

When the contents of all twelve crates are inside, she hands him a wad of bills. He takes them and turns back to the truck. As she goes into the store for the last time the Kleenex she'd dried her tears with falls from her pocket. He must see it in the corner of his eye, because he turns quickly, and picks it up before the wind can take it. The man slips the tissue into his pocket. I feel how kind it is, his act of humility, to pick the tissue up for the crying girl and take it away, so it doesn't blow down the street and out to sea.

As if feeling my eyes on him, the man looks around, slowly surveying the street. When his eyes light on me he smiles, amused. 'Hey,' he says. 'Who you hiding from?'

I come out from behind the house, bashful.

8

'You want to take a ride? Help me get the next load from the dock?'

He indicates the passenger seat in a careless, amiable way. People around here don't seem to talk much but they like to do small kindnesses.

'I can't,' I say, regretful. 'I have to wait for my dad.'

He nods slowly, and then he gets in the truck and it roars away, up the street, in the direction of the ocean. I wish I'd gone with him now. It would have been fun to see the dock.

Someone says 'boo!' and I jump.

The boy from the beach says, 'You took off pretty quick the other day.' He looks even more relaxed and golden than I remembered. 'I'm Nat,' he says. 'Nathaniel.'

'Like Hawthorne?'

'My last name's Pelletier.'

'I meant, Nathaniel Hawthorne the writer.' He looks uncomfortable. I go on quickly, 'I'm Wilder. It's a weird name. You can call me Will.' I've been waiting to try 'Will' out for a while.

'Nah, it's cool. Like a wrestler or something. You're wild, but I'm wilder!' He bares white healthy teeth in a snarl. It sits oddly on his friendly features.

'I'm *Wildah*,' I repeat, and really it doesn't sound so bad, the way he says it. Like something from a play.

He punches me on the arm, fake mad and I laugh and he grins. 'Don't worry about Harper,' he says. 'She's rich so she doesn't need manners.'

I laugh again because he seems to be joking, but I think, *she really didn't seem to have any.*

'You want to swim with us later? We're going late this afternoon. We'll make a fire, sit out.'

I hesitate. I want to go but I'm scared too. I don't really know how to talk to people.

I start to tell Nat no, just as my dad comes out of the post office and beckons to me.

'I've got to go,' I say.

'We'll come by the bay around five,' he calls after me, and half of me is so happy that he seems to want to be friends, and the other is unnerved because it all seems to be settled without my doing anything at all.

I won't hang out with them, I know better. I'll pretend I'm busy when they arrive.


Nat, Harper and I sit on the sand, silent and a little awkward, watching the tide go out. The wet sand of the bay is slick and grey. It's obscene like viscera, a surface that shouldn't be uncovered. Behind us on the beach, the bonfire smokes half-heartedly. As it turns out, we aren't any of us much good at lighting fires. Harper looks even more beautiful in the long, low light. She has the smooth, angular face of a fairy or a cunning child, I think, and then immediately wish I could write that down to use later. I feel the beginnings of stirring in my chinos and after that I purposely don't look at her again. I feel her presence next to me, warm like a small sun.

'I'm sorry,' Harper says. 'I was horrid the other day.'

'Oh, no problem,' I say, cautious. 'I mean, it was just kidding around.' That's always the best thing to say to people who might hurt you. It takes the pressure off of them.

'No, it was mean. I get these moods. I try not to but I do.' She pauses. 'It was also somewhat confusing; you have very unusual—' She pauses, and I feel sorry for her; she's trying not to be rude again.

'I know,' I say. 'I get it all the time.'

People form opinions of me quickly because of the way I look. My eyes are very big, which is supposed to be good. But they're too big, like a bush baby's. And they're pale. So pale it's hard to even tell what colour they are. They almost blend in with my skin, which is also really pale. I'm planning to get a tan this summer – to look more like a regular guy and less like some kind of insect.

'Yeah,' Nat says. 'The guy who lived here before you had the same eyes, the same – colour.' He squints and leans away, looking at me. 'You look like a younger version. He swam here in the mornings too.' He pauses. 'He was nice, we talked sometimes. He liked taking pictures of the coast around here.'

'I thought he died,' Harper says. 'Are you a ghost?'

'That was my Uncle Vernon,' I say. 'He *did* die.'

'Hey, Harper.' Nat's voice is easy but she looks up and flushes.

'Sorry,' she says. 'I get a bit personal sometimes.'

'It's OK. I didn't know him. My dad calls it the Harlow look. Big bug eyes, white skin.'

I risk a surreptitious glance at Harper. Her skin is white too, but creamy, scattered with golden freckles. She looks like a human being, at least, whereas I'm aware I kind of don't. She shivers and I want to give her my sweater but I don't. I've seen it done in movies, giving a girl your sweater, but I've never done it myself, or really even spoken to a girl, and I feel shy.

'Where do you go to school?' I ask them.

'Edison High, in Castine,' Nat says. 'We live on the shore.' I've seen those houses on the shore. They're bleached silver, roofs often patched with aluminium.

Nat wears ragged denim cutoffs and a faded Red Sox t-shirt that's too big for him. I feel the hot poke of shame. The kids at Scottsboro call me poor so often I've got used to it – my mom takes the pants on my uniform down each year instead of buying me new ones. I get a bursary for schoolbooks. But I am reminded now that I'm not poor.

Harper says, 'I'm starting boarding school in the autumn.' She sighs. 'It's a good one, and I'm so bad at school. I probably won't last long there. I'll probably end up at *Fairview*.'

I've heard of Fairview. It's where rich people dump their daughters when there's nowhere else left.

'I belong at Fairview really,' Harper says gloomily. 'It's a crap school for people who are crap at school. Everyone knows it. Even I know it.' She frowns and pokes the sand with a stick. 'I want to go home.'

'Oh. Well, goodbye.' My heart sinks. But I've had an hour with her.

'I mean to the UK.'

'I don't think you'll make it by dark,' Nat says.

'Funny.' She sighs. 'I don't want to go to boarding school. I'm going to miss Samuel so much.'

'Who's Samuel?' I keep my tone casual, even though jealousy is a hot lance in my side. I can't tell if I hide it well or not.

'Oh. My dog,' Harper says. 'He's a dachshund. He's small but he doesn't act like a small dog. He's got dignity. They're giving him to the housekeeper, or that's what they say. It's probably a lie. Mama's probably having him put down. He's so lovely. He always knows when I'm scared. He always comes.' She gets up and dusts her palms free of sand. 'I suppose I do have to go now. It'll be dark soon.'

'Walk you back?' Nat says.

'Better not,' she says. 'They wouldn't like it.' They exchange a look. I burn with envy at the natural intimacy between them. Once again I wonder if they're doing *it*.

We both watch her pick her way up the path in the fading light, crest the clifftop, and vanish into the purple sky.

Nat settles back down into the sand. 'Harper got kicked out of every school in England.'

'What for?'

'What not for? Everything. She *mistrusts institutionalised authority structures*.' His mimicry of her cut-glass tones is pretty good.

'Have you two known each other long?'

'A couple years. Her folks come out every summer.'

'Is – are you two, like, involved?'

'No.'

'I thought maybe you were.'

'No. But I'm in love with her,' he says.

'What?' It is a shocking thing to say out loud, like someone taking off their clothes in public.

'I said, I'm in love with her. I'm going to make her love me, one day.'

'But you don't just – *tell people* stuff like that.' My fists are balled. I can't hang my anger on anything rational, and that makes me angrier still. 'That kind of thing is private, you keep it to yourself . . .'

'Maybe you do, or try to,' he says with a sudden flash of anger. 'But you're not so good at it. You look at her all the time when she isn't looking. But you can't even look her in the eyes; it's embarrassing. Like you've never seen a girl before.'

'You're not getting anywhere either,' I say. 'How long have you been thinking about, like, holding her hand?'

'I'll still get further than you,' he says, confident, and I know he's right.

Before I can think my palm hits his cheek with a crack. He puts his hand up to the red print mine has left behind. 'Did you just *slap* me?' he asks slowly.

I rear back as his fist comes at my face and the punch lands on my breastbone just above my heart. My chest explodes into pain and I gasp. I go for him now, raining blows on his face and chest and everywhere I can reach. I'm not great at fighting but I don't think Nat is either, because neither of us lands many good ones. But he gives me a black eye and I get him one on the side of the face.

We fight until we cough sand and it's in every crevice of our bodies, until we're panting and exhausted. Neither of us seems likely to win so we just kind of stop by common consent, roll away from one another and lie on our backs, spitting grit.

'Sorry.' I hesitate. 'I really thought you two were – you know – together.'

'Nope,' he says. 'We're friends.' He sighed. 'I thought at first you and me could be friends.'

'I know,' I say. 'I thought that too. But it can't work if both of us are in love with her.'

'I think we have to be,' Nat says. 'Friends, and in love with her.' He's right, it isn't possible to stop either thing.

'We can't fight all the time.'

'We have to work out some kind of, like, agreement.'

'OK,' I say, thinking. 'So, rule one, no cheating, no going behind the other's back. We have to agree that from now on, neither one of us tries to get her. Agreed?'

'And we can't ever tell her about it,' he says. 'That's a rule too. Deal?'

'Deal.' I shake his hand.

He touches his cheekbone with a tentative finger and winces. 'Good thing my dad's night fishing. Sleeps in the day. He won't see me in the sun 'til a week.' He pauses. 'That was fun, though. Good fight.'

We kick sand over the smouldering remains of the bonfire and go up the path.

'See you tomorrow,' he calls behind him.


I'm apprehensive about my parents seeing my black eye. I needn't be, as it turns out. My mother puts arnica on my face and makes tutting noises.

'It's OK,' I say. 'We're friends now. Me and Nat.'

'You usually make friends by roughhousing?' she asks, amused, and I realise she thinks it healthy for a boy my age – *roughhousing*.


The next day Harper and Nat are at the white fence after breakfast.

Harper stares at my eye. 'Gnarly,' she says, then, very English, 'What a shiner.' A sour scent hangs about her.

'Like I said,' Nat says, 'I stumbled, grabbed Wilder and we both wiped out. Rolled down the path.' Turning to me he says, 'We're going out on the boat. It's down on the water.'

Harper picks her way down the shale path with exaggerated care. 'Mustn't slip,' she says as if to herself, shooting me a look under her lashes.

The boat bobs on the water in the morning sun. She's chipped and scraped all over, and you can see every colour she's ever been painted, her past written on her like a record. *Siren*, reads the shaky black lettering on her stern. The outboard motor at the back leaks a narrow trail of oil into the water.

There are only two life jackets so after some argument we agree that the only solution is for none of us to wear one.

'One dies, we all die,' I say. It's pleasing.

'Seems like you two are doing a pretty good job at killing your-selves,' Harper says. She watches me with bird-like focus. She takes off her big, clunky gold watch and puts it carefully in a Ziploc bag, then stows it in the locker beneath the bench.

The little outboard engine chugs against the waves. We put her nose out into open water, go out of sight of land, looking for great white sharks. When navy-blue water surrounds us in every direction Nat stops the engine. We take turns jumping off the side into the deep, gasping with shock at the cold, our breath coming fast, picturing monsters moving slowly in the depths below us. We don't see any sharks and soon it gets to feeling lonely, nothing but water everywhere. When we sight the shoreline again we yell with relief, as though we've been adrift for many days.

We make our way slowly up the coast, passing houses perched on cliffs, hillsides rugged with dark pine forest, green meadows studded with ox-eye daisies. On a lonely stretch we surprise a family of seals sunning themselves on flat rocks in a sheltered cove. They watch us, tranquil, with their strange round eyes but don't move. They know we're no threat – we're part of the ocean now.

Harper talks about Grace Kelly. She loves Grace Kelly. It's like the words fill her to breaking point and have to be released. It seems almost an impersonal act, her talk – a mechanical release not meant as communication. 'Such control,' Harper mutters to the sea. 'As an actor, as a woman. She told the truth all the time, but she was a castle of her own making. No one could reach the real her. It was perfect. She made herself safe in a dangerous world.'

'Harp?' Nat touches her gently with his foot and she starts.

'Sorry,' she says. 'I just think actors are holy, you know?'

Harper talks about her dog, too. 'The thing I miss most about Samuel is the way he protected me from my dad,' she says. Then she sits up abruptly and scans the cliffs. 'Do you think the Dagger Man is watching?'

'Ah, we don't need to talk about that,' Nat says. A rare flash of discomfort crosses his friendly face. 'It's freaky.'

'I think he's watching. I think he's waiting for us to come ashore somewhere really remote and then he'll come for us, quick as a shadow, holding his dagger above his head . . .' She raises a fist behind her head as if to stab. Her red hair falls about her face, which has become dark and frightening.

I ask, 'What are you talking about?'

'The guy who breaks into houses round here,' Harper says. 'The Dagger Man. Don't you know? You're not local, so I suppose no one tells you anything.'

I don't point out that owning a large house you visit for a month a year is hardly being local. 'You tell me, then.'

'It happened last year,' Harper says. 'There were break-ins. Always visitors, no one local. But the thing is—'

'—he takes pictures of people asleep,' Nat says. 'It's not as big a deal as she's making it sound.'

Harper says, 'He only takes pictures of the kids. And it *is* a big deal. They think he does it to children because they'd be easier to overpower if they woke up. Then he leaves. Like I said, he doesn't take anything, that they can tell. The family don't even know they've been broken into, even.'

'So how—'

'He sends the photos to people,' Harper says. 'The Polaroids. At least, that's what I heard my dad say. The police, the families. Sleeping children. And they say that in the Polaroids there's a kind of dagger at the child's throat. It happened to the Masons, and the Bartletts, I think some other family but I don't remember who. Anyway it stopped when summer ended. But everyone's wondering if it'll start again.'

'We're not kids,' I say. 'We're probably going to be ok.' Unease is all through me. And some other feeling, too. I stare at her hand, which often squeezes her knee or thigh for emphasis, or as if for stability. Her nails are bitten to the quick and she has an old, greying Band-Aid wrapped around her thumb. There are tiny golden hairs on her legs, which occasionally catch the midday sun like fine wire. When I look up, Harper's eyes are fixed on me.

'His name,' Harper says dreamily, looking at me. 'I think of it as all one word. Daggerman, daggerman . . .'

'Don't. . .' I feel like something's going to happen if she says the name a third time.

'Got one!' Nat yells from the front of the boat and we both jump as if waking from a dream.

Nat pulls the writhing fish from the hook and hits it against the prow until its brains spray out in the bright air. Its body is long and beautiful and bloody. 'Striper,' he says, putting the fish in the cold box, laying the pole carefully down in the bottom of the boat.

We pull into a tiny white beach, no more than a spit of white sand. Nat finds oysters growing waist deep on the rocks beneath the surface. He opens them carefully with the oyster knife. 'My dad carved this,' he says proudly. 'Cool, huh?' The handle of the oyster knife is walnut, worn smooth with use, chased with a pattern of tiny fish. 'He gave it to me for my birthday when I was, like, seven.'

'My dad would never let me have a knife,' I say, enviously.

'He's pretty cool,' Nat says. 'He catches seals sometimes, in the shark rig. That's why he always keeps a boat hook in the *Siren*. What you do is come up beside it, knock it out with the hook, snare it in the shark rig, then pull it along beside the boat for a time, until it's ready to do whatever you want. Then you take it somewhere else on shore to finish it.'

Without hot sauce or lemon the oysters are disgusting but I still eat two. We build a fire from driftwood. We're a little better at it, this time, don't put too much wood on at once to start. We gut the sea bass, wrap it in aluminium and cook it on the coals. The fish's flesh is charred to black in some places and almost raw in others, but we devour it anyway. Spider crabs scuttle near on delicate legs. We throw them the fishbones and they swarm over the skeleton, picking it clean. We lie on our backs on the warm white sand, watching the thin corkscrew of smoke rise into the air. The sun burns above and our skins grow pink and sore.

'This is the best day of my life,' I almost tell them – but I don't. I want to keep all this life corked tight inside me, bubbling and dangerous.

Harper pulls a bottle of Jim Beam out of her bag. It's maybe a third full and we pass it between us, sputtering as the heat strokes down our gullets. 'You might as well tell me,' Harper says into the quiet. 'Why you fought.'

'We didn't fight.' I'm dreamy with whiskey. 'Nat fell on the path, took me down with him.'

'Whatever. You're both terrible liars.' Harper holds up the empty whiskey bottle. 'Let's spin it,' she says.

My heart crawls up my throat into my mouth, a warm lump. I've never played spin the bottle, never kissed anyone. I wonder what it would be like to kiss Harper. I wonder if I'm going to throw up. Nat's watching me. I wonder, through a white haze of panic, what this means for our deal.

'Harper,' he says, but she hisses 'sssssssh!' and glares at him.

Harper puts the bottle on a flat rock in the middle of the three of us. She spins. The bottle gleams and whirls like a propeller in the glare. It slows, then comes to rest. The top points at me, and the other end points out to sea.

'You have to kiss the ocean,' she says.

'But those aren't the rules—' I start to say, helpless, then decide to leave it. Maybe I misunderstood the rules; it's not like I've ever played before. Harper would know how to play better than I do. 'Spin again?'

'No,' Harper says, squinting at me. 'These are our rules, Wilder. You have to kiss who it says.'

Standing up is like being a kite, I'm billowing around on the end of a string. How much whiskey have I drunk? I go to the shallows where they wash bright over the pebbles, turning them into jewels. 'Nice to meet you,' I say to the sea. 'That's a lovely blouse you're wearing.'

The water rushes in over my feet. 'Right down to business, huh,' I say, resigned. 'Whatever you say, ma'am.' I kneel and kiss the sea. It kisses me back, stroking my mouth like a cool tongue. I imagine for a moment that it's salty skin beneath my lips.

'More tongue!' Harper yells. 'Give her more tongue!' And I realise she's had even more to drink than I have.

The game is that we have to make out with whatever object the bottle tells us to. Nat embraces a rock passionately. Harper drapes herself in seaweed, spitting and gagging.

'The bottle is the rule,' I say to her, sententiously. 'The only rule. More tongue.' She pushes me hard and I fall backwards onto the sun-warm shale, laughing so hard I feel like I'll die.


We wake with our feet in the water. The tide is almost in; we have to swim out to the boat with clothes and bags held above our aching heads, the waves slapping salty and cold into our open mouths.

Harper sits at the back of the boat, staring at the water. Her hand trails in the cold blue.

'I don't know how Harper does it,' Nat says. His voice is low, under the cover of the engine and the waves. 'Whenever we play that game it only ever lands on like, a tree. Or a rock.'

I pause in the middle of pulling on jeans. 'You guys play spin the bottle – just you two?'

'Pretty dumb, huh?' He sees my face. 'Not anymore,' he says quickly. 'Now we wouldn't play without you, Wilder.'

By the time we make it back to Whistler Bay we're moving through a swamp of exhaustion.

*

That night I float above my bed, hot and strange, like the sun has entered my body. I can still feel the boat dipping under me, moving with the waves. *This is what life is really like*, I think. *It's this intense.* Then I stumble out of bed and run down the narrow cold hallway to the bathroom, and throw up violently, chunks of half-cooked fish riding on a hot torrent of old Jim Beam.

In the morning my parents leave early for some craft fair or maybe a seafood market, or maybe sightseeing, I don't know. I groan and turn over. 'No,' I say through the pillow. 'I'll stay home. Do some vacation reading for school.'

'Well all right then,' says my dad, pleased. I drift back into the dark, head pulsing.

At last, at about ten, I wake up properly. The day is already noon-hot outside. I make coffee and go out into the sun with a fistful of granola in my hand.

Harper's sitting on the grass outside the gate. She looks drawn and I suspect her night was even worse than mine. I feel a stab of excitement. She came to find me.

'How long have you been here?' I ask, casual. 'You should have knocked or yelled or something.'

She shrugs. 'I'm not in a hurry,' she says. 'Just bored. Nat's got chores. Can I have some coffee? Can I hang out with you today?'

I am excited and terrified at the prospect of spending the day alone with her. 'OK,' I say. 'Yeah, I mean, sure! We can stay here, if you like. My parents are out.'

She nods. 'It's nice to be near a house sometimes,' she says. 'I'm kind of tired of the sea.'

I hold out my hand. 'Want some breakfast?' We eat dry granola from my open palm.

We climb into the branches of the maple. We're just kind of sitting here, awkward, and I'm searching for something to say when she reaches across towards me with a twig.

'What really happened between you and Nat?' She pokes my thigh. 'I think you were fighting. Does he like me?' I think I hear longing in her voice.

'I got questions for you too,' I say. 'Why was that bottle of whiskey you brought on the boat two-thirds empty?'

We glare at each other. I cave first. 'Sorry,' I say. 'I'm being a dick. I've never had a friend who's a girl before. In fact I've never had friends before.' I stare at the ground, waiting for her to say something crushing and smart, or just leave, maybe.

'I don't have any friends except Nat,' Harper says, matter of fact. 'Everyone hates me. All year I wait for summer when we come here. What's your excuse?'

'You first,' I say. 'Why does everyone hate you?'

'I'm not good with people.'

'Why? Truth for truth.'

Harper goes pale and waves her hand, like, *no*.

'Come on,' I say. 'Your British is showing. What are you afraid of?'

'Nothing, stop it.' She brightens. 'Do you have anything to drink?'

'My parents don't drink.' There's a bottle of sweet vermouth on the shelf in the store cupboard. My mom likes a small glass with a lemon slice before dinner. I'm not giving it to Harper. When I look again she's crying. She does it in complete silence, tears gleaming on her face in the dappled shade of the tree.

'Oh . . .' I slide down from my perch in a panic and go over to her. I reach up to where she sits in the crook of a branch. I don't know what to do so I kind of pet her side, like you would a pet a horse.

She shifts away from my touch. 'I just really miss Samuel,' she says thickly.

'Your dog.' I'm pleased with myself for remembering.

'He was so kind and good. He looked after me. He would only eat French fries if they had mustard on them. Isn't that weird?'

'I'm sure he's a great dog,' I say. 'I'm sure he's happy, wherever he is.' I wonder if her parents have already had the dog destroyed. She's talking about it in the past tense today. Could they have done it that quickly?

'Let's just hang out,' she says, tired. 'OK, Wilder?'

'OK,' I say.

So that's what we do. We find a backgammon set in the cupboard beneath the stairs and she teaches me to play. I'm terrible at it.

'Frick,' I say as I lose another game to her.

'You can say fuck, you know. I'm not your mum.'

'Uh,' I say, feeling shy. 'But then I might get used to it and say it in front of her by accident.'

'You are such a weird guy.' She sounds approving.

'We crawl inside and eat Cheez Whiz on crackers in front of the TV. It's old, there's a constant rainbow sprawl in the corner of the screen, but eventually we find a movie to watch, something about a friendship between two bartenders. And only once does that peculiar electricity roar up my spine. Only once, all afternoon.

'Do you ever wonder if you're imaginary?' Harper asks dreamily, putting her head on my shoulder. 'Not a real person?'

'You're real,' I say, every sense alive.

She yawns. 'I'm so sick of this movie.'

'I thought you hadn't seen it before.'

'I hadn't.' She starts. 'Sorry, I'm falling asleep. I'd better go.'

'Let me walk you.'

'Why? Nothing's going to happen to *me*,' Harper says.

She still sounds kind of out of it so I start to insist – but then she gets mad so I back down.

I watch from the window as she goes along the clifftop in the low light.

I'm putting away the Cheez Whiz when I notice the bottle of vermouth is gone. When did she take it? While I was in the bathroom?

I'm afraid my parents will notice, but when they get back they're distracted, unnerved. Not, for once, fighting. There's a problem in Castine. Someone went swimming this morning at dawn, and she hasn't come back. A local business owner who has lived here all her life. The coastguard is out.

'I hope they find her,' my mother says, face white. 'Christy's the most neighbourly soul in Castine, everyone says so.'

'No swimming outside the bay, sport,' my father says to me, placing a hand on hers. I try not to notice that she flinches. 'If you go out in the boat with your friends you stay in the boat. Always take a spare can of gas. The riptides around here are lethal.' His spectacles reflect the lamplight and his beard is messy from the wind.

'I have to see my friends.' I'm anxious but it comes out sounding mad. I'm afraid he'll tell me not to go.

'Just be careful,' he says. 'Did you get any reading for school done today?'

It takes me a moment before I recall my lie of the morning. 'Oh, tons,' I say. He looks so happy that I hug him tightly.

Dad pats me gently. 'I've got to pick up that spare part for the mower,' he says and slips out the front door. My mom's eyes follow him.

He comes in late; the sound of the front door opening blends with my dreams.

Some days Harper's busy with her parents or in trouble for something or other and it's just Nat and me. On those days we talk about her feverishly, about her eyes and hair and how cool she is. We talk about how we'll never love anyone else but her. We feel closer to one another for it. It's strange maybe but it bonds us, being in love with her. It lends security to the whole thing. It means we can be doubly sure that nothing will ever happen.

At first I lend Nat my favourite books. He's such a great friend and if we could only talk about books together he'd be *perfect*.

'But do you *like* Tom as a character?' I ask, as we wade out through the pools at low tide. 'Did Dickie deserve to die?'

'No one deserves to be murdered,' Nat says, handing me a shrimping net.

'I'm not sure,' I say, thinking of school. I feel disappointed. I don't think he even read the book.

'Periwinkle snail,' Nat says, showing me a small shell with a beautiful curve. Inside I glimpse a delicate, shining thing. 'You can cook and eat them,' he says.

'Are – is that what we're going to do?'

'Are you hungry?'

'No.'

'Then no.' He puts the snail gently down in the tide pool.

I don't know much about his home life, or even exactly where on the shore he lives – he keeps that to himself. He always comes to the cottage to collect me, and won't come inside, even when my parents ask him to. He seems most comfortable outdoors, under the sun, beside the ocean.

I never once, throughout our friendship, see him indoors. Until that last time.

We walk together along a cool pine trail. Nat carries the BB gun over his shoulder. We're supposed to be shooting rabbits but I secretly hope we don't find any. Sometimes we stop to line pinecones up on logs and shoot them. I'm pretty good for a beginner.

It's a long, sunlit day. I give Nat half the sandwich I have in my pocket because he didn't bring anything. To my relief we don't see any rabbits. He teaches me to recognise plants – trees and flowers. 'City boy.'

As we near home, we stop in the sloping meadow above the bay where you can see over the beech tops down to the sea, which is bright aching blue today. A stream runs through it, chattering. We drink with cupped hands. Dandelion clocks whirl up around us as we sit down in the grass.

'My folks are fighting a lot.' It feels good to tell someone.

'What are your parents like?' Nat asks.

'They're OK,' I say, surprised. 'My dad is kind of a dork.'

'Do you guys like, hang out?'

'Sometimes,' I say. 'Not as much as we used to.'

'I miss my mom. She ran away and left us. It's OK,' Nat says, seeing my face. 'It was a long time ago.' He opens his battered Velcro wallet. 'My dad doesn't know I have this. He wouldn't like it.'

A woman with a shock of shaggy blonde hair, that her son will later share. She's in a bar, pink with beer and the warmth of the room. Nat has folded the photograph in two, so it fits in the clear plastic sleeve in his wallet where the driver's licence is supposed to go – so that he sees her every time he opens it, I guess.

'She's called Arlene,' Nat says. 'I wonder where she is, sometimes.'

'Maybe one day you'll go find her,' I say. 'Go into the big wide world.'

'Nah, I won't leave. Why would I?' He gestures at the sea, the meadow, the summer sky.

'You feel about this place like Harper does about her dog,' I say. 'She misses it a lot, right?'

Nat shakes his head. 'She doesn't have a dog. Never did.'

'What do you mean?'

'It's not my story to tell.' And I can't get him to say any more than that. Instead Nat says, 'My pa's letting me off chores again tomorrow. We can take the boat. Harper and I will call for you at seven.'

'In the morning?' I'm incredulous.

'We have to get out early to hit the god weather.'

'The good weather?'

'That's what I'm saying.'

I'm nearly sure it wasn't what he said.

I shiver, and everything goes a little dim, as though there's a cloud over the sun.

Nat's watching me. 'What's up?'

'I've got to get home. My mom's expecting me.' My dad probably won't be there. I know that. He's not home much, these days.

But it's not that. I just suddenly don't like this place. I don't know why. It's a beautiful meadow full of flowers overlooking the sea, what kind of person doesn't like that? But I can't wait to get away from it. I feel like I might throw up.

He slaps me on the back in a friendly way and I don't stop to say goodbye. I hurry down towards the sea and Whistler Cottage.

As soon as I'm through the beech trees and back on the cliff path I feel better. There's no way I can explain the feeling that overwhelmed me just now. Like a hand was squeezing my insides. *Get a grip, Wilder*, I tell myself. *Just a place*. But I hated it. I felt like it was looking at me.

The early morning is grey and flat, pressing down on the horizon. In the bottom of the boat is rope, a grappling hook and the oyster knife. My eyes return to them again and again, as we push out of the bay and around the headland.

'What are those for?' I ask eventually.

'We're going somewhere special,' Harper says. She seems worked up, her eyes glassy. I realise that she's been drinking. I feel unease for her, but it's also a little exciting. She's troubled and needs my friendship. Once again there's a stirring in the depths of me.

The sea tosses and spits, black with rims of white.

'This doesn't seem like good weather,' I say.

'It's god weather,' Harper says. 'It's the best weather to see the god in.'

'What god?'

'She's just kidding around,' Nat says. 'Harper pretends she thinks something lives in the back of the cave. And when you call her, especially when the weather's rough—'

'She wakes up,' Harper hisses, eyes on the horizon. 'The woman in the sea. The god.'

I'm scared and I think about telling them to take me back, but I don't want to in front of Harper. Perhaps this is what they've been planning all along – befriending me to lure me here as a sacrifice. My palms slip and slide where I grip the side of the boat.

'Hey,' Nat says, gentle. 'Relax. It's just a trick of sound and light on the water. There's nothing really there.'

'Why take the knife if it's not real?'

'To be scared,' Harper says. 'Being scared is fun. But you have to make it feel real – to be properly afraid.' She puts her hand on mine. 'Don't worry. It's play-acting, I promise. But you have to *commit*.' Her hand squeezes mine urgently. 'We're going to find Rebecca.'

I can tell she wants me to ask, so I do. 'Who's Rebecca?'

Harper smiles. There's just a hint of slurring round her consonants. 'So, like, twelve years ago there was this young actress named Rebecca who was just about to have her big break. She was going to play an Olympic swimmer in some big Hollywood epic. She came up here for the summer to practise, tested herself every day, swimming further and further from shore.

'Rebecca was married to this perfect guy. Every day at dusk, her husband hung a light out for her at the end of the pier, a lantern with a blue bulb, to guide her home. She'd swim to the pier and he'd pull her out of the water, and rub her down in a big fluffy towel, take her inside to warm up and draw her a bath and give her a glass of wine and make dinner and they'd go to sleep.

'One day at dusk, he went down to the pier and hung the blue light. He drew her bath as usual and poured a glass of wine ready for her. He waited patiently. He waited and waited, but Rebecca didn't come. Night came, the stars came out, and she still didn't come.

'As for Rebecca, she swam towards the blue light, looking forward to her bath and her dinner and her warm towel and her warm husband. She felt happy, knowing she was near home. Her limbs had that nice heaviness that comes with tiredness, knowing that you'll rest soon. But the minutes passed and the light didn't seem to be getting any closer. The tiredness in her arms and legs was turning to heavy weight. But she swam on. She was starting to feel afraid.

'The night got dark. But somehow, she couldn't get any closer to home. The blue light stayed there, in the distance. Rebecca swam harder and harder, her breath coming in gasps. She tried not to think about all the big shapes moving far below her, how small her body was in the big black sea. She strained and swam towards that little pinpoint of blue. Still, it didn't come any closer. Rebecca felt the tears running down her face, into the cold sea around her.

'Now it was completely dark, except for the blue light shining in the distance. When she looked up, there were no stars, no moon. Solid black. And the sound of the water was different. It sort of lapped, and echoed.

'Rebecca saw that she wasn't in the open ocean anymore. There were stone walls on both sides of her and over her head. She was in a cave. And ahead was the blue light, reflecting on the shining black walls, on the water. She was crying really hard, now; her body was exhausted and she was afraid. She turned and swam again, swam for her life, into the dark, away from the blue glow. But her fingers met stone. There was no cave mouth. She was alone under the rock and the tide was rising. She knew she was going to die. The blue light pulsed and brightened, like it was enjoying itself. Finally, at last, it came nearer. She stopped swimming, but still the blue light approached. It wasn't one light, she saw now, but two. Eyes that shone in the dark like St Elmo's fire. It came closer and closer. She clawed again at the wall, looking for any opening that could save her. Under the water, she saw the body of the thing was vast, filling the cave like ink spreading in water. Rebecca was surrounded by the god. It tugged lightly at her limbs. Then it took her, drew her down and down and away for ever. It took her and they became part of each other – Rebecca and the god.

'She's strong, though. Even though she's dead, Rebecca never, ever stops trying to find her way back to shore, back to her life and her husband. But all that swimming makes her hungry. So if you feel something grab you by the leg, beneath the water, you'd better say your prayers. Rebecca's got you.'

A pleasurable shiver runs between my shoulder blades and down each vertebra.

'You feel it?' Harper's eyes are bright and fixed on me.

'Is any of that story true?' I ask Nat.

'People do drown out here,' Nat says. 'Like Christy Barham who owned the fishmonger. Everyone's pretty sad about that. And there was a woman called Rebecca who disappeared years ago. Or they say so. Maybe there wasn't and they've just got used to saying it. Harper made all the rest of that stuff up.'

'OK then,' I say. 'Let's go wake the god.'

'Are you afraid?' Harper whispers.

'Yes,' I say and she quivers with pleasure. I finger the wicked, long blade of the oyster knife. 'But if she's dangerous, we'll get her with this.' I fumble and almost drop the knife overboard.

'Careful,' Nat says, anxious. 'That was a birthday present. My dad still borrows it sometimes, he'll know if I lose it.'


We moor the boat to a tall rock like an obelisk. Beyond is a narrow channel lined with rock. The water swells are steep peaks and falls like a rollercoaster. At the end is a dark mouth in the cliff. A cave.

'My dad showed me this cave when I was little,' Nat says. 'It's kind of special.'

The water lashes white against the cave mouth.

'Is this safe?' I ask, with a strong return of my unease.

'We've come here loads of times,' Harper says. Her gaze is fixed on the opening to the cave.

'Not when it's been this rough,' Nat says, reluctant. Harper looks at him in surprise, and then with fury.

'You stay here then.' Before we can move or reply she's gone over the side, into the heaving flanks of the ocean. The thunder of the sea is so loud in the narrow channel, I don't even hear the splash.

'I think we have to go, now,' Nat says. He wriggles a broad elasticated band onto his head. It has a light fixed to the front. 'Don't forget the knife.'

'Wait—' But he's gone too. I'm alone in the boat.

I take a deep breath, grab the oyster knife and jump. The water seems colder, saltier than on that first day. It feels solid, like a hard hand slapping my face.

The temperature plummets as we come under the rocky ceiling, the quality of sound changes. Light plays all over the cave walls and roof. The cave narrows to a tunnel. We move into single file. Here the ocean breathes up and down; the swell throws us against the rough walls, leaving bloody scratches. I raise a hand – my fingers just graze the rough stone overhead.

The swell lifts us gently. The tide is high and rising. I try not to imagine our legs from below, kicking tiny in the black. The narrow tunnel opens up into an echoing space. We're inside the cliff now, I can feel the weight of rock above our heads. I can't see much until Nat's headlamp blinks on and he shines it around.

It's large, the cave, it goes back and back. It's loud, too, like being inside an engine. A big stone looms over the lashing water. The top of the rock is flat, just about big enough to stand on.

'Let's call her up!' Harper yells, her voice echoing and eerie.

'Yes!' Nat yells. His voice is filled with a strange energy. 'The cave is filling up,' he says, coming up beside me. His head torch is blinding. 'Right up to the roof. So let's make this quick.'

'Tell me what we're doing.'

Harper's face is just a gleam of wet cheek. She swims close. 'Some say she's that woman who drowned. Some say she's always been here. We call her Rebecca but who knows what her real name is? She tries to kiss you.' Her face is close to mine, now. 'If you let her kiss you, it's the last thing you'll ever do.' Her breath fills my ear, runs down the spaces of me. Despite the staleness that lingers, it lights my groin with fire. 'She wraps you in her arms and drags you down with her, into the cold depths of the sea. You drown, but in ecstasy.'

32

Here, now, in the cold dark cradle of the water, it feels real. I see what Harper means, now, about commitment to the story. I feel Rebecca below us, waiting.

Nat says, 'I think Wilder should call her.' I can't see his expression; his voice is friendly, but some feeling emanates from him.

'Why?' I ask.

'You don't want to?'

'I'll do it.' I don't want Harper to think I'm not committing.

'Get on up there, tiger,' she says. I hand her the knife and swim over to Nat.

He helps me up onto the rock with the flat top which sticks up out of the waves. 'I'll hold your arms,' he says, taking a wide stance. 'You lean forward and tell your secret.'

He takes my arms in a strong, solid grip. I lean forward slowly, testing. My breath comes shorter as my arms go taut, pinned behind me.

Harper's voice carries over the water. 'You have to tell a secret. The god only comes for those.'

'I don't have any secrets.'

'Everyone has secrets.'

She's right, of course. I could tell them the big one. The one I've been slowly realising, this past year, about myself. For a moment I'm exhilarated. *I'll do it*, I think.

I don't know how to say it, this new idea – that it might not be just girls that I like. But these are my friends, I'll find the words.

'Fine,' I say to Nat. 'Lower me down.' I lean out, perilous, over the water – like a ship's prow. I hear Nat grunt with the effort of holding me back. There are rocks down there, under the shining surface. Suddenly, I realise that I can't move. My arms are pinned behind me, my muscles and chest are burning.

I forget about the secret or anything but getting back up. The pressure on my lungs and ribcage becomes unbearable. I'm having trouble breathing. I gasp, 'Up, up!' Water laps at my face. I think, *he wants to suffocate me.*

'Pull him up, Nat, pull!' I hear Harper's voice as if I'm already underwater. 'This was a stupid trick.'

'I'm trying!' Nat yells and as he does his grip on my arms slips and the black water rushes up. It closes over my head, a sharp rock scrapes along my side. The sea presses on me, smothers me like at school, like the sweatshirt they pressed to my face to stop me yelling. Water dashes cold into my throat. I choke and cough, manage to turn my head and grab a breath.

Four hands scrabble at my slick flesh; Harper's grip is as strong as a monkey's, her fingernails dig into my arms. But I slip down through their hands and inhale more mouthfuls of cold salt. Harper and Nat scream at each other – *I can't pull him up! Let him go! The rocks!*

Someone grabs the back of my shorts and hauls me up away from the water, onto the narrow rock platform. There's not enough room for three here and Harper falls. Nat staggers, holding me; I cling to his wet flesh, breathing fast.

'Sorry, Wilder,' he says in my ear. 'Sorry.'

'You brought me here as a trick,' I say.

'Harper was meant to be waiting underwater for you,' Nat said. 'And then she'd burst up and kiss you. It was supposed to be funny. It was supposed to—'

'Don't be angry, Wilder!' Harper calls from somewhere below. I ignore her.

'I was yelling at you to pull me up, but you wouldn't, you made me stay down, I couldn't breathe—' I hear the sounds coming out of my mouth, I understand that they're words but I can't connect them to meaning. Fear and adrenaline course through me in strong, black pulses.

34

I shove Nat and we both fall into the black. The cold sea closes over my head. I break the surface to the sound of screaming; it echoes on the cave walls, seems to ricochet off the water. At first I can't tell where anything is – up or down, or where the screaming is coming from. Then I see the sun dancing on the waves, a narrow band of blue day at the end of the tunnel, and I strike out hard, heading for the light. I hear the others following behind. The rough roof is even closer over my head and I don't have any breath left for screaming, I'm breathing too fast, hyperventilating as I reach the bright blue. Harper and Nat are behind, calling to me, but I don't wait.

The rising water has narrowed the cave mouth to a slender crescent of light. We were nearly out of time. I dive below the surface and swim out – when I break up into the sun I just bob there, clinging to a barnacled rock, letting the day stroke my face.

My muscles seem to have dissolved into liquid. I can barely pull myself up and into the boat. Shock, I guess. Nat tries to help but I push him away.

'I couldn't hear you, Wilder,' Nat says. 'By the time I realised . . . I swear. I'm sorry.' He shivers, looks smaller than usual, hunched, hair plastered flat to his head.

I just shake my head.

We go back along the coast in silence, to the sound of the motor and the lapping of the sea. Harper touches my leg. 'It was only supposed to be a bit of fun,' she says. 'It went wrong.'

I can't look at her. It's like the day we spent together never happened.

I leap out at the mouth of Whistler Bay, not waiting for the boat to reach the shallows. 'Wilder,' Nat calls after me.

I swim hard for the warmer shallows. The sea now seems unfamiliar, a big spreading thing waiting to kill me. I can't wait to get to land. I think, *yes. There's something in these waters that eats people.*

It's fun to feel fear, Harper said. Is it more fun to make others feel it?

When I reach the shore and turn they're still there, watching from the boat. 'We nearly died back there,' I call. 'You realise that? How could you both be so stupid?' Then I yell, 'Frick you both.'

I turn and go up the path. Friends can break your heart, it seems, just like love.


In the next room, my mom and dad are hissing at one another again. It's been bad these last couple of days. The car starts in the middle of the night and my dad isn't here some mornings. I was so dumb to think that a vacation by the sea would fix things between them. I've heard Nat and Harper's voices at the door, too. I told my mom to say I wasn't home. I never want to see them again.

'Don't you dare,' my mother says furiously to my father. 'I'll deal with it.' The door to my room flies open. 'Come with me, Wilder.'

I groan and pull the covers over my head. The sheets and I have the same musty smell, as though I have fused with them in some way.

The darkness is whipped away and I lie in the blinding light. I cover my eyes.

My mother's hand is firm about my wrist. 'Come on, monkey,' she says. 'I've got you new swimming shorts.'

The wind and the day feel sharp, like my skin is being scraped off. I follow my mother's slim shape down to the water. The towels she carries flutter in the wind.

On the shore I shiver in the breeze. My new shorts are slightly too large, but bright blue with a pattern of anchors on it, like something you'd buy a kid.

My mother wades out of her depth, swims out a couple of strokes then turns. 'The water's fine, Wilder. Come on.'

'I don't want to.'

'Do as I say, please.' There's an unfamiliar steel in her voice. 'When did you last have a shower, monkey?'

The water slips over me. And it is nice – somehow comforting to be a small shape in the vast sheen – to be reminded of my smallness by the large world.

Mom ducks beneath the water and comes up red-faced and breathless. Her hair is a wet mop, her face bare of makeup. I rarely see her like this. She's always so neat, every hair in place. We bob.

'Your friends have been calling for you,' my mother says.

'They're not my friends,' I say.

'What happened, Wilder?'

'They played a trick on me. A prank. It was mean.' Some obscure residual loyalty prevents me from telling her what it was actually like – about the water covering my face, about gasping for air. I know they didn't really mean to hurt me. I know that. But they tricked me and it hurts so bad I could die.

'It's difficult, being sixteen,' my mother says. 'You don't know what's a big deal and what isn't. I remember.'

'It's a big deal to me,' I say curtly and turn to go ashore. I've done as she asked, haven't I?

'Stop a moment.' She sighs. 'Your father doesn't want me to tell you this. But I think I have to. I had a – thing – where I went to bed for a time. It started when I was about your age. I felt this great weight on my chest and I just couldn't get out of bed.'

'For how long?' I'm fascinated. My mother rarely talks about herself.

'Six years, on and off.' She takes a deep shuddering breath, as if feeling that weight on her chest again. 'It was like seeing the world from far away, through dark glass. There were five of us to support, you know, us kids. My parents didn't know what to do with

37

me. That generation buttoned everything up. They'd never heard of depression.'

A darkness, a coldness seems to pass over me with her words. A shadow covering the sun.

'A doctor gave me pills to take,' she says. 'And they helped, eventually. Or maybe I just got used to it. I don't know which. I got out of bed and got that job at the high school, and of course I met your father. But I missed lots of summers like this.' Under the water, her hand finds mine. 'I don't want you to miss anything, Wilder. Ever. I want you to be happy. I think if I'd resisted it from the first, if I'd never let it start, I might have been able to fend it off. So, can you try? Can you try to be happy for me?'

'Yes,' I say, determined. I have never seen her cry before, it's awful. Her face is pink and shiny.

She hugs me, and I cling to her; her flesh is cold and slippery against mine in the water. *Like a corpse*, I think before I can stop the thought.

'I don't know if Nat and Harper will come over again,' I say. 'Maybe they won't.'

'They'll come,' she says, stroking my head with a cool hand. 'Kids are optimists.'

And Nat and Harper do come, just like my mom said they would. When I answer the door they look startled and unprepared. We all stare at the ground, awkward. We've all seen too deeply into one another; it's hard to come back up to the regular surface of things.

'Let's go to the beach,' I say.

It's better down by the sea; if we feel shy there's always something to kick at or pick up or look at. The sea lying in the background like it's watching over us or something. The afternoon is dying so we start to build a fire.

'It was a really dumb joke,' Nat says suddenly. He kicks at the sand and draws a semi-circle with his toe. He throws an armful of drift-wood, white like bone, onto the pyre. The tide is going out, leaving a network of glassy pools in the dusk.

Harper says, 'It went too far.' Her eyes are red and I realise she's been crying. 'We just wanted to give you a little scare, just for a second. Then Nat couldn't get you back up.' She shivers. 'It was so scary.'

I am glad they're sorry. But it feels disappointing somehow. The glamour that surrounded them is cracked open. They're just kids like me, after all.

Nat says, 'The fire's ready.' He lights it carefully with a lighter and tinder of dried grass. It glows red and curls in hot filaments, then licks up flame. Beyond its warm circle the sea stretches out into the dark. I think about how big and old the world is compared to us. We're just little fires burning in the night.

'We'll never lie to you again,' Nat says. 'I swear. It was so dumb.'

'I swear too,' Harper says. Her hand slips into mine. 'We've decided,' she said, 'that you get two forfeits.'

'What do you mean?'

'At any time, you get to ask one of us to do something. And we have to. It's for ever, it doesn't expire. We could all be like, eighty, and we would still have to do it.'

'Anything?' I ask.

'Anything,' Nat says urgently.

'Ha,' I say. 'You don't know what torture I can devise.'

Harper laughs even though it's not a great joke. We watch the fire leap and crack.

'I know we made it all up,' Harper says. 'But I was afraid – in the cave. I kept seeing things – like pictures – like writing on the dark. I'm so sorry, Wilder. It was all my idea – I thought that you liked me.' She's bright red, now. 'I thought maybe you'd tell us that, as your secret. Then I'd come up from below and pretend to be Rebecca and kiss you. I thought it would be fun. No, I didn't think.'

'We're not very good at pranks,' Nat says. It seems funny to me, because it really was the worst practical joke, and I laugh a little, weakly.

'I want to tell you something.' Harper takes off her big wristwatch and hands it to me. 'I don't have a dog,' she says.

'Harper, I couldn't—'

'I'm not giving it to you, you idiot. Look on the back.'

The engraving on the back of the man's watch she wears says *Samuel*.

'Sam, my brother,' she says.

'Why would you pretend it was a dog?'

'I like talking about him,' Harper says. 'But it's kind of a bummer to keep talking about your dead brother. It's a way of talking about him and not talking about it, both at the same time.

'He was only a little older than I am now when it happened. He took a corner too fast on his motorbike. Maybe that's why I feel so weird this year. Soon I'll be older than he ever was. He only ate fries with mustard. He always knew when I was upset.'

I pat her awkwardly. I have to learn something better to do when women cry. It seems to be happening to me a lot lately.

'We don't have to go on about it,' Harper says, smoothing her hair. 'I just thought – after what we did, you know, in the cave – that you deserved the truth.' She sighs. 'You can bring dead people back sometimes, with witchcraft, you know. I tried to bring him back but it didn't work.' She sways, watching something we can't see. I realise she's drunk again. 'What was the secret you were going to tell, Wilder?'

'I didn't have one,' I lie. 'What about you Nat? Anything you want to share?'

'Uh,' Nat looks anxious, as if he doesn't want to disappoint. 'I don't know?'

'Natty,' Harper says, amused. 'The world's open book.'

'No,' he says, stung. 'I have stuff.'

'Like what?' I ask.

'It doesn't matter what,' he says after a pause, with some dignity.

We both look at him and smirk.

'What?' The annoyance on his honest, handsome face just makes it worse. One of the few things that irritates Nat is being laughed at. Harper giggles, which makes me laugh. By the end Harper and I are rolling around in the sand, coughing.

'Why is it funny?' Nat keeps saying. 'I don't get it.'

We don't stop for a long time.

It's the kind of laughter that only comes to kids, I think. Grownups are too used to the absurdity of the world.


The days that follow are golden and quiet. We go out in the boat again when we can, but we're careful. We don't go in any caves, and we avoid the open ocean, hug the coast with its sheltered coves. I can't stop thinking about Christy Barham who went missing while swimming near Castine.

I cut off the legs of a pair of my jeans to make denim shorts. As I get more tanned and haircuts become a distant memory, I enjoy how much like Nat I'm starting to look. I imagine that people might mistake us for brothers. I even start flattening my 'a's a little when I talk – before his look tells me that I'm not doing it right.

I think about my forfeits. I want to choose carefully. In the meantime, I'm trying to come up with something we can all do together that's a little dangerous, a little out there. I feel like it'll make us all equal again.

I have my big idea as I'm helping my dad clean out the tool shed behind the cottage, and I come across cans of spray paint. They're old and rusty and I wonder if they work. But when I depress the nozzle a jet of bright green shoots out, making a rough circle on my bare leg. I blink in surprise, and then it comes to me.

'Can you get the boat tonight?' I ask Nat. We're roasting marshmallows on the coals of our dying fire. I have to go up the cliff path for dinner with my parents, soon. But I'm hoping this is just the beginning of the night.

'Yes,' he says. 'My dad's been on the water all day, he'll be sleeping. As long as we're back by sunrise? That's five-thirty, for you folks from away.'

'I can come too,' Harper says. 'I'll pretend to go to bed early.'

'Oh,' I say, 'you're assuming you're invited?'

She punches me absentmindedly, then pulls her warm marshmallow out into a long string of goo. Before I realise what's happening she has placed it gently on my head, where it clings stickily to my hair.

The porthole swings open silently, letting in the warm night air and the song of the rocks below. I slip out into it.

'Let's go south some,' I say. The spray paint rolls around in the cooler where I've stashed it. 'Where's a place with a big seawall cliff, where lots of boat traffic passes?'

'Penobscot Point, I guess,' says Nat. 'What are we doing?'

'You'll see.'

The point is a sleeping tiger against the night. The cliff wall rears beside us. It's fairly smooth, perfect for my purposes.

I stand up in the boat, wavering with the bobbing of the water. I don't want to risk a flashlight. Trusting to instinct, I take out the can of green paint.

'Wilder,' Harper's voice. 'What are you doing?'

I spray my message on the cliff in the dark. I can only hope it will be legible. I write in capital letters, swaying with the movement of the boat.

A swell tosses me off my feet and I fall into Harper's lap with a yell. From the clifftop above, there's a spurt of yellow – a light coming on. Nat guns the outboard engine and we speed off as a man yells indeterminate things, a torch raking the dark waters around us.

'What did you do?' Nat says, when we slow up out of sight. 'What did you write, Wilder?'

'I wrote "THE DAGGER MAN WAS HERE".'

'What?' Nat says on an indrawn breath. 'What did you do that for? Ah, shit.' Nat rarely swears.

'It's from the story,' I say, surprised at his intensity. 'The one you made up about the Dagger Man. Like the thing in the cave.'

'That story's not made up,' says Harper quietly. 'It's real. Wilder, you shouldn't have done that.' The dark reveals a lot. It's harder to hide things in your voice. Harper's afraid. Not the kind of shivery dramatic fear she likes, but the quiet, real kind.

I feel uneasy for a moment, but I quash it quickly. 'It's just some graffiti, right?' But I wish I'd known it was real. That he's real.


There's a picture of my wavering graffiti on the cliff wall in the paper the next day. The fishing boats saw the message at first light. I have brought the Dagger Man back from the dead. Harper brings the paper over to show me. She climbs high into the maple above me as we talk. She always needs to be doing something. It's not so weird, I tell myself. But I can't help the feeling she's like a lookout up there, scouting for danger.

I stare at the headline.

'Don't be scared, Wilder,' Harper says from above. 'I mean, it was pretty stupid of you. But people will forget about it eventually.'

'I'm not scared,' I say, absentminded. I can't stop staring at the picture. And it's true, I don't feel afraid, just kind of numb.

If I'd paid attention to the local paper my father got delivered every day, I would have known that the Dagger Man was real. If I'd listened to the conversations in the general store in Castine instead of zoning out and thinking about stories, or maybe Harper's skin, maybe I would have heard talk about the happenings last summer. Maybe if I hadn't been so desperate to move on from what had happened in the cave, and had asked Nat and Harper questions, I would have understood what was truth and what was fiction. I'd assumed it was one of their made-up stories, like Rebecca.

'Maybe let's do normal things for a while,' Harper says. 'Daylight things – things regular teenagers do.'

'No problem. I never, ever want to do anything like that again,' I say. I feel slightly sick, like I've eaten something bad.

'Hi, Mr Harlow!' The leaves shudder as Harper waves energetically at my dad who's at the open kitchen window. He waves back. Despite my misgivings about letting them meet her, my parents like Harper. It took me a while to understand that they think she's my girlfriend. I let them; it makes me feel good. They don't know Nat so well, especially as he doesn't like to come inside. He's shy of parents, I think. I've never met his dad, Mr Pelletier.


I decide to journal today; no more wasted time on pranks and sneaking out at night. I'll write, read a great book, get my dad to take me out in the car, do some practice on these quiet roads, get ready for my test in the fall. Normal things like Harper said.

I pull on clothes. My mom's outside hanging laundry on the line. She just shakes her head when I ask where Dad is. Her mouth is a narrow line around the clothes peg. When I look down the hill I see the car is gone.

I go to kick my brain into action with caffeine. As I'm hunting for the coffee I see there's something propped against the window, behind the little aloe vera plant Mom keeps there. I pull it out. It's a Polaroid – a fuzzy image taken in bad light, but it's clearly the view from the window of the cottage, out to sea. There's the cliff, with the sugar maple in the background. There's a shining path of light across the ocean. The sky is dim, perhaps a storm's coming. There's also a long pale shape across the bottom – a finger, I think.

It sets off a weird train of thought in my head. How many people around here own a Polaroid camera? Harper's voice is in my head. *Daggerman.*

'Vernon loved that thing,' Dad says gently, and I jump. I didn't hear him come in. 'We used to go on walks together, find stuff to shoot.' He sees my face. 'You OK?'

'Yeah, it just made me think about the thing with the – with the kids.'

'Don't worry, sport. All that Dagger Man stuff happened last summer. It's over now. Just some drifter who's moved on. Neighbourhood kids playing around, maybe.'


That afternoon I try to read in my room. Instead I think about Harper. A sharp, deafening tattoo breaks into these thoughts. It's hammering, coming from the side of the house.

When I go out to investigate I find my father putting restrictors on all the windows, so they don't open more than a couple of inches. He reinforces the door to the cottage with mortice locks. 'Finally getting around to it,' he says to me cheerfully. 'Just so your mother doesn't fret. Better safe than sorry.' The local paper lies beside him, open at the picture of my handiwork on the cliff. I suddenly realise how distinctive my handwriting is – even when I'm spray painting in the dark. My 'M's have soft curves at the top instead of sharp triangle points. Dad follows my gaze; his eyes rest gently mildly on the picture, and then on me.

'Hooligans,' he says in a resigned voice. 'Don't think any more about it, Wilder.' He takes up the drill and the last screw goes home. He tests the window, makes sure it only swings open a hand's breadth.

'We're all safe and sound now,' he says and picks up the drill. He wanders on to the living-room window. 'Nothing in or out,' he says through a mouthful of screws.

I watch him pick up the drill, humming some old French song. Serge Gainsbourg maybe. He likes all that stuff.

My mom brings out the big box of Uncle Vernon's Polaroids from under the stairs. I'm bored so I sit with her and look through. Maybe I'm not bored. I wouldn't admit it but I want to sit near my mom for a little bit.

'You've grown three feet just this summer,' she says. 'Oof, and I can hardly get my arm around these broad shoulders!'

'Come on, Mom.' But I'm surprised to find, sitting next to her, that she has a point. Either I'm taller or she's got smaller. I hope it's the first one.

Uncle Vernon's photos are really pretty bad. There are so many of them, too. The still lifes are even worse than the landscapes.

'What do you think this is?' Mom holds up something pink, striated with lines of light.

I tip my head to one side. 'It's a hand over the lens. Fingers, anyway.'

A bag full of groceries, a blurry foot striding along a sidewalk, a tabletop with nothing on it labelled 'my pen' in shaky ballpoint. There's a stifled sound from beside me. My mom has a hand over her mouth.

'Mom?' She makes that little smothered woof again. Then she takes her hand away and releases a short shriek of laughter.

'It's *art*, Mom,' I tell her as she lets out those little barks. 'Have some respect.'

She screams and slaps me weakly.

'What's up, folks?' My dad beams from the doorway.

'Oh not much,' Mom says, wiping her eyes. 'Wilder was telling me a joke.'

She knows Dad wouldn't like us making fun of Uncle Vernon. Taking the piss, as Harper would say.

But in the following days I catch her sometimes with a gleaming look on her face. Once at the dinner table she snorts mashed potato in the middle of some conversation. She meets my eye and I know she's thinking about Uncle Vernon's 'art'.


Unbelievably, August is here – and then it's halfway done. The summer is coming to an end.

It's the hottest day of the year so far, deep in the dog days. My father and I take refuge from the heat under the maple. The leaves shush gently in the breeze above our heads. One or two leaves are turning already, taking on a deep, burnt orange hue.

My father has the *New York Times* over his face, his breathing regular. I fidget. It's only an hour until I meet Nat and Harper on the pine bluff. The time I spend away from them has begun to seem vague and unreal. My last days here have become unbearably precious.

The cottage goes on the market in the fall and I'll never come here again. Some other family will come and live here. Some other teen-ager will watch the stars through the porthole, listening to the sound of the stones singing in the bay below. Where will Uncle Vernon's pictures go? I somehow can't imagine that we'll take them back to the city. They'll probably get thrown out. For some reason this both-ers me intensely. The new kid will probably be really cool, maybe have his own car. Nat and Harper will like him more than me.

The newspaper moves gently with my dad's breath. *If he died*, I think, *would I inherit the cottage?* Or Mom would, maybe. I'm nearly seventeen; they couldn't make me go back to school.

I start. My father is sitting up, watching me. How long has he been awake? 'Summer's nearly over. You keeping up with your summer reading? Fall semester will be here before you know it.'

'Yeah, I'm on top of it.' I'm not. The thought of Scottsboro turns in my gut like a knife. Sometimes I feel like I'm not in love with Harper, but with Harper and Nat as a pair. This thought makes me feel uneasy and excited in equal parts. Other times I wonder if you can be in love with a place, just like with a person – this stretch of coast, the bright long days here where you can lose yourself. It's private, this part of the world. Like each cove or copse is a secret.

'You know, the rental market's not bad in these parts,' my father says.

'Good for the rental market, I guess?' I'm furious that he can be so casual when my heart is breaking.

'You've really come out of your shell here, Wilder. This life seems good for you.'

'It is.' I wait, heart beating. You can't hurry my father. Ever. I've tried.

'It's a little nest egg, too. Uncle Vernon got quite the return on it. So what we're thinking is,' he places his large, hot hand on my shoul-der for a moment, 'we could keep it. Not sell it. We could come out here every July. Rent it out the rest of the time. What do you say?'

My heart's pounding. So I just hug him quick and hard.

I skid down the path to the sea to tell my friends.


It feels like no more than two heartbeats before my last day arrives. We spend it by the water as usual. Afterwards Nat starts to build a fire on the beach but I say, 'I'm over bonfires on the beach.' I want a fire, really, but I can't stand it, that this is the last one.

Harper and Nat both look at me and I see they understand. That makes it worse in a way. 'Ugh, so boring,' I say, turning away. Then, staring at the ground, 'Sorry.'

Harper's hand is cool on my sunburned shoulder. 'Let's go up to the meadow?'

'Yeah,' Nat says, 'I'm bored of the beach too.' I love them both so much.

It's cool and green as we go under the trees; sunlight and shadow chase across our faces.


The meadow looks beautiful. Black-eyed Susans peer from the long grass, which stirs in the late afternoon breeze. The air is full of butterflies, birds sing in the nearby copse of beech. *Cuckoo, goldfinch,* I say to myself, thinking of the first day we came here. I didn't know the names of these birds or flowers then.

One thing's the same though. I hate it here, no matter how pretty it is. Every time I sit a little voice in my head goes, *no, not there.* I don't want to say anything – it's better not to go to our favourite places today. Better put the sad memory here, in a place I don't like.

Harper sits on a log and produces a bottle of Havana Club

from her bag. Her parents don't keep tabs on their liquor cabinet. They really should. As I drink she watches me with a combination of interest and amusement. 'What is it with you and this spot, Wilder?'

'I don't know,' I say, shifting on my feet and swatting at the midges that swarm above the grass. Is the itching I feel from them, or coming from inside me? 'I feel like someone died here or something.'

'Someone died almost everywhere,' says Nat, practical.

'I've thought of my forfeit,' I say. 'But I don't know if it's possible.'

'We have to do it,' Nat says. 'That's the rule.'

'Well, this one's for Harper, because you live here.'

Harper raises her head and looks at me. Her red hair is bright, the colour of flame, her skin pale, and for a second it seems like a different person is looking out from inside her. 'Go on,' she says.

'You have to promise to come here every summer, even when we're grown up. All three of us have to get together.'

'Sure,' says Nat, eagerly. 'Sure.'

'How can I promise that?' Harper asks, exasperated.

'I don't know. But you swore. So you have to.'

'Do the thing,' Nat says.

'But . . .' She sighs. 'OK. Maybe. If that's what you really want, Wilder. You both have to do exactly as I say. But first I need some stuff. Give me a couple minutes.'

We trade tiny sputtering sips as we wait for Harper. We're talking loudly about dirt bikes so we don't hear her soft approach through the meadow.

'Do you know what this is?' We jump. She holds a plant, uprooted, shedding loose soil. It's twisted, looks like a withered white carrot, maybe, or a ginger root. Harper grips the stem through a handkerchief, because she doesn't want to get dirty, I assume.

We shake our heads.

'Hemlock. Don't touch it, not even a little. So we're going to put it in the spell, to make the promise last to death and beyond.'

I shiver. 'Is that really – cool, Harper?'

She just shakes her head as though she's too busy for me and scans the land. She goes to a place a little ways away where the earth dips, forming a natural bowl.

Nat puts a warm hand on my back. 'She'll be OK,' he says quietly. 'She gets like this sometimes.'

Harper fetches stones and lines the dip in the ground, making a fire pit. She builds a cone of dry twigs and sticks. Then she puts the hemlock at the heart of it, handkerchief and all. 'Blood,' she says, without turning around. 'We need blood. From all three.'

We both step forward and give her our hands. I can't even see what she holds that does it, but there's a feeling like a click and a moment later our fingers drip crimson.

'Don't waste it,' she says, impatient. 'Put it on the fire.' So we all hold our dripping hands over the wood and kindling and watch it become spattered with red.

Harper puts a match to the fire which crackles up right away. It's been a dry summer. She pushes us upwind of the smoke. 'Don't go near it,' she says. 'The hemlock's burning. I don't know if it's danger-ous to breathe it in.'

'Maybe don't burn it if you don't know stuff like that?' I say, nervous.

'Oh be quiet, Wilder.' She smiles and I blink. For a second it looks like she has too many teeth. 'We have to stay here until the fire dies,' she says. 'So that the spell works.'

'Also to make sure we don't set the woods on fire,' Nat says. He becomes more and more comfortable the weirder things get, I've noticed.

'I'll put something in the spell that will help you with school,

Wilder,' Harper says. 'It'll stop anyone bothering you.' She hugs me. It's unexpected. Usually she shies from touch like a cat. Except Nat's.

'I'll miss you,' I say. 'Can you put something in to help you get sent back home, away from school?'

She shakes her head. 'That's the one thing about magic,' she says. 'You can't do it for yourself. Only for other people.'

'Where do you get these rules?' Nat passes her the Havana Club.

'I just know them.' She looks sad and drinks. When she passes the bottle to me it's got a lot more air at the top. Harper wants to believe in something so badly. In Rebecca, the cave, in magic. Whatever is available. I really love her right now, and also kind of want to shake her, yell at her. But I don't do any of these things. She takes my hand and squeezes it.

The little bonfire gives off heavy plumes of smoke. It billows like thick liquid on the still evening air. Some of the wood must be damp. I hope it smoulders on for a long time. I don't really believe that Harper can stop what happens at Scottsboro. I don't think we'll always come back here every summer. So I want to make it last – the fire, this moment.

# *Pearl*

Pearl's first memory of her mother is her voice raised in the wind, calling. They were on a mountaintop, Pearl doesn't know where. She was little, her legs hurt, her ears hurt because the wind was strong. She was crying, stranded on a crag a way away from her. She didn't know how to get down and go to her mother.

Her mother strode across the rocks, leapt over gaps like a deer. When she got to Pearl she bent and put both hands over her daughter's ears, warming them. 'Hold on,' she said.

Pearl wrapped her arms around her mama's neck and her mother picked her up and folded her inside her jacket. Then she put her down and led her down the mountain. It seemed to take hours. 'You're OK, you're cool,' she bent and said into her daughter's ear. 'You're as cool as a long drink of water.' And Pearl giggled and felt better. It always calmed her down, this saying of her mother's.

Maybe it wasn't a mountain. It was probably a hill. It probably took a minute or two, not hours. But every time Pearl thinks of her mother, she remembers being saved.

She's named after her mother's favourite jewel. She has never felt equal to it – has never felt valuable, since her mother went.

You can't get to know people after they're gone. All you have are memories, moments, and that doesn't make a whole person.

Pearl was five. It was a bright, gleaming morning. They were staying in Castine up the coast, and they came down to the sea each day with a picnic. They already had a favourite spot, a little cove where the rocks made this weird sound when the wind blew in from the sea. Pearl's daddy would explore the rock pools with her, swim, make sandcastles.

While they did this Pearl's mother swam out for forty-five minutes or so. There was a cove by a sea cave where she stopped, got out and stretched, and then went back in for the return. She did it every day. By the time she got back, they had set out lunch on the blanket. Afterwards they would get in the car and go home, feeling sea-dazed and lovely.

Nothing about that day was different, at first. They drove along the green roads to the sea. Mama put a hand to her ear and said, 'Oh, dammit, I've lost one of my earrings.'

'It'll be back at the bed and breakfast,' Pearl's daddy said. 'We'll find it later.'

They parked, climbed the hill and descended the path on the other side. Mama was strong and tall in her black bathing suit and swimming cap; she seemed made for the sea, like some kind of dolphin or fish. They had chosen this beach specially because it had soft sand for Pearl to play in, not like most of the rocky ones around here.

'See you at lunch.' Pearl's mother strode into the water, struck out and soon was just a black skull, bobbing in the waves.

Daddy paddled with Pearl, then got hot and retired to the shade of the cliffs. He napped briefly with a hat over his head. She explored the farther pools, making sand angels in the wet slurry by the water-line. Mama would be back soon, and they would have lunch.

Pearl wanted her sandwich. Daddy woke and started dressing the salad, humming. Crushed garlic, a spoonful of mustard, lemon juice, white vinegar, olive oil. Mama was very particular about her salad dressing. Daddy made it fresh just before eating, every day.

Pearl fell down in the damp sand once more and scrambled her arms and legs. Suddenly there was a searing agony on her breast-bone, like fire, the worst pain she'd ever felt. She thought she was dying. Her scream came from very far away. She was paralysed with pain.

Cheek in the damp sand, chest on fire, she watched Daddy's feet racing closer, sending up sprays of sand. He picked her up and the pulsing pain got worse. If she looked down, she could just see a red welt on her chest, above the line of her bathing suit.

He scooped cold handfuls of sea water over the red mark, then carried Pearl over to the picnic cooler and poured white vinegar over it. The tide of pain receded, and he hugged her carefully and rocked her. Pearl cried even harder then. The comfort was worse than the pain somehow.

'It was just a jellyfish,' he said. A dead one buried in the sand, probably. 'Don't worry kiddo, it's over now.'

But it was only just beginning.


They waited but Mama was late, so Daddy let Pearl eat her sand-wich. Something round and hard was in her mouth. She spat it out and excavated it gently from the bread, peanut butter and jelly. It was a single earring. It must have fallen in somehow while Mama was making the sandwiches.

Mama didn't come back. The red welt on Pearl's chest healed and every day it did was another day she was gone. Daddy kept up hope, but Pearl knew it wasn't a jellyfish she had felt there in the sand. It had been her death. She was only five but Pearl knew. Rebecca had drowned, swum too far out, and left them.

Sometimes her mother talks to Pearl in the night. She learns to keep herself awake, so she can hear her. It always happens the same way, Rebecca's coming. It starts with the sound of the wind, roaring in Pearl's head, just like that day on the mountain. And then Rebecca's warm hands close over her cold ears. Then she hears her voice muffled by her hands. Pearl loves her touch but she always wishes she would take her hands away so she could hear her mother clearly. But Mama never does. She only ever says one thing.

*Stay cool, sweetheart. Cool as a drink of water.*

Pearl keeps the lost earring in her locket. One day the other one will show up, she knows that too, just like she knows it won't be a good day when it does.

# [ ]

Heat
Hat
What

Here
Where

Ham
Am

Hit
Hi
Is
I

# The Dagger Man of Whistler Bay

*From the unpublished memoir by Wilder Harlow*
*June, 1990*

I get to Whistler Bay first – I take the train to Portland then a bus to Castine and a cab out to the cottage. My parents are coming tomorrow but since they had some adult stuff to do in the city we agreed I could come straight here and spend the night alone. I'm nearly eighteen, after all. Totally an adult.

I haul my bag up the hill. I haven't brought much. All I need are shorts and t-shirts, flip flops, sneakers. Swim shorts. Harper arrives next week. Nat's coming to the cottage tonight. I wrote to him weeks ago via the Castine post office, the way he told me to, and let him know I was coming. I don't have his address. When I passed through Castine earlier I found his reply waiting, just as he promised I would, written in careful, childlike cursive: OK. *I'll bring dinner.*

I think of all the things we'll do. I'm glad Nat and I get to catch up before we see Harper. It'll give me a chance to test the ground. I'm kind of nervous about whether the agreement we made still holds. Isn't a year enough to change everything? Because I'm determined to get a girlfriend this summer, and part of me hopes against hope that it could be Harper.

And if the agreement does hold, it will give us a chance to get tight again, me and Nat, before she comes. So I won't be tempted to break our pact.

I hope this logic is sound. It's all so confusing.

There's a figure ahead on the path, silhouetted against the sky. A tall man. He crests the hill and stops, leans against the white garden gate. I wonder who this guy is and what he wants – my heart sinks at the prospect of having to deal with some kind of adult business, when all I want to do is dump my bags and be ready for when Nat comes to get me. I'll tell him to come back tomorrow after my parents get here.

The man turns around in the warm sunset. He holds up a hand in greeting. He's even more handsome than I'd remembered. It's Nat.

We hug briefly and then stand back, examining one another. 'You're, like, a foot taller,' is all I can say.

He smiles. 'You too, Wilder,' he says politely.

Until this moment I'd been so proud of the three and a quarter inches I've shot up this year.

Nat pokes me. 'Go on,' he says, impatient. 'Dump your stuff and come down to the water. I've got beer.' His cheekbones seem even more pronounced beneath the stubble.

I drop my bag in the kitchen. I lean against the wall and breathe, without turning on the lights. Through the kitchen window the sunset is a greenish line on the horizon over the ocean. I know Nat's waiting for me out by the gate – I can almost feel his impatience through the walls. Still, I take time to go into every room of the cottage. For some reason it feels important that I fill the house with my presence, my breath, make it mine again. It's like magic, the kind of thing Harper would do. I wonder how much she's changed, this past year.

The house seems to breathe back at me, a long, slow breath of relief.

I slip into swimming shorts, grab a sweater and go out into the dusk. I'm home.

On the way down to the sea Nat stops. 'Wait,' he says. 'Follow me.' He leaves the path, wincing at the sharp rocks on his bare feet.

The long grass of the meadow is pale in the moonlight. A shimmering fractured moon shines from the sea below. I still don't like it here.

'Come on,' I say. 'What's the hold-up?'

'I got to get something.' Nat shines a flashlight on a tumble of stone by a small escarpment. He reaches a careful hand into a dark crevice and withdraws a six-pack of beer. 'My hiding place,' he says. 'I leave stuff here sometimes. You can help yourself when you want,' he adds. 'Just don't drink it all, OK? I have to pay that dumb Sonny at the auto shop five bucks each time he buys it for me. Or catch him lobster.'

On the beach we build a fire and Nat pokes the potatoes under the greying coals with a stick. He's proud of making the dinner himself, of doing something to welcome me home.

We're still being a little cautious with one another, he and I, getting used to it all again. Because it's the same as last summer, but different too, like looking at two exposures of a photograph.

'You look older,' he says, echoing my thought. 'When I saw you coming up the hill in that blazer, those Oxfords.' He smiles at me, tentative. 'I didn't recognise you. And you looked at me like I was a stranger. Time to eat.' He takes the oyster knife from his belt and plunges it into the blackened carcass of the potato. Steam shoots up into the night sky. 'Potatoes make everything OK,' he says, appreciatively.

The potatoes are too hot so we hack them apart with the knife, stabbing at the flesh with the forks I brought from the cottage. Nat takes a small aluminium parcel from the cooler and unfolds it carefully. A small pale pat of butter. He handles it carefully, divides it between the potatoes with precision. I feel a start of guilt. I could have bought butter in Castine or Bar Harbour, any of the towns I passed through on my way here, we could have bathed the potatoes in it until they dripped gold. But he wanted to do this for us. I'm not always smart about people but I have enough sense not to try to help.

Nat finishes his potato and starts to eat the skin so I do the same. It tastes charred and chewy.

I look up and my flesh walks on my bones. A girl stands at the edge of the firelight, pale as a lily, her eyes two pits of shadow.

'I thought we were meeting at the point,' she says to Nat. 'I been waiting an hour.'

'I forgot.' Nat's shoulders hunch with guilt or maybe resentment. He holds out the remains of his baked potato on its bed of blackened tinfoil. 'You hungry?'

She takes it from him and sits, starts to eat with long delicate fingers. 'Who's this?'

Nat says, 'Wilder. Wilder, this is Betty.'

'Hi,' I say.

Betty looks at me for a moment before turning her attention back to the potato skin. 'Let's go,' she says to Nat when it's finished.

'Hey,' Nat says. 'Wilder just got here.'

She wipes the back of her hand across her mouth then licks it. Her lips still have a buttery sheen. 'Let's go.'

Nat turns to me and shrugs as if to say, *what can you do?*

'You go ahead,' I say. 'Good to see you, man.'

'I'll come by tomorrow,' he says.

Nat and Betty walk away into the dark. She puts an arm around his waist. As they go I see her lift his t-shirt and trace the small of his back with an index finger. I flush and look away.

I pick up the bottles, our trash, then I fill Nat's cooler with seawater and pour it over the remains of the fire. Steam hisses, the stink of charred wet wood sits heavy on the clean night air. I go up to the cottage and dry the cooler, put it by the door, so I can remember to give it back to Nat tomorrow. I change into pyjamas, brush my teeth and use that facewash that's meant to prevent zits. I sit up in bed with *The Heart is a Lonely Hunter* open in front of me. I don't take in a word of it. After a while I turn off the lamp and lie in the dark, the sound of the sea coming in with the moonlight. But I don't sleep. Ever since Betty appeared out of the dark on the beach, my heart's been beating so big and splashy that I can hear it in my ears. Nat has a girlfriend now. He's not in love with Harper anymore.

Faintly, from down in the bay comes a long, narrow high note – and then another. The stones begin to sing. The wind must have changed.

The next day my parents arrive shortly after 10 a.m. They come in quietly and seem surprised to find me awake and reading in the kitchen, the cottage neat and orderly.

'We were afraid you'd have some buddies round,' my father says. 'Have a party.'

I shrug. 'I just saw Nat. We went for a swim.'

'You're a responsible kid, Wilder,' my mom says. Maybe it's my imagination but I think she sounds a little disappointed.

*

A week later I sit in a low crook of the maple, facing out to sea, trying to get into Carson McCullers. I keep a pencil behind my ear but don't make any notes. I read the same sentence a hundred times, it feels like.

Suddenly everything goes dark. There are hands over my eyes, cool fingers stroke my eyelids. My heart hammers. I go very still, which is sometimes how I deal with danger.

'This is how you die,' a voice breathes in my ear. Something narrow slides across my throat. I know it's my pencil, I feel it slide out from behind my ear, but still my breath hitches, my throat goes dry.

I grasp a narrow wrist. I feel a thick metal watchband on it. The hands are small, I can tell that now. I stick my tongue way out and by straining, I just manage to lick the heel of one of her hands where it sits on my cheek.

Harper leaps away. 'Gross,' she says. 'Ugh.' Then she grabs my book and licks it, drags her tongue all the way down the page I'm reading, watching me as she does it. 'Now we're even.' The page is divided by a wet trail, as if a slug has crawled across it.

'Welcome back, Harper,' I say.

'Thanks.' She tosses my pencil over the cliff.

'I need that,' I say.

'No you don't. You're bored of reading. You want to come swimming with me.'

Unlike Nat and me, Harper doesn't seem to have changed at all. She looks the same – that wide gaze, that impossible almost blood-red hair. She doesn't look older or taller. Maybe she really is a fairy. Love fills me as I look at her. She's not a fairy. She's just herself.

I prop *The Heart is a Lonely Hunter* open with stones so it can dry out in the sun and we go down to the beach.

First we go up to the meadow that makes me afraid of death, to get a beer from Nat's secret stash in the rock. When I put my hand in it's warm and damp like a large mouth. I wait for the jaws to close on my arm, take it off. I can almost hear the crunch of bone, feel the hot gout of blood springing from my shoulder.

There are four bottles in the hole. I offer one to Harper, but she shakes her head.

'Not for me.'

She seems different. Her eyes are clear.

We wade in, bob pleasantly in the water. I'm so happy to see her, I can't keep my eyes off her face.

'How's the new school?' I ask.

'It sucked. I'm not going back. I missed a lot of class this year.'

'Are you—'

'Yup,' she says. 'It's Fairview for me.'

'I thought that was just a joke,' I say.

'In typical fashion, that joke has become my life.' I'm ready to be upset for her, but she smiles. 'It's OK, Wilder.'

'You do seem – OK.'

'Yes. I missed school because I went to – well, a place for troubled young ladies who self-medicate. A very expensive place, of course. I don't want to talk about it, Wilder. It worked, that's all.'

'OK,' I say. 'Do you miss it? Is it hard – not to?'

'Drink? Actually, it's a relief. I mean, it's boring, but it's much less stressful. I have coping mechanisms. They teach you those.'

'Like what?'

'Hobbies,' she says, suddenly shy. 'They encourage us to develop interests – knitting, basket-weaving.'

I'm trying to stop my smile but it just breaks through all the same.

'What?'

'I'm imagining them trying to make you like knitting.'

'I know!' She laughs. 'I told them I already had a hobby – witch-craft. It's really interesting, you know. More like psychology than anything else.' She strokes the water with gentle fingers. 'I miss him less when I'm with you. My brother. Samuel.'

'Good.' I want her to be OK, so badly.

'I guess you remind me of him.'

And suddenly I'm not enjoying myself anymore. I swallow to rid my mouth of the sudden sour taste.

'Let's get Natty out tonight,' Harper says, flicking the water with her fingertips. 'I haven't seen him yet. He must be busy with his dad. He usually finds a way to say hi on the day I arrive.' She nibbles a nail. 'I got here yesterday; he's slipping.'

'Yeah, he does seem busy.' I'm not sure whether to mention his girlfriend. I think *no, don't*, because it feels like a violation of the agreement, I'm not sure why, and then the moment's gone, I've waited too long and missed it. 'Come by tonight,' I say. 'We'll sit out, the three of us, catch up.'

Harper turns her eyes on me now, gives me once again that intense focus. I had forgotten what this feels like, the completeness of her attention – it's almost narcotic. 'How are you doing, Wilder?'

'I'm OK,' I say, surprised to find that I mean it. 'It was . . . an OK year.' And it was. Solitary. Lonely, even. But quiet. I studied, read, wrote. The guys who made last year so terrible seemed to forget about me this year.

'Yeah, I know,' Harper says. 'You owe me. Big time.'

'Oh, really?'

'I did magic to stop them bullying you, Wilder.'

'Well, thank you.' I cup my hands and throw water at her head.

She dodges it, effortless. 'Nice try.'

'You want to see me really try?' I launch myself at her.

I wish Harper would cool it with the magic stuff – it makes me uneasy. It's like a tiny clinging remnant of old Harper, who's so desperate to feel, who drinks in the mornings, who makes Nat play tricks on me in a dark cave that nearly kill us all.

Nat comes by shortly after she leaves. 'How's Harper?' They keep missing one another; it's like one of those old British farces – in one door and out the other. Also, it occurs to me, I haven't mentioned she was here – how does he know? Has he been watching us?

'You haven't seen her yet?'

He shakes his head.

I have the feeling of life being just a little out of sync. It's disquieting but also somehow exciting – in the past Nat and Harper were the core of our friendship, a unit, an indivisible pair. Now they seem severed, adrift. Everything is reorienting – with me at the centre.

'Come by tonight,' I tell him. 'Then we'll all be here together.'

My parents are going out to dinner so Nat, Harper and I will hang out at the cottage. I get soda out of the refrigerator, load a cooler with cans to show them that's what we're going to drink. And we will, I tell myself, or at least Harper will, so it's only two-thirds a lie.

My dad is wearing his dumb cufflinks made of Coke-bottle caps, with a safety pin glued to the back. Uncle Vernon made them for him as some kind of joke when they were little.

'Dad, do you have to wear those? They are *so* embarrassing.' I'm anxious that maybe my friends will see them.

'I think they're cool,' he says, striking a pose.

I am almost in an agony of dread. 'Just *go*,' I say. I walk out with them to the gate.

'Hey.' Nat melts out of the dusk. I feel again that quick moment of unfamiliarity. Who is this tall man? Nat looks like he's been running. His shirt is half unbuttoned, a fine sheen of sweat covers him, though the night isn't that warm.

'Hey,' I say. 'Mom, Dad, you remember Nat.'

'Sure,' my dad says, holding out a friendly hand to shake. Last year Nat was a kid, now he's a guy my dad shakes hands with.

Nat just stands there, looking confused. He stares at my dad's hand like he's never seen a hand before. Then I see that he's staring at the cufflinks. I was right, he's horrified; they're so dorky.

'Nat,' I say, and he starts.

'What?' he asks. 'Wilder?' Then he shakes himself like a dog and takes my dad's hand. 'Good to see you again, sir.'

Harper comes up the path. My mom gives her a hug and Harper goes pink. Her eyes stay on Nat the whole time.

'Have fun, you kids,' my mom says, breathless. She pushes an imaginary strand of hair behind her ear even though there's no wind. She's excited about dinner.

'You too!' I say, 'You *crazy* kids.'

They go down the path. We hear the car start and drive away.

'Hello, Natty,' Harper says.

Nat ignores her, frowning – and I see with surprise that he's shaking the tiniest bit. Harper sits down with a thump and puts a hand to her cheek like it's warm.

'Did you get sunburn today?' I ask her. She doesn't look burned but it's getting dark so I can't be sure.

She shakes her head. 'You OK, Natty?'

'Sure.' Nat flicks the nails of his thumb and index finger together. I've learned that this means he's lying about something.

Nat takes a beer out of each pocket and offers one to Harper.

'No,' says Harper with an edge in her voice. 'Natty. I wrote you. I don't do that anymore.'

67

'Come on.' There's something strange in his voice. 'Wilder's having one.' Though I haven't said I will.

'No,' she says. 'Stop it.'

Nat hands the beer to me but I shake my head. I don't want to make things harder for Harper.

'Fine,' he says, tips his head back and drinks it all. Then he raises the second one and drinks that too. His brown throat moves as he swallows. He wipes his mouth. 'Spin the bottle?'

I look at him. 'I thought—'

'What, Wilder?'

I can tell he knows I'm about to mention the pale girl. So I don't. 'No spin the bottle for me,' I say. 'You have to take me out for dinner before we get to the hot stuff.'

He looks at me, sullen. 'You took all my beer, Wilder. I had to get more at the gas station. You're not supposed to clean me out.'

'I didn't,' I say, startled. 'I took one this afternoon, that's all.'

'Don't be mean, Nat,' says Harper.

'Aww, you guys can eat it,' Nat says.

'What's that mean?' I ask.

'Yeah, what?' Harper says. 'Did you mean to say suck it, Natty? Or maybe suck it up?'

He says, confused, 'Eat it. That's an expression.'

'No,' I say.

'No,' says Harper.

'Shut up,' Nat says, but he's smiling.

And it feels like things will get easier from hereon in, but then Harper screams. A pale shape hovers behind the gate, tall and slender as a candle flame.

'What are you doing here?' Nat says, annoyed. 'Don't follow me around.'

'I was bored,' Betty says, walking into the light.

'Hi,' Harper says.

Betty looks at her but says nothing. She just stands there. Nat gets up abruptly.

'See you guys tomorrow.'

Their footsteps fade down the path. 'What is up with him?' I ask. 'He was being *seriously* weird.'

Harper shrugs. 'Get the backgammon board,' she says. 'This'll be nice – the two of us.'

My heart jumps painful and hard inside my chest.

Harper stays for two games then she says she's tired. I walk her as far as the point. She is quiet as we go but I feel her, like always, as a warm sun at my side. I think about what it would be like to take her hand, to touch her in some way, but it seems impossible. She's wrapped in her own isolation. When we come in sight of her house she stops.

'I'm OK from here.'

'But I should take you all the way ...' I don't want to leave her; I want to find some little thing to hook into her attention so she notices me.

'The less parents know, the better,' she says. 'Mine aren't very trusting. Maybe,' she adds in a spurt of honesty, 'I haven't given them much reason to be.'

I can't help feeling she's just taking the first opportunity she can to be alone. To get out of my company.


I walk back along the cliff, under the moon, flashlight off. It's been a strange evening and I'm filled with a frustrated energy. I almost wish for an accident; I want some kind of damage done to something or someone, even if it's myself.

Whistler Cottage rears out of the dark. My parents' car is still gone. As I turn the corner, I see that light is pouring from the living-room window, glowing red through the drapes. Someone is in my house.

*Dagger Man*, I think. I shake myself, that's dumb. But someone's in my house, someone who shouldn't be.

I go quietly down the side of the cottage and get the rake that leans against the wall. Holding my breath, I open the door and slip across the dark kitchen. Someone is sitting on the couch; I can just see the top of a dark head. I raise the rake. It's the heavy kind with teeth.

The head starts to turn and I get a really good backswing going. I ready myself for the blow, for blood.

My mom screams. Her pale face is startled. 'My god, Wilder!' she says. 'What are you doing?'

And I swing wide so the rake hits the couch harmlessly. But I am almost crying with panic at how close I came to hitting her over the head with the vicious metal jaws.

'Why are you sitting in the dark?' I ask.

'I was waiting for your dad,' she says.


After I've put the rake back outside I find her in the kitchen.

'Let me make you some tea,' I say. 'I know that raspberry-leaf stuff you like.' We take cups into the living room.

'I wondered where you'd gone,' she says. 'All the lights were off.'

'I walked Harper home. Where's Dad?'

'He had a little indigestion. I think it was the lobster roll. He always orders it, even though he knows what it does to his insides. He dropped me off, went to find a pharmacy.'

'An open one? Around here?'

'The guy in Castine lives above the store. Apparently he opens up if he's in a good mood, and you ask nicely.' She smiles; I can tell she's tired.

As a guy you're not supposed to think about stuff like when your mom has her time of the month and so on, but it's not like I can ignore it; she gets quiet and pale and lies down a lot.

My sleep is filled with uneasy visions and the scent of stale beer.


Both my parents are still asleep when I get up.

The day is already warm though it's barely eight. I eat a pop tart as I head down the hill. I'm going towards the woods for a change. It's nice to be alone. In the city and at school I feel lonely, even though in those places I'm always surrounded by people. But here, being on my own just seems right.

On the road below the house I see there's something white – either paper or plastic, I can't tell, lying in the middle of it. Litter dropped by someone, or blown here on the wind. I feel a sense of outrage. This is my place, people don't get to leave their trash lying around. I hurry down to get it.

The breeze lifts a corner, flips it. The thing tumbles down the road a couple of feet. I hurry to pick it up. As I draw closer I see what it actually is. The fluttering square is a photograph, a Polaroid, face down. My mom's been looking at Uncle Vernon's 'art' again, I guess – one must have blown away.

I pick it up, looking forward to seeing which of Uncle Vernon's bad attempts at photography has made a bid for freedom. The one of the pine tree where the tree is at a drunken slant? The one of the sea where a big thumb obscures the left-hand corner of the photo? The one with a figure standing in complete darkness, except for one bright point like a star? Mom and I think this is a self-portrait taken in the mirror, but the flash got confused by its own reflection, and didn't go off.

But it isn't any of those.

The face is white, washed out by the flash, as pale as if they're

71

lying on a mortuary slab. Boy or girl, it's hard to tell. They're curled up with a fist under their chin; a tendril of hair, blond or brown, lies on their cheek. The curve of their small ear is perfect.

The sheets have a pattern of teddy bears. The pyjamas are yellow with rockets on them which might suggest it's a boy – or not. Girls like rockets too. There's no comforter thrown over the small frame, which sends a lance of fear through me. I think this is recent. It's been way too warm for covers at night for the past week.

And I guess he doesn't always put the knife at their throats, not always. In this picture, the long, shining blade is by that small pink ear, perpendicular. It almost rests against the lobe, just by the place where the ear joins the skull. A slight movement, a quick twitch and it would be off. I imagine the ear coming free like a pinch of pink cotton candy pulled from the stick.

Maybe it's an old picture, I tell myself. Maybe it's been lying in a ditch or caught in a tree for months and the wind just blew it into the road yesterday.

But the Polaroid isn't old. Its shiny surface is pristine, the image sharp and unfaded. The white strip at the bottom is unblemished. I knew that was a vain hope.

I drop the photo quickly. But I can still feel the touch of it on me. Thinking quickly, I get a small rock and weigh it down. The edge still moves slightly in the stiff breeze, but the rock stays firm.

I run up the hill towards the cottage, yelling for my dad, my mom, and just 'help, help!'

They run down towards me, faces white.

'A picture,' I say, breathless. 'A Dagger Man picture. It was lying there in the road. He must have been here!'

My mother's mouth sets in a grim line. 'If this is a joke, Wilder—' she says. But her tone is frightened.

'Are you sure, sport?' my dad says.

'Please hurry,' I say, agonised. 'Please.'

'I have to respect my knees on a downhill, Wilder,' Dad says, reproving. 'You know that.'

As we near the bottom, I see the little white square, still held fast under the stone. I run the rest of the way.

I get that unpleasant feeling in my fingertips as I turn the Polaroid over, slowly. Behind me I hear my mom's indrawn breath.

Teddy bears, rockets, shining blade.


Dad comes with me to the little police station at Castine. 'But I just found it on the road,' I say over and over. My fingerprints are on it, of course, so they have to take those for elimination. They ask my dad if he touched the picture. He tries to remember.

'Did I?' he keeps asking me, bewildered. 'Did I touch it, Wilder?'

I can't remember if he did or not. My memories of everything that has happened since are static, single scenes. A stack of bright still moments with no narrative. Like a stack of Polaroids.

They take my dad's prints too, for elimination.

I'd thought it might be exciting, being at a police station and involved in a real crime, but after the first surge of novelty it's not. It's long drawn out and boring and scary all at the same time. Throughout the questions and the taking of the report and the fingerprinting all I can think about is that kid in the picture. There are three or maybe four cops in the station, two old guys, a woman. I can't keep their names straight in my head.

'Is it the Abbott girl?' I hear one of them ask. 'The younger one. The Abbotts who took the Salter place this summer?'

'Looks right.'

'Ayuh,' the older man says.

The woman's notebook sits open the whole time, and every so

73

often she writes something in it very, very quickly. It can't be more than a word or two. It never seems to be in response to anything particularly significant that we or they say. Maybe she's making a grocery list. I guess cops have lives just like anyone. They must get their milk from the store in town, like everyone else. Watch TV at night, kiss their families. Normal stuff.

But I see the woman officer biting her lip. Her eyes are miles deep. Nothing's quite normal, or will be ever again. Not for us, because we've seen the Abbott girl sleeping. We've seen those long lashes, the teddy-bear sheets, the fist curled so trustingly under the chin. He has made us see through his eyes, and we can never forget it. To this day, I can't.

As we leave I glimpse the page the woman cop was writing on in her notebook. Over and over the page is scrawled with *stay calm stay calm stay calm.*

I just want my mom to hug me now, and I'm not even embarrassed about it. I've had enough of adult stuff – even the adults have, it seems.

The next day the woman cop is on the dirt road behind the cottage. She places yellow markers gravely at certain points. A photographer comes. Someone else in a white hazmat suit. They don't find anything good, though. I can tell by the forlorn slump of their shoulders. My parents and I watch from the window. The place doesn't feel like ours anymore.

The cop picks up an object with gloved hands, produces a plastic Ziploc bag and drops it in. It looks like a cigarette butt. Reality and imagination blur and shiver. Did *he* drop it? I feel crazy, because I imagined the Dagger Man smoking, in exactly that spot, and it makes me feel responsible, like somehow I've created him or am controlling him or something.

'I'm going down there,' I say.

'What do you mean?' my father asks. His beard is particularly wild today, a good indicator that he's upset. 'Just let the authorities do their job, Wilder. No need to interfere. We've done our part.'

'I'm just—' I look around wildly for inspiration. 'I bet she could use a cup of coffee.'

I carry the steaming coffee delicately down the hill to where she stands, lips pursed in a thoughtful pout. Her face is broad, her eyes too, black like buttons. She looks like one of those old-fashioned dolls knitted from wool.

'Hm?' she says, thoughtful, taking the mug of coffee from me. Then she starts. 'Oh. Hi again. Thanks. You put sugar in it?'

'No.'

'Good.' She drinks the coffee in two swallows. It must be very hot but she doesn't show it, just wipes her mouth with the back of her hand and hands me back the coffee cup.

'Do you think you can catch him?' I ask.

'How do we know it's a him?'

I shrug. 'I think it's a him.'

She sighs. 'Me too.' I still can't recall her name so I look at her name tag which reads *Trooper Harden*. I do it covertly, but her bright button eyes follow my gaze.

'Yes, I've heard all the jokes,' she says. 'You can just call me Trooper.'

'Um, OK.' Right away I can't stop imagining some of the jokes and I feel myself going pink.

'You're freaking out,' she says with certainty. 'I get it.'

'Please can you tell me the truth,' I say. 'I need to know. Would he get a long sentence, if they caught him? I'd freak out less if I had some facts. No one will tell me anything.'

'You're a kid,' she says. 'Don't need to be worrying about this stuff.'

'I'm seventeen.' I take a deep breath. 'I could be tried as an adult, for example.'

She looks at me with her black round eyes. 'So you could,' she says. 'OK then. Facts. They're thin on the ground, right now. But OK. Breaking and entering is a Class B crime – if we can prove it. Then we've got him for taking a picture of a kid which is – what? Child endangerment, sure. Violation of privacy? Probably. And there's the knife. He might get eighteen months. When really, he should be put away forever.

'So even if we figure out who's doing this – maybe nothing much even happens. But we have to try anyway. We *are* trying. Can't wait until he does something worse. Because he will. In the end. That factual enough for you?' She takes a card out of her pocket and hands it to me.

'You gave us one of those last night,' I tell her. 'A card.'

'And I'm giving you another one now. Put one by the telephone, keep one on you. You call us if you see anything else. I mean, anything.'

'Do you think he'll come back here? Like, retrace his steps trying to find it?'

'Maybe. But we'll keep an eye on you. Get a patrol car to swing by in the evenings. You're not his usual type, thank goodness. Good you don't have kids in the house.' She thumps her heart with a clenched fist. 'Oof. I drank that coffee too fast. Couldn't sleep last night, so I was keen for the caffeine. Anyhow, I'm parked up the road a ways.'

I watch her go, feeling strangely bereft.


He must have dropped the Polaroid in the night or early morning, not too long before I found it. That picture wasn't in the road yesterday evening.

Will he come back for it?

That night I lie in bed listening to the sea, the crickets, some night bird calling in the dark. At length I hear it, faint, the sound of a car approaching in the lane below. This is unusual; the road is really quiet. *It's the patrol car*, I think, *they're checking up on us.* I imagine Trooper Harden's serious face behind the wheel, her button eyes scanning the woods for dark figures. Even the memory of her makes me feel safer. I think about getting up and going to the kitchen window, which overlooks the road, to watch her pass. But I don't.

Because what if it's not Trooper Harden. What if it's him?

'Watch your step,' someone says and I blink, startled out of my thoughts. I'm walking tightrope along a groyne that's sunk into the tarry shingle of the oily beach that skirts Castine like a dirty fingernail.

My mom is running errands in town and I've come down to the shorefront. There's not a lot to do here. It's a place for work – rusting hulks stand up on hurdles, yards of net festoon the pontoons. It smells like gasoline and bloody fish. It's not like Rehoboth or Coney Island, not built for fun.

'Watch yourself,' the voice says again, more urgent, but I've already lost my balance. My foot sinks into a pile of slimy seaweed. The ground has a spongy swollen texture and I sink further and further. I yell; all the memories of old black-and-white movies and Sherlock Holmes books run through my mind like tickertape, all those stories I ever heard about quicksand. Struggling makes me sink deeper, and I fall forward. My hands sink into the soft, stinking stuff; I can't help thinking of it as rotten fruit. I'm gasping; each panicked breath seems to send me deeper, deeper; it clings and sucks at me.

A firm hand grasps my shoulder and hauls.

'You OK?' It's the fisherman with the blue eyes who picks up Kleenex. 'Got a little stuck there?'

I smile, embarrassed.

'Come aboard and have a soda,' he says.

His boat bobs off the little jetty.

The boat smells like gasoline but also like carbolic soap. It's very clean. My mom would approve. 'It's like a house,' I say. It reminds me of Whistler Cottage – so neat, everything in its place. I imagine living here, never coming to shore again, just living surrounded by peaceful blue, no people, no worries. No school.

'A floating house,' he agrees, pleased.

Two metal canisters sit on the countertop in the tiny galley. One says *tee*, the other *cofee*. He gets the soda from the cooler. The bottles are still frosted. He lifts the caps from them with a *pop*. The precision of his gentle brown fingers is wonderful to watch.

'Wilder,' I say. 'Sorry, I should have said before.'

'And I'm Mr Pelletier, I guess, but only the bank calls me that. Alton, or Al, to my friends.' He sees my face. 'You know my son. You're a friend of Nathaniel's.'

'Yes,' I say. 'Sorry, I didn't realise.'

'He's not proud of me,' Mr Pelletier says. 'Well, children should want to be more than their parents. It's only right.'

I don't have anything to say to that. To cover the silence I take a deep swig of soda. I cough and it streams out my nose.

'Can I keep the bottle caps?' I ask when I can breathe again. They make me think of my dad and those dorky cufflinks. Maybe I could make my dad another pair; his have gone missing.

'Sure,' he says. 'Why?'

'It's kind of hard to explain, but it's a present for my dad.'

'That's good,' he says, approving. 'Love in a family. That's good.'

The bottle caps make little cold nuggets in my palm.

'You want to see the shark rig?'

I do.

The shark rig is a hydraulic pulley, the line gleams with wicked hooks. I shiver as I look at it.

'I know,' he says. 'Cruel-looking thing. Honestly, I'm losing my stomach for shark fishing, these days. They've got smart eyes, sharks. Last time I got a whitetip I put him back. I could see his pain. Now, bluefin. That's a different story. They're some sons of bitches. I'll drag a bluefin along on the line for as long as I need, no regrets.'

I laugh. He shows me lobster pots, and the tooth he keeps around his neck from a great white. 'Nathaniel gave me this,' he says. 'He's a good boy. Didn't catch it, found it on the beach. But you won't tell him I told you that.' His thumb strokes the tooth. 'He's a real good boy. He's growing up. Not home so much, these days.' He brightens. 'I've got some squashed-fly biscuits,' he says. 'Made with real flies. I get you one.' But I see the flash of sadness on his face. There are certain unmistakeable expressions, no matter how quick they pass. Nat's father is lonely. I think about how my father doesn't seem to want to be around us at all and what a waste it is.

The squashed-fly biscuits are buttery, falling apart at the touch. The 'flies' are plump raisins. 'I'm the baker since my wife left,' Mr Pelletier says. 'This is my gram's recipe. Someone should keep making it, I thought. Can't let a good thing go to waste.'

'When did Nat's mom leave?' Then I quickly say, 'Sorry.'

'It's all right.' Mr Pelletier crumbles another biscuit between his fine fingers. 'Seventeen years ago, now that's a long time, isn't it? Arlene had just birthed Nathaniel. What kind of woman leaves her newborn child? "I'm not coming back," she told me, and I said, "Fine. Let me keep the baby. Raise him right."' He stops. 'She'd fallen back into some bad habits – things she swore she'd quit, when we married. So I let her go and Nathaniel stayed with me, and we've been just fine, us two, ever since.' Again that look crosses his face. 'I just wish he spent more time at home.

I look at my watch. 'Shoot,' I say through a mouthful of crumbs. 'Sorry, Mr Pelletier. I have to go.'

But when I get back to Main Street my mom's car is gone.


I ride in the flatbed of the truck which is great and Mr Pelletier drops me at the foot of the hill.

My mom is drinking raspberry-leaf tea on the couch when I come in. 'Where the hell were you, Wilder? I waited an hour in town.'

'Sorry,' I say. 'I met a friend.'

'You never do that to me again, you hear? I was worried sick. *Sick*. You ungrateful boy.' Her voice drops from a yell to a whisper and she leans back on the couch, pale.

'Are you OK, Mom?'

'Yes,' she says. 'I made sandwiches for lunch but there aren't any left. There's cereal if you're hungry. No milk though, your dad's gone out to get some.'

'Of course he has,' I say.

I grab a handful of dry cereal. I kind of like it like this anyway. And I'm full of squashed-fly biscuits.

'Don't eat it like that,' my mother says, annoyed. 'And don't use that tone about your father. Have some respect.'

'Fine,' I yell. I slam the door on my way out.


I stomp along the cliff path. The wind cuts in sharp, it's cold and miserable. Everything is just fricking *crappy*.

Ahead of me is a hiker dressed in neon yellow. The wind is against them, they don't hear me. I can tell, just from the relaxed set of their back, a glimpse of their profile as they turn to look out to sea, that they think they're alone.

*I could run at them*, I think. *Catch them off guard. I could push them off the cliff – watch as they bounce off the crags, become a little limp yellow figure, and then vanish into the roaring surf at the bottom. Fricking yuh!*

I can't tell if it's a man or a woman yet. I speed up, close the distance between us, my sneakered feet quiet on the rocks. *If it's a woman*, I think, *I'll let her live. If it's a guy—*

The hiker turns seawards again. This time a ponytail comes out of the collar of her jacket, and flies free in the wind.

*Ha, she lives.*

I'm on the section of path that winds along below the meadow, I can tell, because I get the bad feeling. Ugh. I really hate that place. But I'll put up with it; I want a beer from Nat's hidey-hole. He keeps accusing me of stealing them – so I may as well do it.

I hear something like a hoot in the meadow above. As I move through the trees I see a shape in the long grass ahead that doesn't make sense. It looks like a monster. Limbs, eyes. I squint and come closer. I use the same quiet feet I used for sneaking up on the hiker.

It writhes. Those breathy sounds come from it. Hoot, hoot. So this is why I get a bad feeling here. I knew, somehow, that something terrible would happen in the meadow.

I stare, but my mind will only take in isolated detail. Hair red as an alarm, the ragged hem of denim cutoffs. His hand on her back, brown on white. Her shirt has fallen off her shoulder.

Nat's eyes meet mine over her shoulder. They are unfocused and then sharp. Her back is to me, she doesn't see. Nat and I look at one another for a moment and then I turn away and go down the hill. Nat has broken our deal.

I climb the maple tree and stare out to sea. The sea doesn't care about stuff like love, does it. The sea doesn't even know about promises, so it can't break them.

I don't hear my mother calling me for supper. I start and yell as she tugs on my sneaker toe. My father is not home again. We eat macaroni cheese from a box. I can't finish it, even though it's my favourite.

I know what Harper would say if she knew about the agreement Nat and I made. I know she'd hate it. Would she hate it enough to stop whatever is happening between them? I could find out. And I know he's still seeing Betty. I can ruin it all with a word.

I have the power now, I tell myself. But it doesn't feel like that.


I lie awake with the porthole window cracked open as wide as the restrictors will allow. The Dagger Man can't get in that way – I'm starting to suspect he doesn't need to.


The boat engine idles, the sea beckons. We're going out to one of the little rocky islands. Harper wants to watch the seals.

Nat's shorts only have so much life left in them; they're frayed almost halfway up his thigh. I swallow as I remember the long grass tickling them, the hooting sounds.

'No,' I say. 'Let's not go to the island. I want to go to the god again.'

'What?'

'I have a secret to tell.'

'Wilder—' says Harper, annoyed. She really wants to see the seals.

'It's my forfeit,' I say. 'I'm calling it in.'

'We have to, Harper,' Nat says.

The boat speeds out of the bay.

'You OK, Nat?' Harper asks.

'Sure.' But he's lying, doing that thing where he flicks the nails of his thumb and forefinger together. A tic, you might call it.

'What's going on?' Harper asks me. I raise my eyebrows and cup a hand at my ear, like the engine's too loud even though we usually yell over it. Harper sits back, watching me with narrowed eyes.

The boat bounces on the waves like they're solid matter, the sun grows hot. The growing day refuses to reflect my mood, is set to be burning bright.

The tide is halfway in, the cave entrance visible, like lips politely parted. We swim into the dark. I hold the long shining blade of the oyster knife carefully. Behind, the half-moon of daylight beckons. It would be so easy to turn around, swim back out into the warm air, the light.

'Come on, slowpokes,' I call. 'Hurry up.' Cold salt washes into my mouth and I cough.

In the big chamber water trickles down the cave walls, shining. It's quiet in here today, still as looking glass.

'Hold me up,' I say to Nat. 'I've got something to say to the water. A secret.'

'Please, Wilder,' he says. 'Please don't.'

'My forfeit, remember?'

He climbs up behind me and takes my arms.

Nat lowers me, down, down until I'm almost kissing the water. I welcome the pain in my arms, my back. I feel like crying.

I take a deep breath. I'll ruin it for him. For both of them. They deserve it.

'I think my father is the Dagger Man,' I hear myself say. It's not the secret I intended to tell; this bursts out of me instead. I'm so tired and worn out.

Harper says, 'What?'

Nat gasps and staggers. One of my arms slips through his hands, slick as wet rubber and then he only has me by one hand. We both swing perilously over the sea. Then Nat's grip slips, he drops me and I fall headlong.

Beneath me, below the surface of the water, something swirls and comes hurtling towards me, breaks the shining skin and screams into my face. The sound ricochets around the cave, high and ear-splitting. I see her arm reach out.

Someone's hitting me in the face and stars explode behind my eyes. *Stop*, I try to say, *stop*, and push her away but she keeps coming. Nat is yelling, he tries to put himself between us. I flail backwards in the water, and suddenly there's the smell of tin. I'm no longer holding the knife – where is it? Somewhere Nat is moaning, a bad sound that echoes off the water, the stone walls.

We get Nat out of the cave somehow. The light is blinding, a blow to our eyes. There's a trail of crimson in the water behind us, leading back into the dark. It looks like red cloth rippling beneath the surface.

'Sharks?' Harper whispers.

I don't want to think about that.

'How bad is it?' I ask.

Nat groans and lifts his hand. The knife has gone right through it, silver as a beam of light.

I climb into the boat and Harper pushes him while I pull. We try not to jog the knife where it protrudes but we're scared and clumsy. Nat is openly crying now which is hard to take. Eventually we're all in and I start the motor. Nat has gone extremely pale. Dark red gouts of blood continue to pulse from the wound. The knife is in the heel of his hand, almost, and I suddenly think of wrists and veins – how close is the knife to these things?

'Tie a tourniquet round his wrist,' I say to Harper. 'Try and stop the bleeding.' I'm just repeating words I've seen on TV shows, it's the only guide I have.

Harper rips off the bottom of her t shirt, and Nat groans and tries to push her away. She ties it tightly, and the bleeding slows some. But maybe that's bad too? Maybe the hand will go dead? I don't know what to do.

'Where do we go?' I yell at Harper. 'Where's the nearest hospital, or phone, or whatever?'

'I don't know!' Her voice is so high it's almost inhuman. 'Just follow the mainland back towards Castine and stop at the first house we see!'

I don't know how to drive a boat so our progress is slow and stuttering. It's incredible how little attention we paid to the houses on the trip out here. It hadn't seemed important. Now the empty shore passes in endless, agonising minutes. I have the brief conviction that everyone in the world is gone and we're the last three left, that we'll go on and on forever, Nat crying, Harper holding him and whispering, 'I'm sorry, Natty, I'm so sorry.' Then she whispers, 'I love you.' He doesn't reply. I see he has passed out. She cradles him carefully, trying to protect his wound from the jolting of the sea. Still the coast crawls by.

Eventually there's a distant glare ahead on the shore, a couple hundred feet inland maybe. As we approach, I see that it's a big, modern house made mostly of glass. A long boardwalk leads up to it, fenced with white. I pull the *Siren* into the pebble beach, leap out. Running up the beach is like running in a nightmare; time and again I sink, ankle deep in the sand. I think of Rebecca, swimming forever towards the blue light. But eventually I reach the walkway. The boards are good under my feet. I go full pelt but still it seems to take forever, the world dipping and swaying as if I'm still on the waves.

A startled couple are pouring their first cocktails of the day when I burst onto their pool deck, wet and bloody and wild-eyed, as if I've just been born from the sea.

Harper and I wait while they work on Nat. The urgent care centre at Castine is a small building, mostly used for getting things out of toddler's ears and tetanus shots. But Nat needs blood, there's no time to take him on to Belfast or anywhere else.

We curl up on some hard, plastic orange chairs. Occasionally someone goes out for coffee or the receptionist goes to the parking lot to have a cigarette and the doors wheeze open and closed like bad lungs.

'Why do you think your dad is the Dagger Man?' Harper asks. Her eyes are wide in her pale face.

'Little things,' I say. 'But when it's all put together it feels like – a lot. I found something. It was a picture of the Abbott kid, a Polaroid.'

'Where?' she asks sharply.

'Right by our house, on the road. There's no one else for miles – why would anyone be out there? My dad came out here every summer without us, to visit Uncle Vernon,' I say. 'So he was here at the right times. Plus, he disappears at night. There's always some excuse – he's looking for a pharmacy, or we've run out of milk, but it's a big fricking coincidence.' I clear my throat. Weird how even now this is embarrassing. 'Plus things with the Dagger Man happen at a certain time of the month. Like, my mom's time of the month. I don't know . . .'

'Serial killers operate on lunar cycles sometimes,' Harper says. 'I read that.'

'He's not a serial killer.' It's awful hearing it out loud. 'But Uncle Vernon liked to take Polaroids. Maybe they did it together, Dad and Uncle Vernon. Maybe he killed Uncle Vernon.' I put my head in my hands. 'Oh god, maybe he is a serial killer. There's something bad going on, Harper.'

'Do you really think it's him?' There's an odd note in her voice. It sounds like – but surely cannot be – relief. But she's scared too. I've spent a lot of time pretending not to be afraid – at home, at school, so I recognise when people are doing it.

'I don't know. I'm freaking out.'

'Do you think Nat will be OK?' she whispers into my shoulder.

'Of course he will.' But I don't know. His skin was the wrong colour when the ambulance arrived. By the time they carried him in here it was like there was no one in his body anymore.

The glass doors wheeze open. Outside, the sun is throwing low pale light across the parking lot. *Dawn*, I think, then realise, *no, sunset*. It doesn't seem possible, but it's still the same day.

'Hey, you two,' Trooper Harden says. She's holding a coffee taller than her head. 'Rough day? You stay here a moment. I'm going to need to talk to you for the report. Then I'll get you back to your parents.' She goes through the swinging doors to the ward, whistling something.

'We have to tell her,' Harper says. 'About your dad.'

I start to talk but she puts a finger over my mouth. 'Stop,' she says. 'This is a very important moment. Whatever you're going to say – think about it before you speak. Those words will be there forever, you won't be able to forget them. So make sure they're not something you'll regret.'

It's like she can see right into me. I had been about to say, *you can't tell anyone.* But that would be wrong. I've seen the little pink ear, the fist curled under the chin, teddy bear sheets. Whatever my dad is, he's dangerous. I can't let it go on.

I take a deep breath. 'OK. You're right. I'll tell her.' Panic rises. 'I mean, I don't have any proof or anything but—'

The doors to the ward swing open and Trooper Harden comes out. She's different. Her eyes are flinted and sharp. They don't even look round anymore, but have narrowed to wicked points.

I start to get up to talk to her. It's now or never. I know that if I think about it I'll find a reason not to.

Trooper Harden points at me with a sharp finger. Everything about her is suddenly sharp. 'You sit right back down,' she says. 'Neither of you moves a muscle until I say.'

I sit down. She mutters into her radio, watching us the whole time with those sharp eyes.

'What's happening?' I whisper to Harper. 'Do I still talk to her about my dad?'

'No, Wilder,' she says. 'You don't need to.' Her face is twisted with feeling.


It's the oyster knife stuck through Nat's hand that does it. Trooper Harden recognises it from the Polaroids. The picture I found in the road, of the Abbott girl – it doesn't show the handle. The Polaroids of other kids were never released by the police, but in them, the knife is clearly visible. The handle is distinctive; it was hand-carved by Nat's father, Alton Pelletier, from local walnut.

There is one, single microscopic millimetre of hair caught in the knife between the handle and the blade. It's the Abbott girl's hair. It must have been trapped there somehow when he snuck into her room. They think maybe the Dagger Man cuts some off while they're sleeping.

We have been using the Dagger Man's knife to shuck oysters and pry the lids off cans.

The police search the Pelletier property down by the sea. What they find there makes everyone forget about the Dagger Man, because it's worse, much worse than anyone could have imagined. The world breaks apart and we are shattered, all three. I don't think I've truly been whole since.

It was never the tide which was dangerous to swimmers around here.

In the Pelletier place, there is a cellar. The walls of that cellar are lined with carpet, which is stained rich and dark with old blood. Buried in the corner in a cigar box, the police find treasure. A driver's license bearing the name Christy Barham, wrapped in a tissue, stiff with tears. A plastic tortoiseshell barrette. A keyring with the word *Daytona* on it. A wallet-sized picture of a young woman with purple hair. A single pearl earring which is identified as having once belonged to a woman who went missing, presumed drowned, ten years ago. Her name was Rebecca Boone. All these objects are rusted or speckled with blood. Alton Pelletier's fingerprints are all over them.

They find cord from the shark rig, miles and miles of line, spikes with shining wicked hooks. They find Alton's aluminium fish box, six feet long and two wide. Alton made it himself. It seals tight with metal clips. There are traces of human blood inside.

The fish box was how the women were removed from the house after the end. That's how the police think it happened, anyway. No one will ever really know. It must have been a relief to them – the end.

Sometimes I wonder about that time when I drank soda with him – was the fish box on board that day? Was it empty? Was it full?

Alton Pelletier is arrested.

Both Nat and Alton's fingerprints are on the oyster knife. They

89

both used it at times. *For what?* My mind repeats over and over. *For what?* Nat's voice repeats in my ear at night – *snare it in the shark rig, then pull it along beside the boat for a time, until it's ready to do whatever you want.*

Harper and I spend the next day on the narrow bench in the police station, as they interview us – together, separately, and then separately again. The small rooms are hot with late summer. We want to go home but we can't. We tell them, over and over, about our cave, and why we went there, everything we ever saw Alton Pelletier say or do, everything Nat ever said or did. I am so tired the world seems to ripple before my eyes.

As I look up a ghost is passing. But it's Betty, her pale face stained with tears. When next I look up, Harper is gone from my side.

I stagger out into the blinding light of the street, looking around wildly. 'Getting some air,' I say vaguely when someone tries to stop me.

Harper and Betty are standing very close together on the sidewalk. 'What did you tell them?' I see that Harper is holding Betty's little finger in what looks like affection. But the tip of the finger is turning purple.

'What did you tell them?' Harper says again.

'I told them the truth,' Betty says. 'Where to look – behind the skirting board in the living room. Now let me go or I'll hook your eyes out of your skull.'

Harper breathes fast, her face mottled red. She releases Betty's finger. 'Nat told me you were a snoop,' she says. 'He told me you saw his dad hiding that stuff. Don't lie about it. You know it wasn't Nat's.'

Betty looks at her. 'Yeah,' she says slowly. 'That's why he chose you. You still believe his lies. I can't anymore. You take care now.' Betty goes, holding her sore finger gently.

'She's the liar,' Harper says. Her eyes follow Betty down Main Street. 'Oh god.' Her mouth opens wider and wider into a rictus, an upside-down laugh. Tears gleam on her face. 'We've only had a few months together,' she whispers. 'Me and Nat. This can't be how it ends.'

I put an arm around her tentatively.

'Don't touch me, Wilder,' Harper says, savage. 'I never want anyone to touch me again.' Then she bends and vomits neatly into a sewer grate.

In the living room at the Pelletier house, in a hollow behind the skirting board, they find different items. A small sneaker, a brown apple core gnawed at by milk teeth. A ring made of candy, a t-shirt with Road Runner on it, still stained with egg from long-ago break-fast. Each thing is neatly Scotch-taped to a Polaroid photograph of a sleeping child. There are no fingerprints on any of these objects – as if they have been handled with gloves.

In the same hiding place, they find my father's Coke-bottle cuff-links. How they got there, whether Nat or Alton took them, no one knows.

Nat hovers, unconscious, between life and death. They don't move him from Castine. He lost a lot of blood. They think he'll lose his right hand. We're not allowed to see him; we don't know whether he'll live or not.

I don't know what to hope for.

The local papers report it, then the nationals. Alton Pelletier, Nathaniel Pelletier. The names are all over. The sound of them, the way they look on the page, is beautiful. Kind of reminds me of the coast around here, up and down, rising and falling.

I wouldn't have said it could get worse, but it gets much, much worse.

Three days later I stand on the clifftop in the dusk and watch the boats pass the bay, their blue lights flashing and faint. They're searching the caves along the shore with diving teams.

They search all night. I don't sleep. I stare at the ceiling, listening to the boat engines tool up and down the coast, sometimes a distant hum, then a near growl in the bay below. Then as pink light steals in the window, they fade west and don't return. They've found something.

I get up and go out into the dawn. I jog west along the headland until I see the coastguard boats. They bob in the narrow channel that leads to the cave entrance. The obelisk shines black in the morning light. I knew, somehow, it would be here.

I watch, hidden behind the jagged rocks of the headland. Two divers splash in. I wonder if the god will eat them.

The two divers come up and dive again, come up and dive again. They bring up detritus from the cave floor, unrecognizable things festooned with seaweed. Then, at around 11 a.m., they both surface at the same time. They're holding something between them. A guy on board lowers a winch with a platform on it. They lower the platform into the water, and the frogmen do something with chains. An engine churns, the chains go taut, and it begins to rise from the water. It's a metal barrel – an oil drum. Rusted orange, sides pitted with salt and time. One of the guys in a wetsuit takes up a crowbar.

'No,' I whisper aloud. 'Don't open it.' I know he has to, but I know he shouldn't – I have the feeling, the one that comes on like sickness, the one I sometimes get up in that beautiful meadow above Whistler

Cottage. My breath comes short, there are black blossoms all over my vision.

The guy very carefully inserts the crowbar beneath the rim and pries open the top of the drum. The metal lid comes away slowly, stickily, with reluctance. He looks down at the contents, puts his hand slowly over his mouth, walks to the side of the boat and vomits into the waves.

After twenty minutes, another drum is hauled from the deep. The divers lug it up to stand beside the first one on the deck. The drums are both crusted with weed and shellfish; they've been there a while. But I feel like I can smell what's inside anyway, even from here.

And another barrel comes out from the water, and another, and another one after the other. Then there's no more room, and a second boat arrives. They load all the new drums onto that. Eight in all. I learn later that the police think that there was once one more drum; they found the broken end of its chain. Somehow the oldest, the first drum was loosed, was swept gently out to sea by the tide, fell off the deep ledge of the sea shelf and into the deepest black.

By the end of the day both boats sit low in the water, heavy with their cargo of dead women.

Rebecca Boone has come home at last.

I read how her drum is the first one to be found, wedged into a crevice in a deep pool, concealed by floating weed. The oyster knife matches the marks on her bones. She was also the first to die, over a decade ago.

Then they followed the chain and found the next oil drum, and then the next. The bodies are intact – some of the drums are still watertight. These women have different marks on their bones – from a cleaver or an axe, they think.

Two more recently dead women 'deglove' as they are removed from their drum. I don't know what it means at first; I say it to myself a couple of times. It's a beautiful word, something a Victorian lady might do as she comes in from an afternoon stroll.

It's when skin becomes detached from underlying flesh and tissue – happens with drowning victims, or bodies that have been submerged for a time. The two women slip out of their loose skins as they are taken from the drums.

The police think that many of the oil-drum women were summer visitors reported missing over the years, presumed drowned, taken by the tides. But the tides aren't the dangerous thing around here, it turns out. All have blunt trauma to their skulls. The theory is that Alton got near them as they swam, stunned them and took them to the Pelletier house. When it was over he stored them in the drums, in the cave.

They identify two of the women quickly. The first is Rebecca Boone. Christy Barham is in the last drum. I saw her crying, once. Her murderer picked up her Kleenex. I wish I knew why she was crying that day outside the store but I never will. No one will, because Christy Barham is gone.

I dream about it sometimes. Their waterlogged grey skin sliding off them into a pool on a white tile floor somewhere. But in my dreams the women rise up out of their old hides. In my dreams they're new and pink, smooth as a young hand fresh from a satin glove. They walk away, leaving their old selves behind. I don't know where they go, the dream always ends there. I hope it's somewhere nice.


When we fetch the paper from town, there she is on the front page – Rebecca. She's real – not a monster or a story. I take it into the garden to read; it somehow seems better to do it outside. I can't stop staring at Rebecca's picture.

Rebecca leans against a windowsill in a garden on a sunlit day. Crimson flowers, tulips I think, bloom in the window box behind her. One hand shades her eyes from the sun and her arms are brown and corded with muscle. A swimmer, for sure. She's small, athletic, slighter than I'd expected, her face thin with an earnest look. She has big dark eyes and curly hair the colour of ripe straw. Dyed, maybe. It haloes her face like a dandelion, or the rays of the sun. There's a look in her eye like she knows, somewhere deep down, that her time will be cut short. It's strangely common, I have found, with photographs of the dead. It's there in their faces – what's to come. But of course that can't be true. It's us who are left behind who see it. Who put it there.

I think about Rebecca's family and what they must be feeling. They thought she'd drowned, presumably mourned her. Her kid would be about my age. Their past is rewritten, now. Time travel really does exist. Certain kinds of knowledge can change everything, even if it's already happened.

I think about my mother, how she tidies her hair when she's excited, even if it's already perfectly tidy. I remember how when I was little every time she went someplace nice she wrapped bread-sticks in a napkin and brought them home for me. I would wake to her silhouette, open my mouth and she'd feed me tiny pieces, whispering all the time how much she'd missed me.


Two weeks later the news comes that Nat is awake. I'm helping my dad paint the white fence. The phone trills from inside.

'I'll get it,' I say and go in. 'Hello? Harlow residence.' My mom taught me this dumb way to answer the phone when I was little, I guess she thought it was cute, and I can't seem to shake it now, it's a reflex.

'He's conscious,' a voice says. They take a quick inhale. A cigarette.

'What?' I've never heard her voice on the phone before, it takes me a minute.

'Nat, Wilder.' She's impatient. 'Nat's awake. We should go to see him together.'

'Harper, when did you start smoking?'

'Tomorrow, two p.m.,' she says, and I can hear it in her voice, how close she is to breaking. 'That's when visiting hours start.'

'OK.'

She hangs up without saying goodbye, leaving me holding the dead receiver.

I go out and take up the paint brush again, dip it in the can.

'You OK, sport?' My dad's concern is almost too much; his warm hand on my back makes me want to cry. It's so good to be able to love him again.

'Uh, yeah, Dad.' I shrug him off. I draw a long sleek line of paint along the scarred wood. It glistens white in the sun.


I'm at the hospital the next day at two. Harper is late. I wait for her for ten minutes outside, and then I go in by myself. I worry that all this has started her drinking again. But there's nothing I can do about that right now.

There's a state trooper outside Nat's room.

I don't know what I expect. Nat looks sick, but ordinary. He's grey, thin. His hair hangs lank around his pale face. He's lost all that golden glow. I realise in this instant that I was never in love with Harper, not really. It was a way of measuring myself against him.

I give Nat the book on rare coral fish that my mother got for me at Christmas. I think, liking the sea, that Nat will appreciate it. He looks at the cover and shivers. I put it back in the bag right away, stung with remorse. What a stupid idea.

I think Nat is feeling something similar, or maybe he sees my thoughts in my face because he says, 'Sorry, man. I'm so sorry.'

'It doesn't matter,' I say. 'I'm sorry about your hand.'

The stump is blunt and white in its bandage. It looks unfinished and is startling in the way that unfinished things are. I wonder what they did with the hand once they took it off. Burned it?

'It's going to be rough, getting nets in with one hand. But maybe that won't be a problem. Maybe I'm going to jail.'

'You didn't know, did you, Nat?' I say in a rush. Again I see Alton Pelletier's eyes, warm and blue, as he picks up a used Kleenex from the ground. I hear his voice. *Squashed-fly biscuits.*

'I can't talk about it,' Nat says. 'Don't ask me that.' Tears leak from the corners of his eyes. 'I'd rather be dead than go to jail – always inside, always locked up in a room, no sea, no sky. Like this place but worse.' Nat closes his eyes, weary as death, and turns his head to the wall. 'I always thought what a weird story that was, to tell me about clubbing a seal and hooking it in the shark rig.' He is crying now. 'He told me never to go down to the cellar, Wilder, that it wasn't safe.'

I think about how small the Pelletier house is. The cellar isn't deep. I think about how sound travels, even through bloodstained carpeted walls.

'He told you the cave was special,' I say.

'I didn't know why. *It's a place of reflection*, he said.'

'We swam right over them,' I say. A row of drums, connected like a daisy chain, deep beneath the water.

Nat moans softly. I have so many questions for him but they all make me feel sick. I picture him in the dark of Whistler Cottage, taking my father's cufflinks from the nightstand as everyone sleeps, breathing gently. Is that how it happened? I wonder why they were found with all that kids' stuff.

97

I stagger up, sending the plastic chair flying.

'Wait, Wilder,' Nat calls. 'Come back! I have to tell you something!' I run on down the linoleum corridor.

Sometimes, on the edge of sleep I still hear it – my friend's voice, asking me to come back. I can't help wondering what he wanted to tell me – I think I'm better off not knowing.

I crouch on the sidewalk outside the sliding doors of the little Castine urgent care centre. My heart is expanding and contracting, too big then too small for my chest. I gasp. Pain runs up and down my ribs. I know I'm dying.

Someone grabs my bicep and yanks me upright.

'Breathe,' Harper says. 'Just bloody breathe, OK?' She takes something out of a paper grocery bag and hands the bag to me. 'Here. Use this. I've seen it on TV.' The brown paper crinkles uselessly in my hand. 'You breathe into it,' she says scornfully as I fumble with it. Relenting, she takes it and holds it to my mouth. 'Here. In, out. In, out. Slowly, OK?'

I do as she tells me and strangely it seems to help.

'I don't know what's happening to me,' I say when it seems to have passed.

'You had a panic attack,' she says, lighting a cigarette. 'I've had a few, these last weeks.' She takes a deep drag and a woman coming out of the hospital doors frowns and flaps her hand in disapproval at the cloud of smoke.

'Are you OK?' I ask.

'You really messed everything up,' Harper says. 'Everything was all right until you came here. It was under control.'

I tremble again, this time with anger. I am swamped in sticky rage. 'What Betty said, the other day. Did you know? Did you fricking know about the stuff behind the skirting board? The pictures.'

'How can you ask me that,' she says, going flat against the worn hospital brick. 'I didn't know.'

'But you suspected.' I can see she's upset but I'm so angry, this has to be someone's fault.

'Maybe,' she says, and now she's crying, and I feel like such a rat.

'I'm sorry,' I whisper.

'We have to stick together, Wilder.'

I feel kind of unreal and I lean on the wall beside her. We both slide down to sit on the warm sidewalk. Harper gnaws her lip. 'I didn't *know*. But there were little weird things. Nat wasn't allowed to go home some nights. He had all these stashes of blankets and beer and food along the cliffs for the nights he had to sleep out. One morning I got up early and found him sleeping on the porch at my house.' She smiles through her tears. 'I thought it was romantic, but maybe it was just raining. He seemed to think it was normal. "My father needs his space," was all he ever said about it.'

'Those pictures, the Polaroids of the kids,' I said. 'Did Nat take them?'

'Alton's the murderer,' Harper says. 'He must have taken the pictures too.'

'They seem like two different things,' I say. 'The photographs of the kids and the murders. The cops think so. There's one up there, outside his room.'

She shakes her head. 'Just shut up, Wilder.'

'That story you told, the blue light, the monster . . .'

'A story. We make them up all the time.'

'But Nat *knew* she was there, Harper. He knew she was in the cave.' Nat's voice, the pride in it. '*My dad showed me this cave when I was little.*'

'Yes, he was a kid. He was a kid when that woman was killed, Wilder.'

'I know he couldn't have done . . . that.'

'You should feel sorry for him, being raised by a – you know.'

'What did it do to him, being raised like that? Maybe Alton was, like, training his replacement.'

Harper stubs out her cigarette, takes me by the neck of my t-shirt and pulls my face close. I think, though it's crazy, *she's going to kiss me.*

Instead she says through bared teeth, 'That's not how it was, Wilder. You won't go telling people that, will you?'

'No,' I say. My stomach writhes.

'OK,' she says. 'You remember.' She sighs. 'Goodbye. I don't think we'll see each other again.' Now she does kiss me – briefly, on the cheek. 'You're a sweet kid. Weird though.' She takes the paper bag from me and replaces the object in it. Aluminium foil glints in the afternoon sun. Something for Nat. *Is it a snack*, I think blankly, before her words sink in.

'What do you mean?'

'My parents don't want to come back here,' she says. 'Understand-ably. And nor do I.'

'Harper . . .'

'It's for the best. Nat's everywhere I go, here.' She goes into the hospital and the doors swish closed behind her.

Harper's right, I don't see her again – her family leaves the next day. No one tells me where they go. Sometimes I wonder if Harper ended up at Fairview or not.

I only wonder later what she was taking to Nat – the object wrapped in aluminium foil. A longish shape like a cigar but tapered, more like a carrot.

Maybe the way we three all loved one another these two summers will never happen again for me. Maybe I've had my share of love.


After I get home I sit on the cliff. The wind is up, and the whistling from the stones below is high and needling in my head. I suddenly realise how horrible it is, how it's the sound of wind in a cave, the sound of a metal drum dragging across the sea floor.

I shut myself in my room to get away from it. My parents are packing up for our departure tomorrow. Their voices are raised in their bedroom, querulous. They let me be. Everyone wants to get away from here. The thought of murder hangs over the bay like the scent of decay. I pack my things in ten minutes, leaving the little cabin room as bare and neat as I found it.

Everything is finished, here. The city waits, and then school. I wonder if I can survive it. But at least I'll be away from the whistling, and the sea.

I don't think I realise yet that you never get away from that kind of thing.


The air-conditioning unit roars. I'm in my room, staring at the wall. Outside, New York steams. The radio drones on. At around noon, the sidewalks will be so hot, you can fry an egg on them. Some team is playing baseball tonight.

My father is in the doorway. I start. He never comes to my room and my first thought is that there must have been a disaster, some bereavement.

'Is Mom OK?'

'I thought you should hear it from me,' he says. 'Nathaniel Pelletier died a couple of days ago.' First thoughts are often correct, as it turns out.

I feel that peculiar rearrangement of time and space that happens when you hear of death. 'Who killed him?' Harper's face is before me, a clever, cunning child.

'No one killed him. He had a cardiac arrest. It happens. His wound was infected, he'd developed sepsis. You run a high enough

101

fever – the heart just stops. Maybe it's for the best,' he says, putting a hand on my shoulder. 'They're still finding things in that house, the cellar. They think the two of them might have done the killings together. Father and son.'

His hand squeezes my shoulder. From this angle I could bite my father's index finger off. For a moment I actually feel it, the crunch of bone between my teeth.

I turn back to the wall, shaking. I feel the give in the bed as my father sits down beside me.

'I know he was your friend, Wilder.'

'Nat wouldn't have hurt anyone,' I say. 'Wouldn't have.' If I keep saying this, it might come to feel true.

My father sighs. 'Maybe he was a good kid deep down. But there seem to have been other parts that were . . . darker.' I can feel him thinking. 'I don't see any reason why you shouldn't know this,' he says, 'and maybe it will help. Alton Pelletier wasn't Nathaniel's father, you know. Couldn't have been, with the blood types. They weren't even related. In Castine they say the mother ran off to the city one summer. Alton went after and came back with the kid. He said the boy was his; she was bad news and he'd taken him from her. No one had reason to doubt him. She was a troubled woman. But no, it turns out wherever Alton got the boy, he wasn't his son.'

'So Nat was – what? Kidnapped? His mother might've been looking for him the whole time?'

'Maybe, sport.' My dad hugs me and that makes me really feel it – how terrible it is that my friend is gone. I think of Nat as he was, kind and golden like a young lion. Or Nat as I thought he was. Whatever the truth of him, it's all gone now.

'I thought it was you, you know,' I say into my dad's shoulder. 'The Dagger Man.'

'What?' he says quietly. 'Why the hell would you think that, Wilder?'

'You were out at weird times in the night, acting guilty, telling lies. You've been different these last couple years. I thought at first it was 'cause I'd grown up – but it's not just me that's changed.'

His face collapses. 'I'm sorry you were worried, sport.'


I can't stop thinking about Nat. Did he know he was a stolen kid? Did he think about running away, finding his family? I feel so bad for him. Then I feel cold because I think, *bad things give birth to bad things*, and they're often the same kind. Kids who were stolen might think about stealing kids. So Nat might have thought about that, or at least about sneaking into their rooms and looking at them while they sleep, like maybe someone once did to him. Maybe he thought about taking them.

Maybe he just wanted what they had, those kids. A home, a bed with a nightlight in a house where they slept safely with their family. I can understand that. I can almost feel it, twisting in my own gut – the longing he must have felt. Longing can become the urge to punish, even at seventeen I know this. Did Nat think about punishing those kids?

Or maybe everything I'm thinking is wrong and it was all Alton.

I hear the front door click. My dad going out. It's his birthday today. None of us are really in the mood for a celebration, but I do have a surprise present I made for him.

I've found a new way of dealing with my panic. The apartment is quiet. My mom must be napping. I go to the kitchen and look around for a suitable thing. I pick up a chopping board. I feel the weight of it, the heft. Then it seems natural to raise the board high and bring it down on my knee. Pain radiates up my thigh, down my calves, a hot racing stream, and it helps so much, feels so right, that I do it again. I remind myself to be careful. *My parents will have questions if I can't walk tomorrow.* I hear the crack as the board hits my leg as if from very far away. Black flowers bloom before my eyes. *Again,* I think, *just one more.* There is a whistling all around, and I recognise it as the song of the rocks, in the bay, when the wind is in the east. I hear Nat's voice in my pulsing head. *Good fight.*

When I look up my mother is standing in the doorway watching me, and her face is white like flour, blank as if there's no one behind it. Or a stranger behind it. She holds her bottle of sweet vermouth by the neck. Her nail scratches insistently at the label.

'Are you OK?' I ask.

'I can't do this,' she says, her voice high and small. 'I can't be in charge of this. It's not right, leaving me all alone to handle these problems.' She takes a ladylike sip from the bottle.

'Mom?' I whisper. I get up on aching legs and stumble towards her.

'No!' she says. 'I can't help you. I shouldn't be asked to.'

'No one's leaving you alone.' She's upset, it's terrible.

'Oh yes he is,' the stranger who is using my mom's face says. 'Your father is leaving us for a woman in Canada. He's down the block right now, calling her from a payphone. They met in Maine during one of those summers he spent with Vernon. She's not the first, she won't be the last.'

The front door opens. 'Hey, sport,' my father calls. 'How about going out for pizza? It's my birthday, after all.'

My mother throws the vermouth bottle at the wall where it shatters in a spray of glass.


'We agreed we wouldn't tell him,' my father says. 'Not right now. He's been through so much.' My mother has made herself as small as possible in the big armchair by the window. 'I won't lie for you anymore,' she says. She covers her eyes with one hand. I can only see her mouth, which is twisted into a horrible shape, a shape no mouth should be, one corner impossibly high, lips white and gone against her pallid face. Vermouth paints the wall in a long wet stripe and sweetness hangs heavy in the air.

'Dad,' I say. 'It isn't true, is it?'

'I . . . it wasn't meant to go like this,' he says, helpless.

'What's her name?' I ask. I don't know what difference it makes but it feels important.

'Edith,' my father says, then with a gleam of pride, 'she's named after Edith Piaf. That fancy French singer. Her mother is a quarter French.' It isn't Serge Gainsbourg he has been humming all summer, after all.

'I'm sorry, Wilder,' my mom says. 'I'm sorry.' She takes her hand away from her eyes and I wish she hadn't; the mouth was bad, but the eyes are worse. 'You were always slipping up,' my mother says to my dad, pleading now. 'You'll get bored of her like the others.'

My dad starts to cry. 'Edith's different.'

'It's OK,' I say automatically. 'It's OK.'

'If you're going,' my mother screams, 'then go! Stop dragging it out!'

'Please, Sandra,' my father says. 'Please, not like this.'

I take the Coke-bottle cufflinks out of my pocket. I tried to make them just like Vernon did. I even put a little dent in one of them, like the ones that ended up in the Pelletier place.

'Here,' I say. 'Happy birthday.'

He doesn't take them so I go to the kitchen and put them down the garbage disposal. The machinery grinds and screams. Something is happening to the room. The world goes very slow and dark, narrowing to a pinpoint of light which is vanishing into the distance.

'Wilder?' I hear my father say somewhere. The dark hole of the garbage disposal is like the mouth of a cave.

'You know,' I say, 'I think I would have preferred it if you'd been a serial killer,' and then everything is gone.

That is my first episode. Deep breathing can lower the anxiety, and medication dampens it all down to a neutral grey. But nothing stops them altogether. Stress brings it on, as do dark, enclosed spaces – and anything that looks like a lit window in the night, or daylight through a cave mouth.

My father leaves the next day, and I don't see him again until after he's married.

I go back to school and it seems so obvious to me, now, that this life is all there is. I'll finish Scottsboro and then become a teacher.

I do what I do best for the following year – stay low and survive. I get good grades. I'm offered a full scholarship to the liberal arts college I've always wanted to attend.

My father doesn't sell Whistler Cottage. He gives it to my mother in the divorce. He goes to live in Canada. I don't visit. He writes.

His new wife Edith has two teenage sons who blame him for the collapse of her marriage. He can't seem to keep teaching jobs, keeps falling victim to cutbacks. He doesn't feel at home in Ottawa, he misses New York. I think he misses us, too, but there's no way for him to admit that. When we speak occasionally on the phone he sounds so tired I almost feel sorry for him.

The income from my mom's job plus rental from Whistler Cottage keeps us going. The bay becomes a point of interest for people who are into all that stuff – murder. Dark tourism, they call it. It's always rented out for months and months in advance. So we do OK from it. My mother starts scrapbooking, and I'm glad she has a hobby but I worry about it. She cuts out endless pictures of birds and flowers from magazines. No people.

I don't think people should live by the ocean. It's too big to understand.

I think of it, sometimes, the empty Pelletier place – the deep cellar, its walls lined with bloodied carpet, doors crisscrossed with yellow tape, dust gathering on the boards. What ghosts walk there? I hope none. They deserve rest.

I think of Nat's kindness to me, a stranger and a lonely kid. He was my first, my best friend, and now he's gone. I will never know who he really was. And I can't help the feeling that Whistler Bay isn't finished with me yet.

[ ]

Cone
Done
Don't

Set
Let

Turn
Tern
Ten
Hen
Her

Set
Met
Meet

Ace
Race
Grace

# Wilder and Sky

*1991*

My dad drops me at the front entrance to my dorm, unloads my suitcase and stuff from the trunk. It sits in a forlorn messy pile. Mom would have known how to pack things so the cord of the lamp didn't get tangled, the book covers didn't get creased. I hope she's OK. I hope they're treating her right. She gets scared in new places.

Dad claps me on the back. 'Proud of you, sport,' he says.

'Thanks,' I say. 'I can take it from here. You've got a long drive.'

I accepted the ride from him – I had to, Mom was having a bad day – but I don't want him to think he's forgiven.

When he paid for gas just after Allentown a picture dropped out of his wallet. A confused-looking woman with grey hair in tight curls. She's smiling and wearing white. Edith, on their wedding day. I handed the picture back to him without comment.

Now he looks sad and lingers a moment. 'I'll help you get it all up to your room.'

'Really,' I say. 'I've got this.'

He nods, claps me on the back once more, gets in the car. I want to watch him drive out of the gates but I don't. I'm alone. I have to learn to deal with it.

I look around. Grey squirrels are chattering in the bare trees. There's a sound of water from somewhere. The sky is bright and clear. I feel like I can smell the mountains nearby. I wanted to get out of the city for college. And I wanted to be inland, as far as possible from the sea. There's only a small stretch of lake shoreline in Pennsylvania, and I find that comforting.

I take a deep breath and start to drag my suitcase up the steps one by one. Someone jostles me with their shoulder.

'Sorry,' the guy says. He's my age but tall, thin, his chestnut hair messy. He has a big nose and big dark eyes like a horse. He drags an old-fashioned steamer trunk up the steps by its handle.

'He's so clumsy!' his dad says. The dad is kind-looking with a big grey moustache and suspenders. 'Help your fellow student, Sky,' he says to the guy, who dumps the steamer trunk at the top of the stairs and comes back down.

'Oh, OK.' He lifts the other end of my suitcase.

'I'm fine,' I say.

'It's no problem.'

We're up the stairs in no time. 'All set?' the messy-haired guy asks, dusting his hands. People swarm around us down the corridor; we are a rock parting a stream.

'Completely,' I say, smiling, filled with alarm, and they're gone.

The hallways are so loud, full of yelling and people dragging suitcases and carrying pot plants. By the time I've finally fought my way to the bulletin board, found my room allocation, gotten lost in the maze of corridors twice, my heart is beating really fast.

I look at my watch. It's just 11 a.m. and I'm supposed to have them with food, but I take my anti-anxiety pill anyway. I do the deep breathing the counsellor at Scottsboro taught me.

Most of the college is built of old, mellow stone. My room is in the new wing, a network of breeze block and brown and green linoleum. The air is thick with the scent of instant noodles, mingling with the odour of meatloaf from commons. I find room sixteen through a thick fire door which slams loudly behind me, up a steep set of stairs, at the end of a long corridor. This can't be possible, but I feel like the corridor narrows, that the walls converge to a point. The handle of sixteen rattles; it's loose and there's a dent in the lower part of the door as though someone has tried to kick it in.

I go in, then start, because someone's already here – a guy lies on the bed by the window, tossing a tennis ball up and down. He watches as I drag my suitcase in, panting. The window overlooks the back of the kitchens. It lets in a grey, partial light. The smell of noodles in here is almost overwhelming.

'I'm Wilder,' I say.

'Doug,' he says. He's pink, thickset. An athlete, I would guess. Football maybe.

'Shitty room,' Doug says. 'Isn't it?'

'Oh, it's OK,' I say, suspecting some kind of trap.

'This is where they put the full scholarship students,' Doug says moodily. He throws the tennis ball hard against the wall. *Thwock.* His hair is wiry sand. *Maybe they group us by appearance*, I think. The weirdest-looking ones room together.

'Someone's come at our door with a steel toe,' Doug says. 'You see that?'

'I guess we scholarship types are an angry bunch.'

111

Doug stares at me, his face motionless. Then he gives a short hah. 'OK, you're funny.'

'Thanks,' I say.

'Maybe this will be OK,' Doug says. 'I like a funny guy.'

I put my fists on the sides of my hips and make a face like Groucho Marx, do a quick softshoe. I feel sorry for me and Doug – that we're both so grateful for my bad joke.

That night as I lie in bed, the scent of weed drifting up from the yard below, listening to the kitchen staff laughing, relaxing after their shift, I think, *well, I got through Scottsboro. I just have to do four years here. I get the grades and then I'll be free.*

I wonder when you stop marking time, as an adult – when life starts. What would I even do with it if I had the freedom – live?


It happens sooner than even my worst expectations – as in, the next day, in the middle of my first class. Everything's normal at first. I have a bad phone call with my mom after breakfast – she's in a manic phase – but I'm still excited for Introduction to Gothic Architecture. I want to study something real and solid, like buildings. Not stories or books.

I find the room, a seat; I have the correct books. Getting these things right feels like such a victory that maybe I relax my guard a little too much.

The professor has something on his tie, oatmeal maybe, there's a strong scent of coffee and bad breath in the room. But he's a good teacher. We're talking about the gothic, about architecture and the sublime; it's all very interesting. He pulls down the screen over the whiteboard.

He gets out a projector and even then I don't realise, don't worry. *I'm OK,* I think, pleased.

My first pulse of panic comes when he goes to the light switch, and the room goes dark. But no, it's just visual aids, surely this isn't a problem. I breathe deeply. The girl sitting next to me flicks a quick glance in my direction and moves an inch or two away.

The projector throws the image up onto the screen – an elaborately carved arch, with daylight behind. The archway glows like a lighted doorway, or a cave mouth.

That's the last I thing I know; dark comes down over me like a soft blanket, like night falling sudden on the sea.


His is the first face I see when I wake up. We're on a bench, outside in the cold air and the merciful sunshine. From somewhere behind us there comes the sound of the river running.

He's not looking at me, is frowning down at a paperback. He is familiar, though I can't in this moment recall why – messy hair the colour of turning beech leaves, dark russet. His eyes are big and dark. *It's very striking, that colouring*, I think vaguely, and the word strike must set off some kind of word association in my head, because now I remember where I've seen him before.

'You again,' I say. 'From the steps outside the dorm yesterday.'

'That's right,' he says, soothing. 'Hi. You're back.' He looks closely. 'Are you back? Really, I mean.'

'Yes.'

He looks into my eyes a moment longer. 'OK. Because you kept saying you were OK, earlier, when I could tell you weren't.'

I don't want to know, but of course I have to. 'What happened? What did I do?'

'You got up and left class. You seemed kind of confused, so I followed you.'

'Oh.' I'm relieved. 'That's not too bad. Sometimes I start—' I clear my throat. It's rough and sore as though I've been yelling. 'Sometimes when I get upset I have memory gaps.'

He is still looking at me closely. 'That must be scary.'

'Embarrassing,' I say, and I start to get up from the bench. 'Better get going.'

'Woah,' he says, putting out a hand that seems to simultaneously support me and restrain me. 'Hold on. Class is finished, in fact it finished a while ago.'

'How long?'

'An hour or so?'

'And you stayed with me all that time?'

'Sure,' he says.

'You didn't have to do that, I would have been fine.' I can't stand that he feels sorry for me.

'I'd got the point the guy was making,' he says. 'Gothic arches. Very gothic. Arches. Completely arched. No reason to draw it out.'

'That was nice of you I guess.'

'I thought someone should stay with you. So I told the professor I knew you. That we were old friends from back home.'

'Resourceful.'

'That's me. Can you walk? We should get you to the medical centre.'

'Please don't,' I say. The thought of roofs and walls and enclosed spaces is enough to speed my breathing up again. 'I can't handle being inside right now. I – just can't. Please don't ask me to explain.'

He nods and doesn't say anything, goes back to his book, which is great. His presence is relaxing. Most people's thoughts poke out of them, even when they're not talking, when they're trying not to bother you. Maybe especially then. His don't.

I find my pill case in my jeans pocket and take my afternoon medication early. After a moment's thought I take another one.

'I'm Sky,' he says. 'Well, not really. My name's Pierce. But I've decided to start over at college.'

'My name's Wilder.'

'Like Thornton Wilder.'

'Yes.'

'I feel my role as concerned citizen is to get you to a healthcare professional.'

'I just want to stay outside,' I say. 'Please.'

He looks at me, assessing. 'OK,' he says. 'Let's play a game. My dad used to make me do this when I came home late, so he could bust me if I was drunk. If you get this right we can go to the river and forget about the sick bay. If you mess up you have to come with me to medical, no complaints, no questions. OK?'

I think about it. 'What's the game?'

'I'll give you a word, and you have to change one letter, to make it into another word. You can substitute, move, remove and add. But only one letter. OK?'

'OK.'

He pauses. 'Indicate. So you see, what you do is—'

'Vindicate,' I interrupt.

'Very good, a quick study! Hmm. Fiend.'

I smile. 'Friend.'

'Oh, yeah, clever. But I can keep it going.' He smiles back. 'Fried. Are you good to walk?'

I am.


The river is cold, dark brown and rushing, the trees bare and spectral with a couple of clinging crimson leaves. Fall is underway early this year. Crows sit like sentries on the branches, black against the aching blue skies. It feels like there are too many of them. Why are there so many – and why are they so still, so silent? I shiver.

Sky takes off his jacket and holds it for me, expectant.

'You need to keep warm, you're in shock.'

I think about arguing, but in the end I just turn around and slip my arms into it because he's right, I am cold. It's tweed, expensive. The fabric smells of him, like bergamot and lemon, like a fragrant cup of hot tea. Earl Grey maybe.

'Wilder,' Sky says. 'That's an unusual name. Where have I heard that recently?'

My heart sinks. I shrug. 'I have no idea.'

Our names were in the newspapers – mine and Harper's. My mom was mad, but there was nothing to be done because I was over sixteen. I'm really hoping Sky doesn't remember where he heard it.

'We must have met in another life,' Sky says. 'Or a dream.'

'Ream,' I say absently.

'Team,' Sky says. 'I like you, Wilder, we should room together.'

'You don't really know me,' I say. 'Besides, I already have a roommate.'

'Do you like him?'

'Not particularly.'

'Mine eats egg salad sandwiches in bed. It's awful, I want to get rid of him anyway. So it's settled.'

Black wings burst forth from a bare tree, the still dark sentries become a ragged cloud of cawing. One black feather drifts down on the air, sidling, riding the eddies of the cooling day.

I jump. 'What scared them?'

'A cat? A fox? Or nothing, probably,' Sky says, soothing. 'It's just some dumb old crows being melodramatic.'

A giant black shape wheels on a thermal above our heads. The smaller birds scatter out of its path.

'Ah, wait, that one's not a crow,' Sky says.

'Raven,' I whisper.

'Craven.' I can hear a smile in his voice. 'You need someone to take care of you. I'm pretty sure you weren't supposed to take two of those pills together.'

I know he's only joking, and it might be a weird thing for a guy to say to another guy, but the thought of someone taking care of me is seductive in its strength.

But I can't get into the habit of depending on anyone. My mom got dependent on my dad and look what happened there.

'I don't think we can change our roommates now,' I say coldly. 'It's too late.'

I walk away quickly and don't look back.


My roommate Doug is talking on the payphone at the end of the hall. I recognise his hunched back, his corrugated hair.

'He's so weird-looking, too,' Doug says as I approach. 'Bug-eyed. Creepy.'

I flush and hurry past before he sees me.


It comes to me again that night, the dream.

It goes like this – I am swimming in the sea. I become aware that something is tugging on my leg. I'm not afraid; it's a game Harper and I are playing. She swims under and tugs my leg, then swims off before I can catch her. It's like underwater tag, I suppose. I don't know where we've come from, in the dream, or what we're doing there. There's no land in sight, just navy-blue water stretching out in every direction. No boat. No one else.

The tug comes again on my ankle and I dive beneath the surface to try and tag Harper.

But I was wrong, Harper's not here. I see, however, that I'm not alone. The thing tugging at me is a chain which is fastened to my ankle. It leads down into the depths. I follow it down, breathing easily in the glassy deep.

The first oil drum looms out of nowhere, too suddenly for me to back away. It's Rebecca, this one, of course, her blonde dandelion hair floating beautiful and white in the murky water.

I follow the chain on, I have to, it's the logic of the dream. Here's woman five. Her skull is bare, she didn't have any hair left when she was found – they were never sure exactly why. They think maybe it was burned off.

I'm gasping as I try to swim, muscles burning, but every time I pull away a current hauls me back towards it, the terrible daisy chain of oil drums hanging there, silhouetted against the waterlight. There are nine drums, of course, not just the eight they found. The last one is Harper. Her skin has slipped off her flesh. It floats by her like a dress rippling in the current. Degloved.


I wake myself by yelling.

My roommate Doug says, 'What the hell?'

'Sorry,' I say. 'Bad dream.'

'Come on,' he says, thumping the pillow with a fist. 'It's the third time in a week, man. Come on.'

The girls in the room next door are thumping on the walls with something, a shoe maybe. They're pretty sick of me too. They're French, foreign students come for the American college experience. I don't think they expected to be woken by so much screaming during this first week of their US visit.

I fumble for the paper and pen I keep beside the bed. I get my folder of clippings out of the cubby. I take everything out into the corridor. The hallways in this building are always reassuringly floodlit, night and day.

I flick through the clippings, scanning them. At length I have what I need, and I turn to a clean page in the notebook. I start to write the list, hands shaking.

*Rebecca Boone loved semi-precious stones. Turquoise, lapis, pearls.*
*Woman two had a pale band on her finger, where a wedding*
*    ring probably once sat.*
*Louise Dominguez had five children.*
*Elaine Bishop was very short. Her hair was dyed purple.*
*Woman five had a hip replacement but it was done in Mexico so*
*    they can't trace her.*
*Carla Yap had recently had a small tattoo removed from her*
*    hip. It once read* adam.
*Maryanne Smith had unusually white, healthy teeth, with no*
*    fillings.*
*Christy Barham ran the fishmonger in Castine. Her favourite*
*    city was Paris though she never went.*
*      They never found woman nine, although they think she*
*    died first. Her barrel drifted off.*

I refer back and forth to the newspaper articles as I write, to make sure I've got everything correct.

Gradually, as the list goes on, my breathing steadies, my hands stop shaking. This is the only way to keep the dream from taking me: I nail myself down with facts. I make them warm people once more. My mother hated it, my habit of clipping all the stories about each victim from the paper and keeping it. I hoard them, treasure each one like a priceless jewel. I have to; each fact about the oil-drum women is a delicate thread that tethers me to sanity.

Now I put all the clippings back in the binder. I like this binder, it has a picture of Aphrodite coming out of the waves on it. I keep the articles in plastic sleeves to preserve them but even so the newsprint's getting blurred with use. I'll go to the library tomorrow and look through the microfiche for recent articles. There might be something that I don't have, some little human detail. New information still comes out, though in trickles now. They identified Rebecca Boone and Christy Barham right away, but they only worked out it was Carla Yap a couple of months ago.

I worry about woman nine. Is she still lying lonely on the deep sea floor, year in and year out, with no one to make her real? I think about how every family whose mother or daughter or wife or sister went missing near Castine must feel. They may never know whether she's still down there or not, in the deep, curled up tight in her drum.

I never dream about Nat.

The next day I come back from class weary as hell. I didn't get back to sleep last night, I just watched dawn come in at the window, rising grey over the backs of the kitchens. All I want to do is collapse onto my bed and never get up again. I can miss art history in the afternoon, I tell myself. I can get someone's notes later.

Doug's stuff is gone. A steamer trunk sits at the foot of the bed. Instead of his aggressively non-ornamental black-and-white checked comforter, the bed is draped with a bright wool throw. I can tell it's expensive. A copy of *In Search of Lost Time* sits open on the nightstand. A green fountain pen with a gold nib lies across it. I can see that the page is closely tattooed with notes and underlining in emerald-green ink. I peer closer.

'Hey, roomie,' someone says from the doorway. It's Sky.

'What the hell? Where's Doug?'

'I told you I'd work it out. It wasn't difficult. Doug has had enough of you, I'll be honest. He wasn't difficult to persuade. My assigned room is pretty nice, too, overlooks the main quad; he was only too happy to swap. Even after I told him about the egg salad sandwiches.'

'You had no right to do this without asking me,' I say.

'I just figured neither of us was happy with their roommate—'

'It's creepy – moving in with someone without asking.'

'I thought you'd be happy—'

'Happy you gave up your big room on the quad to move in here, above the kitchens.'

'Well—'

'What's your name again? Sky? It's a real novelty for you, right? A big joke. You'll enjoy slumming it here with the scholarship students until you get bored, and then you'll bribe Doug to get your old room back. You'll feel all daring and tell your friends about what an adventure you had with the poor students, the kicked-in door, maybe say something about how you don't really *see* things like class or race. *It's not me who's rich, it's my parents.*' The anger lights up parts of me I never knew existed.

'I'm not like that,' he says.

I go close to him, look into his face. 'You are exactly like that. I know you. I went to school with hundreds of you. And I don't intend to spend college being patronised by you.'

'Sorry,' he says. 'You're right. I shouldn't have – sorry.' He opens the trunk and stuffs the throw back in. 'I'll talk to Doug. I'll be gone first thing tomorrow morning.' His big dark eyes are hurt.

'Good,' I say, icy.


The water is deep and dark. I spit, my mouth is full of cold weed and small snails crawl over my face. My rotting hand reaches for the circle of light, the top of the barrel. Trapped, I scream and the water rushes in. My skin begins to slip from my body as I fight my way free of the barrel that holds me.

'Woah,' someone says; a warm arm wraps around me in the freezing water. I scream again and gasp awake.

I am in my room, trembling, drenched in sweat; it is pooled everywhere. Sky is holding me, pale with shock.

'Get off me,' I say, 'get off!' My throat is hoarse. How long was I screaming? He gets up. I lean over and fumble with the bedside table but my fingers won't grip. I can't get it open.

Sky reaches and opens the drawer. 'What do you need?' he asks.

I point to the pills in their plastic bottle. He twists the cap off, shakes out a pill. My hands are still shaking so he puts it in my mouth and holds the glass for me. My teeth chatter on the rim.

I say, 'I have to – I have to—' I gesture at the notepad, the folder of news clippings with Aphrodite on the cover. I have no idea how I would explain what I have to do now, so it's lucky Sky doesn't ask.

He puts the binder on the bed, opens it. 'I'll leave you to it.'

'Don't go,' I say. 'Please.'

'OK.' He goes back to his bed, picks up *In Search of Lost Time* and starts to read – green pen in hand, making the occasional note in the margin. He seems focused, doesn't seem to be paying me any attention at all.

*Rebecca Boone loved semi-precious stones. Turquoise, lapis,*
*pearls . . .*

At last I'm calm again, or the closest I get to it these days.

'What are those?' he asks. 'The clippings.'

'Nothing,' I say. 'Just research for a project.' Then, dreading it, 'You can put out the light now.'

'How about,' Sky says, 'we keep it on? I got some reading to do.'

'Sure, whatever.' Relief floods my body. 'Look, about earlier—'

'You were right,' he says. 'Simple as that.'

Sky doesn't sleep. I listen to his quiet breathing. It's regular and deep. With that and the scratches of the pen it sounds like . . . 'Like a horse barn at night,' I say, hazily.

'Hmm?' he asks quietly.

But I'm drifting.


I wake to the sound of the alarm. I lie there blinking in confusion. This is more sleep than I've had in days.

Sky is quietly brushing his hair before the mirror. It springs back immediately into its original shape.

'See you tonight, man,' I say and turn over.

'See you tonight,' he says after a pause.

So Sky stays.


I get an envelope from my mom the next morning. Inside are twenty or thirty pictures of flowers carefully cut out from magazines. Her medication is pretty heavy but they let her use safety scissors.

I understand what she means, even though there's no letter.

The payphone at the end of the hall is free, and the hall-way deserted for once. I lift the receiver gently. There's only an alarmed beeping. I see that the tongue of the cradle is stuck in the upward position, meaning the phone is off the hook. Someone has jammed it there with pink bubble gum. I grimace and hook the gum out in gooey strands with the tip of a pencil.

It makes me think of marshmallow in my hair, warm from the fire, hair red as an alarm. I know she said she wasn't going back there but I can try, can't I? I just want to hear her voice.

I still have it written down in my address book, the phone number for Harper's house on the bay, the big white one on the hill. I'm nervous, my fingers are clumsy and I keep misdialling. But at last I get it right.

For the first ten rings or so I can imagine that someone might pick up. But they don't. On and on it goes, but no one answers. Even after forty rings or so I can't hang up. I don't know what I thought would happen. I imagine the trill echoing through empty rooms. What a lonely thought that is, a phone ringing in a vacant house.

We've broken our promise to each other. Nat, Harper and I will never all be together at Whistler Bay again.

I replace the receiver with shaking hands and do my breathing. It doesn't help this time. No one told me that grief would feel so much like fear.

I wait until I'm ready, then I take a deep breath and pick up the receiver to call my mom.


There's a hollow tree stump at the summit of Pursing Hill. Sky and I meet there most days after class. From here you can just see the foothills of the Appalachians to the south, blue against the grey cloud.

'Why did you choose to come here?' I ask Sky. 'You probably could have gone anywhere.'

He doesn't answer, and I see that a rare flush is spreading up from his neck.

'I want to do the writing program when I finish undergrad,' he says. 'The MFA. They say you have a better chance of getting in if you do your bachelor's here – especially if you major in English lit. So that's my plan.'

The college has a graduate writing program. Occasionally, essayists or a novelist comes out of it. It's very highbrow and exclusive. We don't have much to do with them, but occasionally we see the writing students drifting around campus. They look stressed and like they need a shower.

'Oh.' I'm surprised. Because Sky doesn't seem that interested in the English lit seminars. He always wants things to be literal. He's still reading *In Search of Lost Time* after two months. *Maybe he really likes it*, I tell myself. *Maybe he's rereading it.*

'I write short stories sometimes,' Sky says. 'I want to write books.' His face is almost scarlet. He turns away towards the wind, which is the bracing November kind. I look away, too, let him have his privacy. We're good at that, he and I.

'Writing things down purifies them,' he goes on. 'This world is so hard. We need something better. We need books.' He scuffs his foot through the dry grass. 'I don't know if I'm the one to write them though.'

'I bet you write well,' I say, loyally.

He shakes his head. 'No. I don't. It's like – when I put my pen to the page all I can hold in my head is a single word at a time. There are no – it doesn't build anything. Ugh. I'm so blocked I can't even describe my own block. Whatever. Let's talk about something else.'

'I guess you found something money can't buy, rich boy.'

'You *asshole*,' he says, delighted, and grabs me in a chokehold.


At commons, Sky can hardly keep his eyes open. He yawns. All his sounds are gentle. But he looks tired, his nose seems particularly aquiline against his drawn face. I know he doesn't get much sleep because of me.

'Hey, Sky,' a girl says, passing. 'How was your weekend?'

'Hey,' he says back, easy. 'It was good.' I've noticed that everyone seems to know Sky already – people tend to say hi like he's an old friend.

When we get back to our room, I start putting stuff in a backpack.

'What are you doing?' he asks.

'You can have the room to yourself tonight.'

'You don't have to do that—'

'I wake you up almost every night. Afterwards I get back to sleep but you don't. It's not fair, you'll fail your classes.' I take a deep breath. 'Maybe you could write if you got some rest.'

'Wilder I'm fi . . .' His sentence is broken by another long yawn. 'But where would you go?'

'Not your problem,' I say. 'Maybe I'll get laid.'

'Who's the lucky lady?' he asks, smiling.

'Sleep well,' I say.

I close the door on the rest of his protests.


I don't really have a plan so I sit in the library until it closes, and then I go to the movie theatre in town. I get a ticket for the 1 a.m. showing of *The Last Picture Show*. I watch it, nodding gently. It's dark and I'm the only one in the audience, but the people on the screen feel like company, so I do sleep a little.

After the movie finishes I walk back to campus. A couple of windows are lit high up in the main quad. One swings open as I watch, releasing a blast of laughter. The coal of a cigarette glows brightly. A long ponytail swings in silhouette, a burst of Pearl Jam fills the cold air, before everyone says *shhh*. The cigarette arcs and falls like a red star into the dark and the window slams shut, cutting the laughter off, closing me out in the night once again.

I wonder what would happen if I knocked on their door. *Sounds like a party.*

But I won't knock, I know that.

The dark heads are silent behind the glass, they move in silent shadow theatre. I stay for a moment or two to watch. There is a power to it, observing them like this. I wonder if this is what he felt – the Dagger Man.

There's a shed behind commons I've noticed where the lock is loose – so I knock the lock right off it with a rock. I hold my breath after each blow but the night stays quiet, no one comes.

I crawl into the sawdusty interior. Woods and forests loom out of the darkness, painted on flats. This must be where they store the props for the theatre department. I sit on a dusty golden throne upholstered with red plush. The gold paint flakes gently onto my clothes, into my hair. My watch hands crawl slowly round the dial.


I sneak in at about 6 a.m.

Sky is reading in bed, the book upside down. He wears striped pyjamas. His skin is flushed, his hair damp. Has he just had a

127

shower? He doesn't seem surprised to see me; he must have heard the heavy fire door at the foot of the staircase open.

'Hi, Wilder,' he says, turning *In Search of Lost Time* back the right way up.

'Did you sleep?'

'I did,' he says. 'But it was weird, being here on my own. I missed you. Buddy,' he adds quickly.

I get into bed and am instantly asleep – in fact I sleep right through my first econ class. I wake late and panicking. My pillow is covered in sawdust and paint chips which have fallen from my hair in the night.


I buy a padlock for the prop shed and keep the key. Now at least I have somewhere warm to go on those nights.

To a casual glance, the shed door looks undisturbed. If someone tries to open the padlock with the old key, obviously there will be a problem. But I think it'll be OK; the play is *Waiting for Godot* this semester. The director has set it among a regiment of US marines deployed to Vietnam. They're not using much scenery, it's just a blue backdrop and some sand.

I'm still getting more sleep overall than I have done since the bad summer so I don't mind. I figure the occasional night of this is a fair trade-off.


I can't find a pen anywhere so without thinking I open Sky's bedside cubby. A pair of little eyes stare at me from the dark and I gasp, heart hammering.

It's a small doll, made of something dark and wiry. Hair. Horse hair? It's finer than that. The eyes seem to be made of bone – when

I look closer I see that they're two small human teeth. I pick it up. There's a strange weight to it.

'What are you doing?' Sky is pale, his eyes wide. I put the doll back in his cubby and wipe my hands on my pants. I'm embarrassed, as if I've been doing something intimate.

'I didn't mean to – I was looking for a pen.'

He gives me a tight smile and offers me a ballpoint from his pocket.

'What is it?' I ask. 'The doll?'

At first I think he's not going to answer. 'It's magic,' he says. 'For the destruction of my enemies.' I can't help laughing, the words sound so strange in his gentle voice. Then I see his face.

'What is it, Sky?'

Sky sits down heavily on the bed. 'Something happened to me when I was little. I don't remember it, but my parents were really freaked out. And my mom swears it changed me. That I was different, afterwards. My parents are Bible people, you know? There's no room for any kind of different in our house. So when I was thirteen my parents sent me to this place. A camp. It was supposed to fix me.' He shivers. 'It's called reparative therapy, as in – *oh, I'm broken, I need repairing.*'

I've heard about those places. There was a *New Yorker* article. 'What did they – do to you?'

'They used to – no, it doesn't matter. That's not the story. It was winter and we had to sleep in these wooden huts, me and the other boys. It was so cold. In the mornings they let us into the bunk house where the counsellors slept, to do chores – make the beds and so on. It was heated so we all used to take as long as we could to make each bed – to get the numbness out of our fingers.

'I remember thinking, if it's possible that life can be this

129

guilty and hard and sad, then it must be possible for the opposite to exist. Possibility. Magic, I suppose. So I decided I'd grow up, learn to do that magic, and punish all of them. I started taking the hair off the counsellors' pillows and braiding it together. People actually shed a lot of hair over the course of three months.' He picks up the doll. 'And I made this. The teeth are mine – two milk teeth I kept.' He puts the doll gently back in the cubby. Even after he closes the door, I can still feel the teeth-eyes watching me. 'I don't know why I keep it. Comfort for a lonely, sad kid.'

'I know someone who used to do magic like that,' I say slowly. 'Or said she did. It never worked for her.' I think of the doll, its teeth-eyes, its horrible hair-body. 'Has it worked for you?'

'Not yet,' Sky says. 'Come on, let's get out of here.' His composure has returned – his face once more wears an expression of benign confusion. 'Let's go to the woods. I think it's going to snow.' He pauses. 'Maybe they did me a favour, in a way,' he says. 'That place forced me to know who I am. And I swore I'd never let anyone hurt me like that again.' He squeezes my shoulder. 'Be fucked up, be free. Right?'

We go up onto Pursing Hill into the cold, and it does snow, it lands in stars in his hair and lashes. Moments afterwards they're gone, vanished in the warmth of him.


The flashlight shines into the dark, waves lap up, lick the cave walls. Harper's hand reaches out from the oil drum.

*Don't*, I say. *Please.*

*It's OK, Wilder*, Harper says. *It's safe. We're all degloved now.*

I turn over into blinding light. There's the scent of sawdust, of paint. I'm not back in the cave, I'm in the prop shed – and someone's shining a flashlight in my face. Behind I can just see a dark figure.

'What the hell?' A male voice. The security guard noticed the new lock at last.

I leap up and scramble backwards over some peeling battlements. The figure follows, the torch beam dances crazily. I've cleared a way through the old cottage frontages, the forests and plywood city skylines, in case this very thing happens. I'm familiar with it, can pick my way through in relative darkness. The security guard can't, it seems. I hear the report of bone on wood and a gasp of pain. I stumble around behind him, weave through the Egyptian pyramids and out into the night.

I can hear the crash of scenery behind me as I run through the main quad, around the back of the kitchens and up towards my corridor. I back into some bushes, out of sight of the quad, and stop to catch my breath. I'm bent double, laughing and panting, trying to do it quietly. I can't wait to tell Sky, it's the kind of thing he'll appreciate.

The heavy fire door swings. Someone comes down the stairs that lead to room sixteen. He has a kind face, a grey moustache. Unease crawls down me. I know him, recognise him right away. There's only one room up that staircase.

Why is Sky's father here – coming out of our building in the middle of the night?


Sky's hair stands upright in a russet crest; he looks childlike, startled. 'He's got some legal problems, he was kind of – a bad dad. My mother doesn't want me around him. When she found out he dropped me here at the beginning of the semester, she got a restraining order. He's not allowed near me. They'd send him back to jail if they knew he was coming here. But I can't not see my dad, can I. Even though he's bad?'

'But you could meet anywhere, Sky—'

'You won't tell, will you, Wilder? Swear you won't tell.' The expression on his face is sad. Even though I know that Sky is lying about his father, I don't say anything. The story doesn't make any sense. It's somewhat comforting to know that he's so bad at deceit. We respect each other's privacy.

I sit down on the bed. 'I had the dream,' I say.

Sky comes to sit next to me. 'Again?'

'Again.'

He pauses and I can feel him thinking. Then he says, 'Wilder, do you want to tell me what happened?'

'I can't.'

'You listened to me yesterday. Now it's your turn. It will help, I promise.'

'OK.' I take a deep breath and go to the binder with Aphrodite on it. At the back is a special folder. I take the pages out. I've been working on it on and off in the odd hours between classes and studying.

'You know,' I say, 'I used to write a little fiction. Short stories mainly. But I stopped after—'

*Oil drums in a daisy chain. A hand, reaching.*

I take a deep breath. 'After something that happened to me last year. It really messed up my head. That's when it all started. The dreams and so on.

'But I got the idea to start writing this after something you said the other day. Writing things down purifies them. I thought I'd give it a try. So this isn't fiction, it's – well, you'll see what it is. Here.'

He takes the pages from me, wondering, scans the title. '*The Dagger Man of Whistler Bay*, a memoir by Wilder Harlow.'

He reads. I flip quietly through a book, trying not to watch him. I think about leaving the room but that seems worse somehow. There's nothing I can do now, it's out of my hands.

I can tell when he's near the end; it's like I can feel the story moving in him as he reads.

Sure enough, he's on the last page when I turn back. He puts it gently on the stack. He's looking down, I can't see his face.

'So that's why I'm so weird,' I say into the silence. In the spirit of honesty I add, 'Actually, I was always weird. But I'm much weirder now. Not in a good way.'

'I had heard your name before,' Sky says. 'I knew it. You were one of those kids.'

'Yes.'

'What are those for?' he asks, pointing at the newspaper articles.

'It's everything I can find about them,' I say. 'The women.'

'You always read them after you have nightmares.'

'It helps, I don't know why. It makes them real. Helps me remember they were people. Not just nightmares.'

'Oh, Wilder,' he says, and when Sky looks up I see that his mouth is stretched down. He wipes the back of his hand across his nose. He's crying hard, really ugly crying.

'It's OK,' I say, desperate. 'Sky, please don't.'

I put an arm around his shoulders. He flings his arms around me like a kid and holds me tight. 'I'm so sorry,' he says in my ear. 'That all those things happened to them. To you.' We stay like that for a moment, I can feel his heart beating against my chest. I suppose he can feel mine, too.

Sky pulls away and slips a hand behind my head. His gaze is on me, we're inches apart; it's like being in a beam of sunlight. I can smell his tears, mineral on his skin.

'Reading that was like being inside you,' he says. I try and shift out of the floodlight of his gaze, but he clamps a hand down on my leg, pinning me in place. He's strong.

'Was it true, that secret you were going to tell them in the cave?' he asks. 'When Harper and Nat tricked you.'

'I don't know,' I say.

'I think you do,' he says gently.

So I look right back at him, relax into his grip. I give in to whatever's going to happen. He must be able to hear my heart now; it's deafening, my pulse going like a series of detonations in my ears. *I know how it's going to feel*, I think vaguely – but what is 'it'?

His eyes hold mine for endless heartbeats. Then Sky pats my arm. 'Thank you for showing me that, Wilder. You should keep writing it.'

He gets up, goes back across the room to his bed. I watch, hypnotised, as he gets under the covers and reaches for the light. The places where he touched me feel cold now, chilly handprints on my flesh.

'Wilder?'

I realise that Sky is asking me something and I shake myself. 'Sure,' I say. 'What?'

'You OK to sleep without the light tonight?'

I nod.

With a click we are plunged into darkness.

'Never,' I whisper into the dark. I wait. 'Sky? Never.'

'Not tonight,' Sky murmurs.

'OK, I'll go again. Never. Ever. Fever.'

'Mmph,' Sky says and turns over. 'Shut up, would you?'

He's quiet after that, I don't know if he's sleeping.

I don't sleep for a long time; I stare into the dark. I replay the scene over and over in my head. I feel the light whispering touch of fear – fear or something else.

*Fear. Ear. Near.*

I feel like he's been inside me, too.


The next day I'm busy. I'm behind in class and have things to turn in. In the daylight what happened last night seems even more unsettling and I don't know what to feel. I stay late in the library, as late as they'll let me, until they turn the lights out at midnight. I won't admit to myself that I'm avoiding Sky, staying out until I think he'll be asleep.

When I come back to the dorm he's not there. A piece of paper lies on my bed. It's a photocopy of Christy Barham's eulogy, from a column in a tiny local paper. I've never seen it before. It's written by someone who loves her, you can tell. It really brings her to life – I learn that sunflowers were her favourite flower, I read about her closeness with her sisters. I remember her, how kind everyone says she was, how alive she looked that day I saw her, the day Alton Pelletier picked up her Kleenex and put it in his pocket. But even this memory feels helpful, like it's knitting my recollections, my mind back into a whole again, instead of keeping them separate, like Polaroids.

I hold the photocopy to my chest for a moment in relief. Then I slide it carefully into a new plastic sleeve and clip it into the binder safely with the others.

Sky doesn't come back and I drift. I wake to the click of the door as he slips in. It must be late. Has he been avoiding me too?

I listen as he undresses silently in the dark. I think about saying something about the article, about thanking him, but I can't summon any words. He gets into bed but he's not asleep, I can tell. We lie there, listening to one another breathe.

I'm shivering in the quad, waiting for the accommodation office to open to register for vacation residence. I get here early, but I'm not the first. The French girls are here. Some other exchange students, and a couple of shy-looking kids I've never seen before. Everyone who can't get home over the holidays and everyone who doesn't want to. Snow lies in dirty drifts against the stone walls. We all shift from foot to foot, shove hands deep into pockets for warmth.

'I think you should go and see him,' Sky says.

I look up. Sky and I haven't seen each other much for the past couple of weeks. First it was Thanksgiving, and I went back to the empty New York apartment. I spent the holiday watching the parade on TV and eating baloney sandwiches. He went to his mother in Connecticut.

Since our return to campus we have rotated around one another, avoiding long conversations. It has been surprisingly easy, actually. I suppose this is how most people are with their roommates. But I'm lonely; I see how much I've come to rely on him, even in this short time.

'What are you talking about?'

He looks at the queue impatiently, then grabs me by the elbow and tries to pull me out. 'Sky,' I say, standing firm. 'I'm in line, I'll lose my place when they open.'

Sky taps the shoulder of the French girl in front of me. 'Pardon,' he says sweetly. '*Est-ce-que vous pouvez garder sa place en ligne? Pour un instant, seulement.*' He smiles.

She smiles back. 'OK,' she says. Her accent is adorable; I feel like I love her for a second. But when she looks at me the warmth disappears. I get it. I've cost her a lot of sleep.

Sky drags me across the quad, up the west steps and into the hallway leading into commons. It's deserted, breakfast finished an hour ago.

'So I've been thinking about it for a while,' Sky says. 'That you should go and see him in prison.'

'Who?' But I know who.

'Alton.'

'Why?' I feel the world reeling around me.

'To ask him why he did it. Who Nat really was. To *see* him.'

'Why would he tell me that?'

'Maybe he won't,' Sky says. 'But it's the only chance you have. And at least this way you'll know you tried. You could finish that memoir you started. Give yourself an ending. Endings aren't always a bad thing. Endings help you move on.'

'I wouldn't even know how to – how do people contact prisoners? What prison is he in?'

'I don't know, Wilder,' Sky says. 'But there must be a way. What I do know is that you can't go on like this. What you're living is not a life.'

It's on the news later that night. We watch it in the dirty TV den; Sky holds the remote firmly out of reach of the guy who wants to watch a pool tournament. 'Hey, man,' he says, 'just give us a minute, OK?'

The guy goes 'huh' once, then seems to relax into friendliness. He throws his hands up, like *what can you do?* I've noticed that Sky has this effect on people.

When I look back at the screen he is staring back at me – Alton Pelletier. I get a cold shock because he looks just the same, kindly and calm. I don't know what I expected – for his inside to show on the outside, somehow.

'The grieving mother of Christy Barham has implored Pelletier to meet with her, to disclose the identity of the remaining victims or to reveal the location of any other bodies. Pelletier agreed to meet with her, but today, changed his mind and withdrew visiting permission. Mrs Barham was turned away from the prison, head hanging. And Alton Pelletier keeps his silence.' Then the arrest photo comes up again. Mr Pelletier looks at me. His eyes, the kindness they hold.

'He's bored,' Sky murmurs. His eyes are narrowed at the screen. I don't think he's talking to me. 'He's bored. That's why he changed his mind about seeing her.'

'If he's bored, why not see the mother?'

'He wants her to feel his power,' Sky says, absorbed. His eyes are bright and fixed on the TV. 'He offers her hope, makes her come to the terrible decision to visit him – and then after all that, he turns her away at the last minute. Imagines her pleading.' Abruptly he turns to me. 'I think it's worth a shot. I think you should write to him.'


Someone has gummed up the payphone again, and I resignedly take a pencil out of my pocket and scrape it off. At last, when I hear a dial tone, I take the card out of my wallet. I'd forgotten about it until today. The edges are as sharp as the day she gave it to me. If I'd remembered the card I probably would have thrown it away. I went through a stage of tossing everything that reminded me of that time, including all my journals and writing. I was afraid that it would prove difficult to recall events for my memoir, but instead it's been flowing out of me, as if all I ever needed was to open the door (*pry open the lid with a crowbar, the diver's face, vomit floating on the waves*).

Sky hovers beside me. 'OK, Wilder?' He puts a hand on my shoulder. It's the first time he has touched me since that night, and even in the middle of everything else I feel it again, that weird twist of the gut. *Could be fear*, I tell myself. *Could be.*

*Maybe she's moved or been promoted*, I think. Maybe she's on vacation.

'Hello?' Trooper Harden's voice is the same, too. I hear her take a sip of something, imagine the steaming mug in her hand. She sounds genuinely pleased to hear my voice.

'Heya, Wilder!'

It rushes in with almost painful clarity, the memory of the first time I heard my name said in that accent. The voice that said it. This is almost too much and I have to focus, hard, to get the words out, to explain what I want.

'It isn't a good idea,' she says. 'You know that, right?'

'It's – isn't there some program that organises meetings like this? What do they call it, reconciliation?' Sky mouths the words at me and I repeat them into the receiver. 'Victim-offender dialogues.'

'Not for you,' she says. 'That's for families of the victims.'

'Isn't there any way?'

She takes a deep breath. 'You could write to him,' she says. 'He gets a lot of letters. Might read it, might not. Might answer, might not. Might grant you a visit, might not.'

'OK,' I say. 'Where do I write?'

'I'm not going to do this for you, Wilder,' she says, suddenly decisive. 'You want to get on that merry-go-round – you can. All that information is available if you want it. I don't think you should. I helped search that house after his arrest. I saw what was there. That kind of knowledge buries its way inside you.'

'OK, Trooper,' I say. 'I understand.'

'You can call me Sergeant, now.'

'I'm glad,' I say. 'You deserve it.' On a whim I say, 'What's your first name?'

'Wow,' she says, amused. 'OK, fine. It's Karen.'

'That's – a nice name.'

'It's not, and we both know it. Listen, I'm moving up in the world, to homicide. So I won't be here much longer.' She pauses. 'It took it out of me, that case. I need a change of scene.'

'Where will you go?'

'West. Washington State. The weather's still cool out there, I like that.'

'I wish I could have a change too,' I say. 'I can't leave it behind.'

'You're just a kid,' she says. 'Go be a kid.'

'Too late for that.'

'I hope not. You take care now, Wilder.' And the line is dead. I put the receiver back in the cradle, as gently as if it were a small sleeping animal.

'She won't help,' I say.

'Brave,' Sky says, squeezing my shoulder again.

'Rave,' I answer.

'Cave,' he says quietly. 'Don't worry, we can do it without her. I'll take care of everything. I promise, this will be good for you.'


Sky finds the name of the prison, fills out the visit request form, writes the letter. The whole thing seems to be spiralling further and further from my control, but I let it because I know that Sky is right. I'm not really living, haven't done for some time, not since it happened – and I want to be alive again.

He gives me the letter to read, but I don't want to look at it longer than I have to. I sign at the bottom of the page and Sky takes it away.

140

*

I check my mail cubbyhole after breakfast each day but there's
nothing. *The truth.* I've been given the faint, pale hope that it
might be found. But weeks pass. No reply comes and nothing
happens. I realise that I have been counting on an answer, on
some kind of resolution. Because it is too late for me to be a
kid.

I meet Sky at commons as I do every evening. Darkness falls like a
stone; it's the time of year you can feel winter reaching out for you
with a cold hand. I'm hungry but I don't want to eat – the smell of
meatloaf fills the cafeteria. We woke up to it this morning, drifting up from the kitchen. Smelling my dinner all day tends to put
me off it. It doesn't seem to bother Sky. The food here is simple –
chilli, mac and cheese, pot roast on Sundays. Most of the students
seem happy with it. Rich people like to eat like children. I'd have
written that down, once.

Sky digs into his meatloaf, unquestioning. The way it crumbles makes me nauseous. His book lies beside his plate, green pen
keeping his place. It looks like the same place it was yesterday. He
asks, as he does each evening, 'Any mail today?'

I know he's only trying to help but a hot feeling comes up. 'No
there isn't,' I say. 'I wish you'd stop fricking asking.'

'Sorry,' he says, and goes back to *In Search of Lost Time*. He
underscores a passage with vivid green ink. He's got another book
open beside it, which seems irritating, for some reason. I pick it
up. A biography of Proust.

'What's this?' I ask. A red feeling is trickling into me.

'Just doing some background reading alongside my reading,' he says cheerfully. 'I've been thinking about autofiction lately. You know, a kind of fictionalised memoir, a hybrid of a novel and an autobiography. Like this.' He points at *In Search of Lost Time*.

'Why are you thinking about that?' I ask. The red is filling me, it rises up and up.

'For you, Wilder,' he says, surprised. 'So that you can write about what happened.'

'Stop telling me what to do.'

'Someone has to.'

I pick up the copy of *In Search of Lost Time*. Its cover is so stupid, some abstract pretentious design. Sky has marked various passages with little pieces of paper and green ink. There are so many, he must have pored over that book. The red has filled me; it tips over.

'Are you ever going to finish reading that book?' My voice is raised. I'm yelling. Everyone in the cafeteria is looking at me. I don't remember getting up, but I'm on my feet, leaning over Sky, who's looking up at me with alarm. 'Every time I see you you're reading it, but you never get any further in. It's enough to make a person crazy,' I say. 'Constantly making notes, always reading that book – no one has actually read that book, you realise? – it's not going to make you a writer. You know what makes you into a writer? Writing. Why don't you focus on that, instead of asking me the same question over and over!' My fist is clenched. 'You'll use any excuse not to try, so you don't have to fail—'

Sky is on his feet. 'OK,' he says. Then he picks up his book and goes. I'm left standing alone in the cafeteria. All the eyes are on me and I feel terrified. I've pushed away the one person who was really trying to help me.

\*

142

When I come into our room, he's writing, not notes in *In Search of Lost Time* but in a notebook. Lines of green cross the page. 'See?' he says. 'I'm taking your advice.'

'I'm so sorry,' I say to him. 'I can't understand why I did that.' But even I know that sometimes you're yelling at yourself.

'It's OK, Wilder,' he says. 'I hated that book. I only kept going with it because I thought I should. Because I thought it might be useful to you somehow.'

'I know. I'm so sorry.' I pause. 'I guess I've been tense, waiting for a reply. I started to believe in it, you know?'

'We'll just have to find another way to get you a life.' He smiles. 'I'll finish up my notes in the hallway if you want to get some sleep.'

'No.' I say. 'I like the sound.' And I do, it's soothing. I drift off to the scratch of the fountain pen.

I hoped Alton Pelletier could give me peace. Maybe I thought if the story was finally finished, I could be free.

It's not just closure, though. The truth is, I have got into writing it all down – what happened those summers. The act of it has woken the story up again. It's scratching to get out. I need an ending not just for me, but for my book. But there isn't going to be any *deus ex machina*, no dramatic confrontation with a murderer.

'You haven't seen your dad recently,' I say.

Sky looks up. 'What?'

'Your dad. He hasn't been to see you in a while. Did – did your mom find out? Is he OK?'

'He's sick,' Sky says briefly. 'And we had an argument.'

'Oh, sorry to hear that.'

'It's OK,' Sky says. 'We'll make up again, we always do.'

*

I walk up Pursing Hill through the snowfall, towards the hollow tree stump. Sky's leaning against it, bent intently over something. His hair is a shout of russet. He's not even wearing a coat.

'You must be freezing,' I say.

'Hm?' When he turns to me I see that one eye is ringed with dark plum. There's dried blood under his nose; in the cold it has darkened to purple.

'My god. Who did this?' I ask. 'Sky, are you OK?'

He waves an impatient hand. 'I had a big fight with my dad,' he says.

'I thought you hadn't seen him—'

'I lied,' he says, impatient.

This hurts badly. I take a deep breath. 'You never see him again,' I say, shaking. 'You promise?'

'OK, fine, but—'

'I mean it, Sky.' My voice trembles with anger. 'If someone hurts you like that you don't see them again ev—'

'Wilder, shut up for a second.' Sky takes something out of his pocket, hands it to me. It has a prison postal mark. 'Look. He replied.'

'You're opening my mail?'

'It got mixed up with mine.'

I turn the envelope over and over in my hands. 'Did you read it?'

'Yes.'

'I can't do it, Sky.'

'You have to, Wilder. There are enough secrets in the world. Bad families, bad fathers. Let's light up the truth.'

My heart is filling with lead. I don't want to take the letter. The moment I take it, this will be real.

Snow falls on the envelope, leaving little damp marks. I take it and hunch over, protecting it with my body. Snowflakes settle softly on my back.

His writing is just like Nat's. That's the worst part. I breathe through that.

The next visiting day is Christmas, Alton Pelletier writes. It should be then because he's being moved to a supermax some time in the new year, he doesn't know when. After that, only relatives and his legal counsel can visit.

I fold the letter into my pocket and take Sky's hand. 'Come on, it's cold out here.'


Back in our room I clean his face as gently as I can. When I hurt him he winces but doesn't make a sound, like a child who has been told to be brave.

'You can't go alone,' Sky says.

'I don't know if I'll go at all.' But we both know I will.

'I'll drive,' Sky says. 'I've got the car in the lot, I never use it.'

So we both stay at college. I worry about Sky giving up his Christmas – seeing his mother, going back to that white Palladian mansion in Connecticut that I've seen in pictures, missing out on roaring log fires, on holly and food and carolling.

'Sure, sure, all that good WASPy stuff,' he says cheerfully. 'It will keep until next year. I'd rather be with you.'


I call my mother.

'Hello, monkey,' she says.

'How are you, mother dearest?'

She laughs. 'Getting better all the time. Looking forward to Christmas. Shall I make a turkey or a ham? I'll make those sweet

145

potatoes with marshmallows that you like. So disgusting.'

First, she said she'd be out by Thanksgiving, but that didn't happen. I've spoken to her doctor; she won't be out by Christmas.

'Do you know,' Mom says, 'they won't let us play checkers here? They're afraid we'll swallow the pieces. Would you believe it?'

'You don't play checkers.'

'I know that,' she says, 'but I'd like to have the option.' The medication she's on has made her very talkative. Or maybe it's her condition. She doesn't really sound like herself but it's better than the quiet she sinks into sometimes.

'Looking forward to your visit next week, monkey,' she says. 'We can make holiday plans then.'

'Mom,' I say. 'I have to talk to you about something.'

'Oh, sure.'

'I think – I'm staying here for the holidays. I'm going to visit Alton Pelletier.'

I hear her gum snap. 'Are you insane?' she says crisply.

'I have to do this.' I lean heavily against the scarred wall by the payphone. Someone has carved a line of question marks here. They grow in size. The last one on the end at the right is as big as a hand. Someone else, or maybe the same person, has scribbled the question marks even deeper into the drywall with black ballpoint.

I trace a question mark with a finger. It leaves a faint black stain – it looks like fingerprint ink. I remember the police station in Castine. Maybe it *is* fingerprint ink. Maybe the stain has stayed in me all this time, beneath my skin, only to break the surface now like (*an oil drum*) a dolphin.

'What happened that summer ruined our family,' my mother says. 'Why would you want to go back over it?'

'I have to face it,' I say. 'And I think our family was ruined before that summer.'

'I know what this is.' Her breath is fast and erratic. 'You're going to see your dad instead, aren't you? Choosing him over me. No one chooses me.'

'No!' I say, cursing myself. I shouldn't have mentioned Alton. She gets upset.

'Listen,' she says, 'I'm tired. Better get some rest. You take care, monkey, OK?'

'Mom—' I swallow. 'I can't wait to see you next week.'

'Why don't we hold off on that visit, Wilder. I really need my peace and quiet, you know?'

'I want to come—' I say eagerly. But there's a gentle click and she's gone.

It's just an expression, isn't it – heartbreak? But in this moment I actually feel my heart snap inside me like too-taut piano wire.

So that's how I come to spend Christmas with a murderer.


Sky's car turns out to be long and black and shining with headlights that look like big eyes. I don't recognise the logo on the front.

'What is it?'

Sky says a long word in French. 'It's embarrassing,' he says. 'People always look at it, and I'm a terrible driver.'

I hadn't even known Sky had a car and I think how strange that must be, to own something so expensive and beautiful, and never think it worth mentioning.


Sky wasn't lying: he is a really bad driver. The car is a stick shift, and there's a loud grinding noise whenever he changes gear as well as a strong scent of rubber whenever he steps on the clutch.

We drive north, the Appalachians disappear behind us. New

York seems flatter, greyer than even I remember. The winter landscape is bleak as we approach the prison. I feel it as we get nearer the sea and it makes me nauseous.

The prison is a monolith of concrete behind fences and razor wire. It looks so like what I had expected a prison to look like that I'm almost surprised. We come to a halt in the vast parking lot near the gate. White lines stretch out in endless rows. It's nearly empty. Everyone's home, full of holiday turkey and potatoes. I take a deep breath. Sky and I look at one another. 'Shit,' I say, because I can't think what to say.

'Hit,' Sky says.

'It.' The game calms me as it always does. Sometimes I wish I could talk like that always, the structure is so pleasing.

'Here.' He hands me a wad of dollar bills.

'What's this?'

'You can buy stuff from the vending machines. I suggest you get a lot. Treats. He's bored.' He pauses. 'Get your hair out of your face, Wilder.' He tucks my hair, which is getting pretty long I guess, behind my ears. The path of his fingers leave warm traces on my cold skin. 'Clean hair not obstructing the face. Didn't you read the handbook?'

'No,' I say, fear rising up to the brim. What am I doing? Sky softens.

'You'll be fine,' he says. 'Just remember, you can leave. You have all the power.'

The waiting room smells like bleach, like a crime scene.

Each layer deeper that I penetrate they take something from me. My name, at the gate. Then at the next checkpoint someone takes my sweater away – it's beige and looks too much like the colour of the inmates' uniforms. My possessions are stripped from me as I journey inwards towards him. It's like being prepared for sacrifice.

And at last, at the centre is a high-ceilinged room with tall windows. It feels like a museum. A couple of families are seated at the tables. It's quiet like in church.

'Table sixteen,' someone says. I sit down where I'm pointed. I keep my hands on the broad metal table as instructed. A baby stares at me with owlish eyes, over a woman's plaid shoulder.

He's just there, suddenly, unassuming, smaller than I remember. His skin is paler; he's not spending so much time on a boat these days.

'Hi, Mr Pelletier.' My stomach lurches. But what am I supposed to call him? He was my friend's father, and my elder. Now he has become someone else – a number, a person who gets called only by his full name on the TV.

'Hi there, Wilder.'

His voice is the same: dry, characterless. There's something crimson in his hand and my mind is buzzing so hard I can't focus at first; it's red, very red and I think – *blood?* But it's a small square of red felt. He rubs it gently between finger and thumb and yawns.

'Sorry,' he says. 'I didn't sleep last night.' And I recognise the look of the habitual insomniac – all hollowed out behind the eyes. Until Sky and I started rooming together, I had it too.

'Me neither.'

'So, how are you doing, son?' He's relaxed, friendly, like we ran into one another at the store.

'Not bad, thanks,' I say.

'You must have graduated by now. In college?'

'Yes,' I say. 'Near Philadelphia.'

'Inland.'

'I wanted that.'

149

He rubs the little square of felt between his fingers again – sees me looking. 'I just like the feel of it between my fingers,' he says. 'What do you call it, the texture. That's a thing I miss – textures. There's not too many here – metal and cement, plastic – oh, and slop. That's the food. Nothing from the natural world. Wood, water, sand. I took it all for granted, all that time, touching those things. I never knew how much I'd miss it. I go to the supermax next month,' he says. 'They tell me it's only rock outside and concrete inside. Your hands only ever touch two textures. Oh, three including your own skin.'

I watch the red felt in his fingers. I think about some of the things his hands must have touched. 'Did you never think you were going to get caught?'

'We can get into all that later,' he says gently. I flush as if I've been caught out. 'Gum helps me think.'

I jump up, fumble the wad of dollar bills from my pockets. They're damp, somehow. The vending machine has a dent in the side of it, where someone's kicked it. It is chained to the wall. My hands shake so hard I can barely feed the limp bills into the slot. They come out again with a taunting whir. But at last, a jumbo pack of Big Red falls into the well.

'I'm thinking you have questions,' Mr Pelletier says. The scent of cinnamon chewing gum drifts over the visiting room, making me think of girls at school dances. Then I think of oil drums. *Breathe*, I think grimly. *Just breathe. Breath. Wreath. Wrath.*

Alton waits, watching patiently, as if he understands what I'm feeling and sympathises.

'I wanted to ask where he came from,' I say. 'Who was he? Nat.'

'He was my son,' Alton says gently.

'His blood type says he wasn't.'

'Oh, his mother couldn't take care of him,' Alton says. 'Drugs, you know. And I wanted a child.'

'Did she – the mother – just give him to you?'

'Now, what could you mean by that?' Alton says, smiling. 'You got a lot of questions. I got questions too.' His fingers rub the felt. Faster. 'Thank you, son,' he says. 'For coming to see me. It's like having a part of him back.'

And I know what he means because it's the same for me. He has brought Nat back. I know they're not actually related – even so I can see my friend in the greying gold of his hair, the warmth of his blue eyes. His laugh has the same hesitant quality as his son's did, like he's just done something he's shy about. The way he says my name. It's so painful and I want it, more of it, all I can get.

'Remember that hole in the cliff with the beer?' Alton says. 'He was so proud, thought it was his secret. I used to raid it all the time when I was short. I even put some bottles back there, once or twice. For fairness. He get mad at you for taking it?'

'Yes,' I say. 'Sometimes. That was you?'

'Ayuh,' he says, and he looks so mischievous and pleased with himself that I snort a laugh before I remember.

'OK,' I say. 'I don't want to talk about him anymore.'

'Sure. How you holding up after everything?'

'I have to carry on. So I just – eat it.'

'Eat it,' he says, smiling. 'That's funny. That's something Nathaniel used to say.'

'I think he meant "suck it up".'

'Even I know that expression,' Alton says. 'Why did he always get it so wrong?'

'I don't know.' I realise that I'm smiling – not at Alton, at the memory, but still – and even worse, he's smiling too. *Remember who this is*, I tell myself. The trouble is that it's so difficult to associate this slight man with those kind eyes with what happened to the oil-drum women. But then I catch the tiny movement of his fingers, always working on that red, red felt.

'All I want to do is talk about him,' Alton says. He turns that wide, magical stare on me. 'It's hard, being in here, being without my boy.'

'I miss him,' I say. Before I realise, hot tears are making tracks down my face. 'Everything's so messed up.'

'He was good at listening to other people's problems,' Alton says. 'You and he were friends.'

'I just – I have all these things in my head,' I say. 'There's someone I – have feelings for – and I don't know what to do about it. I have these dreams . . .'

'You can talk to me,' Alton says. 'After all's said and done, I'm a father. I'll lend an ear.'

I feel it, his warmth, drawing me in. I could tell him anything. Anything at all. And he'd understand, because he's not a person, really, he's a thing. *It's safe here*, his eyes seem to say. I let the longing in, let it fill me. Just for an instant.

'I'll never tell you anything,' I say, real quiet.

Alton takes a long, slow breath and leans forward. 'Well, that's a shame. But I'll tell you something, Wilder. I'm innocent.'

'What do you—'

'It was all him. My son. I was trying to protect him. I feel like you'll understand that. You're smart.'

'You – you mean he took those pictures of the children?'

'Oh, yes. That too. And he did those terrible things to those poor women.'

'It's not possible. He was too young to have done that to anyone—'

'Yes, he was a boy, just five when he found her in the cave,' Alton says dreamily. 'He was only starting to lose his milk teeth. The first one washed up there, he came across her, but I think that's where he got the idea. And he kept her a couple days so he could practise on them with that knife. I made him that knife, you know. He used to sneak it out all the time. I let him. He kept a boat hook in the *Siren*. Used to brain seals with it. More practice. He practised until he was good and ready – he was a patient boy. When he was twelve he took his first one. The women in the water, he used to call them.' Alton peers at me. I know it's just short-sightedness, but it looks as if he's squinting against the sun. As if the Maine summer follows him everywhere, even here. There's a little snapping sound. He's flicking the nails of his forefinger and index finger against his thumbnail, just like Nat used to do.

'You're lying,' I say.

'You know that I'm not. You've thought about it.' He rubs the felt between his fingers; it almost squeaks with how hard he rubs it.

I understand what Alton is doing, now. He's storing up memories, to sustain him in the concrete. I'm a texture like sand or water. I breathe deep. In, out. I won't let him take me like he took Nat. Instead, I'm going to take Alton, use him for my memoir – my book.

'You've got those wants,' he says softly. 'Those urges.'

'What do you mean, urges?' *How does he know my secret?* I am filled with panic. The closest I've ever come to telling anyone was that day in the cave with Nat and Harper, and even then I never said the words.

'Those wants you told me about, in your letter.'

Now I really have no idea what he means.

A long beep sounds overhead. Around us visitors start to push their chairs back. Neither of us moves a muscle. Alton says, 'I'll write you. You tell me about these urges and I'll tell you about Nathaniel. You can fill his place, be a son to me.'

'No,' I say.

'I'll tell you who he was. Where he was from.'

I know I'm being manipulated. I know it's a trick. But the thought of having an answer pulls at me.

'We're allowed to hug when you leave,' Alton says. His eyes are mild but the challenge lies in the air between us.

I take a deep breath and step in. His arms go around me, tightly. 'Good to see you, son,' he says in my ear, and the words are powerful sweet gusts of Big Red. But under the cinnamon chewing gum Alton smells of nothing – as if he doesn't have a body at all.

It takes a long time to get out of the prison; I have to do it layer by layer just like I went in. The guard who took my beige sweater has no memory of it, and it's nowhere to be found. But at last I'm back out in the parking lot. Sky gets out of the car and starts to come towards me but I wave at him to stay put. I'm dizzy, can't handle a moving target.

I make it to the car OK and lean on the warm hood, surrounded by misty clouds of my panting breath. Sky's hand is on my back. 'That bad, huh?' he says.

'Oh,' I say. 'It was fine.' Then I realise I'm going to throw up, so I do, right there by the car. Sky keeps a hand on my back.

'You're OK,' he says. 'You're OK, Wilder.' When at last I'm all done he asks, 'How about we get in the car so we don't die of exposure out here?'

The heater is blasting, the soft leather seats smell so great and it's so wonderful not to be in prison anymore that I start crying. Sky gives me a pill, baby wipes for my mouth and Kleenex for the tears. He really came prepared.

'He didn't do the murders,' I say. 'Nat. I know that now, at least. They might not be father and son – but they're still father and son, you know?'

'I don't get it, Wilder.'

'Just now Alton told me Nat was a murderer. But he was lying.'

'How do you know?'

'Nat used to do this thing when he lied,' I say. 'He used to flick the nail of his thumb and forefinger together. 'Alton just did the exact same thing.' The car starts shaking, but then I realise it's me. 'He didn't do it, Sky. Nat didn't hurt those women.'

Sky takes a deep breath. 'That's great. And the Polaroids of the children?'

'He said Nat took them, like everyone thought.'

'Was he lying?'

I pause. 'I don't know,' I say at last. 'No. I think maybe Nat did do that.' There's a peculiar buzzing in me. 'Thank you for making me come, Sky.' I'm so relieved. Years of doubt are lifting from me, because I know I'm right. Though it's a strange, partial vindication: oh, my friend *just* took pictures of sleeping children. Just that. No big deal.

Sky hands me his green fountain pen and a notebook. 'Write it all down,' he says. 'Everything. What he said, how he looked, how it smelled. Everything. Quickly, before you forget.'

So I take the pen from him and we sit there in the desert of the prison parking lot with snow falling all around and I write. At length I slow and stop midsentence. The pen trembles over the paper, a drop of ink falls, makes a perfect emerald circle on the page.

Sky watches me. 'What is it?' he asks.

'I can't write it,' I say. 'It's too fricked up.'

'Don't be afraid of fucked up,' Sky says fiercely. 'Embrace it. Fucked up will save you. Fucked up will set you free.'

I take a deep breath. 'In there, he called me son. And just for a second it felt so good.' I don't tell Sky how I almost told Alton Pelletier what I feel about him. I don't tell him about the hug. I keep all that for the story.

The snow starts suddenly outside Albany, a storm of white feathers whirling on the road ahead. Sky drives fast to try to beat it, but it's heavy before we get another ten miles. I feel like it's Alton's will, somehow, clogging our escape.

'We can't go any further in this,' Sky says. 'We have to find somewhere to spend the night.'

We crawl past a motel with a vacancy sign outside, and then another one. 'There's one,' I keep saying, 'you missed it,' but Sky refuses to stop.

'Not that one,' he replies, again and again.

At last, when the road is almost impassable, a sign looms out of the dark. *Oak Lodge Guest House*, it reads.

'Ah,' he says, pleased. 'Here we go.' This place has a drive, not a forecourt. The roof has actual gables and there's a wrought iron storm lantern over the door. No vacancy sign here.

'Sky,' I say in panic. 'I can't afford this.'

'Don't worry about it, Wilder, we're celebrating. Wait here. Keep the car running and pray they have a room.' Sky gets out and strides inside. He's back in under five minutes. 'They have one left,' he says with quiet triumph. 'I think you'll like it.'

Everything in the honeymoon suite is the colour of heavy cream. There is a fireplace hung with fir cones and little lights. I suddenly remember that it's Christmas. I understand why Sky hustled us past reception. The bed is an expanse of satin. The windows have triangular leaded panes, there's a mahogany vanity, a tub with feet, which is something I've only ever seen in movies, and there are chocolates on the pillow.

'Wow,' I say, then, 'I can't afford this. I really mean it.'

'Don't worry about it, and I really mean that. We don't have a choice, anyway. You want to get back out on the road?'

The world through the window is a maelstrom of white.

'Exactly,' Sky says. 'Scotch, I think.'

He orders scotch and steaks. I wait in the bathroom when the guy delivers it. I feel uncomfortable about him knowing that we're sharing this room. Its opulence is suggestive, meant for romance. Everything covered in velvet or linen or cotton, the wood too shining, the bed too soft, too easy to touch, stroke, lie on. Such richness (*such textures*).

Through the door I hear Sky joking with the waiter. I assume he tips him. I stare at the bathtub on its little feet. I think about my friend Nathaniel Pelletier. I wonder if he remembered anything of who he really was, or if sometimes he dreamt about it, the time before – those dreams everyone has sometimes – of being little again. I hope he did. Warm arms holding him, a crib, a blanket, the knowledge of safety.

'You'd better tell me now,' I say to Sky when we're done eating. I'm ready, or as ready as I'll ever be. 'Tell me what you wrote in that letter. The one I signed my name to. He asked me about my urges. At first I thought he meant – what did you say to him?'

'Just – what we agreed,' Sky says. 'You read it.'

'Don't lie to me.' My fists are clenched. 'What are these urges I have, Sky?'

'OK, I added one thing before I mailed it. One sentence at the bottom of the page. It was no big deal.'

'What?' I hold myself in check.

'I told him you felt like doing things like that yourself, sometimes.'

'What?' My heart is in my ears, booming.

'You heard me.'

'Oh my god.' The room swims for a moment. I breathe deeply. 'You had no fricking right to do that, Sky.'

'It worked, didn't it?' Sky is tired and cold and frightened too, his usual calm is deserting him. 'He wouldn't have agreed to your visit if I hadn't. He hasn't allowed anyone else. He needed something special. A connection to you.'

I'm frightened because I felt it, in there opposite Alton. I felt the connection, and it wasn't Sky's doing – not altogether.

'I'll never forgive you,' I say.

'Let's sleep on it?' he says, weary. 'It's been a hell of a day.'

'I'll go ask them for another room,' I say coldly. 'I'll sleep in the car – whatever – but I'm not staying here with you.'

'Please don't.' Sky lifts his head and looks at me. 'Please, Wilder.' He comes and takes my hand. He places it flat on his chest, over his heart. I can feel it, his pulse through my palm, beating into my arm and all through me, his heartbeat.

'Please,' he says again and I realise: *he's scared of losing me.*

'You messed up big time,' I say.

'I know.'

The tip of my little finger grazes the warm skin of his neck, where his top button is undone. I push him away, shove against his heart until he's at arm's length. Not hard, I want to feel it, the muscle and bone of his shoulder under my hand. Sky recoils but then straightens. He leans in closer, and closer. He's taller than me but only slightly, our eyes are almost level.

He reaches and removes my glasses, puts them down gently on the desk. Now he's a blur of cheek, red stubble where he missed a spot shaving, pale skin. His clavicle is an elegant triangle.

'You're staring,' he says.

'You're worth staring at.' What a dumb thing to say. A blush scalds my face.

'So are you.'

'Don't be an asshole.'

'I'm not. These big eyes . . . I've never seen eyes so big.'

'Why was your dad coming out of our room that time, Sky? Why did he hurt you?'

He pauses. 'It's complicated. What do you want from me?'

'An answer.'

'You have all the answers you need, Wilder. It's all here.' His fingers leave hot trails on me, burning pools where they linger. 'Is this what you thought Alton meant by urges?'

My heart, my whole being thrums with his closeness. But I'm stubborn. 'I hate being lied to,' I say.

'It's complicated,' he says. 'Please let's not talk about it. Let's be you and me, alone here. Let's pretend the rest of the world is gone – dead or exploded or something.' His hand, strong and gentle on the back of my neck.

I think I knew how this would end when I saw the room, maybe I knew when we decided to take this trip.

'I've never done this before,' I say.

'With a guy.'

'With anyone.'

'We'll figure it out,' he says, and he's right.


Sometime in the deepest, blackest hours as the snow piles high against the windowpanes, he twists my neck back and pulls my ear to his mouth. 'Do it now,' he says. 'What you always wanted. Pretend I'm Nat.'

I push him away.

'Sky,' I say, 'that's really, really messed up.'

His eyes are dark gold in the low light. He says, 'Fucked up will set you free, remember? Don't be scared, Wilder. It will take the pain away.'

The human heart is deep and dark with many chambers. Things hide down there.


I wake as night breathes into morning. The sky has cleared, the light of a crescent moon glows on the snowfall outside. The light falls through those old windowpanes onto Sky's face.

He's difficult to describe, physically, because he's always animated. He moves quickly between states and expressions, as though always escaping from one or fleeing another. The only time you can really see what he looks like is when he's asleep.

With that odd colouring he gives the impression of handsomeness but he's not really, his features don't add up. The nose is too big, the mouth a little crooked. Unlike most people he looks older when he sleeps. I can see lines and grooves of care that his restlessness hides when he's awake. The lines are deep for a face so young.

There's just enough light to see, now. Dawn is coming in, turning the dark world pink. I get my binder out of my bag softly. I take Sky's pen from the table and start to write. I put everything down, including what we just did. It's all going to be part of the book. Writers are monsters, really. We eat everything we see.

When it's written I lie back down. I test my mind and feelings gently, like someone putting weight on an injured leg for the first time since it healed. *I'm alive again*, I think. My eyes close. I hadn't realised how heavy the weight was on my heart until it was gone.

A hand wanders through my hair. There's a stinging pain in my scalp. 'Ow!'

Sky's awake, eyes on me. He holds a dark tuft in his fingers.

I clutch the smarting place on my head. 'Sky, did you – did you pull my hair out?'

He grins.

'Is it for the hair doll?'

'No,' he says. 'You're not my enemy, Wilder. I'm going to put this in a box and keep it.'

'You're a strange person.' Neither of us can stop smiling. Through the window the day is gold and blue. I can almost smell it, the cold clear air.

'It's late,' I say. 'They must have ploughed the roads. Should we get going?'

He shrugs. 'I've got nowhere to be.'

'Um.'

'Yes, Wilder?'

'Is this what it's like for everyone?'

'No. Never, actually.' And Sky's dark eyes go big and scared, he reaches for me hard, everything gets hazy, and through the rough sweet ache I think, *oh I see, we really are in trouble.*

Abruptly I push him away. 'Wait, what happens now?'

'You mean this?'

'Well – yeah. With us.'

'I don't know,' he says into my mouth, words warm with his breath. 'I don't know, Wilder, shut up. Please, just . . .' The sunlight pours over us, it seems to come from everywhere and I think, *so here it is at last and I –* but I don't finish the thought.

Love.


When we get back to college, Sky drops me out front. 'I'm starving,' he says. 'You go get us a place for dinner. I'll meet you in commons. Got to put the car in the lot.' His finger grazes the back of my hand gently. The touch runs right through me.

'OK,' I say.

After a minute he says, 'I think you have to get out of the car to do it, Wilder.'

'Sure,' I say. I can feel how stupid my smile is, so wide it almost hurts my face. 'I'm going.'

I go to commons and I save two places. It's early, there's plenty of room. Someone's made a token effort with holiday decorations – there are wreaths and ivy on the walls. I think they're plastic, but it still looks green and glossy. There's a small plastic tree in the corner with lights, paper chains. I feel festive. I look for mistletoe and then feel flushed. A few more students trickle in as I wait.

Sky's taking a while, and I wonder what's keeping him. Maybe there was a problem with the car – a tyre or something? I don't know much about cars. Time passes, and still no Sky. To hell with it, he can catch up when he gets here. I take a plate and load it with food. They have sweet potato with marshmallows.

*I'll call my mom later,* I think, to wish her happy holidays. And I'll call my dad. Everything will be OK. We can move on. We don't have to be chained to the past anymore. We can all be free.

The hall empties out. They start to put the food away so I quickly grab some turkey and bread for a sandwich and wrap it up in napkins. Sky will just have to make do, it's all I can sneak out of here. He never seems to care what he puts in his mouth anyway. I think about what happened last night and his mouth and suddenly everything feels very hot again. I feel transparent, like anyone who looks at me can see what I'm thinking.

Someone taps me on the shoulder. Time to go, they have to clean up.

I carry the sandwich carefully across the quad and up the stairs. The fire door hits my shin painfully as it swings closed, but I don't care.

The door to our room is slightly ajar. Maybe Sky fell asleep. We didn't sleep much last night.

I push open the door. The room smells strongly of turkey from the nearby kitchen. The bag I took up to the prison is neat and dead centre on my bed. Sky's side of the room is bare. All his stuff is gone. I look in the cubby. The little doll with teeth for eyes is gone. His closet and cubby look dingy, slightly dirty, in that way empty things do.

A folded note lies on his pillow. I seize it and open it with fingers that can't quite seem to grip (*degloved*). All this is becoming slippery as a dream.

The note reads, in ink as green as grass:

*Thanks for everything.*

A terrible idea is dawning. I hunt through my bag. Panting, I tip the contents out onto the bed. The folder containing all my notes, my writing and my clippings is gone.

I raise my head – are there stealthy sounds on the stairs below? Almost as if someone has been hiding in the showers so they could sneak past the door and down the stairs? As if someone was waiting there, watching, so they could see me one last time.

I hear the fire door click shut downstairs and I run. By the time I get down there no one is in sight. I run across the main quad and out back to the parking lot. There's no sign of Sky or his car. A faint scent of exhaust lingers in the air.

My anger is a ragged red scar in my chest. I'm not sleeping, the dreams are back. I keep the light on at night. The empty bed on the other side of the room gapes like a missing tooth.

Weeks pass, stretching into months. Time is blank.

Someone shakes me by the shoulder. The professor has oatmeal on his tie. There's a slide of a gorgon projected on the screen. It's architecture and the gothic, the class where I first met Sky. For a moment I think I really have slipped back in time and he's about to take me outside, sit me on a bench and teach me a word game. I look around, some feeling soaring in my chest like pain.

The hand shakes my shoulder harder and I look up. The hand belongs to a woman I vaguely recognise from the admissions office. 'If you could come with me, Mr Harlow,' she says, 'the principal would like to see you.'

'What?' I say. 'Why?'

The professor is staring, has stopped his lecture. Everyone else is staring too, the students, all those eyes, it suddenly starts to feel like every eye is a needle in my skin.

'OK,' I say to her. 'Let's go.'

I've never been in the principal's office before. It is panelled in mahogany. The windows are as tall as the ceiling, sunlight plays on the crystal of the chandelier, sends little motes and rainbows scattering across the walls. It's bigger than the room I shared with Sky, it smells like leather; I am sure right away that it never smells like chicken soup or meatloaf in here.

The principal is a woman with hair that looks like it's been cast in metal. She stands up behind her desk, which seems to me to be the size of a bus.

For a second I wonder if I am in love with her, she looks so authoritative. Maybe she can undo this mess.

Someone else stands, too. This man wears a pale suit and has shining russet hair, tamed into strict submission. He looks very like Sky.

'Young man,' he says, 'I understand you roomed with my son. Perhaps you can offer an explanation as to where he might be.'

'No,' I say. 'This is not his dad. It's a trick.'

'It's not a trick,' the man says, cold. 'I am Pierce's father.'

'Pierce?' Then I remember that Sky's real name is Pierce.

A dark crack is opening up inside me. I say to the principal, 'Sky's father has a grey moustache. Not so tall. Kin— I mean, different eyes.' This man has no moustache and does not look kind at all. But he looks very like Sky. The dark crevasse in me grows and widens. I'd known that the kind-eyed man wasn't Sky's dad – since that night I saw him sneaking out of our room. But unwelcome truth is always a cold sharp shock, no matter how prepared you think you are.


Mr Montague peels quails' eggs with his fingers. After that he has a steak which he cuts with a long, shining knife. I try not to watch. Knives like that still make me nervous sometimes. I order a burger which I eat with my hands.

Sky's father asks me questions in a way that suggests no one has ever refused to answer him.

'But maybe he's dead,' I say, feeling almost hopeful.

'He used the credit cards in New York last week,' he tells me.

'Maybe someone stole them and killed him.'

Mr Montague looks at me with a sudden distaste then shakes his head. 'He was always running away when he was young,' he says. He pats his lips with a linen napkin white as snow. 'We had to lock up the silver at night. He kept trying to steal it. Read about someone doing that in a story, I suppose. What was he going to do with sterling silver spoons? Pawn them? He was six. Always hopping from one idea to the next. My son is a disappointment to me, but I love him. He just does whatever rubs off on him. Oh god,' Mr Montague says, 'I don't know what's happening to this country. I thought, *as long as his obsession with this writing thing continues – then at least I know my son is safe*. I wish I knew where he was now.'

'I'm sorry,' I say, feeling a twinge of sympathy.

'He had a bad experience when he was young. It warped him, I'm afraid to say. Perversions.'

I put down my burger. It seems too fleshy, too bloody all of a sudden. My sympathy has evaporated.

'His unhealthy interest in murder developed as his perversion got worse,' Mr Montague says, wiping blood from his chin. 'These unsavoury excitements are all interlinked. He told me he wanted to be called Sky, of all idiocies. We have been Pierces since the Boston Tea Party.' He looks at me, assessing. 'He must have been very excited by you.'

'What?' I feel hot and transparent like blown glass.

'He is always reading about that case – doing research for his novel. I don't understand that kind of book,' Mr Montague says, signalling for the check. 'I like biographies. There's a very good one of Truman which just came out. Why did Pierce want to write, or anyone want to read about, those murders in Maine? The oil-drum women.' Mr Montague leans forward. I smell meat on his breath. 'He keeps working on it, but it never goes anywhere. It's an obsession. We never should have told him what happened to him up there. That's what set it off, of course – the perversion.'

'What happened to him?' My breathing comes faster, I feel black nibbling away at my edges. 'Where?'

'You're an odd fellow,' Mr Montague says, thoughtful. 'Are you odd on the inside, too? Did you lead my son astray, I wonder?'

I'm going to black out if I stay here. I get up from the table and push my way out of the hotel. When I hit the fresh air I break into a run, and I don't stop until I reach the college gates. I don't go in, however, but find myself walking onwards, into the March afternoon.

I go up Pursing Hill to the hollow tree stump, to our place. Sky and I always meet here. Or did. Even months later, I have trouble thinking about him in the past tense. The trees are green, tight catkins are unfurling. Spring will be here soon. I think of his hands on me and snow piling up against leaded panes, sunlight flooding the room. He never existed, Sky, I have to realise that. He was just some rich kid's invention.

Sky knew who I was the whole time. He encouraged me to write it all down, what happened those summers on the Bay, so that he could steal it. I was research.

I know that I will have to write fast. Sky will be finishing his book too. This can be part of the story too. This betrayal. I'll get my ending.

In the following weeks, I try to write – but the words seem to slip away. The order things happened in has become unclear. Even the faces are fading in my memory. Why don't I have any pictures of them? Harper, Nat.

Writer's block isn't being unable to write, I discover – it's being unable to feel. And my body, my mind, my hair and legs, my very fingernails are all taken up with anger.

I stare at the page.

Writing, I think. *Writhing.*


Pursing Hill turns green. There are golden orioles in the trees. Later, they'll move on north I suppose. Maybe up to Maine, to those woods by the sea.

At last, in my empty dorm room, I write to Alton Pelletier. His transfer has been delayed by some kind of red tape, and I've nothing left to lose. *Tell me who he was,* I write. *Nat. I have to know.* Sky did this. He dug deep, uncovered all these longings then left me exposed, an open grave.

He sends back a brief note. *Come next weak. I moov end of Jun.*

It brings back memories almost painful in their intensity. Not great letter writers, either of the Pelletiers.

I spend the last of my textbook money on a train ticket to New York, to the city nearest the prison. I don't know how I'll get there from the station. Take a taxi? Walk? The journey will take twice the time it did in the car with (*don't say his name, don't even think his name*).

I get up on the morning of the visit at 5 a.m. Once more, I haven't really slept. Before I set off, I go to the payphone and call as instructed to confirm my visit.

'The prison is closed to visitors,' a bored voice says.

'But I've booked the visit,' I say stupidly. 'I'm authorised.'

'Not today.'

'Is it rioting?' I ask. 'I've read when you cancel visits it's because of rioting.'

'Are you next of kin?'

I close my eyes, Alton's voice in my ear. *You can fill his place, be a son to me.* 'No,' I say.

'Visit is cancelled, that's all.'

I replace the phone. A soft pad of bright pink gum is stuck to my ear.

I fell for it just like Christy Barham's mother. I picture Alton's gentle smile. I guess I should be grateful that I didn't get all the way to the prison before he changed his mind.

I don't find out until that evening that Alton Pelletier is dead. The news reports it. Alton was set to repair the cracks in the pavement of the yard. He ate handful after handful of wet cement as he worked, without the guards seeing him. When he was sent back to his cell at the end of the day, Alton stuffed his mouth with his bedsheets to muffle his screams as the cement set hard inside him.

I can't know, but I am convinced that this is Alton's last message to me. *Eat it.* And I feel a strange grief.

*It's OK*, I keep telling myself. *I can still write it.*

But I can't. Everything I put on the page is hieroglyphics. I wonder where Sky is, where my binder is, what Aphrodite is looking out at right now. He took the most important parts of me away when he went.

My mom is no better, so I stay at college over summer break and get a job in a bookstore. Pennsylvania is hot and still, and empty of students the town feels like a place I don't recognise. I long for classes to start again, for people. I drift across the parched quad like a ghost. I have more episodes. The stress even starts to affect my eyesight – I develop a blank, pale spot in the centre of my left field of vision. Stress, I suppose.

'Shall I come visit, son?' My dad's voice on the phone.

He's a loser and a dork and I hate him, of course, but I'm lonely – and he's my family. A flush of love spreads through me and I open my mouth to say *yes, please come, Dad*.

'Edith and I – well, we're not getting on so well,' he goes on. 'Might not be working out.'

'Frick off,' I say and hang up.


The parcel arrives in September, wrapped in brown paper, just before the semester starts. It's ungainly and takes up most of my cubby hole.

I don't wait to get it back to my room – I tear it open.

It's a typed manuscript. *The Sound and the Dagger*, reads the title page. *By Sky Montague*. I snort in disbelief. I flip through with trembling hands. A line jumps out at me.

*I don't think people should live by the sea*, it reads. *It's too big to understand.*

'No,' I say aloud. 'It's not possible.' He wouldn't, he couldn't.

There is a letter tucked into the pages, written in that vivid green.

*Whistler Bay, Maine*
*1st September 1992*

*Dear Wilder,*

*Well, here it is, I finally wrote something, like you said. I shouldn't have tried to make you tell this story when you clearly didn't want to relive those things.*

*I'm writing this looking at the late summer sun on Whistler Bay. Strange to be back. I haven't been here since it happened – it's beautiful, I'd forgotten.*

*I wasn't being honest with you, or myself. This is my story, too – you'll see, when you get to page ninety-two.*

*A publisher has accepted the book, it comes out next year. But I want you to see this final draft, with all my mistakes and corrections. I'm trying to tell the truth these days.*

*I had to leave quickly Wilder, or I wouldn't have had the courage to go at all.*

*Go live your life. Be fucked up. Be free. You might not believe this, but—*

*With all my love,*
*Sky*


Grimly, I turn the cover page and start to read. The manuscript is full of green notes in the margins, crossings out and passages corrected with white-out. *Indecisive*, I think. Always trying to be liked.


I finish *The Sound and the Dagger* in a day. During the first couple of pages I alternate between horror and floods of warm relief. It isn't too well written. I scoff with ashamed glee at each dangling participle. Then every so often I come across a line lifted right from my memoir and my hands clench as if around a throat.

The plot is all too familiar.

The story is told backwards, from the perspective of the hero Skandar. Skandar meets Wiley at college. They become friends.

Wiley reveals his traumatic past to Skandar, and they become lovers. It's kind of sweet, actually. It seems like a coming-of-age story at first. But then the book shifts into the past.

The bullied protagonist Wiley arrives at the summer cottage above a bay named Looking Glass Sound. He befriends two local kids. They sit on a tiny beach eating striper cooked over a fire. Wiley and Nate are both in love with Helen. After a terrible accident in a sea cave, Nate is wounded. His father is arrested for being the serial killer known as the Lifeguard (it's ironic) who abducts women swimmers, tortures and murders them. He stores their bodies in barrels, sunk in the pools of a sea cave.

It's not the thoughtful, truthful memoir I wanted to write. It's horror. It's – schlock. It's obscene. Worst of all, Sky turns Rebecca, a real woman who died, into a kind of Hammer horror ghoul. She's dark and voluptuous and drowns in a long red dress – who goes swimming in a long red dress? There's a bloody wound on her shoulder, from where she was caught in the shark rig the Lifeguard uses to catch swimming women. Her ghost becomes a kind of siren, luring swimmers out into the riptide.

I think of the real Rebecca, the one I've looked at so often in newsprint – blonde, slight, sunlit, leaning against the windowsill, framed by tulips. 'I'm sorry,' I whisper to her.

The other characters don't fare much better. *Helen was slender, with a bright silver streak through her blood-red hair. He could see the age in her young eyes.*

Yuck.

*Anton had eyes like the black behind the stars, and hair that lay flat on his head like an oil slick.* He carries a boat hook everywhere (it's a red herring).

*Nate was whip-thin, brown as tanned leather, with a smile that twisted up at the corner.*

Skandar, our hero, is of course tall and self-deprecating. His hair is always tousled, a cloud of auburn.

Then there's Wiley. *Wiley's eyes were so small they seemed to disappear into his face like a mole's. Even in sleep, there was always a suppressed rage about him. Nothing makes a man so angry as knowing that he's part of the wallpaper.*

I shake with anger as I read.

Sky somehow knows things I never told him. He mentions the blood running down into the seawater pooled at the bottom of the boat and turning it crimson. I didn't mention or write that – I'm certain of it. He talks about the shape of Helen's leg, the down on it that *gleamed in the sunlight like fine wire*. I didn't tell him that either. It's like he's been hunting around inside my memories. *Can someone do that?* I think wildly. *Take thoughts right out of your head?*

I wish once more that I could kill him – but kill him a year ago, the day we first met, so I would never have to feel this.

I reach page ninety-two.

# The Sound and the Dagger
## by Sky Montague

*Page 92*

'I don't really remember it,' Skandar says. He kicks his sneakers off as they reach the stream. He ties the laces together, slings them round his neck and wades into the fast brown water. Wiley waits patiently on the grassy bank. He hates cold water.

'It was years ago. I was just a little kid.' But Skandar does remember and Wiley knows it.

'Tell me,' he says.


Skandar was excited because he was eleven, and what kid isn't excited to go to the beach for the summer? The house was white and beautiful. The sea was right there below – right there! There were sharks in ocean, he could tell. He was really into sharks.

The holiday was strained at first because his mom and dad were still mad at each other.

It had all started when Sally took him to the store. Sally was NOT his mom, she was the nanny, but she did all the mom stuff like snacks and playing tag and looking under the bed and in closets for monsters. At the store, Sally let him choose his own toy once a week. And the one he chose wasn't good, apparently, not one for boys. But Skandar loved his new doll – she had shiny hair and a string you pulled in her back that made her say, 'I'm pretty!'

The night he bought the pretty toy, Skandar woke to yelling and got out of bed. He followed the voices down the hall. He held his blanket tightly – he had brought it with him for protection. He stood outside the door and listened.

'It's a little girl's doll!' Daddy said. 'Sally can't control him. She's no good. I won't take her on vacation.'

'It was just a goddamn doll, the kid didn't know what he was doing. Kids are not rocket scientists,' Mommy yelled. 'I'm not going without a nanny.'

Mommy was mad because who was going to look after the kid in the middle of goddamn nowhere? She worked hard goddamn it, organising the DAR benefit last month had nearly killed her. Mommy was very loud and Daddy hated that. Usually Mommy being loud was enough to change his mind.

But this time Daddy said, 'Then we'll stay here for the summer,' and Skandar could tell that he meant it. It wasn't just about the doll, he knew that. It was all the other things, the secret things he knew he wasn't supposed to feel. His daddy could see he wasn't right inside and never had been.

Skandar crept back to bed. He thought very carefully about what to do. He wanted Mommy and Daddy to be happy, and he wanted to go on vacation.

So the next day he went to his daddy in his study and said, 'Can I have one more toy this week?'

Daddy looked up from his piles of paper and said sharply, 'You've had your toy this week.'

'I threw that one away,' Skandar said. 'It was a toy for a little kid and for girls. I beat it up to pieces and I threw it in the woods. Now I want an action man. I want an action man with a gun. Sally can take me to the store. Please may I?'

'All right, son,' Daddy said. He patted Skandar on the head. And Skandar played with the action man and the gun for the rest of the week, especially in the evenings after Daddy came home.

So they went on vacation after all and even Sally came after all and she had a little room next to his own room and both rooms had windows that looked out onto the sea. It was great.

Skandar played with his action man on the beach, running up and down, *pow pow*. By the end of the first day he was so tired he nearly fell asleep in his lasagne. Sally put him to bed. He got the pretty doll out from his secret place in his suitcase and slept with her cradled in his arms.

He woke to a flash. *Lightning*, he thought, but there was a person behind the lightning. A hand reached, and the doll was pulled gently from his hand. Skandar saw a figure, the monster behind the lightning. It seemed really tall, and then straight after, he thought it might be a kid, like him. Something shone in its hand – a beam of light, a knife. Skandar felt the cold grip of fear on his guts. He understood right away that this was also him. His other half, the bad stuff inside him coming out. This was Bad Skandar, Shadow Skandar, who wanted to do wrong things. The knife came closer, closer. Something brushed the top of his head. A hand.

Skandar lay frozen in the dark, as Bad Skandar softly stroked his hair.

Skandar closed his eyes and began to scream. When he opened them again the lights were on, Bad Skandar was gone, the curtains were fluttering in the breeze. The open window showed a black square of night. Mommy and Daddy were there. They all looked at the Polaroid which lay on the floor, then back at Skandar. So many eyes. Mommy picked up the Polaroid. It showed Good Skandar sleeping. Something shone at his neck. Her hand covered her mouth, her face was pale like white butter. 'What did he do to you?' she asked. 'What did he do?'

Everything in the bed was wet. Skandar was ashamed; he wasn't a baby, he hadn't wet the bed for years. But the other thing was worse. Daddy was staring and Skandar looked down, following his eyes. He burst into tears, because now Daddy knew he was a liar, and that Bad Skandar was real.

The doll lay on the floor where Bad Skandar had dropped her. Daddy picked her up. 'I'm pretty,' she said in a tinny voice.

They went home the next day and never reported it to the police.

It is years before Skandar understands what really happened that night – when the newspapers start publishing stories about the Dagger Man of Looking Glass Sound.

Wiley kicks off his sandals and wades into the stream to where Skandar stands. His pants are wet to the knees but he doesn't seem to notice. 'I'm sorry,' he says.

'I imagine him sometimes,' Skandar says. 'The Dagger Man. I can't help thinking of him as Bad Skandar, still, out there, alone in the night. I feel sorry for him.'

Wiley's hand comes to rest on Skandar's back. For Skandar the world narrows down to Wiley's palm, warm through the thin cotton.

'It messed me up,' Skandar says.

'It's OK to be messed up,' Wiley says. 'Being messed up sets you free.'

Wiley takes off his glasses and puts them in his breast pocket. His eyes are small but very grey like pinpoints of light. He puts his hand on Skandar's hip, then slides it gently under his t-shirt, up his stomach and chest. His palm comes to rest over Skandar's heart which beats like a drum. All the world stops, they are at its still centre. The stream is gone, everything is gone except Wiley's hand, and his breath soft on Skandar's neck.

# Wilder

The Polaroid falls to the floor, loosed from the pages. It's faded now, but I can still make out the features of a sleeping child with messy russet hair. A thin, shining thing hovers by his throat. The shade of the hair, the nose is familiar. The thick lashes on closed lids. It's Sky, of course. I'd know him anywhere.

My heart twists. Sky is so little, in the picture – so easily harmed. I think of them both – Nat and Sky, two messed-up kids in a dark bedroom. This moment, this flash of connection between them before I ever knew either of them existed.

Anger settles back in with its hooked barbs. 'No,' I mutter through clenched teeth. 'That does not give you the right.' I am close to blacking out. But I have to finish reading, I have to know it all.

After his father's arrest, Nate kills himself. It emerges that he had been sneaking into children's bedrooms and taking photographs of them as they slept. He is the Dagger Man of Looking Glass Sound. Back at university Wiley's behaviour is becoming more and more erratic, and his obsession with Skandar more unhinged. So our hero comes to suspect the truth: that Wiley was the Lifeguard all along, and Nate's father was innocent.

Wiley flees from college and Skandar pursues him back to Looking Glass Sound, where they have a confrontation in the cave where the barrel women were found. Wiley attacks Skandar, who kills him in self-defence. The ghost of the first barrel woman, Rebecca, pulls Wiley down into the depths of the ocean. At the end Skandar and Helen realise they're in love. The story ends.


I stand up, unsteady. My breath comes fast, there are bright and dark spots on my vision. I need air. I stumble down the stairs, out into the cool evening. I can hear ravens on the wing above me. The Polaroid is still in my hand, I realise. I throw it as far as I can. It flutters down onto the college lawn.

I wipe my eyes angrily with the back of my sleeve. I take a deep breath. 'Frick you, Pierce,' I shout aloud to the empty quad. I flex my hands, imagine the feel of a throat in them. 'Frick you, frick you!' I yell. Birds scatter like black confetti on the sky.

Right away I go and pick up the Polaroid again, wipe it clean of dew. I have to keep it. Preserve it. Every time I feel my anger dim, I tell myself, I will look at this again. Sky thinks *this* gave him the right to steal my story.

'I should have killed you,' I say aloud. 'It's mine.' Or it was mine. I feel it slipping away from me already. There's no point in trying to write anything now. Sky has emptied me out.


I understand, cool and clear, what I have to do. I'm going to find Sky. I'm going back to Whistler Bay.

# *Pearl*

Pearl is making a tuna sandwich. She plans to drink a glass of milk with it. Simple pleasures. She's happy. Summer's ending and the city feels uncommonly alive. It's a sunny, shining nickel of a New York day.

She sees Harper's number come up on the caller ID display and her heart leaps. *Forgiven,* she thinks. Harper isn't exactly speaking to Pearl – but today seems like a day to believe in things.

She licks tuna from her thumb and answers.

At first, she thinks she's made a mistake because the voice on the other end sounds nothing like Harper. It's cracked, heavy with breath. A ghost's voice. Harper is crying.

'What's the matter?' Pearl asks. 'Oh, Harper, what's wrong?'

When Pearl hears that he is dead, she sits down on the kitchen floor.

In her ear Harper says, 'You did this.'

Pearl realises that the floor is wet. Milk spreads in a cool ghostly pool about her. The carton is broken, nearby. She must have dropped it. She realises with a start that she's still holding the phone and she puts it back on the wall cradle carefully. There's no one on the other end anymore. Harper hung up some time ago. The kitchen smells of tuna fish and so do her hands. Why? Vaguely she remembers the sandwich she was making when she answered the phone. For the rest of her life even the smell of tuna will make her retch.

Pearl thinks about the fact that he is dead. It has been a long time since she felt this kind of pain – since her mother died, in fact. She observes it with detached interest. She wishes she had a notebook and a pen. It's fascinating.

After a certain amount of time she wipes her face – interesting, she hadn't noticed she had been crying – and mops up the milk with paper towel.

'If ever there was a time for witchcraft,' she says to her quiet apartment, 'it's now.' That stuff doesn't work, it never has. Pearl tried it for her mother. She used her pearl, the one she kept from her earring. It didn't work.

But that was more than ten years after she died. Time must make a difference, mustn't it? He's only just gone – freshly dead. She thinks hard and starts to laugh. Of course. She knows where she can always find him – even in death.

Pearl goes to the living room. *The Sound and the Dagger* stares at her from the bookshelf. The cover is unnerving. A boat hook, a night sky over the sea. Blood-red lettering. Somehow that double 'G' in *Dagger* bears an uncomfortable resemblance to a pair of eyes. He's scattered throughout this book. She can use it.

Pearl goes to the cocktail trolley. She takes the knife she uses for cutting lemons and pierces her finger with the tip. It hurts even more than she expects and she dimly recalls some fact about grief exacerbating physical pain. She lets her blood trickle into a wineglass. She pulls the cork out of a random bottle and takes a swig of wine. She swills it around her mouth then spits it into the glass. She's not planning but acting on instinct now, using objects she finds to hand. It's the same kind of hypnotic state she gets into when she's writing.

She knows what she needs next. She takes the doll carefully from the drawer by her bed. Its tooth eyes stare, blank. She takes a couple of precious strands of his hair from the lock she keeps safe. She wraps the letter around it. She takes the chewing gum from the same drawer. For a moment she lets it rest in her mouth. It's cold, hard, holds no memory of his mouth.

In the bathroom, she opens *The Sound and the Dagger*. She finds a part about him and traces the words carefully in blood and wine, with a needle. One line will be enough, she thinks. Pearl puts the book, the doll and the hair in the bath tub and pours over blood and wine. It's thick, viscous, she doesn't like it; there is something alive about the mixture, as though it's gestating. The book's a special advance copy; it's a shame really, but magic has to cost you. She takes the pearl out of her locket. Real magic costs you a lot.

She pushes the pearl into the centre of the doll, like a heart, or a belly button. Then she opens the book so the pages catch better, and strikes a match. At first the pile smokes sullenly, so she squirts on some paint stripper she finds under the sink – magic is like this, it always provides – and then it crackles up, bright and stinking. The hair fizzles with a fecal stench. The bathroom is full of smoke and Pearl's head swims. She thinks, peacefully, *so this is the real magic – this is how I join him.*

She is dimly aware of the cracking of wood and shouting. Someone has broken down the door of her apartment. But the floor grips her like a magnet and she can't move. There are legs and voices all around, kind hands raise her and someone directs white foam at the burning pile in the bathtub.

'Are you crazy, lady?' someone asks, shaking her, before someone else stops them. They're pulling her up, and she sees the bathroom for what it is now: a death chamber with smoke-blackened walls.

As they pull her away Pearl struggles and frees an arm, manages to reach into the smouldering debris in the tub and grab the cracked, blackened pearl from the wreckage. Its surface is charred and rough. It will never be bright again. Neither of them will. There is no such thing as magic or witchcraft; he's dead and will stay dead for ever.

'I love you,' she whispers. But she can already feel it – his absence in the world.

# Wilder, Day One

As soon as I hear he's really dead, I get on the train. I don't drive anymore. Emily used to cry over it, my declining eyesight. The truth is, I kind of like it – this gradual blurring, the world fading into white.

Sky went sailing, just struck out to sea and never came home. It was like one of his stories, everyone says. It's like *The Sound and the Dagger*.

He dies in stages – first of all he goes out sailing and doesn't come home. Dark comes and he's still gone. The next day, the coastguard is called out, they comb the shore. The hospitals are checked. On the fourth day, his boat is found washed up on a sandbank. On the fifth day, a severed finger is caught in a net by a trawler north of the point. It's wearing Sky's ring. It has his fingerprint. He's presumed dead. Rescuers give up the search.

At dusk they announce it on the satellite news channels – Sky Montague is dead. Only then do I let myself believe it.

Lost at sea. A romantic end; he would have appreciated it. I would have preferred he'd died of something involving a rash. I imagine it – the sea all around him, navy-blue and cold, clutching him tighter, pulling him deeper and deeper into its folds. I wonder if parts of him are keeping her company, the last, lost oil-drum woman, where she lies on the ocean floor.

Maybe it suits him after all – that death.

*The Sound*, Sky's boat was called. He could never get away from that first book.


I buy a can of beer from the automated vending machine when it comes trundling down the aisle. There's not much left on the credit card I suspect – but I'm celebrating, after all.

The manuscript of *The Sound and the Dagger* sits on the seat beside me, tied up with string and carefully enclosed in Saran wrap. His letter is on top, encased in a plastic sleeve. Each time the train rounds a bend I hear the book shift on the seat, as if it's whispering to itself.

I kept it, of course I did. I make myself read it sometimes to keep the fires fresh. The hurt. You have to coax anger along, otherwise after a certain time it dies.

I have a published copy of *The Sound and the Dagger* in my briefcase, too. I might need it for reference. But it's the manuscript that grips me. All those frantic green corrections, the little crusted islands of white-out, hiding Sky's first, corrected thoughts. Sometimes I think about scraping them off to see what lies beneath.

He wrote other books after *The Sound and the Dagger*. I think people only bought them because they loved that first damn book so much. He got the keys to the kingdom because of that book. He conned everyone into thinking he was a writer, when all he was, was a thief. I find my hands tightening into fists.

'Fuck you, *Pierce.*'

A woman across the aisle looks at me in alarm and I realise I'm muttering the words aloud. A beam of rose-coloured light passes though the carriage, through the woman, surrounding her head with a holy corona, all the shades of a summer dawn.

I'm finally finishing that journey I started thirty-one years ago. I'm going to Whistler Bay to kill Sky. I didn't do it back then of course. I got as far as New York City before I lost my nerve. I got off the train and headed back to Philadelphia. Part of me has always been glad I did. Another part hates myself for my cowardice.

With the new maglev rail, the journey takes half the time it did when I was seventeen. But it's the same: train to Portland, a bus to Castine and a cab out here.

'Nice to see you again,' the cab driver says, which adds to the unreality of it all. He's no more than twenty, must be mistaking me for someone else. I see a soap playing on a little screen set into the dash. Was he talking to the TV? This must be a lonely job.

I expect it to be different somehow – the hill less green, the house less neat and perfect. But Whistler Cottage looks just the same, white like a gull perched up there. I'm the one who's different.

I get out of the cab down in the road. There's the spot, right there, where I found the Polaroid of the Abbott girl.

I try to notice my feelings as I climb the hill (that's more diffi-cult than it was, there's a difference right there). I notice that I feel sweaty and maybe hungry. Big moments are like that sometimes. You wait for the burst of feeling but actually you just kind of want a snack.

In the kitchen, I lean against the wall and breathe.

'Hello again.' I feel my sixteen-year-old self stirring. Time travel. Dusk is falling but I don't turn on a light. Through the window the sun sinks, a copper ball on the sea. Exhaustion creeps up my limbs. It's been a long day and I head for the bedroom, feeling my way along the walls with fingertips. I need to get used to the house.

I could sleep in the master, I suppose, but I don't want to. That's my parents' room. They have both been dead for years, but they still follow me almost everywhere. Or that's what it feels like.

The room is smaller than I remember. There's a soft blue blanket folded at the foot of the single bed. I open the porthole. The restrictors my father put on all those years ago are long gone. I breathe the night air and wait. The sea whispers, faint. It sounds like pages shuffling. A seal barks. I lick a finger and test the breeze. The wind is in the east.

A moment later it comes, mournful and high. The stones are singing and I feel it, at last, that I'm home. I listen for a time, despite my tiredness. I think, *if heartbreak had a sound, it would be just like this*. I imagine what the stones might be saying about me – Wilder Harlow, come back to Whistler Cottage thirty-three years later and just as many pounds heavier, almost blind, to write this book. This time I won't fail.


In the night I wake to a sound like scratching. I close the porthole but the sound continues. I know it's just a branch on a windowpane somewhere down the side of the house – but it sounds like a pen, writing on paper. I recall that first night Sky moved into my dorm room, when I had the nightmare. How he comforted me, kept the light on so I wouldn't be afraid. I fell asleep to the sound of his pen scratching across the page. For a moment there's a beat of warmth in me.

But what was he writing? Skandar's story probably. My warmth evaporates. I imagine that vivid green ink scrawling all over the cottage, the bay, the sky, like marker pen on transparency. Him, marking my stuff. My house, my past, my place. Me.

A long chorus line of small, elven figures dances across the dark before me. They doff their scarlet caps in unison. Their bright eyes flash.

It's called Charles Bonnet syndrome and it often accompanies macular degeneration. That pale spot that developed on my vision during college has been spreading for years. Now the centre is almost entirely white and gone. At the moment I can still see fairly well on the peripheries. The fancy Manhattan doctor Emily took me to told me to prepare myself for a long, slow descent into blindness.

What no one expected were the visions.

The first time I had one, Emily and I were in a restaurant. I saw a wisteria plant growing up the waiter. It captured his waist in its twisting grey branches, spread its delicate purple blossoms all over his head.

The fancy Manhattan doctor thinks that the only thing that prevents this from happening to everyone is the brain being forced to process sight all the time. When there's no more work to do, it goes rogue.

'Try and see this as your mind playing, being free, now that it's not so busy with sight.'

And I did for a second, I really did try to think of my coming blindness as freedom, as an extra ability. Then I felt like kicking him in the nuts.

Anyway I've gotten somewhat used to it. The visions don't frighten me anymore. I can usually tell what's real and what isn't.

*

In the helpful light of morning I do a quick inventory. I have the credit card I took from Emily's wallet and some cash. Not much. It will be enough.

The cottage is decorated in a way I don't recognise. Who chose all this stuff? The bright rag rugs, the white cotton, the rattan furniture. Everything neat and clean. I can't associate it with the grumpy man I speak to on the phone at the rental agency.

Sometimes he mentions 'a girl from town who comes in to help', so I guess she picked all this. I like it.

Uncle Vernon's terrible Polaroids are gone, disappeared somewhere over the years. I kind of miss them. The refrigerator's the new kind with the voice controls and the store cupboards are stocked. Even the instant macaroni cheese I used to like is here. As a teenager I ate it by the bucket. I feel like someone's looking after me. Like maybe Whistler Bay is glad I'm back.


OK. Begin. Time to really kill him.

I get out my old Remington. *Laptops are for taxes and satmails*, I tell myself. *Typewriters are for writing.* The truth is that it's difficult for me to see the screen on a laptop. Typescript on a white page is easier.

I pull my desk out under the old sugar maple. It has grown so tall – it's the only thing around here that looks bigger than it used to. Thirty-three years will grow and shrink you in unexpected ways. I make instant coffee in a pan, on the stove, add milk and take it outside. The coffee's too hot and I burn my lips. Overhead, the leaves whisper.

I couldn't come back here after *The Sound and the Dagger* was published. Not after Sky started renting the big house each summer. The one Harper's parents used to own. What an imagination he had, everyone says so. What a book it was. Even the families of the oil-drum women felt he really captured the atmosphere of the place. The feeling. Their grief.

I still remember how I felt when I first saw a photograph of Sky, here – standing on Main Street in Castine, in front of the place the fishmonger used to be. Christy Barham's old store. It's a VR café now. The kids love them, I hear. I don't get it. Who needs virtual reality when you have books?

Anyway, I was at the dentist, I opened a magazine and there he was, staring at me, hair tousled, russet. It was the summer the book came out. That was a bad one – hot in Pennsylvania but also burning hot inside me, like there were handfuls of coal in my stomach. That day I had an episode in my class on Faulkner. It was, as it turns out, me who lay dying. On the floor. Of the classroom. Bad joke, never mind.

After that Sky came up to the bay every summer. He became famous for it. People used to come here from all over the world, hoping to run into him.


I've had years to think about my time with Sky. There's not a moment I haven't pored over and analysed. And I know why he read *In Search of Lost Time* obsessively throughout the semester, alongside that biography of Proust. He was working out the mechanics of it – how to blend my writing, my truth with his egotistical schlock.

No one knows the truth but they will soon. I have to be smart about this. You can't libel dead people, of course, but you also can't be too careful. I want it published, and widely. Also, even if it can't bother me, I don't want people to think I'm petty. Also some of the stuff that happened might be difficult for Emily to take.

Autofiction indeed.

I stare at the great white expanse of page. I realise that I don't want to start. *Don't go there*, as my students say.

Snow on windowpanes, his touch, sunlight everywhere. *Fucked up will set you free*. I've nailed the first part. Soon, with any luck, I'll be free.


It's not working. I can see it all, glowing in my mind like stained glass. Why can't I write it?

The maple tree whispers. A neon-yellow cloud of songbirds burst from the sea. They drag bright golden script behind them – beautiful, flowing calligraphy. *Wilder, Wilder, Wilder* it says over and over. I close my eyes and count like the doctor showed me. I take deep breaths. When I open my eyes again they're gone.

Even the birds I hallucinate are writing. Why can't I?


I start up, with the sense of someone having just left or maybe touched me gently before running away. Is the gate swaying in the wind? Is there a scent, some acrid tang in the air?

There's a breeze up so when the sound comes again it's still faint enough to be imagination. My first thought is *the stones?* I test the wind with a licked finger, but it's blowing from the south. The next time it comes I'm sure – it's a human voice, calling from the cove below. And on the third I can even make out the words.

'Help, can someone help me?'

I go to the edge as quickly as I can, shade my eyes and stare at the glittering water below. I can just about see a black shape

– a head perhaps, bobbing. It dips beneath the gleaming skin of water, and then reappears. 'Please,' she shouts. 'Help!'

The ground gives with a squelch as I hurry out of the gate. Sand and shale scatter in my wake as I go down the narrow path to the sea. When I reach the little beach I see her more clearly, out at the mouth of the bay where the grey cliffs stop and it turns to open water. Pale face framed by dark hair, slick on her head.

The woman waves with a frantic arm as she disappears beneath the surface once more. I kick my shoes off in the sand and plunge fully dressed into the water. She shouts something indistinct. I think she's getting tired.

'I'm coming!' I yell.

I gasp as the freezing sea reaches my heart. I strike out in a crawl, wheezing with the deathly cold. The waves slap my face, my mouth is filled with frigid salt water. She must have a cramp. Or maybe her leg is caught in something beneath the surface? Old fishing net or something similar. That happened to a child just down the coast a few summers ago; I read about it. I see that she's right next to a pale blue buoy; maybe she's tangled in its rope.

I can make out her features now. A heart-shaped face, full, beautiful lips. She's wearing something dark, not a swimsuit, I don't think. Her shoulders are sharp and shapely through trans-lucent dark linen.

The dress slips off her shoulder and for a horrified moment I think she's wounded. But then I see she has a large birthmark, roughly the shape of an apple with one bite taken out of it, spread-ing dark over one shoulder.

She gasps and spits a jet of water. The dress isn't black, I see, but blue, darker with the water. It billows and floats about her. Her skirts balloon on the waves. So she went in the water fully clothed. That's not a good sign. People don't generally get in the sea in long dresses when everything is going well. But maybe she fell off a cliff or a boat or—

A roller dashes me directly in the face. I cough and sink. For a moment I drop below the cold green horizon. Water rushes by my ears, into my nostrils. I kick up and break the surface, gasping.

She's gone. I can't see her anywhere. She must have grown tired. I've got to be quick. I redouble my efforts, muscles burning with the unexpected strain. When I reach the blue buoy I take a deep breath and dip beneath the surface, peering for a glimpse of fluttering blue linen. There's nothing but clear, still sea.

I'm no longer out of my depth, here. The middle of the bay is deeper than the narrow mouth, which is protected by an underwater sandbank. So when I sink my feet into the soft bottom, the water only reaches my waist. Even if she's much shorter than me, she should have been able to stand here comfortably. Where is she? Frantic, I plunge down again and again, peering in every direction. There's good visibility for some distance. The current isn't strong; I should be able to see her, or at least that billowing blue dress, even at a distance, even beneath the water.

Fear is washing through me, colder than the sea. There must be a riptide somewhere; it caught her, pulled her under, out into the open ocean.

I flail back to the shore and stumble up the path barefoot. From the clifftop, I can see the buoy bobbing on the ocean. No waving arm, no blue-clad form floating face down. She is simply gone – not drowned, because where is the body? – but vanished. I run inside, grab my cellphone and dial 911. The operator is soothing but seems to me unhurried so my voice rises higher and higher in frustration.

'Sir?' she says. 'I need you to breathe?'

It feels like forever, but actually someone is here within the hour.

The coastguard shouts as he rounds the headland in a boat with an outboard motor. I think I expected something more official. As the sun sinks lower he combs the cove and the open sea beyond, but finds nothing. He comes ashore as darkness takes the bay. He's older, with that skin you see round here, cured brown by being on the sea.

I wonder if he was on that boat that day, the day the oil-drum women were found.

'Are you sure it was a person?' he asks. 'Could it have been a plastic bag floating on the surface? The water plays tricks on the eyes.'

'I'm sure,' I say. 'She was calling for help – I saw and heard her quite clearly.'

'Well,' he says. 'The only access way to this cove is to come past your cottage up there, right?'

'Yes.'

'She would have to have come straight past you.'

'That – yes, that's correct.'

'Unless she fell overboard from a boat. And nothing of that nature has been reported.'

'All right,' I say, irritable. I recognise what he's doing; I do it to my worst Great American Lit students all the time – make them state the facts out loud, logic themselves out of their own bad assertions.

'There's always one or two called in each year,' he says. 'Mermaids, sirens. People want to believe those things.'

'It's got a soul of its own, this place,' I say.

'That it does,' he agrees, looking at me with a flicker of interest.

'Were you here when the oil-drum women were found?' I ask.

His expression goes cold. 'You make up that story about a woman drowning so you could call me out, talk to me about that? You got a lot of nerve.'

'No,' I say, horrified. 'Of course not!'

'We get your kind round here all the time. Be aware that you can be charged for making a false report and wasting coastguard resources.' I wonder if this is true.

'She was *there*,' I say. 'I saw her and heard her.'

'You take care,' he says in a tone that says he hopes I don't.


After he leaves I watch the moon on the cove for a time, before the night chill drives me indoors, shivering. I'm really upset. I didn't hallucinate her, I know that.

My condition is strictly a visual one. You don't hear or feel anything, the doctor was very clear on that.

And I heard her voice. *Help.* I always know what's real and what isn't, I tell myself.

The thought that pokes at my mind, like a tongue at a bad tooth is – *I know her somehow, that woman.* I hope she's not dead.


In the kitchen, in the warmth of the range, I take off my wet clothes wearily. I mustn't ruin them, I only brought a couple things with me. Emily is the one with the money. My heart gives a sad little dip. Divorce is such a sundering. Plus, expensive. I can save her that.

After lots of searching and opening and closing of cupboards and once, accidentally shutting myself into the closet under the stairs, I find a wooden rack. I spread the wet clothes over it and put it in front of the stove to dry. Even with the terrible day I've had, I feel a little pleased with myself for having solved this domestic problem.

I gasp myself out of a shallow sleep, fighting the sheets, trying to dispel the dream of being smothered in wet blue linen. I am flooded with that same sense of recognition which visited me earlier tonight – about her, yes, but more – the whole scene is like something I've seen or dreamed: the dress billowing in the cold sea, her cry for help, my cold rescue attempt. I stare into the dark, my heart drumming in my chest. Who was she? Where did she go? And how do I know her? It eats at me until dawn puts pale fingers through the shutters and it's time to start the ghastly business of the day all over again.

A pattern of dashes and diamonds rolls black over the dawn sky.

My pants, underwear and shirt have dried into solid crisp shapes, which still hold the form of the rack after I lift them off. I think they are still wearable. The belt is ruined. The wet leather has shrunk and hardened to the consistency of rock.


I call Emily.

'Yes, Wilder, what is it?' She sounds like she's in a restaurant or some busy place, which is strange: she hates to go out before noon. Or maybe it was me who hated it. That's marriage – you grow into one another like that.

I say without thinking, 'Hello, darling.'

An awful silence falls, a deep plunge of horror and regret. Someone has to break it, so I do. 'I wanted to ask you something.' At least my voice sounds relatively normal, no sign of the hideousness inside me. 'I had a strange exchange with a girl in Castine the other day; she seemed to know me, but I couldn't place her.

I was wondering if she was a girl from the city, maybe? Or from around here and maybe we met her in the city . . .'

Emily takes a breath. 'Describe.' That was a bad moment, but she could never resist gossip.

'Mid-twenties, dark hair, attractive, large birthmark on her shoulder.'

'We don't know anyone like that.' She's eating something as we talk, I can hear it – there's a fullness, a wetness around her words.

'She was wearing a blue dress,' I say. 'She looked kind of like something out of an old Italian movie.'

'Rings no bells,' she says.

'Well thanks for your time,' I say frostily. 'I won't keep you from your lunch any longer.' Though it's barely ten o'clock.

'It sounds like something out of that book you hate.' She takes another bite of whatever it is.

'Emily—' I had thought I was annoyed with her, but it's so easy to mistake one feeling for another. My chest feels spongy, soft with longing, 'Can I come home?'

She clears her throat, that sound I know so well. It has nothing to do with actual throat clearing. It means she's nervous. *Oh no. Ask me anything but that.*

'Where were you that weekend I was in the Hamptons?' she asks.

'We've been through all this.'

'You're still lying.' I feel her withdrawal, cold like an open window in winter.

'It's not a lie!' I'm shouting, I realise.

'Wilder, you need to think about your condition. You need to make preparations.'

'These are my preparations. Writing a book.'

'I can't look after you if you won't look after yourself.' The words have the crack of tears in them. 'I don't think we should speak for a while.'

'Fine.' I hang up before she can reply. I feel so mad I have to walk around the little square of garden three times before I can breathe evenly again. But it's welcome, the hot red rush.

The thing about anger is, you mustn't let it drop or you might find out how you really feel.

As I sit down to work it arrives, diamond-sharp and perfect – the title. The book will be called *The Sound Revisited*.

Oh *dear*. What an awful – what a truly *terrible* – name for a book. It's amazing how good bad ideas can seem in the night. The blinding shaft of light that turns out to be nothing but a mirror-trick.

I try to write. Again, no good. Every so often I cast my eye down at the bay, expecting to see a dash of blue in the water, linen fluttering and trailing like a sea creature. I start at the wind in the trees, on my skin. But all is quiet and the bay remains clear and shining.

In the afternoon, I have a visitor.

I'm staring hard at the sentence I've just written. I've been staring so long it looks like cuneiform.

I look up and she's there, leaning over the white gate, smiling at me. A woman – a reassuringly solid one, this time. She must be cold; there's a bite in the breeze but she wears a voluminous cotton blouse, baggy pants of some rough fabric and a straw sunhat. She's weather-beaten, which speaks of life round here, but the accent doesn't.

'Wilder Harlow.'

'Yes? How can I help you?' I'm so glad to speak to someone, anyone, to escape from staring at that one line of typescript.

The woman looks at me for a second and then says, 'Everything OK with the cottage? To your liking?' She's British. There will be a story there, no doubt. Maybe I'll ask her in for a cup of stove coffee. There's something I like about her.

'Oh, yes!' I say. 'Everything is great in the cottage, thank you.' I realise that this must be the girl from town who 'comes in to help.'

'I stocked the kitchen with your favourite things. I even found some of that disgusting instant macaroni cheese you used to like.' She sighs. 'That was a million years ago. I imagine you don't like it anymore.'

'I do still like it,' I say. 'Some things never ever change and one of those is macaroni cheese. But you—' A terrible suspicion is dawning. She takes off her hat, and her hair is grey, but there's something about the shape of her head, and then I see that the grey is streaked with red.

'Oh my god. Harper?'

She smiles.

I go to the fence, give her a pat on the shoulder and an awkward kiss on the cheek. Her face is still broad, her wide gaze that of a child. But she's missing that air of cunning, of assurance that enveloped her when she was younger. Age strips us of our certainties, I suppose.

She takes my face and turns it this way and that. It's a weird thing for someone to do, who is to all intents and purposes a stranger. But it doesn't feel weird. I can't stop looking at her either, tracing the lines of her old self in her adult face.

'I'm so sorry,' I say. 'I don't see so well.'

'Well, you've not changed at all,' she says, which I know to be untrue, but she has the grace to sound sincere.

'Yes, it's a pity.'

She starts to laugh then stops abruptly, watching me. 'Do you have everything you need? They only told me you were coming at the last minute, I had to stock the cupboards quickly.'

'Why were you stocking my cupboards?'

'I help people out with things round here – cleaning, cooking, shopping. Taking care of the summer houses in the winter, and so on. It's easy enough, mindless.'

I feel the sting of awkwardness. 'But you – what happened?'

'To all the money, you mean?' She smiles. 'My family and I – we had some differences of opinion. They don't speak to me anymore. And I don't want to speak to them.' She sees my look. 'Those were hard years, after it all happened, Wilder. I fell back into some bad habits. And picked up some new ones. They decided they'd had enough. I can't blame them, really. I was pretty vile.'

'Where are you living?'

'Down on the water, up from Castine.'

'Near—'

'I couldn't afford much. It's the old Pelletier place. Or it was. It's mine now.'

Horror is all through me. 'Harper, why there?'

'Don't, Wilder,' she says, quiet and firm. 'It's the right place for me. It reminds me of him. Besides, I've made it nice.'

There's something extra upper class, something brittle about her Britishness, now. I've observed this in some of them who settle in the US. Their accents become more pronounced, their speech becomes more and more liberally peppered with those quaint phrases, as if they're afraid their identity will be fatally diluted by contact with us.

'I thought I'd never see you again,' I say. And at the same time she says 'So, I've come to call.' We're both awkward and hectic, we can't get the cadence of conversation going.

'No, no change in you whatsoever.' Harper unlatches the gate, uninvited, and comes into the garden. She leaps up into the arms of the maple and sits in the crook of the tree. The leafshadow chases across her face. She hasn't really changed at all, I realise.

'Come on in,' I say. 'Have a seat. Stay a while.'

She grins and just for an instant I am quite in love with her again.

'Why are we back here, both of us?' I ask. 'Why are we such gluttons for punishment?'

'Maybe everything we do after the age of sixteen is just a kind of rehash.'

Silence falls between us. There is too much to talk about.

Harper reaches out her foot and touches me lightly on the knee with her toe. 'Welcome back, you old git.'

'Thank you.' I am oddly moved.

'I've read one of his books,' Harper says. 'Not *that* one, another one. What was it called? *The Wallaby*?' I feel a punch of resentment. Sky's everywhere, it seems.

'*The Platypus*,' I said. 'I don't really read horror. Not my thing.'

'The one about the man who accidentally kills everyone he loves. I thought, "this is a lonely person". Did he mean to show how lonely he was – in the book?'

'Hey,' I say to change the subject. 'Do kids still come out here to swim?'

'No, I mean, I don't think so. There are far better beaches on the other side of town. Didn't you know him? Sky Montague?'

'We were at the same college, at around the same time, many years ago. I wouldn't say I knew him.'

'It must be strange – someone you went to college with, getting so famous.'

'As I said, I really didn't know him.'

'We saw him round here sometimes. Our local celebrity. No one seems to have spoken to him properly though. Seems like the more famous you are, the fewer friends you have.'

'By that logic, I must have thousands of friends.'

'Yes, you're swimming in them.' Harper looks around. 'You're alone, Wilder? No wife or children?'

'No.'

'Autumn's well underway. Winter comes on fast in these parts.' She pauses, watching, but I don't answer. 'If you're planning to stay that long you might want to think about putting the storm shutters up again, insulating the pipes, getting some tins in for power cuts and so on.'

I don't take the bait. 'Thanks for the advice.'

'Well, home for tea, I suppose. I'm off, you old plonker.'

'See you later, you old, old—' But I find that I am bent double, gasping. The world becomes vague and I fall to my hands and knees. The ground seems spongy, too soft for support and I think, *this isn't real, none of it is, it's not right that such pain can be real.*

'All right. Come here. You're all right.' She sits me up gently; her understanding is more than I can bear. The fist in my chest squeezes ever tighter. I touch a hand to my cheek – it comes away wet. I'm crying, it seems. This is terrible – what is happening? Harper comes up close, far too close. The concern on her face is appalling.

I realise that I haven't been touched by another living being in days – not since it happened. That's a wonderful thing about marriage – the casual, day-to-day intimacy, those little glancing moments of closeness. Fingers grazing as I hand Emily a dish, wet with suds. A kiss planted on the top of my head as I squint over an exam paper. Brushing past one another in the narrow hallway as we hurry in opposite directions. One becomes so quickly accustomed to it – the thousand touches that make up a day.

'What's wrong, Wilder?'

'I don't know how to start my book,' I say. 'And I think I saw a ghost.' I watch in fascination as a bright green frog leaps gracefully from her shoulder.

'Wilder,' she says. 'You – don't seem too well.'

'I didn't imagine it.'

'Ghosts don't exist,' she says gently. 'They're just your mind telling you things you don't want to know.'

Her words land like tumblers falling into place. I stare at her. 'You're a genius, Harper.'

She makes a sound of disgust.

I hardly hear her leave; I'm bent over the typewriter. The keys fly. That's it.

Autofiction. *Tell all the truth but tell it slant.* That's what my unconscious mind was trying to tell me when it showed me the drowning woman. It was a kind of waking dream, perhaps. Or maybe (and I would never admit this to the coastguard) I did mistake some floating debris for her . . .

The reason she seemed so familiar, the woman, is that she looked a little like Sky. Different colouring, but even so, there was something about the nose . . . anyway, here's the thing.

The book isn't about Sky, it's about *Skye.* A woman. It unlocks everything and resolves all those pesky issues of libel. It solves the other problem, too, which I've been worrying over – how to write *around* those certain aspects of what happened between us. They don't belong in this book, which is all about the theft.

You know, I can see her – Skye. I can even hear her voice. It's as if she's been waiting down in the dark all this time – for me to bring her up, into the light.

How about simply *Skye*? I kind of like that. I'll set it in 1991 – exactly as it happened.

# *Skye*

She gets her chance the first day in class. The room has that particular smell of new textbooks and marker pen. The professor has oatmeal on his tie and an air of despair.

Skye sees him right away. In her head, he's just *him*. He's not a person, doesn't get a name. He's just a force she's chasing, a long-sought destination.

She doesn't sit right by him, of course not. She doesn't approach. She's not an idiot. She sits in the row behind. She watches the back of his neck. It's an overlooked area, the back of the neck. It is very expressive. His is no different.

He is very pale, and the flush that steals over it is revealing. He flushes a lot. Not from embarrassment, she realises, but from tension, a particular kind – the effort of keeping things together. Skye recognises that.

The professor puts a transparency on the projector, an arched window with stained glass the colour of jewels. A unicorn, wings, a sword. The dark classroom becomes a cave with a mouth of vivid light. No sooner has Skye had this thought than she draws in her breath and looks at him.

She is right, he has had the thought too. In the dim she can see his head is bowed, neck thrust forward like a vulture's. His breath is heavy, like someone just falling asleep, but that's not what's happening. He gets up, arms outstretched like a blind person. He seems drunk, can't get out of the raked seating of the lecture hall. He pushes hard past a girl who cries out – not from hurt, but surprise. He makes an anguished noise and shoves harder past legs, hands groping for purchase on the desk, sending books and pens flying.

Skye gets up quickly. The light flares all around; the professor has turned it on. 'Young man,' he says to Wilder. 'Please sit back down.'

Wilder waves his hand and then covers his mouth with it. Skye realises what is about to happen, and slips out of her seat. In an instant she is by his side, holding his elbow.

'I know him from home,' she says. 'It's a panic attack. I'll take him outside. He'll be fine in a little while.'

She manages to get him to a bench in the sunshine on the other side of the quad. She can hear the river rushing somewhere behind them.

In the end he doesn't throw up. He leans back, turns his face to the sun. He seems exhausted.

It's strange being near him, this person she has thought so much about. He looks alien in photographs – with those pale eyes, barely grey or blue, almost the colour of his white skin, made whiter by the contrast of very dark hair. In photographs those protruding eyes look menacing. In person he just looks young. Somewhat fragile. He opens his mouth, gasps. She sees he has gum in there. She realises he might choke so she hooks it out quickly with a finger. It's bright pink. She sits there with it on her finger, still warm. After a moment's thought she puts it in her mouth. For a moment it tastes of him, clean and slightly alkaline. Then it's just a piece of gum. She tears a piece of paper from her notebook and wraps it up, puts it in her pocket.

When she looks back at him he's watching her.

'Hey,' she says. 'You OK?'

'You again,' he says. 'We met on the steps outside the dorm the day we got here. You were with your dad.'

She nods. 'That's right.'

'You didn't help.'

'No, I guess I'm not very helpful,' she says.

'You've been helpful to me,' he says, awkwardly. 'Thanks.' After a moment he says, 'I'm Wilder,' and offers a hand to shake.

She takes it. 'Like Thornton Wilder?'

'Yes.'

'I'm Skye.'

'It suits you,' he says, and smiles. 'You have very shiny hair, like a horse's hide.'

'Thank you.' She smiles back, the widest and sunniest of smiles, one that comes right up from the depths of her. *Oh no*, she thinks, torn between exhilaration and horror.


She says to Elodie, '*Je peux payer.*' Elodie nods briefly. They haggle a little but it's a deal easily done. She moves her stuff into Elodie's single room. She can feel his presence through the wall.

It's located in what the more affluent freshmen call the orphanage – this is the wing where they put the scholarship and exchange students. It overlooks the kitchens and everything smells like meatloaf. No one parties hard in the orphanage – these students are here to work. The rooms are small, cramped; there's only room for one bed in most of them.

Skye's allocated room is way better, on the front quad. She shares with a hockey-playing girl who eats boiled eggs in bed but the room is warm and good and smells like beeswax and cleanliness so on top of the hundred dollars Skye gives her, she doesn't think Elodie is getting a bad deal in the trade.

Sometimes as Skye lies here at night she can feel him through the wall, breathing, those big lantern eyes lidded in sleep. She knows he doesn't lock his door at night. She knows the sound of his lock, a stiff sludgy click. She has memorised it, along with all his sounds.

She runs through when she hears it, the dream. He's sweating, eyes open and staring, not seeing this world. He doesn't seem surprised, or even aware of a strange girl in his room.

She puts an arm around him the way one would a child. She feels it as he slowly returns to his body.

'I need this,' he says and reaches into his bedside cubby. It's a binder with a picture of Aphrodite on it. Inside are newspaper clippings, each one encased in plastic.

Skye's breath seizes in her throat. She knows each one, could recite each article from memory. She doesn't say anything.

He stares at the clippings. 'I expect you think I'm a weirdo, reading about murders after I have a nightmare.'

'No more than me,' she says honestly. 'When I can't sleep I plan my suicide.'

'Really?'

'Really.'

'What did you go for?'

'Drowning,' she says. 'It's pretty painless.'

'What about hemlock?' he asks. 'Totally pain-free. And it grows

209

everywhere. It looks kind of like a carrot.' After a pause he says, 'I didn't know you were next door. That's a weird coincidence.'

She shrugs. 'Sometimes the universe moves in your favour,' she says. 'Just once in a while.'

Their smile holds, the warm feeling dips and grows. He looks down, suddenly abashed. 'I'm OK now,' he says. 'You can go.'

'I can hang out a little,' Skye replies. 'What's that?' She reaches out. Behind the clippings at the back of the binder there are lined pages. Typing, not newsprint.

He flushes and she feels the sudden lurch of intimacy. 'I'm writing something.'

He covers the pages quickly with newsprint. She knows she has to read whatever this is. On the one exposed corner she reads: . . . *is hauled from the deep. The divers lug it up* . . . The top of the *l* key is missing. It looks like an *i*.

He looks at her for a moment. Then he slowly pulls the pages from the binder and hands them to her.

Her heart beats fast – how can it be this easy?

'This is why I have the dreams,' he says, shy. 'You've been kind, you deserve to know why you're getting woken up all the time. If you want to.'

*The Dagger Man of Whistler Bay*, the title page says. *By Wilder Harlow.*

She reads like someone starving, keeping her face neutral. By the time she's finished, dawn is coming in over the kitchen and she can smell sausage.

'Thank you,' she says to Wilder. She kisses him once on the cheek. He starts but permits it.

She goes back to her room and gets out her pen, fills it with her favourite grass-green ink. She writes it all down quickly before she forgets any detail of what he wrote. But not just that – what he said, what she said back, the shape his knee made, crooked beneath the sheet, the particular sheen of sweat on his brow, carried from the dream back into the waking world. How he didn't flinch or react to her physical presence at all, even when she sat on the bed and leaned close to test him. To breathe him.

Being right next door to him is good; the walls are so thin they feel at times like porous skin. But it goes both ways. He can hear her too and she needs privacy. She needs company at night sometimes.

She has learned to do her crying elsewhere, in measured bursts. That's private, too. Sometimes she sits in coffee shops with her Walkman, earphones in. Then she cries. People don't question it so much if there's something playing in her ears. But what they don't realise is that she's not sad, all that was burnt out of her long ago – she's gone. What they're looking at is the charred case for her rage.

If he's next door she becomes alive, a trembling mast, every fibre alert for his movements, his coughing. His dreams. Observing someone so closely – it's very like being in love. No wonder she gets the two confused, she tells herself.

It's just transference. Wilder is the gateway. It's not him she really wants to be around. This is stray love, orphaned love, vagrant love looking for a home – for its belonging place. She knows all this.

But she finds herself thinking of his hands all the same – and laughing a little in the middle of a test, when she thinks of how he can't bring himself to say the word *fuck*.

'I've been thinking about you,' she says the next day. She hears him catch his breath. They're lying on her bed with their legs propped up against the wall. Her feet rest on a Pearl Jam poster, right on Eddie Vedder's face.

'What were you thinking?'

'You could try sleeping somewhere else,' she says. 'If you have enough nightmares in a room they kind of sink into the walls. Try different places.'

'Like where?'

'There's this storage room for old props,' she says. 'Try sleeping somewhere like that.'

When she sees him the next morning he's letting himself into his room, shadowy eyes haunted.

'The security guard nearly caught me in that old shed this morning,' he says, almost mad at her, and she can't stop laughing.

'I didn't think you'd actually do it,' she says.

'Oh, frick you. I need a shower.'

'Did it work, though?'

'I didn't have any dreams,' he says reluctantly.

So she can make him do it again.


She's got a lot of material, but she needs more, she tells herself. She doesn't know what that *more* is, until they see the news item on the big TV in the common room. Alton Pelletier is refusing to see visitors. He won't see Christy Barham's mother. And here, she realises, is the perfect end to her book.

'I think he would see you,' she says to Wilder. He is even paler than usual; he's holding back a panic attack.

She looks at him carefully, sees how close he is to the edge.

So she decides not to push it, not just yet. Not like this. At some point, she couldn't identify it, he has transformed from *him* into Wilder.

In her room Skye stretches lazily and listens to Wilder clattering next door. Undressing, getting ready for the trek to the spider-ridden showers. Her bed still holds the warm contours of her most recent visitor. She found him at last call in a bar in town the night before, didn't need his name. She took his credit card from his pants pocket on a whim, but she knows she can't use it. Too easily traced back to her. So it's the hunt today.

She picks a café on the other side of town. It's in a bookstore, which is good – those kinds of people tend to be absentminded. Easily lost to the world.

In the store she spends a moment drawing her hands along the spines in her favourite section. The covers are dark, on these shelves. The titles shine out like neon lights. These books tell the truth about life. The horror.

Skye has spent everything she has on the plan so she has to supplement her funds. And she has to be strategic. Never steal from students, never near the college. Cash where possible. She sees him across the room. Big, mid-forties, the pouched face of someone who drinks their feelings.

She drops her notebook at his feet as she passes. 'Oh, sorry,' she says. 'I'm such a klutz.'

Skye manages to walk fairly normally across the quad, holding a pile of books in front of her face. Getting to her room is a relief.

After that she sits and waits. Not long now. Wilder always comes by after his English Lit class.

He knocks and opens the door all in one instant. They've got a familiar way between them now. Skye would know it was Wilder without looking up, even if she wasn't expecting him. She can smell him the way wild animals smell prey.

She feels the shock run through him when he sees her face. The rusted trail of blood down her philtrum, the lush velvet of the bruise around her eye.

She'll hold it inside her forever, the feel of the brick against her back, the smell of the dumpster, the sound of traffic fifty feet away, in another world. The expression on the guy's face, the almost comical surprise when she asked him to hit her. He was reluctant at first. 'Honestly,' she said. 'You'd be doing me a favour. It's for a science project.' Who would believe such a thing? She picked well; she sensed it in him.

The moment, the flicker in his face, when he realised he enjoyed it.

She wasn't sure he would stop so in the end she ran, spatters of blood flying from her nose behind her. She's not even sure he ran after her. It was a valuable lesson. Power turns on a dime, can be exchanged or lost in an instant. She will be more careful in future.

But when he finds his credit card is gone he won't report her. There is that.

'Who did this to you?' Wilder says again. She realises, in surprise, that he is close to tears.

'I had a fight with my dad,' she whispers into his ear.

Wilder's horror, his indrawn breath, sends shivers of excitement down her. His arms are warm and good. She puts her cheek against his even though it hurts. Just for this moment, she allows herself to feel this, and nothing more.

He cleans her face tenderly but clumsily. The wet cloth stings on her bruises.

'You must never see him again,' he says. Skye has persuaded him, just, out of reporting it to the police.

'I think you should write to him,' she says. The lamplight is low. Despite the Advil her wounds pulse in her, aching. With him so close, with such attention to her physical being, she's getting mixed up. It's almost like that other feeling, that low level hum, that need.

'Write to who?'

'Alton Pelletier.'

His being goes still. 'Why would you say that?'

*Careful*, she thinks. *Tread carefully*. This afternoon's experience has left her wary. Of course Wilder won't hit her. Of course he would never. But things turn on a dime, don't they?

'Men who hurt people shouldn't get away with it,' she says, fierce. 'I'm too much of a coward to even hold my dad to account. But Alton . . . you could ask him who they are. The women they haven't identified. You could make him confront himself. Hold him to account.'

'He wouldn't tell me any of that,' Wilder says. The cloth he's holding is stained with her blood.

'But he might.'

'Just leave it, Skye,' he says, because he knows she's right. Somehow, they both know. Alton will see Wilder. If he asks the right way.

[ ]

Hello
Hell
Help

# Wilder, Day Four

*Skandar reached his hand out to the woman. Her dress billowed about her in the water. 'Reach for me,' he said urgently. 'Reach for my hand.' The woman opened her mouth as if to scream. Her throat opened wider and wider. He saw, too late, that in her mouth was a tiny, lit-up scene – a family picnicking on a beach.*

*'Who are you?' he asked, desperate.*

*'Rebecca,' came the answer. Her voice was the grinding of metal on stone.*

*The Sound and the Dagger*, by Sky Montague

I'm up with the dawn – I fetch the typewriter, pull the table outside under the maple, facing the bay. It's been an excellent, excellent couple of days, and I feel this will be another one. I admit, it's turning into more of a novel than I had anticipated. She seems to be running away with the story, Skye.

I always had this feeling, this knowledge that after Sky died, I would be able to write again. I hoped, I prayed it would be true, and it is.

I love typing on the Remington, love the sound of it, the rattle and clack as thoughts make their way through my fingertips and become fixed on the page. I know I should get it fixed but I like the broken *l*. It's been that way for so long, it feels like part of my personality now.

I'll do it as soon as it's finished. How, though? The oven range is the kind that's always on. Even if I knew how to turn it off, it's not gas. So that's out of the question – no Sylvia Plath for me.

I've measured the drop from the most robust branch of the maple tree – I don't think it's high enough. Besides, I don't know how to tie those noose doodads you always see in the movies. I can't stand knives and blades and blood and that kind of thing so strike that from the list. Suffocation? Duct tape, a plastic bag over the head? I don't trust myself not to change my mind.

The obvious answer is out there through the window, lapping at the cliffs below, of course. The sea. But ever since I saw the woman I've known it won't be the sea. What if, after I load my pockets with stones and wade into the deep, I open my eyes, and come face to face with her? Blue linen billowing about her face, arms reaching for me. What if I'm wrong and she is a ghost? What if I die but she keeps me here, trapped forever in her arms, listening to the whistling of the bay? Odd how some things are more frightening than even the prospect of death. So no Virginia Woolf, either.

It will be pills, I suppose. I have Emily's prescription, grabbed as I was leaving the apartment. The box has a reassuring number of warnings on it. I'll get some vodka, too, to help things along. And perhaps I'll sit in a full bathtub? I don't know, it all sounds so stressful.

I won't leave a note – I'll call Emily just before I do it and give her my instructions. Maybe I'll get the answering machine – that would be best, really.

*

'Our time has run out, Wilder,' Emily said. As though time were milk in the refrigerator and we needed to go to the store. I knew she meant it; she never calls me Wilder, but Will. That never sat right to me – the name always felt like a kind of disguise. It has been stripped from me now; she hasn't called me Will since we parted. It sounds cold in her voice – *Wilder*.

These days *Wilder* makes me think of an oldish man in a bow tie – then I catch a glimpse of the bow tie at my neck, feel the beginnings of a paunch and realise with a dull thud, *but that's me. That's what I am.*

Why don't they make recordings of someone breathing? I miss the sound in the night. There can be comfort in a disguise. Being who you are can be lonely.

This evening is cool. The little kerchief of lawn is covered in red leaves. I rake them and make a small bonfire on the cliff, away from the maple's spreading limbs. Smoke climbs into the dusk in a spire. Like a signal, out to sea.

There's a shout from down in the bay. I run to the cliffside and peer over. Two kids kayak past the cove in neon lifejackets. They're laughing. Is there something behind them? A dark head perhaps, bobbing in the water? I strain and lean forward and for a terrible second I lose my balance. The long rock fall pulls at me.

I gasp and grab clumps of turf, steady myself. I nearly went over. *That would be a way to do it*, I think. But how certain could I be that I would die? I imagine lying at the foot of the cliff, maimed and broken, until I die of exposure or someone finds me.

No.

*

Dinner is macaroni cheese, very delicious, though there is a little purple fire burning in the middle of the plate.

Afterwards I sit with the green fountain pen and paper. I practise all night, using his writing in the manuscript for comparison. The pile of paper is growing at my elbow. The ink is as green as grass, as green as wickedness.

It's kind of, how would you put it, character work. Actors do the same thing. I find it helps me get into his mindset, remembering things Sky said, writing them down with the kind of pen he used, imitating his penmanship as closely as possible. It brings stuff back. Odd little moments. Notes from the dead to the living.

*Fucked up will set you free*, says one. I pick up another note. *Getting close now*, it says. The next one just says, *I'm here*.

'No you're not,' I say aloud. 'You're nowhere. Dead. Gone.'

I leaf through the MS of *The Sound and the Dagger*. Every time the past comes up to tap me on the shoulder, and I risk feeling anything but rage, I read the descriptions of Wiley.

*Even in sleep, there was always a suppressed rage about him. Nothing makes a man so angry as knowing that he's part of the wallpaper.*

I replace the page with a shaking hand. No matter how many years pass, those words will always be a wound to the heart. Did he really think of me that way?

'I'm not part of the wallpaper,' I say aloud. My voice is startlingly loud in the quiet kitchen and I realise how long I've been alone.

Something flutters from the table. One of my green notes. *I'm sorry, Wilder.*

This one is particularly well done. I've really captured his handwriting, the wild scrawl. But of course this is the impossible note – it says what Sky would never write. He was never sorry for what he did.

# Wilder, Day Five

*Helen wore the pain of the past on her like an extra skin. Her hair was red as an alarm.*

*The Sound and the Dagger*, by Sky Montague

I come to, realising I can't see the page in front of me anymore. I don't know what time it is but dark is almost here. My fingers are numb with cold.

Have I made myself too likeable? But Sky must have liked something in me. Surely I have to start there. Am I making Skye too unlikable? That also needs thinking on. People forgive male characters for that – everyone loves an antihero. Less so with women, I've noticed.

I grab a coat and go into the garden. The moon is a silver dime, the sea shines black and white and broken under its beams. But clouds are gathering close in the distance. The air is icy. I feel the past around me.

As I get older I see more and more how fluid a thing time is. There are so many ways to slip in and out of it. The wonder is that we ever stick in the now.

You can't write someone you can't feel for. Telling the story from her point of view makes it, oddly, mine. I have to know her. Sky's voice is in my mind, clear through the years. *Reading that was like being inside you.* The air smelled of snow that night too.

I stop. A voice calls from down in the bay.

'Help,' she calls. 'Help!'

I grab a flashlight, run down and shine it onto the water of the cove. It's still and black as oil (*oil drums*). 'Help!' the voice calls faintly. But there's no one there.

I run inside and slam the door.

*Ghost*
*Host*
*Most*

Taking the word apart makes me feel a little better. Because of course she wasn't a ghost. She was a manifestation of my creative self.

A little nagging voice in my depths.

*So why does she need help?*

Problems this morning. The typewriter ribbon is beginning to run out. I can tell because when it gets worn the ink fades from black through all the colours of the spectrum. Right now it's a kind of deep green. I know from experience that it will turn blue, then grey, then fade altogether.

I swear I brought a replacement with me from New York but I

can't find it anywhere. I turn my drawers and briefcase inside out. But there isn't one. How irritating.

I give up on the hunt for the typewriter ribbon and take a notebook outside. The pages whip cheerfully in the wind.

My writer's block has lasted thirty-two years. I've tried, believe me. I've written many, many failed books. Failed or not, each book has a different nature and they like you to respect that, as you write them. You can't hustle a slow, deliberate book for instance, and you have to write that jaunty little comedy in a sidewalk café. In that respect Skye's character is perplexing. It requires me to see everything backwards, as if the camera had turned around to shoot the scene from another angle. The book is a mirror and I am stepping through the looking glass.


Even half asleep I recognise the sound. I think, *oh, they do make recordings of breathing after all. I am loved. Being loved tells me who I am.* I struggle towards consciousness, fighting off the black slumber that holds me. *That's not a recording.* I feel it, the warmth of a body at my back, one arm flung over me. A sleepy hand strokes my chest. I'm filled with a joy so sharp it makes me gasp. The hand trails up over my arm, my shoulder and taps me twice, as if to say, *follow me. Wait*, I think, *wait, I'm coming.*

Moonlight reflects on the snow outside. I'm filled with new feeling, the world is new.

I turn to face him, to pursue. The porthole casts a pale circle on the bed, a spotlight. His back is so familiar, that russet head. I pull his shoulder and turn him to me. Beneath the sleek hair there is no face, just a green S.

I wake shuddering. It hurts to pull myself away from that old grief, away from the memory of snow on windowpanes. None of that stuff is going into the book, of course. It's really not the story. The story of *Skye* is the theft.

Anyway that's often what writing is, isn't it? What you leave out.


In a way, I'm sorry he took the matter out of my hands because I meant to kill him one day – Sky. At least, I think I did. I used to fantasize about it. I would plot his end, the way I plan my own now.

I plan every detail. It goes, as they say, a little something like this.

I wait until Emily's out of town. She loves the Hamptons at this time of year, says it's less vulgar than at high summer when just anyone goes.

I take the train to Portland, the bus to Castine and then a taxi out to the cottage. The taxi is the risky part, but surely with the glut of visitors I won't stand out too much. The cottage is vacant, I've made sure of that. I feel a rush of homecoming, as I climb the hill and see the cottage perched on the hill above me, a white gull.

The catch is loose on the porthole window on the seaward side. The rental agency is always complaining about it. I open the window and slip inside. I don't do it with the grace I once did – perhaps I even stick a little, around the middle. But a few heaves and I'm through. The house greets me with dim silence.

I know Sky's habits, I've read about them often enough. He talks endlessly to journalists about his 'process'.

Every morning in the dawn he takes a walk from Harper's house (that will always be how I think of it, no matter how often he stays there) along the coastal path, which leads past Whistler Cottage. I wait.

When the time comes I go out to the maple tree, watch as

ribbons of mist melt into silver above the sea. I'll know him when he approaches, even with my sight failing. There are some things that fix forever inside you. His tread, the way he breathes. I can feel him like a storm coming.

A figure approaches, dark on the mist.

I step out from behind the tree and smile. He hesitates, and then recognition spreads all through him. He stops short and neither of us speaks for a moment. What will happen?

'You got old,' he says.

'So did you,' I say, though I can't really see him in detail. I can make out the silver streaks through his russet hair.

'I missed you,' I say quietly.

'I—' he says, at a loss for words, for once. 'I . . .'

I go to him slowly. I take his head in my hands and kiss his crooked mouth. His breath is soft on my cheek. Our lips part and I gently, softly pass the hemlock, the thinnest, merest sliver of it, into his warm mouth with my tongue.

We walk on together for half a mile or so before we both begin to stagger. Sky grabs my arm. I feel the surprise all through his body, feel it turn to fear.

Of course, this is idle thought. I couldn't write my book if I were dead.

I drift gently into sleep, thinking of other ways I would have done it.

*Ayuh*, says a voice. A dark figure stands in the corner of the room. His eyes are large and black. In his hand, there shines a boat hook. He takes one step forward into the stormlight. *You from away?*

Water drips from his rubber coat, his boots, pools on the floor. Fish blood trails down his jacket, a spray of brains.

I turn the light on, gasping. I feel the blackness threaten to take me, in a way it hasn't, not for many years. *Breathe*, I tell myself. *Breathe*. It had Alton's words in its mouth, but it wasn't him. The eyes were different – pitch black where they should be blue. And he never wore that wet weather gear that I saw.

Even so, it runs through my mind. *Maybe he's not dead.*

So I check it on the satellite news archives on my phone, tapping the keys with shaky hands, waiting anxiously for the results to load. There it is, in black and white. He killed himself by swallowing cement. The virtual news archive is a wonderful thing. *Eat it*, I whisper to myself, staring at the lit square of the screen, where the cursor pulses. I should feel better but I'm still shaking.

I go down to the kitchen and I take up a heavy cast-iron skillet. I haven't done this in years. Living with someone prevents you, in general. But it always used to calm me down.

I raise the skillet and take aim. Then I slam it into my leg. Yes, that's it. I do it again and again. Crack. The flesh smarts, reddens, then numbs. My legs sing with pain; I hit myself harder. I can hear my own panting, hear the blows on flesh, but it seems far away. I do it and do it and do it, until all the world sings and I am the only thing that exists, right at the centre of everything.

There will be bruises tomorrow. But there's a still place at my centre now. I feel clear.

It wasn't Alton, I tell myself again, and this time I believe it. He carried a boat hook, sure. But the face was different. The voice was wrong. His eyes, especially, belonged on a different man. They weren't warm blue in a leathery face. Those black eyes, that white face – they were those of a stranger. He looked a little like

Sky too, I realise. No surprise there; Sky is rarely far from my thoughts these days.

It was just my mind, making pictures on the dark. Old fears, reaching long fingers up from the pit of the past. Did I really expect that there would be no consequences, when I decided to open the coffin of the past and poke at its corpse?

Ooh. Good line.

I go to the typewriter. The keys fly, deafening, hypnotic. The world vanishes.

# *Skye*

When Wilder wakes up on a Sunday morning, he usually knocks on Skye's wall to rouse her. Then they take a walk together – a long one that helps fill the short winter day.

Skye is up early, transcribing her notes. She writes all her observations down in shorthand with her green pen, while Wilder's not looking. Normally she writes in her copy of *In Search of Lost Time* – it looks like she's making notes on her reading. If she doesn't have that with her any surface will do – her takeaway coffee cup, her bus ticket. Once she untucked her shirttail to scribble *sexually ambivalent* on it, then tucked it in quickly when he turned around. When she gets back to her room she adds it all to her big file.

Alton's letter is open on the bed beside her. Skye developed the habit of going through Wilder's mail early on – this morning it paid off. She knew what it was right away: it's stamped with the name of the prison, the sender's name on the back in black and white.

*Dear Wilder,*
*It was a pleasure to get your male. Of course I remmember*
*you.*

*First thank you for being strait with me. Second do not be
ashamed of your urges. If they are your true feelings then you
are just being honust with yourself. What is normal anyway?
You are and always have been a good frend to my son and I
know he was fond of you.*

*I wuld be OK for you to visit if it is soon. they say they move
me next month an I dont think there will be receeving visiters
at the new place. We can go over old times. I would be happy to
answer your questins if I can. I feel like if you are being honest
with yourself like this, then it makes me think I can do the
same. We can continue to write after I am moved. We will get to
know each other more.*

*Thank you for your kind words about Nathaniel. I mist my
son very much these last months. You know they dint even let
me see him before died.*

*Yrs*
*A. Pelletier*

Skye holds the letter with her fingertips. In the corner, the writing paper has a little cowboy on a rearing horse. She feels like it
will burn her or poison her. She's sorry she made Wilder write.
She doesn't need to put him through this, she has what she needs.
She's going to destroy the letter, but first, she's going to copy it
out, word for word.

She puts the letter in the drawer in her bedside table, beside
the doll of human, copper hair. Teeth for eyes. Her own baby
teeth, actually. A single, unset pearl for a navel.

She starts at the sharp rat-a-tat-tat of knuckles on the thin room
divider. She doesn't answer; lets him wait. After a minute he knocks
again. Again, she draws out the pause. Then she knocks back.

They open their doors at almost the same moment, like in one of those British farces. His scarf covers the lower half of his face, making his eyes look even larger and less human than usual.

They've established a regular route around the top of Pursing Hill. It's bleak in winter, the trees bare, the crows cawing their ragged secrets to one another. Skye prefers this to a beautiful landscape, to sunshine. This kind of weather doesn't demand happiness from her. It's relaxing.

When they reach the fork in the path and she starts along their usual route, he touches her elbow. 'Let's go the other way today,' he says.

'Why?'

'I want to show you something.' Briefly, hysterically, she wonders if he's going to kill her. She often wonders this about people. More often than she should, she guesses. It's a side effect of spending all your time thinking about murder.

Each bramble and branch carries a fine burden of snow. Glossy ice frames the leaves. Even with the grim steel bowl of sky overhead, it's beautiful.

Wilder bends double every now and again, peering into the undergrowth.

'What are you looking for?'

'You'll see,' he says. He's excited, she can feel it coming off him in waves. His pale skin has rare colour, flushed to the shade of pale peony. He looks almost living, for once. She resists the urge to touch his cheek.

He shouts with happiness, crouching over a thicket of thorns. She can see there's something coming out of the ground there, a frilly, lacy fall of startling green.

'What is it?'

'The day we met you said that when you were scared in the night, what made you feel safe was imagining killing yourself.'

'Right.'

'By drowning.'

'Wilder—'

'I told you I had a better idea. Look,' he says and takes something from his pocket. It's a page ripped from an encyclopaedia.

'You can't do that,' she says, amused. 'They're library books – for everyone, you know?'

He points to the picture, and to the little fall of green. 'This is the same plant, right?'

'It could be.'

'It is,' he says triumphant. 'It's hemlock. It matches the picture. If we pull it up, it'll look just like this. A white carrot. Now you always know it's here.'

'Why would you show me this?'

'No one can stop you doing it,' he says. 'If you really want to. But I thought, maybe – if you know where the plant is, you'd always have the plan ready. You could always feel safe.'

It makes an odd kind of sense. She stares at the green fronds in their ice casket. Absentmindedly, she reaches to touch it.

He makes an alarmed sound. But her fingers stop short of the ice. Would it be enough to kill her, this casual contact? She doesn't know.

'It's my present to you,' Wilder says.

'It's the weirdest gift I've ever heard of.'

'Do you like it?'

'I like it.' She's overwhelmed. It's horrible and perfect.

She steps forward – slowly so as not to startle either of them – and puts her arms around him. After a second, his close about her. It's strange being so close to someone; they stop being a person and

232

become a series of impressions. Breath on her cheek, the faint smell of peppermint from his toothpaste, warm skin grazed with stubble. The blurry pink curve of an ear. A heart, beating through cloth.

'I wrote to him,' Wilder says into her ear. She's kind of drunk on his breath. 'Alton. I asked to go see him.' She knows that this is Wilder's real gift to her. Of course, she already knows he's done it, but she is moved.

*Wilder is just a character*, she reminds herself. Just part of a book. But she tightens her arms around him anyway. She wants to give him something back but can't think what.

Then it comes to her, the thought, spined and exciting. She could show him her story.

'Let's get inside,' she says. 'I want to show you something.' It comes out breathy, suggestive, and he looks startled. She laughs. 'I mean – not like that. Let's go.'

She's going to take the risk of showing him this part of herself.


Skye offers the pages shyly. She tries for indifference but she doesn't know how well she pulls it off. She has been working on this for days, feverish, crouched over the keyboard.

'It's called *Pearl*,' she says. 'I'm working on a series of stories about murder.'

He takes the pages with a big smile. 'Oh, wow. I didn't know you wrote stories, Skye.'

'I mean, a little . . .' She hates herself for the hesitation in her voice.

'Do you want me to stay here while I read it?'

She can't decide which is worse, him reading it here in front of her or somewhere else, feeling something she can't see.

'Might as well stay,' she says. 'I've got studying to do anyway.'

She stares at the physics textbook. Every fibre of her is attuned to the scratch and turn of the page. It's seven printed pages and she counts as he finishes each one. When the last one turns, she waits for him to say something. She stares unblinking at the graph before her, eyes watering. Still she waits.

At last, she has to look up. He's smiling but something is wrong. Badly, badly wrong. He doesn't look transported, thoughtful, like he's just been on the journey she laid out so carefully. He looks – and this is interesting, because she has never seen this expression on his face before, and she makes a point of noting all his expressions – he looks embarrassed.

'So,' she says lightly. 'What did you think?'

'It's really evocative,' he says. 'You've got a really good use of language.'

'Right,' she says, the crevasse opening wider and wider before her. 'Listen, be honest, I can take it. It's helpful to know if something's not working.'

'It's so bleak,' he says. 'So – dark.'

'That's kind of the point.' Her smile is a wooden board nailed to her face; it's cement.

'Writing about that stuff – you know, murder and so on – you have to try and not sensationalise it.'

'It's life and death,' she says. 'Those are sensational things.'

'Maybe it's just a matter of practice,' he says, and the dark crevasse swallows her whole. She sees that he thinks he owns it, what happened at Whistler Bay. He thinks it's something that happened to him.

'One day I'll write about you.' She's going for a playful tone but she hears the glassy, hectic edge in her voice.

Wilder looks nervous. 'What?'

She realises that this was an unwise thing to say. Truth is leaking out of her. Too late to take the words back.

'Writing is power,' she says. 'Big magic. It's a way of keeping someone alive forever.'

'Why would someone want to live forever in a book?'

'Maybe they don't. Maybe the writer keeps them prisoner.' She leans in, puts her lips to his ear. 'You can trap someone in a book, their soul – make a prison of words. A cage.' It's something she vaguely remembers from somewhere. Something about trapping a soul in an object.

'Wow, Skye,' he says, nervous. 'Every time I think you can't get any creepier . . .'

'Nearly time for commons,' she says. 'Let's go. Maybe there'll be meatloaf again. Yum.'

'Skye,' he says. 'Hey, I'm sorry. Don't be upset.'

'Why would I be upset?' she asks. He opens his mouth but she suddenly can't handle whatever's about to come out of it.

He calls after her as she heads down the hall, asking her to wait, but she doesn't turn. She wants him to feel the distance between them, the indifference of her back.


He finds her later in the rec room. All the sports guys are squabbling over the remote, everyone wanting different things. Basketball, baseball. She catches an eye, smiles a little. The guy smiles back, then topples over as his buddy tackles him, tall as a felled tree. She'll find him later tonight. Maybe.

'Skye,' Wilder says. She starts. How long has he been there? 'I'm sorry.'

'For what?' she says, smiling.

'You left in such a hurry . . . I thought maybe you were upset.'

'Nah,' she says. 'I just really wanted to catch the beginning of this – she squints at the TV – 'inning? First half? Rally?'

He smiles back, relieved that she's decided to make a joke of it. 'Dramatic stuff. But I really am sorry if I said something to – you know, upset you.'

And she thinks, *you will be.*


She seals Alton Pelletier's letter with Elmer's glue and slips it back into his mail slot early the next morning. She practises her face for when he shows it to her. She was being dumb, before, trying to spare him. She needs to see this through. The effect on him is irrelevant.

Even so, she sees it when they meet for noon commons. His face is like paper; as if someone has placed a very thin Wilder-mask on top of an open wound.

He jumps and drops his fork. Peas spill all over the table, grey-green. A girl with a ponytail makes a point of shifting her chair further away from them. Though that might not be about the peas.

'You OK?' Skye asks.

'Sure,' he says. 'Just jumpy I guess. Maybe there'll be thunder later.'

She nods and says nothing. She feels a mean little razor-slice of pleasure. *Pretty sensational stuff, isn't it, Wilder? After all.*

*

He tells her through the wall, as though he can't bear to look at her – as though looking into her face will make it real.

'Night, Skye,' he says.

'Night, Wilder.'

'Skye? He wrote back,' says his muffled voice. There is a long pause. 'I don't think I can do this.'

'You can,' she says. 'I'll be with you every step of the way. I'll even drive.' She wonders if she's still mad at him, whether she even was, really. She strokes the wall gently with her fingertips. Her feelings are getting all tangled up in the pretence. Surely it was all an act, to make him feel guilty. His opinion on her writing doesn't mean anything to her.

The prison is vast, though not as big as the parking lot which stretches out like the great plains in the falling snow.

'I can't do it,' Wilder says, and he does look like he's going to throw up. She doesn't try to persuade him. She takes him tentatively in her arms. They've started doing that more and more in recent weeks.

'Give me your loose change,' she says. 'Your keys, wallet. They'll stop you otherwise. Just take your ID. And – wait' – she reaches in back – 'you'll have to change that sweater. Your one's tan, they don't let visitors wear beige or orange.'

'Why not?'

'It's too close to the colours of the inmates' uniforms. They might mistake you for someone who belongs there, and never let you out.' She smiles but immediately sees she's made a mistake. His skin turns a pale green.

'You have to do this for Nat,' she says. 'Remember? It's the last chance to find out the truth.'

He nods. She doesn't say that name too often, knows how powerful an effect it has on him. But they are in the endgame, now.

Skye stares at the prison through the windshield. He's in there. Odd to think it.

She called the inn from the payphone before they left, to confirm her reservation. It's on the route back to college, and she picked it because it's romantic, because she wants to make it special, and because they were the only ones who had a room available on Christmas Day. It's starting to snow. She hopes they'll make it to the inn – and part of her hopes they won't. She's strangely frightened of what she plans to do.

Wilder is a tiny figure in the distance; he grows larger slowly through the whirling snow. She gets out and runs to meet him. He leans on her all the way back to the car, pausing once to throw up. His vomit disappears, sinks into the white.

In the warm, she makes him write it all down. She has pen and paper waiting for exactly this. The snow is falling thicker, thicker. *Just write*, she wants to scream; she knows they're running out of time, soon the road as far as the inn will be impassable. But she needs him to get it down while it's all fresh in his memory. So she keeps an iron hand on her feelings, doesn't hurry him, doesn't let him see her panic at every hesitation, every pause of the nib on the page.

They drive into snowfall almost as solid as a wall. He keeps suggesting that they stop at motels they pass. It would be the sensible thing to do.

'No,' she says again and again, 'not that one, not that one.' The car has chains on the tyres but even so she knows she's cutting it dangerously close. She can barely see the road through the snow, falling like a rain of ash.

But at last, with a feeling inside like a shout, she sees the inn ahead.

'I can't afford this,' Wilder says over and over, and she thinks, *god, how many times can my heart break?* But there are no more choices left, now.

'It's OK,' she tells him. 'Stay in the car while I see if they have room.'


The honeymoon suite is just as opulent and ridiculous as the photographs in the brochure promised. The bath has feet. She knows they need to be taken outside themselves, given scenery.

They also need booze. Whiskey and steak together make a heady, rich haze in her head.

'You put something else in the letter,' he says. He's mad but she knows where this is going, it's the helpless snapping of the trapped animal.

So she tells him. He backs away from her, eyes impossibly wide.

'I'll take the couch,' Wilder says, and she puts her hand over his heart. It beats hard under her palm.

'Please don't,' she says, making her eyes soft. Genuine vulnerability is a luxury she can't afford but she knows how to perform it. Enjoys it. Sometimes, like now, she even feels a flutter of the real thing. She flings her arms around him and taps his shoulder, like someone saying *follow me*. And Wilder does. They figure it out gradually. She thinks maybe he hasn't been with a woman before.

'Pretend I'm him,' she whispers into his ear. 'Pretend I'm Nathaniel Pelletier.'

Skye pretends, too. She pretends to be her real self, the person she was before all this.


Skye stays awake, watches him in the glow of the moon, reflected on the crystalline snow.

When he stirs she quickly arranges herself on the pillow, her own hair spread, to give him the pleasure of watching her sleep.

She probably won't have any room in her life for romance or anything after this, so she wants to enjoy it while she can. He watches her, she can feel it.

As dawn comes in pink she can hear the scratch of the pen on paper. *Yes,* she thinks, full of joy, *that's right, that's it, write it all down for me.*

At length, when day has come in full, she leans over and yanks out a pinch of his hair. Wilder yells and she grins at him.

Later Skye wraps the soft inky black lock tightly in a piece of paper and puts it at the bottom of her makeup bag. She allows herself this one indulgence. Something to remember him by.


The drive back to college is quiet. Sometimes, she thinks, you can actually feel happiness taking up space, almost see it. Like a balloon hanging in the air.


'Go get us a place in commons,' she says and he goes quickly, glad to do something for her.

She waits until he's fully out of sight. She tucks his wallet into his backpack with all his overnight stuff. She takes out his folder, the one with Aphrodite coming out of the waves. She can feel the words pulsing in it. She's desperate to open it, to go through it, but she resists. She puts the folder carefully into the back seat behind her. Skye was going to let him keep it – she knows most of it off by heart. But she has decided not to. It belongs to her, not Wilder. She has earned it.

*I'll write it the way I want,* she thinks, fierce. Like a wound in the chest.

Then she leans over and opens the passenger door. She puts

Wilder's backpack out carefully onto the kerb. It will probably be OK there until he comes looking for her – the college is full of rich kids, after all – and people are mostly honest.

[ ]

Won't
Don't

Moss
Muss
Must
Rust
Trust

Herd
Her

Donut
Don't

Dust
Rust
Trust

Hem
Them

Whelp
Help

Held
Help

Heap
Help

# Wilder, Days Six through Ten

*Nate wore his ragged clothes with style. He gave the impression of being made of natural things – wood and sand worn smooth by the tide.*

*The Sound and the Dagger*, by Sky Montague

I wake to the sound of breath. No hand caressing me, this time. Instead I have the sense that I am being pummelled and stretched, pulled by firm hands into agonising, geometrical shapes. I scream but no voice comes from my throat. Instead, an infernal scratching – horrible, like rats' claws on stone, like bone grinding, like the creak of a bough before it breaks. Or like a pen scratching on paper.

I hit the floor with a crack.

In the morning I have a bruise all down one side, purpling and fresh as thundercloud. Some of it is yellowing and greenish, as though already healing. There's something horrible about that and I pull my shirt down, wincing.

The yellowish green parts of the bruise have a distinctive shape. Almost like the double curve of a snake.

So today I type one-handed, nursing my aching arm. I punch out a letter at a time, peering at the keyboard askance, as though afraid to look directly at it. There's a kind of familiarity to it, this expression, and I wonder why – then I realise. It's Sky's expression. It's how he used to look when he was concentrating.

I'm wearing him like a skin.

I went to see the movie of *The Sound and the Dagger* they made, oh, years later. Of course I did – who could resist? They mixed up the timeframes – it all happened in college in the film. It lost some of the youthful naivete of the story, but it lent it some depth and complexity. I watched as handsome Skandar went to the cave alongside Wiley, Helen and Nate. Somehow the fact that there were four kids in the boat, not three, made me maddest. It hammered home how he had added himself in.

The actor who played Wiley looked just like me at that age. And the actor who played Skandar looked exactly like Sky. Memory and film have merged together over the years. The mind is faithless. So now when I recall that summer all that I can see before my mind's eye is the movie – Helen, Nate, Skandar and Wiley in that boat, on the bright sea. He has even taken my memory.


How could I have forgotten Sky showing me his short story? Maybe I wanted to gloss over it, because he was so offended. I hated it when we fought. But of course things escalated after that. He realised I was a better writer – that he had to move fast.

Strange how memory is flooding back now. I've unlocked the

past. It's all falling into place. It's like being a detective, hunting through a mystery. Of course, you only need a detective when there's been a crime. The murder of my life, I guess. My career.

Reading back today's pages, something else starts tugging at my memory – but I can't grasp it. Something about the hemlock being shaped like a carrot? For some reason I keep seeing Harper's face. It'll come to me.


I'm getting a sweater from the closet when I see it, a white edge, sticking out through a crack in the boards at the back. I can see half a cursive letter, written in that snake-green ink. I know what it is, of course, or at least I have a terrible feeling.

'Come on,' I mutter, fingertips scrabbling and pinching at the paper. 'Come on.'

I get the toolbox and lever the back of the closet open with a crowbar. The wood yawns, gives and breaks. I wipe the sweat from my brow.

The note reads, *Missing you, missing y.*

The y trails off in a long tail, as though the writer was interrupted. Ink bright green as grass. It looks wet. 'Sky?' I whisper, even though it's not him. It can't be.

'Enough,' I say aloud.

I see something lying in a shadowed corner. White, green ink. I pick the note up with shaking hands.

*Miss you badly today. S.*

The end of the slip of paper looks singed, burnt, which for some reason is terrifying. It's as if the note is telling me what to do with it.

I set a match to the notes, watch as the writing disappears, goes up into flame. Ash whirls out into the air, over the sea, and is gone.

'You can't get me,' I whisper out loud. 'You're not here, Sky. You're dead.'

I regret it immediately because now that they're gone, I have an awful creeping doubt that they ever existed. I know that I've been getting too close to him, going inside him. Am I maybe becoming him?

Shivering, with the bedclothes pulled up to my neck, I wait for sleep. It's dark outside the window. At least I think it is. Comets of green fire stroke across the horizon.

It's bright today and very cold but I don't want to be in the cottage. I put on my hat and muffler, two pairs of socks and the boots Emily got me for hiking in the Catskills. I drag the desk outside.

The morning goes well and I eat lunch outside too, the last box of mac and cheese. Is this my last mac and cheese ever? I'll tidy the cottage before I do it. I don't want people to think I was losing my mind. I need them to take the book seriously.

I check my faculty satmail too – if I don't, they might get concerned. A colleague might send a police officer to do a, what's it called, a welfare check. I know this, because Emily did it once, when she was in Cabo and I didn't answer the phone for a couple of days.

Footsteps break up my thoughts. Harper comes into view, heavily laden. A bucket, cloths, scrubbing brushes, cleaning products.

I smile and wave and then take in her burden with a terrible lurch of embarrassment. 'The cottage doesn't need cleaning,' I say. I can't let her in there.

'Wilder,' she says. 'I haven't come to scrub your bloody floors, OK?'

'Where are you going?' I indicate her load.

'Doing public service. Want to help?'

I want company, so I nod.

The wind roars as we go down the cliff path together, then once we're down in the arms of the bay it falls still. The stones aren't singing today, thank goodness. Though is there the odd faint note over the quiet rippling water? I close my eyes and breathe.

We pick our way over the pebble spits that reach out across the cove. 'Here,' Harper says.

I don't see it until I turn back, landwards. On the cliff something drips, green. In shaking, sloppy letters, the cliff walls spell out one word in green paint. *Murderer*. I feel sick and faint for a moment. 'Who could have done this?' I ask Harper. 'Did they come up the path – no, it must have been by boat.'

From the land the message is invisible, hidden from sight on the sea-facing cliff wall below. If you were passing in a boat however, you would see the word *Murderer* written in brilliant green on the cliff. Directly above it, you would see the sugar maple and my desk where I sit each day to write. *Murderer*. A warning for only those on the ocean, who will know to look for it.

'Is that a joke?'

She looks at me. 'What's funny? It's just some local kid's tag.'

'Why would they choose that?'

'Maybe they think it sounds tough? Cool?'

'It's for me,' I say. 'It's a message.'

'I don't think it is, Wilder.'

'Who then? You?'

She ruffles my hair, absent. 'You've got to run a comb through this. It's frizzy as a carrot top.'

I suddenly feel cold. *Carrot*. The memory's been tugging at me since I wrote about the day I found the hemlock on Pursing Hill . . . I showed it to Sky. But who was it, who first showed *me* hemlock?

'Harper,' I say. 'Have you been leaving little notes in my house? Little notes written in green ink? You were always one for games.'

She says, tight, 'I have no idea what you're talking about.'

'What really happened to Nat, Harper?'

'He's dead, Wilder, as you well know.'

'You had a paper bag with you that day I saw you outside urgent care – it had something in it wrapped in aluminium foil. A thing you took to Nat. What was it?'

'I don't know, Wilder. A joint? A snack? Nothing important. Why would you bring this up now? That was all years ago.'

I gesture at the cliff. 'Maybe this is about you, not me.'

'Maybe what is about me?' Harper says. She sounds puzzled. 'Wilder, it's just some kids messing around.'

'Maybe you've learned it's best to keep your enemies close. So they don't start to figure out what you really are.'

Harper smiles at me. Her smile is too big. It grows long enough to wrap around her head, almost, and she has so many teeth, I see that now, how could I not have seen it before? How wide that slash of a smile is – too broad and toothy to be human.

I stumble up the cliff path, blinded by panic. I can't hear whether I am pursued or not, over the clatter and my panting – I don't turn to look.


I'm shaking, though I feel better with the cottage door shut behind me. I remember again the carrot-shaped object that Harper took into the Castine urgent care centre, when she went to see Nat all those years ago – just before he died of sudden heart failure.

I imagine villagers with pitchforks. *Heart failure*, they would say. Like Nat. *The sea got him*, they would say. Like Sky.

I take up *The Sound and the Dagger*, flipping the pages with trembling hands. I find it quickly. Sky did use the scene where I spray-painted THE DAGGER MAN WAS HERE on the cliff. But he transformed it. In the book, local kids congregate on the beach below Wiley's house. They don't believe Anton is responsible for the murders. They know better. They spray, on the cliff below, the word: *Murderer*. A secret message that can only be read from the sea.

I look cautiously out of the door, and then peer over the cliff. Harper's gone, somehow, though I didn't hear her pass on the path.

I go down to the beach. The cliff wall gleams, freshly scrubbed. I smell detergent. But there are still traces of green paint on the rock. My sleep is uneasy, filled with the sound of the front door blowing open, as it sometimes does. But every time I get up, it's locked.

Disaster, this morning. There's no more coffee in the can.

Maybe there's a secret stash. Emily always does this – hides stores of nice or necessary things like chocolate or toilet paper – so that when we think we've run out we have the joy of realising there's actually more. I miss her.

I hunt through the shelves. None to be found. Right. I'll have to get to the store somehow. I can go without food and sleep, I can live without love if I must, but I cannot carry on without coffee.

*

I walk to the main road and stick my thumb out. There's a wind up, I wish I'd brought a warmer jacket. Cars roar by. No one seems likely to stop. Who can blame them? No one hitchhikes anymore and who's going to pick up a dishevelled middle-aged man with odd protruding eyes? I accept defeat and take out my cellphone to call a cab.

Behind me, a car pulls over onto the verge and comes to a halt. 'Wilder Harlow,' calls a voice. The passenger is a neat-looking elderly woman. Even my peripheral vision is slightly fuzzy today; lack of sleep I guess.

'You don't recognise me, huh.' The voice is familiar. Voices don't change the way faces do. Voices come from inside us, and the inside never changes as much as the outside.

'Hi, Trooper Karen.' I'm actually really happy to see her.

'It's detective, now,' she says. 'Or was. Now it's just Karen. Jump in.'

'Oh,' I say. 'I don't know . . .'

'Come on,' she says, 'it's perfectly safe.'

I climb nervously into the back seat beside her. She pushes the start button and the car moves away smoothly.

I try not to look forward, where there should be a steering wheel, dashboard, driver's seat. I'll never get used to driverless cars.

Karen Harden smiles and pats my hand. 'It's been a minute.'

'You came back to Castine,' I say.

'Oh yes. Once you're from here, you're from here.' The fall land rushes by.

'Are you with the police, here?'

'I'm retired. It's good to do nothing, you know?'

'No,' I say, honestly. 'I don't know.'

'What you doing back here?'

251

'I'm writing a book,' I say.

'Lots of writers come out here these days,' she says, nodding. 'Terrible thing that happened to that poor man. You know, I would have asked more questions about that death.'

'We've got vandals out by the cove,' I say, to change the subject. 'Kids.'

'I saw. It made the paper.'

'Did you know him?' I ask suddenly, without meaning to. 'Sky Montague. What was he like?' For some reason I want to know what kind of man he became.

Trooper Harden purses her lips, thinking.

'Distant,' she says eventually. 'Kind, though. Always had a word for people who wanted to say hello. They came a long way, some of them. I thought he was sad.'

Castine is bustling; I realise it's a Saturday. Karen Harden drops me outside the general store. This has changed since my day. What used to be a small family-run business is a branch of a big chain, now. The green lettering above the storefront gleams in the fall sunlight. It's made to look like handwriting.

'You OK?'

'Sure,' I say quickly, tearing my eyes off the green sign. 'Thanks for the ride. It was good to see you.' I slam the car door and hurry away.

Inside the store I pick up a pound of coffee and then I go to the news stand. It's not on the front page of the local, but it's on page five. A picture, must have been taken from a boat.

There's the cottage, the bay. I can even see my writing desk under the maple tree if I squint. A tiny splotch. Underneath, the cliff is spray-painted. I peer closer. The childlike letters are orange, not green. They read: *Mickey222*

I check the date of the paper. There's no mistake: it's today's.

I buy the paper and go out onto Main Street. I keep looking at it in the daylight to see if the headline changes. It doesn't. The Saturday crowds mill around me. Someone jostles my elbow.

'Watch it,' I say – perhaps too sharply – I turn and catch a flash of blood-red hair. Harper. It's her. I'd know her anywhere, that upright back, her walk, as though she'd walk right through anyone who gets in her way.

'Harper!' I yell. But she's gone, hidden behind a family on the sidewalk, father harried-looking, dragging two kids by the hands. The dad gives me a dubious look as I hurry past.

I run up the street, ducking and dodging people. At last, I think I see a glimpse of red turning a corner into a narrow back street, just by the old fishmonger. By the time I get there, there's no sign of Harper. I put my hands on my knees and pant, a shooting pain rushing up my arm. Careful, I think. Got to finish the book first.

I use precious minutes on my cellphone plan to call a cab to take me back to Whistler Bay. It only occurs to me as I wait under the green store sign for it to arrive, sweating, that Harper must have dyed her hair back to its original colour. The other day her hair was mostly grey.

The storm wakes me. Lightning judders in the sky outside, the glare so bright, everything in the bedroom in black and white. Beside me, soft breathing. I reach out for the breath, longing. *Oh, let me undo it. Be here. Be you. That hand, stroking my chest.*

She's standing beside the bed, the woman from the sea. Water pours from her hair and clothes. The blue of her dress is dark as wine in the electric light, but I can see the birthmark on her bared shoulder.

'Who are you?' I whisper.

Her mouth opens and water pours forth in a long straight stream, shining in the flickering light. It looks as if a knife is being thrust down her throat. She is choking and screaming through the water, but still it comes, hitting the bedclothes and the floor with a blow, the strength of a fire hose, spraying a fine mist of droplets on impact. Above her rictus mouth, her eyes implore me. *Help*, I hear in my mind, clear as a bell.

I fall to the floor. Moisture seeps into the sheets twisted about my ankles. My face comes away from the boards wet. The floor is dotted with gleaming pools. I lick my lips and taste salt.

*Help*, she says in my ear. The odour strengthens. Wet linen and salt water and the slightest note of rot. On the floor something glistens. A wet, sandy footprint. Slowly, I look up.

There she is above me, stretching out flat across the ceiling.

*Help*, she says, and something drips onto my shoulder.

'Who are you?' I say again. I hear the tears in my voice but inside I'm echoing with fear.

She raises a finger. I can see it's bent at an angle, as if it's been broken. She starts to trace letters on the air. They shine green and luminous, like light through clear water.

*Rebecca*, she writes with her maimed finger; the word shimmers like a sunlit sea.

I think of the young, blonde, sporty woman from that long-ago picture in the paper. I take out my phone and search the satellite newspaper archive. The picture comes up quickly. There she is, Rebecca Boone. I breathe a sigh of relief. I was right. Whatever this is, it's not her – nothing like the thoughtful, young woman leaning against the windowsill.

'You're lying!' I say. 'You're not her.'

The thing hovers above me.

'Maybe you're looking for someone else?' I say. 'Your family? I'm definitely not the right person.' Do ghosts do that? Dial and get the wrong number, as it were? 'Who are you?'

She points again to the name, *Rebecca*.

Oh god, I'm lying on the wet floor arguing with – what?

*Run*, I think, *just get out of here*. My legs won't obey me at first; I crawl with her at my back, towards the front door. If I can just get to the air, the light—

Something white lies on the doormat. I unfold the note with trembling hands.

*Don't hate me, Wilder.*

*S*

The vile, snake-green ink seems to gleam.

A sudden twinge of pain comes in my side, and I double over.

I pull up my shirt, wincing. The thin line of bruised flesh is deep yellow, healing to a murky green. I look from the note, to my side, and back again. The bruise is now shaped like a calligraphy S, the same shape as Sky's initial, on the page.

My stomach drops down into my bowels, and I think for a moment I am actually going to empty them right here and now, into my pyjamas. I scream.

When at last I run out of breath, she's gone. I look around the room wildly, open drawers and look under the bed, but the dead woman is nowhere to be seen.

I have a terrible idea. I need to test it.

I hunt in my briefcase for my published first edition of *The Sound and the Dagger*. I read this version years ago but it doesn't seem real to me, the way the manuscript does.

Fingers trembling, I flip to the description of Rebecca.

*He was halfway out to the drowning woman and Skandar could make out her features now. A ragged, chalk-white face. She wore something blue, though not a swimsuit. Her shoulder blades were sharp and starving though translucent blue linen. A birthmark spread over one shoulder. The girl seemed like she was breathing too fast, and he worried she might exhaust herself. She looked half-dead already. There was a scent of rot in the air.*

*'What's your name?' He had heard that being called by your name in times of stress was calming. You remembered yourself.*

*'Rebecca,' she answered faintly in a cracked voice like pepper being ground. It was the most frightening sound he had ever heard. No human voice should sound like that.*

I've read the other description so many times, in Sky's first draft, I forgot he changed this description for publication. It's the dress that fooled me – Rebecca's dress in the manuscript of *The Sound and the Dagger* is red. The thing I see is dressed in blue. And she has a birthmark on her shoulder, not a wound.

For some reason my hands expect the manuscript of *The Sound and the Dagger* to be soft, mouldy and rotten. But it's dry to the touch, just a pile of papers.

I flip through them at the kitchen table – I find myself swatting with my right hand at an area behind me, as I used to when I could feel Emily trying to read over my shoulder. I turn and stare at the kitchen. Empty. Or at least it looks empty. I turn the pages with trembling hands. Here.

*He was halfway out to the drowning woman and Wiley could make out her features now. A heart-shaped face, full, beautiful lips.*

*She wore something red, voluminous, that spread about her like*
*a bell in the water. Her shoulders were sharp and shapely though*
*translucent linen. The cloth slipped, and he saw she had a wound*
*on her shoulder, red and bloody like a bite from an apple. The girl*
*was breathing too fast, and he worried she might exhaust herself.*

*'What's your name?' he called. He had heard that being called*
*by your name in times of stress was calming. You remembered*
*yourself.*

*'Rebecca,' she answered faintly.*

But the description didn't always read like this. The page is covered with rough patches of white-out.

I wonder, I wonder, I wonder. I get a sharp knife from the drawer. Delicately, gently, I scrape away at the white-out. Soon the table is covered with little dusty white flakes. I can't believe we used to write like this – so painstakingly. After a few minutes I have completed my excavation. I carefully blow the last particles of white powder from the page. There. Just as I thought.

Rebecca's red dress was originally blue in the manuscript he sent me, just like the published version. Sky was always one for changing his mind.

I dab quickly at the manuscript page with white-out, blowing on it impatiently to speed the process. At long last, it's dry. I scribble over the description of her dress, replacing blue with red again, returning the birthmark to a wound.

I need her to come back, to test my theory. I wait, hair rising in quills on the back of my neck. Every shadowed corner of the kitchen seems to hold eyes.

The smell comes first. A taint of rot on the air. My heart slows, begins to beat cold and sludgy in my chest. Even though I'm waiting for her, even though this time I want her to come.

She's here, skirts dripping. I avert my gaze, looking without looking. Rebecca moves rapidly to and fro, shivering in and out of existence. I can see, even in the corner of my eye, that her dress has changed to a deep, dripping red. I can smell the blood from the wound on her shoulder.

I scratch at the white-out again and watch her from the corner of my eye.

A dark stain creeps up the hem of Rebecca's skirt. She opens her mouth in a silent rictus. I can't hear her but I can tell she's screaming. The hem of her dress change to a deep, blue, the colour of the ocean. Her blood dries and flattens into a birthmark on her shoulder.

The blue creeps up her skirts, to her waist. When it reaches the place where her heart would be, she puts her hand protectively over the place. Slowly, inch by inch, the blue inches up her red dress. She cries in silence. She reaches out a hand, imploring me to stop. It's not an easy thing, being rewritten. But you can always play around with a first draft.

I'm not being haunted by a ghost – I'm being haunted by a book. More specifically, by the characters from *The Sound and the Dagger*.

That's why only I could see the word *Murderer* in green on the cliff face. Why Harper looked so young, when I saw her from a distance in Castine. It wasn't Harper. It was Helen.

A high giggle escapes me, rolls out and out. I laugh and laugh and I can't seem to stop, even though it aches and I can't breathe and my eyes water. The world has gone insane, or maybe I have. I don't know which answer is worse. Another possibility, of course, is that I am already dead. A ghost, in some kind of fever dream of an afterlife. Oh god – please don't let me be dead.

# [ ]

'It will work this time,' Grace says. 'Because you'll use me.'

'Sit down and be quiet.' She is too eager to give me her blood. The knife opens a crevice of red in her skin.

'Careful,' I snap. 'I don't want to call an ambulance.'

I take the bowl. It's stainless steel where it should be silver, but I'll make do. This will be the last time. The last chance.

Her blood hits the bowl with a patter like rain.

I pierce my finger with a sharp knife, wincing. I've done this a hundred times, but habit doesn't dull pain. *It will work this time*, I tell myself. It will. It has to.

I let my blood join hers in the bottom of the bowl. There is a light *plink* as the drops fall. I mix in the wine and seawater. In the past I used water from the bay. I knew it wasn't good enough. So this time, I made myself go there. It remembers, that water.

The stone ceiling was alive, reflecting the endless patterns of light. The pools spread out in the black, a dark mirror-land. I felt like they were there – all of them – watching from their rusted drums. Then I shook myself. They were gone, long gone. *Get it and go*, I told myself.

The touch of the water was cold as death. I scooped it up in a plastic bottle – not very magical but it got the job done.

Somewhere near the back, something stirred. I knew I was imagining things but I ran for the water, swam for the light, before I could be forced to know.

I'm nervous. This is big magic. I've never done anything this big before. And it's been so long.

I take the hair and drop it into the bowl. I'm breathing harder than I should be. The surface of the mixture swirls unpleasantly with each breath.

'Come into this ink,' I ask. 'Be bound by it.' Nothing happens, but often you don't know if magic is working until later.

But of course it won't work. None of this stuff really works, I know that, deep down. It's just a way of putting a tiny drop of your will into the great black ocean of the universe. Sometimes it's just too hard to lose what you love.

'Keep him. Bind him.'

The tears are here before I know they're coming, spilling almost painfully down my cheeks. I lean forward and let them drip down my face, off my chin and into the spell. Real tears are big magic too. You can't plan for them, in witchcraft. They either happen or they don't.

I grind the singed and blackened pearl to dust with a pestle and mortar. I add it to the mixture. Now, it's time.

I pick up the bowl, stomach already churning. The scent of wine rises, but there's an edge to it, a bloody salty undertone which makes my stomach heave.

I turn my head away, take a deep breath and hold it. I drink from the bowl. It tastes fleshy and human on my tongue. I immediately run for the bathroom. Blood and wine mingle uneasily in my throat, my tongue seems coated with it. I half spit, half heave into the toilet bowl. I don't think I have to swallow it for this to work, do I? Anyway I just can't.

With the rest of the liquid, I trace the first words of the book carefully with a needle. There. It's begun in blood. This book isn't finished yet. I think that's the key.

But nothing's happening. Surely there should be some sign? I flip through the printout sadly.

He won't be back. I'll never see either of them again.

And there it is.

```
Hello
Hell
Help
```

'Hello,' I whisper.

'Did it work?' She takes my hand and love stirs in me, strange and painful.

'Thank you,' I say to her.

'I'm yours,' she says. 'All I want is to be near you. Have I earned that?'

'Yes.' I'm crying. It has been so many years since I've let myself feel this – opened these dark places to the daylight. It's painful.

I look again at the words on the page. I still can't believe it.

'It worked.'

And now I open my mouth and let out a scream, so all the dead can hear – we'll be together again at last.

# Wilder, Day Eleven

I don't remember writing that section with the witchcraft. I must have been playing around with that idea Sky put in my head all that time ago, about trapping people in a book.

I must have been.

Great start this morning because I think she's gone – a wonderful moment. I check the corners of my bedroom, the ceiling. I get out of bed, looking for the icy wet footprints she leaves in her wake. But the floor is bare.

Hope rises. Maybe she's gone for good. Maybe she got bored, found somewhere else to be or died. Can whatever she is die?

But when I open the bedroom door she's there in the hallway, waiting, floating, blue dress billowing. I think her face is getting whiter and more decayed each time I see her – lips a deeper blue. This morning something has been nibbling at her ear. There's a ragged place where the left lobe should be. Has that always been there?

She follows close behind as I go to the bathroom. I don't turn around. I have a theory that she gets more detailed the more I look at her. Little things, like the mother-of-pearl buttons on her cuffs, which weren't there yesterday. She doesn't follow me into the shower. She waits politely outside the door.

In the kitchen I edge around Rebecca carefully to get to the kettle. It's not good to touch her. Not good at all. I won't make that mistake twice. My body goes cold when I think about it.

You're not supposed to be able to touch them, hear them, smell them – Charles Bonnet hallucinations. But of course, even doctors make mistakes.

Something falls around me in drifts. The ashes of my life. No, snow. It's snowing. I become aware that someone is shaking me and I get ready to scream. Can she touch me now, Rebecca?

'Hey,' says Harper's voice. 'Come inside.'

Even if she is a murderer, I am so happy to see a person. I cling to Harper as we go inside.

'I can tell that it's all going to sound insane,' I say. The coffee steams in my hands.

And I'm right, it does. Harper gives me that look I give my undergrads when they lie clumsily to get an extension on their term paper. There's pity in it. 'You're saying a character from a book is haunting you.'

'From Sky's book,' I say, desperate. 'Not just her, either. Look.' I go to the cutlery drawer. I've started keeping the notes I find around the house. I've grown to dread that vivid green. 'Look. It's his handwriting! They're everywhere! I'm getting notes from a dead man! Explain that.'

'They don't look very threatening,' she says. '*Happy reading?*'

'It's cruel,' I say. 'That's what it is.'

'You've been under a lot of strain,' Harper says. 'I don't think being alone out here is good for you.'

'I didn't imagine it,' I whisper, once again quite close to tears. 'Look.' I pull my shirt up. The S-shaped bruise hurts, bad as ever. 'This bruise won't fade – it turned that awful green, and now it just stays that way.'

'Wilder, it's a bruise.'

'The shape of it! It's an S.' I hold out a note. My hand shakes. 'It's the exact same shape. His writing. His signature. He's *here*. *He signed me.*'

She says, gently, 'You were flinging about some pretty wild accusations the other day, Wilder. Are you OK?'

'I don't know,' I say. 'I'm seeing things. Or I'm not. I don't know!'

'They used to call it a nervous breakdown,' she says. 'I like that better than any of those scientific terms. Because that's what it feels like, doesn't it? Like everything in you is broken.'

I can't believe Harper's right. Because her being right would mean I have truly let go.

'And the notes?'

'Maybe you wrote them and forgot,' she says. 'Maybe you brought old notes with you and have repressed it. Maybe someone's messing with you. I don't know, but I'm a logical woman and I do know there's a logical explanation for everything.'

'Everything? Even your hair being red again?'

'You saw a girl with red hair,' she says gently. 'Your mind filled in the rest. We see what we want, Wilder.' She kisses me on the cheek. 'You call me if you need anything, OK?'

I follow her to the door. Snow falls on Harper's red and silver

264

hair, swirls around her face, and I think, *how beautiful she is*. Her hair is caught by the wind. In that moment it looks like red skirts billowing in water and I almost scream.

I stride about the garden vigorously in the building wind, with fine, freezing rain misting my face. Clouds are boiling in the distance. 'Come out, show yourself!' I yell at the sky. I yell it again and again, until my throat is hoarse and dry from that stormy air.

A herd of deer graze peacefully on the surface of the bay. Their eyes are deep red. Heavy stripes of indigo race across the sky.

And I'm forced to ask myself, was Harper really here at all?

# Wilder, Day Twelve

*Skandar froze in horror as he bent to pick up the thing that lay on the doormat. It was an aging Polaroid photograph of a child asleep. Skandar reached for his younger self. A small hand rested gently against his cheek.*

*Only one person could have put it through the mail slot. The person he gave it to, all those years ago.*

*'Wiley,' he whispered.*

*He felt the breath then, on the back of his neck.*

The Sound and the Dagger, by Sky Montague

My head pulses gently where it rests on cold metal. I feel Rebecca's dead gaze move over me and I hold my breath. But today she must have other business, because she moves on. I feel her recede, go elsewhere.

It's so cold. My teeth are actually chattering. The light is grey and low, clouded. Below, the bay is cool steel. The sun is going down, or maybe coming up?

When I sit up, the typewriter keys spring up with a cheerful click. They have left imprints on my cheek, neat rows of square red recesses, as though I am now ready for the placement of fingers. I unspool the pages with trembling hands.

I don't remember writing this. Magic seems to be making its way into this book. Or maybe it started with magic, because there is a worse possibility than all of this. I'm not being haunted by a book. I'm *in* a book.

'You can trap someone in a book, their soul – make a prison of words. A cage,' Sky said that long-ago day. It seems outlandish, farcical. But what if he found a way to do it?

A soft sound at the kitchen door and my heart stops. But it's just the mail.

When I glance at what lies on the doormat, I freeze, quite literally; my body grows icy cold. I don't think those are letters.

I go close, even though I don't want to. I have to, because I am in a plot, aren't I? I have to do what the writer wants, and no writer wants me to turn away, to never look at these terrible things.

My face is peaceful on the pillow, one hand curled under my cheek, skin pale as a corpse in the glare of the flash. It's horrible.

My fingers tremble as I reach for them. But I stop short, I don't touch. Because if I touch, and these are real, I'll know this is really happening.

Footsteps on the path outside. Someone running away. I look out of the window. I just glimpse the back of a shaggy head of hair. It looks like a teenage boy, tall and whip-thin.

I throw open the door and yell after him. 'What?' The air seems to vibrate with danger. 'What do you want?' But there's nothing but the faint mineral tang of the sea.

Sky is here. He's all around me. Because they're all just part of him, aren't they? The ghosts never existed until he wrote them. Nothing is real here, except *The Sound and the Dagger*.

Her breath is rotten on the back of my neck, stinking of death and the endless sea. 'Leave me alone,' I whisper.

Behind me I hear a sound like the belly of a snake on the earth. Or like the scratch of pen on paper. I close my eyes. 'Please,' I whisper, 'please leave me alone.'

I start and choke. Coughing, I put my finger into my mouth. The paper is moist, sodden. I manage to unfold it with careful fingertips.

The green ink is wet, the words blurred, as if they're out of focus. But I can read them, all right.

*Burn*
*Urn*
*Turn*
*Tarn*
*Earn*
*Earl*
*Pearl*

# *Pearl*

*Summer 1990*

They pull Pearl out of Domestic Management to tell her. After ten years, Pearl's mother has come home. Not drowned after all – that would have been better. They have made an arrest.

They take Pearl to the principal's office – Pearl has been there in the past but it seems different now. They are acting like they're the ones in trouble. The counsellor is there and the nurse. Pearl wonders if they think she's going to attack them.

'She doesn't seem to be taking it in,' the principal says to the nurse.

'Shock,' said the nurse. 'I'll take her pulse.' The nurse's hands are a little damp, as if from nerves.

Pearl thinks of Rebecca lying in a cave all those years, alone, under the water. They were right, she isn't taking it in. Weirdly, it's the Polaroids she can't stop thinking about, the ones of the sleeping children. She hopes those little kids are OK. She wonders if it made its way into their dreams, somehow – the click, the flash. The nightlight shining soft on closed eyelids.

The principal's voice sounds distant, as if underwater. 'Your father will come and collect you as soon as he can. Thursday.' She's wearing the blush-coloured twinset and pearls today. Sometimes she wears a smart pantsuit. There's something in her eyes on those days, a little secret smile, maybe. Pearl can tell she feels daring on pantsuit days.

The bell screams its warning and she jumps.

'You had better get back to Domestic Management,' says the principal. 'Your classes will keep you from thinking too much.'

She hears the words just fine, but the underwater thing is getting worse. The office shivers and ripples. The sound of wind rises in Pearl's head. Or is it waves beating against a cave wall?

This all happens on Monday, she thinks, but it might have been Tuesday. Afterwards it bothers her that she can never be completely sure.

Around Pearl, girls are sewing, darning. They are all supposed to be homemakers by the time they leave school.

Muriel slips her hand into the waistband of Pearl's skirt. There's a little puppy fat there. Muriel pinches hard with strong fingers. Pearl's eyes water.

'Don't cry,' she said softly. 'You'll get in trouble.' This is a genuine warning. Crying is regarded as showing off. Pearl gets that the way Muriel acts towards her isn't personal. It's the way it is.

'What did the principal want?'

'My uncle died,' Pearl says at random. The truth is precious, not everyone deserves it.

Muriel leaves her alone for the rest of the period. An uncle is distant enough. Everyone has an uncle. The discovery of Pearl's mother's body, stored by a serial killer in an oil drum, probably would have made Muriel feel uncomfortable. People are unpredictable when they're uncomfortable.

That night Pearl tries to summon the mountaintop, her mother, waits for her voice, her warm hands on her head. Tonight, surely, of all nights, she will come. *I'm trying to be cool, Mama*, she thinks. *Cool as a drink of water.*

Her mother doesn't come.

There are whole chunks of memory missing around here, for Pearl. The funeral, the weeks after, the return to school. They're not faint or repressed or anything. They're just gone.

Nothing, really, for months – until the day the new girl arrives at Fairview.

Pearl can already tell there's something different when she gets to history class. There's a warmth in the air. A brightness. And there's someone sitting in the usually empty seat beside Pearl's. The girl has a round childlike face with innocent eyes, red hair like a shout.

Pearl knows her name, of course she does. She has seen her picture in the paper. She feels everything rearrange – the classroom, her organs, the world.

'Hello,' Harper says. Of course, she doesn't know who Pearl is. Pearl's picture wasn't published in the newspaper.

If you summer in all the same places, and send your kids to all the same schools, then yes, of course sooner or later they are going to bump into one another – Pearl and the girl who helped find her mother's body.

Pearl opens her mouth to speak. She doesn't know what she's going to say.

Harper plays with her Fairview pin, turning it nervously in her fingers.

Muriel beats her to it. 'Don't pay any attention to Moony Boony,' she says to the new girl. Moony Boony is what Muriel calls Pearl, on account of her last name being Boone. 'Her uncle died months ago. She's still being weird about it. I'm Muriel.'

'Harper,' says the new girl.

Muriel reaches out. 'Let me help you with that pin.'

Pearl thinks about warning the new girl, but it's too late. The pin sinks into the ball of Harper's thumb. The girl's lips part silently but she doesn't make a sound.

Muriel nods approvingly and turns away. The history lesson begins.

Pearl watches the new girl take the pin from her thumb. The silver needle is crimson and shining. She senses Pearl's eyes on her and looks up. Looking Pearl right in the eye, she puts the sharp bloodied end between her lips and sucks, leaving the pin shining and silver and clean. She fastens it neatly to the lapel of her blazer.

'Ew,' Pearl whispers, fascinated. 'You drank your own blood.'

Harper checks the front of the classroom. The teacher is frowning at the blackboard.

She leans in close to Pearl. 'Don't let your blood fall just anywhere,' she whispers in her ear. 'With each drop, you leave a part of yourself there. Who's the giraffe?'

'Muriel,' Pearl whispers, exhilarated. Muriel hurt her but Harper doesn't care. She's found a way to keep her power. She can breathe again, in the new girl's presence.

'Come for a walk after classes?' she asks. Pearl's heart races until the new girl nods.

The rain falls in dull sheets around the bleachers, hammering on the metal like applause. A spider runs up a gossamer rope. It's his place, down here, it's not for human girls – but that's OK, Pearl hasn't felt like a human girl in some time. Harper hands her a bottle from her satchel.

The burning swallow tells Pearl she's alive.

'What?' Harper says. 'Are you sad about your uncle?'

'I have to tell you something,' Pearl says.

Harper's eyes get bigger and bigger as Pearl talks, and she puts her head in her hands as though Pearl's story has physical weight, as though it is filling her skull with lead.

'Bloody hell.' Harper touches Pearl's shoulder, just once, and Pearl wonders how she knows how badly Pearl wants to be touched right now – but that a hug is smothering.

'In future,' Harper says, 'if you want them to leave you alone, tell them your dog died. People really care about that.'


Harper got it from a book originally, the magic. It was given to her when she was a kid, so it's a book for kids. The book has a badly drawn cauldron on the cover and a woman with long hair floating on the wind, with a sprig of something in her hand. There's a lot of stuff about balance and the earth and Gaia. Harper doesn't care about that. She's interested in the good stuff that makes people fall in love with you or rot their living flesh or change the colour of their eyes, maybe.

There isn't enough of that in it. Pearl and Harper abandon the book.

You have to invent witchcraft in the moment, they discover.

There's no such thing as an actual spell. Nothing ever works twice. They can tell they're doing it right when the world goes all blue at the edges and sound drops away, and it's just them, and whatever they're focusing on. A bloody slip of paper, a piece of bark to which they've whispered a wish. Blood, mixed with the dirt from a girl's shoe, to make her get her period in front of everyone on the soccer field. Names written on a piece of paper with a date on it. Something bad will happen on that date, to that person. They don't specify what. That's up to the universe.

Pearl grits her teeth and picks up a fine strand of Muriel's hair. All around her, in the dark, sleeping girls breathe.

The scissors make a quiet crunch as they close. It's so loud in the dark. But Muriel sleeps on.

Harper takes Pearl's hand and leads her silently. They glide like ghosts down the rows. Someone turns over and groans and they stop in terror, arrested like statues with joined hands. But no one wakes. Pearl feels the power of it. They could do anything to the sleeping girls, anything – to their necks and ears and vulnerable eyes.

They sneak out the loose window on the ground floor – the catch doesn't sit flush to the frame, Harper noticed this her first day. Pearl would never have thought of looking for such a thing. 'Years of experience,' Harper says cheerfully. 'That's partly what magic is – knowing what to look for.'

The night air is silky on their faces and they run, hearts pounding, through the rain to their spot under the bleachers which will, they figure, hide the flame from anyone looking out into the dark.

They burn the hair in a silver bowl (trash can lid) under a full moon (probably, though it's hidden behind the evening drizzle). They ask for her to be expelled.

Nothing happens to Muriel, but she has a small cropped place on her head the next day. She keeps touching it, puzzled.

Harper is friends with the man who works at the gas station a mile away. She walks there most days. Walks are allowed, they're healthy for young ladies. It's only later that Pearl wonders what kind of friendship there can be between a seventeen-year-old girl and a middle-aged man. Harper always comes back with sweet-sour breath.

Sometimes Pearl sees Harper doing her own private magic. She whispers to a flower or a bird or a cloud. 'Tell her I love her,' Harper whispers. Pearl knows who Harper's talking to. Nathaniel Pelletier died before he knew.

It's sad, but it was sensible, Pearl thinks. What person in the world would have let a teenager carry that baby to term?

'Do you think he blames me for not keeping her?' Harper says sometimes, staring wide at Pearl. 'Do you think he knows now? Do you think he's with her?'

Pearl shivers at the thought of Nathaniel Pelletier looming above them somewhere in the sky, with a crying ghost baby in his arms.

'I was getting better before it all happened,' Harper says. 'Now it's too late for me. I've gone too far into the dark.' She picks up a moth whose wings are sodden and gently places it high on a strut of the bleachers so its wings can dry.

'That's not true,' Pearl says. 'We have plans.' She squeezes Harper's hand. They do have plans. They're both going to be famous artists or writers or painters. They do spells for it with moss and bird bones, burning the hair off their arms with a thrilling sizzle.

'Success,' Harper whispers.

'Success,' Pearl whispers back. 'We can do anything we want.'

'I'm going to be a film star like Grace Kelly then,' Harper says, batting her eyelids. 'Grace Kelly doesn't do all the stupid things I do. I'm going to be in the cinema.' She sighs. 'I love her.'

'Movies are so weird though,' Pearl says. They have recently shared a small yellow pill Pearl found while going through Muriel's purse, which she does on a regular basis. It's starting to kick in. 'They're traps, for moments in time.' The edges of the world pulse pleasantly.

'You can make a trap out of anything; a painting, or a word,' Harper says. Her head droops like a wilting flower. 'You can send a soul out into a star, imprison it on the head of a pin.' Her consonants jostle softly against one another. 'Anything can be a prison.'

Pearl nods, she knows what Harper means. Prisons are all around, if you choose to look. Out on the dark hockey field some small animal moves. The last of the rain falls in silver knitting needles through the night.

'Where does it come from?' Pearl whispers, as everything pulses blue around the edges. 'Magic.'

'From everything,' Harper says sadly.

They are nearly caught coming back into the dormitory. Pearl has trouble getting Harper back in the window. Harper has lost control of her limbs and she's angry. She hits Pearl in the face, leaving a red welt. Pearl gets Harper to the bathroom in time, before she throws up. After this Harper goes to bed, docile. Pearl cleans the bathroom. The streaked tile is red as murder; the smell follows her, clings to her hair. But it's all done in time for morning bell.

Harper sleeps through her classes the next day and gets grounded. No more walks to the gas station. But they can't prove anything which is good. Girls are expelled for that kind of thing. Pearl is worried about Harper. Harper arrived late in the year and missed a lot of school – she isn't keeping up in class.

Harper apologises to Pearl a hundred times. 'I'm so sorry,' she keeps saying. 'I won't do that anymore.'

'It's OK,' Pearl says. 'It's OK.' She strokes Harper's hair.

'I'll make it up to you,' Harper says. 'I'll do anything.'

'Tell me about it,' Pearl says. 'The cave.'

She feels Harper go cold in her arms. 'I can't do that,' she whispers. 'Please, don't make me.'

'It's the only thing I want,' Pearl says. She feels a cold hard place in her being exposed. She didn't know she could be this person.


Harper and Pearl sit under the bleachers. There are more spiders here now, it's their season; they hang like bombs about to drop. She and Harper are witches, Pearl reminds herself, so spiders are their friends. Out on the field, the lacrosse team slop and slide through puddles, mud. It seems to rain all the time at Fairview.

'What's it like?' Pearl asks. 'Look, smell.'

Harper thinks carefully. It makes Pearl love her – that she is answering with such care, even though Pearl is making her. 'It's behind a rock,' she says. 'That looks like an obelisk. A narrow channel leads to it. Inside it's kind of beautiful. Water playing on the ceiling and so on. At low tide it's a cave with places to sit. I used to just go there to think. With – Nat. It smelled like a tin can, but clean, you know. Not bad. At high tide it's like an underground lake.'

'Do you still miss him – Nathaniel?' A worm is writhing, pink at her feet. Pearl knows that normal girls would be afraid. They'd jump up and make expressions of disgust. But that's why she and

Harper like it down here. They don't have to pretend to be normal.

'I miss him,' Harper says. She stares at the worm. 'But I'm afraid of my memories. They're scary.'

Pearl feels sick and she realises, looking at Harper's pale face, that Harper does too. It costs Harper every time she relives this, Pearl knows. But she can't stop asking, either.

'Tell me about the other one,' Pearl says.

'Wilder. He tagged along after us and we let him. He was a sweet kid, I guess – weird though. Big bug eyes. Grey or blue I think, hard to tell, they were just so – pale. Too much going on inside them – like they were blank and busy at the same time. He had this . . . this want in him. For what, I don't know, but it was frightening – strong. I don't think he even knew what it was he wanted.' Harper shivers. 'If I had to pick the one who did stuff like – what happened – it wouldn't have been Nat. It would have been Wilder.'

Pearl nods. He haunts her like a light in the corner of her eye, this person, Wilder, like a light that goes out as soon as she looks at it.

'Tell me about the last day in the cave.'

'Pearl,' Harper says. 'I don't want to. Please, no more.'

Pearl takes a soda bottle out of her coat pocket. She walked to the gas station yesterday and had a good talk to the man there. 'Here,' she says to Harper.

Harper takes it, and Pearl hates that she's seen that moment in her friend's face just now – she stopped being a person, for a second.

'You started out in god weather,' Pearl says.

'We picked Wilder up just after dawn,' Harper's voice is steadier now. She holds the soda bottle tightly.

Pearl knows that if she fills in enough details, if she knows enough, then finally she will understand, she will be healed. She'll hear her mother's voice in her head again, the way she used to. Back when she had just drowned, out at sea, and had not suffered those unspeakable things in the dark, before her death.

'I want to kill him,' Pearl says, when Harper's done.

'I know you do.' Harper knows that Pearl means Alton Pelletier.

'Let's do it,' Pearl says. 'We can do it with the blood.' Excitement floods her, hot and itchy. It's the kind of excitement that will eat her up, she knows that. It's not good for her.

'What do you mean?'

'Kill him.'

'Pearl . . .'

'We'll use magic,' she says. 'You were there in the cave, you swam over her bones. And I'm of her blood too. So we're all connected.'

Harper's hand is kind on Pearl's shoulder. She knows what Pearl wants to say, but can't. Words are very powerful in themselves, and if she says it, puts it into the world with her breath, the idea will be there and Pearl will have to deal with it.

*Maybe if we kill him she'll come back.*

It's impossible, of course, and Pearl can't handle facing that, the impossibility. So she doesn't say it.

As they creep out from under the bleachers Pearl steps on the worm, grinds it beneath her heel. *It's kinder this way*, she tells it silently.

\*

In the following days, she can't stop looking at Harper's pale skin, thinking of the blood that runs under it, and the blood that runs under her own.

She knows, of course she does, that it's just nonsense, a game. A

279

way of protecting her mind from sadness and fear. But at the same time she knows that it isn't.

Harper cuts herself with a scalpel dissecting a frog. She throws the Band-Aid into the trash after biology. Pearl stares at it, thinking of the spell she would invent, which will link her with her mother, using her blood.

Pearl looks up and sees Harper watching. She knows Pearl is thinking of taking the Band-Aid out of the trash. She understands Pearl really well. People always think she talks too much, but Pearl knows why she does that, the incessant stream of words. She does it because she notices too much, and it's too much for her to take, all these things she sees. Sometimes she has to shut it all out with talk or gas-station wine.

Pearl knows, if there were such a thing as a witch in the real world, it would be Harper.

'Don't, Pearl,' she says. 'Let it go.'

'Let's go out tonight,' Pearl says. They're walking from Biology to Chem. The halls stink of mud and wet leather. 'Let's take some of Muriel's toenail. I bet I can do it without waking her up.'

'Not tonight, Pearl.'

'I took a walk to the gas station yesterday,' Pearl says.

'No!' Harper says. She almost yells it and a couple of girls look back at them. She lowers her voice. 'Not tonight, maybe never.'

Pearl starts to shake. 'What does it look like, Harper, the cave?'

'I meant it, Pearl.'

She looks at Harper, stunned. The sound of roaring waves almost drown her voice.

'I won't do that anymore,' Harper says. 'It's not good for you – and it's not good for me.'

'But I need it,' Pearl said. 'I need you to tell me—'

'We both have to move on. Get a life.'

Pearl scratches at Harper's face. Harper grabs her wrist in a strong grip. 'I'm sorry,' she says, and she sounds it.

Pearl shrugs. 'You're right,' she says. 'Sorry. Went kind of crazy there for a second.'

Harper hugs her and Pearl hugs her back. Pearl knows her really well, too. She knows how deep she has to hide the feelings, so Harper won't see them.

Once or twice, some nights, it seemed like Harper half woke as Pearl stood over her. Pearl held her breath and was still, and soon enough Harper turned over and Pearl thought she had fallen back to sleep. But she wonders now if she really did.

No one knows who tips off the principal but during the search they find wine under Harper's pillow.

Harper stands there for a second, looking at the bottle. Then she looks up at Pearl, and her smile is sad, not angry.

Harper's parents come for her the next day. No one is allowed to say goodbye. Pearl watches from an upstairs window as Harper gets into the car, pale, looking somehow half her usual size. Pearl wonders what will happen to Harper. Where will she go? Who will she become?

She pulls the doll out of her pocket. It's made mostly of her braided hair, dull brown. But the coppery red strands from Harper's head give it a metallic appearance in places. She took it slowly, hair by hair, over many nights as she slept. Pearl got the idea from what they did to Muriel.

The little blank, braided face stares up at her. The doll seems to absorb all the light, a patch of dark in the bright day. There's a narrow swipe of rust across the doll's face, where Pearl wiped Harper's blood, from where she scratched her.

'I don't need you anymore anyway,' she whispers as Harper's car draws away with a crunch on the gravel. But she knows it's a lie. She needs Harper more than anything.


Pearl doesn't know, even now, whether she really once thought she could kill a man or raise her mother from the dead with a doll of hair. She isn't sure what she thinks now. Panic rises. Who is she without Harper? She's alone, alone, all all alone.

Pearl breathes deeply. *Cool*, she thinks. *Be cool as a drink of water.*

When she opens her eyes she knows what she's going to do. Maybe she has always known. It might take some time. It might take years. But she'll get it done.

# Wilder, the Last Day

Rebecca hums, darkens and fades in the corner. I've stopped changing her in the text – at first I did it for fun, but it stopped being fun. She suffers when I do it. It's cruel, I see that now.

She's rotting badly; ribbons of flesh are loosening from her face, floating free on the unseen tide. It feels good to have given her a story. It feels like justice somehow. I've found reasons for all the things that are happening to me. I snort a little amused snort to myself because *Skye* makes way more sense than what's happening in real life.

I reread *Skye* as the sun rises. It's not too long – more a novella than a novel. I can't tell whether it's any good or not, it just is. Some of it I don't recall writing.

Time to finish my story, too.

I box up my typewriter. I put *Skye* beside it, with a brief note. No explanations, just instructions. I asked Harper to come over for lunch.

She'll find the note. I hate to do this to her but there's no one else.

So Sky found a way to trap me in the book. It's obvious to me now. I've seen Helen, on the streets of Castine. Rebecca follows me faithfully. Even Anton has paid me a visit. Skandar strokes my chest at night. Nate put Polaroids through my mail slot.

The cast of *The Sound and the Dagger* is all around me and there's only one character missing. Where's Wiley? There's no Wiley, because it's me. I'm in the book.

I put on a coat. It's due to snow later. Then I take it off again. It's a nice coat; Emily bought it for me. I don't want to spoil it. Someone might want it after.

I make my way behind the cottage, up the hill to the meadow. The air warms as I go. The meadow is covered in wildflowers. There are birds on the wing. Spring has crept in close without my noticing. But that can't be right, it's far too early. The birds are summer birds, chickadees, cuckoos, goldfinches. The meadow is covered in nodding grass, starred with daisies and black-eyed Susan. The copse of beech trees is in full leaf. The ground beneath them is carpeted with violets, yellow and purple.

It isn't spring, it's summer, a blue and gold summer. I walk through the weather of *The Sound and the Dagger*. The bay below is a different shape, the beach wider. Seals luxuriate on warm rock. It's not Whistler Bay. It's Looking Glass Sound.

Sky's original manuscript is under my arm.

Rebecca drifts behind me, blue skirts making no impression on the young grass. In the sunlight her suppurating flesh is a horror. Her eyes are blank as pearls. Maybe I can give her some peace. I mean to try. She may not be real, but she can feel pain, all right.

Should that fact have some kind of meaning – tell me something about life? Perhaps it should, but I don't know what.

Ahead of me, he's walking – Nate. Thin brown legs brushed by long grass. Denim cutoffs worn to a softness so thin that you can almost see his shorts under. One hand trails beside him, stroking the switchgrass.

I bend to breathe it, the warm earth. A daisy nods at my fingertips. I see that something is wrong with my hands. They're smooth – the knuckles don't have those maddening, fine tufts of hair that seemed to appear as if by magic on my forty-fifth birthday. No age spots, the nailbeds are pink. Young.

I put my hands to my face then my stomach. I'm thinner; I can feel the firmness of stomach muscles, ribs, cheekbones. My hair is thick, the forelock that hangs over my brow is silken, dark as pitch.

I see it up ahead, the treeline, the branches shushing and murmuring in the summer breeze. A wood pigeon calls, a cuckoo. It's warm, so warm I feel like I could just lie down here in the sunshine and fall asleep. In a way that's what I'm going to do.

In the trees, the light filters through all strange, a summer green. First, I clear a space in the grass and gather sticks for kindling. I brought lighter fuel and pretty soon the fire is crackling merrily. I put the manuscript of *The Sound and the Dagger* on the fire. The pages catch and curl, then roar up in a gout of flame.

Nate, Skandar, Anton and Helen stand in a circle, watching me. Their eyes are hollow places. Rebecca hovers, her mouth opens wide. Even though it's silent, I can tell it's a scream.

'I'm sorry,' I whisper. 'Just a couple moments longer.'

Her jaw extends lower and lower; her mouth is a long black place, a doorway opening. When I look I see there's a tiny lit-up scene inside her mouth – a family, picnicking on the beach. A mother, a father, a little girl.

'Did you eat them?' I ask her, 'Oh, god, please don't eat me.' Her hands reach rotten for my neck. Her white eyes stare.

The book is almost gone. I kick the crackling red pyre. *The Sound and the Dagger* flies apart and as it does, the book ghosts explode in a shower of red sparks. There's a smell like bad meat cooking. Rebecca goes last. As she burns, her hair goes blonde and curly. She seems to get smaller, slighter, more athletic. She has revealed herself at last. It's difficult to read her expression in the moment before she disappears, but I hope it's relief.

Soon the book is no more than a storm of ash, floating on the wind. I pick a posy of wild tulips in her honour and lay them on the remaining ashes. A crimson poppy nods among the grass. A squirrel chatters overhead, racing from branch to branch. There's so much growing life.

The other thing grows here, too. I find it again without too much difficulty, even with my eyesight – it's like it wants to be found. Green fronds. I start to pull my sleeve down over my hand, to grasp the stem, and then stop. What would be the point of that?

This is the right ending. I've finished the story, I've burned the past. There's nothing left for me. I'm an aging failure. Sooner or later, I'll go blind.

Still, I hesitate for a moment.

The weekend Emily was in the Hamptons I went on the satweb to find, what do you call it these days, a date. And I waited, and waited, and the guy didn't even show. But she came home early – I wasn't there, like I said I was.

Emily knows me really – I think she's always known. The funny thing is, she might have listened, if I'd talked to her about everything. About Sky and desire and all those things that float in our darkness, like lights on the water. Too late now. It's all too late.

I take the hemlock in a firm grasp. The stalk is spongy, it gives at the pressure of my grip and the sap comes away sticky on my hand. I pull it right out of the ground. The root is like misshapen fingers. It looks evil. I don't even shake it free of dirt. There's no point in that, either. I close my eyes and bite. It tastes sharp and fresh, not like poison at all.


I wait. The sun rises higher over the sea. Nothing happens. I shove more hemlock into my mouth, chewing furiously, trying not to gag on the dirt. My suspicion turns to certainty. I start laughing, around mouthfuls of wild carrot.

I spit out the last soily mouthful and get up. This isn't my ending, apparently.

A sound on the wind. I turn my head sharply.

'Are you there?' I whisper. 'Rebecca?' But she burned up – there is only the wind.

*Help*, comes the voice.

'What do you want from me?' I shout.

'Here,' comes the voice. 'Help. I'm in here.' Slowly, I turn my head. It can't be. But it is. The cliff is calling. It's coming from the hole in the cliff that Nat kept his beers in.

I go to the hole. 'You're not real,' I tell it. 'You're not talking.'

'Please, give me your hand,' the hole says to me. 'Please.'

I don't want to but I do, just to prove to myself that I'm right and this is all some kind of dream. Maybe his ghost left me a beer, I think, hysterical. I wait to feel the smooth shape of a glass bottle.

'I'm in so much pain,' moans the hill.

'Nat?' But it's not his voice. Darkness creeps up my arm like ink. I remember this feeling, that the hole is a mouth preparing to close on me. Further, further, I insert myself into the rock, the land. I think of snakes and spiders and rats, and all the things that live in holes. I gasp and brace myself, preparing to feel fur, the smooth scales sliding past my fingers. But there's only rough rock.

Maybe the hemlock worked after all. Maybe I'm dead. How would I know? I am up to my shoulder, buried in the cliff.

A hand closes around mine. Fingers grip like a vice. The earth has hands. I gasp and struggle.

*Help*, says Rebecca from inside the earth.

Even though I don't want to, I bend and look into the rocky passage.

Fingers grip mine, dark with dirt and blood. I can see crescents of nail, black with earth. From the back, a gleam in the darkness. An eye blinks. I am in a dream. The meadow is looking at me with its shining eye.

I scream then, a raw sound that comes from the very pit of me. It fills the air with jagged noise.

'You found me,' the voice says again, and it's not Rebecca. Not a woman at all.

I stop, weak.

'Sky?' No sound to the hallucinations, I tell myself again. There is supposed to be *no sound*.

So I have finally gone mad. This is it.

'Wilder? Oh, Wilder, it's you.'


It takes a day for the rescue crew, working with pickaxes and drills, to widen the hole in the cliff and drag Sky out. He is thin almost beyond recognition. His left hand is wrapped in muddy, dirty fabric. He can't stop shaking and sticking his tongue out, as if he's still trying to lick the runoff from the stream which trickles down the cave walls.

Nat's hidey hole leads down, down into the bowels of the hill. At the bottom is a chamber. There's a narrow underwater entrance from the cove, which was closed by a rockfall. In it is a metal barrel, surface rough with time. She has been found at last – the missing oil-drum woman.

They identify her by her fingerprints. It's Arlene Pelletier, Nat's mother. She never left Whistler Bay, after all.


'I kept going towards the light,' Sky says.

His room is quiet, there's only the soft whir of machines. I don't know what they all do. There's intermittent gentle beeping. Behind the door comes the muted sounds of a hospital at night.

Sky couldn't feed himself at first, but he got his nasogastric tube out yesterday and he opens a tub of apple sauce. The noises of enjoyment he makes while eating it are almost obscene.

'You want me to leave you alone with that?' I ask.

He looks frightened. 'No,' he says, 'please don't leave me alone.' I'm sorry right away that I teased. He's still pale, almost as pale as his white-bandaged stump. They couldn't save the hand. What was left of it.

'I didn't mean it,' I say, touching his remaining hand. 'And you don't have to talk about it if you don't want to.'

'I want to, Wilder. It's wonderful to have someone to talk to. To have you here. Mmm.' He makes an appreciative noise and sticks his tongue into the applesauce pot.

'Almost three weeks with nothing but crabs,' he says. 'Have you ever eaten a live crab in its shell, Wilder? It's horrible.' His voice is still hoarse. He spent days yelling, calling for help beneath the hill.

'But I could always see it up on the scree – that little square of light. I crawled as far as I could each day. Sometimes that was only an inch. Never seemed to get closer, so sometimes I thought I was imagining it, the daylight. But at night I could see stars too and I thought, well, I could be dreaming the day, but not both – sunlight and starlight. I don't know why I was so convinced of that, it doesn't make much sense. You narrow down, when you're trapped in the dark like that. You reduce everything to a couple of certainties.'

He found the cave when he was anchoring his boat in Whistler Bay one night.

'What were you doing there in the dark? Or,' I pause. 'At all?'

'Well,' he says, looking sheepish. 'Sometimes, when I'm up here, I go to the cottage at night. If it's empty, I let myself in. The latch on that porthole window is really loose. You should get that fixed.'

'Good to know,' I say dryly. 'Why?'

'I leave you notes,' he says, suddenly shy. 'Just in case you ever come back here. Not long ones, just a word or two. I hide them around the cottage.'

'Like behind skirting boards and the backs of drawers?'

'Yes.'

'That,' I say, 'is as creepy as hell.'

He smiles. 'It sounds it, now I say it out loud . . . I've been going through a hard time, these last couple years. Been thinking about things I could have done differently.' He pauses. 'And I thought it was romantic. At the time.' We look at one another.

'So you were in the cove—'

'Right,' he says hurriedly. 'The anchor was stuck on something so I jumped in to get it, and there it was, this little dark hole, a cave – I could see the rim of the opening, just above the surface.'

'It doesn't make sense,' I say. 'How could we not have known? How could we not have seen it?'

'The tides have changed in the last thirty-three years. The sea levels are different. Anyway, I swam in. And I found her, the oil drum, wedged in the rock. I tried to get her out and that's what did it. When I moved her, the rockfall came. It was so loud, everything was crashing around me, I thought I was going to die. When it was quiet again I was surprised to find myself alive. Later I started to wish I wasn't.

'I took a pretty good blow to the head. When I woke up, my hand was buried under these sharp rocks, up to the wrist. I was in so much pain. I couldn't see, but I could tell I'd lost a finger. It felt like it was on fire. I could smell blood.

'When the tide came in it half-filled the cave. The water rose as high as my chest. The next day it was higher, nearly up to my shoulders. I knew if I stayed there too long, I'd drown. I had to get free. The knife was in my belt. I'd brought it with me, in case I needed to cut the anchor loose.' He stops, swallows. 'Still, it took me three days to get up the resolve to cut it off,' he says. 'My hand.

'I made a tourniquet out of everything I could tear off my clothes. Managed to get my belt off. It took longer than I thought it would. I couldn't do much at one time. Had to saw through in stages. But I was getting weaker and weaker, and I couldn't – get through the bone.'

I feel lightheaded. 'How did you—'

'I remembered that dream you used to have. In the end I just – pulled, and the skin came off like a glove.'

'Oh my god,' I say, heat rising in my throat. *Degloved*.

'It saved my life,' he says. 'It was interesting, in a way, looking at my hand without any flesh. I wrapped it up in what was left of my shirt but I knew I'd never see it again, one way or the other. I wonder if the rest of my hand is still down there – I wonder if the crabs are eating me, now?'

'How can you smile?' I say, shivering. I picture a bloody glove of flesh, trapped in the rock.

'I'm happy,' he says, surprised. 'I'm alive when I was sure I'd die. And you're here. I've always hoped I would see you again.' He touches my hand lightly with his good one. 'I could hear your voice, Wilder. I thought I was dreaming – thought it was death coming for me. I called out to you. Again, and again.'

'I heard you calling for help. I thought you were a ghost.'

'Host,' he says.

'Lost,' I say.

Sky bows his head. His messy russet hair is streaked with grey. 'Everything got so messed up between us,' he says.

'Yes, totally fucked up.'

'Don't you mean fricked up, Wilder?' He raises his head and looks at me with the trace of a smile.

'No,' I say. 'I don't.'

'What I don't understand,' he says, 'is what you were doing there. I'd only just crawled within reach of the hole. If you'd been any later I think I might have been dead. I was so nearly dead as it was. How did you get there just then?'

'I don't know,' I say. 'But somehow your book led me there. I can't explain it. *The Sound and the Dagger* brought me to you.'

'That's . . . nonsense, Wilder.'

'Maybe nonsense is all we have left.'


The doctors and nurses all fall in love with Sky. Even twenty pounds underweight, his skull cadaverous, his smile is as warm as ever.

'He's such a fascinating man. You two must have such interesting conversations,' a nurse says to me, breathless.

'Oh, I'm sure we will,' I say dryly, looking at Sky.

Somehow, there is no question that he will come to Whistler Cottage when he's released from hospital.


I wake with his arm flung over me, his warmth at my back. I yawn and prepare myself to face the morning chill. It's still dark out. The winter is a hard one. Snow falls, and a couple of times the power has gone out for an hour or so.

Sky makes a complaining sound and taps my shoulder, like, *be quiet*.

'Sh,' I say. 'No need for you to get up yet.' We took to sharing a bed for warmth, after the heating cut out one night.

Sky's a lot better but he's still weak. I cut up his food, I help him dress and brush his hair for him.

'We could go somewhere else,' I say when I bring him oatmeal. 'South. California. Wouldn't that be better?' The light is coming in over the sea.

'I hate California.'

'Oh,' I say. 'Well, I'm sure California started it.' He's been touchy, these last few days.

I have his arm halfway into a cardigan when he stops me, impatient. 'I'm not going to apologise to you for what happened back then,' he says. 'You know that.'

'Oh,' I say. 'I do know. Believe me, I know the kind of monster you are.'

'It didn't belong to anyone, that story. It was as much mine as yours.'

'Whatever you need to tell yourself,' I say. I draw the sleeve

293

very gently up his maimed arm. He is healing well but he still feels pain there, in the missing hand. 'Do you remember that first architecture class?' I ask, absent. 'You—'

'I gave you my coat,' he says.

'It was so warm,' I say. 'From you. It was like being inside your skin.' And suddenly we're aware: of the sea murmuring outside, of the maple with its shushing leaves, and most of all we're conscious of space and time and skin, our bodies, my hands on him.

'The thing is,' I say. 'You did cure me, in a way. I never had a panic attack again after that book was published. I was too angry.'

'There's a package for you in the bottom drawer of the dresser,' he says. 'I had it sent over.'

She's unchanged by time, a little faded maybe but I still recognise her – Aphrodite, coming out of the waves. The pages are crisp, the typescript greenish with age. It's strange to hold it in my hands again. *The Dagger Man of Whistler Bay.*

'You kept it.'

'Of course.'

'I've been trying again,' I say. 'Writing.'

'I need to know you're not going to try that other thing again, Wilder – that stunt with the hemlock. Can you promise me that?'

'You're only alive because I tried to do that. Imagine if I hadn't been there.'

'I need to know.'

I look at his face, obscured by bright blue worms, writhing. The white patch is spreading fast over my vision.

'I'll be blind soon,' I say bitterly.

'There are worse things than blind. Promise me.' His hand is warm on my cheek.

*

I see the visions for a couple months longer – little parades of elf men marching up the lampshades. Beautiful bright fronds waving in the air, like live corals in the tide. Nothing from the past, though. That part seems to be done.

Winter comes. In Castine they say that the Pelletier place stands empty, now – Harper is gone, no one seems to know where. I'm glad. It feels like some spell has been broken, releasing her from this place. Perhaps we can all move on, now.

My sight deteriorates sharply. Darkness begins to fall. As soon as Sky can move around, he has to start looking after me.

I feel the spring come in, rather than see it. It's late afternoon, too warm in the kitchen because the oven has been on. Sky opens the door, even though it's bitter-bright. I smell cold spring tides, the waking of the land. There's a tractor working in a field some-where. A blackbird sings in the woods behind. Sky is writing something. I hear the scratch of his pen. It makes me think of a warm horse barn at night. The timer goes and he gets up. The oven opens, there's a brief faint pulse of heat.

'Scoot your chair in,' he says. 'Dinner's here.' I move carefully – I'm still getting used to the dark. I think, *ordinary things are wonderful.*

'Salmon is at twelve o'clock,' Sky says. 'Peas are at nine. Potatoes are kind of three to six. Do you want watercress sauce? This is an old family recipe.' I don't tell him I heard him open the carton. I let him lie to me about little things, sometimes. I know he needs it.

Sky describes where the food is on the plate, so I know what I'm eating. In return I cut his potatoes up for him. He hasn't had his prosthetic hand fitted yet. We like to eat early, before the light goes, because I can still kind of see the sunset if it's red enough, and besides, that's what we prefer – so who cares that it's the time when old people sit down to eat?

I almost manage to stifle the stray thoughts that scratch at me in the night, while Sky sleeps beside me. Nat and Sky both lost a hand. It's symmetrical. Neat. Almost like someone's written it.

I think about our three names, us kids, as we were. 'Wilder,' I whisper to myself sometimes. 'Nathaniel, Harper.' We're all named after writers. It's too much of a coincidence. *Harper. Wilder Harlow.* The names chime together. The kind of thing that would never happen in real life but it might happen in a book.

I take a deep breath. Such thoughts lead nowhere. I have to start trusting sometime. This. Him. Just because I can't see him doesn't mean he's not there.

'Can you, Wilder?' Sky says, breaking into my thoughts. I can tell he's struggling with the sauce and I find the bowl with careful hands and spoon it over his salmon. The scent rises, creamy. Scent has become a tapestry for me. There's so much more of it than I'd ever thought, when I had my sight. It's a book in itself.

'We're a fine pair, aren't we?' Sky says, cheerful.

'I don't think I ever got over it,' I say, suddenly putting down the bowl of sauce with a crack. 'I never got over you leaving.'

There's a long silence. One terrible thing about being almost blind is that you can't scan people's faces. You have to learn to read silences, to breathe the feelings coming off people's skin. But I can't read this one. I don't know what he's thinking.

'I miss you,' I say. 'I have done ever since. The missing, it's worse than pain. It lives inside me, it eats me like a parasite. I won't be able to bear it if you leave again.'

'I have an idea,' he says, at last. 'If we both stay in the same place, we won't miss one another. What do you think?'

There's a crash that shakes me, goes right into my gut.

'That damn door,' Sky says. I hear him get up and close it, but it breaks free again and hits the wall with a crack.

The wind roars in, pushing like a bully, tearing at my hair and clothes and all the doors in the house slam and the windows are rattling hard in their frames. Sky's hand finds mine, he flings his good warm arm around me. We are breathless, clinging to one another.

The wind whistles through the house, lifting objects in its path. Is everything floating? I picture it, furniture and beds and tables and chairs and us, all being sucked out of the door, flung out over the wide terrible sea, dropped into the deep, lost forever. 'Am I blowing away?' I ask Sky. 'Is the house still here?'

Sky holds me tighter. 'It's the wind,' he says. 'Just the wind, darling.'

And with his words I feel the ground beneath my feet again, and I can smell that blue-green mineral tang in the air. I take his earlobe gently between my teeth and tug. There will be snow before nightfall.

*The End*
*Whistler Bay, Maine, 2011*

# *Pearl*

## 2011

Pearl Boone finishes writing the book as first light spreads over the sea. The words pulse on the screen in front of her.

### *Whistler Bay, Maine, 2011*

Her head aches, she feels scared and sick. First draft done. It's not finished, but it's there.

It's bold, it experiments with form, it's metafiction. All that crap the critics like. It sold well, *The Sound and the Dagger*, but no one really respected it. They'll respect this, she hopes. Then she thinks – *why, after all these years, do I care?*

Through the window, the sea is steel grey, lashing white. It's cold out there; all she wants to do is curl up in front of the TV. But she can't, she has a promise to keep. She goes there every time she finishes a book.

She puts on boots, a sweater, a jacket. The wind blasts her face. Castine is quiet, cold, asleep for the winter. She can't stand the sight of so many boarded-up storefronts. They remind her of death, somehow. Pearl strikes out along the rocky shore, spirits rising. She'll be a different person now she's put it all down on the page, she's sure. She'll be free. But then, she feels that every time she finishes.

It's just ten minutes' walk from town but it could be another world. The tarry beach, littered with tide debris. Empty plastic bottles, the odd shoe, fragments of net. And the old house itself, hunched on the shingle, as though keeping a secret.

Layers of paint peel to show the bare wood silvered grey with time. There's an empty KFC bucket hung on the gatepost. The one remaining pane of glass winks in the early sun like a gleaming eye.

*Sun*, she thinks. *Sin*. That old game her dad made her play when she came in drunk. *She was here*, she thinks, as she always does. It's a sacred place for that reason. She died here, they think. Rebecca Boone. Pearl doesn't go into the hows of that, lets her mind cover it with merciful velvet black. But she feels the power of the house. It's the last place her mother was alive, and so Pearl is connected to her here.

She tests herself but she knows her limits, these days. She never goes in. People do, all the time. Kids keep breaking into the house looking for ghosts – as kids have done since there were first kids. Nor does she go out back to the seaward side, down to the little pier where the boat used to dock.

Pearl has been on to the town council, time and again, to tear the place down, but it keeps getting snarled up in zoning and red tape. They don't admit it, but the house is a tourist attraction. Pearl can see them from the boat sometimes in the summers, walking in a long line, single file along the narrow beach at high tide, to see the place where women were killed. The shingles on the roof are all gone. People take them. The roof is ribbed and bare like the skeleton of a whale.

Sometimes Pearl imagines them, these shingles, sitting on mantlepieces or bedside tables or stored in shoeboxes in teen-agers' bedrooms. Do people like sleeping in the same room as a roof shingle that once absorbed the sound of women dying? The council filled the cellar with earth, at least. At least they did that.

Pearl turns to start the trek back to her car, and then she stops dead. There's a sound on the air, it's unmistakeable. Weeping. *Don't be coming from in there*, she thinks. *Anywhere but there.* But she understands right away with a heavy sinking that there's a child crying in the old Pelletier place.

The tearful moan comes again, from inside the house. Maybe it's not a child, but an adult. *Maybe they came here to be upset in private*, Pearl tells herself. Maybe Pearl is actually bothering them and she should just go—

'Are you OK?' Pearl calls.

'My foot is stuck,' a small voice replies.

*Shit*, she thinks. 'OK, keep still. Don't move. I'm coming in.'

The doorway is still standing but Pearl doesn't like the look of it. There's something creepy about opening a door to a place that's open to the sky. She steps through a hole in the wall.

'Where are you?' But she sees the leg dangling from the ceiling, bloody. The girl was exploring upstairs and stepped on a rotten place. The boards parted like butter left out all night.

'Coming,' she says, suddenly finding it difficult to breathe.

The stairs are OK; someone has laid new boards over the old rotting ones, hammered them into the joists. *Sure, great*, Pearl thinks. Make it easier to access this death trap.

The door to what was once Nathaniel's bedroom has come off its hinges. It leans against the wall. She's in there, sitting back on her haunches. One leg is plunged into the hole in the rotted board. There's blood on the old wood and everything swims around Pearl for a second. *More blood*, she thinks. *The house feeds on it.*

'I fell through,' the girl says unnecessarily. She's got a fierce chin, copper hair. Her eyes are wide with fear.

'I see that. Does it hurt?'

'A little.' She winces as she says it. A fresh thread of blood runs damson-dark across the boards.

'I'm going to help you,' Pearl says calmly. 'But I need to get some stuff from my car. Can you hold on? Don't move while I'm gone. Stay completely still. Can you do that?'

'I think so,' the girl says. Her pupils are dilated, black suns. She's in shock.

Pearl runs back along the beach, heart hot in her throat. She could see the white of bone amidst the crimson mess of the girl's leg. She calls 911 as soon as she hits cellphone reception. They'll be out as soon as they can. It might be an hour; it's treefall season, the roads are bad.

She grabs the hacksaw from her trunk. Everyone keeps one of these handy this time of year – fallen branches block the roads sometimes. She takes a blanket from the back seat and opens the little first aid kit she keeps behind the spare wheel. Looking at the contents, she feels the give of fear. A roll of gauze, antiseptic, ointment for insect bites. She thinks of the open mouth of flesh in the girl's leg. It's a kit for nicks and scrapes, not wounds where the bone peeks out like a shy smile.

'We'll work with what we've got,' she says aloud to herself.

She must run pretty fast back across the shore; she doesn't remember doing it but suddenly she's there, blinking in front of the ruined house.

She climbs the stairs carefully, looks at the girl trapped in the floor, at the ragged splintered gap. She doesn't step across the threshold into the bedroom for now. No use both of them going down.

Pearl thinks. She examines the door, which leans against the wall. Unlike the floor, it seems sound. She lays it gently down on the floor, over the rotted boards. If she crawls out onto it and reaches out her arms, she should be able to touch the girl.

'I'm going to slide you this saw,' Pearl says, 'can you grab it? Reach with your arm, don't shift your weight. Try not to move your leg.'

'OK.'

'Then I'll crawl over to you.'

The girl grabs the handsaw by the blade as it whistles past her. One of its sharp teeth pierces her finger. A drop of blood rises. A princess in a fairytale. It seems so insignificant compared to the gaping wound in her leg – but all wounds are significant, aren't they? Pearl feels her thoughts getting wild, panic is sending up its little red tendrils.

*No*, she thinks. *Be cool. Be a drink of water.*

She takes a deep breath and lowers herself onto her belly. Down here she can smell the Pelletier place. She's kissing distance from its bones, its body.

Pearl crawls slowly across the door. Her sweater rides up and she feels the sand and dust scrape her flesh, feels the filth of the place touch her. *Doesn't matter*, she thinks again. It's kind of her mantra. *Doesn't matter, doesn't matter.*

The boards creak beneath her and she catches her breath, feels the fall, sees her death. But the boards stay sound.

When she gets to the girl she sits up very slowly, one movement at a time. Pushes up onto her hands. Turns over. Lowers herself into a sitting position. When she's done it and she and the girl are face to face they smile at each other, goofy with accomplishment. The girl reaches out and squeezes Pearl's hand briefly.

'OK,' Pearl says, 'Here goes.' The saw bites and drags in the old, splintering wood, which is riddled with soft spots. It releases the scent of rot as she cuts. The texture is that of something dead that's been lying out.

'Ow,' Pearl sucks her finger.

'Are you OK?' The girl looks terrified. Pearl can understand that. A drop or two of her blood falls, marks the girl's faded, filthy jeans and she sees the girl losing her colour, sees the white creeping into her face.

'I'm Pearl. What's your name?' she asks.

'Gracie.'

'That's a nice name,' Pearl says.

'I'm going to change it.'

'Why?'

'My mom gave it to me.' Gracie wriggles her nose, uncomfortable. 'She didn't want me, so why should I be who she wanted?'

'Mine was murdered,' Pearl hears herself say.

They both kind of take that in for a moment.

'I changed my name from Pearl to Skye while I was in college,' Pearl says.

'It's a nice name, Pearl.'

'I guess.'

'Why'd you change it?'

'I was feeling pretentious that day. Maybe I was tired of being me. I changed it back later.'

'You write the books,' Gracie says. 'I know you.'

'Yes.'

Gracie's face contracts with pain. The anaesthesia of shock is wearing off.

'My best book was my first book,' Pearl says quickly. 'I think they've all been crappy since then.'

Gracie smirks, the way young people do when grownups try and be cool by swearing in front of them.

'It was about what happened here,' Pearl says. 'This town. This place. Or at least, Whistler Bay, up the coast. But I changed the name. I called it Looking Glass Sound in the book. It was about the murders.'

'I know,' Gracie says. 'I've read it. I've read everything about them.'

'Of course you have,' Pearl says. She knows Gracie is young, tries not to let the anger rise in her. Why must people come here like this? To stare, to imagine the suffering. It's like they're feeding the house, keeping it alive. But then isn't that what she's doing herself, in a way?

'Where you from, Gracie?'

'All over,' Gracie says, and Pearl feels the heaviness behind the words. She sees the signs. Hands clean but nails dirty, a collar of grime at her neck. It's a quick gas station wash, one where you act fast and don't take off any clothes. Her t-shirt is three sizes too big. The one foot Pearl can see is shod in a dirty sneaker, the disintegrating sole bound onto the shoe with duct tape. Homeless, probably. Definitely poor. Pearl's anger dies down as quickly as it flared.

'How old are you, Gracie?'

'Nineteen.'

Pearl's heart gives a tug. It's so young.

'All done,' Pearl says. She has cut a circle around Gracie's leg with the hacksaw. She hopes this is the right thing to do. If she can lift the leg out within its tight corona of boards, maybe they can get out of there without hurting her too much.

'Like a cookie cutter,' Gracie says, looking at Pearl's handiwork. Her eyelids flicker and her head dips for a second as if she's sleepy. Pearl doesn't like that.

'Just like a cookie cutter,' she replies. She sticks a metal ruler in at various points around the circle and gently, gently as she can, applies pressure, lifting. She hears dust and detritus falling to the kitchen floor downstairs. Gracie moans and winces.

'I'll stop,' says Pearl, suddenly terrified. 'This was a bad idea.'

Just then a piece of floor falls away, and Gracie and Pearl are looking down into the kitchen through a jagged hole. Gracie lifts her leg tentatively. Her ankle is still encased in a collar of wood, but she is free.

Pearl slips her arms under Gracie's and slides herself backwards inch by inch across the door, pulling Gracie with her. She can feel the girl's ribs working as she breathes. She can tell that she's trying not to panic.

Once they reach the door of the bedroom and are back on fairly solid footing, they just sit for a second. Pearl feels almost euphoric. 'We did it,' she says, wild.

Gracie sinks back against her, as if relaxing. Pearl realises that she has passed out.

From below comes the sound of running footsteps. Voices call from the beach. Help is here.


The little emergency room in Castine is quiet. Night is falling. Pearl sits on the uncomfortable orange seats and waits.

They close the wound in Gracie's leg with a flap of skin. Otherwise, if left exposed the bone would become dry and brittle. To Pearl it seems so strange and logical – that the best way of treating damage is to cover it up.

Gracie has no insurance. They treat her, but she can't stay.

'You can come home with me,' Pearl hears herself say. She's startled. It's the last thing she wants, she tells herself. 'Just one night.'

*

The stones are whistling below as they reach the cottage. The sugar maple is crimson in the fading light.

Pearl bought the cottage off Wilder's mom after his death but she doesn't come here much. She came this year, to write the book. Harper still lives on the bay, in her white house that looks like crème pâtissière. Pearl feels a moment of guilt that she made her Harper character live in the old Pelletier place.

Pearl and Harper don't speak, haven't since the day, all those years ago, that she heard about Wilder.

'What's that sound?' Gracie says. She's a slip of white in the dusk. She's using old wooden crutches, which were all the hospital was willing to part with.

'It's just a trick of the wind,' Pearl says. 'Don't worry.' She can't tell if Gracie is worried or not. The girl has a still surface. Pearl recognises that. It's a way of protecting yourself from others – of hiding the deep warm things that are happening inside.

Gracie is almost asleep but Pearl warms soup from a can and makes her eat it with crackers. 'I've never been much of a cook,' she says, apologetic and slightly defiant. 'But you've lost blood.'

'It's good,' Gracie says, and eats. When she's finished she says politely, 'Thank you for dinner.'

Pearl puts her to bed in the room with the porthole. She goes to close the window; the night air has a bite to it at this time of year. 'Leave it open,' Gracie says. 'I like the noises the stones make. Hooting. It sounds like owls.'

'I suppose it does,' Pearl says. 'I never thought of it like that before.' All this time she thought the stones sounded like mourning or destruction. But maybe they've sounded like owls all along.

*

Pearl wakes completely in an instant. The house is quiet and at first she can't think what disturbed her. But then it comes again.

The unmistakeable ding of her laptop. The sound it makes when you scroll to the end of a document. It's irritating but Pearl has never been able to work out how to stop it.

She gets up silently, moves down the corridor lightly on the balls of her feet. For a moment, oddly, she thinks – *Wilder?* But he's dead.

Gracie's head is silhouetted by the bright screen. She's hunched, reading. Pearl can see what it is on the screen, what she's reading with such absorption. It's the manuscript of *Looking Glass Sound*.

'What the fuck are you doing?' Pearl asks, cold.

Gracie jumps, startled. 'I didn't hear you coming,' she says.

'I can see that.'

'I know I shouldn't have – I know—'

'I think you'd better get out.'

'Please, let me explain.'

'People like you should be ashamed of themselves.' Pearl gets them, occasionally, these people. They make their way out here to see it for themselves, the real-life inspiration for Looking Glass Cottage, for *The Sound and the Dagger*. At first, she had been flattered. Then she was annoyed and eventually, after someone quietly removed some of her laundry from the line outside and took it away with them, she was scared. She had the sign for Whistler Cottage taken down, the one that used to point up the sandy path to the house. It sort of worked. In Castine they don't answer questions about her anymore, won't direct people to the house. She's become a source of pride to them, something to be protected. Like a favourite pet, maybe.

The girl's eyes are glassy with tears. But there's also an air of resignation to her, which affects Pearl more. She's used to being kicked out into the cold night.

Pearl sits down. Gracie hovers, uncertain of her fate.

'Is Gracie really your name?' Pearl asks.

'Yes!'

'Did you come here to meet me?'

'No. I mean, I hoped—'

'Did you fake all that, being trapped, to make me bring you here?' She knows it doesn't make sense, Gracie couldn't have engineered it all. But she's scared, angry. She took this girl into her home.

'No,' Gracie is in tears. 'I came here because of my dad,' she says. 'My dad was from here. He was – he had something to do with that old house. I wanted to see it.'

The world slows down for Pearl, as it does in moments of shock. She curses herself. How stupid she has been, how blind. 'Your mother,' she says. 'Who was she?'

Gracie looks up slowly and for a second Pearl is terrified. There seems to be a flicker of light behind her eyes. She just shakes her head at Pearl.

'Who – *is* she?' Pearl asks.

'I think you already know,' says Gracie. A strand of hair falls over her cheek and Pearl sees how it's red in the lamplight, as red as an alarm. Pearl sees Gracie's mouth tighten up into a bud. She's trying not to cry.

'She won't see me,' Gracie says, loud and heartbroken, her face red. 'She told me not to come here.'

Pearl pushes Gracie gently away. 'You have to leave in the morning,' she says, making her tone as cool as she can. 'First thing.'

Before Pearl knows what's happening Gracie is crying on her shoulder. Her head is cornsilk under Pearl's hand. She feels Gracie's snot and tears sinking into the shoulder of her cotton pyjamas. Gracie's back heaves with sobs; Pearl can feel her heartbeat and the breath moving through her thin ribs. She's touched Gracie more in the last day and night than she has touched another person in years. *No*, she thinks, fierce – *I didn't come all this way, build all this armour for myself, only to feel this now.*

'I'm sorry I looked,' Gracie says. 'I know it was wrong. I just wanted to read what you were writing about him. And her. All I have is this – this *asking* inside me. Like a pulse, every second. Would he maybe have loved me? Even if he was bad,' Gracie wipes her red eyes hard with the back of her hand. 'Bad people can still, like, love you. I would have taken that, maybe. It would have been better than this.'


Pearl lies awake most of the night, listening. She wonders if Gracie will try to leave in the night, maybe with her wallet or laptop. She almost hopes she will. Wallets and laptops can be replaced. She would prefer that to having to act.

She recalls the doll she made all those years ago out of Harper's hair, Wilder's gum. A pearl from her mother's earring as round as a little bellybutton. Wrapped in the letter from Alton Pelletier, from Wilder's stolen folder. Did she really think she could bring back the dead, with witchcraft? It isn't real and never has been. Ghosts are just that: traces, memory. Nothing lasts.


When she ventures out of her room into the kitchen in the early, grey morning, Gracie is there, crutches and backpack leaning against the kitchen table.

'You can take some food with you,' Pearl says. She wonders what she has. She offers Gracie the box of pop tarts.

'I want to make you a deal,' Gracie says, determined.

'There's no deal here,' Pearl replies. 'You go.'

'I read your book last night,' Gracie says. 'Most of it. It's weird.'

'Great, thanks,' says Pearl.

'I mean it's weird to write a book that's all about your first book.'

'It's just what happened,' Pearl says. 'I mean, I tried to see it from his side.' Why is she justifying herself?

'What happened to him in real life, your friend?'

'I don't want to talk about that.'

'You need your ending.'

'The book has an ending. Sky and Wilder are happy together. The end.'

'I mean you need an ending for you. I have something I think you'll want.'

Pearl walks to the door and opens it. The day is grey, blustering. A wind whistles in. 'Time to go.'

'It's good, I promise,' Gracie says. 'It's something my mother left me. It's the only thing she sent with me to my adoptive parents. She wrote that I deserved to know about my dad.' She takes a deep breath. 'It's my only precious thing but I'll give it to you if you let me stay.'

Feeling pulses through Pearl. She tells herself it's shock, but she knows, really, that it's excitement. 'Fine,' she says, reckless. What is she agreeing to? 'Show it to me. You can stay for a couple days.'

Gracie takes an envelope out of the front pocket of her backpack. It's grubby and soft with much handling. She opens it carefully, slowly. Pearl wants to grab it from her but she doesn't. Instead she wipes her hands carefully with a cloth and takes the picture by its edges.

Pearl recognises it from Wilder's description – this picture, which once lived in Nathaniel Pelletier's wallet. She looks at the woman in the bar with her hair a shock of shaggy blonde, that her son will later share. She's pink with beer and the warmth of the room. She looks happy. She doesn't know that she's going to disappear soon. Pearl knows who she is. It's the woman they never found. The one they think might be the missing oil-drum woman.

Nat's mom.

An anonymous arm drapes over her shoulder, hands and face both hidden from view. The photograph is a Polaroid, folded in half.

Pearl unfolds it with shaking fingers. There he is.

The man's face is obscured by a thumb, broad and blurry and pink. Pearl can guess at the identity of the photographer. Wilder's uncle Vernon never got much better at it.

The man's wrist is now visible, however. He's wearing cufflinks made of Coke-bottle caps. Pearl thinks of all Wilder's mom's insistence that Edith was not the first affair. She thinks of Wilder's instant affection for Nathaniel Pelletier, how they gravitated towards one another. They say siblings who were separated at birth, or never met, can recognise one another if they meet later in life. Even if they're only half-brothers.

She looks at Gracie, feeling wild.

She missed it at first because Gracie has that red hair – but Pearl can see it now. The pale eyes, almost the same colour as her skin. The eyes are large, slightly protuberant. The Harlow look.

'Go put your stuff back in the bedroom,' she says briefly to Gracie and turns away. Now it's her turn to make a call. She hopes Harper answers. They haven't spoken since that day the milk spilled all over the kitchen floor, the day Pearl set a fire.


Pearl has decided to call the book *Looking Glass Sound*.

She uses Wilder's memoir as a beginning. She still had it in the safe at her New York apartment – that binder with Aphrodite on the front, containing his careful handwriting, telling the story of that summer. So, once again, she went back to those dog-eared pages. This time, she typed it up word for word.

The college part is pretty accurate, she didn't change much there. Trying to imagine his feelings, looking out through his eyes – it was a kind of salt-sweet torture. She made herself go inside him. Reliving it was like catharsis, but also cannibalism. Going to see Alton Pelletier. Her flight, leaving him, disappearing with his writing. She changed her own gender, of course – became Sky. It made sense – after all, she did the same in *The Sound and the Dagger*, years ago, when she made herself into Skandar. It's a disguise, this change, it makes her feel safe. Otherwise those books are just windows into her pain.

Maybe she made Sky and Wilder too romantic. She wants Wilder to have some happiness, even if it's only imaginary – even if it's just in a book.

Wilder is dead. He never got old, never married, never became a professor. Pearl most enjoyed that part of writing the book; it gave her pleasure to give him those things. It was good imagining him three decades later, a slightly grumpy older man. Pearl had a harder time imagining the technology in twelve years' time – she's never been much good at all that science-fiction stuff, all the critics say so.

In *Looking Glass Sound* she uses actual passages from her first novel, *The Sound and the Dagger*, to haunt her fictional Wilder. Just as the events that inspired it haunted him, all those years ago.

Wilder's story ended here, on Whistler Bay. Or up in the meadow on the hill above the house, anyhow. He must have got the idea from Harper all those years ago – hemlock. It grows up there. She has imagined it a thousand times – his last moments.

She forces herself not to think of what she knows about hemlock. The burning, the pain, the loss of muscle control, the drooling and convulsions.

Pearl still remembers the last thing Harper ever said to her, before she hung up, which was the last time they ever spoke.

'You did this.'

Pearl gave him a better ending. Wilder goes to the meadow surrounded by summer flowers. But in her version he finds Sky beneath the earth, and there's a happy ending.

And since she has been writing, it feels as if this version – though she knows that this doesn't make sense – has become true. She can imagine Wilder happy in this house, with Sky. She has felt – no, known – these past couple months, that he's really OK. Through some thin membrane, in another world, Wilder is alive and well. At times when the barriers are thin she feels him here. In the kitchen, pushing past her, absentminded, to get a can from the store cupboard. Lying by her in the night, breathing. Sometimes when she wakes up just before dawn, she even thinks she hears the clack, clack, clack of his old Remington in the kitchen.

But this is mere wishful thinking of course. Pearl's new book is just that. A book. And Wilder is dead. Gone these nineteen years. Some days Pearl doesn't even think about him at all. Not once.

She saw it in his face that morning in the lodge, with the bath with the feet. The night they spent together after seeing Alton Pelletier. She saw that what she felt was not returned. It wasn't that he didn't like women. But he didn't love Pearl, not like that.

Sometimes she tries to persuade herself that what she did to him wasn't payment for this fact.

Sandra Harlow left the final pages of Wilder's journal on the table at Whistler Cottage. They were the first thing Pearl saw when she opened the door to her new house. Pearl doesn't know whether

Sandra left them as a comfort for Pearl, or an accusation.

Pearl used them, too. Over the years she has pored over every word. Now she's using them in her new book. *Monsters, aren't we all, writers*, she thinks. *We eat everything we see.* The end of Wilder's memoir has always struck her as odd. He says he's coming back to Whistler Bay – which he did. He doesn't sound sad, but angry. He must have found he couldn't write his revenge novel. Writers' block follows you everywhere, as Pearl knows.

Sometimes she wonders what happened to that typed draft of *The Sound and the Dagger* she sent to Wilder. Her fictional Wilder burns it, in *Looking Glass Sound* – but really, it's never been found.

The fire roars and licks at the night sky. The quiet sea is full of stars. Somewhere in the dark, a seal barks.

Pearl waits, looking out for her – but of course the moment she takes her eyes off the path, bends to pour herself a drink, Harper appears silently. Suddenly she's just there, behind the fire.

She's older, of course she is. Red hair streaked with grey. But her face is unlined, as wicked-looking as ever. Firelight plays on it, makes holes of her eyes. All the beginnings to this conversation that Pearl had ready are gone from her head.

'Hello, Pearl,' Harper says. 'It's been a while.'

Pearl takes a deep breath. 'I thought you had an abortion, Harper,' she says. 'Back at school, you always let me think that—'

Harper goes pale and still. 'She's here, isn't she?'

Pearl nods. There's such sorrow in Harper's face. 'I found her wandering round the old Pelletier place.'

'I told her not to come.' Harper sits down suddenly in the sand. 'I can't see her,' she says. 'This is a trap. How could you do this to me?'

'Have a drink,' Pearl says. 'You need it.' Then she flushes, remembering.

But Harper isn't listening. 'I should have known she'd find me.'

'There's more.' Pearl hands Harper the Polaroid. It's in a clear plastic bag, now. Like an evidence bag, Pearl supposes.

Harper looks briefly and says, 'She's a girl in a tight spot. She wants somewhere to stay. Maybe she just saw what you needed and gave it to you.'

It's been years, but Harper and Pearl still see to the heart of each other. Maybe if you know someone this deeply once you can never lose it. 'No more lies, Harper,' Pearl says gently. 'Nat's gone. You don't need to keep his secrets anymore. Is this the picture Wilder saw in Nathaniel Pelletier's wallet?'

Harper nods. 'Vernon gave Nat the photograph, said it was of his mother and his real father. Vernon always thought it was wrong that Nat didn't know who his dad was – but he'd promised his brother never to tell anyone. So he kept giving Nat these little hints. When Nat saw Wilder's father wearing those bottle-cap cufflinks that evening at the cottage, he realised. He stole the cufflinks and hid them with his Polaroids behind the skirting board.' Harper takes a deep breath. 'The last time I ever saw him was at the hospital that day – the day I told him I was pregnant. I think he wanted our child to have something from their past. But of course the police found the cufflinks. All he had left to give was the photograph.'

'Did anyone else know?' Pearl's heart beats fast and strong.

Harper shakes her head. 'Nat was afraid of what Alton might do if he realised. But he knew his time was running out, one way or another.' Harper wipes her eyes fiercely. 'So that day in the hospital, he asked me to tell Wilder that they were brothers. And I was going to, I swear I was. But I waited, and waited, then it was too late.' Harper pauses. 'I found him. Wilder. Did you know that?'

315

'No,' Pearl says, shaken. 'I'm sorry. How did he seem to you, before—' She's trying to find a way to ask whether Wilder seemed likely to kill himself. 'From what he wrote in his memoir, it seemed like he was coming back here to write his revenge novel. But I guess something changed his mind.'

'He was angry,' Harper says.

'With me.'

'With you. But very – alive.'

'He might have a niece,' Pearl says. 'We'll be certain once we have the DNA. Gracie's agreed to it – I have some of Wilder's hair.'

Some strong feeling comes from Harper. 'Where did you get that?'

'I took it the morning after we—'

'You should have told me you had it,' Harper says. In the fire-light she's pale with anger.

'What does it matter?' Pearl asks, her own anger rising. 'The things you keep to yourself, Harper! Did you never want to find her? Your daughter?'

'Don't you judge me, Pearl.'

'You're the one judging me,' says Pearl. 'You've blamed me for his death for so long – years, Harper, nearly twenty years – but it wasn't my fault!'

'You took a vulnerable, traumatised boy and used him,' Harper says. She ticks the items off on her fingers. 'You pumped him for information, you slept with him, you made him relive that trau-matic past, just for your book – just like you tried to do to me.' Their faces are so close that Pearl thinks, *will she bite me?*

There is the sound of footsteps on the cliff path and they both turn their heads sharply. A slim figure comes out of the dark.

'I didn't know where you were,' Gracie says to Pearl.

'We decided to have a fire on the beach,' Pearl says. She breathes deeply, trying to calm herself. 'This is my fr— this is Harper.'

Pearl feels the air move and change as Gracie and Harper look at one another.

'I don't have anything to say to her,' Gracie says. She grabs a marshmallow from the bag and skewers it.

'These things take time,' Pearl says. The hurt on Gracie's face is too much to bear. 'You two need to get used to each other. You can do that, can't you, Harper?'

But Harper isn't listening. She's watching Gracie's features dancing in the firelight, watching her eat the long pink strings of marshmallow. Feeling eyes on her, Gracie looks up. For a moment Wilder looks out, pale, through Gracie's eyes. How could Pearl not have seen it before? Then Gracie tips her head back and he's gone, instead it's Nathaniel Pelletier who turns a leonine head up to look at the moon overhead.

Pearl is about to say, *do you see now? Harper, did you see that?* But there's no need. Harper's face gleams with tears. 'It worked,' she whispers. 'The magic. All three of us made it back here in the end.'


Gracie goes to bed after three hotdogs and most of the marshmallows.

'I'm going to credit him, you know,' Pearl says to Harper. He wrote some of it. I might even say he co-wrote it.'

'What are you going to do about her?' Harper asks.

'I don't know,' Pearl says. 'I thought maybe she could stay here when I go back to New York. For a time, anyway.' She doesn't know how Harper will react to this.

'If she does decide to stay,' Harper says, 'I'll look in on her.'

'You could have her to stay some night,' Pearl says.

'Maybe.'

317

'OK,' Pearl says.

Harper looks at Pearl in surprise. Pearl tries to stem the tears, push it all back in, but the ugly things are bulging up from the depths, closing her throat.

'I loved him,' Pearl says. 'I wanted him, and oh god, I was so fucked up back then. I didn't know how to deal with it all. I did it, I killed him like you said.'

'No,' Harper says quietly. 'I was angry when I said that. You were young. You were grieving. It was Alton Pelletier who killed Wilder. He never got over what happened. He never got over Nat.'

'I like to walk up there sometimes,' Pearl says, after a moment. 'Do you want to come?'

The path winds ahead like a snake's back, cinder-black and silver. Harper and Pearl stumble a little, laughing some. Pearl feels light as a feather, unlike herself. They could be back at school, walking across the hockey field under the bright moon.

The meadow is white-lit and broad. The moon is a lamp, glowing under the sea.

Pearl doesn't know exactly where they found him. She has never wanted to know. But now she sees Harper looking, staring really hard at the ground beneath a handsome beech tree. She thinks, *oh, there*, and she starts to cry all over again because it's a peaceful-looking place, comfortable, with some pale stars of night jasmine opening just now, nearby, and she's glad it happened in a peaceful place. There's so little to be glad about but there is this – this one small thing – that he died surrounded by flowers with the sea shining blue before him.

'Why did he come up here to do it?' Pearl asks. She has often wondered this. 'I thought he hated this place.'

'Maybe that's why he chose it,' Harper says. 'It's difficult to leave if you're surrounded by the things you love.' Harper breathes deeply; the night air is filled with spring. 'We would have done magic here, once, wouldn't we?'

'Being old kind of takes the magic out of things,' Pearl says. 'It's sad.'

'But also a relief.'

'Also that.'

'I gave up witchcraft, after Wilder died,' Harper says. 'It was too hard to keep hoping it would help. Too hard to take every time it failed. Part of me died with him. I know it's the same for you.' Harper touches Pearl lightly on the arm. 'It's good to see you again.'

Pearl is moved. She squeezes Harper's hand. Harper goes tense and Pearl thinks, *I've gone too far*, but Harper's attention is elsewhere. She calls suddenly, 'You can come out, Gracie!'

The girl comes out from the dappled shadow of the beech trees.

'I heard you talking about magic,' she says. 'I'm a witch too, you know.'


Gracie dances down the path ahead, surefooted in the moonlight. *I've gotten old*, Pearl thinks enviously – *old and afraid before my time*. Harper stays close to Pearl. Every so often, Pearl swears her feet leave the path. She glides beside Pearl, toes grazing the sandy shale.

*I need some sleep*, Pearl thinks. She's seeing things.

'I want you to have something,' Pearl says to Harper when they reach the house. 'Just a second. Wait here.'

She goes to her bedroom and takes the lock of hair from the locket where she keeps it, in the drawer with her mother's pearl, the blackened sphere that was once set into her mother's earring.

She recalls Wilder's expression of sleepy bewilderment and annoyance as she tugged the hair out of his head.

There's not much left but Pearl divides the dark, silky strands into two. Strange that this slender strand of hair can provide answers to so many questions. She'll keep half for the DNA testing, but half should go to Harper. On impulse she opens the box where she has kept the pearl for thirty-two years. She looks at it in moments of high tension. She finds it calming.

The pearl is not there.

Pearl breathes. Gracie, maybe. Or maybe not. Perhaps Pearl didn't put it back one night. Maybe it rolled down the back of a drawer. Not everything is someone's fault. She thinks for a moment, tests the old deep wounds – and realises, to her surprise, that it's all right. She doesn't need it anymore. Maybe Gracie needs it more. Time for new things.

Harper and Gracie are standing together, silhouetted against the moonlit sea. Gracie is whispering urgently to Harper. Their heads part quickly as Pearl comes back.

'Here.' Harper's hand is soft, smaller than Pearl remembers. She expects everything about Harper to be tough and hard but it's not, of course. Harper lost a lot, too.

'You must miss him,' she says. 'Both of them.'

She folds Wilder's hair into Harper's palm. 'For you,' she says. She pauses. 'You know, after you called me that day, the day he died – I tried to do magic with his hair. Like that stuff we used to do at school. I thought I could bring Wilder back to life with it. I burnt my mother's pearl. The only thing of hers I had left.'

'Well,' Harper says comfortingly, after a pause. 'Maybe it will work. Maybe you'll be together again one day.'

Pearl laughs and hugs her, and after a moment Harper returns the hug.

'He'll be waiting for you when you're ready,' Harper says. 'Wilder.' Pearl is surprised. She hadn't thought Harper religious. But they've both changed.

'I'm glad we're friends again,' Pearl says. 'You're the best friend I ever had. I'm sorry I didn't know it, back then.'

'Oh god,' Harper says. 'Neither of us knew anything. We were idiots. But sometimes we do get second chances.'

It's odd, Pearl thinks, how you can feel things, in the darkness. She can tell that Harper is smiling. She feels a great weight lifted, a burden she has carried for many years.

'Please don't go yet,' Gracie says to Harper, and it's so strong, the longing in her voice, that Pearl can almost see it on the night air like a colour.

'I'll leave you two to talk,' Pearl says.


Pearl tries to sleep but her mind is a lightning storm. She can hear the low murmur, out on the cliff, of Harper and Gracie talking. In the end Pearl gets up. She gets the Aphrodite binder out of the closet and sets it down on the kitchen table, strokes it gently with her fingers. It feels different now, something to be treasured, not a reminder of guilt. She opens it and spreads the pages of *The Dagger Man of Whistler Bay* out over the kitchen table. That broken typewriter key – it drives her nuts every time.

*I don't think people should live by the ocean. It's too big to understand.*

*But what else can we do,* Pearl thinks, *except keep coming back here again and again and again, trying to understand?*

Pearl reads, sinking into the blue and gold of that summer.

\*

Her attention is snapped by a raised voice out in the night. 'I don't know if I can do it.' There is such suffering in Harper's voice.

Gracie says something back. Pearl can't make out the words but there are tears in them. She hastily focuses on the pages before her. Some things are private.

Later when the eastern sky is touched with the first gauzy light, Pearl hears Harper's steps fade away past the cottage and down the hill. A moment later Gracie comes quietly into the kitchen. She has been crying and her cheeks are red, but her eyes are bright stars.

'I'll make you a hot chocolate.' Pearl can't think of anything else to say but it seems to be the right thing because Gracie holds her tight and buries her face in Pearl's shoulder.


Pearl wakes with a gasp. Blue snowlight is coming through the porthole window. Someone is breathing beside her.

Ah, there you are, she says, and flings her arm over him, stroking his chest. Tap tap, she goes, as in, *follow me*. He turns towards her, but as he does he is gone.

Waking is like being torn apart.

*It's not Wilder*, she reminds herself. And he's definitely not a ghost. Ghosts don't exist. It's a dream she has sometimes, that's all, of a night twenty years ago, when she was young and Wilder was alive. She hardly knew him, really. It's been so long since they talked, since they touched – and what did it all mean anyway?

*One day I'll be an eighty-year-old woman*, Pearl thinks. *And I'll still be sad, missing this nineteen-year-old boy.*

\*

Pearl stands under the maple, looking out at the Sound. *No*, she corrects herself. *Whistler Bay.* It's easy to get confused. The water looks back at her in a sheen of steel. The stones are quiet. It's time to get back to life.

'You OK?' Harper asks.

'Do you love her?' Pearl asks in a rush. 'I know I'm hardly the maternal type but please, don't let her stay like this, for you, if you know you can never really love her back.'

'That's my daughter, Pearl,' Harper says softly. 'Don't interfere.'

'OK,' Pearl says. 'I won't.'

Harper and Gracie have been growing closer, these last few weeks. Long walks along the coast path. Every so often Pearl comes home to find the kitchen haunted by faint scents – woodsmoke, resin, herbs. Harper is back to her old tricks, then. It's harmless enough, Pearl supposes. Wicca, white witching, whatever you call it – polite magic, stripped of the urgency and blood of bygone ages.

Sometimes Gracie and Harper go out at night under the waning moon. Once or twice Pearl has woken to faint screams coming up from the bay. Pearl is glad that Harper is reclaiming that part of herself. And it's good that she shares it with Gracie.

Gracie will stay and look after the cottage when Pearl's gone – it suits everyone. Mother and daughter can continue to weave the delicate web of their relationship, and Pearl gets a resident caretaker.

Gracie wanders out of the front door, chicken leg in one hand. She has the manuscript of *Looking Glass Sound* in the other. Pearl printed out two copies, one for Gracie and one for Harper. She can see that the title page has smears of chicken grease on it.

'Won't you be lonely?' Pearl asks Gracie again.

Gracie still puts everything she owns in her backpack each night and uses it as a pillow. Not because she's afraid that Pearl will steal things, but because she's used to doing it. She needs time to get used to being safe.

'I'll be alone,' Gracie says. 'Not the same. Anyway, I have Harper.'

Harper looks over at her daughter briefly and a quiet ripple of feeling passes between them.

'All set?' Gracie asks Pearl.

'All set,' she says, trying not to ask what Gracie thought of the book.

Gracie grins. She's good at hearing what people don't say. Survival instinct, Pearl supposes.

'I don't understand,' she says. 'You made Wilder do stuff for you for the book. You kind of used him.'

'Yes,' Pearl says.

'But he was your friend. You like, loved him. That didn't stop you?'

'Why should it?' Pearl asks, genuinely puzzled.

Gracie thinks about this. 'I like how they find her. My grandmother. The last barrel woman, hiding under this cliff. Can you imagine if it was true?'

'I don't think they'll ever find her now,' Pearl says gently. 'We don't even really know if that's what happened to her. That cave under this hill doesn't exist. I made it up.'

Gracie shrugs. 'I like the little chapters you put in that are only word games.'

Harper turns, looks at Gracie with a smile.

'What?' asks Pearl.

'You put in chapters that are just, like, words.'

'No,' Pearl says. 'I mean, I mention the word game I used to play with my dad but—'

'Well you put columns of words in,' Gracie says, puzzled and a little hurt. She seems to feel that she's being accused of lying, somehow. 'It's right there. And you made it look like a typewriter wrote them. That's cool too.'

'Gracie, you have to stop.' Sometimes Gracie gets anxious when Pearl's about to leave a room or the house, and she invents excuses for her to stay. 'I have to go, I'll miss the New York flight.'

'No.' Gracie shoves the bundle of pages into Pearl's hands. 'I mean it. You must have forgotten, or something. Take it. Look, you'll see that I'm right.'

Pearl takes the pages from her.

'Can I have the other chicken leg?' Gracie does this too, she asks for permission to eat food, as though it were being rationed.

'Of course,' Pearl says, absent, flipping through the pages. Gracie dances back into the cottage.

Pearl stops flipping. Her heart stops too.

```
Won't
Don't

Moss
Muss
Must
Rust
Trust

Hem
Them

Whelp
Help
```

```
Held
Help

Heap
Help
```

She didn't write this. She knows she didn't.

According to Pearl's dad's rules, the game had a structure. The last word of each group should make a message.

Don't trust them
Help
Help
Help

'I must have written it and forgotten,' she says aloud, wild. 'I must have done.'

But the top of the '*l*' is missing, leaving it looking like a drunken '*i*'. The letters are slightly greenish, as though the typewriter ribbon is running out.

'Wilder?' Pearl whispers, looking around her in a flood of – what? The sea and the sky shimmer, as though about to answer back.

Harper is watching her. 'Yes, he's in there,' she says. 'I put him there. I used the hair you gave me.'

The sky goes dark as dusk. Harper's eyes are as silver as the last of the light on the sea.

Pearl sees that she has never really known her at all because the look on her face is not of the woman she knew, or even really a person at all.

'You wanted to live forever,' Harper says gently. 'You both did, you and Wilder. That's all writers really want, whatever they say. Now, you can – here, in the book. I have your blood so after you die you'll go in too. You'll be together forever, walking through the pages.'

'How do you have my blood?' Pearl's flesh moves like the sea around her bones.

'Gracie. You bled on her jeans when she was trapped in the house, the day you took her in here. And she brought it to me – as well as your mother's pearl.'

'Gracie wouldn't. I tried to help her—'

'You tried to make yourself feel better. And she was using you to be near me. She's my daughter, mine.' Harper pauses. 'You're a monstrous person, but books are cages for monsters. You both deserve it, you and Wilder. You put all my pain there on the page without a thought. Those women who died – they don't deserve to be used by you. It was stealing, Pearl. She was your own mother, but you left her out of the story. You focused on the killer and his son instead.'

'This doesn't make sense,' Pearl says, desperate. 'Wilder died years ago. I only gave you his hair a couple of weeks ago.'

'If I had used a stone or a tree to trap him in – no, it wouldn't have worked. But books don't work like that. They are outside time. They are everywhere.'

'But—' Pearl's mind is a furnace. She feels the black pulse that comes from Harper. Every part of her shouts, *danger, get away.*

Harper sees. She smiles. 'That's right,' she says, gentle. 'Get in the car and drive. And don't come back here. This is my place. I thought you understood that. Why did you come back? You thought it was all about you, but this story has been about me, the whole time. You never thought about me, any of you. The things I had to – no one knows what I had to do, what I went through.'

327

Harper's face is pink and twisted with tears.

'Nat would have hated prison,' she says though clenched jaws. 'I couldn't let that happen to him. He took those pictures of those children. He told me, I made him tell me. He wanted forgiveness, so I gave him that – then I fed him. It was best.'

Harper looks up at Pearl. Her face is a screen of tears. 'Do you know what it's like – to kill someone you love?' Her voice is strangled, wet with tears. 'It's more than love can stand. I found a way we can all be together again. Nat, Wilder and I. We can go back to before it all happened.' Harper takes a deep, gulping breath. 'I messed up badly before, but I've finally fixed it.'

# Harper

She's almost ready.

The bay glistens, the meadow is golden in the low light. Harper smells the warm earth. It's been a dry summer. That's good. Hemlock grows stronger in the sunshine. Her heart is drier than the earth. Harper knows she has to take herself to the edge for this one. The last one.

The windows of Whistler Cottage were open as she passed. Some visitor. She ducked her head and hurried by. She doesn't want to attract attention.

She unpacks the items one by one. The silver knife, the gleaming fresh seabass she bought in Castine. There has to be something from the sea and Nat liked to catch striper. Carefully, she unwraps the sweater that swaddles the jar of tincture. The liquid is blood red, for some reason, she doesn't know why; maybe she did something wrong.

She found it in the *King's American Dispensatory* in her father's library – the instructions.

*. . puck it moderately in a conical glass percolator, and grad-ually pour diluted alcohol upon it, until one thousand grammes of tincture are obtained . . .*

Luckily, she was always OK at science. Harper didn't have a percolator so she used a coffee pot. She broke it afterwards and hid the pieces in the trash, enclosed in three layers of garbage bags.

She unscrews the jar and carefully stands the knife in the liquid. The whole blade should be covered in it.

Harper came back to watch over the bay as its guardian. She has the strong impression – this could be wrong, though, so much magic is guesswork– that it asked her to. Sometimes she thinks it's watching her back. Or else she's mad. Either way, she's been here since Fairview, in that empty white house. It's like time stopped for Harper. Even Pearl has gone and done something with her life. Harper read about it in the paper – the book. Harper hasn't drunk, though. There is that. Not for two years.

'Haven't I done well, Natty?' she says aloud. She talks to him sometimes. Maybe someday he'll answer.

'Harper?'

Harper turns, flesh thrilling. She hasn't even started yet – but she knows that voice.

Wilder stands knee deep in the nodding grass, looking hesitant. He has a leather satchel slung over his chest. Harper opens her mouth to say hello. Instead, she says, 'Someone has fallen in love with you since we met last. I can see it.' And she can, the gleaming light of it all over him. 'I didn't know you were back.'

'I just got here,' Wilder says. 'I was looking at the sea and think-ing about you – about the past. Then I looked up and there you were outside. So I followed. Forgot my glasses on the table, but I wanted to catch up with you. I didn't realise you were coming here.'

'You still hate this meadow?' she says, smiling. 'You used to say it was like someone died here.'

'Weirdly, I don't feel like that today.' He smiles too. 'I've grown up, I think.'

He looks at the fire she's built. The knife. She carved the handle herself, from walnut. The pattern of fish on the walnut handle is a little clumsier than the original. But it looks very similar.

'What are you doing?' Wilder asks slowly.

'I'm practising,' Harper says. She takes a deep breath. 'I think I can bring Nat back. But there's something else I need, and I can't get it yet. So I'm doing a trial run.

'Of?'

'You think all this is rubbish.'

'It doesn't matter what I think.'

She sighs. And she does want to tell someone; she worked really hard at getting this just right.

'Here's the knife – it's not the one Nat used but it's as close as I could make it. We're in a place where Nat gave his blood, remember? The forfeits. So the spells will be linked by blood and place and ownership. But I need to have the object to put it in. And it has to be this specific one. It's a book about you know, everything that happened, written by – well, that doesn't matter. It's called *The Sound and the Dagger* – it's published next year. Until then, I'm going to practise the rest of it. I have to get everything right. I think there's only one chance.' Harper looks out to sea. She doesn't want him to see her crying.

'I know it's stupid,' she says. 'I know I can't change anything. But I have to have some purpose. Some hope.'

Wilder looks at her. Silently, he opens his satchel and takes out a wad of pages. The title page reads: *The Sound and the Dagger*. 'You can do it now,' he says.

'How did you—' Harper feels the world disintegrate around her.

'She heard it from me,' Wilder says. 'Our story. We ended up at the same college.' He shakes his head. 'Pretty strange, right? That I turn up here with exactly the thing you need, just when you need it.'

'That's how it works,' Harper says. 'Magic. Is it – what are we like, in the book?'

'It's more about her than us, I think. You're called Helen, in it. Look. Here. I'm Wiley. She put herself in it, too – a character called Skandar.'

'Ugh,' Harper says.

'She's a low-down thief. I came up here to find her.'

'Are you going to kill her?' Harper is interested.

'I'm going to forgive her,' Wilder says with dignity.

Harper bursts out laughing. She laughs even harder at the look on his face. 'You don't change. I've got a better plan.' She holds out her hand. 'Give it to me.'

He hesitates.

Something breaks inside her. 'Give it to me, Wilder! Even if you think this is all crap, even if you think I'm insane – just humour me. OK?'

Her hands shake as she takes the manuscript. 'You'll enjoy this next part. I'm going to burn it.'

'Harper . . .'

She smiles and squeezes his hand. 'We can talk afterwards,' she says. 'There are things you should know, things I promised Nat I'd tell you.' She has failed to keep so many promises. But she can make it right.

Harper places the manuscript on the pyre. She takes the knife out of the jar and shakes it free of liquid, careful not to let the drops fall near her. She pours the rest of the tincture on the kindling at the base of the pile. It's mostly alcohol, it will act as an accelerant. She drops the match, and flame leaps up, pale in the sunshine, as though it's been waiting eagerly for this moment.

She raises the knife to her throat. A scratch would be enough, she thinks, but she's not taking chances.

'What the hell are you doing?' Wilder says, horrified. He lunges for her, she ducks out of his grasp. 'Harper, don't!'

'Don't try and stop me, Wilder,' she says, shoving him away. 'It needs my blood. I can bring Nat back in the book. I'll still be alive, I'll just be – in there. I'll be Helen.'

Wilder doesn't answer. He stares down at the long, deep bloody scratch that has opened his forearm.

Harper goes cold with horror. 'I'm sorry,' she says. 'Oh, Wilder. I'm so sorry.'

'It doesn't hurt,' he says. 'It should hurt. What's on the knife, Harper?'

'Tincture of hemlock,' she whispers.

'Oh god,' he says. 'Call 911. You can run down to the cottage . . .'

She knows there isn't time. The tincture is already in his body, riding on his blood.

'I'm scared. What's going to happen?'

'It'll be fine. I can fix this.' Harper's heart pounds. He's messed up the spell, she doesn't know what to do now. She can't fix this. Around them, red, burning fragments of paper float on the air.

'I don't want to die,' Wilder looks young and very afraid.

'Sit down,' Harper says. There's a handsome young beech tree nearby and she helps him sit with his back against the trunk. She hopes that keeping him still will slow the poison.

Wilder starts to cry. Harper reaches for him but he flinches away from her. He can feel her true self now, the vast darkness of her. 'Don't touch me,' he whispers.

'Whatever you want,' Harper says, smiling. She keeps the smile pinned to her face and the tears far, far back, stinging her throat. There must be a way – there must.

'Wait,' she says to Wilder.

She runs to the pyre. The book is nearly gone, it is roaring flame. She holds her breath and reaches in, manages to grab a white fragment of page. She stamps on its glowing edges. It's a scene between Wiley and the guy called Skandar. *Messy russet hair, big nose. Kind.*

*How creative, Pearl*, she thinks. *Making your main character a male version of you. Ugh, fine.* It will have to do.

She sharpens her mind and heart. To her terror and amazement, the feeling is coming upon her. Witchcraft is about to happen. The world goes blue and blurry at the edges.

She smears the singed page with blood from Wilder's wound. She bites the inside of her cheek until it bleeds, then spits that onto the page too.

When she's ready she says, 'Open your eyes.'

Wilder's eyes are vast, dark, pupils fully dilated by the poison. 'Who are you?' he asks. 'Am I dead?'

'You're Wiley.' Harper hears her voice, deep. She touches her throat, feels the stubble, the unfamiliar bump of an Adam's apple. Her shoulders are broad now. Powerful. Is this what it's like? She tries not to think. She has to believe it, he has to believe it. They have to get into the book.

She leans in, lets him feel her breath on his mouth, parts her lips. She gently touches them with hers. The gasp he takes is as long as her soul; they breathe each other in. She tastes his tongue, clean like minerals. When she grasps Wilder's hand she sees her own is unfamiliar – large, long-fingered.

'Put your hand on my heart,' she says.

Wilder thrusts his hand inside her shirt, buttons fly through the air. He places his hand on the strange flatness of her chest, over her heart. Harper stops thinking and lets the magic take over, lets it batter her like an avalanche. The world is a mess of colour around the fixed point of one another. Every part of her is focused on Wilder's breath, his mouth, his heartbeat. She tries to push their breathing, beating hearts into the book.

For a moment, the meadow shivers around them. The bay below is a different shape, there are seals on the warm rocks. *It's working*, she thinks. She and Wilder aren't beneath a beech tree, but standing in a sunlit brown stream. She's Skandar, and he's Wiley.

It only lasts for a moment. Wilder's lips spasm and go cold under hers. She feels it as he begins to die.

Harper pushes harder but it's no good. The blue light at the edges of things begins to dim. She feels her hair lengthen, her face narrow and smooth. She returns to herself.

Wilder is looking up at her, mouth frozen, eyes glassy with fear. The tiniest spark of life remains – and he's gone, his eyes are blank. She knows it didn't work. The page she holds is just a page.

Even though she knows it's useless, Harper shakes and calls to Wilder. She screams and beats his dead chest with a fist. The body that housed him grows slowly cool.

Harper strokes his dark hair. 'It'll be all right,' she whispers into his ear. 'I swear I'll fix it.'

# *Pearl*

'I thought it was me who killed him,' Pearl says blankly. 'But it was you.'

'It was an accident,' Harper whispers.

'A life wasted for something that didn't even work,' Pearl says, her heart clenched with sorrow.

'I think you can only do it with a book that's not completely finished.' Harper almost sounds pleading. 'But most of all, I think it needed Gracie. She's all three of us, you see. Me, Nat and Wilder. Blood of our blood. Now we can all be together, do it all over again.'

'But that would be awful, to go through it all again,' Pearl says.

'I can't wait to see them,' Harper says.

Pearl says slowly, 'You put my mother's pearl in.' Her breath is short.

'Yes, you'll see your mother.'

Pearl thinks she might faint. She groans.

'I don't understand you, Pearl. You should be thanking me—'

'It means she'll die again, Harper. And again and again.'

'You'll get used to it. Though it's a shame you made Rebecca come back as a ghost in this book – her ghost suffers so much.'

Pearl looks at her hands and thinks of them wrapped about Harper's throat.

*No.* Harper's voice thunders in Pearl's skull. Pearl clutches her head.

Harper wipes her tears away, businesslike. 'Don't write about Whistler Bay anymore,' she says. 'It's not for you. That's two books we'll all have to live through, now. Try writing something different. Try writing lots of different things. Live and love – listen and watch. Then put it all into the worlds on the paper. That will give you more room to roam – when the time comes. You write them, so you're in all of them. We're just in the ones you decide to put us into.'

'This isn't possible,' Pearl says, weak. 'You're trying to scare me.'

'Maybe,' Harper says. 'Maybe not. Since you don't want to join us here, I would try to live as long as possible and make as many worlds to live in as you can.'

Her smile stretches slowly into a grin. It grows wider as she reaches for Pearl, who tries to scream but she can't get the breath. Harper's arms enclose her and Pearl feels it, the great dark smiling power of her, the old suns and moons and constellations turning within. How could she once have thought her harmless?

'Let me go,' she whispers, her insides twisting. 'Please, I'll do what you want. I'll go and never come back. I'll write about other places.'

'Pearl?' Gracie is saying, worried. 'Harper?' She stands in the doorway, chicken leg in hand. Her teeth gnaw the bare bone. Pearl flinches.

'Harper is using you, Gracie,' Pearl says. 'She just wants your blood.' She knows it's a cruel thing to say.

Gracie shakes her head. 'She's my mother,' she says, simply.

Harper watches Gracie with a slight smile – something burns in her eyes. Pearl sees, startled, that it's love. It passes between

337

mother and daughter, a bright, gleaming moment.

Harper turns back to Pearl. 'You're pretty low on gas,' she says politely, 'but you'll make it to the highway.' Pearl doesn't ask how she knows. That dark vastness pulses behind Harper's eyes – she taps Pearl lightly on the arm with one finger. The nail is dry, sharp and light.

Pearl gasps and flinches from the touch. She turns and runs down the hill, sliding and slipping on the shale path, feeling the weight of eyes on her back, her neck.

She slams the car door shut, sealing herself in. She breathes deeply, taking in the smell of leather, the comforting sweet tang of an old slushee in the cupholder. These are real, ordinary things. But power crawls on the back of her neck like flies.

The engine starts first try and Pearl sobs with relief. The car tears away in a spray of grit and shale. She reminds herself to breathe and the road steadies somewhat before her. *Don't look back*, she thinks, *do not, do not*, but in the end she can't resist, it's as if her neck is being cranked round by a handle. As she nears the turn she flings a glance behind her.

Up on the hill two figures are silhouetted, black against the sky. Pearl knows it must be Harper and Gracie, but for a moment the sun dazzles her eyes. It could be two boys on the cusp of manhood, standing arm in arm, to watch her leave.

[  ]

Wont
Won
Yon
You

Hart
Hare
Are

Fear
Ear
Hear
Her
Here

Tooth
Sooth
Soot
Toot
Too

# Acknowledgements

My wonderful agents are fearless champions for my books and deserve far more praise than I can give them here. First thanks as always must go to the magical Jenny Savill, who always wields her power for good. Thank you to all at Andrew Nurnberg Associates: Michael Dean, Barbara Barbieri, Rory Clarke, Lucy Flynn, Juliana Galvis, Halina Koscia, Ylva Monsen, Andrew Nurnberg, Sabine Pfannenstiel and Marei Pittner.

To the wonderful Robin Straus and Danielle Metta at the Robin Straus Agency – thank you – you've changed everything for me.

All thanks go to my wonderful UK and US editors Miranda Jewess and Kelly Lonesome O'Connor – I can't sing your praises highly enough. This book was quite the journey – thank you for your trust, your patience, your seemingly inexhaustible creativity and resourcefulness.

I am so grateful to the mighty Viper team for their brilliance and hard work – Andrew Franklin, Drew Jerrison, Flora Willis, Claire Beaumont and Niamh Murray in particular. In the copy edit, Hayley Shepherd's eagle eye saved me, as ever, from error.

To the amazing Nightfire coven in the US: Alexis Seraala,

Devi Pillai, Michael Dudding, Jordan Hanley, Sarah Pannenberg, Kristin Temple and the rest of the fantastic team at Tor Nightfire and Tor Books – thank you. I feel very fortunate to be published by you.

The beautiful, dramatic covers for 'Looking Glass Sound' were created by Steve Panton in the UK and Katie Klimowicz in the US.

For long talks, support and kindnesses too numerous to mention, my thanks to Emily Cavendish, Oriana Elia, Kate Griffin, Virginia Feito, Essie Fox, Lydia Leonard, Craig Leyenaar, Anna Mazzola, Andy Morwood, Thomas Olde Heuvelt, Natasha Pulley, Gillian Redfearn, Alice Slater, Holly Watt, Belinda Stewart-Wilson, Rachel Winterbottom and Anna Wood.

To my lovely parents Isabelle and Christopher, and to Antonia, Sam, Wolf and River – you are always in my heart.

My darling Eugene Noone, you are in every book I write, and you are missed.

# About the Author

Catriona Ward was born in Washington, DC, and grew up in the US, Kenya, Madagascar, Yemen and Morocco. She read English at the University of Oxford and spent several years working as an actor in New York. When she returned to the UK she worked on her first novel while writing for a human rights foundation, then took an MA in Creative Writing from the University of East Anglia. Her first novel, *Rawblood*, was published in 2015 and won the August Derleth Award for Best Horror Novel in 2016. She won again in 2018 for *Little Eve*, which also won the prestigious Shirley Jackson Award. In 2021 she published her bestselling novel *The Last House on Needless Street*, which was both a Richard and Judy Book Club and BBC Two *Between the Covers* Book Club pick. It was awarded the August Derleth Award in 2022, making Ward the only woman to prize three times. She lives in London and Devon. Find her on Twitter @Catrionaward.